DATABASE
MANAGEMENT
WITH WEB SITE DEVELOPMENT APPLICATIONS

Part IV **Manipulating Relational Information**

...ontent with Relational Algebra

...ting database tables gives you a clear
...gramming and provides the vocabulary
...guage.

...Database Content and Structure

...pers use to describe database applications
...wledge of SQL will be the key to your success

...eb Sites

...n the Web with HTML

...e for representing information. You will learn
...hat uses style sheets to create an environment
...es.

...een Users and Servers with

...and Web applications combine to create
...velop programming skills by studying, writing,
...grams.

...plications for the Web

...L, HTML, and Web applications, database
...nple and powerful.

...jing Web-Database Interaction

● **Chapter 13**   **Designing an Interactive Web Site**

Studying a complete example of a complex information system, from
requirements to conceptual data model, to relational database, to Web site
design and SQL programming, solidifies your understanding of information
systems.

● **Chapter 14**   **Implementing BigHit Online in ASP and JavaScript**

Developing complete Web applications in a systematic and careful fashion,
together with experimenting with a fully functional online Web site, increases
your understanding of the software development process.

● **Chapter 15**   **Advanced Issues in Web Site Design and Implementation**

The possibilities for further study are endless. You will learn how to enhance
reliability and security in your applications, while sharpening your Web and
database knowledge and programming skills.

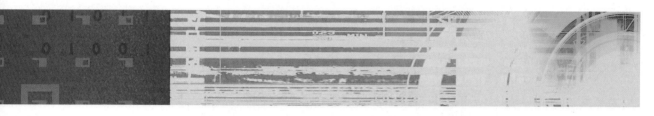

DATABASE
MANAGEMENT
WITH WEB SITE DEVELOPMENT APPLICATIONS

GREG RICCARDI
Florida State University

Addison
Wesley

Boston San Francisco New York
London Toronto Sydney Tokyo Singapore Madrid
Mexico City Munich Paris Cape Town Hong Kong Montreal

Acquisitions Editor: *Maite Suarez-Rivas*
Project Editor: *Katherine Harutunian*
Executive Development Manager: *Sylvia Mallory*
Development Editor: *Lauren Keller Johnson*
Production Supervisor: *Marilyn Lloyd/Juliet Silveri*
Production Services: *Kathy Smith*
Composition and Art: *Gillian Hall, The Aardvark Group*
Cover and Text Designer: *Leslie Haimes/Janet Theurer*
Design Supervisor: *Regina Hagen Kolenda*
Marketing Manager: *Michael Hirsch*
Manufacturing Supervisor: *Evelyn Beaton*

Cover imagery © 2003 by Digital Vision

Library of Congress Cataloging-in-Publication Data
Riccardi, Greg.
  Database management with Web site development applications /
  Greg Riccardi.
      p. cm.
   Includes bibliographical references and index.
   ISBN 0-201-74387-6
   1. Database management. 2. Web site development. 3. Application
   software—Development.   I. Title.

QA76.9.D3 R517 2003
2002071654–dc21   2002071654

3 4 5 6 7 8 9 10–QWT–0403

To Ann, Mary, Christina, and Elizabeth

Contents

PREFACE   xvii

Part I **Introduction to Information Technology
and the World Wide Web   1**

● **Chapter 1 INTRODUCTION TO INFORMATION AND DATABASE SYSTEMS   3**

  1.1   What Are Information Systems and Databases? 5
  1.2   Why Are Databases Important? 6
  1.3   How Do Databases Represent Information? 8
  1.4   Who Works with Database Systems? 9
  1.5   How Do Databases Support the World Wide Web? 10
  1.6   What Database Concepts and Terms Do You Need to Know? 11
      1.6.1   Schemas and Instances 11
      1.6.2   Database Query Operations 12
  Interview Philip Greenspun, Applications of Yesterday's
          and Tomorrow's Internet 14
  Chapter Summary 15
  Key Terms 15
  Questions 16
  Further Reading 17

● **Chapter 2 INTERNET INFORMATION SYSTEMS   19**

  2.1   Components of the Web 20
  2.2   Web Pages and HTML 20
  2.3   Web and Information Servers 24
  2.4   A Close Look at a Sample Web Site 26
      2.4.1   Information Content of a Web Site 26
      2.4.2   A Customer-Information Web Page 27
      2.4.3   Purchasing Videos from a Web Page 28
      2.4.4   Recording a Purchase in a Database 29
  Interview Jakob Nielsen, Business Benefits of Usability 30
  Chapter Summary 32
  Key Terms 32
  Questions 33
  Problems 33
  Further Reading 33

Part II   **Designing and Specifying Information Systems**   **35**

● **Chapter 3**   **REPRESENTING INFORMATION WITH DATA MODELS**   **37**

    3.1   Data Models 38
       3.1.1   Types of Data Models 38
       3.1.2   Database Schemas 38
    3.2   Discovering and Specifying Information Requirements
        and Technology 39
    3.3   Organizing Information 40
       3.3.1   Entities, Entity Classes, and Attributes 40
       3.3.2   Key Attributes 43
       3.3.3   Constraints on Attribute Values .45
       3.3.4   A Closer Look at "Null" 46
    3.4   Relationships and Relationship Types 48
       3.4.1   Modeling Relationship Types and Instances 48
       3.4.2   Relationships Are Not Attributes .49
       3.4.3   Constraints on Relationship Types 49
       3.4.4   Higher-Degree Relationships 51
    3.5   **Case in Point:** Determining Entity Classes, Attributes,
        and Relationship Types for Video Sales .53
    Interview Marc Caruso, Using SQL to Solve Customers' Needs 56
    Chapter Summary 57
    Key Terms 57
    Questions 58
    Problems 58
    Project 59
    Further Reading 59

● **Chapter 4**   **DATA MODELING WITH ENTITY-RELATIONSHIP DIAGRAMS**   **61**

    4.1   Entity-Relationship Modeling 62
    4.2   Entity-Relationship Diagrams 62
       4.2.1   Entity Classes and Attributes 63
       4.2.2   Relationship Types and Constraints 64
    4.3   Modeling Video Rentals 66
       4.3.1   Modeling Rentals as a Relationship Type 66
       4.3.2   Modeling Rentals as an Entity Class 66
    4.4   Roles in Relationship Types 69
    4.5   An E-R Model for BigHit Video 72
       4.5.1   Recording the History of Rentals .72
       4.5.2   Employee Roles and Cardinalities 74

4.5.3 Purchase Orders and the True Meaning of Video 75

4.5.4 Employees, Time Cards, and Pay Statements 77

4.6 Object-Oriented Data Models 78

Interview Peter Chen, On the Birth of the Idea
for the E-R Model 81

4.7 **Case in Point:** E-R Model for Video Sales for BigHit Video . . .83

Chapter Summary 86

Key Terms 86

Questions 86

Problems 87

Projects 87

Further Reading 87

Part III   **Designing and Creating Relational Databases**   **89**

● **Chapter 5**   **DEVELOPING RELATIONAL MODELS**   **91**

5.1 Introduction to the Relational Model 92

5.2 A Closer Look at Relation Schemas and Keys 94

5.3 Translating E-R Diagrams to Relation Schemas 94

5.4 Representing Entity Classes as Relation Schemas 95

5.5 Representing Composite, Multivalued, and Derived Attributes 96

5.5.1 Composite Attributes 96

5.5.2 Multivalued Attributes 97

5.5.3 Derived Attributes 99

5.6 Representing Relationship Types as Attributes 100

5.6.1 One-to-Many Relationship Types 100

5.6.2 One-to-One Relationship Types 101

5.6.3 Representing One-to-One Relationships by
Merging Entities 103

5.7 Representing Many-to-Many Relationships as Tables 103

5.8 Representing Weak Entity Classes 104

5.9 Representing Inheritance as Tables 107

5.10 **Case in Point:** Relational Model for Video Sales for BigHit Video . . .110

Interview Sandy Charron, Steps Through the Design
and Implementation of a Database 113

Chapter Summary 115

Key Terms 115

Questions 116

Problems 117

Projects 118

Further Reading 118

● **Chapter 6** **DEFINING RELATIONAL DATABASES WITH MICROSOFT ACCESS** **121**

6.1 Creating an Access Database 122
6.2 Creating Tables in Access 123
   6.2.1 Entering Attribute Values into an Access Table 126
Interview Sandy Charron, On the Critical Stage of
   Requirements Gathering 127
   6.2.2 Modifying Attribute Values in an Access Table 128
6.3 Creating Forms from Tables 128
6.4 Configuring Access for Multiple Users 131
6.5 Specifying Relationship Types in Access 135
6.6 **Case in Point:** Creating an Access Database for BigHit
   Online Video Sales 138
Chapter Summary 139
Key Terms 140
Questions 140
Problems 141
Projects 141
Further Reading 141

● **Chapter 7** **IMPROVING RELATIONAL SCHEMAS AND NORMALIZATION** **143**

7.1 Redundancy and Anomalies in Relation Schemas 144
7.2 Functional Dependencies between Attributes 146
7.3 Superkeys and Keys 149
7.4 Inferring Additional Functional Dependencies 150
7.5 Determining Keys from Functional Dependencies 152
7.6 Normalization 152
7.7 Third Normal Form (3NF) 153
Interview David McGoveran, Data Normalization 155
7.8 Boyce-Codd Normal Form (BCNF) .156
7.9 **Case in Point:** Normalization of a Car Registration 157
Chapter Summary 161
Key Terms 161
Questions 162
Problems 162
Further Reading 162

Part IV **Manipulating Relational Information** **163**

● **Chapter 8** **MANIPULATING DATABASE CONTENT WITH
RELATIONAL ALGEBRA AND MICROSOFT ACCESS** **165**

8.1 Manipulating Information in Relational Databases 166

8.2   Projection Queries 166

8.3   Selection Queries 171

8.4   Product Queries 175

Interview Judy Bowman, SQL As It Is Practiced 177

8.5   Queries with Multiple Joins .182

8.6   Combining Relational Operations 184

8.7   Defining Complex Queries with Microsoft Access 185

8.8   Applying Set Operators to Tables 187

       8.8.1   Union 187

       8.8.2   Intersection 188

       8.8.3   Difference 190

8.9   Creating User Interfaces in Access 190

8.10   **Case in Point:** A Video Rental Checkout Form 195

       Chapter Summary 198

       Key Terms 199

       Questions 199

       Problems 200

       Projects 200

       Further Reading 201

● **Chapter 9 USING SQL TO MANIPULATE DATABASE
CONTENT AND STRUCTURE   203**

9.1   Creating Queries in SQL 204

       9.1.1   Simple Select Statements 204

       9.1.2   Simple Join Queries 207

       9.1.3   Outer Join Queries .207

       9.1.4   Queries with Multiple Relational Operators 210

       9.1.5   String Pattern Matching and Ordering Results 214

       9.1.6   Expressions, Literals, and Aggregates 215

       9.1.7   `Group by` and `having` Clauses 216

       9.1.8   Nested Select Statements 218

       9.1.9   Set Operations 220

9.2   Modifying Database Content with SQL 221

       9.2.1   Insert Statements .221

       9.2.2   Update Statements .223

       9.2.3   Delete Statements .223

Interview Peter Chen, The Importance of Theories
That Solve Business Problems 224

9.3   Creating and Manipulating Table Definitions with SQL 225

       9.3.1   Creating Tables and Defining Attributes 225

       9.3.2   Key and Foreign Key Constraint Specifications 226

       9.3.4   Default Values, Nulls, and Constraints 227

       9.3.5   Adding, Removing, and Modifying Attributes 228

9.3.6 Schemas and User IDs 228

9.3.7 Drop Statements 228

9.4 The Rule of 90/10 229

9.5 Case in Point: SQL Statements for BigHit Online Video Sales 229

Chapter Summary 232

Key Terms 233

Questions 234

Problems 234

Projects 235

Further Reading 235

Part V   **Creating Interactive Web Sites**   **237**

● **Chapter 10**   **PRESENTING INFORMATION ON THE WEB WITH HTML**   **239**

10.1 The Architecture of Web Sites 240

10.2 Introduction to HTML 241

10.3 A Closer Look at HTML Documents .241

10.4 URLs, Anchor Tags, and Document References 245

10.5 Presenting Information in HTML Tables 247

10.6 Controlling HTML Table Format with Style Sheets 249

10.7 Using External Style Sheets and Style Classes 253

Interview Jakob Nielsen, Better Design for a New Medium 254

10.8 Case in Point: Defining a Style for BigHit Online 256

Chapter Summary 260

Key Terms 260

Questions 261

Problems 262

Projects 262

Further Reading 263

● **Chapter 11**   **CREATING INTERACTION BETWEEN USERS AND
SERVERS WITH ASP AND JAVASCRIPT**   **265**

11.1 The Architecture of Dynamic Web Sites 266

11.2 Designing HTML Forms for User Input 267

11.2.1 Creating a Customer Information Form in HTML 267

11.2.2 Understanding Browser-Server Interaction with HTTP 269

11.3 Writing Web Applications in ASP and JavaScript 271

11.4 Processing Forms with ASP and JavaScript 275

11.5 Using Objects in ASP and JavaScript 278

11.5.1 Strings in JavaScript 279

11.5.2 The `Request` and `Response` Objects in ASP 280

Interview Philip Greenspun, On Starting a First Business
and the Use of Database Applications 281

11.6 Using Objects and Methods to Improve Code 283

 11.6.1 Defining Functions That Produce the Page Header
  and Footer 283

 11.6.2 Creating and Manipulating Objects 284

 11.6.3 Using `with` Statements to Simplify Code 286

11.7 **Case in Point:** Writing JavaScript Code for BigHit Online 287

Chapter Summary 290

Key Terms 291

Questions 292

Problems 293

Projects 293

Further Reading 293

● Chapter 12 DEVELOPING DATABASE APPLICATIONS FOR THE WEB   295

12.1 Connecting to Databases with ASP 296

12.2 Executing SQL `select` Queries with ASP 298

 12.2.1 Fetching and Displaying the Customer's Name 298

 12.2.2 Gathering Rental Information from Three Database Tables . . .299

12.3 Creating Objects from Queries 301

12.4 A General Purpose Query Execution Script 303

Interview Victor Vianu, Database Ideas for Tomorrow 308

12.5 Inserting New Customer Information 308

12.6 Handling Quote Marks in SQL Statements 312

12.6 Debugging ASP and JavaScript 313

12.7 **Case in Point:** Adding and Updating Customers in BigHit Online . . .314

Chapter Summary 318

Key Terms 319

Questions 319

Problems 320

Projects 320

Further Reading 321

Part VI   Developing and Managing Web-Database Interaction   323

● Chapter 13 DESIGNING AN INTERACTIVE WEB SITE   325

13.1 Components of the BigHit Online Web Site 326

13.2 Data Modeling for BigHit Online 327

 13.2.1 Evaluating the E-R Diagram 327

 13.2.2 Improving the E-R Diagram 329

13.2.3 Using Weak Entity Classes for Many-to-Many
Relationship Types 330

13.2.4 Modeling Shopping Carts and Wish Lists 332

13.2.5 Modeling to Support Searching for Movies 334

13.2.6 Final Evaluation of the Conceptual Model 334

13.3 Relational Model for BigHit Online 337

13.4 Creating an SQL Database .340

Interview Mary Riccardi, Merging the Needs of the
Client with the Ability of the Technology 341

13.5 Web Site Design, Pages, and Flow 342

13.5.1 Login and Customer Information 342

13.5.2 Shopping Carts, Searching, and Selecting Items 343

13.5.3 Checkout and Receipt 346

Chapter Summary 349

Key Terms 349

Questions 349

Problems 350

Projects 350

Further Reading 351

Chapter 14 IMPLEMENTING BIGHIT ONLINE IN ASP AND JAVASCRIPT   353

14.1 Viewing Source Code and SQL Statements 354

14.1.1 Displaying ASP Source Code in a Web Page 354

14.1.2 Recording and Displaying the Application Log 356

14.2 Login and Customer Information 358

14.3 Searching and Adding Items to a Shopping Cart 361

Interview David McGoveran, Transaction Processing
and Performance 367

14.4 Checkout Processing 367

Chapter Summary 371

Key Terms 372

Questions 372

Problems 372

Projects 373

Further Reading 373

**Chapter 15 ADVANCED ISSUES IN WEB SITE DESIGN
AND IMPLEMENTATION   375**

15.1 Forms Checking with Client-Side JavaScript 376

15.1.1 Validating Form Data 376

15.1.2 Calling the Validation Function During Form Submission 380

15.1.3 Installing Form Validation in ASP Scripts 380

15.2 Error Handling in Server-Side JavaScript 381

15.3 Transactions and Transaction Management 384

    15.3.1 Example of Concurrent User Interference in BigHit Online . . .385

    15.3.2 Database Transactions 385

    15.3.3 Using Transactions in BigHit Online 387

    15.3.4 General Theory of Database Transactions 389

    15.3.5 Transaction Management in ASP with SQL Server 389

    15.3.6 Analyzing Interference with Concurrent Updates 390

15.4 Backup and Recovery from Failures 392

    15.4.1 Backups and Checkpoints 393

    15.4.2 Transaction Logs 394

15.5 Security in Information Systems 394

    15.5.1 Security in Database Management Systems 395

    15.5.2 User Authorization for Database Servers 396

    15.5.3 Protection of Database Objects 396

15.6 Stored Procedures and Functions 398

Interview Victor Vianu, Database Research and the Web 400

Chapter Summary 401

Key Terms 401

Questions 402

Problems 403

Projects 403

Further Reading 403

REFERENCES   405

INDEX   409

Preface

Database Management with Web Site Development Applications comprehensively covers the core database concepts for the design, creation, and manipulation of relational data. Thus it is ideally suited to the core introductory database course for many students. The topics are discussed in the context of how databases are used in businesses and Web sites. The presentation includes analysis of requirements, conceptual modeling, definition of the relational model, relational database design and normalization, creation of databases, and the manipulation of relational databases in relational algebra, in Microsoft Access, and with SQL.

My vision in writing this book was twofold. First, I wanted to give students a practical way of learning the basics of how information is specified, acquired, and managed using database technology. I aimed to cover the core information that any first database course should offer:

- Determining the information requirements for a system
- Specifying those requirements
- Developing a relational database to store the information
- Using the SQL language to manipulate databases

The other part of my vision was to introduce these topics in a motivating, realistic context so that students could understand how information is used to support businesses and other organizations. I thus present the principles of database management in the context of two business-oriented examples: BigHit Video Inc., a traditional brick-and-mortar video rental business; and BigHit Online, an online video sales company. These examples are followed from the initial requirements through the data modeling and database development and finally to the development of complex working Web sites.

To further motivate students and to provide them with additional practical knowledge, I also include a detailed presentation of how to create a database-driven Web site. As the book develops the BigHit Online retail sales site, additional topics are introduced and students learn to:

- Design Web sites to interact with users
- Construct Web pages with HTML
- Design and implement their own dynamic Web applications
- Use database management systems to manage the information content of Web sites

Motivating Students to Learn

For teachers, the Web provides an opportunity to engage students in learning the fundamental principles of information management. It's not hard to convince learners that the Web cannot exist without database systems. Anyone who looks at a Web search engine or an online retail Web site knows that vast amounts of information are stored behind the scenes. If we convince students that they can learn how information is managed in Web sites—that they can even learn to develop their own sophisticated Web sites—they will be excited. If we get across to them that they cannot understand or develop Web sites without a thorough understanding of database management, they will want to learn.

One theme of *Database Management with Web Site Development Applications* is that database management and the Web are inextricably linked. As we learn about the Web, we are learning about information management—about collecting, managing, and distributing information. As we learn about database management, we are learning the fundamental principles that support good Web site development.

Audience and Prerequisites

This book is designed for IT, MIS, and mixed-majors courses with no computer programming or math prerequisites. It takes on the significant challenge of presenting material whose understanding requires both technical skill and precision to students who may be unfamiliar with the need for either. Among the book's major goals are emphasizing the need for precision in the specification of information systems and developing each student's capability to be precise.

With this information and these skills in hand, students will be prepared for additional study in database management, information systems, computer science, and Internet technology. Additionally, the material in the book provides an excellent foundation for entry-level employment in Web site design and management.

Coverage and Organization

This book is divided into 6 parts that take the reader from an overview of information systems and Web sites, through the principles that underlie database systems, and into Web site development. Part I is an overview of all of the material of the book. Parts II, III, and IV cover data modeling, relational database design, and manipulation of relational databases. Parts V and VI present the basics of Web pages and Web sites, and a detailed look at building complex Web sites and database applications.

In Part I, before encountering the details of database system development, students are introduced to information systems with overviews of what they are, why they are important, and how people create and interact with them. Students are also shown how information system requirements, relational databases, and Web servers work together to produce dynamic Web sites. The early coverage of these topics sets the stage for the study of the principles of database management.

The presentation of the specification, design, and implementation of databases is primarily contained in Parts II, III, and IV. Students begin in Part II (Chapters 3 and 4) by learning about the importance of data modeling and then about how to develop precise specifications of information content. Part III (Chapters 5–7) shows how to transform data models into relational database schemas, create databases, and normalize database schemas. Part IV (Chapters 8 and 9) completes the traditional database material by concentrating on manipulating databases with relational algebra, Query by Example, and SQL.

The coverage of Web site design and implementation continues in Part V (Chapters 10–12). Students learn a very simple style of using HTML to present information and of using cascading style sheets (CSS) to control the look and feel of a Web site. They move on to a discussion of using Microsoft Active Server Pages (ASP) and JavaScript as a programming environment for developing Web applications.

Web-database interaction is developed using the Microsoft Active Data Objects (ADO) library. Students "learn by doing" as they read about applications development and practice modifying existing applications and writing their own.

By the time students have studied Parts I–V, they will be capable of analyzing system requirements, designing and creating databases, and designing and implementing complex Web sites. The "Case in Point" section that ends each chapter gives students detailed examples of how to apply what they've learned, using the text's BigHit Online example.

The final part of the book, Part VI (Chapters 13–15), draws from all of the principles of information systems presented in the first twelve chapters to create the BigHit Online system. Chapter 13 begins by analyzing system requirements and then develops the data models and database for the system. The Web site design is presented as an SQL application by showing exactly what SQL statements must be executed to create and process each Web page. Chapter 14 takes a very detailed look at Web applications in JavaScript. It discusses many new programming ideas and demonstrates their usefulness. Chapter 15 addresses a number of issues that are crucial to making databases and database applications reliable and secure.

The presentation of Web development applications in the book is entirely self-contained. All necessary information is presented in the book and the book's companion Web sites (details below). Additional materials are available through the Addison-Wesley ftp site to assist instructors in setting up the necessary Web server support for class projects and to help students install the Web server tools on their own computers.

Features of This Book

The basic premise of this book is that many students learn best when they work from the specific to the general. Chapters begin with a compelling example of the material. The example is decomposed into its basic parts and each part is explained. In this way the principles emerge from the details in a natural way.

Some special pedagogical features are built into each chapter to help to communicate, and get students involved with, the content of the basic database course—beginning with two continuing examples:

- **A running example, Big Hit Video Inc.**, shows how database principles apply to businesses. This study brings the basic concepts to life in the context of information management for a brick-and-mortar video rental company. Throughout the BigHit Video example, readers dissect an existing database to learn about database design, SQL, and the Entity-Relationship model. All of the elements of the BigHit Video information system are available online for both instructors and students—the E-R diagrams, a sample Access database, sample SQL queries, and a working Web site.

- **A second running example, BigHit Online**, investigates a retail Web site. This fictitious Internet business that sells movie videos is featured in each chapter's concluding "Case in Point" section, and it is also the basis for the hands-on discussion in Chapters 13–15 of developing and managing Web-database interaction. This example allows students to apply database concepts by building an online video sales store one step at a time. The BigHit Online example helps students to understand how the design decisions that they make early on affect the later development process.

   The entire BigHit Online system is available on the book's Web site. Both students and instructors can see the E-R diagrams and database schemas. Each Web page on the site has a link to source code of the application that generated the page. Even the SQL statements that are used by the Web applications can be seen in Web pages. Students and instructors can download the entire Web site, including a sample SQL Server database, for local installation.

Each chapter concludes with exercises organized into questions, problems, and projects, as follows.

- **Questions** require students to read and understand the chapter and to draw conclusions. In many cases, students are asked to consult references (Web sites or books) that allow them to expand on the topics of the book.

- **Problems** are applications-oriented in that they involve design or implementation of topics from the chapter, and they generally require more time and effort than the questions do.

- **Projects** present step-by-step information system developments that contribute to the BigHit Video, BigHit Online, or Movie Lovers information systems. Each chapter's projects ask students to apply what they've learned in the chapter to create an ever larger piece of an information system.

  Instructors should consider choosing one of the three information systems and assigning a project from that system for each chapter. In developing their own solutions to the projects, students will be challenged to study the principles of database systems in more detail. They will solidify their understanding of the material by applying it to real system developments.

  The BigHit Video and BigHit Online systems are described in the book in ways that leave many parts incomplete or overly simplified. Projects encourage students to evaluate and extend the simple systems of the book to create their own more realistic systems.

  The Movie Lovers projects encourage students to invent an information system and a Web site for movie fans. A prototype implementation of this information system is available to instructors, but is not available to students directly. The Movie Lovers projects are described in general terms in the book, and each instructor is able to tailor projects to students' needs by providing them with more or less of the prototype implementation.

  The project supplements that are available to instructors are designed to make it easy to assign and evaluate student projects. This is especially important for the Web site development projects when students will create their own Web sites using infrastructure tools that can be downloaded from the Web.

Each chapter includes additional features aimed at providing real-world applications of the text concepts and additional details on core database theory.

- **Key Concept** boxes call attention to essential information and emphasize important principles. Some Key Concept boxes go beyond the scope of the core course to provide more information on the underlying theory. Topics highlighted in the Key Concept boxes include the Hypertext Transfer Protocol (HTTP), storing information in memory and disk, and naming foreign key attributes.

- **General interest sections** cover topics that enhance chapter material by taking readers beyond the main narrative. Examples include discussions of the history of the Internet and the World Wide Web, and the evolution of database systems.

- **Interviews** with working professionals give insight into the future of information systems and into the realities of working in the field. Each chapter includes an interview with an information professional. The interviews focus on the importance of fundamental database concepts and on-the-job learning to successful careers in information systems.

- **Key terms** emphasize the importance of using proper terminology. Each key term is shown in boldface when it is introduced in the text. A precise definition of each new term appears at the end of the chapter in which the term is introduced.

Possible Course Outlines

Database Management with Web Site Development Applications will support a variety of one-semester courses for students from any discipline who are interested in information management and the World Wide Web. No computer programming background is assumed.

The audience for the book includes students in both two-year and four-year colleges and universities. This book can be used for required database courses for students in majors that rely on information management and is also suitable for elective courses taken by students looking for an interesting way to learn about the Web and to fulfill computer competency requirements.

Instructors can use the book as the foundation for several possible courses:

- **A traditional database course** that covers chapters 1–9. These chapters contain plenty of material for a one-semester course, including details about how to use Microsoft Access as a database applications programming environment. Students could use Access or any relational database to create databases and develop their skills in SQL programming.
- **An applications-oriented database** course that covers the material in Chapters 1–9 in about one-half or two-thirds of a semester. The remainder of the course would be an in-depth study of Web pages and Web application design and implementation. Student projects would typically involve designing and implementing a database in the first part of the course, and using JavaScript to develop Web applications in the second part.
- **An applications-oriented database course with integrated Web development** that covers Chapters 3–7, which address conceptual modeling and relational databases, in parallel with Chapters 10 and 11, which address basic Web pages and Web server programming. Students could begin using HTML for developing Web sites early in the course and experiment with ASP and JavaScript while learning the traditional database material. The treatment of database applications and SQL in Chapters 8 and 9 could be combined with the database programming of Chapter 12. Students could write Web applications with database interaction during this part of the course. The final part of the book could be covered while students were finishing their semester projects.
- **A Web development applications course** that quickly covers parts of Chapters 3–9 and spends the bulk of the semester on the database and Web applications of Chapters 10–15. This course would be particularly important for students who know about databases and want to learn about dynamic Web sites.

In addition, this book potentially can be used for other courses, including an introductory course on information technology or information studies, or a liberal studies elective or computer literacy course for general interest students.

Supplementary Resources

This book comes with companion Web sites (http://www.aw.com/riccardi and http://www.web4data.com) offering a variety of supplementary materials online.

For students and instructors:
- Sample databases for experimenting with Access and SQL.
- Detailed instructions for installing the book's companion Web sites on student and instructor computers.
- BigHit Video and BigHit Online examples, fully functioning Web sites with all source code. The code can be used and viewed on the Web site or downloaded for local installation.

For instructors only:
- Solutions to text exercises
- PowerPoint lecture notes
- All of the text illustrations
- A test bank of sample exam questions
- Access to all software required to install and administer the example Web sites and databases, and detailed instructions about installing and using the sites.

- Resources for the Movie Lovers information system. The full implementation includes E-R diagrams, sample databases in Access and SQL Server, a fully functioning Web site, and all source code.

The Movie Lovers Web site gives film fans opportunities to view information about movies, to record their opinions of movies and movie people, and to keep track of their own movie experiences. This site has been implemented in full detail with E-R diagrams, relational models, sample databases in Access and SQL Server, and complete Web applications. This site is not available to students directly. Instructors are free to create student projects by providing as much detail as is appropriate for their students. Students could begin with the simplest sketch of the Web site, or a detailed description, or could even begin each piece of the project with the implementation of the previous project that can be found on the book's instructor-only Web site.

Instructors should contact their local Addison-Wesley representative for access to the instructor-only materials.

Acknowledgments

First, I would like to thank my acquisitions editor, Maite Suarez-Rivas, for her unfailing support and encouragement. She listened to my proposal, believed that we could make an impact, and put together a team of thoroughly professional people to produce the book.

I can't say enough good things about the editorial and production teams of the Computer Science group of Addison-Wesley. Executive Development Manager Sylvia Mallory helped keep us focused on introductory students. Laurie Johnson was invaluable as the developmental editor and first student of the book. Katherine Harutunian, the project editor, has now helped and supported me through three books. I am particularly grateful to Katherine for producing the interviews that appear in the book. The design and production process greatly benefited from the contributions of Patty Mahtani, Marilyn Lloyd, Regina Kolenda, Kathy Smith, and Jennifer Pelland. Mary Riccardi designed the Web site logos. Thanks to all of you.

This book was extensively and thoroughly reviewed by Professors Michael R. Bartolacci of the Pennsylvania State University at Berks and Lehigh Valley College, Russell Fish of the University of Washington, Kevin R. Parker of Idaho State University, Harry Shasho of Towson University, Mark W. Smith of Trident Technical College, and Peter Wolcott of the University of Nebraska at Omaha. Their suggestions were invaluable. My thanks also to go to those who contributed with their reviews of selected chapters, including Professors Barbara Beccue of Illinois State University, Chris Fernandes of Union College, Dana E. Madison of Clarion University. of Pennsylvania, Madhavarao Raghunathan of Bowling Green State University, Santosh Venkatraman of the University of Arkansas at Little Rock, and Peiling Wang of the University of Tennessee at Knoxville. The book is far better because of these insightful reviewers.

My experiences teaching database systems and working with both students and faculty at Florida State University have been most helpful to me. I am particularly thankful to Professors Lawrence Dennis and Lois Wright Hawkes. My thanks also go to Mike Heidmann and Tracy Ball, students at the FSU London Study Centre, who used the book in draft form.

My greatest debts are owed to my wife Ann and daughters Mary, Christina, and Elizabeth. They have supported me through long hours and tense deadlines. I owe all of my successes to their support and encouragement.

About the Author

Greg Riccardi is Professor of Computer Science at Florida State University, a faculty associate of the Florida State University School of Computational Sciences and Information Technology, and a research associate of the e-Sciences Research Institute of the United Kingdom. Professor Riccardi's research interests include Grid computing, Web portal technology, scientific databases, and distributed object computing. He received the President's Award for Excellence in Undergraduate Teaching in 1997 from Florida State University.

DATABASE
MANAGEMENT
WITH WEB SITE DEVELOPMENT APPLICATIONS

PART I

Introduction to Information Technology and the World Wide Web

In Part I you will learn about information systems and database systems: what they are and how they are used. The emphasis is on how information is used in the Internet and the World Wide Web.

Chapter 1 introduces the Internet and the World Wide Web, as well as information systems and database systems. Specific examples of systems help to convey how important these systems are to businesses and individuals. This chapter includes an overview of the structure and content of database systems. We examine how people interact with these systems and what their jobs are like. We also encounter the BigHit Video company, a fictitious video rental and sales company that is used for many of the examples throughout the book.

Chapter 2 presents a detailed introduction to how information and database systems support the World Wide Web. It begins by introducing the basic structure of Web browsers, Web servers, and information servers. It then takes us through a sample Web site that allows customers to purchase videos from BigHit Online.

The two chapters in this section form the basis for all of the rest of the material in the book.

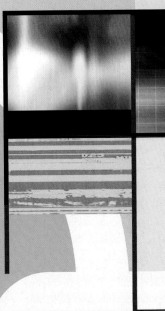

CHAPTER 1

Introduction to Information and Database Systems

In this chapter, you will learn:

- What information and database systems are
- What the Internet is and how it has been used to create the World Wide Web
- How information and database systems support the World Wide Web
- How database systems benefit organizations
- What database management systems do and how they represent information
- What database management systems consist of
- What people do who work in information systems
- How database systems are used on the Web

The emergence of the World Wide Web as a tool for communication among individuals and organizations has revolutionized not only computing but also our work and personal lives. Before the mid-1990s, computers were tools used largely by businesses, government organizations, and educational institutions. Since then, the Internet and the software tools that support the Web have enabled people to use computers in whole new ways—with remarkable results.

Businesses use the Web for sales, marketing, and many other kinds of communication. For example, e-mail has almost entirely replaced paper memos, especially in companies with employees all over the world. Firms use the Web to disseminate information among their employees, as well as to partners, customers, and the general public.

Individuals use the Internet to look up information as well as post information about themselves, communicate with friends and family, and shop. You may have used the Internet to search for information on your studies, on your favorite music or books, or on the latest movies. You may have also built your own personal Web site at Yahoo or HotMail, and put links on your pages to encourage your site visitors to access other sites.

All these activities have revolutionized commerce and communication. For example, consider eBay, an Internet auction site. eBay lets individuals and businesses buy and sell all sorts of items. To do that, eBay must keep track of all its buyers and sellers, as well as the millions of items that are available on the site. But the company must do much more. It has to provide a way for bidders to make offers and find out if their bids are winners. It must also keep track of a huge volume of information, ensure its accuracy, and present it to customers in appropriate ways. Finally, as a service to its customers, eBay provides both chat rooms and e-mail exchanges between individuals.

How does eBay manage all this? It depends on computer **information systems**—collections of software applications and computer hardware that store and manipulate information.

Concept

The Internet and World Wide Web

The **Internet** is a loose and dynamic collection of computers that are connected by a variety of networking devices. Figure 1.1 illustrates some of the ways that computers can be connected. The Internet was born in the 1960s as a U.S. Defense Advanced Research Projects Agency (DARPA) project to allow computers in the Defense Department and universities to exchange information using telephone circuits and switching devices. The initial development focused on designing and manufacturing switching devices and creating rules for the way computers would communicate using these devices. The initial network, called the ARPANET, was used on a large scale beginning in 1972.

Soon after communication between computers was a reality, electronic mail emerged as a valuable tool to improve communications between people who were working on ARPANET. More and more institutions joined the ARPANET and the pioneers recognized the need to expand the network and make it widely available.

The work on wide-area networks (WANs) was accompanied by the development of local-area networks (LANs) to allow interaction between computers and people within an organization. The primary LAN system now is Ethernet, which allows computers to communicate at high speeds at distances of up to a mile.

The combination of LANs for local interaction and WANs for interaction across longer distances is what we now call the Internet. By the early 1980s, most universities and research organizations and many companies had joined the Internet and were using a variety of software systems to interact.

In 1980, Tim Berners-Lee, a scientist at the European Center for Particle Physics (CERN), proposed a notation for linking documents together. In 1987, Apple Computer introduced the Hypercard system, which exposed many people to the advantages of linked documents. By 1990, Berners-Lee had developed a strategy for applying his linked documents to the Internet. He called his documents *Hypertext* and developed software that allowed readers of a document to fetch related documents by clicking on links. He called his system the **World Wide Web**. CERN researchers were scattered all around the world, and Hypertext gave them a wonderful new tool to communicate.

In the early 1990s, researchers at the National Center for Supercomputing Applications (NCSA) at the University of Illinois launched the development of a new browser called Mosaic. In March 1994, some of the masterminds of the Mosaic project created the Mosaic Communications Corp, which later became Netscape, and the new Internet economy took off.

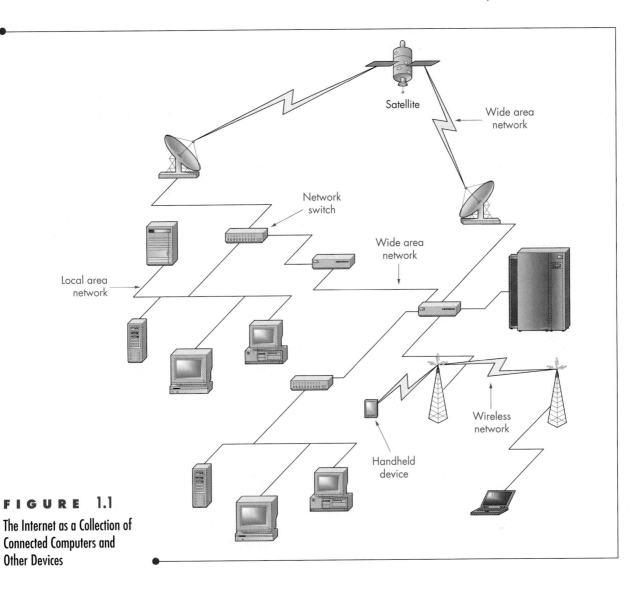

FIGURE 1.1

The Internet as a Collection of Connected Computers and Other Devices

WHAT ARE INFORMATION
1.1   SYSTEMS AND DATABASES?

In the past, the human brain was the only information system around. We still use our brains to take information in, store it, interpret it, and retrieve it. But we are limited in how much we can remember and how quickly we can make decisions. Computers, with their capacity to handle huge volumes of data and process them speedily, have helped us overcome these limitations. The computer systems at Amazon.com keep track of millions of sale items and millions of customers. When the capacity of those systems is exceeded, they can simply add more computers.

That doesn't mean that creating the software that enables a computer to process information is easy. Indeed, information management is one of the most challenging aspects of software development. To develop an effective information system, software engineers must determine what kind of information will go into the system—for example, names, addresses, and credit card numbers for customers, description and price for products. They must also give a precise definition of that information and develop ways by which the computer can create, maintain, and protect the information.

But where—and in what form—does all this information actually exist in a computer? It goes into a **database management system (DBMS)**, which is the combination of software and hardware that allows people to organize and store information. A **database**, or **database system**, is the system that results when users add specific information to a DBMS.

Users of a database store crucial information—from customers' names and suppliers' prices to sales history and procurement records—update that information and make it readily available to whoever needs it. The people who work with databases are responsible for many of the benefits that computers have offered all kinds of organizations.

In today's technology-intensive economy, most organizations around the world—whether they are for-profit, not-for-profit, educational, or governmental—could not stay competitive or achieve their goals without database management systems. Thus, no matter what career path you envision taking (or may be embarking on now), knowledge of information systems and database management can help you make important contributions to your organization's success. And if you decide to start up your own business, that knowledge will prove just as important. Finally, if you want to learn how to design and implement database systems and database applications, you can feel confident that your skills will be in demand in many different industries.

This book focuses on the role of information management in computing and the database-management technology that supports it. As you work your way through the chapters, you'll learn a great deal about Internet applications, including the World Wide Web. Why the focus on the Web and on databases? The Web has become a major resource for people who want to look up information, buy or sell products or services, and communicate with others. And much of the software used to operate Web sites also controls the interactions between Web servers and databases.

1.2   WHY ARE DATABASES IMPORTANT?

To get a sense of just how important databases are, let's explore their impact on commerce. Consider two retail-sales giants: the Wal-Mart Company, the world's largest retail-store chain, and L. L. Bean, a major mail-order clothing and sporting-goods retailer.

Both of these companies use database systems to record details about sales. They then analyze that information to make decisions about how to run their business and sharpen their competitive strategies. Although both companies share common activities, they use their database systems in markedly different ways—and with different goals in mind.

For example, Wal-Mart, like many retail businesses, uses electronic cash registers connected to database systems to record every item that customers purchase in every store. Each time a customer goes through the check-out line, Wal-Mart's systems record exactly what he or she bought, how many units, and at what price. Computers also document the customer's total purchase, and his or her means of payment. The company then uses all of that information to assess the individual store's—and the entire corporation's—performance. By recording the details of each purchase, Wal-Mart can take a closer look at the following crucial aspects of its business:

- Sales of individual products

  How does the daily number of a particular product sold compare with the number of units in inventory?

  How, if at all, do sales of specific and similar items vary seasonally?

  How do sales of similar items with different features compare?

- Market-basket collections (all items in a single purchase)

  What are the average and variation in total purchase amount?

  What are the average and variation in number and price of items?

  How do sales of different items in a single purchase compare?

- Customers

  What is the average customer's buying behavior?

  What are individual customers' preferences?

By analyzing sales of individual products, the company can determine how much stock it needs to purchase to ensure a ready supply of available products. For example, this kind of analysis may reveal that light-colored bathing suits sell better in mid-summer than they do in the spring, or that people buy more charcoal on Thursdays than they do on Mondays. Armed with this information, the retail store can make better use of its inventory and its capital.

Market-basket analysis can shed light on the combinations of items that customers typically purchase during one visit to the store. Wal-Mart uses this information to organize the sales floor. For example, if the company discovers that people often buy milk and bread in one purchase, then putting the bread in the front of the store and the milk in the back may encourage customers to go to the back of the store. By wandering through the rest of the store, they might see other items they want to buy.

Wal-Mart probably has little interest in tracking individual customers' behavior, because the company has so many millions of them. However, whenever a customer pays for a purchase by check or credit card, the store records that information and could use it to identify the purchaser if he or she comes back.

L. L. Bean differs from Wal-Mart in several key ways. For example, it has far fewer customers than Wal-Mart does, and it stores much more information about those customers. L. L. Bean records each customer's name and address and directly associates that information with each purchased item. This matching lets the company customize the distribution of its catalogs. For instance, someone who buys camping equipment will receive the outdoor catalog. This database system also lets L. L. Bean's salespeople personalize their interactions with customers. For instance, if a sales clerk knows that a phone customer has purchased several polo shirts over the past few years, he might point out that the shirt is on sale. L. L. Bean can thus offer individualized service to its customers by responding to their individual profiles.

Wal-Mart can extract only so much customer information from its sales data because of the sheer size of its databases. The store collects multiple terabytes (that is, a million million bytes) of sales data every single year. Managing those data, making sure the information is accurate, protecting it from access by competitors, and devising ways to analyze it and distribute the results all take time and money. Wal-Mart conducts these activities because they result in significant improvements in customer satisfaction and business profitability.

Clearly, database systems perform vital functions for companies. Not surprisingly, as business competition has stiffened, the field of database management has experienced phenomenal growth. Microsoft sells more than 1 million licenses for its Access DBMS each month. Oracle Corporation has become the second largest software company in the world by specializing in DBMSs. Economists estimate that nearly $10 billion is spent directly on database software each year and that the Oracle leads Microsoft and IBM in total database revenues.

1.3   HOW DO DATABASES REPRESENT INFORMATION?

Database professionals draw a sharp distinction between data and information. By **data**, we mean a collection of bits (a **bit** is a single binary digit, either 0 or 1). By **information**, we mean data that have a specific meaning. A value such as 8505551212 stored in a file on a computer is a form of data. To give that datum meaning—that is, to turn it into information—we would need to describe its type (for example, a number; character or letter; string of characters; and so forth). We would also need to give it a name (such as `phoneNumber`) and identify a context in which the name has meaning; for example, the directory information number for Tallahassee, Florida.

Here's a more comprehensive example: If we know that bytes (a **byte** is 8 bits) 1003–1022 of a computer file have some specific value, then we have the bytes' *data content*. If we know that those bytes hold a 20-character string that represents the last name of a customer, we have their *information content*.

As an important first step in building a software system, a software developer defines a **data model**, which describes what kind of information will be included and how that information will be structured or organized. One way is to create a diagram that shows all of the kinds of data that will be present in the system. Database management systems enable software developers to transform such specifications into databases that can maintain that information content.

Let's take a closer look at database management systems. DBMSs consist of data combined with software that lets people store, manage, and retrieve the information in the database. DBMSs have the following basic components:

- **The physical database:** a collection of files containing the data content
- **The schema:** a specification of the physical database's information content and logical structure
- **The database engine:** software that lets people access and modify the database contents
- **The data definition and manipulation languages:** programming languages, such as Java or **SQL (Structured Query Language)**, that let software developers define the schema and access the database.

Although these components make up a basic DBMS, a special kind of DBMS has emerged in recent decades: **relational database management systems (RDBMSs)**. An RDBMS is a DBMS that stores all data in the form of tables. A table's rows represent database objects, such as customers, and its columns represent the characteristics of those objects, such as customer number, last name, and first name.

For example, the table shown in Figure 1.2 might be part of a database for the BigHit Video Company, a fictitious chain of video rental stores that you will encounter throughout this book. Each row represents a customer, and each column represents an attribute of those customers; in this case, account number, last name, and first name. The figure also reveals the table's *schema*, or structure; in this case, the table's name ("Customer") and a list of column names.

The *table creation statement* goes further than the schema, specifying the type of information (integer, character) that goes in each column. The table itself contains the column definitions and a set of rows. In this case, each row represents information about a single customer and contains a value (whether an integer or a string of characters) in each column. By executing the table creation statement, the software stores the schema inside the DBMS.

How might people in an actual organization interact with the company's database? Typically, individuals have desktop computers on which some database application program, possibly Microsoft Access, has been installed. That application program interacts with the company's DBMS through a client-server interface, as illustrated in Figure 1.3. In a **client-server system**, the application—that is, the client—stores infor-

Customer table

accountId	lastName	firstName
101	Block	Jane
102	Hamilton	Cherry
103	Harrison	Kate
104	Breaux	Carroll

Logical description (Schema): Customer (accountId, lastName, firstName)

Table creation statement: create table Customer (accountId integer, lastName char(20),firstName char(20))

FIGURE 1.2

Customer Table for BigHit Video

mation in its memory as objects. The server executes on another computer and stores information in its memory as tables. Among other benefits, this separation of client and server allows the server computer to be kept in a secure, central location and the client to be located elsewhere.

A typical scenario is that someone—perhaps a manager or sales representative—decides he needs to look up information in the database. He opens the database application on his desktop computer and chooses a specific request from a menu. The application then presents the request for information, or **query**, to the server in the form of a statement in the SQL language. In response to the request, the server extracts the required information from its tables and sends it to the application in a standard format, such as a Web page.

Through the application, a user can also submit requests to modify the database contents and schema. The server processes these requests only if they are consistent with that user's access privileges.

1.4 WHO WORKS WITH DATABASE SYSTEMS?

People who work with database systems possess a variety of skills and knowledge, and can perform a wide array of tasks. Some of them are **end users**—for example, managers and salesmen whose jobs require them to access and use information from a

FIGURE 1.3

Client-Server Interaction

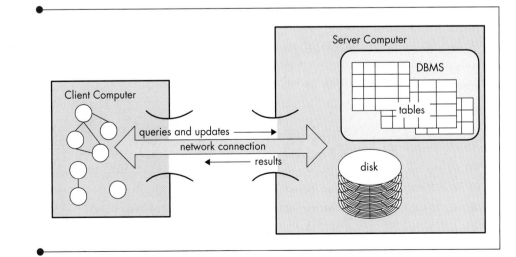

database. *Casual users* make occasional use of the system, but have little or no training. They might access the system through simple user interfaces, such as a Web browser, but they would not typically modify the database content. *Sophisticated users* have more familiarity with database systems and might be allowed to modify the structure as well as the content.

Other people who work with database systems are specialists, and include:

- Database designers
- Applications developers
- Web-application developers
- Web-site designers
- Database administrators

Database designers are software professionals who specify information content and create database systems. They begin by consulting with end users to determine what those users need from the database and how they want to use the system. Then they gather documents, such as sales receipts and customer account applications, and other examples of the information content that the system will contain. Next, they produce a detailed description of the structure of that information; for example, an Entity-Relationship diagram. They then translate this document into a data-definition language (such as SQL) and use it to construct the actual database.

Applications developers create applications that extend the functionality of the database system. These applications interact with the database to help users accomplish specific tasks, such as analyzing information or recording the sale of a video.

Web-application developers create Web pages and devise means for processing information content through the Web.

Web-site designers are responsible for the "look and feel" of Web sites and for specifying their information content. Based on their knowledge of how people interact with computers, Web-site designers work with graphics and images to design attractive and easy-to-navigate pages.

Database administrators control access to database systems, maintain data accuracy and integrity, and monitor and improve database performance.

1.5   HOW DO DATABASES SUPPORT THE WORLD WIDE WEB?

Clearly, effective Web sites depend on information management—especially in today's world of ever-changing Web-site content. Each day, organizations such as The *New York Times* Company and CNN publish huge quantities of new information on the Web. Almost all of it is created by software that draws on information stored in databases. Likewise, to engage in electronic commerce, companies must collect information from customers and manage inventories and other records using databases. Anyone who wants a future in Web-site development or management must have a working knowledge of database systems.

Databases support Web sites in several ways. Specifically, they:

- Maintain information that is published in the site
- Track the ways in which site visitors use that information
- Track the number of site visitors and customers
- Store information collected from input forms such as requests for customer addresses
- Store the structure and content of Web pages

Figure 1.4 shows a simplified Internet Explorer window that is displaying a page from BigHit Video's Web site. BigHit's database contains information about customers, videos, rentals, and much more. This page displays information about a specific cus-

FIGURE 1.4

Reservation Form for BigHit
Video Web Site

tomer (Jane Block) who has visited the Web site to reserve a videotape. The page shows her account number, name, and address, as well as a link to a page where she can modify that information. The page also lists four movies that are available for rent. The customer has selected one of the four. When she clicks the **Reserve** button, the displayed information is sent to the Web server for processing. The request for account number 101 to reserve a copy of the movie *Annie Hall* is then recorded in BigHit Video's database.

You'll learn more about the contents, purpose, and implementation of the BigHit Web site in Chapters 9–13.

1.6 WHAT DATABASE CONCEPTS AND TERMS DO YOU NEED TO KNOW?

To truly understand database systems, you need to master a number of concepts and technical terms. Most of these terms are English-language phrases. However, many of them have a specific—and sometimes completely different—meaning when used in the field of database systems. We'll begin with definitions and examples of some of the most important terms. We'll then define additional terms in subsequent chapters. You'll also find a list of key terms and their definitions at the end of each chapter.

1.6.1 Schemas and Instances

To understand database systems, you not only need to master some technical terminology; you also must make a clear distinction between a database's structure (the schema) and its contents (its *state* or **instances**). We create the foundation for understanding the information by defining the structure of the database, but we store the information itself in the instances.

Figure 1.2 showed the schema of a customer table and four instances (rows) it contains. The schema of the table specified that each customer has an account ID, a last name, and a first name. Each row contains facts about things that exist outside the database. For example, the first row of the table in Figure 1.2 represents the fact that the customer with account ID 101 is named Jane Block.

Both the schema and the instances are stored in the database. In creating the database, the database designer adds only the schema information. At this point, there are no instances. Once users begin accessing the database, they add instances. Thus, the database changes as users enter and retrieve information.

The database schema not only defines the types of information that will go into the database (integer, character, etc.); it also specifies limitations, or *constraints*, on that information. For example, a schema might stipulate that a particular value—such as account ID—must be unique within a table. If a user tries to create the same account ID for two different customers, the database system will detect an error and refuse to create the duplicate account.

A relational database also represents relationships between objects. For instance, once Jane Block has reserved a copy of the movie *Animal House*, an instance in a reservation table records the relationship between that customer and the movie, as illustrated in Figure 1.5. The third row of the table depicts this relationship. If Jane Block cancels the reservation, the database system deletes the relationship instance from the table. You'll learn more about how databases represent relationships in Chapter 5.

1.6.2 **Database Query Operations**

Relational databases depend on a variety of *query* operations that let users and administrators fetch information; update it; and create, change, and delete tables. Often, a query asks the system to pull together information from multiple database tables. For example, suppose a manager at BigHit Video wanted to know what movies Jane Block has reserved. To provide this information, the server must fetch the account ID for Jane Block from the customer table and then gather all the rows of the reservation table that contain that account ID. The server might also process this query by first searching for all customers with the first name of "Jane" and the last name of "Block," and then searching for the rows of the reservation table that have the same account ID.

Query operations are handled by special programming languages, of which Structured Query Language, or SQL, is the most widely used today. The query asking for all the movies that Jane Block has reserved would look like this in SQL:

```
select movieTitle from Customer, Reservation
    where Customer.accountId = Reservation.accountId
    and lastName='Block' and firstName='Jane'
```

The query consists of a request to display (select) the movie title for those reservations that have the same account ID as a customer whose last name is "Block" and first name is "Jane." You will learn all about SQL queries in Chapter 9.

FIGURE 1.5

Reservation Table Showing Relationships Between Customers and Movies

Schema: `Reservation (accountId, movieTitle)`

accountId	movieTitle
101	Annie Hall
165	The Thirty-Nine Steps
101	Animal House
453	Annie Hall

History of Database Systems

In the earliest days of computers, data were stored on media such as paper tape, punched cards, and magnetic tape. People could access these data only in the order in which they were stored. The earliest information-management efforts therefore centered on structuring information in files and finding efficient ways to put that information in order by one or more attributes.

In the early 1960s, the first general-purpose database management systems were introduced—with great success. The Integrated Data Store (IDS), developed by Charles Bachman at General Electric, was a major impetus behind the development of the first standard data models by the Conference on Data Systems Languages (CODASYL). Bachman also introduced methods for precise specification of data models. The development of larger and less expensive disk drives and memories made it possible for people to store vast quantities of data on computers and to improve access to that information.

In the middle to late 1960s, IBM introduced a product called the Information Management System (IMS) that added data communication capabilities to large-scale databases. The company's collaboration with American Airlines led to the development of the Sabre airline reservation system—the first database system to support large numbers of concurrent users and networks for database access.

All of the major computer manufacturers produced successful database systems in the early 1970s. The study of database systems also became a major academic and research area. E. F. Codd introduced the relational model, which formed the foundation of database theory. C. J. Date published his first book [Date75] on relational databases in 1975. Peter Chen showed how diagrams could be used to describe data with his Entity-Relationship model. You will learn about Entity-Relationship models in Chapter 4.

The relational model catalyzed significant interest among businesspeople and researchers. By the late 1970s, it was challenging the large commercial database systems for primacy in the market. The work of the System R group at IBM showed that relational databases could provide the flexibility that applications required—without sacrificing performance. In particular, this group demonstrated the effectiveness of client-server models, showed that databases could handle large numbers of concurrent users and vast amounts of data, and proved that automatic optimization of user queries could enhance database performance.

The early 1980s saw the emergence of several software companies that developed and sold relational database systems. Earlier, computer manufacturers had developed database systems. Now, companies such as Oracle, Ingres, Sybase, Informix, and others showed that it was possible to develop hardware-independent systems with no sacrifice in performance. These companies played a major role in the emergence of a large, independent software business that served commercial markets. The 1980s also witnessed the advent of the PC, as well as the PC-database systems Dbase, Paradox, and others.

In 1985, a consortium of database companies published the first standard for SQL. The standardization of data definition and data manipulation languages boosted the credibility of the fledgling database software industry. Data managers could now afford to buy reliable relational-database software for their companies.

The 1990s saw relational database systems rise to dominate the market. Oracle has become the second largest software company in the world, and IBM's DB2 product has driven the company's own non-relational database software out of the market. Vast amounts of research—both industrial and academic—have pushed the quality and applicability of the relational model far beyond anyone's expectations.

Current hot topics in database systems include object-oriented databases, distributed databases, and databases that store geographic and multimedia information. With the continued advance of the Internet, the World Wide Web, and wireless computing devices, we can expect to see database technology reach new milestones as well.

INTERVIEW

Photo courtesy of Elsa Dorfman.

PHILIP GREENSPUN
Applications of Yesterday's and Tomorrow's Internet

In the mid-1990s, Greenspun founded the Scalable Systems for Online Communities research group at MIT and spun it out into a $30 million (revenue) open-source enterprise software company. The ArsDigita Community System software package is best known for its support of public online communities, such as photo.net, which started as Philip Greenspun's home page and grew to serve 150,000 users educating each other to become better photographers.

CURRENT JOB I'm retired, but every other semester I volunteer to teach "Software Engineering for Web Applications" (6.171) at MIT. After class, I use any questions that the students might have had to improve the online textbook that we use for 6.171, http://philip.greenspun.com/internet-application-workbook/

FIRST JOB I was 14 years old and computer programming was one of the few occupations where a young kid could earn a reasonable salary. My first programming job was writing Fortran code for Pioneer Venus in 1978 at NASA's Goddard Space Flight Center.

EARLY YEARS OF THE INTERNET Throughout the 1980s and early 1990s, I built collaborative computer applications that ran over the network (Ethernet and ARPAnet in the early years). These never went very far because they would only run on one kind of computer. Furthermore, all the users of the application had to have the same kind of computer and operating system. The sight of NCSA Mosaic running on a Unix workstation in 1993 was a revelation: Here's something that can make these multiuser applications practical.

My first Web project was a simple 210-page book with 250 photographs: *Travels with Samantha*. By making the book commentable I discovered what makes the Web more powerful than print: the ability to represent multiple perspectives gathered from the readers. The photographs in the book spawned a lot of questions about photography. I built database-backed systems to make it easier for me to answer readers' questions, but it turned out that Reader A would answer Reader B's question without any intervention on my part. My site became an accidental online community.

ON BUILDING APPLICATIONS A word processor is great for a novelist and a spreadsheet is great for an engineer working by herself but by and large the most useful applications of computers are those that facilitate people working together.

The desktop applications that we see every day are built by teams of 10–20 programmers at a tiny handful of companies such as Microsoft. By contrast, custom collaborative information systems are demanded by virtually every group of people working together in a modern organization. None of these applications are as famous or widely used as Microsoft Office, for example, but collectively they occupy a lot more programmer and user time.

RELATIONAL DATABASES AS A TOOL FOR TODAY'S IDEAS Every project that I've worked on since 1993 has involved an RDBMS! On photo.net, for example, the Oracle RDBMS is used to support user registration, content management, user comments, discussion forums, and site administration. Having everything in one database makes it easy to produce a page showing all contributions from a particular user. This is important for establishing accountability in an online community.

> **"A word processor is great for a novelist and a spreadsheet is great for an engineer working by herself, but by and large the most useful applications of computers are those that facilitate people working together."**

CHAPTER SUMMARY

This chapter gives an overview of the field of information systems, including how information systems and databases contribute to the economy, how databases represent information, what roles people fulfill in information systems, and how database systems enhance software applications.

Businesses rely on database systems to store crucial information, to maintain its accuracy, and to make the information readily available. Managers analyze this information and use it to make operational and strategic decisions. The growth in revenues of database software companies testifies to the economic importance of information systems.

Database system developers make a clear distinction between the way information is used and the way it is stored. They thus have created easy-to-maintain systems and robust, flexible applications. The client-server architecture provides an additional layer of independence between the database systems that store the information and the software applications that use it. A database management system (DBMS) comprises data, its structure, and software. The software supports access to the data, modification of its structure, protection and security for the system, and interaction with database client applications.

People who work with information systems are specialists. They may be users, database designers, applications developers, Web designers, or database administrators. No one person needs to know everything about a system, and each specialist can contribute in his or her own way.

Database systems are exerting an enormous impact on the World Wide Web. A large percentage of Web content is stored in such systems, and Web servers act as database clients. The development of software that supports Web-database interaction is a major theme in this book.

A relational database system (RDBMS) represents information as a collection of tables. A row in a table represents a single object of a specific type. A column represents an attribute of an object. The contents of a table are the set of all objects of that type.

Current strategies for designing and developing leading-edge information systems come from many years of industrial and academic research and development. Today, the relational model dominates the database industry, and specialists expect it to continue to do so for years to come.

KEY TERMS

Applications developer. A person who designs and develops applications that extend the functionality of a database system.

Bit. A single unit of information that is either true or false, on or off, 1 or 0.

Byte. A sequence of 8 bits. A single text character is stored in one byte.

Client-server system. A system made up of two or more components, in which the client makes requests and the server listens and responds. The client-server interaction typically takes place across a communications network, such as the Internet.

Data. A collection of bits that represent some value or collection of values.

Data model. A description of what kind of information will go into a particular database and how that information will be structured or organized.

Database, or **database system.** A combination of software, data, and computer hardware that implements a specific data model. A database system uses a DBMS and is combined with application programs to create an information system that has a specific purpose.

Database administrator. A person who controls access to the database system, maintains data accuracy and integrity, and monitors and improves database performance.

Database designer. A software professional who specifies information content and creates database systems.

Database management system (DBMS). A combination of software and data storage that provides the means to create and maintain database systems.

End user. A person whose job requires access to the information content of a database system.

Information. Data that have a specific interpretation or meaning.

Information system. A collection of software applications and computer hardware that store and manipulate information.

Instance. An object, or collection of values, in a database system.

Internet. The worldwide network of computers that includes strategies for naming and locating specific computers and transferring information among them.

Query. A request for some of a database's information content.

Relational database management system (RDBMS). A DBMS that implements the relational data model. RDBMSs typically use SQL as their interaction language.

Schema. *See Data Model.*

SQL (Structure Query Language). A standard language for defining the structure of relational databases and manipulating their contents.

Web. *See World Wide Web.*

Web-application developer. A person who develops software that generates Web pages and processes a Web site's information content.

Web-site designer. A person who creates the look and feel of a collection of Web pages.

World Wide Web. The combination of the Internet and a variety of access protocols that enable people to publish, collect, and organize information.

QUESTIONS

1. Describe three different aspects of a typical retail business that require collecting and maintaining information. Describe the basic content of the information that must be maintained.

2. Using a Web browser, connect to the home page of a retail Web site such as llbean.com, amazon.com, or ebay.com. Evaluate the Web page to determine the major categories of information that are being displayed. One category may be a list of links to other Web pages, another might be a list of the top sellers. List three other distinct categories that are included in the page.

3. Using a Web browser, connect to the home page of a Web news site such as nytimes.com, usatoday.com, or zdnet.com. Evaluate the Web page to determine the major categories of information that are being displayed. One category may be a list of links to other Web pages, another might be a list of the top stories. List three other distinct categories that are included in the page.

4. Package shipping companies offer package tracking on their Web sites. You can see examples at www.ups.com or www.fedex.com. Using one of these sites as a reference, describe what information must be kept by the company in order to respond to tracking requests. Describe what the employees of the shipping company must do in order to collect this information and maintain it.

5. What is market basket analysis? How does it differ from the analysis of individual product sales? What information can be extracted from market basket analysis, but not from the analysis of individual product sales?

6. Describe information that is appropriate to be stored in a database for BigHit Video, Inc., as introduced in Section 1. Suppose that the first analysis of its business requirements has concluded that the company needs to keep information about its employees, customers, transactions, stores, and suppliers, as well as about its collection of videos and music. Your assignment is to analyze the information requirements for storing information related to a particular topic. Prepare a list of attributes of your topic that should be kept in a database. For each attribute list the topic, your user ID, the attribute name, the attribute type, and a comment that describes the attribute.

   a. Employees

   b. Customers

   c. Stores

   d. Inventory of videos

   e. Rentals of videos

   f. Sales of videos

7. Consider a database system that maintains information about someone who loves to watch and analyze movies. This person wants to keep track of all of the movies that he has seen and associate a rating (one to four stars) with each review. On occasion, he wants to write a review and keep that in the database.

   a. What information about each movie should be kept in the database? Give an example of the information for a particular movie.

   b. What information should be kept in the database to record the viewing of a movie? Give an example.

   c. Give an example of a report that could be created from this information that shows some aspect of the person's viewing tendencies.

FURTHER READING

The history of the Internet is described in detail in a variety of Web sites and books. Tim Berners-Lee's book *Weaving the Web* [Ber1999] offers many insights. Gregory Gromov's *History of Internet and WWW: The Roads and Crossroads of Internet History* is a Web presentation (http://www.netvalley.com/intval.html) that covers the period from 1995 to 1998. The bibliography lists many other Web sites that you can consult for background. The role of information management in commercial organizations is covered in much more detail in management information systems textbooks such as those by Stair and Reynolds [St2001], Jessup and Valasich [JeVal1999], and Gupta [Gup2001].

Information about the role of database systems and the Internet in the world wide economy can be found on any number of Web sites. Look at www.internetindicators.com and news.com.com for details.

CHAPTER 2

Internet Information Systems

In this chapter, you will learn:

- How Web browsers and Web pages interact
- What HTML is and how it works
- How the Internet supports the Web
- How Web servers interact with database systems
- How information is published in Web sites

You're probably familiar with the World Wide Web. Perhaps you use a Web browser such as **Netscape Navigator** or **Microsoft Internet Explorer** to access various Web sites. And you might use search engines such as Google or Yahoo to find sites of interest. To stay up on the news, maybe you consult the on-line versions of news-media sources such as the *New York Times, USA Today,* or CNN. You may also use e-commerce sites such as eBay or Amazon to compare prices and buy anything from sporting equipment and kitchen appliances to books, CDs, and DVDs. And of course you probably use a variety of Web sites for the sheer amusement or entertainment they offer.

In this chapter, you'll learn how Web sites present information to your browser and how databases provide information content to Web sites. We'll begin with an example of a simple Web page and take a quick look at how Web site designers use the HTML language to present information on such pages. Then we'll consider a simple example how a BigHit Video customer might use a Web browser to buy movies on BigHit's Web site.

The BigHit Video example lays the foundation for understanding the basic features of databases and Web servers. By working with this example, you'll see how information is stored in databases and how a Web server can extract that information for display as **Web pages**.

2.1 COMPONENTS OF THE WEB

Figure 2.1 depicts the basic organization of a typical system that supports the use and maintenance of Web sites. This system consists of three components:

- The **Web browser**, which formats and displays Web pages.
- The **Web server**, which sends Web pages to browsers and lets site visitors enter and request information. The Web server accepts requests from users and either processes the requests directly or sends them on to the remaining system component, the information server.
- The **information server**, which accepts requests from the Web server and uses its stored information to respond appropriately. A database system is a typical information server.

Web browsers are computer programs that run on a user's computer. Microsoft Internet Explorer and Netscape Navigator are the two most prominent browsers, but several others are available.

Web servers are computer programs as well. Web servers can be run on almost any computer, but are typically run on computers that are available for access through the Internet. The Microsoft Internet Information Server (IIS) is a Web server that is distributed with the Windows operating system and is widely used. The most widely used Web server is the Apache server, which is developed and distributed by the Apache Software Foundation. This server is freely available and runs on almost every computer operating system.

An information server is typically a collection of programs that respond to a variety of service requests and provide a way of storing and accessing information. Information servers typically support database system access, through a DBMS such as the Oracle DBMS or the Microsoft SQL Server. A server may also provide access to file storage, multimedia libraries, and other application programs.

A **database server** is a kind of information server. It stores information in the form of database tables. Web servers and other applications connect to the database server and send queries and updates to it for processing. As you'll see in the later sections and in later chapters, the ability to store and retrieve information in database servers is an essential aspect of Web-site development.

2.2 WEB PAGES AND HTML

Figure 2.2 shows the home page for BigHit Video's Web site. For demonstration purposes, we've made this home page a lot simpler than most of the home pages you've

FIGURE 2.1

The Web-Services System

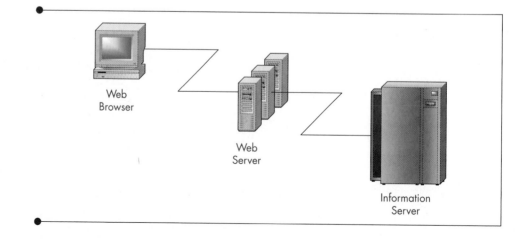

Web
Browser

Web
Server

Information
Server

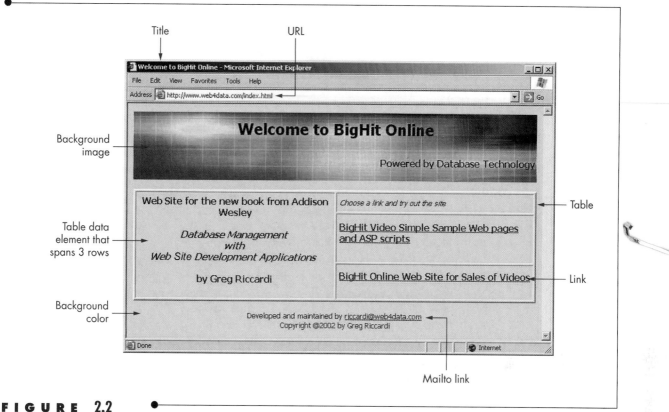

FIGURE 2.2

BigHit Video Home Page

seen on the Web. The figure is annotated to highlight several basic page components: specifically, the title of the page, the address of the page, an image for the background of the header, links to other Web resources, and text that is displayed in a table. You'll build on this basic understanding in later chapters of this book.

Web pages can include simple formatted text as well as images, links to other Web pages, buttons, input elements, and many other features. For example, in Figure 2.2, the title banner at the top of the page is an image. The links to other Web pages are underlined.

A reference to a Web page is represented by a **URL (Universal Resource Locator)**. You can think of a URL as an address or location that tells a browser where to find the requested page. The URL of the Web page shown in Figure 2.2 that is displayed in the browser window at the top of the figure is

```
http://www.web4data.com/index.html
```

      Protocol   Host machine   Name

Try typing this into your browser's address field.

A URL always begins with a protocol description—usually `http` (Hypertext Transfer Protocol), a colon, and two slashes. The protocol description `http://` tells the browser that the referenced document will be found on the Web. If you type the name of a Web page into the browser URL field and omit the protocol, the browser will add it for you.

The rest of the URL, the part after the protocol, contains the name of the host computer and the name of the resource. We use the term *host computer* to refer to the computer that is running the Web server that serves this page—in this case `www.web4data.com`. After the host computer name comes the document name, which in this case is `/index.html`. You'll see more examples of URLs in the next few sections and in Chapter 9.

The World Wide Web Consortium (W3C)

The World Wide Web Consortium, or W3C, was organized in October 1994 to promote ideas supporting the Web and its related technologies. As one of its main activities, the W3C develops recommendations for a variety of Web languages, including HTML (Hypertext Markup Language). The consortium also provides a forum for individuals and organizations to propose Web technologies and to comment on and modify one another's proposals. In addition, the consortium produces technical reports on emerging technologies, open-source software, and recommendations that would interest various standards agencies.

Goals of the W3C include providing a vision for the development of the Web, designing standard technologies to support the Web, and ensuring that Web technologies remain open to use by everyone. Everything developed under the umbrella of the W3C is freely available.

The consortium's work comprises five domains:

Architecture, to develop underlying Web technologies such as **HTTP (Hypertext Transfer Protocol)**; this is the strategy used by browsers and servers to communicate.

Document Formats, to develop and standardize languages such as HTML.

Interaction, to improve people's interaction with the Web.

Technology and Society, to address social, legal, and public-policy concerns related to the Web.

Web Accessibility, to help people with disabilities use the Web.

The consortium publicly carries out and documents its work through the Web site at http://www.w3c.org and through public meetings. W3C's Web site contains a wide variety of documents that describe the organization's goals and activities.

Web developers create Web pages by writing precisely organized instructions in HTML and storing them in files. An **HTML** document contains **tags**—combinations of text and special symbols that delineate sections of a Web page and define their contents and formatting. An HTML tag consists of a tag name and other text surrounded by the symbols < and >. The tags describe the logical structure of the document and how it should be formatted for display in a browser.

Figure 2.3 shows a portion of the HTML document that produced the page depicted in Figure 2.2. You can see the full page definition at the URL given above. The line numbers are not part of the HTML document; they're included here to help you quickly identify particular lines. Line breaks and most spaces have no significance in HTML documents. As with the line numbers, we've inserted line breaks and indentations in Figure 2.3, to make it easier for you to read and understand the code. Many developers use breaks and indentations to make their documents accessible to others who may want to read them. In Figure 2.3, we've highlighted code sections of particular interest.

You'll learn a lot more about HTML in Parts V and VI of this book. For now, you will need just a basic sense of how tags define Web-page elements, create links between pages, and enable site visitors to enter and retrieve information.

Line 1 of Figure 2.3 contains two tags. The first one (`<html>`) has tag name `html` and marks this collection of lines as an HTML document. The second tag on line 1 (`<head>`) has tag name `head` and marks the beginning of the section of code that creates the header, or title, of BigHit's home page. Each tag has a corresponding **end tag** marking the end of the document; for example, `</html>` in line 23 marks the end of the HTML document, and `</head>` in line 4 designates the end of the header section. An end tag has the same tag name as its corresponding beginning tag, except that it's preceded by a slash (`/`).

```
1   <html> <head>
2   <!-- Home page for BigHit Online Demonstration Site-->
3      <title>Welcome to BigHit Online</title>
4   </head>
5   <body bgcolor="#c2e1e7" link="black" vlink="black" alink="black">
6      <font face="tahoma" "size=14px">
7         <center>
8         <!--lines for heading with image omitted -->
9            <table width="715" border=2 cellpadding="5">
10              <!-- lines for first row omitted -->
11              <tr><!-- second row -->
12                 <td><h3>
13                    <a href=" http://www.web4data.com/bighit/index.html">
14                       BigHit Video Simple Sample Web pages and ASP scripts
15                    </a></h3></td>
16                 </tr>
17                 <!--lines for third row omitted -->
18              </table>
19              <!-- lines for footer omitted -->
20           </center>
21        </font>
22     </body>
23  </html>
```

F I G U R E   2.3

Portion of the HTML Document
That Produced Figure 2.2

The rest of the head section contains a comment tag (line 2) and the title of the page (line 3). An HTML comment is a tag that starts with **<!--** and ends with **-->**. Comments are ignored by browsers. The text between the **title tag** (**<title>**) and its end tag (**</title>**) appears in the title bar of the browser window. Line 4 marks the end of the head section.

Lines 5 and 6 create much of the look of the page. Line 5 begins the body, that is, the area of the document that is displayed in the browser window. Line 6 defines the font that is used for text throughout the document.

The **body** tag in line 5 includes its tag name plus additional text that defines several *attributes*. An attribute in an HTML tag is a name and value separated by an equal sign (=). The attribute value is usually enclosed in quote marks (**"**). The quote marks are not always required, but it is good form to use them consistently.

The **bgcolor** attribute defines the background color of the page. The value **#c2e1e7** defines the light blue color of the page as a hexadecimal value, that is, a value in base 16. Hexadecimal numbers are expressed using the digits (0–9) plus letters a–f. Each pair of characters in the value is the intensity of one of the colors red, green, and blue. The red value is **c2**, or decimal 194, and is about 80% of the maximum intensity of 255 (hex **ff**). The green value is **e1**, and the blue value is **e7**. The larger the value for each color, the brighter that color appears. White is **#ffffff** and black is **#000000**.

Tables in HTML are used to organize information into rectangular rows and columns. The middle of the page has a table, defined in lines 9–18, that has two columns and three rows. The source code for the first column has been omitted. Each row of a table is contained within table row (**tr**) begin and end tags, as in lines 11 and 16 for the second row. The table data elements are contained between table header (**th**) or table data (**td**) begin and end tags.

The table element in lines 12–15 contains a reference to another Web page. The **anchor tag** (a) in line 13 defines a link to the document called `bighit/index.html` through the value of the `href` attribute. The text of the link appears on line 14 between the begin and end tags.

When a browser is displaying a Web page, the HTML source document can be seen by selecting `view source` from the view menu bar. At this point, readers might find it very useful to experiment with modifying this page. Feel free to save the document in your own Web site. Then any modifications that you make can be displayed in your browser.

The HTML documents that describe Web pages that are familiar from news and shopping sites are much more complex than that given in Figure 2.3. However, it is possible to understand HTML documents by remembering that the document is divided into simple text and tags and that a tag-end tag pair delimits a portion of the document and describes some aspect of that portion, such as formatting or linking.

For now, it is sufficient to know that Web pages are described by HTML documents and to know the basic structure of HTML.

2.3 WEB AND INFORMATION SERVERS

A Web server is a computer system that responds to requests for Web pages and submissions of information. The server responds by processing requests from the browser and returning a new Web page to the browser. The browser then displays the page for the site visitor. Figure 2.4 illustrates the interaction between a browser and a Web server.

Figure 2.4 illustrates what happens when a site visitor types the URL `http://www.web4data.com/index.html` into his or her browser window. The browser sends the URL to the Web server named www.web4data.com and waits for a response. The Web server recognizes the URL as a reference to a file stored in its file system. It fetches the file from the file system and sends it back to the browser.

With simple requests for Web pages—requests that use URLs such as those you've seen in the above sections—Web servers typically respond by finding an HTML file that satisfies the request and sending the file back to the browser for display. When users ask for Web pages that contain images, multimedia clips, and other non-HTML *objects*, servers also find and return these objects in similar ways.

In large and frequently updated sites, an information server generates much of the content automatically. For example, in the case of the *New York Times* Web site, the

FIGURE 2.4

Processing a Site Visitor's Request for a Web Page

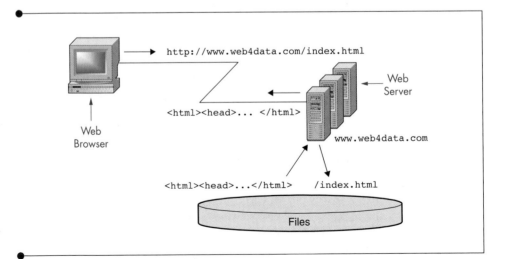

same electronic versions of newspaper articles that are used to create the paper version of the newspaper are also used to generate the Web-site content. If you direct your browser to the *New York Times* home page at http://www.nytimes.com, you'll see that the page includes a date (titled "UPDATED") that indicates the date and time the page was created. The page is not up-to-the-minute, but rather generated periodically—perhaps once or twice per hour. The pages will be updated more frequently when the content changes rapidly, such as during major news events.

Figure 2.5 illustrates how software located in an information server creates Web pages. Some unknown source, a user or a computer program, issues a request to generate a page. In response to this request, the information server generates the HTML text that created the page and sends that HTML document to the Web server to be stored in its file system. The Web server can then satisfy requests for the page in the same way that was depicted in Figure 2.4.

Browsers can also issue requests for Web pages that aren't stored in files, but that the Web server must generate dynamically, such as when a user issues a search request to the Google server. These sorts of requests often include information provided by the user, such as key words or phrases.

Concept

The HTTP Communication Protocol

A *communication protocol* is a strategy that specifies how two or more things are expected to interact. Protocols are used in all kinds of communication. For instance, an expert in social manners would tell us that when two people meet for the first time, the proper protocol involves an exchange of names and a handshake. Joe says his name, Jane says her name, and then they shake hands.

The HTTP protocol is similar in that it specifies what the Web browser tells the Web server and what the browser can expect to receive in response. The details can be found in Web sites and reference books (see the Further Reading section for examples). The basic protocol is for the Web browser to collect information from its user, format it in the proper style, and send it to the Web server. The server receives the information and creates a Web page that is sent back to the browser.

The HTTP protocol specifies in detail how browsers and Web servers interact, especially in cases where the response page must be dynamically generated. You'll hear much more about HTTP beginning in Chapter 11.

FIGURE 2.5

Creating Web Pages from Information Servers

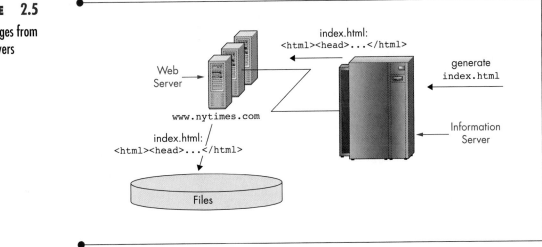

HTTP, or the Hypertext Transfer Protocol, is a protocol (see the Concept box) that is used to create interactions between browsers and servers. HTTP specifies the way that information is transmitted to the server, the way that a program on the server responds to the request, and the way that a response is transmitted back to the browser. The details of HTTP are covered in detail in Chapter 11. The next section provides some examples of how HTTP is used to create interactions between Web servers and databases.

We'll delve much more deeply into the role of Web, information, and database servers in later chapters.

2.4   A CLOSE LOOK AT A SAMPLE WEB SITE

Now that you know the basic structure of Internet information systems, you're ready to look more closely at a simple Web site. The example we'll use is, again, from the fictitious BigHit Video company. In this section, though, we'll limit our exploration to BigHit's on-line video-purchase Web site. We'll begin with an overview of the site's information content and examine how that information is stored in BigHit's database. Then we'll proceed to the Web pages that let BigHit's customers buy videos and the Web-server and database-server activities that support those pages. While you read this section, you should go to the site, login as a new customer and buy some videos. Investigate the behavior of the site and think about how you might improve it.

This section presents a basic overview of the interaction between Web pages and databases. It gives you a glimpse into core concepts that you'll learn more about later, including how information is represented in database tables and how developers use the Structured Query Language (SQL) to extract information from databases and modify a database's contents.

All of the pages shown in this section are dynamically generated by programs that execute within the Web server in response to HTTP requests from the browser. The user is presented with a Web page that has a button or other link. Clicking the button or link initiates a request to the Web server. The Web server responds to each request by executing a specific software application that has been written by the Web developer (your author!) and installed in the Web server. In this section, we look at the activity of each of these programs, one at a time. We refer to these programs as **Web applications** and the resulting Web pages as **dynamic Web pages**.

2.4.1 Information Content of a Web Site

The information in the video-purchase part of BigHit's Web site can be divided into three types: customers, videos, and purchases. *Objects* of these types—that is, information about specific instances of these types—are stored in tables in BigHit's database. Each table defines a specific list of **attributes** for each object; that is, values of characteristics such as the last name of a customer or the date of a purchase.

Figure 2.6 contains sample tables. Note that in the `Customer` table, each customer is represented by a row. Customers' account IDs, names, and addresses are stored in the individual cells of the rows. The table's column headings (e.g., `accountId` and `firstName`) contain *attribute names*. In the `Customer` table, the row containing all the information about Account ID 101 is an *object* of type `Customer`.

Note that in the `Customer` table and in the `Movie` table, no two customers have the same `accountId` and no two movies have the same `movieId`. `AccountId` and `movieId` are *unique identifiers*, or *keys*. The `Sale` table in Figure 2.6 shows how keys store information about connections *between* objects. For example, each row in the `Sale` table connects a customer to a movie. The first row, for instance, records the sale of 1 copy of a VHS tape that has the movie ID number 123 to a customer with

Sample `Customer` Table

Value of attribute `firstName` · `city` attribute · `Customer` object

accountId	lastName	firstName	street	city	state	zipcode	balance
101	Block	Jane	345 Randolph Circle	Apopka	FL	30458	0
102	Hamilton	Cherry	3230 Dade St.	Dade City	FL	30555	3.47
103	Harrison	Katherine	103 Landis Hall	Bratt	FL	30457	30.57
104	Breaux	Carroll	76 Main St.	Apopka	FL	30458	34.58
106	Morehouse	Anita	9501 Lafayette St.	Houma	LA	44099	0
111	Doe	Jane	123 Main St.	Apopka	FL	30458	0

Sample `Movie` Table

`Movie` object

movieId	title	genre	length	rating	dvdPrice	tapePrice
101	The Thirty-Nine Steps	mystery	101	R	29.95	19.99
123	Annie Hall	romantic comedy	110	R	19.95	10.99
145	Lady and the Tramp	animated comedy	93	PG	13.95	7.49
189	Animal House	comedy	87	PG-13	39.95	9.49

Sample `Sale` Table

`Sale` object

accountId	saleDate	movieId	quantity	format	cost
104	Jan 16, 2002	123	1	VHS	19.95
103	Jan 25, 2002	189	2	VHS	39.90
101	Jan 27, 2002	145	5	VHS	99.75
101	Jan 27, 2002	123	3	VHS	59.85
101	Feb 21, 2002	101	1	DVD	19.95
101	Mar 5, 2002	145	1	VHS	9.49
101	Mar 5, 2002	145	1	DVD	23.95

FIGURE 2.6
Sample Database Tables

the account number 104 on January 16, 2002, for a cost of $19.95. We can look in the `Customer` and `Movie` tables to see that Carrol Breaux bought *Annie Hall.*

2.4.2 **A Customer-Information Web Page**

A customer enters BigHit's Web site by typing the site's URL into his or her Web browser. The initial page (not shown here) allows the customer to enter an account ID and a password and click a button to login. A Web application executes in the Web server, validates the login, and generates the customer information page as shown in Figure 2.7.

The page in Figure 2.7 shows information about BigHit's customer Jane Block. The information is organized as a table. In this table, each row corresponds to an attribute from the `Customer` table in BigHit's database. The Web application running in the Web server extracted the values for the attributes from the database through the following request, or *query*, written in SQL. The developer of the Web site wrote the program that created and executed this query.

```
select * from Customer where accountId = 101
```

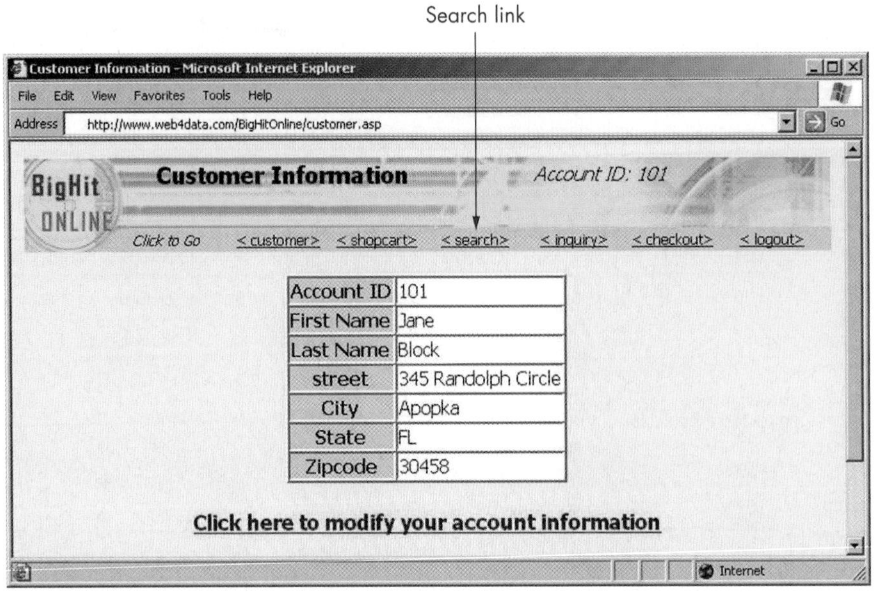

FIGURE 2.7

A Customer-Information Page

This SQL statement asks the database server to retrieve all the attributes for the row of the `Customer` table whose `accountId` attribute has a value of 101.

By clicking on the link at the bottom of the page in Figure 2.7, Jane Block can jump to a page that lets her modify information about herself, such as her address.

Once Jane is ready to purchase videos, she must enter the search area of the Web site to find the videos that she wants to purchase. She does this by clicking on `<search>` at the top of the customer-information page.

2.4.3 Purchasing Videos from a Web Page

To make it possible for customers to buy videos through its Web site, BigHit must provide a way for customers to search for and display information about particular videos. Figure 2.8 shows an example of a page that a customer might see if he or she searched for comedy movies. For now, we are omitting the details of searching for videos. The page includes places where the customer can enter a purchase quantity for each video. In this case, the customer has indicated that she wants to buy one copy of a videotape of *Animal House* and one copy of a DVD of *Duck Soup*.

The page in Figure 2.8 displays information that comes from the `Movie` table in BigHit's database. The Web application extracted the information from the database by creating and executing the SQL query shown below:

```
select movieId, title, genre, rating, dvdPrice, tapePrice
from Movie where genre like '%comedy%'
```

This SQL statement selects specific attributes of the `Movie` table for all rows in which the value of the `genre` attribute contains the word `comedy`. The only attribute from the `Movie` table that is *not* included is the movie's `length`.

The `DVD` and `Videotape` columns of the table in Figure 2.8 contain input elements that let customers indicate how many copies of each movie they want to buy. These elements are connected to the `Buy` button shown at the bottom of the page. When a customer clicks on `Buy`, the Web browser collects the quantity information and delivers it to BigHit's Web server as part of a request to display a new page. For now, we'll skip the details of how the information is delivered. Instead, we'll get right to what happens in the database when a customer submits a request to buy movies.

F I G U R E **2.8**

A Purchasing Web Page

2.4.4 Recording a Purchase in a Database

In processing a customer's request to purchase videos, the Web application records the purchase in the database; presents a receipt to the customer; and, of course, initiates billing and shipping of the videos. Figure 2.9 shows a sample receipt. The table at the top of the page gives an overview of the purchase and includes the total cost of the two videos that customer Jane Block has purchased. The table at the bottom lists the details of the two videos the customer has purchased.

To create this receipt, the Web application must first add the details about the sale to the `Sale` table in the database. (See the third table in Figure 2.6.) That is, when the customer hits the `Buy` button, the Web application lets the database know that account ID 101 has purchased one copy of the VHS version of movie 189 and one

F I G U R E **2.9**

A Receipt Generated by a Web Site

copy of the DVD version of movie 987. The last two rows of the `Sale` table are repeated below:

accountId	saleDate	movieId	quantity	format	cost
101	Mar 5, 2002	189	1	VHS	9.49
101	Mar 5, 2002	987	1	DVD	23.95

The Web application tells the database to record this information in the table by creating and executing the following two SQL statements, one for each new row:

```
insert into Sale values (101, 'Mar 5, 2002', 189, 1, 'VHS', 9.49)
insert into Sale values (101, 'Mar 5, 2002', 987, 1, 'DVD', 23.95)
```

Once the database server processes these SQL statements, the Web application can extract the information for the receipt. You might have noticed, however, that the information in the table at the bottom of Figure 2.9 comes from more than one database table. Specifically, the title and price come from the `Movie` table; and the format, quantity, and total cost come from the `Sale` table. Note, too, that both tables in the receipt include the customer's account ID. The ability to draw data from different database tables and combine them into one table is one of the valuable features of SQL.

SQL provides a way of combining two or more tables with a single select statement. The following statement shows one way of getting the information presented on the page.

INTERVIEW

JAKOB NIELSEN
Business Benefits of Usability

Jakob Nielsen is Principal of Nielsen Norman Group, a think tank focusing on human use of technology and on how to make technology easier to use. *Internet Magazine* wrote about this author of *Designing Web Usability*: "Long regarded as the 'king of usability,' Jakob Nielsen is the man people turn to when they want to know what makes a good Web site."

CURRENT JOB Except for the "business deals" and "manage my team" parts of my current job description, I am doing almost the same today as I did in my first job twenty years ago: running studies with users and developing methodologies and guidelines to improve the usability of user interfaces and hypertext systems.

FIRST JOB I studied CS at Aarhus University in Denmark. They hired me the day I graduated as a researcher and assistant professor.

SUCCESS ON THE INTERNET Usability is very important, even though it's obviously only one of the issues that determine success on the Internet or com-

puters in general. Price is another very important parameter: If an e-commerce site has too high prices, people won't buy. Fulfillment costs are a third important matter: If it costs more money to send out an order than you make from that customer, then the site will never be profitable, no matter how easy it is to use.

USABILITY AND THE BOTTOM LINE All usability can do is increase the amount of usage and number of sales; it can't make the sales profitable if the company's cost structure is wrong. However, I should add that usability can decrease the cost of customer support substantially by making it less likely that users make mistakes and more likely that

```
1  select Movie.movieId, Movie.title, Sale.format, Movie.dvdPrice,
2      Movie.tapePrice, Sale.quantity, Sale.cost
3  from Movie, Sale
4  where Movie.movieId = Sale.movieId and Sale.accountId = 101
5      and Sale.saleDate = 'Mar 5, 2002'
```

Each output row is made of attributes from a row of the `Movie` table and a row of the `Sale` table (highlighted text on line 3), where the `movieId` values match (highlighted text on line 4). Further, we are asking for only those rows in which the account ID is 101 (customer Jane Block) and the date of the sale is March 5, 2002. These are exactly the rows needed to print the receipt. This is quite a complicated SQL statement. You can be sure that once you've studied SQL statements in Part IV of this book, you'll find this one easy to read and understand.

As you might imagine, a Web site that handles video sales is quite a bit more complicated than what we've covered here. You'll learn more about the details of such sites in Part VI of the book. In addition, you'll get a closer look at SQL and other aspects of manipulating database content in Part IV.

In the next chapter, we'll turn to the first steps in developing an information system: determining the information required and creating precise specifications for each type of information.

they can find the answers to their questions on their own. Similarly, usability can reduce those parts of the fulfillment costs that relate to shipments that go to the wrong address or that have to be returned because the customer didn't understand the product correctly based on the information on the Web site.

USABILITY AND THE SOCIAL PERSPECTIVE
Usability is also very important from a social perspective, if we want to include all members of society in the world of the future. For example, it is hard to get a good job these days if one cannot use a computer, and most office jobs involve some use of the corporate intranet. If the design doesn't work well for users with disabilities, then an employee with a disability will not be able to do well in the job. Similarly, for government Web sites, it should be politically unacceptable to release a design that senior citizens have a hard time using— whether for the simple reason that all the text is tiny or because the user interface is too confusing.

USABILITY AND THE CUSTOMER
Poor usability definitely drives people away. Life is too short for difficult Web sites. Users have been burned enough

"For the masses of e-commerce sites, the fact remains that they do the majority of things wrong from a usability standpoint... Life is too short for difficult Web sites."

in the past by bad sites, so most of them have concluded that if a site is too difficult on the first few pages, then it will probably not be worth an extended stay. So they leave. Leaving is the one thing that's easy on the Web. E-commerce uptake is much depressed because of bad design. For example, consider the list of 207 design guidelines for e-commerce user experience which I published recently (www. nngroup.com/reports/ecommerce). In analyzing a group of mid-sized e-commerce sites, we found that they only followed 37% of the usability guidelines on average. The biggest sites scored better: For example, Amazon.com complied with 72% of the usability guidelines, which is a very good score—you can never expect any site to do everything I say since there are always some special considerations on any Web site. However, for the masses of e-commerce sites, the fact remains that they do the majority of things wrong from a usability standpoint. We tested a total of 496 attempts by people to use e-commerce sites, and the users succeeded in accomplishing the tasks in 278 cases, for a success rate of 56%. Thus, e-commerce sites should be able to approximately double their sales if only they were easier to use.

CHAPTER SUMMARY

The World Wide Web comprises information stored as HTML documents, Web browsers, Web servers, and information servers. People use browsers to access the Web and navigate among various Web sites and pages. Each time an individual types a URL into the browser and hits the Enter key or clicks on a link or button, the request goes to a server for processing. The Web server accepts requests from users and either processes the requests directly or sends them on to an information server for processing.

A Web page is defined by an HTML document and displayed by a Web browser. HTML uses tags to delineate sections of a Web page and specify how those sections will be formatted once they're displayed.

Web servers form the center of the Web system. Servers receive requests for pages and other Web objects and deliver those objects to browsers. Servers also receive requests for information processing and either perform the processing or deliver it to a separate information server.

Web pages include forms, defined by a variety of tags, that let users enter information that the Web browsers can then send to a server for processing. Web pages typically use forms for specifying key words for searching and entering personal information.

An information server is a computer and software system that stores, retrieves, and processes information on demand for other systems. Information servers are independent of Web servers and may be used by any other computer system. Much of the complexity of creating and maintaining Web sites is located in information servers.

A database is a collection of information organized into tables. Each row of a table defines an object of a specific type. Columns of tables represent the attributes of the objects. The SQL language lets programs extract information from database tables.

KEY TERMS

Anchor tag `<a>`. An HTML tag that defines a reference to another Web page.

Attribute. A name-value pair in an HTML tag that specifies some information about the tag. Also a column of a database table.

Browser. *See Web browser.*

Database server. An information server that stores information in a database system and responds to requests to retrieve, store, and modify that information.

Dynamic Web page. An HTML document that is generated by a Web server in response to a request from a browser.

End tag. Any one of the HTML tags that starts with `</` and marks the end of the part of the page described by the corresponding begin tag.

HTML (Hypertext Markup Language). A standard method of describing Web pages that is used by Web browsers and Web servers.

HTTP (Hypertext Transfer Protocol). A method of requesting and transferring Web objects between browsers and servers.

Information server. A computer and software system that stores, retrieves, and processes information on demand for other systems. Information servers typically support database system access. A server may also provide access to file storage, multimedia libraries, and other application programs.

Microsoft Internet Explorer. A Web browser developed by the Microsoft Corporation that is available for computer systems that use Microsoft Windows operating systems. Internet Explorer is well integrated into the Windows environment.

Netscape Navigator. A Web browser developed by the Netscape Corporation that is available for almost all computer systems. Navigator is part of the Netscape Communicator package that includes a mail reader, a Web page editor, and other tools.

Tag. A name and other text surrounded by `<` and `>` that describes the meaning of a part of an HTML document.

Title tag `<title>`. An HTML tag that defines the title of a page that is displayed in the browser's title bar.

URL (Universal Resource Locator). A text string that describes the location of a Web page, image, or other Web artifact. A URL may also describe the location of an information service that collects or publishes information.

Web application. A software program that is executed by a Web server to respond to a request from a browser.

Web browser. A graphical computer program that displays Web pages and provides interaction between users and Web servers.

Web page. An HTML document that can be displayed by a Web browser.

Web server. A software system that runs on one or more computers and provides access to Web pages and information services. The server supports a variety of protocols that allow browsers to find and display Web pages and provide information to information systems.

QUESTIONS

1. Use your Web browser to look at the site of the Web Accessibility Initiative (WAI) of the World Wide Web Consortium (http://www.w3c.org/WAI). Use this site to answer the following questions.

   a. What is the purpose of this initiative?

   b. What characteristics of typical Web pages are difficult to understand for people with visual disabilities?

   c. What characteristics of typical Web pages are difficult to manipulate for people with limited motor skills?

   d. How does the WAI propose to make the Web more accessible to people with limited motor skills?

   e. Choose one of the major WAI working groups. What are its mission and goals?

2. Describe how you can personalize your Web browser to control the fonts and colors of displayed pages.

3. What is a URL? Give an example. Then identify the protocol, the name of the host computer, and the document name in your example.

4. What is the difference between a static Web page and a dynamically generated Web page? Give two reasons why a Web-site designer would create static pages. Give two reasons why a designer would create dynamic pages.

5. Go to your favorite Web search engine (e.g., www.google.com) and search for information on Web servers. Write a brief description of how you think the search engine stores its information and how it finds Web pages that satisfy your search criteria.

6. Consider the sample database tables of Figure 2.6. What additional attributes should be added to each table to support the online sales application?

   a. What attributes should be added to the `Customer` table?

   b. What attributes should be added to the `Movie` table?

   c. What attributes should be added to the `Sale` table?

7. The online video sales example of Section 2.4 does not allow the customer to enter a method of payment. How would you add this capability? Be sure to include which pages and tables would be modified and what additional processing would be required.

PROBLEMS

8. Copy the Web page of Figure 2.2 to your own Web directory. Make the following modifications and turn in the URL of your new pages.

   a. Change the title of the page in both the title bar and the heading so that it includes your own name.

   b. Replace the background image of the heading table with an image that you prefer.

   c. Change the links in the right-hand column of the table so that they point to favorite pages of yours.

   d. Modify the page so that the footer includes a reference to your own name and e-mail address.

9. Write an HTML document that uses a table to create a header with an image on the left and a page title on the right. Make sure that the page title appears both within the page and in the header of the browser window.

10. Use an HTML editor such as FrontPage to create a home page for the Web site that you will develop while studying this book. Include links to interesting pages and an appealing color scheme and images.

FURTHER READING

Much of the information about the Web is accessible on the Web, especially on the W3C site (http://www.w3c.org). Many excellent books on HTML are available, including Musciano and Kennedy [MuKe00] and Lehnert [Leh02]. The interaction between the Web and data-bases is the subject of books for both professionals and inexperienced, first-time developers. Look at Friedrichsen [Fri01] for an example of building Web sites using Microsoft development tools.

PART II

Designing and Specifying Information Systems

Now that you have a solid understanding of what you are studying and why, you are ready to start learning the details of how to create high-quality information systems.

In this section you will learn how to identify the information content of database systems and how to create detailed and precise description of that content. After studying these two chapters, you will have a thorough understanding of how to analyze the requirements for systems and prepare a description of those requirements that can serve as the basis of communication between users and developers.

Chapter 3 introduces the idea of a *data model*, which is a precise description of the information content of a database system. You will learn how to recognize the various types of components of a data model. The most important aspect of a data model is that, if created properly, it can be used to build a useful database system.

Chapter 4 continues the presentation of data modeling by introducing the Entity-Relationship (E-R) model, which is a graphical style of specifying information content. E-R modeling is a very effective tool for achieving accurate data models.

After studying Chapters 3 and 4, you will be ready to create your own databases, and ultimately to design Web sites that use databases.

Representing Information with Data Models

In this chapter, you will learn:

- How databases are created
- How to select information to include in your database
- What data models are

- How data models help you specify what kind of information will go into your database and the way it will be organized
- What certain important data-modeling terms mean and why understanding them is vital for building a database

As you saw in Chapter 1, database designers create a *data model* to describe what kind of information will go into a particular database and how that information will be structured or organized. To create a data model, designers interview people who work in the organization that wants the database built, and they analyze the company's existing documents and information systems. Once the designers learn what kind of information the company wants to put in its database and how it wants that information organized, they can then create a data model and use it to build the actual database. In this chapter, you'll learn about a number of different kinds of data models.

In planning a database, it's important to create an accurate model of the information that will go into it. If you make mistakes in your data model, or include too much or too little detail, your database won't work the way you want it to. Making errors during the data-modeling stage would be similar to building a house without first creating or reviewing an accurate diagram of the exterior and interior structure or compiling a list of the materials you want to use. The key is to build a data model that describes all the information you'll want to include in your database, and nothing that it won't need.

3.1 DATA MODELS

Let's consider BigHit Video's database needs. In order to conduct business, BigHit Video must keep track of its videos, rentals, customers, orders, employees, purchases, and stores. Clearly, the company's success hinges on the quality of its information management. The activity that's most obviously crucial to BigHit is the management of rentals: knowing which customer has which video, how much each customer owes, and when the videos are due. Nevertheless, the company has to attend to many other activities, such as keeping track of employees and paying their wages, and purchasing videos for the stores.

BigHit's database designers must translate their understanding of BigHit's database needs into a data model that is written down and circulated to users and developers. The company's managers, application designers, and database designers can study the data model and consider the impact and benefits of various possible information representations.

But what are data models, exactly? In this section, we consider a variety of different ways to describe the structure of databases, how users can view the contents of databases, and how the information will be stored in database systems.

3.1.1 Types of Data Models

A *data model* describes the structure of a database's information content. There are three important kinds of data models, each of which meets the unique needs of different individuals who use or work with a particular database system:

- A **conceptual data model** describes a system in terms that its users will understand such as a diagram that displays the main kinds of objects and their relationships. Information system developers use conceptual models for the initial specification of a database and for communication with users. In fact, once it has been documented, the conceptual model often serves as the contract between an organization and the database developers it hires. As soon as the two parties agree on the conceptual model, the developers build a system that correctly implements this model. This chapter takes a closer look at conceptual modeling.

- A **logical data model** specifies the structure of a database system. For a relational database, the logical data model is a collection of table definitions. Once the developer of the system documents this model, he can use it to create the actual database. The database server uses the logical data model to accumulate and maintain information in the database. Client applications use the model to request access to the database.

- A **physical data model** describes the way in which a logical data model will be represented in storage. The physical model of a relational database is generated automatically from the logical data model. As you will see in Chapter 11, database designers and administrators can modify the physical data model by specifying where certain database objects are stored, how they are stored, and how users might access the information.

3.1.2 Database Schemas

A **schema** is a precise description of the structure of information in a database system. A logical data model provides a schema for a relational database system. However, a database system serves a variety of different kinds of users, each with their own requirements. Each different kind of user of a database system must be presented with a schema that is specific to their requirements.

Databases present different schemas to different users. These schemas can be divided into three levels: the external level, the logical level, and the internal level (see Figure 3.1).

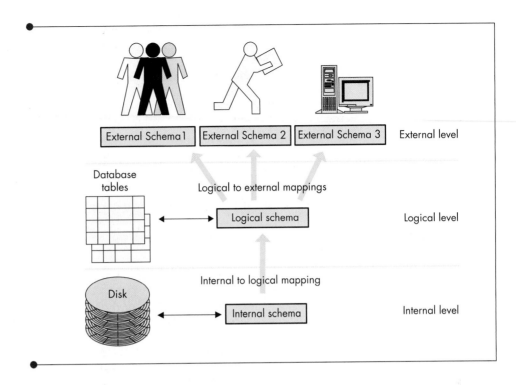

Database end users interact with the system at the *external level*. They see special **external schemas** that give each class of users a view of the database that is tailored to their needs. As illustrated in Figure 3.1, general users, such as people looking at a store's Web site, get one external schema; for example, a list of movies available for sale. Other users, such as the store manager, get a second schema; for instance, daily sales information. An accounting program that prepares statistical reports on annual sales gets a third schema that produces exactly the information needed by that program.

The *logical* level includes the **logical schema**, which sees a relational database as a collection of tables. At this level, the database system maps information from the logical schema to each of the external schemas. Database developers can make changes at the logical level without causing any noticeable effect on the external schemas.

At the *internal* level, the computer sees the database as a collection of files and software. This level supports the logical view of the data. By modifying the internal schema, database administrators can change the contents and structure of the files and improve the system's performance or reliability.

The division of the database system into these three levels enables both developers and users to work within their own levels without having to know the details of the other levels, and without having to respond to changes in the other levels.

3.2 DISCOVERING AND SPECIFYING INFORMATION REQUIREMENTS AND TERMINOLOGY

No database is successful unless the information it provides is (1) important to its users and (2) accurate and complete. However, users may have difficulty specifying their needs at the beginning of the database-development process. For this reason, information system developers often use what's called the "discovery" process to determine the users' requirements.

To discover information requirements, information system developers usually interview people in the organization and analyze current documents and computer systems. Armed with this information, they create a data model that describes what are known as the *objects of interest* that must be included in the database, the attributes of those objects, and the kinds of operations that users should be able to perform.

Attributes are the characteristics that a user wants to see represented in the database. In BigHit's case, attributes would include relevant customer characteristics such as name, address, videos rented, and so forth—but not height, hairstyle, or other characteristics that simply aren't useful to BigHit.

As an important step in this process, developers determine the vocabulary that the users employ to describe their business. The developers then incorporate this terminology into their data model. Utilizing the users' vocabulary often makes it much easier for users to adopt the final database system. In addition, it facilitates communication between users and developers—a crucial factor in the system's ultimate success.

What might the discovery process look like for BigHit Video? The database developer might collect documents such as customer applications, rental receipts, employee time cards, store schedules, and video purchase orders. These information sources would provide insights into BigHit's objects of interest. The developer could then interview employees to gather additional details. Interviews would also reveal how employees and managers view and define many of the company's activities, such as the ways that clerks interact with customers and the system for handling the physical videos when they are returned after rental.

3.3 ORGANIZING INFORMATION

Once you've identified the kind of information you want in a database, it's time to determine how you might organize that information. As you've seen, a **conceptual schema** specifies the content and structure of information that will go into the final database. Ideally, this schema helps users and developers communicate about the desired database and employs the users' vocabulary in a precise way. By reading the schema, users can understand what information will be stored in the system and developers can grasp what they need to do to build the actual system. Once users and developers have written and agreed on the conceptual schema, members of each group can feel confident that they're working toward the common goal of producing a useful database system.

To learn how information in a database is organized, you also need to understand some technical-sounding terminology. Let's explore these concepts below.

3.3.1 Entities, Entity Classes, and Attributes

A database represents characteristics of the objects of interest that the user has identified as important. For example, suppose the user has identified a specific customer as an object of interest. Examples of characteristics of that object might be her first name "Jane" and her last name "Block." In database terminology, objects of interest are called **entities**, and their characteristics are referred to as **attribute values**.

Entities can be further categorized into distinct **entity classes**. All the entities in a particular class share certain attributes. For example, BigHit Video's database contains a `Customer` entity class in which each entity shares the attributes `lastName`, `firstName`, and `address`, among others.

You can think of an entity class as the set of all possible entities of one type that could be represented in a particular database. For example, the `Customer` entity class is the set of all people who might become BigHit Video customers. Of course,

Understanding the Fonts in This Book

You may have noticed that certain words in this book—such as "Customer" and "lastName" in the preceding paragraph—are typeset in a fixed-width (monospace) font. This is done to clearly differentiate the *names* of entities, classes, and attributes from the rest of the text. However, *references* to entities will be typeset in the normal font because they're not the entity names. We might mention a customer who is represented by a row of the Customer table. That is, a customer is a real person whereas Customer is the name of a table in a database.

BigHit's *data model* would not list all the company's existing customers. Rather, it would describe the *kind* of customer information the company would want to manipulate once it began using its database—this is the entity class. The actual database would contain representations of people who have done business with the company; that is, people who are indeed customers—these are the entities.

A key early step in data modeling is to name and describe the entity classes that will be represented in the intended database. Table 3.1 illustrates this task by providing the names and brief descriptions of important entity classes for BigHit Video.

Table 3.1 Some of BigHit Video's Entity Classes

Entity Class	Description
Customer	A customer of the business
Video	An item in the rental inventory
Employee	A person who works in one or more stores
PayStatement	A record of the wages paid to an employee
TimeCard	A record of a block of time worked by an employee at a store
Store	One of the retail outlets of BigHit Video
Rental	The rental of a video by a customer for a specific period and cost
PurchaseOrder	A request to purchase an item
Supplier	A company that sells items to BigHit Video

A Convention for Naming

The convention used for names in this book is consistent with the naming convention adopted in Java, a language used for Web site development. The name of an entity class or attribute consists of a descriptive noun or noun phrase. The first letter of the name is capitalized if it is the name of an entity class; it is lowercase if it is the name of an attribute (a *field* in Java terminology). The first letter of each subsequent word is always capitalized. No underscores are used in names and there are no spaces. Whenever the name of a class or attribute is used in the text, it will appear in a fixed-width (monospace) font.

Each entity *class* has specific attributes or properties that describe the characteristics of that class. The attributes themselves exist somewhat independently of the entity class. In particular, some attributes might appear in more than one entity class. For example, the attribute `lastName` is likely to represent an attribute of both BigHit's `Customer` entity class and its `Employee` entity class. Table 3.2 lists some (but not all) attributes of the entity classes shown in Table 3.1. Each attribute is characterized by a name, a type, a **constraint** or restriction on its values, and a description. Table 3.2 also shows a sample value for each attribute. The combination of type and constraint define the set of possible values (the **domain**) of each attribute. An attribute value must be a member of the domain of the attribute.

Each of the attributes in lines 1–8 of Table 3.2 is a **single-valued attribute**; that is, the attribute has as a simple value and is not described as a collection of values. The first six attributes have character strings as their values. Each has its own form, however, as described in the *Restrictions on Values* column. This column specifies *domain constraints*, or restrictions on the attributes' values. The `title` attribute (line 1) has no restriction on its length or form, but both `lastName` and `firstName` (lines 2 and 3) can have no more than 30 characters. The attribute `email` (line 4) can have no more than 50 characters, and the value of attribute `rating` (line 5) must come from one of the listed values. The `ssn` attribute (line 6) is constrained in length to 9 characters and may contain only the digits 1–9. Attributes `accountId` and `numberRentals` (lines 7 and 8) must consist of integers (whole numbers such as 1094 or 25).

Table 3.2 BigHit Video Attributes

	Attribute	Type	Restrictions on Values	Description	Sample Value
1	title	String	Unbounded	The title of an item	Annie Hall
2	lastName	String	30 characters	The last name of a person	Block
3	firstName	String	30 characters	The first name of a person	Jane
4	email	String	50 characters	The e-mail address of a person	jblock@web4data.net
5	rating	String	'G', 'PG', 'PG-13', 'R', 'NC-17', 'NR'	The rating of a movie	PG-13
6	ssn	String	9 digits (0-9)	A Social Security number	211009008
7	accountId	Number	4 byte integer	The identifier of a customer account	101
8	numberRentals	Number	4 byte integer	Number of rentals for a customer	6
9	otherUsers	Set	Set of strings of 30 characters	Names of other people authorized to use this account	Jeremiah Block Kenneth Block Georgette Heyer
10	dateAcquired	Composite	month, day, year	Date that a video was acquired	January 23 2002
11	address	Composite	2 strings of 30 characters, one string of 2 characters, and one string of 9 digits.	An address that consists of a street, city, state, and zip code	345 Randolph Circle Apopka FL 30458

Storing Information in Tables

Tables 3.1 and 3.2 are examples of two-dimensional structures used to store information. Like this book, relational databases also contain tables. Each table has a fixed number of columns, and each column has a name. Each row has a value for each column, and the meaning of these values comes from the meaning of the column. The values in a row go together to provide information about a single idea or entity. This structure is exactly the same one that relational databases use to store information.

The `otherUsers` attribute in line 9 of the table is a **multivalued attribute**; that is, each value of the attribute consists of a set of strings. The value of this attribute is a collection of the names of people other than the customer who are allowed to use this particular customer's account. This attribute has multiple values in the sense that each name in the set of strings is a value of the attribute. The sample value consists of three names, each shown on its own line. The name "Jeremiah Block" is a value for `otherUsers`, as is "Kenneth Block" and "Georgette Heyer."

The values of `dateAcquired` and `address` (lines 10 and 11) are *composites*; that is, they contain a particular number of values, each with its own type and restrictions. A `dateAcquired` value (line 10) comprises three fields: `month`, `day`, and `year`. The `address` attribute (line 11) is also a composite and contains a `street` and `city` (30-character strings), a 2-character `state`, and a 9-digit `zipcode`. An attribute with composite values is called a **composite attribute**.

3.3.2 Key Attributes

Most entity classes have one or more **keys**; that is, properties that uniquely identify a single entity among all entities within that class. Table 3.3 shows a broad range of examples.

Table 3.3 Examples of Key Attributes

	Entity Class	Key Attribute	Comment
1	Customer of BigHit Video	account ID	This value is assigned by the BigHit Video information system when a new customer is entered into the database.
2	Working person in the United States	Social Security number	Each person who is allowed to work in the United States must have a Social Security number. The U.S. Social Security Administration assigns these numbers on request and ensures that no two people have the same number.
3	Online customer of BigHit Video	e-mail address	Each online user of the BigHit Video rental system must provide an e-mail address to uniquely identify this user.
4	DVD video	UPC number (bar code)	Items that are available for retail sale in the United States have unique Universal Product Code (UPC) numbers. These numbers are assigned by the Uniform Code Council.
5	Book	ISBN number	Every commercially published book has a unique identifier that is assigned by the publisher in cooperation with the International Standard Book Numbering Association.

The first line of Table 3.3 shows a key attribute whose values are artificial; that is, there is no inherent meaning in the value of an account ID. These values are important only in that each one uniquely identifies a single entity within the relevant entity class. The account ID attribute of a BigHit Video customer is completely internal to our system and should be created automatically by the information system whenever a new customer is entered.

A major difference between Social Security number (line 2) and account ID is their origins. The Social Security number of a person is assigned by the U.S. government. The values are external to our information system and are provided to us by the individual customers.

The e-mail address of line 3 is different in that the key value not only uniquely identifies the customer, but also has meaning: In this case, it can be used to contact the person. Hence, the value of this key attribute is not artificial, but rather represents a characteristic of that customer. We must recognize, however, that e-mail addresses change frequently. One characteristic of a good key is that it is not likely to change. Thus, we might want to create an artificial key for the BigHit Online customers.

The UPC and ISBN numbers of lines 4 and 5 of Table 3.3 are a blend of artificial and meaningful keys. As explained in the Concept box, an ISBN number identifies the publisher of a book and the book's title—two meaningful pieces of information. It also contains a check digit, information that has no meaning. In the case of UPC symbols for videos, the 12-digit number includes an identification of the publisher of the video. Similarly, driver's license numbers in Florida contain the driver's year of birth, and automobile identification numbers contain paint codes and other manufacturer information. However, just as with Social Security numbers, when we store ISBN or driver's license numbers in a database, the values are assigned externally to the information system and cannot be changed by it.

The key of an entity class may consist of more than one attribute. For instance, suppose we don't include the ISBN number in our data model, but instead have two attributes: the publisher ID and the title ID. In this case, neither of these attributes *in*

Identifying Products with Bar Codes

Below is the bar code from the back of the book *Principles of Database Systems with Internet and Java Applications*. At the upper left is the UPC symbol, which consists of the bar code and the UPC number below it. Below the UPC symbol is the ISBN number, For books, the UPC symbol contains 13 digits. The first three digits are always 978. The next 9 digits are the ISBN number, and the last digit is a check digit, which bar-code scanners use to promote reliable recognition of bar codes.

An ISBN (International Standard Book Number) uniquely identifies each book. The number consists of 10 characters divided into four parts that are clearly separated by spaces or hyphens. The parts consist of the group identifier (one digit), publisher identifier (three digits), title identifier (5 digits), and check digit (one character). The ISBN check digit is not included in the bar code.

ISBN 0-201-61247-X

Identifying symbols of the book *Principles of Database Systems with Internet and Java Applications* by Greg Riccardi.

itself is an appropriate key. The publisher ID is not unique, because any one publisher may publish many books. The title ID is not unique because each publisher uses the same range of values. It is only the *combination* of the two attributes that uniquely identifies a single book.

Artificial keys may be created even when some combination of meaningful attributes forms a key. For class `Customer`, for instance, we might find that the combination of `lastName`, `firstName`, and `address` forms a key. In spite of this, the `accountId` attribute was added to the class `Customer` as its key. A single attribute key makes it easier to enforce uniqueness. As you will see in Chapter 5, it is also much easier to represent relationships with single attribute keys.

Whenever a table has more than one key, we designate one as the **primary key** and the others as secondary keys. If `Customer` has `accountId` as one key and the combination of `firstName`, `lastName`, and `address` as another key, we would declare that `accountId` is the primary key and the other key is secondary. If possible, the primary key should be a single attribute and its value should be unlikely to change. We choose `accountId` as the primary key of `Customer` because it is a single attribute and because `address` is likely to change.

Some caution is in order in designating our choice of keys. Declaring that a combination of `lastName`, `firstName`, and `address` forms a key of `Customer` restricts the entities that we can store in the database. Suppose two people with the same first and last names and the same address want to be customers of the store. This multi-attribute key declaration will require that they be considered the same customer. In this situation, the data model may limit the applicability of the resulting information system. There will be no way to represent these unusual customers in the database.

The declaration of key attributes for entity classes is a fundamental part of building a data model. A database contains representations of many entities within each entity class. By declaring a particular attribute as a key of that class, you enable your database to ensure that no two entities in a class will be identical.

3.3.3 Constraints on Attribute Values

You've seen that each entity in a class must have a value for its key attribute that is different from any other entity in that class. In this sense, the values of entities' key attributes are *constrained*, or limited.

For example, the `ssn` attribute of the `Employee` class is a single-attribute key. No two employees may have the same value for the `ssn` attribute. This limitation reflects the uniqueness of Social Security numbers. Because two employee entities represent different people, and different people have different Social Security numbers, the `ssn` attribute is an appropriate key for the `Employee` class.

In the case of the `Customer` class, the `accountId` attribute is an artificially created key attribute. No other customer attribute besides `accountID` is guaranteed to be unique. For example, two customers might have the same name or address. Declaring the **key constraint** for the attribute specifies that the database must guarantee the uniqueness of the attribute values among the entities in that particular class. For example, if a BigHit employee tried to add a new customer with the same `accountId` value as another customer, the database system would reject the new customer.

Table 3.4 shows the attributes and constraints of three entity classes for BigHit Video. In this table, the constraints on the attributes are variously described as `key`, `not null`, and `derived` and `currency`. The constraint `not null` requires that the attribute have a value; that is, its value cannot be empty or an utter absence of information. `Derived` means that the attribute is not entered by a user, but rather is derived—or calculated—from some other information. The `currency` constraint of the `balance` attribute means that the value is appropriate to represent a monetary value. This constraint would be interpreted differently in different countries. In the

Table 3.4 Entity Classes, Attributes, and Constraints

Entity Class	Attribute	Constraints or Further Description
Customer	accountId	Key
	lastName	Not null
	firstName	
	address	
	balance	Currency
	otherUsers	
	numberRentals	Derived
Video	videoId	Key
	title	Not null
	genre	
	dateAcquired	
	rating	
PayStatement	datePaid	
	hoursWorked	
	amountPaid	

Concept

Attributes and Entity Classes

It is the database designer's responsibility to distinguish between attributes and entity classes. For example, the `address` attribute of a customer is a composite attribute with several attributes of its own. A designer might decide that an address is an attribute of a customer entity, or that it's an independent entity. For example, the designer could argue that the most important thing to the user about an address is that it represents a lodging or place of business and hence is *independent* of the people who live or work there. Alternatively, the designer could argue that the address is simply an attribute of a person that can be used to communicate with that person. In this case, the lodging or place of business would have no special relevance in the final database. The BigHit Video example running through this book treats customer addresses as attributes.

Unfortunately, there is no simple rule to use in making these distinctions. A designer must decide whether an attribute should be an entity on the basis of whether it is sufficiently important to the database's users or independent of other entities.

United States, `currency` would have two decimal digits and thus be able to represent dollars and cents. In Japan, where the smallest denomination is one yen, `currency` would be an integer with no decimal digits.

3.3.4 **A Closer Look at "Null"**

You can also think of entities as *instances* of an entity class. Each entity is distinguished by its attributes' values. Tables 3.5 and 3.6 show four entities of class `Customer` and five entities of class `Video`, respectively.

Table 3.5 Entities of Class `Customer`

account Id	last Name	first Name	address				other Users	number Rentals	balance
			street	city	state	zip code			
101	Block	Jane	1010 Main St.	Apopka	FL	30458	Joe Block, Greg Jones	3	0.00
102	Hamilton	Cherry	3230 Dade St.	Dade City	FL	30555		1	3.47
103	Harrison	Kate	103 Dodd Hall	Apopka	FL	30457		0	30.57
104	Breaux	Carroll	76 Main St.	Apopka	FL	30458	Judy Breaux, Cyrus Lambeaux, Jean Deaux	2	34.58

Table 3.6 Entities of Class `Video`

videoId	dateAcquired	title	genre	length	rating
115	1/25/98	The Thirty-Nine Steps	mystery	101	PG
145	5/12/95	Lady and the Tramp	animated comedy	93	G
90987	3/25/99	Elizabeth	costume drama	123	PG-13
99787	10/10/97	Animal House	comedy	87	PG-13
123	3/25/86	Annie Hall	romantic comedy	110	PG-13

As you've seen, each entity's attribute has a value. In Tables 3.5 and 3.6, a value may be the special value **null**, which is represented as an empty field. For example, the values of the `otherUsers` attribute in the middle two rows of Table 3.5 are null.

It is not always easy to know what "null" means. In this case, because the attribute is a set of values, *null* refers to the empty-set value. That is, there are no other users for this customer. In other cases, "null" may mean any one of the following:

- **Not applicable:** The attribute is not applicable to this entity and hence should not have a value.
- **Missing:** A value of the attribute exists but is not recorded.
- **Unknown:** The value of the attribute may be either missing or not applicable.

For example, consider an entity class `Person` that includes attributes `spouseName`, `height` and `phoneNumber`. The attribute `spouseName` of an unmarried person would be null because that attribute is not applicable to an unmarried person. But a null value for a person's `height` attribute means that the value is missing, because every person has a height. A null value for a phone number may arise for a number of different reasons. Perhaps that person has no phone (not applicable). Or perhaps he or she does have a phone but the value did not get recorded (missing). The null value in this case could also mean that the person refused to give a phone number, or that the number originally given was wrong or has changed. In this case, the null value would not give enough information for the database users to interpret the attribute.

3.4   RELATIONSHIPS AND RELATIONSHIP TYPES

Now that you've learned about entities and attributes, let's broaden the scope to see what happens when entities are related to one another. Each entity in a database has associations, or **relationships**, with other entities. For instance, whenever a BigHit customer rents a video, a relationship would be created in BigHit's database between that customer and that video. The relationship ends when the customer returns the video.

> **Concept**
>
> ### A Simple Definition of Data Model
>
> A data model contains the definition of the structure of the information in a database and provides us a way of understanding the meaning of the data. A data model does not determine which entities are represented in the database or which relationships exist among those entities.
>
> The data model simply describes the possibility that information of certain specific kinds may be stored in the corresponding database.

Part of data modeling entails defining what kinds of relationships will be important to the database user. Equally important, data models designate the *possibility* of a relationship by defining *relationship types*. An *actual* rental relationship occurs between a specific customer and a specific video. The collection of all *possible* rentals between customers and videos forms a relationship *type*. By defining a `Rents` relationship type as part of the data model, BigHit's database developer lays the foundation for the final database to record *actual* rental relationships *as they occur*.

3.4.1 Modeling Relationship Types and Instances

As you've seen, a relationship between two entity instances in a database represents some association between them. For instance, two people can be associated as parent and child (a parent-child relationship) or as husband and wife (a marriage relationship). Each relationship that occurs is an *instance* of a **relationship type**.

Moreover, each entity plays a specific **role** in the relationship. If two people are associated by a parent-child relationship, one person is the parent and one is the child. That is, the relationship is "parent-child," and the roles of the individuals are "parent" and "child." The name of a role expresses the function of a particular entity in a relationship.

A relationship type represents the *possibility* that one entity in a database may have an association with another entity. A relationship *instance* occurs when a specific entity has an *actual* association with another specific entity. For example, the parent-child relationship type is defined as the possibility of an association as parent and child between an entity in class `Person` and another entity in class `Person`. However, this relationship type doesn't specify that one particular, actual person is the parent of any other specific, actual person.

How are relationship types designated in a data model? Each relationship-type name consists of a verb phrase that can be used in a sentence. For example, you could say, "A customer may rent a video," to express BigHit's `Rents` relationship type. From this, "Jane Block rents 'Annie Hall'" represents a relationship *instance* of the `Rents` relationship *type*. BigHit's database also uses roles as in "Jane Block is the renter of 'Annie Hall'" or "Jane Uno is the manager of store 3."

Constructing such expressions facilitates the discovery process, because this kind of sentence reveals the presence of a relationship type. When a database developer or user employs such a sentence to describe facts about the company, that person is expressing the existence of a relationship type.

Relationships often have their own attributes. For example, a marriage relationship could have a `weddingDate` attribute. BigHit's `Rents` relationship type has the attributes `dateDue`, `dateRented`, `amountPaid`, and `amountDue`.

3.4.2 Relationships Are Not Attributes

Identifying relationships between entities is a major function of any data model. Indeed, relationships receive special attention during the model-building process and are treated separately from entity classes. To maintain flexibility in the way relationships are ultimately implemented, developers follow a strict rule: No *relationship* should be specified as an *attribute*.

The discovery process often unearths characteristics of entities that appear to be attributes but that should actually be relationships. By identifying these situations during the discovery process, database designers improve their chances of creating a more accurate data model—and, ultimately, a more useful database. The following illustration shows examples of how relationships sometimes masquerade as attributes.

Consider Figure 3.2, which shows a rental receipt from BigHit Video. The receipt includes information about the rental, the customer, and the video. The account ID information identifies a specific customer: Jane Block. We've determined that a customer is a separate entity, so presence of the account ID in this document, actually indicates the presence of a relationship between the customer and the rental. The customer's name and address are attributes of the `Customer` entity class, not of the `Rental` entity. Similarly, the video ID and title are attributes of a related `Video` entity. Analysis of this receipt reveals that a `Rental` has *attributes* `dateRented`, `dateDue`, and `cost`, and *relationships* to a `Customer` and to a `Video`. The other fields that appear on the receipt are not attributes of the `Rental` class.

3.4.3 Constraints on Relationship Types

Like attributes, relationship types also have constraints. A **cardinality constraint** on a relationship type puts restrictions on how many of one entity can be related to one entity of the other, and vice versa. For example, when we say that a relationship type is *one-to-one*, we mean that one entity may be related to *at most* one other entity through this relationship type. For instance, the marriage relationship type is one-to-one because each person may be married to at most one other person.

As you've seen, each relationship has two roles. Each cardinality constraint is applied to a single role within a relationship. Thus, the one-to-one constraint on the

---

FIGURE 3.2

A BigHit Video Rental Receipt

BigHit Video

Rental Receipt

Account ID: 101   **video ID:** 90987   **Date:** January 9, 2002   **Cost:** $2.99

Jane Block
1010 Main St.
Apopka, FL
30458

Elizabeth

Date due: January 11, 2002

> **Concept**
>
> ### Attributes and Relationships
>
> A simple analysis of an entity class may result in the classification of some characteristics as attributes when they more appropriately indicate the presence of a relationship type with another class. For example, the Social Security number (`ssn`) and employee name both appear on a pay statement. This fact might lead us to add those characteristics to the entity class `PayStatement` as attributes. We also know that these characteristics are attributes of the `Employee` entity class and that `ssn` is its key attribute. Thus, adding these characteristics to class `PayStatement` as attributes makes them part of both classes.
>
> But this data-modeling process is still incomplete, because attributes of one entity class (`Employee`) are attached to another class (`PayStatement`). We have a duplication of information in the model and the data model does not clearly identify which entity class really owns the Social Security number and employee name. Of course, we know that the Social Security numbers and names are assigned to people and not to pay statements.
>
> We must recognize that the presence of an `ssn` attribute in class `PayStatement` is an indication that class `PayStatement` is *related* to class `Employee`. Therefore, we must remove these attributes from `PayStatement` and define a relationship between the two classes instead.
>
> A crucial step in data modeling is to review user requirements and compare them with what is represented by the model. As in this case, we must make sure that the data model is consistent with the user's intent and that all attributes and relationships make sense in the user's context.

marriage relationship can actually be thought of as two constraints. The role of wife and the role of husband are each constrained to have cardinality no more than one. In other words, for a particular woman, the set of people for whom she is the wife has cardinality no more than one. And for a particular man, the set of people for whom he is the husband has cardinality no more than one. Together, these constraints form a *cardinality ratio constraint* on the `Marriage` relationship type.

There are three types of cardinality ratio constraints:

- **One-to-one.** An entity in either role may participate in at most one relationship, and hence have at most one related entity.
- **One-to-many.** An entity in one role may have at most one relationship, but an entity in the other role may have any number of relationships.
- **Many-to-many.** An entity in either role may participate in any number of relationships.

In addition to the above three constraints, relationship types may have what are known as minimum and maximum, or min/max, constraints. A *maximum cardinality constraint* restricts the *number* of relationships of a particular *type* that an entity may have. For instance, if BigHit wanted to ensure that no customer rented more than 10 videos at a time, it would have to specify the cardinality of the renter role to be no more than 10.

Constraints may also specify a *minimum* number of relationships for a particular entity. A constraint that specifies whether at least one relationship must exist for each entity is often called a *participation constraint*. That is, if the cardinality is "at least one," then each entity must participate in the relationship type by being related to at least one other entity. For instance, a rental must have a relationship to a customer. This is often called a **mandatory participation constraint**. A video, however, does not have to be rented. That is, it may not be related to any rental. In this case, the video has an **optional participation constraint** on its relationship with rentals.

Figure 3.3 illustrates entities related in a one-to-many way through the `Owns` relationship type that represents the ownership of videos by stores. The oval on the left lists the `storeId` attributes of some `Store` entities. The oval on the right lists the `videoId` attributes of some `Video` entities. The rectangle in the center contains a square for each ownership relationship between a store and a video. As the figure illustrates, each of the five relationships connects exactly two entities—one from each class. The first relationship associates store 3 with video 90987 (a copy of *Elizabeth*). This relationship represents the fact that store 3 owns that copy of *Elizabeth*.

The `Owns` relationship type is one-to-many because each store may own many videos, but each video is owned by one store. Each store may have relationships with many videos, but each video has at most one relationship with a store. The store that has no relationships illustrates that participation in this relationship type by stores is optional. Store 5 owns no videos. Each video, however, must be owned by a store and participation by videos in the relationship type is mandatory. Each of the five videos has a relationship to a store.

Figure 3.4 illustrates the many-to-many relationship cardinality ratio, through a collection of 13 `PreviouslyRented` relationships that record the history of rentals. The first relationship records the fact that customer 101 (Jane Block) rented and returned video 123 (*Annie Hall*). The `PreviouslyRented` relationship type is many-to-many because each video may be checked out many times by many different customers. The many-to-many cardinality ratio of the `PreviousRental` relationship type allows each customer or video to be related to many objects of the other class. However, each relationship object (represented here by a black box) still connects exactly two entities. "Customer 101 previously rented video 123" is a relationship and "Customer 101 previously rented video 145" is a different relationship.

Figure 3.4 reveals other interesting information as well; for example, that customer 102 (Cherry Hamilton) rented and returned video 101 (*The Thirty-Nine Steps*) twice, as illustrated by the fourth and fifth relationships.

3.4.4 Higher-Degree Relationships

Up to this point, our discussion has suggested that all relationship types are binary. That is, that each relationship connects two entities and each relationship type connects two entity classes, or one class with itself.

But a company may also have some multiparty, or higher-degree relationships. For instance, a BigHit Video store purchases a video from a supplier. This purchase represents a three-way relationship among the store, the supplier, and the video. Figure

F I G U R E   3.3

A Set of One-to-Many
Relationships of Type **Owns**

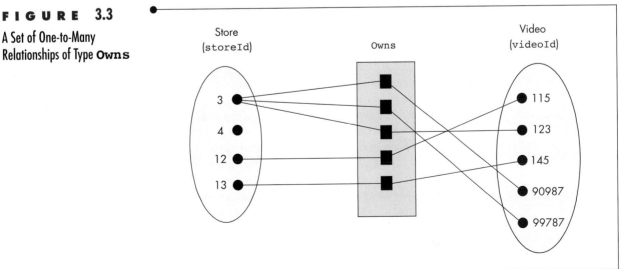

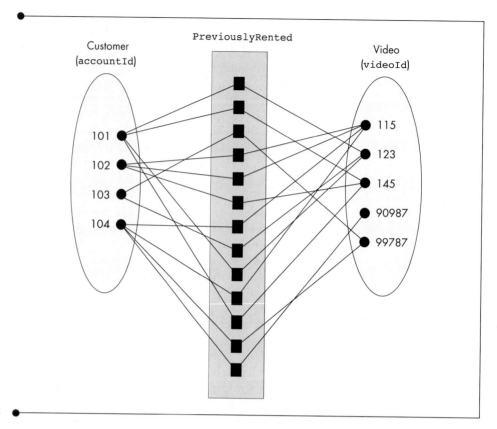

FIGURE 3.4

A Set of Many-to-Many
Relationships of Type
`PreviouslyRented`

3.5 illustrates this three-way relationship type, which we call `PurchasedFrom`. The number of entities that are linked by an instance of a relationship type is called the *degree* of the relationship type. `PurchasedFrom` is a relationship type of degree 3.

The five relationships shown in Figure 3.5 include the purchase of video 548 from supplier Acme for store 3, and the purchase of video 3087 from supplier Mpx for store 12. Each relationship is represented by a black square and 3 connecting lines.

Cardinality constraints are even more confusing with non-binary relationship types. The `PurchasedFrom` relationship type has three cardinality constraints. It is

---

Concept

Relationships, Relationship Types, and Databases

Figure 3.5 emphasizes the difference between relationships, relationship types, and databases. Each `PurchasedFrom` relationship connects exactly three entities and thus represents a single fact about the purchase of one video by one store from one supplier. The `PurchasedFrom` relationship type represents the possibility that videos are purchased by stores from suppliers. The presence of the `PurchasedFrom` relationship type in our data model tells us that we need to be able to record these relationships. Finally, a database contains a particular set of relationships. Each `PurchasedFrom` relationship stored in the database represents a fact about the purchase of a video for a store from a supplier. The database is the repository where information about video purchases is recorded.

A relationship is a fact about real entities, a relationship type is a part of a data model, and a database is the place where particular relationships are organized and recorded.

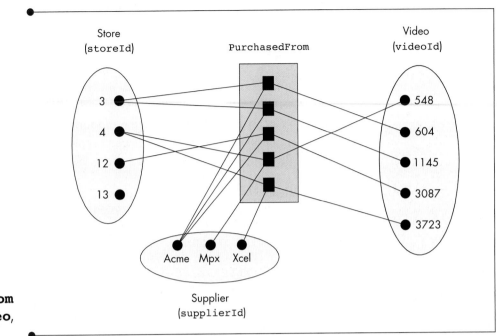

FIGURE 3.5

Three-Way Relationships of Type **PurchasedFrom** Between **Store**, **Video**, and **Supplier**

to-one with `Video` because each video is purchased exactly once from one supplier for one store. It is to-many with `Store` and with `Supplier` because each store purchases many videos from many suppliers and each supplier sells many videos to many stores. Hence, we see that each video has exactly one line in the figure and the stores and suppliers have many lines.

Although relationship types of higher degree occur naturally, they are quite complicated to express and even more difficult to understand and to explain to users. Hence, most developers make the necessary effort to express them as simpler, binary relationship types.

CASE IN POINT: DETERMINING ENTITY CLASSES, ATTRIBUTES, AND 3.5 RELATIONSHIP TYPES FOR VIDEO SALES

The following statement describes some aspects of the BigHit Video information system that was outlined in Section 2.4. The description presents the way that an employee of BigHit Video would understand of the system. The English description may be filled with ambiguities and irrelevant information, together with fairly precise descriptions of real information requirements. This is the type of description that system developers get from their users.

Our job is to analyze the description and make an initial list of entity classes, attributes, and relationship types for the system. We also want to eliminate potential entity classes that are not of interest to the system. Phrases of particular interest have been highlighted in the text below. Different colors are used for different kinds of information.

BigHit Video Inc. wants to create an information system for online sales of movies. People will be allowed to register as customers of the online site and to update their stored information. Information must be maintained about customers' shipping addresses, e-mail addresses, and credit cards. In a single sale, customers will be allowed to purchase any quantity of movies. The items in a single sale will be shipped to a single address and will have a single credit card charge.

A customer will be provided with a virtual shopping cart to store items to be purchased. As each item is selected, it is added to the shopping cart. When the customer finishes shopping, he will be directed to a checkout area where he can purchase all of the items in the shopping cart. At this time, payment and shipping information is entered. Once the sale is complete, shopping cart will be deleted and the customer will be sent a receipt by e-mail.

We must analyze the above description to discover the entity classes, attributes, and relationship types, and also to identify those parts that describe activities rather than information. We also must identify irrelevant information and objects that are outside of the interest of the system.

A simple reading of the description is sufficient to identify entity classes (highlighted in dark pink) `Sale`, `Movie`, `Customer`, and `ShoppingCart`.

Several noun phrases (highlighted in light blue) in the description do not represent entity classes. "BigHit Video, Inc." is the name of the company. Since there is only one entity of this class, it does not need to be included. "People" represents an entity class, but one that is outside the information system. We are only interested in people who become customers. No information will be needed for people who are not customers. "Items" refers to a thing that is purchased and does not identify a new entity class. In essence, "item" refers to a movie.

Attributes of entity classes include those items highlighted in light green. The `Customer` entity class has shipping addresses, e-mail addresses, and credit card information. The description does not make it clear whether a single customer may have many shipping addresses, e-mail addresses, and credit cards. In other words, the description does not specify whether these attributes are single-valued or multivalued. Because the description is not specific, we should consult with an expert at BigHit Video Inc. who is in a position to tell us which of these attributes is multivalued. Of course, BigHit Video is a fictitious company with no personnel. So we must make the decision based on some reasonable analysis. It will be prudent to allow for multiple addresses because people buy for themselves and also buy gifts for others. In contrast, a single e-mail address will suffice. (Can you think of advantages of this decision?) Let's also allow multiple credit cards per customer.

Very little information has been listed to help us specify exactly what attributes are needed for the entity classes, so we need to apply some common sense. For instance, we know that a movie has a title and an identifier, and that a customer has a name and an account ID. Table 3.7 shows an initial list of entity classes and their attributes. You can probably think of more attributes for these classes.

The phrases highlighted in light pink in the description are indications of relationship types that are needed for the information system. The following are some relationship description sentences:

- A sale has exactly one customer.
- A sale has one or more movies with a quantity of each one.
- A shopping cart has exactly one customer and any number of movies with a quantity of each one.
- A customer may make many sales, but can have only one shopping cart.
- A movie can be part of many sales and many shopping carts.
- A sale is shipped to a single address.

From this list of sentences we conclude that the relationship types listed in Table 3.8 are required.

Table 3.7 Entity Classes and Attributes for Online Movie Sales

Entity Class	Attribute	Constraints or Further Description
Customer	accountId	Key
	lastName	Not null
	firstName	
	shippingAddresses	Multivalued composite with components name, street, city, state, zipcode
	emailAddress	
	creditCard	Multivalued composite with components type, accountNumber, expiration
	password	Not null at least 6 characters
Movie	movieId	Key
	title	
	genre	
	length	
	languages	
Sale	saleId	Key
	totalCost	
	dateSold	
	creditCard	Composite with components creditCardNumber and expirationDate
ShoppingCart	cartId	Key
	dateCreated	

Table 3.8 Relationship Types for Online Movie Sales

Relationship Type	Entity Class	Entity Class	Cardinality Ratio	Attributes
Purchases	Customer	Sale	one-to-many	
Includes	Sale	Movie	many-to-many	quantity
Selects	Customer	ShoppingCart	one-to-one	
Includes	ShoppingCart	Movie	many-to-many	quantity

INTERVIEW

MARC CARUSO
Using SQL to Solve Customers' Needs

CURRENT JOB I am a business intelligence consultant, which means that I help companies report and analyze enterprise data.

FROM COLLEGE TO THE WORKFORCE An economics major at Tufts University, I only took a couple computer science courses. I was exposed to Microsoft Access while working my way through school at Ernst & Young LLP, and learned SQL on the job by developing several small database applications. After graduating, that experience prompted me to change careers from finance and accounting to the information technology field.

A RECENT PROJECT One of my projects was to create a Web-based, expense-analysis system for a large networking equipment manufacturer. The goal was to allow the company to manage expenses on a global scale, twenty-four hours a day. In addition to analyzing expense data from the company's general ledger, users also needed to see the detail behind some of the numbers.

Starting with Preexisting Data and Software The client had an existing general ledger system that was based on an Oracle relational database. All the information users required was in this system, but it was at too granular a level to analyze effectively. My task was to transform this data into a format that could be readily accessed by business analysts.

> **"Whether you are a business analyst in the MIS department, or a Java programmer writing software for the Web, chances are you will be required to use SQL often in your career."**

Using SQL to Match a Client's Business Needs For this project, we used SQL to summarize data from the client's general ledger. We then used a custom SQL API to load the data into analysis software. Finally, we used the same API to create real-time SQL calls from the analysis software to the general ledger, which enabled the users to get transaction detail on demand.

The End Result With the help of SQL, we delivered a seamless user interface that relied on the client's existing systems to fulfill a business need. It spared analysts from switching between two applications to view critical data. Whether you are a business analyst in the MIS department, or a Java programmer writing software for the Web, chances are you will be required to use SQL often in your career.

A few phrases in the diagram, highlighted in purple, are about processes or reports. The reference to "checkout area" is to a Web page that is part of the process of selling movies. We need to plan for a way of allowing the customer to specify payment information and confirm the purchase, just as we must have a way to add items to the shopping cart. These procedures will be discussed in later chapters. The reference to a "receipt" is to a document that is produced from information stored in the database. Once the customer has finished the purchase, entities in the `Sale` table of the database will provide the information necessary to create a receipt.

Finally, the reference to purchasing the shopping cart items and deleting shopping carts as part of the sale (highlighted in teal) are also about process, but have significance to the data modeling. From these two facts, we can assume that the shopping cart is deleted when the sale is finalized and that the sale comes from the shopping cart. Thus, the virtual shopping cart acts like a real shopping cart. The customer gets a cart when shopping begins and discards the cart when shopping ends. No customer needs more than one cart at a time. We can conclude that the relationship type between `Customer` and `ShoppingCart` has one-to-one cardinality.

We'll continue the design of this information system at the end of Chapter 4.

CHAPTER SUMMARY

A data model specifies the information content of a system. Many different types of models exist, each with its own purpose. A conceptual model expresses users' and developers' understanding of how the system will work and what it will do. A logical model specifies the structure of the database system and is used to create the actual database. Physical models and representational models give a more detailed specification of how information is stored in computer systems.

Database developers build data models for constructing actual databases. The goal of data modeling is to produce a conceptual description of what information will go into the database and how it will be structured. The data-modeling process exposes design alternatives and enables developers and users to evaluate them. Faulty or incomplete data modeling can make the final database ineffective.

Through the discovery process, developers identify users' needs, the kind of information that should go into the database, and the way in which that information should be structured. Developers discover these things by interviewing the intended users of the planned database and analyzing documents and current computer systems. Developers must translate this information into precise data models. Many of them use the entity-relationship (E-R) modeling method.

An *entity class* represents a collection of similar entities. An *attribute* describes a characteristic of an entity class. An *attribute value* is the value of that attribute for a specific entity in the class. An *entity* is an instance of an entity class. Each entity has a value for each attribute of its class.

A *relationship type* represents the possibility of a particular association between entities. A *relationship* is an *instance* of a relationship type; it occurs when two (or more) entities become associated by the relationship type. Each entity that participates in a relationship has a specific role.

A *cardinality ratio* limits how many of one entity can be related to how many of the other. In a one-to-one relationship type, an entity in either role may participate in at most one relationship. In a one-to-many relationship type, an entity in one role may have many related entities, while an entity in the other role may have only one related entity. In a many-to-many relationship type, an entity in either role may be related to many other entities.

KEY TERMS

Attribute value. The values of a specific attribute for one entity.

Attributes (properties). The characteristics that describe an entity.

Cardinality constraint. A restriction on the cardinality of a role of a relationship. Typical constraints are **to-one**, in which an entity may be related to no more than one entity of the related type, and **to-many**, in which an entity may be related to an unlimited number of entities of the related class. A cardinality constraint may specify a minimum or maximum number of related entities.

Cardinality ratio constraint. A combination of two cardinality constraints, one on each role of a relationship. The three basic types of cardinality ratios are **one-to-one**, **one-to-many**, and **many-to-many**.

Composite attribute. An attribute whose value is composed of a collection of individual fields.

Conceptual data model or conceptual schema. A precise definition of the data requirements of a system that is understandable to both users and developers of a database. This model includes detailed descriptions of data types, relationships, and constraints and is of-ten represented as an E-R model, E-R diagram, or object-oriented model.

Constraint. A limitation on the contents of a database. Data models include constraints on the values of attributes and the cardinality of relationships, among others.

Domain. The combination of type and constraint that defines the set of possible values of an attribute. Each attribute value must be a member of the domain of the attribute.

Entity (instance). An object in the real world that is of interest to the information system.

Entity class. The common characteristics that represent a collection of entities.

External schema. A definition of a user's or application's view of the information content of a system.

Key. A set of attributes of an entity class whose values uniquely identify an entity.

Key constraint. A constraint on the entities of a class that no two different entities can have the same values for a specific set of attributes. This set of attributes is a key of the class.

Logical data model or logical schema. The definition of the information content of a system in a manner that can be used to create a database.

Mandatory participation constraint. A cardinality constraint on a role in a relationship that requires an entity to be related to at least one entity of the related class.

Multivalued attribute. An attribute whose value is a set of values.

Null value. A special attribute value that is different from any value in the domain of the attribute. The meaning of a null attribute value of an entity is ambiguous. It may represent a missing value, one that is unknown, or an attribute that is not applicable to the entity.

Optional participation constraint. A cardinality constraint on a role in a relationship that allows an entity to be related to no entity of the related class.

Physical data model or physical schema. The definition of the information content of a system in physical terms.

Primary key. One of the keys of an entity class that is chosen to identify the entities.

Relationship (instance). An association between two or more entities.

Relationship type. A representation of the possibility that entities of two or more entity classes may be associated.

Role. The function of an entity in a relationship.

Schema. A precise description of one or more aspects of a database system.

Single-valued attribute. An attribute with a single, indivisible value.

QUESTIONS

1. List three reasons why a data model must be created before implementing an information system.

2. What is a conceptual data model? Who is the target audience for a conceptual data model?

3. How do users benefit from complete and accurate data models? How do developers benefit?

4. What is a logical data model? Who is the target audience for a logical data model?

5. How do developers benefit from a logical data model?

6. What is an external schema? How do users benefit from external schemas?

7. What is meant by *discovery* in data modeling? What resources are available to developers in discovering information requirements?

8. Suppose that you are designing an information system for a university. What documents would you use to determine the information requirements?

9. What is the difference between an entity class and an entity? Give an example of each.

10. What is the difference between an attribute and an attribute value? Give an example of each.

11. What is the difference between a relationship type and a relationship? Give an example of each.

12. What is a cardinality constraint? What is a participation constraint? Give an example of relationship types that are one-to-one, one-to-many, and many-to-many. What are the participation constraints on these relationship types?

13. What are the three possible interpretations of the null value for an attribute?

PROBLEMS

14. Consider the following description of an enterprise.

    An auction Web site has items for sale that are provided by sellers. Each item has an opening price, a description, and an ending time. Customers submit bids. The highest, earliest bid submitted before the ending time is the winning bid and the item is sold to the bidder. Each seller must pay the auction company 5% of the winning bid. The auction company wants to be able to analyze the sales behavior of its customers and sellers and so must keep track of all bids and sales.

    a. What entity classes are mentioned in the description?

    b. List seven attributes that will be used in a data model for the auction company.

    c. What relationship types exist between the entity classes of part a?

    d. Give three example entities of each class listed in part a.

15. Create a collection of documents for BigHit Video. Include the following items:

    a. Customer application

    b. Rental receipt

    c. Purchase order

    d. Employment application

    e. Time card

    f. Pay statement

    g. Report on rental activity

PROJECT

16. You will be developing a Web site called the Movie Lovers Web site in stages in this and subsequent chapters. This site is intended for the enjoyment of people who love movies. It should keep a record of movies, actors, directors. It should also keep track of members and allow members to record their movie experiences: dates of viewings, ratings of movies, written reviews, etc.

   a. Draw a sketch of three major Web pages that will be used in your Web site.

   b. For each of the Web pages, list the entity classes that are required to supply the information content.

   c. For each entity class, list its attributes.

   d. Give two example entities for each entity class.

   e. List the relationship types that are required for the entity classes.

FURTHER READING

There are books on data modeling for all levels of readers. Both Muller [Mul01] and Halpin [Hal99] are excellent introductory books. Database textbooks such as Riccardi [Ricc01] and Elmasri and Navathe [ElMa99] devote significant effort to data modeling. More complete treatments of modeling for database professionals are found in Hoberman [Hob01] and Silverston [Sil01].

Data Modeling with Entity-Relationship Diagrams

In this chapter, you will learn:

- What entity-relationship data modeling is
- How to read and draw entity-relationship (E-R) diagrams
- How to represent entity classes, attributes, and relationship types in E-R diagrams
- How to add cardinality and other constraints to E-R diagrams

- How to model video rentals and other BigHit Video information using E-R diagrams
- What inheritance is and how to use it to improve data models
- How to represent inheritance in entity-relationship diagrams

In Chapter 3, you learned what data models consist of and why they are valuable. In this chapter, you'll learn about a special data-modeling method called entity-relationship modeling.

Entity-relationship modeling is a high-level data modeling technique that helps designers create accurate and useful conceptual models. E-R models are best expressed using graphical E-R diagrams. This technique was originally developed by Professor Peter Chen to serve as a tool for communication between designers and users.

Chen recognized the problems that are caused when developers and users fail to understand each other. It is typical for developers and users to think that they each know exactly what the other is thinking. Unfortunately, human communication is not that good. In the presence of misunderstanding, developers build information systems that do not meet user needs. The result is either the total failure of the system that was developed or a major increase in costs as the system is rewritten.

E-R diagrams provide a visual, graphical model of the information content of a system. Developers create E-R diagrams that represent their understanding of user requirements. Users then carefully evaluate the E-R diagrams to make sure that their needs are being met.

Once the E-R diagram has been approved by the user community, the diagram provides the specification of what must be accomplished by the developers. In the presence of accurate models, developers can be confident that they are building useful systems.

61

Without a precise description of the agreement between users and developers, the system is doomed to failure. Our goal, then, is to produce a data model that is understandable to users and that accurately and precisely describes the structure of the information to be stored in the database.

4.1 ENTITY-RELATIONSHIP MODELING

An **entity-relationship (E-R) data model** is a high-level conceptual model that describes data as entities, attributes, and relationships—all terms you encountered in Chapter 3. The E-R model is represented by E-R *diagrams* that show how data will be represented and organized in the various components of the final database. However, the model diagrams do not specify the actual data, or even exactly how it is stored. The users and applications will create the data content and the database management system will create the database to store the content. In this chapter, we'll focus on E-R diagrams; Chapter 5 will take a closer look at how E-R diagrams are represented as tables in a relational database.

This modeling method pays particular attention to relationships—the interactions among entities. Relationships require special treatment in the development of databases, because they are the glue that holds information together and because their realization in relational databases is particularly important. Moreover, an E-R model is usually accompanied by a *behavioral* model, which describes the way that the applications of the information system must behave. Database developers create these two models together.

An E-R model attempts to capture those aspects of the real environment that are necessary for the proper functioning of a business or other system. Not everything about the real environment can be captured by the E-R model. For instance, it will not be possible to design a data model that requires that no employee work more than 40 hours per week. Rules like this one must be enforced through the behavioral model of the system.

The data modeling process is iterative: You start putting some ideas together, then the process reveals some problems in your thinking. So, you go back and rework your ideas. You keep doing this until it all makes sense. In other words, a full, accurate E-R model doesn't just spring fully formed from a designer's mind and appear on paper.

This chapter walks you through a condensed version of the modeling process—including encountering some thinking problems and some dead ends. The primary examples come from the BigHit video rental business. The data model for this business will emerge through a series of decisions and specifications. In more than one case, we will find errors in the model. Fixing those errors will require modifying, or even destroying, E-R diagrams so that the final diagrams represent an accurate view of the video rental business.

As you see these diagrams and draw some yourself, you will recognize the need for E-R drawing tools. Professional information system developers always use E-R diagramming tools. Organizations that are serious about achieving useful systems adopt a variety of software development tools to make their jobs easier and their results more reliable. You can feel confident that your ability to draw these diagrams by hand will easily translate to understanding and using diagramming tools.

4.2 ENTITY-RELATIONSHIP DIAGRAMS

As one important aspect of E-R modeling, database designers represent their data model by **E-R diagrams**. These diagrams enable designers and users to express their understanding of what the planned database is intended to do and how it might work, and to communicate about the database through a common language.

The myriad of styles and conventions for E-R diagramming make it difficult to choose the best one. This book utilizes an acceptable style, but certainly not the only one. Each organization that uses E-R diagrams must adopt a specific style for representing the various components. While studying this book, you should use the style presented by the text. You can be sure that the principles of E-R diagramming are independent of the stylistic details.

4.2.1 Entity Classes and Attributes

Figure 4.1 shows an E-R diagram that describes the entity class `Customer`, as previously shown in Table 3.5. In this E-R diagram style, entity classes are represented by rectangles and attributes by ovals. Solid lines connect attributes to the entity class. Note that the diagram shows only entity class and attributes—it does not describe any particular *instances* of either. The shaded boxes are comments, and would not be parts of the E-R model diagram.

Figure 4.1 illustrates the basic shapes used for describing entity classes and their attributes. In the center of the diagram is the rectangle that represents the `Customer` class. Single-valued attributes `lastName`, `firstName`, `accountId`, and `balance` are shown as ovals with connecting lines. The `accountId` attribute is underlined to show that it is the key of the class.

Additional characteristics of attributes are distinguished by their display. The multi-valued attribute `otherUsers` is shown as an oval whose border is a double line. The derived attribute `numberRentals` is shown with a dashed border.

The composite attribute `address` is shown as the central point of connection for its component attributes `street`, `city`, `state`, and `zipcode`.

You may have noticed that much of the detailed information that you saw in Tables 3.1 and 3.4—such as descriptions of classes, relationships, and attribute constraints—is not shown in Figure 4.1. Instead, this information would be maintained in text form as part of the database specifications, in a table called the **data dictionary**.

FIGURE 4.1

E-R Diagram for Entity Class **Customer**

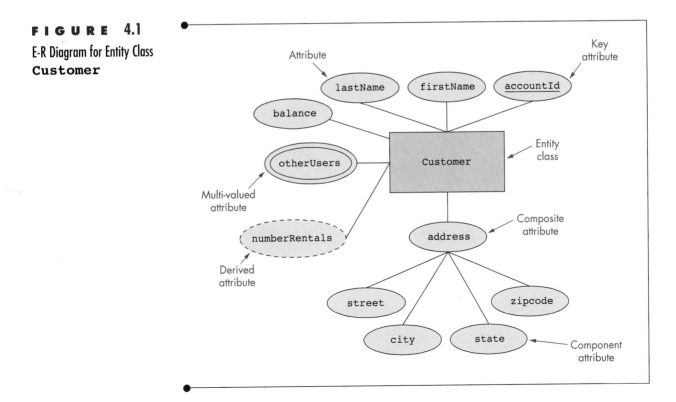

Figure 4.2 shows the E-R diagram for entity class `Video`. It uses the same style as `Customer`. Each of the attributes of class `Video` are simple and single-valued.

4.2.2 Relationship Types and Constraints

Figure 4.3 shows the relationship type `Owns` that connects classes `Store` and `Video`. A relationship type is represented by a diamond and two connecting lines. The name of the relationship is shown inside the diamond. Reading this diagram from left to right yields "a store owns a video." The name of the relationship type is a verb or verb phrase that describes the relationship. The alternate relationship name `IsOwnedBy` is the name of the relationship type when reading the other direction. That is, "A video is owned by a store." You will notice that the attributes of `Store` and `Video` have been omitted.

Additional symbols have been added to the relationship type in Figure 4.4 to express the cardinality and participation constraints of the relationship type. The relationship type is one-to-many. That is, a store may own many videos and a video may be owned by no more than one store.

Cardinality constraints are represented in Figure 4.4 by the symbols `1` and `M`. The symbol `1` in Figure 4.4 means that a video can be owned by no more than one store. The symbol `M` means that a store may own many (zero or more) videos. That is, these

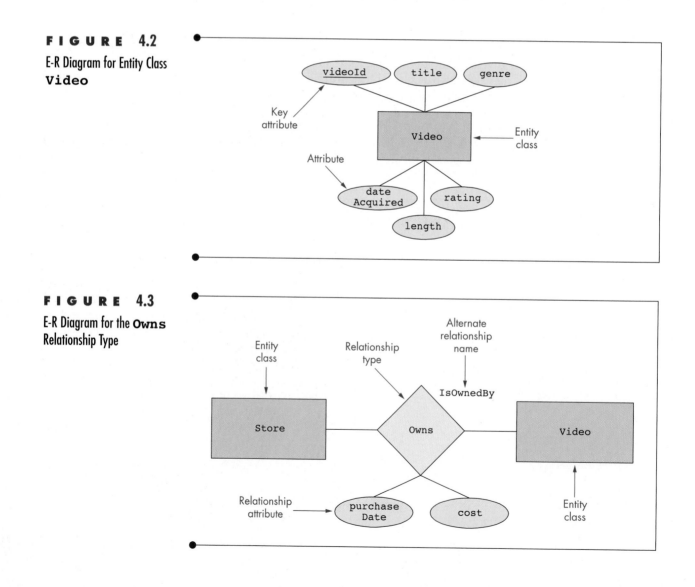

FIGURE 4.2

E-R Diagram for Entity Class
Video

FIGURE 4.3

E-R Diagram for the **Owns**
Relationship Type

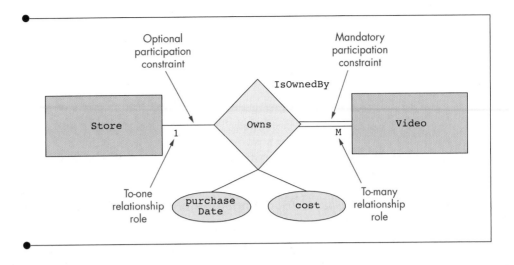

FIGURE 4.4

E-R Diagram for the **Owns** Relationship Type Showing Cardinality and Participation Constraints

two symbols together define the relationship type as one-to-many. The constraint symbols tell you how many entities of the *related* class (the class near the constraint symbol) can be associated with one entity of the *subject* class (the class on the other side of the diamond).

We can best understand the meaning of these cardinality marks by creating sentences to represent the relationship roles. To create such a sentence, name one entity, then the relationship, then the cardinality, and finally the other entity. For example, we could create the following two sentences by reading the diagram from left to right and right to left, respectively:

- A store may own many (M) videos.
- A video is owned by no more than one (1) store.

Again notice that the symbol that tells us how many relationships a store is allowed to have is on the opposite side of the diamond from the store class. The position of the cardinality mark makes it easy to create the sentence that makes the constraint understandable, as shown above.

You've probably also noticed that the constraint symbols can appear either above or below their double lines. They simply must be located near them.

This relationship type also has participation constraints. A store is not required to own any videos, and hence has *optional participation*. A video must be owned by a store and hence has *mandatory participation*.

Figure 4.4 adds these participation constraints to the E-R diagram for the **Owns** relationship type using single and double lines. The line between **Store** and **Owns** is single to specify that a store does not need to participate by being related to (owning) any videos. The line between **Video** and **Owns** (or **IsOwnedBy**) is double to specify that each video must participate by being related to (owned by) a store.

Again we can create sentences to understand the constraints. We add either "may" or "must" to the sentence depending on whether the participation is optional or mandatory. These are the sentences:

- A store may own many videos.
- A video *must be owned* by one store.

The first sentence, about the constraint on stores, has not changed, and the diagram didn't change either, because the line was already single. The second sentence, about the constraint on videos, has changed. The phrase "may be owned by no more than one" has become "must be owned by one." If the cardinality constraint on videos were to-many, the sentence would be "A video must be owned by at *least* one store."

4.3   MODELING VIDEO RENTALS

We are now ready to look at more complex objects and relationships. We will take on the renting of videos by customers. We begin with a description of the classes and relationship types and then produce an E-R diagram.

The rental of a video is an agreement between the BigHit company and a customer that the customer will be given possession of the video for a particular period of time for a particular cost. At BigHit Video, we need to keep track of our videos. We need to know whether the video is currently rented, and if so, who has it and when it is due back.

4.3.1   Modeling Rentals as a Relationship Type

There are two different ways to represent video rentals. The first is to identify the rental as a relationship between a customer and a video, as shown in Figure 4.5. Relationship type `Rents` links classes `Customer` and `Video` in a one-to-many relationship. A customer may rent many videos, but a video can be rented by no more than one customer. Both of the relationship roles have optional participation (connected by a single line) since a customer doesn't have to have any rentals and a video may be unrented, and thus available for rental.

A relationship between the customer and the video is created when the customer rents the video. The relationship is removed when the customer returns the video. This accurately models the movement of the video, the behavior of the customer, and the business rules of BigHit video. The relationship is created when the customer accepts possession of the video. The relationship ceases to be of primary interest to BigHit Video when the video has been returned to the store.

Once the video has been returned by the customer, we will keep track of that previous rental as shown in Figure 4.6. The relationship type `PreviouslyRented` is many-to-many because each customer may have previously rented many videos and each video may have been rented many times. The participations are optional for both customers and videos.

The BigHit information system will create a relationship when a customer rents a video. The relationship will be stored in the database. When the video is returned, that relationship will be removed from the database and a permanent `PreviouslyRented` relationship will be created and stored in the database.

4.3.2   Modeling Rentals as an Entity Class

An alternative view is that a rental is an entity and not simply a relationship. Note that we have been referring to a "rental" as an object of interest. The use of the noun

FIGURE 4.5

E-R Diagram of Relationship Type **Rents**

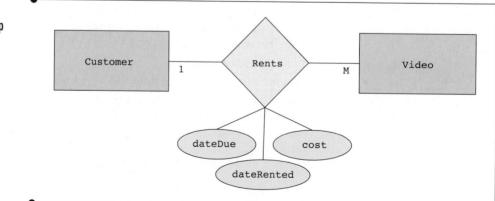

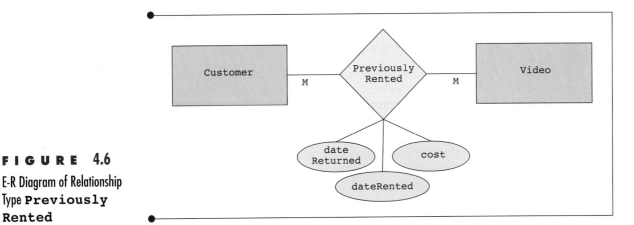

FIGURE 4.6

E-R Diagram of Relationship Type **Previously Rented**

"rental" suggests that we are referring to an entity. You will recall that entity classes are named by nouns and relationship types are identified by verbs. Hence, it is very natural to think of a rental as an entity that has an existence distinct from the customer and video that it connects.

Figure 4.7 shows the `Rental` entity class and its relationship types with classes `Customer` and `Video`. Each rental entity has three attributes: `dateDue`, `dateRented`, and `cost`. The relationship types are called `Has`. This is a name that can be used for a relationship type whose meaning is obvious. These are the relationship sentences for the diagram:

- A customer may have many rentals.
- A rental must have one customer.
- A rental must have one video.
- A video may have no more than one rental.

Thus each rental entity is related to one customer and one video just as it should be according to our understanding of what a rental is.

One difficulty with understanding the meaning of `Rental` entities is the problem of distinguishing between one rental and another solely based on attribute values. That is, what is the key of a rental? None of the attributes is unique and not even all of the attributes together form a unique key. For instance, a customer may rent two different videos at the same time. This may result in two rentals with the same date rented, the same cost, and the same due date. We can only distinguish between the two rentals according to which video each is related to.

We have an entity with no distinguishing attributes that is partly identified by its relationships to other entities. We call this a *weak entity* and class `Rental` a **weak entity class**. Figure 4.9 shows how weak entity classes are shown in E-R diagrams.

Two items in the diagram now have double-lined borders. The border on entity class `Rental` has been doubled to specify that `Rental` is a weak class. The border on

FIGURE 4.7

An E-R Diagram Showing Entity Class **Rental** and Its Relationship Types

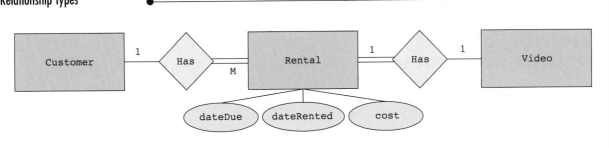

Distinguishing Between Current and Previous Rentals

The cardinality constraint on videos in the `Rents` relationship type of Figure 4.5 shows that we must be modeling current rentals. Each video can have only one `Rents` relationship with a customer. Before the video can be rented by a different customer, the relationship must be deleted so that the video is available for rental.

Obviously a video may be rented over and over. The BigHit Video business depends on collecting money for renting each video many times. However, a major distinction exists between videos that are currently rented to customers and those that have been rented and returned. The record of previous rentals is important for analyzing customer behavior and video usage. However, the current rentals are used to determine where videos are located, who has them, and how much the renters owe in overdue fees. Our data model makes a clear distinction between those two very different relationship types.

The cardinality constraint exposes the distinction between current and previous rentals, and thus demonstrates one of the important features of modeling constraints: Being specific about constraints exposes questions about the meaning of entities and relationships that must be answered in the data model.

Finally, it is worth noting that we can combine the current and previous rentals into a single relationship type, as in Figure 4.8. In this model, a current rental is one in which the `dateReturned` is null. The major problem with this model is that it fails to distinguish between relationships that have a very different meaning and importance to the business, as described above.

This example serves to emphasize that one of the most important goals of data modeling is to accurately express the meaning of information as it is understood by the users of the system. We as developers may prefer the model of Figure 4.8 because it has fewer relationship types. But if it is difficult for users to understand, or if it is inconsistent with the users' understanding of their information, it is not the right model. For BigHit video, Figure 4.8 is less accurate and harder to understand and explain.

FIGURE 4.8

E-R Diagram of a Combined Current and Previous Rental Relationship Type

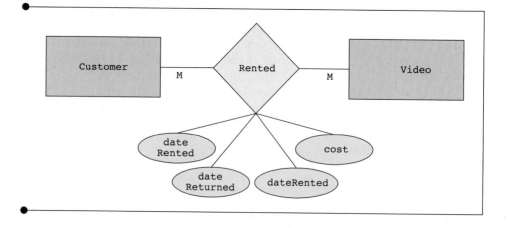

the `Has` relationship type with class `Video` has been doubled to specify that it is the **identifying relationship type** of class `Rental`. This notation means that a rental is identified by its relationship to a video and cannot exist without it. An identifying relationship type is always to-one.

With these two double borders, we have completely specified the nature of the class. No two rentals can be related to the same video because of the cardinality constraint on class `Video`. Thus we can distinguish two rentals by their relationships with videos.

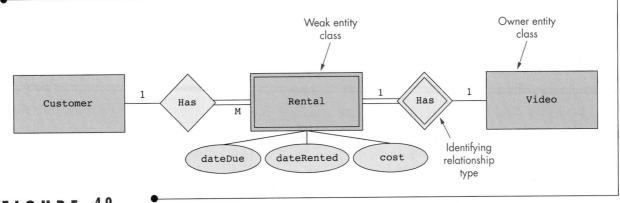

FIGURE 4.9

An E-R Diagram Showing Weak Entity Class **Rental**

The double border on the diamond that relates `Rental` to `Video` also marks `Video` as the *owner entity class*. The related video is considered the *owner* of the rental. Without that relationship, the rental cannot exist. The *key* for a `Rental` entity is therefore the `videoId` attribute, which is also the key for its owner video.

4.4 ROLES IN RELATIONSHIP TYPES

As you saw in Chapter 3, each entity in a relationship plays a specific *role* in it. For example, in the `Rents` relationship type of Figure 4.5, the customer is the renter of the video, and the video is rented by the customer. The customer plays the "renter" role and the video plays the "rented by" role. We'll take a brief break from modeling BigHit Video information and consider some interpersonal relationships among people.

Roles are particularly important in situations where two entity classes are linked by more than one relationship type and where a relationship type links an entity class to itself. For example, consider the traditional marriage relationship. It relates one person to another, as shown in Figure 4.10. This diagram shows the entity class `Person`,

FIGURE 4.10

Relationship Types **IsMarriedTo** and **IsChildOf**, with Role Names

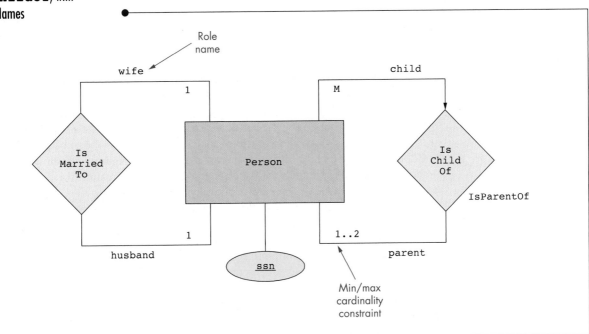

with its key attribute `ssn`, and the relationship types `IsMarriedTo` and `Is-ChildOf`, with their lines and cardinalities. The names of the roles `wife`, `husband`, `child`, and `parent` are shown in the diagram next to the relationship-type lines. For each pair of people related by parentage, one is the child and one is the parent.

Additional information from the figure is expressed by the following sentences:

- A person may be the child of one or two parents.
- A person may be the parent of zero or more children.
- A person may be the wife of a husband.
- A person may be the husband of a wife.

You can create these sentences by reading along the relationship lines in the diagram. Read the entity class, the role, the cardinality of the role, and finally the other role.

Note the unfamiliar cardinality symbol `1..2` on the `parent` line. This symbol means that the child may have between one and two parents. Figure 4.10 also shows the two names for the parent–child relationship. From the child's point of view, the relationship is called `IsChildOf`; this phrase appears inside the diamond. Outside the diamond is the name of the relationship from the parents' perspective: `IsParentOf`. The arrow on the child's relationship line points toward the diamond. This pointing indicates that the name of the relationship inside the diamond refers to this role's relationship name.

Concept

Overspecified Cardinalities

Perhaps you've seen a flaw in the cardinalities shown in Figure 4.10. If every person must have one or two parents, either there are infinitely many persons—or some people are their own descendents. This is a common error created by overspecifying the cardinality of a relationship type. In this case, we must recognize that this relationship type represents parent–child relationships between people whose names will be included in this database. Some people in the database will have parents who are not part of the system. Hence the child must be allowed to have no parent.

Remember: All data models and all databases attempt to represent just a small part of the world. The cardinality of a role need only represent the number of related entities that are relevant to the planned database.

Although E-R diagrams include declarations of cardinality constraints, many other constraints cannot be represented in this format. The E-R diagram for the `Is-ChildOf` relationship type restricts the cardinality of the child so that a child has no more than two parents. However, it does not place any restrictions on which individuals are the parents. According to this model, it is possible for Joe to be a child of Jane and for Jane to be a child of Joe at the same time. The diagram also allows Joe to be a child of Joe! Unfortunately, such nonfactual relationships cannot be excluded from an E-R diagram. Instead, constraints on individual membership in relationships must be written down as part of the E-R modeling process. Developers will consider these later in the database- and application-development processes.

Figure 4.11 shows examples of basic symbols used to draw E-R diagrams. Almost as many styles of E-R diagramming exist as organizations that draw them—and there's no best one. The style presented in this chapter is used by many developers. Each designer works within or for an organization and must draw diagrams using symbols that conform to the style conventions established by that organization. These symbols serve as the primary means of communication between users and developers. The particular style chosen is more important to users than to developers. It must convey a precise specification to developers, but must be easily understood by trained users. Once database designers adopt a specific E-R style, it is their responsibility to make sure their users understand it.

FIGURE 4.11

Examples of E-R Diagram Symbols

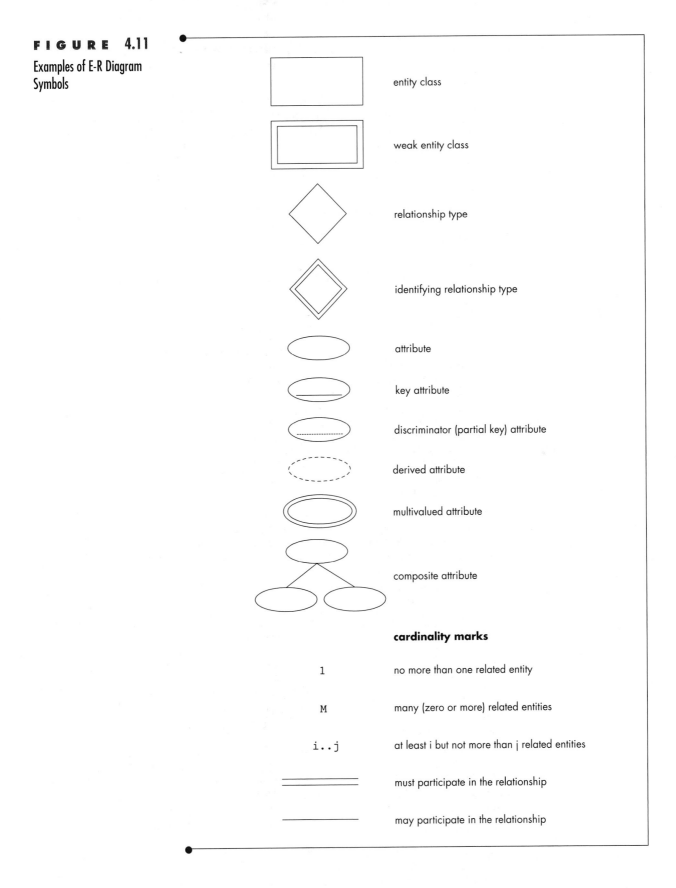

4.5 AN E-R MODEL FOR BIGHIT VIDEO

Now that you've become familiar with the symbols used in E-R modeling, let's see what a more comprehensive E-R model for BigHit Video might look like. Figure 4.12, a conceptual schema, shows one possibility. It depicts all of the entity classes you saw in Table 3.1, along with their relationship types. The diagram is incomplete, because it omits the attributes of most of the classes. You will be invited to finish the attribute and entity-class definitions as part of the exercises at the end of this chapter.

In this section, you'll discover more about what information this conceptual schema can and cannot represent. By carefully studying this diagram, you can gain insights into many issues that arise during the discovery and specification processes. The figure also illustrates how much detail can be specified by an E-R model and how that detail constrains the resulting database.

4.5.1 Recording the History of Rentals

The entity classes `Customer`, `Rental`, and `Video` are shown as related in Figure 4.12. As noted earlier, `Rental` entities represent the current state of video rentals. When a video is returned, the corresponding `Rental` entity is removed from the database.

But what if BigHit wanted to record historical information about its business? For example, suppose it wanted to determine which videos are being rented most often and what types of videos a particular customer tends to rent. The entity class `Rental` does not provide the information required for these analyses.

The entity class `PreviousRental` of Figure 4.13 has been added to record the history of customer and video rentals. The difference between `Rental` and `PreviousRental` lies in the cardinality constraints of the relationship with `Video`. Class `Rental` has a one-to-one relationship with `Video`, whereas `PreviousRental` has a many-to-one relationship. This relationship allows the database to record many rentals of each video.

The entity class `PreviousRental` is a weak entity class with a single identifying relationship. Unfortunately, the related video does not uniquely identify the `PreviousRental`. This property is another difference between `Rental` and `PreviousRental`. Because a video can participate in at most one rental at a time, the rental is uniquely determined by its relationship to the video.

To uniquely identify a previous rental, we must add another attribute to the key. This attribute, called a **discriminator** or **partial key**, should uniquely identify the entity among all those related to a specific identifying entity. In this case, the `dateRented` attribute and the key of the related video together form a unique identification. The `dateRented` attribute *discriminates* among all of the previous rentals for a particular video. The partial key is shown with a dashed underline in Figure 4.11.

This definition of the key of entity class `PreviousRental` may create some problems for BigHit Video stores. In particular, under this definition, a video cannot be rented twice on the same day. The easiest way to eliminate this problem is to change `dateRented` into `dateTimeRented`, an attribute that includes both date and time. If this modification is not appropriate, BigHit's database designer could create an artificial key `rentalId` to serve as the key of the entity class.

But BigHit might also want to allow a `PreviousRental` entity to have no associated customer. As shown in Figure 4.14, the database designer would place a single line between `PreviousRental` and its relationship with a `Customer`. With this cardinality, managers or clerks at BigHit could delete inactive customers and the records of their previous rentals without compromising the company's ability to analyze rental activity.

FIGURE 4.12

An E-R Diagram for BigHit Video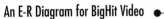

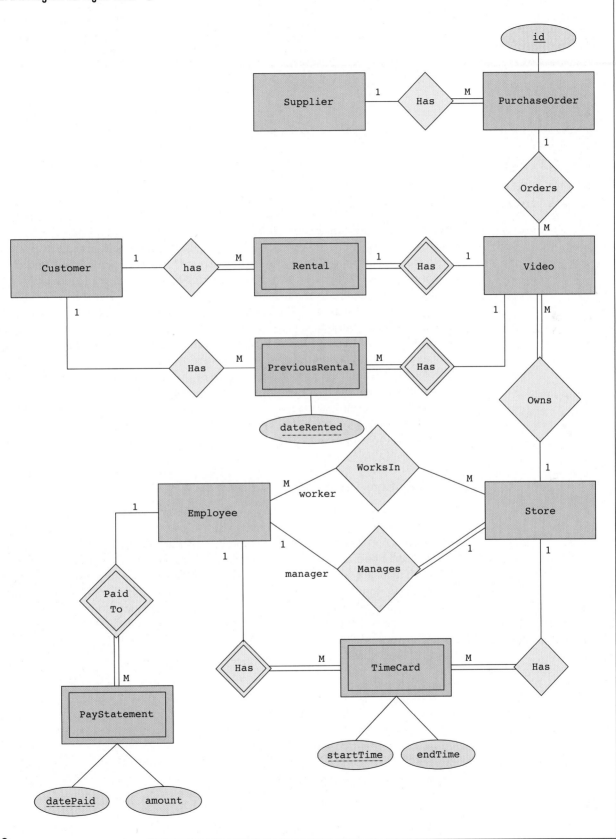

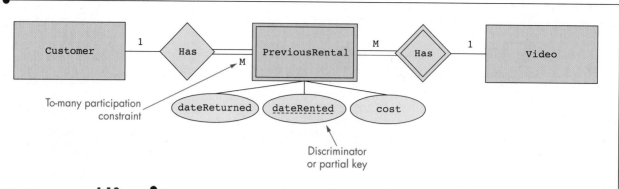

FIGURE 4.13

E-R Diagram for Entity Class
PreviousRental

This strategy for handling rentals and previous rentals with separate entity classes exposes some limitations of E-R models. We have defined the relationship type between `Rental` and `Customer` as one-to-one, which means that a video can have at most one current rental. However, when a video is returned, the `Rental` entity must be deleted and a similar `PreviousRental` created. In some sense, the `Rental` is transformed into a `PreviousRental`. Unfortunately, the E-R diagram has no way to represent this required transformation.

As described in the Concept box in Section 4.3.1, an alternative way of representing rental history would be to have a single `Rental` entity class with a one-to-many relationship type with `Customer`. With this strategy, the current rentals would consist of all rentals with a null return date. However, the E-R diagram would be unable to depict the requirement that there be at most one current rental. A database designer must decide which is most important: ensuring that there is at most one current rental or ensuring that the previous rentals are reliably created by the information system when videos are returned. The model shown in Figure 4.14 is a compromise between these two goals.

4.5.2 Employee Roles and Cardinalities

Now let's look at the relationship types between `Employee` and `Store`. As you might see in Figure 4.15, two such types exist. An employee can be associated with a store as manager or as worker. These employee roles are shown next to the lines that connect `Employee` and its relationship types. This specification allows an employee to be both manager and worker. It also allows an employee to be a worker for more than one store—a usual occurrence in a business that has multiple outlets in one area.

According to the diagram, an employee can be the manager of no more than one store, and each store has exactly one manager. This setup could pose a problem if the

FIGURE 4.14

E-R Diagram for Entity Class
PreviousRental
with Optional **Customer**
Participation

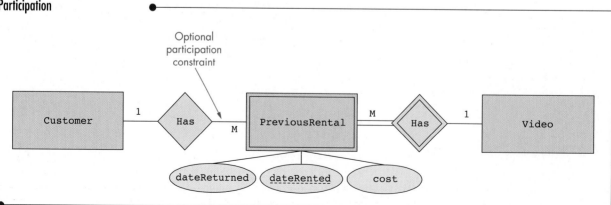

Customer Privacy in the BigHit Information System

The idea of recording previous rentals raises the issue of customers' privacy. Some people may consider it a violation of their privacy for a company such as BigHit Video to keep track of all the videos they've ever rented. Employees of BigHit Video could search the database to find out private information about customers. Public libraries avoid these accusations by keeping this kind of information private. U.S. courts have supported libraries' right to maintain the privacy of their circulation records. BigHit Video is not under the same constitutional constraints. However, it may not even want to record a history of individual customers' rentals.

Removal of the relationship type between `Customer` and `PreviousRental` would make it impossible for BigHit Video to record information about which customers rented which videos.

business needs one person to manage more than one store. For example, if the company fires a store manager, there will likely be a period of time when there is no manager or some other manager temporarily fills the vacancy. The database would be unable to represent this situation. The information system would have to add a fictional employee to the `Employee` class and associate that employee with the store as manager. An alternative approach, as shown in Figure 4.15, would be to modify the cardinalities of the `Manages` relationship type so that a store can have no manager and an employee can manage more than one store.

The precise specification of the cardinalities exposes the kinds of issues that can arise from real business practices. It is users' responsibility to determine whether the E-R model adequately represents their enterprise and meets its needs. It is developers' responsibility to find and expose the questions that always arise as part of the discovery and specification processes.

4.5.3 Purchase Orders and the True Meaning of Video

Let's now take a closer look at how to handle weak entity classes in an E-R diagram. The entity class `PurchaseOrder` could be defined as weak. (Purchase orders refer to BigHit's ordering of videos from its suppliers.) The cardinalities of the relationships

FIGURE 4.15

E-R Diagram for **WorksIn** and **Manages** with Modified Cardinality and Participation Constraints

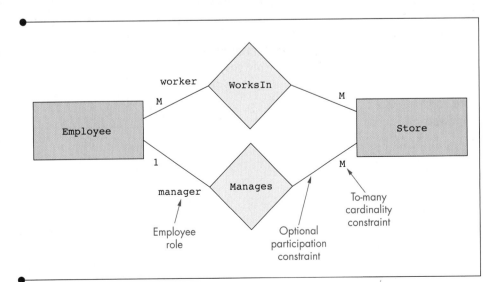

of class `PurchaseOrder` require that a purchase order have a single supplier and at least one video; hence a purchase order cannot exist unless it is related to other entities. This situation typifies a weak class. The natural key for `PurchaseOrder` is some combination of `date`, `supplierID`, and `items`. But in this case, it is much more straightforward to create an artificial key (`id`) and to define `PurchaseOrder` as a strong entity, as is done in Figure 4.12 and repeated here as Figure 4.16.

A weak entity has no key of its own and cannot exist without being related to another entity. Another example from BigHit Video is the entity class `PayStatement`. This class has no key, because many employees may be paid on the same day. However, the relationship type `PaidTo` is a many-to-one relationship that links each pay statement to a single employee.

The relationship between a purchase order and a video indicates that the specific video is being ordered as part of the purchase order. A purchase order can be related to many videos—many DVDs and videotapes may be included in a single order. In contrast, a video can be related to only one order, because it is purchased only once. To create a purchase order, the information system must add an entity to the `Video` class for each item in the order. Each of these video entities is associated with a specific store. When the order is received, a clerk can use the information in the database to determine which store the DVDs and videotapes go to.

This strategy is not the usual approach to purchasing. Typically, a purchase order contains a list of items to be purchased. Each item has some identifying information (for example, a catalog number) and a quantity. In this case, the intention may be to purchase 25 copies of *Lady and the Tramp*. Figure 4.12 would require that 25 entities be created—each with title "Lady and the Tramp," genre "animated comedy," and its own unique value for `videoId`. In turn, each entity would be individually linked with the purchase order. The effect would be an order for 25 items, rather than an order for one item with quantity 25.

This situation reveals a clear mistake in the diagram of Figure 4.16. To be correct, the conceptual data model should have a close correspondence to the real objects that it represents. As it now stands, a `PurchaseOrder` entity is not an accurate representation of an actual purchase order.

We might be tempted to place a quantity attribute on the `Orders` relationship type, as shown in Figure 4.17. Now the purchase order is a set of items, each with a quantity. Yet in this model, the meaning of `Video` has changed. In Figure 4.12 , a `Video` entity represents a specific DVD or videotape that may be rented. In Figure 4.17, a `Video` entity represents a specific title, but not a specific physical DVD or videotape. A video can now be purchased multiple times and may represent more than one physical DVD or videotape.

This problem reveals another error as well—this one in the understanding of the nature of class `Video`. In the E-R diagrams of previous figures, two different entity classes have been confused as the single class `Video`. One class represents the physical video—an object that can be rented, is taken away by a customer, and must be returned before its next rental. The other class represents a more conceptual object—the movie or the catalog item.

FIGURE 4.16

Model of Purchase Orders
from Figure 4.12

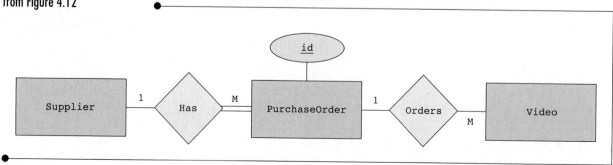

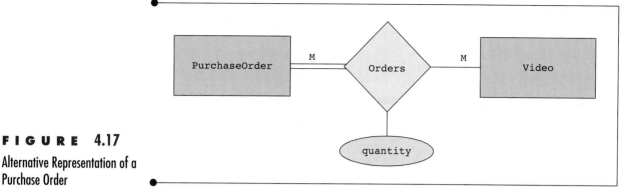

FIGURE 4.17

Alternative Representation of a Purchase Order

Each *physical* video is a *copy* of a specific movie. The movie itself must be represented by another entity class. It is this movie object that BigHit purchases from its supplier and that customers want to watch. After all, a customer doesn't ask "Do you have video number 112376?" He asks, "Do you have a copy of *Lady and the Tramp*?" Figure 4.18 gives a more appropriate E-R diagram for videos, movies, purchases, and sales. In this diagram, a video is designated as a *copy* of a movie. The title, genre, and other attributes that are common to all copies of a single movie are attached to the `movie` entity class. A purchase order consists of many detail lines, each representing the purchase of some quantity of a single movie. The application that handles the receipt of movie shipments will have to create `Video` entities for each new item so that the clerk can enter the DVDs and videotapes into the rental inventory.

4.5.4 **Employees, Time Cards, and Pay Statements**

Are you ready to move on to another aspect of BigHit Video's business? Let's take a look at the entity classes `TimeCard` and `PayStatement` from Figure 14.12, repeated here as Figure 14.19. These weak entity classes record when employees work and what they are paid. In both cases, the entities are not uniquely determined by

FIGURE 4.18

E-R Diagram for Suppliers, Purchases, Movies, and Videos

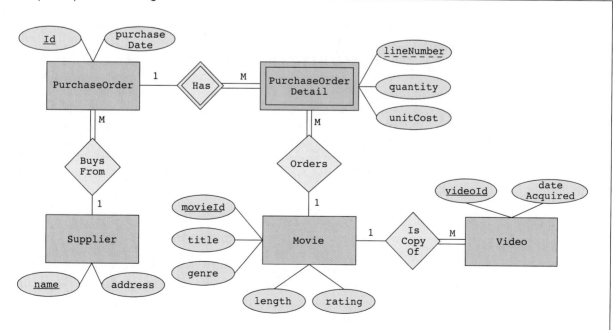

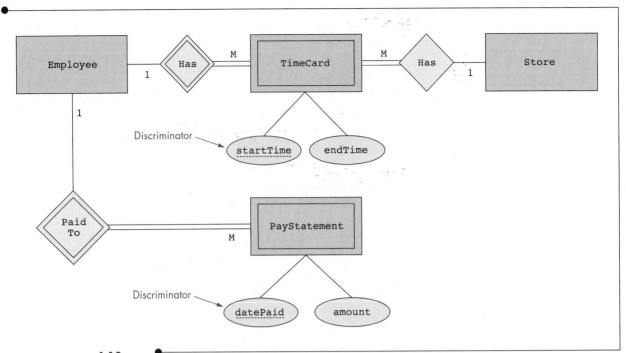

FIGURE 4.19

TimeCard,
PayStatement, and
Their Related Entity Classes
from Figure 4.12

their identifying relationships. For instance, a pay statement is identified by its related employee, but is not unique for that employee. It is the *combination* of the employee's `ssn` and `datePaid` that is unique. Like `dateRented` of class `PreviousRental` in Figure 4.14, the attribute `datePaid` is called a discriminator (or partial key) because it identifies the entity among all of those that depend on the same strong entity.

Each time card is associated with an employee and a store. It records the date and the starting and ending times of a single period of work for one employee at one store. A database based on this E-R diagram cannot represent a situation in which an employee works in two stores with a single time card. Instead, a work period for an employee who begins work in one store and then changes to a different store must be represented by two time cards.

4.6   OBJECT-ORIENTED DATA MODELS

Thus far, we have considered the rentals of videos. But what about the difference between videotapes and DVDs? Should these differences be important to BigHit Video? These questions lead us to the topic of **object-oriented data models**. Such data models allow us to express the idea that a video can be either a DVD or a videotape, but not both. The concepts supporting object-oriented design will emerge from the consideration of these different types of videos. We will also see how E-R diagrams can be enhanced to directly express object-oriented designs.

Not surprisingly, the company must be able to tell whether a particular video is DVD or tape. Customers typically care which format they rent, so the company needs to store them in separate shelf sections. The database designer can easily make arrangements for the database to record the media type of a video by adding an attribute to the `Video` entity class. The attribute media has only two possible values: "dvd" and "videotape."

It is more difficult to represent attributes that are specific to one media. To illustrate, a videotape has a single soundtrack in a specific language and format. The format might correspond to either U.S. video standards or European standards. By contrast, most DVDs have soundtracks in several languages, closed captioning, and possibly even multiple video formats. Figure 4.20 shows one way to add attributes to the `Video` entity class in order to maintain information specific to each media. The `media` attribute records whether a video object is a videotape or a DVD. Tape objects have values for the fields of the compound attribute `tape`. DVD objects have no values for the fields of `tape` but rather have values for the fields of `dvd`.

Unfortunately, Figure 4.20 does not specify any correlation between the value of `media` and the presence of values for `videotape` and `dvd`. We want to ensure that the attributes of videotape have non-null values only if `media` is `videotape`, and the attributes of `dvd` have non-null values only if `media` is "dvd." In order to guarantee accurate information in these attributes, we must make a clearer distinction between objects of these two kinds.

To clearly distinguish between videotapes and DVDs, we can create two new entity classes, one for each media type. We add the appropriate attributes to each class. You may be thinking that the simplest strategy is to replace class `Video` with two classes `Videotape` and `DVD`, as shown in Figure 4.21. But there is significant duplication in the attributes of these classes. And when we try to put these classes into the larger E-R diagram, as in Figure 4.22, an even worse problem arises. We have had to dupli-

FIGURE 4.20

E-R Diagram with **dvd** and **videotape** Attributes of Entity Class **Video**

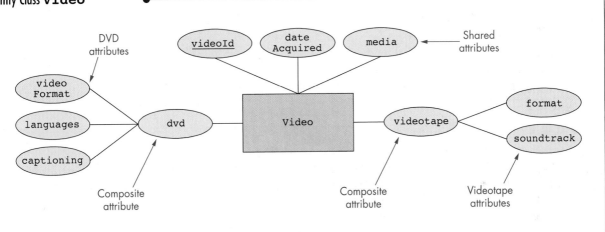

FIGURE 4.21

E-R Diagram Showing Classes **DVD** and **Videotape** as Unrelated Classes

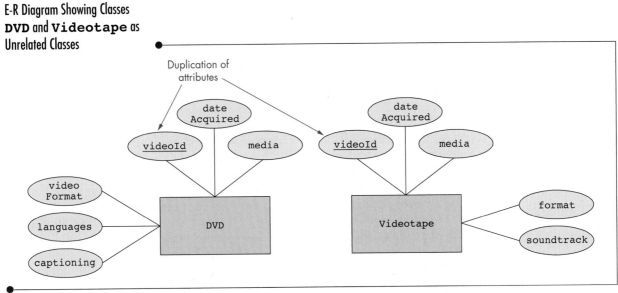

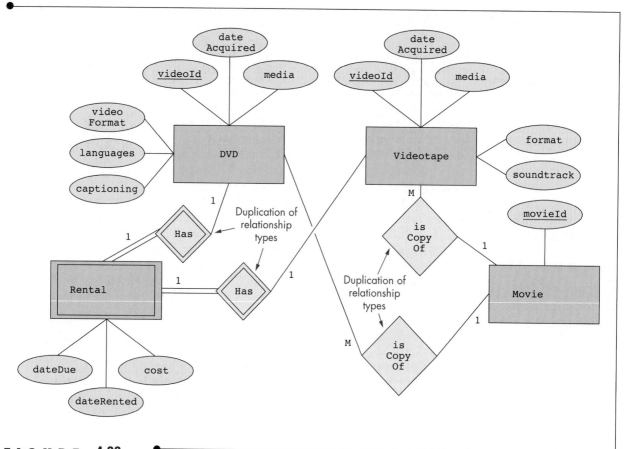

cate every relationship type of entity class `Video`. Each movie has related videotapes and related DVDs. Adding these new classes has created a huge, complicated mess!

The object-oriented approach to representing this information recognizes that there is a commonality between videotape objects and DVD objects. Each one is a video object, has rentals and previous rentals, and has a related movie. Figure 4.23 shows the representation of the three related classes using the concept of **inheritance**, or **is-a, relationship types**. We say that a DVD entity *is a* video entity, and that entity class `DVD` *inherits* attributes from entity class `Video`. Similarly a videotape *is a* video and entity class `Videotape` *inherits* attributes from class `Video`. Inheritance relationship types in our style of E-R diagramming are depicted by the small circles (*inheritance circles*) and their associated lines and arcs. The cup symbols (*inheritance symbols*) point toward the superclass; in this case, `Video`.

Notice that the duplication of attributes and relationship types that we saw in Figure 4.22 has been transformed in Figure 4.23. A DVD has a `videoId`, a `date-Acquired`, and a `media` because of its relationship with a parent video. It also has relationship types with `Rental` and `Movie`. A DVD, as represented by this model, is a member of the entity classes `Video` and `DVD` and has all of the attributes and relationship types of both classes.

The major advantages of including object-oriented features in E-R diagramming are that the is-a relationship is complex and hard to describe without these features, and that the accurate maintenance of entities in classes such as `Video`, `DVD`, and `Videotape` require special treatment by database developers. These additional E-R diagramming symbols allow designers to accurately capture the nature of inheritance in a simple, graphical style. We'll see in Chapter 7 how the translation of inheritance from E-R diagrams to relational databases preserves the structure and the information content of these classes.

INTERVIEW

PETER CHEN
On the Birth of the Idea for the E-R model

Peter Chen published the first paper on the Entity-Relationship Model. That paper was selected as one of the top 40 great papers in the field of computing and remains one of the most cited papers in the computer software field. Today the E-R model is ranked as the top methodology used in database design by several Fortune 500 companies.

FIRST EXPOSURE TO COMPUTING   I changed my major to CS my senior year at the National Taiwan University (NTU). I still feel very thankful to Dr. Richard Chueh, visiting professor at NTU who introduced me to the computer field. After graduating from NTU, I got a fellowship from Harvard, where I studied CS under Dr. Ugo Gagliardi and Dr. Jeff Buzen.

THE EARLIEST CAREER STEPS   I received my Ph.D. from Harvard and joined Honeywell to work on their next-generation computer project. One of my teammates was Mr. Charles Bachman, who is the inventor of the CODASYL/Network data model. Honeywell eventually abandoned our project and a few years later I joined MIT as an Assistant Professor of Information Systems in the Management School.

AN IDEA IS DEVELOPED AND PRESENTED
While at MIT, I received a lot of guidance from Dr. Stuart Madnick and met Dr. Mike Hammer, who was working on data models at that time. It was during my time at MIT that I published the first paper on the Entity-Relationship (E-R) model. A few years later, I moved to UCLA's management school. There, I learned a lot from several experts in the CS department including Dr. Wesley Chu, Dr. Alfonso Cardenas, and Dr. Leonard Kleinrock. An-

> **"It [the E-R model] solves a critical problem of almost any business: How to understand what data and information is needed to operate and manage the business."**

other colleague, Dr. Eph McLean, encouraged me to organize the first E-R conference. We expected a small gathering of 50 people or so. It turned out that over two hundred people showed up. Now the E-R conference is an annual gathering of scientists and practitioners working in the conceptual modeling area and is held in a different country each year.

A THEORETICAL CONCEPT'S EVERY-DAY BUSINESS APPLICATION
Almost every business needs a methodology to organize the ever-increasing amount of data. The E-R model methodology has proven to work very well in practice in almost any kind of business all over the world. It solves a critical problem of almost any business: How to understand what data and information is needed to operate and manage the business. It helps address data issues such as: (1) Assuring that crucial data the business needs is collected, (2) disregarding unimportant information to avoid too much data, (3) organizing data in a retrievable manner, and (4) relating the data obtained. The E-R model helps a business identify and focus on what data it needs and, thus, solves issues (1) and (2). If a business uses the E-R model to guide the design of its databases, it will help to solve issues (3) and (4), particularly using the relationships of data to find the desired information.

The meaning of inheritance in E-R diagrams is both precise and complex. According to the E-R diagram of Figure 4.23, each entity of class `Video` may be a member of either class `DVD` or class `Videotape`. The inheritance diagram also specifies that each entity in class `DVD` and each entity in class `Videotape` must be an entity in class `Video`. Another way of saying this is that the set of all entities of class `Video` includes

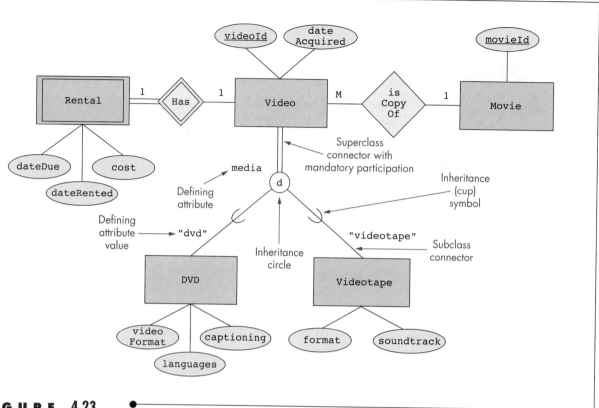

FIGURE 4.23

Object-Oriented E-R diagram for Entity Classes **Video**, **DVD**, and **Videotape**

all of the entities in classes DVD and Videotape. All of this meaning is defined simply by including the superclass connector, the inheritance circle, and the subclass connectors with their inheritance symbols.

Additional features of object-oriented modeling are included in Figure 4.23, as noted by the comments. These features allow us to represent more subtle characteristics of the inheritance relationship as graphical components of the E-R diagram.

Attribute media has been moved and is now placed near the line that connects Video to its inheritance circle, and its allowable values, "dvd" and "videotape," appear near the subclass connectors. This definition of the media attribute and its values combine to specify that the value of the media attribute of a video entity determines whether the video is in class DVD or class Videotape. Attribute media is called the *defining attribute* of the inheritance and the values "dvd" and "video-tape" are the *defining attribute values*.

The superclass connector is a double line in Figure 4.23 to denote a mandatory participation constraint. That is, each video entity must participate in the inheritance by also being either a DVD or a videotape. This diagram does not allow the existence of a video entity that is neither DVD nor videotape. The small "d" in the inheritance circle specifies that the inheritance is *disjoint*. That is, each video entity is either a DVD or a videotape and cannot be both.

A different combination of participation and disjointedness is shown in Figure 4.24, which defines an example of inheritance for employees. As before, the inheritance diagram specifies that an employee may be a supervisor or a clerk and that each supervisor and each clerk must also be an employee. In this case, however, the superclass connector is a single line to express an optional participation constraint. This optional inheritance allows an employee to be neither a supervisor nor a clerk. The inheritance circle is empty to denote that this is *overlapping* (non-disjoint) inheritance. An employee is allowed to be both a supervisor and a clerk. The diagram also allows an employee to be a supervisor but not a clerk, or a clerk but not a supervisor.

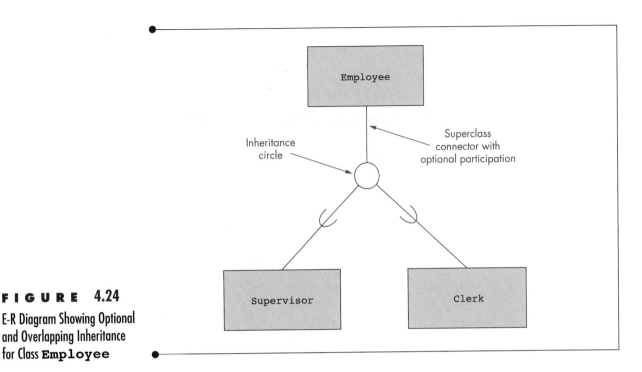

FIGURE 4.24

E-R Diagram Showing Optional and Overlapping Inheritance for Class **Employee**

Inheritance of attributes between classes is an important concept in E-R data modeling. You'll learn much more about inheritance in the following chapters.

4.7 CASE IN POINT: E-R MODEL FOR VIDEO SALES FOR BIGHIT VIDEO

The following statement is repeated and slightly modified from Chapter 3 and describes some aspects of the BigHit Video information system. This time, our job is to take the entity classes, attributes, and relationship types from Chapter 3 and create an E-R model for the system. The text highlighted in green has been added.

> BigHit Video Inc. wants to create an information system for online sales of movies in both DVD and videotape format. People will be allowed to register as customers of the online site and to update their stored information. Information must be maintained about customers' shipping addresses, e-mail addresses and credit cards. In a single sale, customers will be allowed to purchase any quantity of videos. The items in a single sale will be shipped to a single address and will have a single credit card charge.
>
> A customer will be provided with a virtual shopping cart to store items to be purchased. As each item is selected, it is added to the shopping cart. When the customer finishes shopping, he will be directed to a checkout area where he can purchase all of the items in the shopping cart. At this time, payment and shipping information is entered. Once the sale is complete, the shopping cart will be deleted and the customer will be sent a receipt by e-mail.

The analysis of this description in Chapter 3 produced a list of entity classes and attributes and a list of relationships that must be part of this information system. These lists are reproduced as Tables 4.1 and 4.2. The text highlighted in green tells us that there are two kinds of movies for sale. Table 4.1 has two new classes—DVD and Videotape—which are subclasses of Movie, as discussed in Section 4.4.

The representation of this information as an E-R diagram is shown in Figure 4.25. The diagram is a faithful representation of the entity classes, attributes, and relation-

Table 4.1   Entity Classes and Attributes for Online Movie Sales
with Subclasses

Entity Class	Attribute	Constraints or Further Description
Customer	accountId	Key
	lastName	Not null
	firstName	
	shippingAddresses	Multivalued composite with components name, street, city, state, zipcode
	emailAddress	
	creditCards	Multivalued composite with components type, accountNumber, expiration
	password	Not null at least 6 characters
Movie	movieId	Key
	title	
	genre	
	media	Either "dvd" or "videotape" determines subclass
DVD	languages	Subclass of Movie
	videoFormat	
	captioning	
Videotape	format	Subclass of Movie
	soundtrack	
Sale	saleId	Key
	totalCost	
	dateSold	
	creditCard	Composite with components type, accountNumber, and expiration
ShoppingCart	cartId	Key
	dateCreated	

Table 4.2   Relationship Types for Online Movie Sales

Relationship Type	Entity Class	Entity Class	Cardinality Ratio	Attributes
Purchases	Customer	Sale	one-to-many	
Includes	Sale	Movie	many-to-many	quantity
Selects	Customer	ShoppingCart	one-to-many	
Includes	ShoppingCart	Movie	many-to-many	quantity

ship types. The only major improvement is in the participation constraints of the relationship types.

The E-R diagram specifies required participation by having double lines connect certain entity classes and relationship types. Each sale must be purchased by exactly one customer because of the double line (required participation) between `Sale` and `Purchases`. Similarly, each shopping cart must be selected by exactly one customer. A sale must include at least one movie because the line connecting `Sale` and `Includes` is double.

Single lines connecting an entity class and a relationship type denote optional participation. A customer need not have any sales nor any shopping carts. Also, because a shopping cart may be empty, `ShoppingCart` has optional participation with `Includes`.

The representation of the subclasses `DVD` and `Videotape` of entity class `Movie` is exactly that of Figure 4.25.

F I G U R E **4.25**

E-R Diagram for Movie Sales

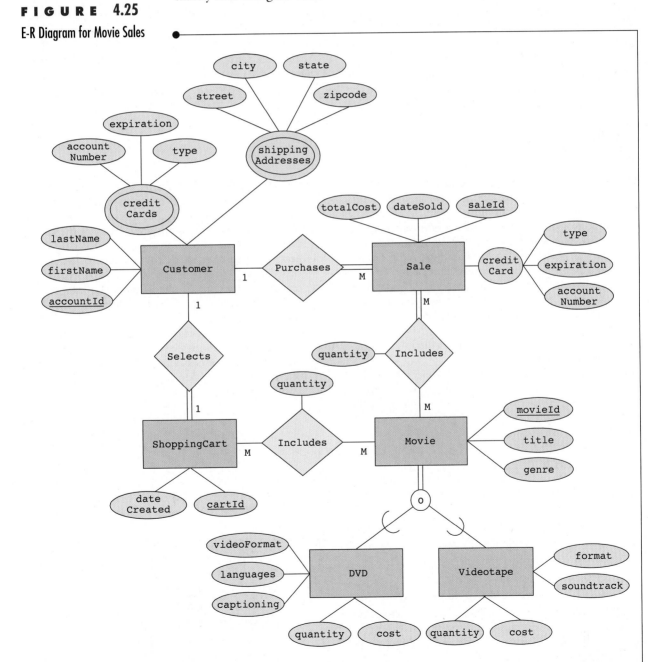

CHAPTER SUMMARY

E-R diagrams are a concise and understandable representation of E-R data models. Diagrams are relatively easy for both developers and users to understand. They provide an excellent way for users and developers to talk about a planned database.

E-R diagrams represent entity classes by rectangles, attributes by ovals, and relationships by diamonds and connecting lines. Each of these symbols contains the natural name of the object being represented. Key attributes' names are underlined. Cardinality marks are placed alongside the relationship lines. Participation constraints are represented by double lines.

Users and developers can easily express and understand the relationship types represented in an E-R diagram by creating sentences through reading the diagram. They state or write the name of one entity class, the participation constraint of its role ("may" or "must"), the verb phrase that states the name of the relationship type, the cardinality constraint of its role

("one" or "many"), and finally the name of the other entity class.

An initial diagram representing the purchasing aspects of the BigHit Video system revealed errors in the data model so far. Designers must make a clear distinction in the data model between a movie and a video, which is an individual copy of some specific movie. `Title` and `rating` are attributes of the movie, but `dateAcquired` and `mediaType` are attributes of the video copy.

Closely related classes such as `Video`, `DVD`, and `Videotape` can be modeled with object-oriented extensions to E-R diagramming. An inheritance ("is a") relationship links the superclass (or parent class) `Video` with each of its subclasses `DVD` and `Videotape`. Each attribute and relationship type of entity superclass `Video` is thus inherited by entity classes `DVD` and `Videotape`. The entities in classes `DVD` and `Videotape` are also entities in class `Video`.

KEY TERMS

Data dictionary. A table that contains the descriptions of classes and the types, descriptions, and constraints on attributes of an information system.

Discriminator or partial key. An attribute of a weak entity class that identifies an entity from among all of those with the same identifying entities. A discriminator is part of the key of the weak entity class.

Entity-relationship (E-R) data model. A strategy for constructing conceptual data models using diagrams that focus on entity classes, relationship types, and attributes.

Entity-relationship (E-R) diagram. A graphical strategy for representing E-R models.

Identifying relationship type. A to-one relationship type between a weak entity class and its owner entity class that helps to uniquely identify an entity of the weak class.

Inheritance (is-a) relationship type. A relationship type in which the subclass (child) is related to a superclass (parent). Each object of the subclass is also an object of the superclass and inherits all of the superclass attributes and relationships.

Object-oriented data model. A conceptual data model that divides objects into classes and supports the direct representation of inheritance relationship types. E-R diagramming supports the inclusion of object-oriented features.

Weak entity class. An entity class with no key of its own, whose objects cannot exist without being related to other objects. A weak entity class must have at least one identifying relationship type and corresponding owner entity class.

QUESTIONS

1. Characterize the difference between the following pairs of terms.
   a. Entity and entity class
   b. Relationship and relationship type
   c. Attribute value and attribute
   d. Strong entity class and weak entity class
   e. Multivalued attribute and composite attribute

2. What is a data dictionary? Give three examples of information about entities and attributes that must be stored in a data dictionary and cannot be directly represented in an E-R diagram.

3. Discuss the relative merits of the E-R diagrams of Figures 4.5 and 4.7. Why would you choose one over the other?

4. Consider the E-R diagram for the BigHit Video enterprise as shown in Figure 4.12. Write relationship sentences, including participation and cardinality constraints to describe the roles of
   a. An employee in a store (2 roles).
   b. A pay statement to an employee.
   c. A store to an employee (2 roles).
   d. A time card to a store.

5. Why are weak entity classes important to conceptual modeling? Give an example (not from BigHit Video) of a weak entity class. What are its identifying relationship(s), its owner entity class(es), and its discriminators, if any?

6. Give an example of a relationship type of degree higher than 2. Show how a weak entity class can represent this relationship type.

7. Consider the E-R diagram shown in Figure 4.18.

   a. Write a sentence (in English) that expresses the role of a supplier in the diagram.

   b. Write sentences that express the roles of a purchase order in the diagram.

   c. Write sentences that express the roles of a movie in the diagram.

   d. Can a movie be purchased from more than one supplier?

   e. Can a purchase order include more than one detail line for a single movie?

   f. Write three more questions like (d) and (e) that ask questions about cardinalities and participation that can be answered from the diagram.

8. Give a list of constraints that apply to "is-a" relationship types that don't apply to all relationship types. Consider participation constraints and cardinality constraints, among others.

PROBLEMS

9. Augment the E-R diagrams given in this chapter with attributes, as follows:

   a. Augment Figure 4.1 by including attributes for information about customer preferences, credit cards, and forms of identification. You may use the customer application from Problem 3.16a as the model.

   b. Augment Figure 4.2 by including attributes for information about videos, including length, rating, studio, and so on.

   c. Augment Figure 4.3 by including attributes for information about stores, including location, name, and so on.

   d. Augment Figure 4.12 by including attributes for employee information, as described in the employee application form of Problem 3.16d.

10. Consider the following description of an enterprise.

    An auction Web site has items for sale that are provided by sellers. Each item has an opening price, a description, and an ending time. Customers submit bids. The highest, earliest bid submitted before the ending time is the winning bid and the item is sold to the bidder. Each seller must pay the auction company 5% of the winning bid. The auction company wants to be able to analyze the sales behavior of its customers and sellers and so must keep track of all bids and sales.

    Draw an E-R diagram to represent this enterprise. Be sure to include all attributes and to identify the key attributes of each class.

PROJECTS

11. Continue the development of the BigHit Video system as shown in the E-R diagrams of this chapter. Extend the model of this chapter by adding additional entity classes, attributes, and relationship types as required. Produce a full E-R model for the system.

12. Continue the development of the Movie Lovers system started in the project of Chapter 2. Draw an E-R diagram to represent the entity classes, attributes, and relationship types of the Movie Lovers system. Include key designations and constraints on relationship types. Be sure to include the following activities:

    a. The system allows people to become members by presenting them with a membership form. Include all appropriate attributes of members.

    b. The system records information about people who are involved in making movies. Each person may take on the role of actor, director, or writer. Feel free to add additional roles. Consider whether these roles should be relationship types or entity classes. Don't forget that there may be many actors, writers, etc., for each movie.

    c. Members should be able to record information about when and where they have seen movies, and make plans to see additional movies.

    d. Members want to record their evaluations of movies both with a rating scheme and by writing reviews.

FURTHER READING

Discovery and modeling of information systems is described in Herbst [Her97] and Teorey [Teo94]. The original paper on E-R modeling is [Chen76]. Several books have extensive discussions of E-R modeling, including Elmasri and Navathe [ElNa99]; Date [Date99]; and Riccardi [01]. Modeling specific to electronic commerce is presented in Reynolds and Mofazali [ReMo02].

PART III

Designing and Creating Relational Databases

Now that you have a solid understanding of data modeling, you are ready to learn to specify and create databases. Relational databases are the best available tool for managing the content of information systems. The structure of a relational database is specified using a logical data model called the relational model. Transforming an E-R diagram into a specification for a relational database is not difficult, but it requires careful attention to detail. The resulting database will be capable of storing all of the information content of the E-R model in an efficient and consistent manner.

In this section, you will learn the basic principles of the relational data model and how relational models differ from E-R models. You will learn how to transform an E-R data model into a relational data model and how to create a relational database to store its information. Finally, you will learn how to ensure that the structure of your databases is of the highest possible quality.

Chapter 5 introduces the relational data model, which is the foundation of relational databases. We look at the details of how entity classes, attributes, and relationship types are represented in the relational model. You will learn exactly how to translate each feature of an E-R diagram into a piece of a relational model. If you pay close attention to detail, this chapter will teach you to be an expert in creating relational database specifications.

Chapter 6 gets even more specific as it addresses how a relational model is used to create Microsoft Access databases. You will learn many of the details of using Access as a tool for storing information. By the end of Chapter 6, you will understand how to create and manipulate relational tables and how to create and use simple forms.

Chapter 7 shows you how to evaluate the quality of relational databases. Specific techniques are included to help you find problems with database specifications and then modify the specifications to eliminate the problems.

After studying Chapters 5, 6, and 7, you will be ready to learn to manipulate the information content of relational databases, and ultimately create Web sites that use databases.

CHAPTER 5

Developing Relational Data Models

In this chapter, you will learn:

- What relational modeling is and why it's important

- How to translate an E-R model into a relational model

- Why translating an E-R model into a relational model is important

- How to refine a relational model to create a sound database

- How to recognize and improve an unsound relational model

In Part II, you learned about data models, with an emphasis on the entity-relationship modeling method. An entity-relationship data model is a conceptual model that takes the form of E-R diagrams. As you saw in Chapter 4, these diagrams specify the kinds of data that will go into the final database and the proposed structure for the data.

The next step in building a database system is to translate E-R diagrams into a **relational data model**, which defines the logical schema for the final database system. The logical schema is based on the representation of entities as rows of tables, and hence is a more restricted data model. The conceptual model specifies the structure of information in a style that is directed at enabling understanding between users and developers. The logical model is aimed at enabling developers to build databases.

A relational data model is a description of a set of two-dimensional tables containing rows and columns. The term **relation** is a mathematical name for a rectangular table of data. Some of the tables you saw in Chapter 3 are examples of relations. You may be familiar with this term from your study of discrete mathematics.

In a relational data model, a table is a logical, rather than a physical, concept. That is, data is organized into tables and can be manipulated as tables, but we do not have to be concerned with how tables are physically stored in the computer. All of our manipulations of relational tables will be based on the table description, that is, on the logical model. The relational data model has many advantages over other strategies for defining databases. Those advantages will be highlighted as they occur in the discussion that follows.

This chapter shows you how to transform an E-R diagram into a collection of relational table definitions. As you'll discover, the translation process can be tricky. You create some tables based on your E-R diagrams, spot some logical problems with your plan, and then revise your tables so that they more accurately represent the data you'll be working with. Thus, you will steadily refine your data model until it's as logically sound as possible. Even though the process can involve some trial and error, there are basic rules for creating good tables. You'll learn about those rules in this chapter. Chapter 7 is devoted to more formal methods of evaluating the quality of relational models and finding ways to improve them.

Note: As you work your way through this chapter, keep in mind the distinctions between the words *relation* and *relationship*. These terms have unique meanings in database nomenclature. A _relation_ is a two-dimensional table of values that represent entities from a specific entity class. A _relationship_, as you saw in Chapters 3 and 4, is an association between two entities.

5.1   INTRODUCTION TO THE RELATIONAL MODEL

A relational model consists of **relation schemas**, which specify the structure of the tables; that is, the structure of the information that will go into the tables' rows and columns. The structure of tables is often called the **metadata** of a database. Each relation schema represents an entity class; that is a type of entity that is of interest to the system. A relational database system includes a relation, or table, for each relation schema. The collection of relation schemas is called the **database schema**. In turn, the contents of a particular relation represent a specific set of entities. We'll see in Chapters 8 and 9 that the relational model is supported by several methods of manipulating the contents of the tables.

Figure 5.1 shows a relation schema and a sample table for BigHit Video's `Movie` entity class from the E-R diagram of Figure 4.18, repeated here as Figure 5.2. The re-

FIGURE   5.1

Schema Definition and Table

Schema: Movie (<u>movieId</u> number, title string, genre string, length number, rating string)

<u>movieId</u>	title	genre	length	rating
101	The Thirty-Nine Steps	mystery	101	PG
145	Lady and the Tramp	animated comedy	93	G
90987	Elizabeth	costume drama	123	PG-13
99787	Animal House	comedy	87	PG-13
123	Annie Hall	romantic comedy	110	PG-13

Column headers contain attribute names

Row is an entity

Cell contents is an attribute

Column is an attribute

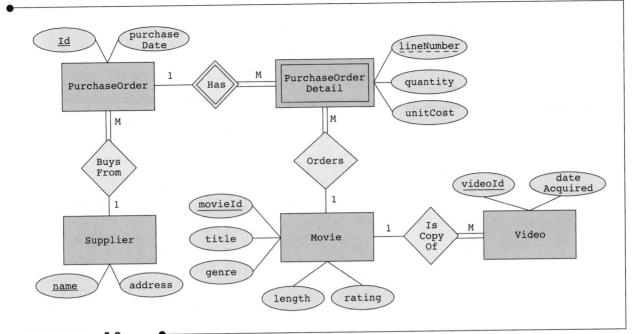

FIGURE 5.2

E-R Diagram for Suppliers,
Purchases, Movies, and Videos

lation schema for the table, shown at the top of the figure, lists the name of the table (in other words, the entity class) and the names of the entity attributes. The table shows the attribute names across the top row. Each of the table's other five rows contains all the attribute values for the single entity represented in the row.

Thus, in a relation, the columns of the table represent data attributes and the rows represent entities. An individual cell within a table contains the value of one attribute of the entity represented in that row. In Figure 5.1, for example, the cell in the third row (not including the header row) and second column contains the value "Elizabeth." This is the value of the `title` attribute of the entity (a movie) whose attribute `movieId` is 90987.

A relational table can also be thought of as a set of rows. Each row represents the values of a specific *collection* of attributes of a single entity. In Figure 5.1, the highlighted row would be an example of an entity. In a table, each row must have a unique set of attribute values. That's because the database will consider any two entities whose values are identical as the same entity. As a consequence, a user cannot add a new row to a table that contains attribute values identical to those of another row.

Attributes in the relational model are always single valued. The composite and multivalued attributes that we use in E-R diagrams must be translated into single-valued attributes in a relational model. The details of the translation are covered in Section 5.3, below. The fundamental characteristic of an attribute in a relational schema is that it must be **atomic**. That is, the attribute has a single value that cannot be decomposed into components.

The schemas of Figure 5.1 include attributes whose types are `number` and `string`. It is easy to see that a number is single valued, but more difficult to conclude that strings are. A string, of course, is composed of a sequence of characters and thus can be decomposed. However, the primary operations for database access to string attributes are string equality, comparison, and concatenation: all operations of the whole string and not its character components. Hence, it is most convenient in the relational model to consider the string to be a single-valued atomic attribute.

Is a Date Atomic?

The relational model provides for attributes of type `date`, which is not obviously an atomic type. A date can be decomposed into components in a variety of ways. The following are all equivalent ways to represent March 26, 2002.

year: 2002, month: March, day: 26
year: 02, month: 03, day: 26,
year: 2002, day 85
year: 2002, month: 3, day: 26, hour: 0, minute: 0, second: 0
milliseconds: 1017118800000

The last value is the number of milliseconds between Jan. 1, 1970 and March 26, 2002: a typical way that computers store date values.

The relational model accepts date as an atomic type in order to most easily support comparing dates (e.g., are two dates equal, is one earlier than the other). We'll see in Chapter 8 that the SQL language supports a variety of date manipulation functions that allow us to extract any of the above components from a date value.

The bottom line is that we declare relational attributes to be atomic and then add functions to allow us to freely manipulate them.

5.2 A CLOSER LOOK AT RELATION SCHEMAS AND KEYS

A relation schema specifies the name of the relation (table), the name and type of each attribute, and the domain of (that is, **constraints** on) the attributes' values. In Figure 5.1, we see simple domain restrictions: `number` for `movieId` and `string` for title. A more detailed schema might include a restriction that the `genre` be no more than 20 characters. Even more specific would be a list of values for `rating`: G, PG, PG-13, R, NC-17, NR. As another example, the domain for the attribute `GPA` for the entity `collegeStudent` would range from 0.0 to 4.0.

As you've seen, a relational table contains information about the various entities within a specific entity class. A relational database consists of a collection of such tables. Hence, the database contains a collection of entity sets. Each entity in a database is part of a specific table and belongs to the entity class associated with that table.

A relation schema must also identify at least one key. As you saw in Chapter 3, a **key** is an attribute (or set of attributes) whose values make each entity unique. A customer number or a person's Social Security number might make appropriate keys. In most cases, the keys of a table are exactly the same as the keys of the associated entity class.

For example, if `movieId` is declared to be the key for the `Movie` schema, then no two rows in the `Movie` table will have the same `movieId` value. Any attempt to add a movie that has the same `movieId` value as another video will result in an error and the rejection of the new movie. Also, any attempt to change the `movieId` of a movie will not be allowed if the new value violates this key constraint.

5.3 TRANSLATING E-R DIAGRAMS TO RELATION SCHEMAS

The goal of this chapter is to learn how to translate E-R diagrams into relational database definitions. To do this, we will examine each component of an E-R diagram. The discussion of the possible strategies for representing each E-R component is accompanied by specific rules to guide translation. In most cases, simply following the rules in the order given will produce an excellent database definition.

The relational database definition is produced in an iterative fashion by following the steps given in the following sections. We begin by choosing an entity class and creating a relation schema for it. We add the attributes of the entity class to the relation schema and define its key. Then we go on to the next entity class. We continue to add attributes and relation schemas one by one until we have applied all of the steps covered in this chapter. The result of this repetitive process is a full database definition that includes everything in the E-R diagram.

The database definition produced according to the steps given in this chapter will be used directly to produce database tables. Chapter 6 will discuss how to create tables in Microsoft Access. Later chapters will cover creating databases with the SQL language.

The following sections cover the E-R components:

- entity classes
- simple attributes
- composite attributes
- key attributes
- relationship types of different cardinalities
- weak entity classes
- multivalued attributes
- inheritance

The discussion of each component begins with a general view of how to represent it, and is accompanied by one or more translation steps. We generate the relational database definition in an iterative fashion by following these steps.

To translate an E-R model into a relational model, the database designer would start by creating a relation schema for each entity class in the E-R model. Hence, the designer of BigHit Video's database would begin by creating one relation schema for customers, one for rentals, one for videos, and so on. The designer would then add attributes to these schemas and identify key attributes for each schema. In addition, he or she would create schemas representing all of the relationships and multivalued attributes (such as other users) shown in the E-R model. In the end, we expect to have more relation schemas than we had entity classes in the E-R diagram.

5.4 REPRESENTING ENTITY CLASSES AS RELATION SCHEMAS

Each strong (non-weak) entity class in the E-R model should be translated into a relation schema whose name is the same as the class name and whose attributes are those of the class. Let's perform this translation on the classes of Figure 5.2. We translate one class at a time and end up with the preliminary schemas of Figure 5.3. The attribute types have been specified as part of the schema. The key attributes have been underlined.

FIGURE 5.3

Preliminary Relation Schemas for the Strong Entity Classes of Figure 5.2

Schema: PurchaseOrder (<u>id</u> number, purchaseDate date)

Schema: Supplier (<u>name</u> string, address string)

Schema: Movie (<u>movieId</u> number, title string, genre string, length number, rating string)

Schema: Video (<u>videoId</u> number, dateAcquired date)

All values for an attribute come from a specific domain, or range of allowed values. This idea corresponds exactly to the definition of attributes in conceptual modeling. Relational models, however, place some restrictions on attribute domains that do not occur in conceptual models.

For example, the domains available in a relational model are restricted to indivisible, or *atomic*, values. That is, each domain must contain some data type that cannot be divided into simpler values. Numbers, strings, and dates, as used in Figure 5.3, are considered atomic because their components cannot be directly referenced. For instance, with an attribute of type `date`, we can easily test if one value is the same date as another value, and easily test if one date is earlier than another, but it will be more difficult to compare the year of two date values.

The following is the first step in translating E-R diagrams into relational schemas.

Step 1: Create Relation Schemas for Strong Entity Classes and Their Simple Attributes

In Step 1, you identify the strong entity classes and their simple attributes in your E-R model and create a relation schema for each. Use these rules:

Rule 1a: For each strong entity class, define a relation schema by the same name.

Rule 1b: For each simple attribute of a strong entity class—that is, single-valued attribute—create an attribute by the same name in the relation schema.

Rule 1c: Define the key of the corresponding relation schema as the key of the entity class. If the entity class key consists of multiple single attributes, the key of the relation schema will be that set of attributes. Underline your selected key attribute in each schema in order to identify the key.

5.5   REPRESENTING COMPOSITE, MULTIVALUED, AND DERIVED ATTRIBUTES

The attributes `address` and `otherUsers` of the entity class `Customer` of Figure 4.1, repeated here as Figure 5.4, should not be designated as atomic. That's because you would want to be able to search for customers from a specific city or zip code, and to be able to ask whether a particular individual appears in the list of other users for a customer account. Treating these attributes as atomic would mean that users of the database would be unable to directly represent these operations in the final database.

The designer would have to provide some additional programming to implement them. For example, suppose the designer specifies `otherUsers` as an atomic string attribute. The individual names of "other users" would be stored within the string and separated by commas. An attempt to determine whether a specific person appears on the list would require a complex pattern-matching operation. An attempt to modify the value would be even more complicated.

5.5.1 Composite Attributes

A composite attribute such as `address` should not be designated as atomic, because it comprises several attributes, each with its own name and type. You would want the database system to represent each component as a separate attribute so that you could search for entities with specific values for those components and modify the components if necessary. Figure 5.5 shows the entity `Customer` with `address` decomposed into its four fields, each listed as a separate attribute. Notice that the attribute `address` does not appear in the schema. Instead, the correspondence between `address` and its four components must be maintained in the *data dictionary* (mentioned in Chapter 3).

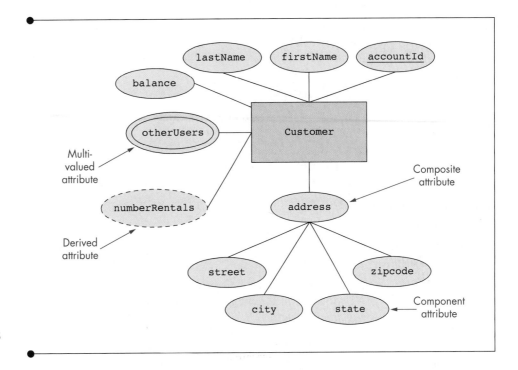

FIGURE 5.4

E-R Diagram for Entity Class
Customer

The translation of composite attributes into simple attributes is described by Step 2.

Step 2: **Break Down Composite Attributes into Their Components**

In Step 2, you break down any composite attributes of the entity class into their component attributes and add those component attributes to the schema as simple attributes. Use these guidelines:

Rule 2: For each composite attribute of a strong entity class, create an attribute in the relation schema for each component attribute. If appropriate, use the name of the composite attribute as a prefix for each of the component attribute names.

5.5.2 **Multivalued Attributes**

A multivalued attribute such as `otherUsers` also should not be designated as atomic, because the value of the attribute for a single entity comprises a set of com-

FIGURE 5.5

A Schema and Table Showing a
Composite Attribute

Schema: `Customer (accountId string, lastName string, firstName string, street string, city string, state string, zipcode string, balance number)`

accountId	lastName	firstName	street	city	state	zipcode	balance
101	Block	Jane	1010 Main St.	Apopka	FL	30458	0.00
102	Hamilton	Cherry	3230 Dade St.	Dade City	FL	30555	4.47
103	Harrison	Kate	103 Dodd Hall	Apopka	FL	30457	30.57
104	Breaux	Carroll	76 Main St.	Apopka	FL	30458	34.58

Schema: `Customer (`<u>`accountId`</u>` number, lastName string, firstName string, street string, city string, state string, zipcode string, `<u>`otherUser`</u>` string)`

<u>accountId</u>	lastName	firstName	street	city	state	zipcode	<u>otherUser</u>
104	Breaux	Carroll	76 Main St.	Apopka	FL	30458	Judy Breaux
104	Breaux	Carroll	76 Main St.	Apopka	FL	30458	Cyrus Lambeaux
104	Breaux	Carroll	76 Main St.	Apopka	FL	30458	Jean Deaux

FIGURE 5.6

Schema Definition and Sample Table for **Customer** with Multivalued Attribute **otherUser**

ponent values. Each value is subject to the same domain, but the attribute has many values. The value of `otherUsers` can be decomposed as a set of attributes, but such a set would not be directly representable in the relational model. That's because relational models contain only sets of entities—not sets of attributes. (Attributes are *part* of entity sets.)

So how might the designer get around this limitation? He or she could add a single `otherUser` attribute and make a new entity for each other user. For instance, suppose BigHit Video customer Carroll Breaux had three other users. Figure 5.6 shows three rows for this customer, each of which has a unique value for the `otherUser` attribute. The key of this schema is the set of two attributes: `accountId, otherUser`.

If you're thinking that searching and updating this customer table would be very difficult, you're grasping two basic principles of information systems. The first principle says that a data model should correspond closely to the real situations it represents. In this case, three entities (rows of the table) represent a single real customer. The second principle says that data models should keep duplication of values to a minimum. Clearly, almost all of the information in Figure 5.6 is duplicated. If Carroll Breaux moves to a new address, a database application would have to change every customer entry for him. This schema is not a good one.

If multivalued attributes cannot be represented as attributes of the containing schema, they must be put in a separate schema. One way to understand the required modification is as a change in the conceptual schema, and then as a relational model. In the E-R model, we could create an `OtherUser` entity class and relate it to the entity class `Customer`, as shown in Figure 5.7. The class `OtherUser` has a single attribute, `otherUser`. The relationship ratio between `Customer` and `OtherUser` is one-to-many. That is, a single customer may have many other users, but another user of an account must have exactly one customer. `OtherUser` is a weak entity class be-

---

Concept

Using a Fixed Number of Values for Multivalued Attributes

Another strategy that might work for representing multivalued attributes is adding a particular number of attributes to represent some of the values. For instance, we could have three attributes: `otherUser1`, `otherUser2`, and `otherUser3`. This approach would limit the maximum number of other users to three and make searching difficult. To determine whether someone is allowed to use an account, we would have to look in all three `otherUser` attributes. In some cases, this strategy works well; in most cases, however, it is unacceptable.

cause it has no key of its own and entities of the class can exist only in relationship to a customer. Thus, the multivalued attribute has become a multivalued relationship.

The best way to represent the `otherUsers` attribute as a separate relation in our relational model is as a schema with two attributes: `accountId` and `otherUser`, as shown in Figure 5.8. The attribute `accountId` represents the relationship between the other user and the customer account. We'll discuss the rationale for this choice more fully later in this chapter.

The details of the translation of multivalued attributes from E-R diagram to relational model are best understood after learning about translating relationships and weak entity classes. Step 7, in Section 5.8 explains exactly how to make the translation of multivalued attributes to relation schemas.

5.5.3 Derived Attributes

A derived attribute, such as `numberRentals` in Figure 5.4, represents a calculation in the database. The relational model does not directly support derived attributes. Hence, the attribute `numberRentals` will not appear in the `Customer` relation schema.

Relational database systems do support derived attributes through the use of defined procedures, however. We'll see examples of this in Chapter 15.

F I G U R E 5.7

E-R Diagram Showing a Separate Weak Entity Class

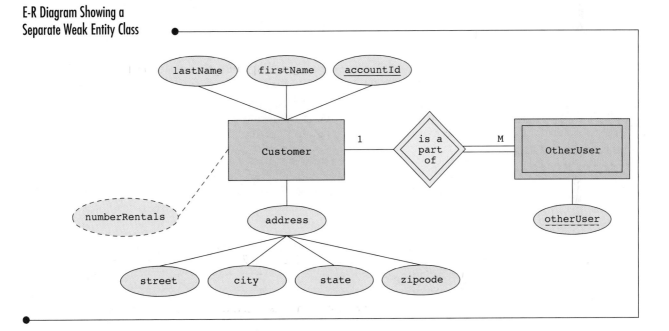

F I G U R E 5.8

Schema Definition and Sample Table for Entity Class **OtherUser**

Schema: `OtherUser` (<u>`accountId`</u> number references Customer, <u>`otherUser`</u> string)

<u>accountId</u>	<u>OtherUser</u>
104	Judy Breaux
104	Cyrus Lambeaux
104	Jean Deaux

A relational model does not specify a special data structure to represent relationships; it has only tables and attributes. Hence, we must represent each relationship type in an E-R model by tables, attributes, or some combination of the two in order to translate the E-R model into a relational model.

5.6.1 One-to-Many Relationship Types

In Chapter 3, you saw that each strong entity class has a key that uniquely identifies its entities. The relational model requires that every relation schema have a key that consists of one or more attributes of the schema. The relational model uses these keys to represent relationships between entities.

For example, consider the `Video` schema shown in Figure 5.9. The attributes of `Video` include the simple attributes `videoId` and `dateAcquired`. In addition, `movieId`, which is the key of entity class `Movie`, and `storeId`, which is the key of entity class `Store`, have been added to `Video`. These attributes represent the `IsCopyOf` and `LocatedIn` relationship types, respectively. The value of the `movieId` attribute identifies the movie of which the tape is a copy. The value of the `storeId` attribute of a `Video` entity identifies the store where the tape is located.

The `storeId` attribute of schema `Video` is called a **foreign key** attribute because its values are keys of another (foreign) schema; in this case, the value of the `storeId` of a `Video` entity is the key of a `Store` entity. The foreign key value of attribute `storeId` of a video identifies a single store where the video is located. This foreign key attribute contains the representation of the `LocatedIn` relationship between `Video` and `Store`. The notation `references Store` is included in the definition of attribute `storeId` to specify that the field is a foreign key that refers to the key of the `Store` table. Similarly the `movieId` attribute `references Movie` specifies that it is a foreign key that references the key of the `Movie` table.

F I G U R E 5.9

E-R Diagram, Schema Definition, and Sample Table for Entity Class `Video`

Schema: Video (videoId number, dateAcquired date, movieId number references Movie, storeId number references Store)

videoId	dateAcquired	movieId	storeId
101	1/25/01	101	3
111	2/5/00	123	3
112	12/31/98	123	5
113	4/5/01	123	5
114	4/5/01	189	5
123	3/25/89	123	3

The value of a foreign key must be the key of a related entity. By including `references Movie` in the declaration of the `movieId` attribute of `Video`, we declare that each `Video` entity must have a value of `movieId` that is the key of some `Movie` entity. The database system will be responsible for enforcing this constraint (restriction) on the values of the `movieId` attribute of `Video`. The constraint is called a foreign key or **referential integrity constraint**.

Because `IsLocatedIn` is a *one-to-many* relationship between `Store` and `Video`, each video is located in a single store, and a store has many videos located in it. We could not add a `videoId` attribute to schema `Store` to represent the `IsLocatedIn` relationship type because that attribute would have to be multivalued.

We can always represent a many-to-one relationship by adding a foreign key attribute to the schema that is "to-one" in the relationship.

Step 3: Create Relation Schemas for One-to-Many Relationship Types

For a one-to-many relationship type, we add the key attributes of one entity class to the other entity class. We add attributes to the class whose cardinality is "to-one." The attributes that represent the relationship type are single-valued because no more than one related entity exists.

Rule 3: For each one-to-many relationship type R between subject class S and target class T, add the key attributes of class S to class T as foreign keys. Name the attributes using the role that S plays in relationship type R. Add the attributes of the relationship type R to target class T.

5.6.2 One-to-One Relationship Types

For a *one-to-one* relationship type, we can add a foreign key attribute to either related schema. The designer must choose one of the schemas in which to include the foreign key. In some cases, one choice is better than the other.

Figure 5.10 shows two alternative representations of the one-to-one `Manages` relationship type between classes `Store` and `Employee` from the E-R diagram of Fig-

FIGURE 5.10

Schema Definitions and Sample Tables for Entity Classes **Store** and **Employee**

(a) Schema: `Store (storeId number, street string, city string, state string, zipcode string, manager string references Employee)`

storeId	street	city	state	zipcode	manager
3	2010 Liberty Rd.	Apopka	FL	30457	145-09-0967
5	1004 N. Monroe St.	Apopka	FL	30458	588-99-0093

(b) Schema: `Employee (ssn string, lastName string, firstName string, managed string references Store)`

ssn	lastName	firstName	managed
145-09-0967	Uno	Jane	3
245-11-4554	Toulouse	Jennifer	
376-77-0099	Threat	Ayisha	
479-98-0098	Fortune	Bruce	
588-99-0093	Fivozinsky	Bruce	5

ure 5.11. The schema `Store` includes the foreign key attribute `manager`. The schema `Employee` includes the foreign key attribute `managed`.

Even this approach raises some problems, however. To illustrate, we know that there are more employees than stores. In Figure 5.10, there are two stores and five employees. Every store has a manager, but many employees are not managers. Suppose we included the foreign key `manager` in the `Store` schema, as in Figure 5.10(a). The value of `manager` then becomes the key (`ssn`) of the employee who manages the store. Each row of the `Store` table will contain a non-null value for `manager`. If the foreign key `managed` is included in the `Employee` schema, as in Figure 5.10(b), its value becomes the key (`storeId`) of the store that the employee manages. Most rows of the `Employee` table will have null as the value for `managed`. As you saw in Chapter 3, the presence of many nulls in a table wastes space and makes the data ambiguous. Thus, we would want to avoid the approach shown in Figure 5.10(b).

Step 4: **Create Relation Schemas for One-to-One Relationship Types**

A one-to-one relationship can be represented as a foreign key in either related schema. The choice of where to put the foreign key is often based on a careful analysis of the expected number of entities in each related class and the expected number of instances of the relationship type. It is appropriate to put the foreign key into the schema where it will have the fewest null values.

Rule 4: For each one-to-one relationship type R between classes S and T, choose one class to be the subject and one to be the target. Add the key attributes of the subject class to the target schema as foreign key attributes and add the attributes of the relationship type to the target schema, just as in Rule 3.

Concept

Naming Foreign Key Attributes

We have two obvious choices for the name of a foreign key attribute. We can give it the name of the key attribute of the related class (`storeId` in schema `Video`) or the role name of the related class (`manager` in schema `Store`). The role name is the ideal choice, but the name of the key attribute is acceptable in many cases.

F I G U R E   5.11

E-R Diagram with Relationships of Different Cardinalities

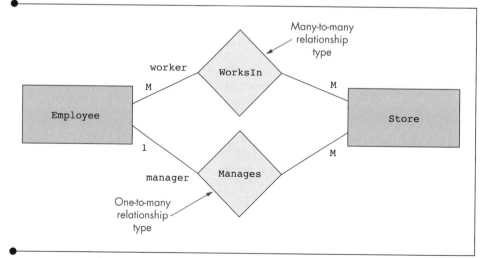

5.6.3 Representing One-to-One Relationships by Merging Entities

Figure 5.12 illustrates a final alternative for representing one-to-one relationships. In this case, the two related entity classes `Employee` and `Store` have been merged into a single relation `EmployeeStore`.

This table also poses some problems. Specifically, it removes the distinction between the two entity classes and has no explicit representation of the relationship. The E-R model identifies two separate entity classes and a relationship type, but the relational model has just one table. This table doesn't draw a clear distinction between employees and stores, even though they are very different entities. It also doesn't clarify which relationship the merger represents. Nowhere in this schema does the term "manager" appear!

5.7 REPRESENTING MANY-TO-MANY RELATIONSHIPS AS TABLES

We can't represent many-to-many relationship types by adding foreign keys to an existing schema the way we do with many-to-one and one-to-one relationship types. A foreign key added to one of the related schemas could not be single-valued, because it must have a value for each of the many related entities. The value of the foreign key would be the set of keys of the related entities.

Instead, we must represent a many-to-many relationship as a separate relation schema whose attributes are the keys of the associated entity types. The table for this schema is often called a **junction table** or a *bridge table*, because it stores information about the connections (junctions or bridges) between related tables. For instance, the `WorksIn` relationship type that you saw in Figure 5.11 can be represented by a relation schema whose attributes are `ssn` and `storeId`. The value of each of these attributes is the Social Security number (`ssn`) of the related person. Figure 5.13 shows the schema definition and a sample table for this relationship type. There are two employees in the table (their Social Security numbers begin with 3 and 5). Employee 3 works in store 3 and store 5. Employee 5 works in store 5.

FIGURE 5.12

Schema Representing a One-to-One Relationship by Merging Two Entity Classes

Schema: EmployeeStore (<u>ssn</u>, lastName, firstName, storeId, storeStreet, storeCity, storeState, storeZipcode)

Table:

<u>ssn</u>	lastName	firstName	<u>store Id</u>	storeStreet	store City	store State	store Zipcode
145-09-0967	Uno	Jane	3	2010 Liberty Rd.	Apopka	FL	30457
245-11-4554	Toulouse	Jennifer					
376-77-0099	Threat	Ayisha					
479-98-0098	Fortune	Bruce					
588-99-0093	Fivozinsky	Bruce	5	1004 N. Monroe St.	Apopka	FL	30458

Schema: `WorksIn` (<u>ssn</u> string references Employee, <u>storeId</u> number references Store)

<u>ssn</u>	<u>storeId</u>
358-44-7865	3
579-98-8778	5
358-44-7865	5

FIGURE 5.13

Schema Definition and Sample Table for Relationship Type `WorksIn`

Step 5: Create Relation Schemas for Many-to-Many Relationship Types

A many-to-many relationship type cannot be represented by single-valued attributes in either of the related classes, because an entity of either class can have many related entities. The solution to this dilemma is to represent the relationship as a separate relation schema. An example of adding a schema to represent a relationship appears in Figure 5.13.

Rule 5: For each many-to-many relationship type R between classes S and T, create a new relation schema R and add attributes to represent the key of S and the key of T as foreign key attributes. The key of schema R is the combination of those attributes. Add the relationship attributes to schema R, as in Rule 3.

In designing representations for relationship types, we are free to use Rule 5 no matter what the cardinality ratio of the relationship type is. A new schema may be employed to represent one-to-many and one-to-one relationship types. This approach may be used when the relationship type is so important that it deserves to be treated as an entity class. In addition, it might be used when there are many fewer relationships than there are entities in the related classes.

5.8   REPRESENTING WEAK ENTITY CLASSES

Weak entity classes cannot be treated in the same way as strong entity classes (Step 1) because they lack their own unique key values. Let's look at the weak entity class `Rental` from Figure 4.9, reproduced here as Figure 5.14. `Rental` has three attributes: `dateDue`, `dateRented`, and `cost`. No combination of these attributes forms a key of the class. A relation schema consisting of only those attributes would not be an accurate representation of the entity class. In particular, if two rentals had the same `dateRented`, `dateDue`, and `cost`, they would be considered the same rental.

However, according to the E-R diagram, each rental must be related by an identifying relationship to a video. Hence, the key of the related video can be the key of the rental. Figure 5.15 shows the initial schema for `Rental`. The key of `Video` is included as the key of `Rental` and is also a foreign key to the `Video` schema.

The general rule for representing weak entity classes is to create a schema for the weak entity class by including foreign key attributes for the identifying relationship types.

We are not done with class `Rental` because the schema has no representation of its relationship with `Customer`. We simply apply Rule 3 (one-to-many relationship types). The resulting schema, as shown in Figure 5.16, includes attribute `accountId` as a foreign key to `Customer`.

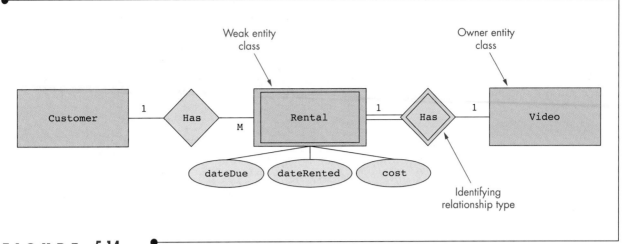

FIGURE 5.14

E-R Diagram for Weak Entity Class **Rental**

You may recall from Chapter 4 that weak entity classes may include partial keys, also called discriminators. Entity class `TimeCard` of Figure 4.19, reproduced here as Figure 5.17, has `startTime` as its discriminator. The key of the schema for `Time-Card` is the discriminators plus the foreign keys. That is, the foreign key `ssn`, the key of `Employee`, and the discriminator `startTime` form the key of relation schema `TimeCard`.

Figure 5.18 shows a schema and a sample table for the weak entity `TimeCard`. Notice that the key of the schema is the attribute set {`ssn`, `startTime`}. The attrib-

FIGURE 5.15

Preliminary Schema and Sample Table for **Rental**

Schema: Rental: (<u>videoId</u> references Video, dateDue date, dateRented date, cost currency)

<u>videoId</u>	dateRented	dateDue	cost
101	1/3/02	1/4/02	$1.59
113	2/22/02	2/25/02	$3.00
114	2/22/02	2/25/02	$3.00
123	12/1/01	12/31/01	$10.99

FIGURE 5.16

Full Schema and Sample Table for **Rental**

Schema: Rental: (<u>videoId</u> references Video, dateDue date, dateRented date, cost currency, accountId number references Customer)

<u>videoId</u>	dateRented	dateDue	cost	accountId
101	1/3/02	1/4/02	$1.59	103
113	2/22/02	2/25/02	$3.00	101
114	2/22/02	2/25/02	$3.00	101
123	12/1/01	12/31/01	$10.99	103

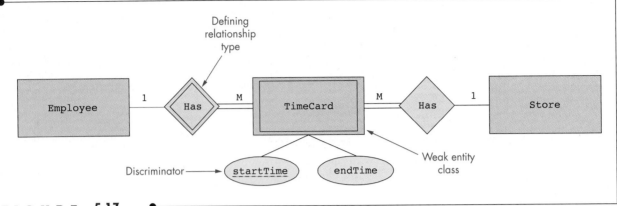

FIGURE 5.17

E-R Diagram for Entity Class
TimeCard

utes `date` and `startTime` are partial keys. From the attribute values, we can see
that no combination of two attributes is unique. The first two rows have identical
`startTime`, and `endTime` values. The last two rows have identical `ssn` and
`startDate` values. Thus, no single attribute forms a key for the schema.

Because the relationship between `TimeCard` and `Employee` is many-to-one, the
attribute `ssn` is not unique in the table and thus cannot be the key of `TimeCard`.
The attribute of the entity class `TimeCard` that combines with `ssn` to form the key
of the schema—in this case `startTime`—is called a discriminator because it provides
a distinction between two rows of the table that have the same value for the foreign
key (`ssn`) field.

Step 6: **Create Relation Schemas for Weak Entity Classes**

A weak entity class cannot be directly represented as a relation schema because it has
no key of its own. Translation of a weak entity class to a relation schema begins with
the creation of a new schema and the addition of the class attributes to the schema.
More attributes must be added to the schema for the identifying relationship types.
The key of the schema is those attributes plus the partial key attributes, if any. Rule 6
formalizes this translation.

Rule 6: For each weak entity class W, create a new relation schema. For each strong
entity class that is related by an identifying relationship type, add the key
attributes of that class to the new schema as foreign key attributes. Declare the

FIGURE 5.18

Schema Definition and Sample
Table for Entity Class
TimeCard

Schema: TimeCard (<u>ssn</u> string references Employee, <u>startTime</u> date,
endTime date, store number references Store, paid boolean)

<u>ssn</u>	<u>startTime</u>	endTime	storeId	paid
145-09-0967	01/14/02 8:15	01/14/02 12:00	3	yes
245-11-4554	01/14/02 8:15	01/14/02 12:00	3	yes
376-77-0099	02/23/02 19:00	02/24/02 2:00	5	yes
145-09-0967	01/16/02 8:15	01/16/02 12:00	3	yes
376-77-0099	01/03/02 10:00	01/03/02 14:00	5	yes
376-77-0099	01/03/02 15:00	01/03/02 19:00	5	yes

key of the schema to be the combination of the foreign key attributes and the partial key attributes of the weak entity class. Add the simple and composite attributes of class W to the schema, as in Rules 2 and 4.

Step 7: **Creating Relation Schemas for Multivalued Attributes**

A multivalued attribute cannot be represented as a single attribute, but rather must be treated as a separate entity. In essence, the multivalued attribute is treated as if it were a weak entity class in a many-to-one relationship with its containing class. The examples of Section 5.5.2 and Figure 5.8 illustrated the application of this step.

Rule 7: For each multivalued attribute M of an entity class C, define a new relation schema M. Add the components of attribute M to the new schema. Add the key attributes of the schema that contains the other attributes of C to M as a foreign key. Define the key of the new schema to be the combination of all of its attributes.

It is possible to create a key for the new schema that does not include all of the attributes. We must declare a key that is consistent with the meaning of the attributes. Examples of more complex multivalued attributes are included in the practical example at the end of the chapter.

5.9 REPRESENTING INHERITANCE AS TABLES

We've dealt with all of the components of E-R diagrams, except for inheritance relationship types and subclasses. Now we're ready to complete the discussion of translating E-R diagrams to relation schemas.

Let's first consider the simplest case of a single superclass and multiple subclasses. Recall that entity classes that are related by the special inheritance relationship are called superclasses and subclasses. The subclass inherits from the superclass. There are three basic strategies for representing inheritance as tables:

1. Create a table for the superclass with its attributes and a table for each subclass with its attributes.

2. Create a table for the superclass with all of the subclass attributes.

3. Create a table for each subclass that includes both subclass and superclass attributes.

Consider the example of DVD and videotape specialization, shown as an E-R diagram in Figure 5.19. This specialization has a single superclass, a defining attribute, and two subclasses. The class Movie and the relationship type isCopyOf illustrate how specialization and relationships interact.

The first strategy for representing specialization as tables is to create a superclass table and three subclass tables. Possible relation schemas for the three subclass tables are shown in Figure 5.20. The key of the superclass (videoId) has been added to each subclass table schema as a key and foreign key. The defining attribute media is added to the superclass (Video) schema table. Note that the relationship isCopyOf is represented here by the foreign key movieId in Video. For each DVD, an entry appears in the Video table and the DVD table. Similarly, a videotape has an entry in Video and Videotape. To access all of the attributes of a single object, a user would have to access a row from the superclass table and a row from each relevant subclass table.

In this strategy, a subclass is essentially treated as a weak entity class whose identifying relationship type is its inheritance relationship type, as with the tables DVD and Videotape represented in Figure 5.20. The attribute videoId is a foreign key to Video and forms the key of each of these classes. Because the specialization is always

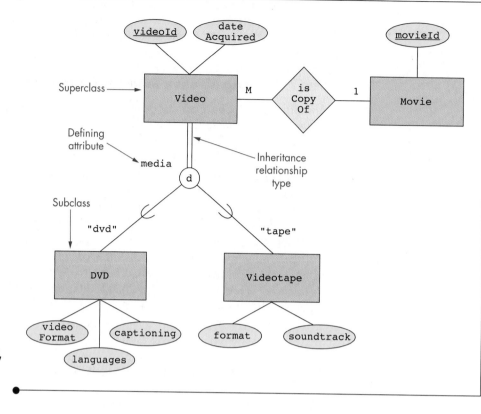

FIGURE 5.19

E-R Diagram of One Superclass, a Related Class, and Two Subclasses

Superclass schema: Video:(<u>videoId</u> number, dateAcquired date, media string, movieId number references Movie)

videoId	dateAcquired	media	movieId
101	1/25/01	dvd	101
111	2/5/00	tape	123
112	12/31/98	tape	123
113	4/5/01	dvd	123

Subclass schema: DVD:(<u>videoId</u> number references Movie, videoFormat string, languages string, captioning string)

videoId	videoFormat	languages	captioning
101	letterbox	English, Spanish	yes
113	letterbox	English, Russian, French	none

Subclass schema: Videotape:(<u>videoId</u> number references Video, format string, soundtrack string)

videoId	format	soundtrack
111	VHS	English
112	VHS	Spanish

FIGURE 5.20

Schema Definitions and Sample Tables Representing Inheritance as One Table for the Superclass and One for Each Subclass

one-to-one, we would not need a discriminator to identify a key of a subclass. The BigHit Video database would include tables for both DVDs and videotapes.

The second strategy, as illustrated by the relation schema and table shown in Figure 5.21, creates a single entity class with all of the attributes, including the defining attribute. To access all of the attributes of a single entity, a user would have to access a row from the resulting table and ignore the irrelevant attributes.

An attribute of an entity is non-null only when it is an attribute of the actual type of the entity. For example, the DVD attributes (`videoFormat`, `languages`, `captioning`) will be non-null only when `media` is "dvd" and the type of the entity is DVD. The videotape attributes (`format` and `soundtrack`) will be non-null only when `media` is "tape" and the type of the entity is `Videotape`.

This strategy poses some problems, primarily because it relies heavily on null values and leaves subclass membership somewhat vague. The example of Figure 5.21 uses attribute `media` to define subclass membership. Suppose we omit this attribute. We know that a video is a DVD if the `videoFormat` attribute is not null, but what does it mean if `videoFormat` is null? Perhaps the video format has not been entered or is not known. Hence, we can't always determine subclass membership simply by looking for null (or non-null) values.

The third strategy for representing specialization as tables is to represent each subclass as a table with all of the attributes of each entity. As shown in Figure 5.22, there is no table schema for superclass `Video`. Instead, the superclass attributes appear in each subclass table schema. Each entity belongs in a single subclass and has all of its attributes in that table. To access all of the superclass (`Employee`) entities, a user would have to access the employee attributes in both tables.

One unfortunate characteristic of the representation shown in Figure 5.22 is the duplication of the `movieId` attribute. In essence, two relationship types are represented in these schemas. There is one relationship type between `DVD` and `Movie` and one between `Videotape` and `Movie`. For access to all of the videos for a particular movie, a user would have to access both attributes. We have recreated the E-R model shown in Figure 4.10 that was found to be unacceptable.

FIGURE 5.21

Schema Definition and Sample Table Representing Specialization as a Single Table with Attributes from the Superclass and Subclasses

Step 8: **Represent Inheritance Relationship Types and Subclasses**

The translation from specialization graph to relation schemas must be coordinated among the entity classes in the collection. Usually, the same rule should be used for all classes in the collection. These entity classes may be represented as separate rela-

Schema: `Video:(`<u>`videoId`</u>` number, dateAcquired date, media string, movieId number references Movie, videoFormat string, languages string, captioning string, format string, soundtrack string)`

<u>video Id</u>	date Acquired	media	movie Id	Format	languages	captioning	format	sound track
101	1/25/01	dvd	101	letterbox	English, Spanish	yes		
111	2/5/00	tape	123				VHS	English
112	12/31/98	tape	123				VHS	Spanish
113	4/5/01	dvd	123	letterbox	English, Russian, French	none		

Schema: `DVD:(videoId` string, `dateAcquired` date, `media` string, `movieId` string, `videoFormat` string, `languages` string, `captioning` string)

videoId	date Acquired	media	movieId	video Format	languages	captioning
101	1/25/01	dvd	101	letterbox	English, Spanish	yes
113	4/5/01	dvd	123	letterbox	English, Russian, French	none

Schema: `Videotape:(videoId` string, `dateAcquired` string, `media` string, `movieId` string, `Videoformat` string, `soundtrack` string)

videoId	dateAcquired	media	movieId	format	soundtrack
111	2/5/00	tape	123	VHS	English
112	12/31/98	tape	123	VHS	Spanish

FIGURE 5.22

Schemas Representing Specialization as One Table for Each Subclass

tions, each with its own attributes (Rule 8a), as a single relation C with all attributes (Rule 8b), or as separate relations, each of which has all of the superclass attributes and its individual subclass attributes (Rule 8c).

Rule 8a: Create a relation for each superclass C using the appropriate rules. For each specialization of C that has a defining attribute, add that attribute to the schema for C. For each subclass S, create a new relation schema. Add the simple and composite attributes of class S to the schema, as in Rules 1b and 2. For each superclass C of S, add the key of C as a foreign key referencing relation C. Declare the key of the subclass relation for S to be the composite of these foreign keys.

Rule 8b: For each superclass C, create a new relation schema using the appropriate rules. For each specialization of C that has a defining attribute, add that attribute to the schema for C. For each subclass S of C, add the simple and composite attributes of S to the schema for C.

Rule 8c: For each subclass S, create a new relation schema. For each superclass C of S, add the simple and composite attributes of C and S to the new schema, as in Rules 1b and 2. Declare the key of the schema to be the combination of the key attributes from the superclasses. For each superclass C that has a partial specialization, create a new relation schema and add all of the attributes of C.

Rule 8a is applicable to every specialization class. Rule 8b should not be used for multiple generalizations (multiple inheritance), and Rule 8c should not be used for overlapping specialization and multiple specializations.

For Rules 8a and 8b, the superclass schemas may have already been created by the application of Rules 1a or 6.

CASE IN POINT: RELATIONAL MODEL
5.10 FOR VIDEO SALES FOR BIGHIT VIDEO

At the end of Chapter 4, we had developed an E-R diagram for video sales, reproduced here as Figure 5.23. Our goal in this practical example is to turn the E-R diagram into a set of relation schemas. We'll take the steps outlined in this chapter, one

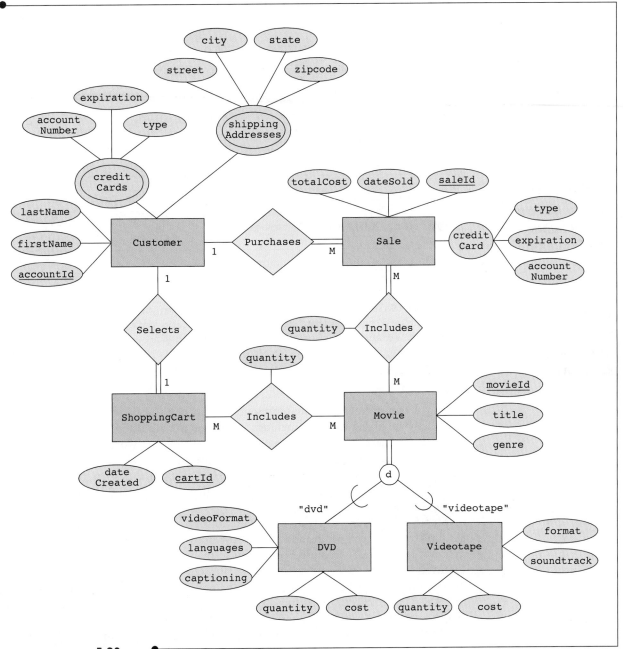

FIGURE 5.23

E-R Diagram for Video Sales

at a time. The schemas will begin with relations for each entity class and will evolve into their final versions.

Figure 5.24 shows the results of applying Step 1 to the four entity classes of Figure 5.23 and their simple attributes. We still haven't processed the many-valued attributes, the relationship types, and the subclasses.

The next step (Step 2) adds the composite attributes to the schema. The only simple composite attribute is `creditCard` of entity class `Sale`. Figure 5.25 shows the new schema for `Sale`. The new attributes are highlighted. The component attributes of `creditCard` are named by appending the composite name to the attribute name.

Step 3 tells us how to represent one-to-many relationship types. The only one-to-many relationship type is `Purchases`. Because each sale has exactly one customer, we add the key of `Customer` to the schema for `Sale`. The result is shown in Figure 5.26. The foreign key that represents `Purchases` is highlighted in the figure.

FIGURE 5.24

Preliminary Relation Schemas for Video Sales

Schemas:

Customer: (<u>accountId</u> number, lastName string, firstName string)

Sale: (<u>saleId</u> number, dateSold date, totalCost number)

Movie: (<u>movieId</u> number, title string, genre string)

ShoppingCart: (<u>cartId</u> number, dateCreated date)

FIGURE 5.25

Schema for **Sale** with Composite Attribute **creditCard**

Schema: Sale: (<u>saleId</u> number, dateSold date, totalCost number, creditCardType string, creditCardExpiration date, creditCardAccountNumber number)

FIGURE 5.26

Schema for **Sale** with Relationship Type **Purchases**

Schema: Sale: (<u>saleId</u> number, dateSold date, totalCost number, creditCardType string, creditCardExpiration date, creditCardAccountNumber number, accountId number references Customer)

Step 4 tells us how to create representation for one-to-one relationship types. The E-R diagram of Figure 5.23 includes one-to-one relationship types Selects between Customer and ShoppingCart. We must choose where to put the foreign key. In this case, a shopping cart must have a customer, but a customer does not need a shopping cart. It is best to add the key of the Customer class to the ShoppingCart relation because the attribute will never be null. Figure 5.27 shows the modification to ShoppingCart.

Step 5 tells us how to create representations of many-to-many relationship types. As directed, we need to create a schema for both of the many-to-many relationship types of Figure 5.23. Because both many-to-many relationship types are called Includes, we must select new names for the schemas. Figure 5.28 shows the new schemas SaleItem and CartItem. The names were selected because each entity in the SaleItem schema represents a single item (a movie) that is included in the sale. The key of SaleItem is the combination of the two foreign keys. Similarly, each entity in the CartItem schema represents a single item that is included in the cart.

FIGURE 5.27

Schema for **ShoppingCart** That Includes a Foreign Key to Represent the **Selects** Relationship Type

Schema: ShoppingCart: (<u>cartId</u> number, dateCreated date, accountId number references Customer)

FIGURE 5.28

Relation Schemas for the Many-to-Many Relationship Types of Figure 5.23

Schema: SaleItem: (<u>saleId</u> number references Sale, <u>movieId</u> references Movie, quantity number)

Schema: CartItem: (<u>cartId</u> number references ShoppingCart, <u>movieId</u> references Movie, quantity number)

SANDY CHARRON
Steps Through the Design and Implementation of a Database

I'm a consultant working for the Central Media Group at Pearson Education. This department produces technology-based supplements for textbooks. I administer a database that tracks the production of online courses and other supplements to textbooks.

DAY TO DAY One of my everyday activities is to keep the database in sync with the needs of its users. Sometimes that's as simple as adding new fields to existing tables, or changing a field's size or other field rules. Other times, the data model needs re-thinking, and I must meet with both management and the users to discuss the requirements before making any major changes to the system. Either way, it's a lot easier than before. In the late 70's we used to design database applications from scratch in the classroom—we didn't have anything like Oracle or SQL.

> **In the late 70's we used to design database applications from scratch in the classroom—we didn't have anything like Oracle or SQL.**

FROM DESIGN TO IMPLEMENTATION

First: Interview the users of the database, in order to sketch out the data model. While designing the components of the database, it's often necessary to go back to the users to clarify the meaning of some data elements and how they relate to the big picture.

Second: Once the "first draft" of the database is complete, it's helpful to populate it with some real data for testing. Create enough records with typical data to test the table relationships and forms, then test a few queries on the data.

Third: The users should be given a chance to experiment with this first version of the database and give feedback on any problems, so the final version can be completed.

Fourth: Populate the database with the real data, which may involve importing vast amounts of data from existing spreadsheets or other formats, or it may be done on a record-by-record basis using the data entry forms.

The last thing to always remember: The database is a living thing that grows with users' ever-changing needs. Each major update to the database requires another phase of the steps above.

Each relationship type has an attribute `quantity`. Each of these attributes is properly included as an attribute of the corresponding new relation schema.

Step 6 applies to weak entity classes. The E-R diagram includes no such classes.

Step 7 tells us how to represent multivalued attributes. Class `Customer` has two multivalued attributes `creditCards` and `shippingAddresses`. Figure 5.29 shows schemas `CreditCards` and `ShippingAddresses`. You will notice that the names are now capitalized since they have changed from attributes to schemas. Each new schema contains `accountId` as a foreign key to `Customer` together with the components of the attribute.

Rule 7 requires that we select a key for each new schema. The key of `Shipping-Addresses` is the combination of all attributes of the schema. The key of `Credit-Cards` is declared to be the combination of `accountId` and `accountNumber`. By this declaration, we declare that the combination of those two attributes is unique and that the key does not require the inclusion of `type` and `expiration`.

Step 8 tells us how to handle inheritance. In this case, we will apply rule 8a, which creates a schema for the base class and for each subclass. Class `Movie`, the base class, was represented by a relation schema as part of step 1 in Figure 5.24. Figure 5.30 shows the schemas for the subclasses.

Some constraints that are in the E-R diagram are not represented in the schema. For instance, the schema does not specify the participation constraint that each movie must also be either a DVD or a videotape. We will have to enforce these constraints in the application programs.

Figure 5.31 shows the full database schema for the E-R diagram of Figure 5.23.

FIGURE 5.29

Relation Schemas for the Multivalued Attributes of Entity Class **Customer**

Schema: CreditCards: (<u>accountId</u> number references Customer, <u>accountNumber</u> number, type string, expiration date)

Schema: ShippingAddresses: (<u>accountId</u> number references Customer, <u>street</u> string, <u>city</u> string, <u>state</u> string, <u>zipcode</u> string)

FIGURE 5.30

Relation Schemas for the Subclasses of **Video**

Schema: DVD: (<u>movieId</u> number references Movie, videoFormat string, languages string, captioning string, cost currency, quantity number)

Schema: Videotape: (<u>movieId</u> number references Movie, format string, soundtrack string, cost currency, quantity number)

FIGURE 5.31

Database Schema for Video Sales

Customer: (<u>accountId</u> number, lastName string, firstName string)

Sale: (<u>saleId</u> number, dateSold date, totalCost number, creditCardType string, creditCardExpiration date, creditCardAccountNumber number, accountId number references Customer)

Movie: (<u>movieId</u> number, title string, genre string)

ShoppingCart: (<u>cartId</u> number, dateCreated date, accountId number references Customer)

SaleItem: (<u>saleId</u> number references Sale, <u>movieId</u> references Movie, quantity number)

CartItem: (<u>cartId</u> number references ShoppingCart, <u>movieId</u> references Movie, quantity number)

CreditCard: (<u>accountId</u> number references Customer, <u>accountNumber</u> number, type string, expiration date)

ShippingAddress: (<u>accountId</u> number references Customer, <u>street</u> string, <u>city</u> string, <u>state</u> string, <u>zipcode</u> string)

DVD: (<u>movieId</u> number references Movie, videoFormat string, languages string, captioning string, cost currency, quantity number)

Videotape: (<u>movieId</u> number references Movie, format string, soundtrack string, cost currency, quantity number)

CHAPTER SUMMARY

The relational data model is used to define logical schemas for information systems. It has a single data structure, the relation, that is used to store the contents of the database. The conceptual data model, defined using the techniques of Chapter 3, can be directly translated into a relational data model. In turn, the relational data model is supported by database management systems that provide operations to support the creation and manipulation of relations.

A relation is a two-dimensional table of atomic values. It consists of a set of rows, each with the same number of fields (columns). Each row represents an entity. Each row of a relation is unique, and each relation has a key set of attributes. There is no ordering of the rows. The structure of a relation is defined by a relation schema that defines the name of the relation and the name and type of each of its attributes. A database schema is the set of the relation schemas for the tables of the database.

A relation schema is created to represent an entity class in a conceptual model. The attributes of the schema include the attributes of the class. The single-valued attributes of the class are directly represented by schema attributes. In contrast, a composite attribute of an entity class is represented by one attribute for each single-valued field of the composite type. A multivalued attribute is usually represented by a separate relation schema.

Relationship types are represented in the relational model by foreign key attributes. A foreign key is a set of attributes in one relation schema that refer to a key of the related schema. A foreign key may be added to one of the related schemas to represent a one-to-one or many-to-one relationship type. A new schema must be created to represent a many-to-many relationship type with foreign key attributes to reference each of the related schemas. As part of this effort, the attributes of the relationship type are placed in the schema with the foreign key attributes.

A relation schema is created for each weak entity class in the conceptual model. This schema contains all of the attributes of the weak entity class plus foreign key attributes for each owner entity class. The key of the schema is the foreign key attributes plus the discriminator attributes of the weak class.

Specialization graphs are translated into relational schemas by creating a schema for the superclass and each subclass, by creating a single schema with attributes from the superclass and all of the subclasses, or by creating a schema for each subclass that includes the superclass attributes.

Each multivalued attribute of an entity class is represented as a weak entity class related to the containing class.

This chapter also summarized the process of transformation of conceptual models into relational models using 8 specific rules.

KEY TERMS

Atomic attribute. An attribute that cannot be decomposed into simpler values.

Constraint. A restriction on the state (or contents) of a table.

Database schema. The collection of relation schemas that define a database.

Foreign key. A set of attributes of a relation schema that reference the key of another schema.

Key. A minimal set of attributes that are unique in a table. More formally, a superkey for which no subset of attributes is a superkey.

Junction table or bridge table. A relation that is created to represent a many-to-many relationship type.

Metadata. The specification of the structure of a database. Also called a database schema.

Referential integrity constraint. A constraint on the contents of a table that requires that the value of a foreign key attribute of an entity must be the key of an entity in the related table. Referential integrity can be enforced by Access and other database systems.

Relation. A set of rows that come from the domain of a relation schema.

Relation schema. The definition of a domain of values.

Relational data model. A data model that describes all data as relations that are two-dimensional tables of atomic values.

QUESTIONS

1. What are the differences between an E-R model and a relational model of an information system?

2. Characterize the differences in the types of attributes in E-R models and relational models. What restrictions are placed on relational attributes that are not placed on E-R attributes?

3. Define the terms *relation*, *relation schema*, *database schema*, *atomic attribute*, *key*, and *foreign key*.

4. Discuss the declaration of keys in the context of the following questions and the table of Figure 5.1.
   a. What does it mean for a column of the table to be a key?
   b. For which columns of the table are all of the attribute values unique?
   c. Is it reasonable to make attribute genre a key? Why or why not?
   d. Based on the answers to a, b, and c, why is it not always possible to infer a key constraint from the contents of a table?
   e. Give some reasons why designers must declare the keys of each table.

5. Under what circumstances can attributes of an entity class in an E-R model not be represented as simple attributes of the associated relation schema? Give examples.

6. How are simple attributes of an entity class represented in a relation schema?

7. How are composite attributes of an entity class in an E-R model represented in the associated relation schema?

8. How is a derived attribute of an entity class represented in a relation schema?

9. Under what circumstances can a relationship type not be represented by attributes in one of the associated relation schemas?

10. How are attributes of a one-to-many relationship type represented in the relational model?

11. Describe three different ways to represent a one-to-one relationship in the relational model.

12. Why is it impossible to represent a many-to-many relationship type as attributes in one of the related relation schemas?

13. When a weak entity class in an E-R model is represented as a relation schema, what is its key?

14. Briefly describe the three methods of representing inheritance as relation schemas. Which one of the three can always be used?

15. Consider the tables of Figure 5.20.
   a. What rows must be added to the tables to represent the addition of a new DVD video for movie 123? Give appropriate values for all attributes.
   b. What rows must be added to the tables to represent the addition of a new videotape video for movie 123? Give appropriate values for all attributes.
   c. Suppose we delete the first row from the DVD table. What other rows of tables must be deleted?

16. Consider the tables of Figure 5.21.
   a. What rows must be added to the tables to represent the addition of a new DVD video for movie 123? Give appropriate values for all attributes.
   b. What rows must be added to the tables to represent the addition of a new videotape video for movie 123? Give appropriate values for all attributes.
   c. Suppose we delete the first row from the Video table. What other rows of tables must be deleted?

17. Consider the tables of Figure 5.22.
   a. What rows must be added to the tables to represent the addition of a new DVD video for movie 123? Give appropriate values for all attributes.
   b. What rows must be added to the tables to represent the addition of a new videotape video for movie 123? Give appropriate values for all attributes.
   c. Suppose we delete the first row from the DVD table. What other rows of tables must be deleted?

PROBLEMS

18. Translate the E-R diagram below into a database schema. Take care in selecting attribute names that will represent relationship types.

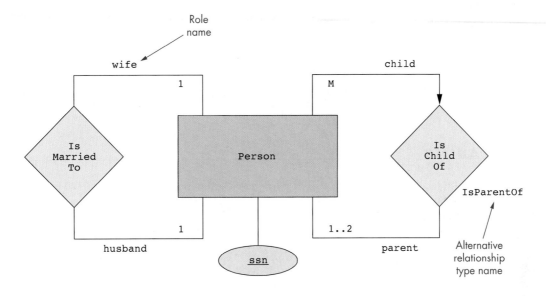

19. Give three different schemas that represent the `IsMarriedTo` relationship type for the E-R diagram of Problem 18. The three schemas should differ at least in the names of the attributes.

Hint: One of the schemas should represent the relationship type as a separate relation schema and not as an attribute of `Person`.

20. Create a relation schema for the following E-R diagram.

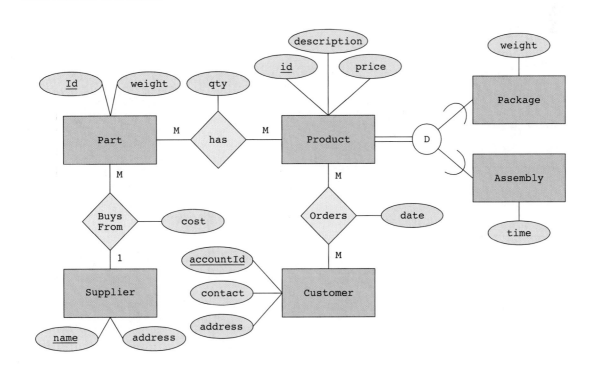

PROJECTS

21. Continue your BigHit Video project from Chapter 4 by translating the E-R diagram that you created for your Chapter 4 project into a database schema.

23. Continue your BigHit Online project from Chapter 4 by translating the E-R diagram that you created for your Chapter 4 project into a database schema.

22. Continue your Movie Lovers project from Chapter 4 by translating the E-R diagram that you created for your Chapter 4 project into a database schema.

FURTHER READING

E .F. Codd introduced the relational model in his 1970 paper in the *Communications of the ACM* [Codd70]. He received the ACM Turing award in 1981 and described his efforts in his award lecture [Codd82]. Many excellent books present significantly more detail on this subject than is given in this text. Codd's 1990 book [Codd90] is his restatement of the relational model 20 years later. Date's book [Date99], now in its seventh edition, is recognized as one of the most comprehensive treatments of the relational model.

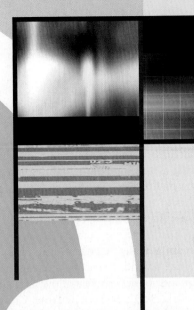

CHAPTER 6

Defining Relational Databases with Microsoft Access

In this chapter, you will learn:

- What Microsoft Access is and why it is valuable
- How to create databases using Access
- How to define tables in Access

- How to specify attributes and constraints
- How to define relationships
- How to specify table displays

In Chapter 5, you learned how to translate E-R diagrams into a relational model. Once you've refined your relational model, it's time to build an actual database founded on the model. This chapter shows you how.

There are numerous tools for creating databases. Graphical user interfaces that interact with multiple database vendors are available from PowerSoft (the PowerBuilder software system) and Microsoft (Microsoft Access). Each database vendor provides a package, often called an *enterprise manager*, that works with that vendor's system. Oracle has an enterprise manager for its Oracle 8i and Oracle 9i, IBM has one for DB2, and Microsoft for SQL Server.

In this chapter, you'll learn how to use Microsoft Access to create and manipulate Access databases. Access offers numerous advantages as a database-construction tool. In particular, its graphical user interfaces allow users to create and modify schemas using point, click, and type; it uses the same basic interfaces and development tools of the Microsoft Office software family; and it can be used to create databases with almost any database server. Access is designed to be used by novice database users, but is also a reasonable tool for more knowledgeable database developers.

6.1   CREATING AN ACCESS DATABASE

A Microsoft Access database is contained in a single file that has a ".mdb" extension. To begin creating a new database, you start Access by selecting it from the `Start` menu. You'll see a dialog with the option of opening an existing database or creating a new one. Choose the option to create a blank database. You'll specify the name of your new database and access will create it and store it as a file on your computer. Figure 6.1 shows what you would see in Access if you had just created a new database called `BigHitVideo`.

After naming a new database in Access, you will use Access tools to create the database tables, enter data into them, and define relationships between tables. As shown in Figure 6.1, Access offers three options for creating tables: `Create table in Design view`, `Create table by using wizard`, and `Create table by entering data`. The create table **wizard** is a sequence of dialogs that allow you to select from sample table definitions and sample attributes to create a new table. Creating tables by entering data presents you with an anonymous table with attributes (Access calls them **fields**) named `Field1`, `Field2`, etc. In this case, you must modify the field names as needed.

When a database user creates a table by using a wizard or by entering data, Access automatically determines the table definition, that is, the relation schemas. You have already learned how to analyze database information requirements and create table definitions through data modeling, so you can enter the table definitions directly. Therefore, in this chapter we'll focus on creating tables in design view. However, we will use the wizard option to define table forms specifying how we want Access to display the database tables.

A Microsoft Access database contains a combination of table definitions, table values, and application programs consisting of queries, user interfaces, and reports. Figure 6.2 shows various windows of the user interface that you could view if you were working on the BigHit Video Access database.

- The *main window* lets you select and display database objects of different types, such as tables, forms, queries, or reports.
- *Table contents windows* show the entities, attributes, and attribute values that are stored in tables and that let you modify the contents.
- *Table design windows* let you create and modify tables.

FIGURE   6.1

Creating a New Database in Microsoft Access

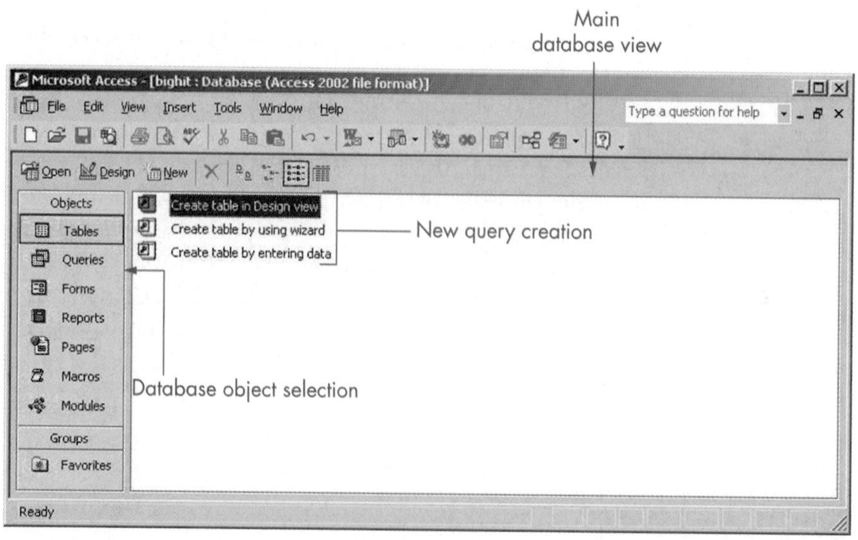

Concept

The Storage of Information in Memory and on Disk

Data used by computer programs can be stored in disk files or in memory. Data stored in disk files is retained when the program stops executing and even when the computer is turned off. Data stored in memory is deleted when the program stops or the computer is turned off.

When a computer program begins executing, it must transfer any data it needs from disk to memory. Programs can only directly access data that is stored in memory. The data is manipulated in memory and must be written back to disk in order to be saved. When the program stops its execution, all data in its memory is lost.

For example, a word processing program reads a document from disk and stores it in memory. The document display is produced from the memory version of the document. Changes to the document are stored in memory and not copied to disk. When the user closes the program, it shows a dialog window asking the user whether to save the latest version of the document.

A database program behaves differently. It reads the contents of the database from disk to memory only when needed—usually a few rows at a time. When data is changed in memory, the database program writes the data from memory back to disk so that even if the program crashes, the database is safely stored on the disk.

The contents of an Access database are stored in a disk file and that file is kept up to date. When Access is closed it doesn't ask the user whether the data must be saved because it already has been saved.

When Access displays the contents of a table on the screen, it is showing what it has in its memory. When a user changes the values of fields on the screen, Access changes its memory contents. However, the disk update does not take place until the user closes the table display or moves to another row of the table. The memory update and the disk update are not completely synchronized.

A general rule of database applications is that to modify data, the application must read data from disk files into memory and change the contents of the memory version. The change to the disk image, that is, the change to the permanent contents of the database, takes place separately.

- *Query design windows* enable you to create special ways of looking at the table contents.
- *Form design windows* enable you to create and modify custom presentations of the contents of database tables.
- *Form contents windows* let you manipulate database tables in a custom layout.

6.2 CREATING TABLES IN ACCESS

The first step in creating a new database is to get a copy of the schema definition that was created using the techniques of the previous chapter. Recall that we began the information system development by analyzing the information requirements and using them to define a conceptual data model as an E-R diagram. Then we translated the E-R diagram into a set of relation schemas. Now we are ready to create the tables that will store the information. Each relation schema will be represented by a single database table.

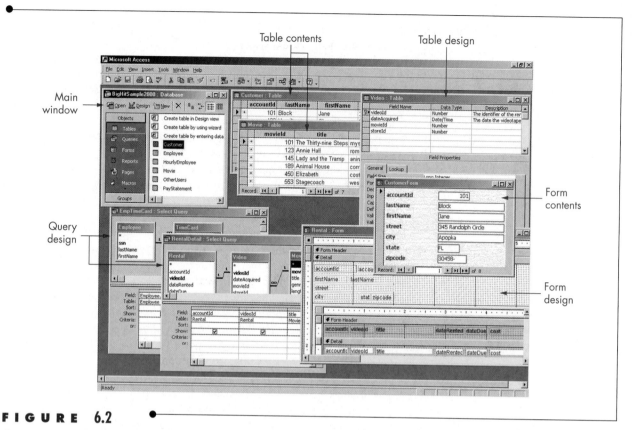

FIGURE 6.2
Elements of an Access Database

As you saw in Chapter 5, each relation schema in a relational data model is represented as a table showing the names of the attributes for the entity class embodied in the table. Access lets you specify characteristics and comments for each attribute.

To create tables for the schemas of the BigHit Video database in Access, we'll begin by clicking on the `Create table in Design view` entry shown in Figure 6.1. Access presents a blank table definition, as shown in Figure 6.3. Each attribute (called a *field* in Access) has a name, data type, and description.

FIGURE 6.3
Design View of a New Table

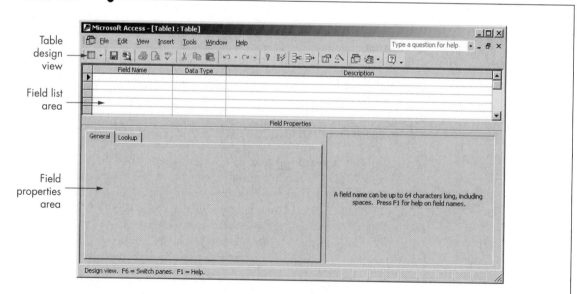

Suppose we wanted to start by creating the `Customer` table. First we would retrieve the schema for the `Customer` table we prepared in our relational data model, reproduced here as Figure 6.4. Then we would enter the `Customer` attributes in the `Field Name` column, enter the data type and description for each attribute, save the table, and name the table `Customer`.

Figure 6.5 shows what the design view of the `Customer` table would look like after we performed these steps. We would define each table from our relational model in the Access database in a similar way.

Note that in Figure 6.5, the `accountId` field is marked as the key attribute, as indicated by the symbol to the left of the field name. To designate an attribute as a key, we select the field and click on the key icon in the toolbar. The icon is shown pressed down in Figure 6.5 because the selected attribute is the key of the table.

FIGURE 6.4

A Schema and Table for **Customer**, Reproduced from Figure 5.5

Schema: Customer (accountId string, lastName string, firstName string, street string, city string, state string, zipcode string, balance number)

accountId	lastName	firstName	street	city	state	zipcode	balance
101	Block	Jane	1010 Main St.	Apopka	FL	30458	0.00
102	Hamilton	Cherry	3230 Dade St.	Dade City	FL	30555	4.47
103	Harrison	Kate	103 Dodd Hall	Apopka	FL	30457	30.57
104	Breaux	Carroll	76 Main St.	Apopka	FL	30458	34.58

FIGURE 6.5

Design View of **Customer** Table

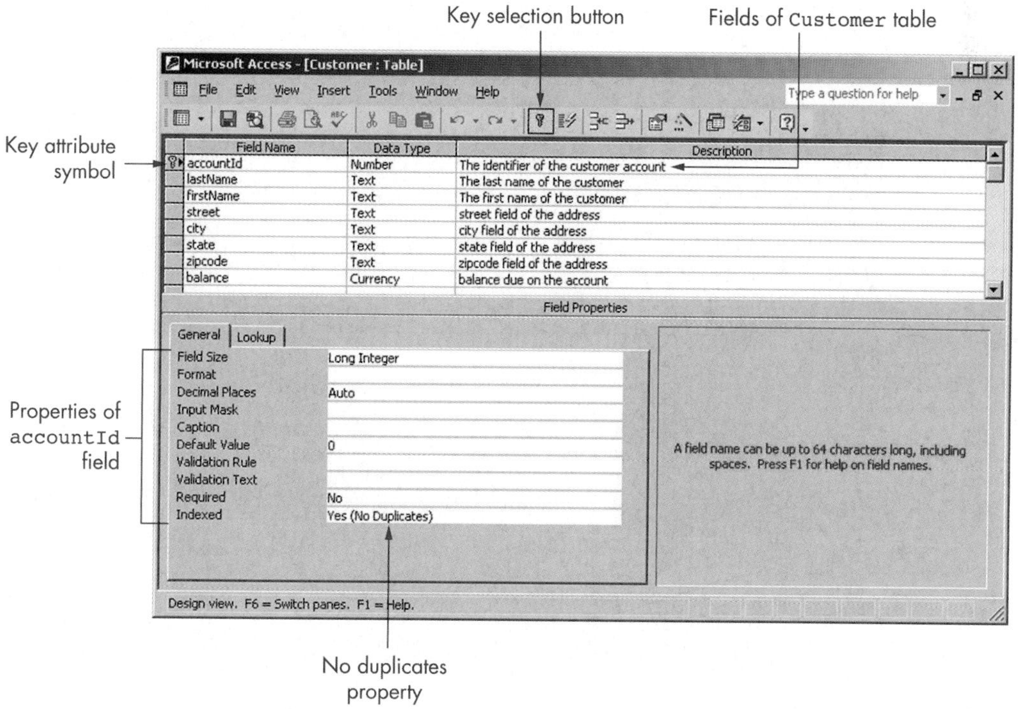

To designate a multi-attribute key, hold the shift key down and click on each attribute that makes up the key. Then click on the key icon once. Figure 6.6 shows the definition of the `PreviousRental` table with a three-attribute key.

The bottom half of the window shown in Figures 6.5 and 6.6 lets you specify default values, default captions for use in forms, validation rules, and formats. In addition, you can specify a default representation for use in forms. These fields will be explained in the discussion on forms in Section 6.3.

6.2.1 Entering Attribute Values into an Access Table

Once we create a table, we can enter rows of attribute values for each entity within the table. To do this, we open the table in **datasheet view**, click on the last line of the table and type the attribute values. Figure 6.7 shows the datasheet view of the `Customer` table with the last line selected and a new account ID. Filling in the rest of values will result in a new entry in the table. To move between rows, we can use the navigation buttons at the bottom of the window. The leftmost button ⏮ lets us select the first row of the table. The rightmost button ⏭ lets us add a new row to the table.

Figure 6.7 shows what the datasheet looks like after several rows of data have been entered. Note that each row of the datasheet contains the attribute values of a single

FIGURE 6.6

Design View Showing a Multi-attribute Key

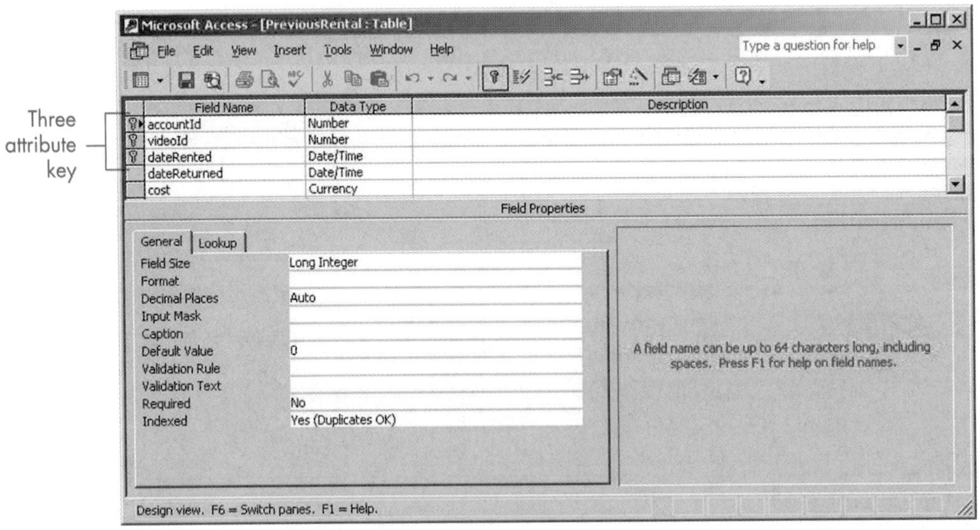

FIGURE 6.7

Customer Table with Four Rows

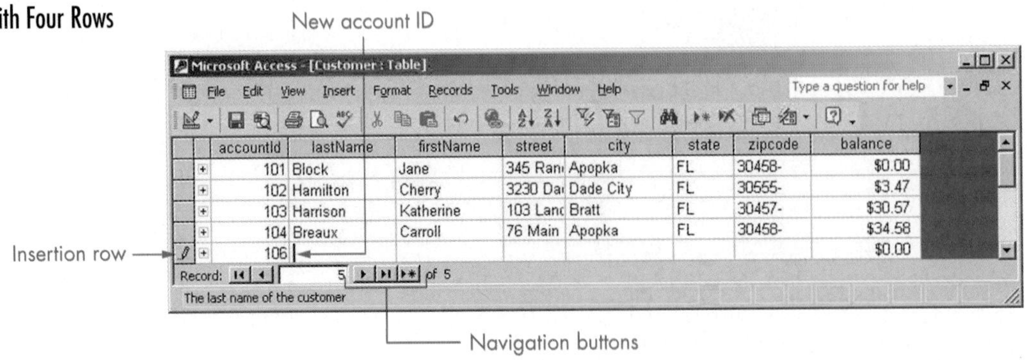

customer, and each column has the values of a single attribute for all customers. In this view, the width of the columns seems too wide for the `accountId` and `first-Name` columns and too narrow for the `street` column. We can adjust the column widths by using the cursor to move the borders between the attribute names.

INTERVIEW

SANDY CHARRON
On the Critical Stage of Requirements Gathering

WHOM TO TALK TO WHEN GATHERING REQUIREMENTS The first folks I talk to are those who are the source of the data. They can give me an appropriate name for each field, determine its format, maximum size, and description, and explain what each field means in relation to their business procedures. Secondly, I talk to those who will be entering the data in the system who can advise me on the design of the data entry forms they'll be using. Finally, I talk to managers and anyone else who has reporting needs to find out what kind of big questions they'll be asking of the database: For example, "give me a list of all products that did not meet their deadlines, or that went over budget last quarter." Chances are, you'll have representatives of all three groups in meetings during the planning phase of the database.

EMPLOYEES USE THE DATABASE IN DIFFERENT WAYS Sometimes different constituencies use the data in different ways, and my job is to find a solution that satisfies all of them. I could spend hours, days, or weeks discussing the requirements with users. This time is always well spent, as errors in the initial design can lead to vast amounts of time later redesigning the structure and adjusting the live data to fit the new structure.

HERE'S AN EXAMPLE PROBLEM A manager asked me to include fields to track the cost of each step of production: coding, QA, other media costs, etc. He wanted a cumulative field for each step in the process; he was not interested in detail, such as invoice dates or individual charges.

SOME REQUIREMENTS GATHERING When I brought this up with the person who would be entering the cost data, I learned that he would need a way to balance the data entered against his monthly totals of charges. So, I planned a data table for invoices where each record would represent a line item charge on an invoice. This way, he could enter invoice numbers, dates, and vendors, which gave

> ❝I could spend hours, days, or weeks discussing the requirements with users. This time is always well spent, as errors in the initial design can lead to vast amounts of time later redesigning the structure and adjusting the live data to fit the new structure.❞

him the ability to reconcile the total amount charged per month according to the database with the total amount paid out each month by the Accounts Payable department. For the manager's needs, I could write code that would add up the individual costs and post cumulative amounts on the manager's view of cost data.

FURTHER REQUIRE-MENTS GATHERING This issue became more complicated when I discussed with a project manager how these costs should be linked to the products produced. I learned that sometimes a single charge would have to be split among multiple products.

AND THE END RESULT From three different users I was given three different needs concerning product cost data. If I had simply incorporated the manager's needs into my data model, the "cost accounting" problem would have been solved quickly, easily, and incorrectly. It took longer to scope out the requirements for product cost accounting and it resulted in a more complex data model; but in the end, time was saved, as it would have been more difficult to change the data model after the database was complete and in use.

6.2.2 **Modifying Attribute Values in an Access Table**

After we've entered attribute values, we can modify a table's contents, again by using the datasheet view. For example, suppose we wanted to modify the city of customer Cherry Hamilton. To do that, we could simply click the mouse on the value we want to modify. Figure 6.8 shows what the datasheet view looks like as we modify the city attribute of the second row of the `Customer` table.

Once we've selected the value, we make the desired change by typing. We can use the mouse or the tab key to move to other attributes of the same row. However, the change we make in the row won't become permanent until we either select a different row or close the table. At this point, Access writes the new values in the row to the database file. This difference between the values displayed on the screen and the values stored in the database becomes particularly important when multiple users are using the same database, as we'll see in later chapters.

6.3   CREATING FORMS FROM TABLES

In Access, a **user interface** is called a **form**. Forms enable you to tell the system how you want it to display a table's contents. The datasheet view of Figures 6.7 and 6.8 are the simplest forms in Access. Other types of forms must be created explicitly by users. You can create forms by first clicking on the `Forms` tab on the right side of the Access database display, as shown in Figure 6.9. The `Forms` tab display includes options that let you create forms using a wizard. Double-clicking on `Create form by using Wizard` will result in the screen shown in Figure 6.10.

To create a new form, you select the table whose display you want to change. In Figure 6.10, we've selected the `Customer` table. The wizard then prompts you to select which fields of the `Customer` table you want the system to display. In Figure 6.10, all of the fields except `balance` have been added to the `Selected Fields` box.

You click the `Next` button, and the system responds with a screen similar to the one shown in Figure 6.11. You can then select the style of form you want. Figure 6.11 shows the **Columnar form** that shows a single row at a time with the fields in columns. `Tabular` and `Datasheet` forms are two-dimensional tables. A `Justified` form, like `Columnar`, shows a single row of the table, but the fields are arranged in rows from left to right and top to bottom. Examples of `Columnar`, `Tabular`, and `Justified` forms are included after the rest of the discussion of the wizard.

The `Datasheet` form lets you modify column widths and formatting, column headings, and the order of columns in a table. Figure 6.8 is an example of a datasheet form.

FIGURE   6.8

Datasheet View of
Customer Table with
Added Entries

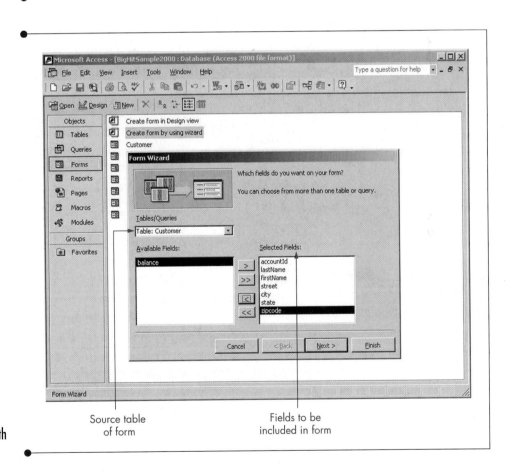

F I G U R E 6.9

Forms Tab in Access

F I G U R E 6.10

Selecting Table and Fields with
the Forms Wizard

Clicking Next in the layout selection window will produce the style selection window, as shown in Figure 6.12. We can select a style to produce an initial background image, color palette, and font for the form. In Figure 6.12, the Stone style has been selected. The Stone style has a raised field for the column labels with red text, among other style characteristics. Figure 6.13 shows the columnar form for the selected fields of the Customer table with the Stone style. Figure 6.14 shows the same fields in

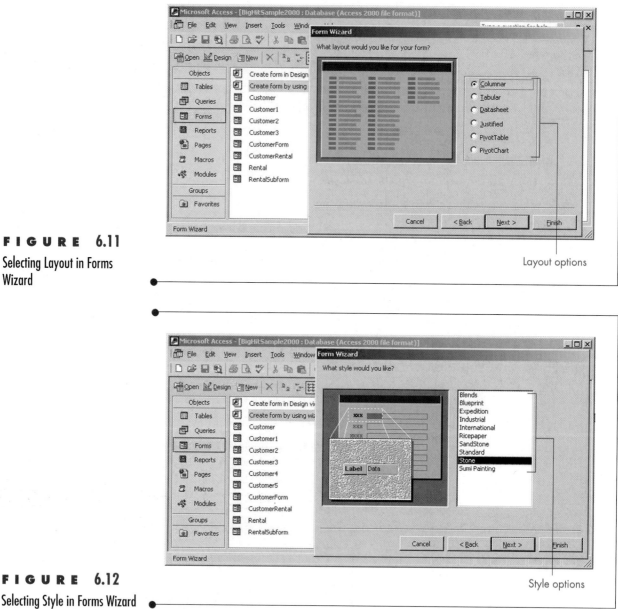

FIGURE 6.11

Selecting Layout in Forms Wizard

Layout options

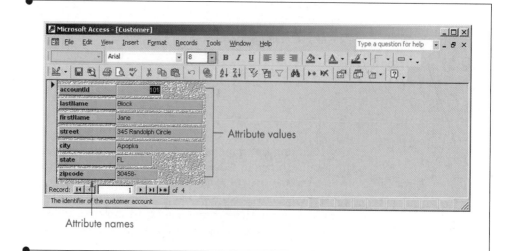

FIGURE 6.12

Selecting Style in Forms Wizard

Style options

FIGURE 6.13

Columnar Form Created by Wizard

Attribute names

Attribute values

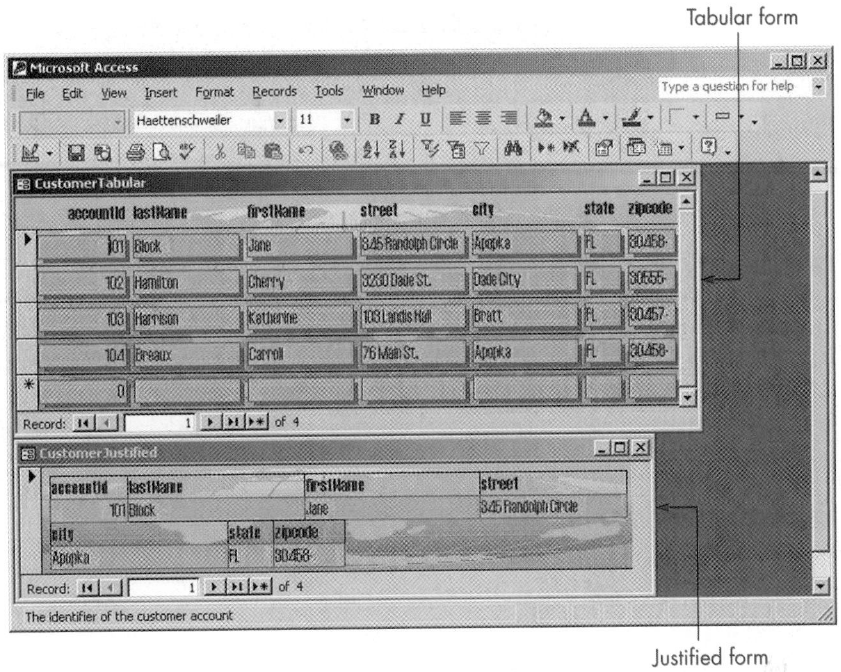

Tabular form

Justified form

FIGURE 6.14
Tabular and Justified Forms with International Style

forms in tabular and justified layouts. These forms were created with the `International` style, which features a globe in the background image.

It is simple to create a form using a forms wizard. The wizard initializes the selected fields and the style of the form. However, all of the properties of the form can be modified with the **design view**, as shown in Figure 6.15. Nothing that was done by the wizard is permanent. So you can use the wizard to get started and then the design view to tailor the form to your exact needs.

The design view of a form lets you create and modify a form's layout and contents. Figure 6.15 shows an example of the design view of the form created by the forms wizard. Using this view, you can change labels, formats, and other form characteristics. You can also add new form elements, such as labels, text boxes, buttons, drop-down menus, lists, and so forth. The **toolbox** in Figure 6.15 has icons representing these elements. In Microsoft terminology, form elements are called *controls*.

You'll see many examples of the use of controls in the more complex user interfaces in Chapter 8, which is primarily concerned with manipulating relational data and creating database applications in Access.

6.4 CONFIGURING ACCESS FOR MULTIPLE USERS

A typical Access database contains data and programs stored in a single file. It is not easy to configure an Access database for use by more than one person at a time. That's because multiple users must share the database file, and programs and data are intermingled. Fortunately, Access provides a tool—called the **database splitter**—that helps address both problems.

The database splitter divides the database into one file, the **front-end database**, that contains all of the program elements, and another file, the **back-end database**, that contains only the tables. Figure 6.16 shows how to use Access's `Tools` menu to select the database splitter tool.

F I G U R E   6.15

Design View Showing Toolbox
and Properties

Form design view   Toolbox   Properties

F I G U R E   6.16

Choosing Database Splitter Tool

The file containing only the database tables is called the back-end database. In the case of BigHitVideo.mdb database, the default name for the new back-end database will be BigHitVideo_be.mdb.

The splitter modifies the original database file by removing the tables and replacing them with links to the tables in the back-end database. This strategy is called **linked tables**, that is, tables that are part of some other database and are not stored directly in the database file. Figure 6.17 shows the table display of the split database. Note that each table name is preceded by an arrow to denote that it is a linked table.

Splitting an Access database gives you an enormous advantage in sharing information. Specifically, each user can have a copy of the front-end database to use to access the same back-end database. Because the front-end database contains all the queries

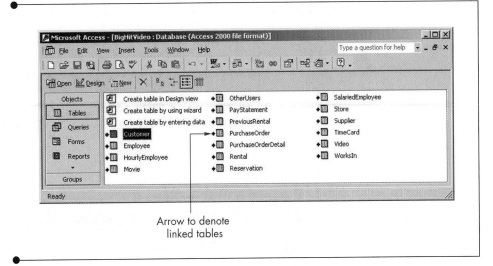

FIGURE 6.17
List of Linked Tables After Database Splitting

and forms, each user can create his or her own forms and queries. Also, query and form modifications made by one user are not imposed on the other users.

You can also create your own linked tables using Access tools. To do this, select `Get External Data` from the `File` menu, and then select `Link Tables`. Access responds with the usual file dialog. Select an Access database file and you'll see a dialog box like the one shown in Figure 6.18.

From the dialog box shown in Figure 6.18, you can select another Access database and then select specific tables from that database that you want to link to tables in your database.

By linking tables, you can also use Access forms and queries to interact with databases stored on other computers. Linked tables do not even have to come from Access databases; they can be housed in other kinds of databases, such as those sold by Oracle and IBM.

FIGURE 6.18
Link Tables Dialog

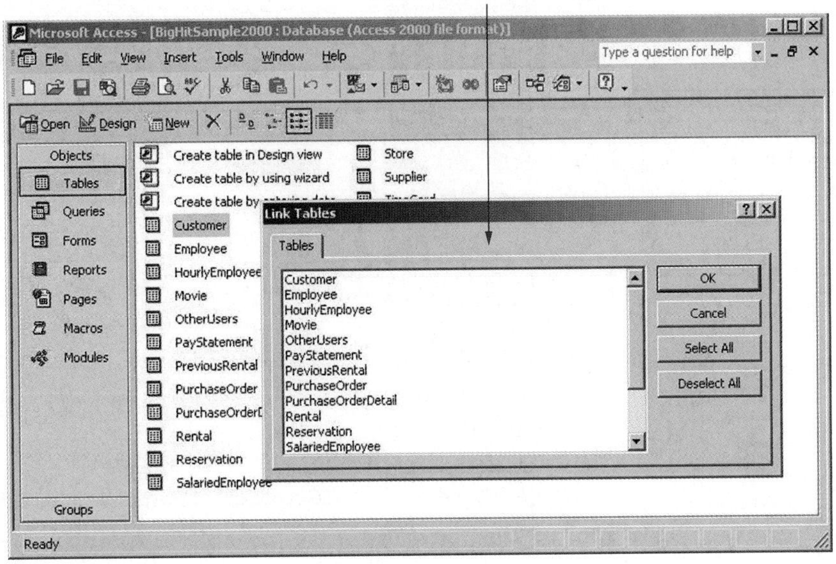

Microsoft Windows has a tool called ODBC (Open Database Connectivity) that lets you link to tables on other computers or in other databases. Once you link an external database to your computer as an ODBC data source, you can use Access tools to create links to the tables of the external database. To use an ODBC data source, simply follow the menu items to link tables, as described above. Then, from the file dialog box, select `ODBC Databases` from the `Files of type` entry at the bottom, as shown in Figure 6.19. The ODBC linking dialog opens (as shown in Figure 6.20) and lets you select an external database. See the suggested further readings at the end of this chapter for more details. Chapter 12 includes instructions on how to create ODBC data sources.

FIGURE 6.19

Choosing ODBC Databases for Linking Tables

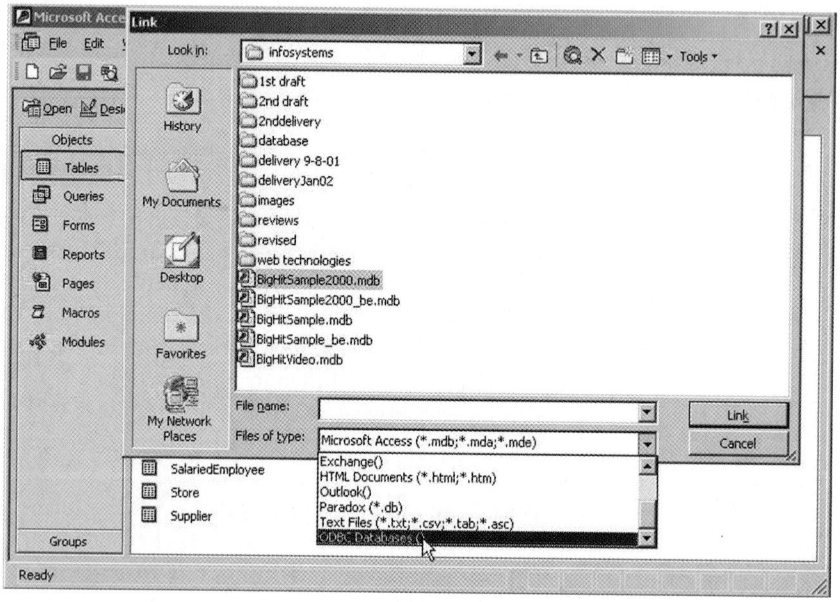

FIGURE 6.20

Selecting an ODBC Database Source

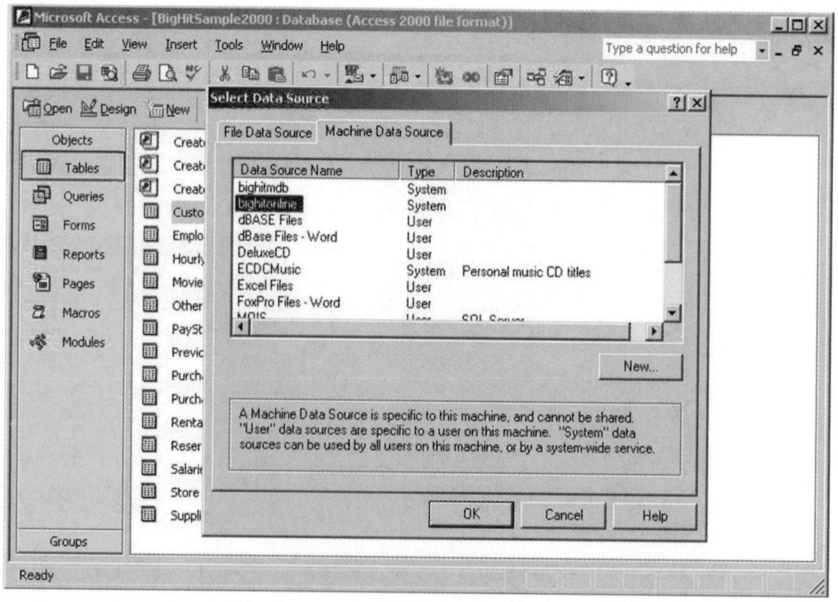

6.5 SPECIFYING RELATIONSHIP TYPES IN ACCESS

Once you've selected table forms and created tables for your Access database, use Access's relationship tools to specify relationship types between tables. The relationship types of the original E-R model form the basis for the specification. You will recall from Chapter 5 that E-R diagram relationship types are represented as foreign key attributes in relation schemas. Defining an attribute as a foreign key introduces a constraint on the schema. Each value of a foreign key attribute must correspond to a key value of the related table. We specify relationship types in Access so that the database system will enforce the foreign key constraints.

To define relationship types, select `Relationships` from the `Tools` menu. Access responds by displaying a blank window and the `Show Table` dialog that lists the tables in the database. Figure 6.21 shows an example from BigHit Video's database. In the figure, three tables, `Customer`, `Rental`, and `PreviousRental` have been added to the relationship window and table `Movie` is being added. You should add all of the tables to the relationship window. You should also move the tables around (by dragging) so that related tables are close together. You can rearrange the display later. The display for each table shows the name of the table and all of its attributes. The key attributes of the table are shown in boldface.

To define a relationship in Access, first consult your database schema. Choose a table that includes a foreign key declaration. For example, the `Rental` schema, as shown in Figure 6.22, has a foreign key to `Customer`. Find that table (`Rental`) and the related table (`Customer`) in the relationship window. Then simply click on the key attribute (`accountId` of `Customer`), hold the mouse button down, drag to the foreign key attribute of the related table (`accountId` of `Rental`), and release the mouse button. Note that the mouse pointer changes shape as it moves.

Figure 6.23 shows the relationship window while the relationship between `Customer` and `Rental` is being defined. The highlighted `accountId` of `Customer` is being dragged to the `accountId` of `Rental`.

FIGURE 6.21

Adding Tables to the Access Relationship Tool

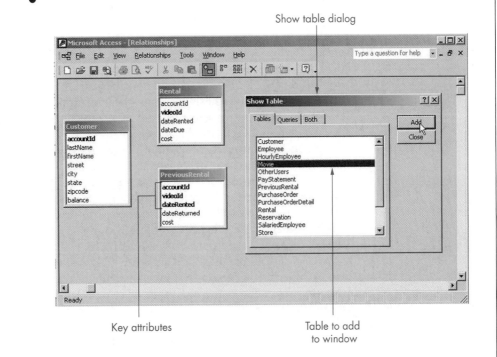

FIGURE 6.22

Relation Schema for
Rental

Schema: Rental: (<u>videoId</u> references Video, dateDue date, dateRented date, cost currency, accountId number references Customer)

FIGURE 6.23

Defining a Relationship

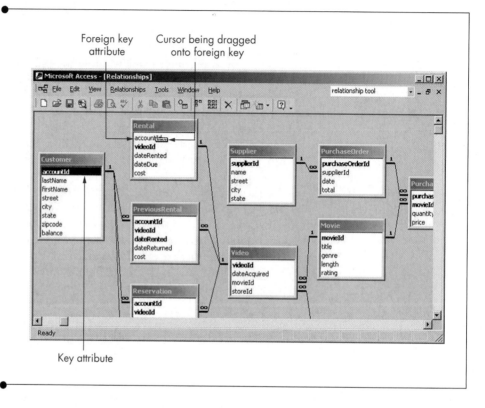

Once you define a relationship in this way, a relationship properties dialog box opens, as shown in Figure 6.24. The dialog box in this figure shows the properties of the relationship between the `accountId` field of the `Customer` table and the `accountId` field of the `Rental` table. At the bottom of the box, the relationship type is specified. We know this is a one-to-many relationship because `accountId` is the key of `Customer`, but is not the key of `Rental`. Hence, one customer can have many rentals, but each rental has a single customer.

An important property of relationships in database tables is that each value of a foreign key must be the key of a related object.

The checked box labeled `Enforce Referential Integrity` in the middle of the dialog tells Access that each value for the `accountId` field of a `Rental` entity must be the `accountId` of some `Customer` entity. For example, the system would not let you enter the value "1" in the `accountId` of a `Rental` unless the database already contained a customer with `accountId` 1.

Access can enforce referential integrity whenever you modify keys or foreign keys. For example, if you changed the value of a foreign key field, Access would check to see that the new value is the key value of some related entity. Thus, a change in the `accountId` value of a `Rental` entity would prompt Access to make sure that the new value is the `accountId` of some row in the `Customer` table. Similarly, when you create a new row in the `Rental` table, its `accountId` must be the `accountId` of some customer.

FIGURE 6.24

Relationship Properties
Dialog Box

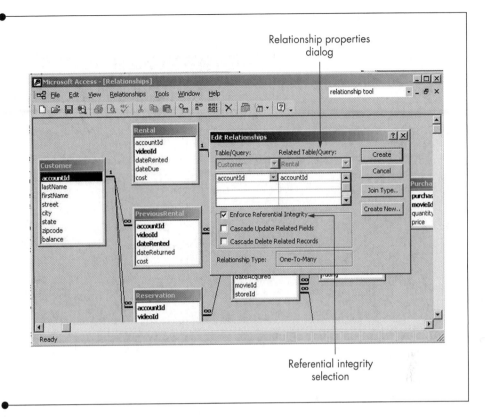

FIGURE 6.24

Relationship Properties
Dialog Box

Figure 6.25 shows examples of defined relationship types. The line between `Customer` and `Rental`, for example, indicates a one-to-many (∞) relationship type between the `accountId` field of `Customer` and the `accountId` field of `Rental`. That is, one customer can have many rentals, but any rental has only one customer. The line between `Rental` and `Video` indicates a one-to-one relationship type between the `accountId` field of `Rental` and the `videoId` field of `Video`.

Enforcing referential integrity becomes somewhat more complicated when you change a key *value*, for instance, the account ID of a customer. You can see in Figure 6.25 that `accountId` of `Customer` (its key field) is related to the `Rental` table, the `PreviousRental` table, the `Reservation` table, and another table that is not shown. Whenever you change the key of a customer, add a new customer, or delete a customer, the system would check all of the related entities of all related tables for violations of referential integrity.

The two items below `Enforce Referential Integrity` in Figure 6.24 tell Access what to do when changes in key values cause violations of referential integrity. Both items use the term "cascade" to indicate that a change in one value may require changes in other values, and that those changes may require yet more changes.

The first item, `Cascade Update Related Fields`, relates to changes in keys. If we check this item, Access will apply a change in the `accountId` of a customer to the foreign key fields of all related items. All of the foreign key fields will be changed. This is called **cascading updates** because one foreign key change may cause a change in a key value, and the system will have to apply the update to all related entities. Consider the relationship between `Customer` and `PreviousRental`. The `accountId` of `PreviousRental` is part of its key and is a foreign key to `Customer`. A change in the `accountId` of a customer causes the `accountId` of that customer's previous rentals to change. This changes the key of the previous rental, which may affect the integrity of other references.

The second cascade item in Figure 6.24, `Cascade Delete Related Fields`, is important when you delete a row from a table. If you check this item and then

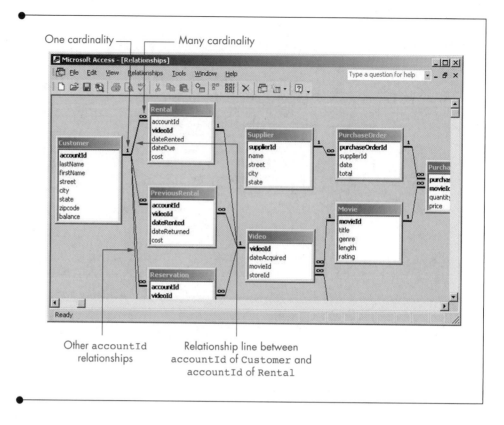

delete a row, Access will delete all the entities that depend on it. Thus, the deletion of a `Customer` entity will cause the deletion of all related `Rental` and `Previous-Rental` entities.

If you don't check these cascade items, Access will disallow any attempt to change a key or foreign key that results in a violation of referential integrity.

CASE IN POINT: CREATING AN ACCESS
6.6   DATABASE FOR BIGHIT ONLINE VIDEO SALES

We take the next step in the development of the video sales Web site by creating an Access database that contains the tables of the database schema of Chapter 5, as shown in Figure 6.26. We first create a new database, then define the tables, and add the sample data values. Finally, we can define the relationship types.

The resulting database is shown, in the relationships view, in Figure 6.27. All of the tables, attributes, keys, and relationships are shown in this view. Further details are available in the Access file `bighitonline.mdb`.

The process of creating the database is quite straightforward. We did the hard part by defining the E-R diagram (Chapter 4) and transforming it into a database schema (Chapter 5). Creating the database in Access is simply a matter of transferring the contents of the database schema into Access using the tools provided for database creation and metadata management in Access.

As promised, a relational database schema is exactly the definition needed to create a relational database. In Chapter 9, we'll see how to represent a relational schema in the SQL data definition language, instead of the informal style of Chapters 6 and 7. Once we have the SQL definition of the database, we will be able to feed that to a database server, which will create a new database without further information.

FIGURE 6.26

Database Schema for Video Sales, Reproduced from Figure 5.27

Customer: (<u>accountId</u> number, lastName string, firstName string)

Sale: (<u>saleId</u> number, dateSold date, totalCost number, creditCardType string, creditCardExpiration date, creditCardAccountNumber number, accountId number references Customer)

Movie: (<u>movieId</u> number, title string, genre string)

ShoppingCart: (<u>cartId</u> number, dateCreated date, accountId number references Customer)

SaleItem: (<u>saleId</u> number references Sale, <u>movieId</u> references Movie, quantity number)

CartItem: (<u>cartId</u> number references ShoppingCart, <u>movieId</u> references Movie, quantity number)

CreditCards: (<u>accountId</u> number references Customer, <u>accountNumber</u> number, type string, expiration date)

ShippingAddresses: (<u>accountId</u> number references Customer, <u>street</u> string, <u>city</u> string, <u>state</u> string, <u>zipcode</u> string)

DVD: (<u>movieId</u> number references Movie, videoFormat string, languages string, captioning string, cost currency, quantity number)

Videotape: (<u>movieId</u> number references Movie, format string, soundtrack string, cost currency, quantity number)

FIGURE 6.27

Database for BigHit Online Showing Tables, Attributes, Keys, and Relationships

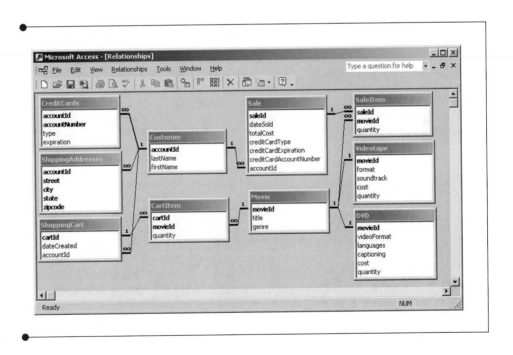

CHAPTER SUMMARY

Microsoft Access is just one of many database tools that support graphical design and manipulation of databases. Access allows us to define and populate tables for our database schemas, and to easily create software that manipulates and displays information. A Microsoft Access database is a combination of table definitions, table values, and application programs that are queries, user interfaces, and reports.

A table in Access can be created using the design view, which displays the attributes of a table and all of their properties. The datasheet view of a table shows the contents in a natural tabular representation. Forms in Access are user interface windows whose information content comes directly from database tables. A columnar form is one that displays the attribute values of a single object at a time. Navigation buttons at the bottom of a form allow users to easily move between objects. The easiest way to create forms is by using the form wizards.

Access databases store both data and programs in files. The default configuration is to have both data and program in a single file. The database splitter tool can be used to separate data and programs into a back-end database containing only data and a front-end database that contains the program elements and uses linked tables to access the data. ODBC tools allow us to use linked tables to access tables that are located on different machines.

Relationship types are represented in Microsoft Access in the relationship window. We are able to specify the cardinality of relationships and whether or not to enforce referential integrity.

KEY TERMS

Back-end database. An Access database that contains only tables and no program elements.

Control. In Microsoft Access, an element of a form.

Cascading updates. The automatic updating of the contents of a foreign key of one object whenever the key field of the related object is updated.

Columnar form. A form that displays the attribute values of a single object at a time.

Database splitter. A tool in Access that divides a database into a back-end database that contains the tables and a front-end database that contains the forms and other application elements.

Datasheet view. The view of the contents of a database table in rows and columns.

Design view. A user interface in Access that supports the modification of the structure of a table, the design of a query, of the elements of a form or report.

Field. Another name for attribute.

Form. A window that provides user access to database information.

Front-end database. An Access database file that contains queries and forms but no tables. The front-end database has links to tables that are another part of the database.

Linked table. A table in an access database whose contents are not contained in the database file, but rather are part of some other Access database or database server.

Toolbox. A small window that contains icons that represent design tools. In Access, form elements (controls) can be created from the toolbox.

User Interface. Any graphical or text display that provides information to users or gives users ways to modify and create database content.

Wizard. A sequence of dialogs in Access that make it easy to create tables, queries, forms, and other user interface programs.

QUESTIONS

1. Give a brief description of how to make the following changes in an Access database.
   a. Change the name of a table.
   b. Change the name of an attribute in a table.
   c. Modify the value of an attribute.
   d. Change the type of an attribute.
   e. Add a table.
   f. Add an attribute to a table.
   g. Create a two-attribute key for a table.

2. Briefly describe the purposes of forms in Access.

3. What is the difference between a datasheet view and a columnar view of a table?

4. List three advantages of splitting an Access database into a front-end and a back-end database.

5. Explain how Access can be used to interact with a non-Access database server.

6. What is the purpose of the relationship tool in Access?

7. How do you configure a relationship in Access so that referential integrity is enforced?

PROBLEMS

8. Create a new Access database and call it Prob78.mdb.

    a. Create tables for these schemas from Chapter 5.

    Schema: `Customer` (`accountId` string, `lastName` string, `firstName` string, `street` string, `city` string, `state` string, `zipcode` string, `balance` number)

    Schema: `OtherUser` (`accountId` number references Customer, `otherUser` string)

    b. Use the Access relationship tool to define the relationships between the schemas.

    c. Create a printout of your relationship window.

9. Create a new Access database and call it Prob79.mdb.

    a. Create tables for these schemas from Chapter 5.

    Schema: `WorksIn` (`ssn` string references Employee, `storeId` number references Store)

    Schema: `Store` (`storeId` number, `street` string, `city` string, `state` string, `zipcode` string, `manager` string references Employee)

    Schema: `Employee` (`ssn` string, `lastName` string, `firstName` string)

    b. Use the relationship tool to define the relationships between the schemas.

    c. Create a printout of your relationship window.

10. Create a new Access database and call it Prob710.mdb.

    a. Add attributes to the following schemas to represent the appropriate relationship types.

    Schema: `PurchaseOrder` (`id` number, `purchaseDate` date)

    Schema: `Supplier` (`name` string, `address` string)

    Schema: `Movie` (`movieId` number, `title` string, `genre` string, `length` number, `rating` string)

    Schema: `Video` (`videoId` number, `dateAcquired` date)

    b. Create tables for your schemas.

    c. Use the relationship tool to define the relationships between the schemas.

    d. Create a printout of your relationship window.

PROJECTS

11. Continue your BigHit Video project using your database schema from Chapter 5.

    a. Create a Microsoft Access database.

    b. Create the tables for your database schema.

    c. Populate those tables with data.

    d. Create a simple form, like that of Figure 6.13, for each of the tables of your database.

12. Continue your BigHit Online project using your database schema from Chapter 5.

    a. Create a Microsoft Access database.

    b. Create the tables for your database schema.

    c. Populate those tables with data.

    d. Create a simple form, like that of Figure 6.13, for each of the tables of your database.

13. Continue your Movie Lovers project using your database schema from Chapter 5.

    a. Create a Microsoft Access database.

    b. Create the tables for your database schema.

    c. Populate those tables with data.

    d. Create a simple form, like that of Figure 6.13, for each of the tables of your database.

FURTHER READING

There are many excellent books about using Microsoft Access, including Irwin, et al. [Irw02] and Feddema [Fed02]. The Microsoft Web developer Web site (http://msdn.microsoft.com/) has many helpful articles and other references. Details about other database design tools are available on the Web as well. Information and references for Powersoft PowerBuilder can be found at http://www.powersoft.com/. Oracle Enterprise Manager for Oracle database servers is described at the Oracle TechNet site http://technet.oracle.com.

CHAPTER 7

Improving Relational Schemas and Normalization

In this chapter, you will learn:

- General strategies for improving database schemas

- The roles of keys and foreign keys in defining the quality of schemas

- The definitions of various normal forms

- How to decompose relations to achieve normal form

- How to define and enforce constraints on database content

We are now ready to consider the quality of the database design and what we can do to evaluate and improve quality. We have already seen that the careful application of the rules given in Chapter 4 results in a database schema that is an accurate representation of the E-R model. A database built from the schema will be able to represent all of the information that was described by the E-R model.

Unfortunately, sometimes a correct and faithful schema may lead to a database that is difficult to use, inefficient to query and update, and hard to understand. This chapter presents some ideas that have been developed to measure the quality of schemas as well as some techniques that can be used to improve that quality.

The general criteria for quality are that each attribute and schema should have a simple meaning; redundant values in tables should be minimized; the presence of null values in tables should be minimized; and spurious or meaningless entities should not be allowed. Fortunately, the translation of a good E-R model results in a high quality database schema, one that has meaningful attributes and schemas, and no meaningless entities.

Most of the problems discussed in this chapter can be avoided with good data modeling. The schemas that were developed in previous chapters are of high quality. In most cases, good data modeling results in good database schemas.

The techniques of this chapter are most useful in system developments where the initial database schema is developed from sample documents or previous systems. A typical example is when a new database development is based on a previous implementation where the data represented in the old system is exactly what is needed in the new. In that case, the old database schema may have problems of the type seen in the chapter. The schema developer's job would be to identify the problems and systematically remove them. This chapter ends with an example of developing a database schema from sample documents. Every step in the development of the schema is included.

This chapter describes the process of **schema improvement**. It shows you how to evaluate the quality of a database schema and identify problems. It also demonstrates how to remove those problems and produce a more useful, higher quality schema.

7.1 REDUNDANCY AND ANOMALIES IN RELATION SCHEMAS

Redundancy—that is, the repetition of information—is a particular problem with relation schemas for several reasons. Most obviously, redundant values waste space because the same information is stored more than once.

A more serious issue is that modification of entities with redundant values is difficult. Several anomalous things happen as a result of modifications of redundant values. By **anomalous**, we mean that changing one row of a table results in unexpected changes or inconsistencies in other rows.

An **update anomaly** is a situation in which an update to one value affects another value. To illustrate this circumstance, Figure 7.1 shows a schema and its contents based on the definition of entity class `Video` from Table 3.6. (In this chapter, schemas list the names of the attributes, but not their types.) The schema is called `VideoMovie` because it contains attributes that represent both videos and movies.

The redundancy in this schema is that multiple copies of the same movie will have the same value for `movieId` and will also have the same values for `title`, `genre`, `length`, and `rating`. The three highlighted rows are all copies of the movie *Elizabeth* and the values of `movieId`, `title`, `genre`, `length`, and `rating` are the same for all three rows.

It is important to the consistency of the database that all copies of *Elizabeth* have the same genre, length, and rating. We saw in Section 4.5.3 that these attributes are more properly considered part of `Movie` and not of `Video`.

FIGURE 7.1

Schema and Contents of `VideoMovie`

Schema: VideoMovie:(<u>videoId</u>, dateAcquired, movieId, title, genre, length, rating)

<u>videoId</u>	dateAcquired	movieId	title	genre	length	rating
115	1/25/01	101	The Thirty-Nine Steps	mystery	101	PG
90987	2/5/00	450	Elizabeth	costume drama	123	PG-13
145	12/31/98	145	Lady and the Tramp	animated drama	93	G
8034	4/5/01	145	Lady and the Tramp	animated drama	93	G
90988	4/5/01	450	Elizabeth	costume drama	123	PG-13
90989	3/25/89	450	Elizabeth	costume drama	123	PG-13
543	5/12/98	101	The Thirty-Nine Steps	mystery	101	R
1243	4/29/94	123	Annie Hall	romantic comedy	110	R

Consider what happens if the length of video 90987 (row 2) is changed from 123 to 127. One copy of *Elizabeth* now has a different length than the other two copies—an anomalous situation. To preserve the consistency of the database, any attempt to change the length of a video must change the length of every other video with the same movie ID. This situation is called a **modification anomaly**.

Two other types of update anomalies are possible: insertion anomalies and deletion anomalies. An **insertion anomaly** occurs when adding a row results in an inconsistency. For instance, suppose we add the row:

114	6/5/01	450	Elizabeth	costume drama	110	R

The addition of this row creates an inconsistency in the length of the copies of *Elizabeth*. The values of `movieId`, `title`, and `genre` are the same as those of the highlighted rows of the table. But the `length` and `rating` attributes (highlighted) for the new row are different. How do we answer the question, "What is the rating for the movie with ID 450?" We cannot be sure whether the row for video 114 (the new row) is correct in stating that the rating is R or the row for video 90987 is correct in stating that the rating is `PG-13`.

An attempt to add a new row to `VideoMovie` must not be allowed if it will create an inconsistency. With this schema for `VideoMovie`, each insertion or update must be checked to make sure that no inconsistency is created in attributes `title`, `genre`, `length`, and `rating`.

A **deletion anomaly** may be the most insidious anomaly. Notice that if we delete video 1243 (the last row of Figure 7.1), we delete not only the `videoId` and `dateAcquired` of video 1243 but also all of the information about *Annie Hall*. Deleting the last video for a movie will result in the loss of information about the movie. The table no longer records the title, genre, length, and rating of the movie with movie ID 1243.

These anomalous situations arise because of the redundancy of the attributes. The `Movie` schema of Figure 5.1 and the `Video` schema of Figure 5.9, repeated here as Figure 7.2, that are derived from the revised E-R diagram of Figure 4.18 do not exhibit these redundancies, because `title`, `genre`, and other attributes that are common to the movie have been moved to the `Movie` schema.

Entity class `VideoMovie` was modified in Section 4.5.3. That is, it was decomposed into two classes: `Video` and `Movie`. The result of the modification was a reduction in the amount of redundancy in the database tables. Such decompositions will allow us to improve schemas by eliminating redundancy.

Professional database designers apply a process called normalization to their schemas in order to ensure high quality and low maintenance costs. **Normalization** is a process of modifying the schema so that it conforms to certain rules called **normal forms**. Normalization is conducted by evaluating a relation schema to find violations of the particular rules, and then decomposing the schema into smaller, related schemas that do not violate the rules.

The next sections take a rather formal, mathematical approach to defining measures of the quality of schemas. The material is expressed in an abstract way, but is accompanied by extensive examples.

FIGURE 7.2

Schemas for `Video` and `Movie`, repeated from Figures 5.1 and 5.9

Schema: Video (<u>videoId</u>, dateAcquired, movieId references Movie)

Schema: Movie (<u>movieId</u>, title, genre, length, rating)

7.2 FUNCTIONAL DEPENDENCIES BETWEEN ATTRIBUTES

In order to fully understand schema improvement, we must adopt some terminology that expresses the basic concepts. The key concept is that of functional dependency between attributes of a schema.

A **functional dependency** is a strong connection between two or more attributes in a table. In particular, one attribute is functionally dependent on another attribute when any two rows of the table that have the same value of the second attribute must have the same value for the first.

In class `VideoMovie` of Figure 7.1 for example, attribute `title` is functionally dependent on attribute `movieId`. In the table, if two rows have the same value for `movieId`, they must necessarily have the same value for `title`. We declare the functional dependency with the following notation. (The name FD1 is not part of the dependency declaration, but is included for later reference.)

$$\text{FD1: movieId} \rightarrow \text{title}$$

Another way of showing the dependencies is with a graphical notation that shows the schema with arrows pointing from the attributes on the left side to the attributes on the right side of each dependency:

```
VideoMovie:                        ┌── FD1 ──┐
                                   │         ▼
(videoId, dateAcquired, movieId, title, genre, length, rating)
```

You'll notice that the arrows don't necessarily point from left to right, but always point away from attributes on the left side of the functional dependency toward the attributes on the right side.

It is also true that attributes `genre`, `length`, and `rating` are functionally dependent on `movieId`. Any two rows with the same `movieId` must have the same value for `genre`, `length`, and `rating`. We express the combination of these functional dependencies with FD2.

$$\text{FD2: movieId} \rightarrow \{\text{title, genre, length, rating}\}$$

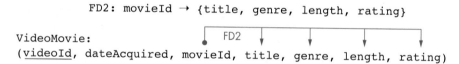

```
VideoMovie:                        ┌── FD2 ──┬──────┬──────┬──────┐
                                   │         ▼      ▼      ▼      ▼
(videoId, dateAcquired, movieId, title, genre, length, rating)
```

The attribute in the left side of the dependency (in this case `videoId`) is called a **determinant** because it can be used to determine the values of the right side attributes.

Suppose we want to determine the title and genre of the movie whose ID is 450. In the `VideoMovie` table, every row with `movieId` 450 has `title` *Elizabeth* and `genre` "costume drama." The question, "What are the title and genre of the movie with ID 450?" can be answered by looking at any row with `movieId` = 450. We do not have to look at more than one row to find the answer.

In general, if the value of attribute A in a relational table uniquely determines the value of attribute B, we say that A *functionally determines* B or B is *functionally dependent* on A. Any two rows of the table that have the same value for A will also have the same value for B. We express this idea as

$$A \rightarrow B$$

A functional dependency is a restriction on the contents of a table: It is a violation of the meaning of the table for two rows to violate the dependency.

Not every rule of the form A → B is a functional dependency. For example, is `movieId → dateAcquired` a functional dependency in the table of Figure 7.1? That is, are there two rows of the table with the same value for `movieId` but different values for `dateAcquired`?

The highlighted rows have identical values for `movieId` but different values for `dateAcquired`. Hence, the rule `movieId → dateAcquired` is not a functional dependency.

Consider the `Customer` schema and sample table of Figure 7.3. Included in a `Customer` table is a set of postal addresses in the United States. The `state` attribute is functionally dependent on the `zipcode` attribute. That is, every address with a particular zip code is in the same state. The arrow pointing from `zipcode` to `state` illustrates the functional dependency.

Functional dependency FD3 can be seen in this table. Accounts 101 and 111 (highlighted in blue) have `zipcode` 30548 and `state` FL, and accounts 103 and 104 (highlighted in red) have `zipcode` 30457 and `state` FL. These are the only rows whose values for `zipcode` match. Therefore, any two rows with the same `zipcode` also have the same `state`. The functional dependency does not imply that any two rows with the same `state` must have the same `zipcode`.

We must be careful when we try to use the contents of a table to figure out which dependencies hold, because a particular table only shows some of its possible values. From the table above, we might conclude that `firstName` determines `zipcode` because accounts 101 and 111 (highlighted in blue) are the only rows that share values of `firstName` (Jane). These rows also have the same `zipcode`. We know from our own experiences that a person's first name does not determine the person's zip code. Thus, the contents of a table are not a reliable guide to declaring functional dependencies.

We declare functional dependencies based on the meaning of the attributes. According to the United States Postal Service, each zip code is associated with a single state and no zip code covers addresses in more than one state. Hence, we can conclude that it is appropriate to declare that `state` is functionally determined by `zipcode`.

How does the table of Figure 7.3 determine a function from `zipcode` to `state`? Given a particular zip code, we can find the state by searching for a row with that value for the `zipcode` attribute and read the value of the `state` attribute.

However, at any particular time, the `zipcode` column of the table does not include every zip code—in this case there are only 7 rows and 5 zip codes. Hence, the function determined by the table is undefined for some numbers in the domain of the `zipcode` attribute. Thus, we can only look up the state for zip code values that belong to customers in the table.

FIGURE 7.3

Customer Schema and Sample Table with Functional Dependency between **zipcode** and **state**

FD3: zipcode → state

Customer:
(accountId, lastName, firstName, street, city, state, zipcode)

accountId	lastName	firstName	street	city	state	zipcode
101	Block	Jane	123 Main St.	Apopka	FL	30458
102	Hamilton	Cherry	3230 Dade St.	Dade City	FL	30555
103	Harrison	Kate	103 Dodd Hall	Apopka	FL	30457
104	Breaux	Carroll	76 Main St.	Apopka	FL	30457
106	Morehouse	Anita	9501 Lafayette St.	Houma	LA	44099
111	Deaux	Jane	123 Main St.	Apopka	FL	30458
201	Greaves	Joseph	14325 N. Bankside St.	Godfrey	IL	43580

When an address is added whose zip code is not already in the table, the function changes to include that zip code–state pair.

Functional dependencies are also declared with sets of attributes. Figure 7.4 shows a more complete set of functional dependencies for the `Customer` schema. Here `zipcode` determines `city` and `state` (FD4), and the combination of `street`, `city`, and `state` determines `zipcode` (FD5). We write these dependencies as shown in Figure 7.4. The determinant of the functional dependency FD5 is the set of left side attributes {`street`, `city`, `state`}.

An investigation of the table of Figure 7.3 shows that the functional dependencies hold. The two rows highlighted in blue have identical `street`, `city`, `state`, and `zipcode` values. Thus, both dependencies FD4 and FD5 hold for those rows. The blue rows have the same `city`, `state`, and `zipcode`, but different `street` values. Thus, for these rows, functional dependency FD4 holds, because `zipcode` determines `city` and `state`. If we look at the first and second rows of the table, we find identical `city` and `state`, but different `street` and `zipcode`. These rows do not violate functional dependency FD5 because they differ in their values for one of the determinant attributes (`street`).

A functional dependency is a *declared* constraint on the contents of a table, much as a key declaration is a declared constraint. As part of the specification of the table in Figure 7.4, we have declared that no two rows with the same `zipcode` value will be allowed to have different `city` or `state` values.

The enforcement of the `zipcode` → {`city`, `state`} dependency in `Customer` requires that every update to a `city`, `state`, or `zipcode` field be checked for consistency. A change in a customer's `city`, `state`, or `zipcode` cannot be allowed unless it is consistent with all other customers who share the `zipcode`. Checking these constraints can be very expensive. You might also notice that the `Customer` table contains significant redundancy: the `city` and `state` are repeated for every row with a particular `zipcode`.

FIGURE 7.4

Customer Schema with Functional Dependencies

```
FD4: zipcode → {city, state}
FD5: {street, city, state} → zipcode


Customer:
(accountId, lastName, firstName, street, city, state, zipcode)
```

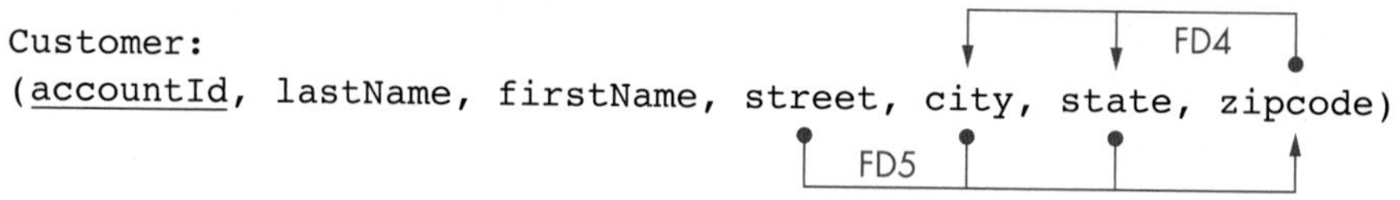

Concept

Maintaining Functional Dependencies

Once the functional dependencies in a database schema have been specified, the database designers and implementers must ensure that those dependencies are not violated. Users of database systems want to be sure that all data in the database are consistent with the functional dependencies. Any attempt to modify the data in the database must be denied if the modification will create an inconsistent state. In the zip code example, every new address must be checked for consistency with addresses that are already in the table. If the table contains a row that shows that zip code 32306 is in Florida, no new row can associate zip code 32306 with some other state.

A major issue with database design is the need to find ways to reduce the cost of maintaining functional dependency constraints.

Key constraints and functional dependencies are closely related. We can exploit our knowledge of keys to gain a better understanding of functional dependencies. This section introduces some notation that makes schema improvement easier to describe and understand.

It is not too hard to see that a key constraint *is* a functional dependency. In the `Customer` schema, for instance, attribute `accountId` is the key, and every other attribute is functionally dependent on it. Figure 7.5 illustrates the way that a key constraint determines a functional dependency. The definition of functional dependency applies directly: No two different rows in the table are allowed to have the same value for `accountId` because it is a key of the table. Hence, if two rows have the same value for `accountId`, they are the same row and therefore have the same value for all other attributes. The key of a relation schema always functionally determines the set of non-key attributes of the schema.

Any functional dependency that includes all attributes of a schema is called a **superkey dependency**. Thus, a **superkey** of a relation schema is a set of attributes that functionally determine all other attributes of the table.

From this definition, we can conclude that a key of a schema is also a superkey. In Figure 7.5, for example, we have a functional dependency that includes each attribute of the schema. The left side (the determinant) of dependency FD6 is a superkey of the schema.

Other sets of attributes may be superkeys. Figure 7.6 shows a dependency between `accountId` and `lastName` as determinant and the rest of the `Customer` attributes as right side. If FD7 is truly a functional dependency, then `{accountId, lastName}` is a superkey.

Is the rule of Figure 7.6 a functional dependency? The answer requires a little logic. Since `accountId` is a key of `Customer`, no two rows of the table have the same values for `accountId`. Thus, no two rows have the same values for the combination of `accountId` and `lastName`. By the definition of functional dependency, FD7 must hold.

Another definition of superkey is that a set of attributes is a superkey if the set contains a key. Since `{accountId, lastName}` contains the key `accountId`, `{accountId, lastName}` must be a superkey.

FIGURE 7.5

Customer Schema with Functional Dependency Between Key and Non-key Attributes

```
FD6: accountId → {lastName, firstName, street, city, state,
zipcode}

Customer:
(accountId, lastName, firstName, street, city, state, zipcode)
        └── FD6 ──┘    ↑         ↑        ↑     ↑       ↑
```

FIGURE 7.6

Customer Schema with a Superkey Functional Dependency

```
FD7: {accountId, lastName} → {firstName, street, city, state,
zipcode}

Customer:
(accountId, lastName, firstName, street, city, state, zipcode)
     └── FD7 ──┘        ↑         ↑      ↑     ↑       ↑
```

We can now give a formal definition of "key" based on the definition of functional dependency. A set of attributes A is a **key** of a relation schema if A is a superkey and any proper subset of A is not a superkey. That is, removing any attribute from a key produces a set of attributes that does not functionally determine the rest of the attributes of the schema. A key is therefore a minimal superkey. The removal of any attribute from a key produces a set that is not a superkey. It follows that any single-attribute superkey is necessarily a key.

Why are key constraints so important? The great advantage of key constraints over other functional dependencies is that database systems support the enforcement of key constraints. Once we tell the database system that a particular set of attributes is a key, the system will guarantee that no two rows have the same value. The database system will refuse to update the database if the requested update would create a violation of a key constraint.

In contrast, relational database servers do not support the enforcement of other functional dependencies. In the next section, we will see how arbitrary functional dependencies can be transformed into key constraints. This transformation greatly improves the quality of relation schemas.

Section 7.4 describes methods for substituting key constraints for other functional dependencies. Rules are defined that identify tables with functional dependencies that are not key constraints. Those tables can be decomposed into smaller tables in which all functional dependencies are key constraints.

7.4 INFERRING ADDITIONAL FUNCTIONAL DEPENDENCIES

Database designers specify functional dependencies that arise from the meaning of the data. However, many less obvious dependencies can be inferred from the ones provided by the designers. Improvements in the quality of database schemas must be based on all of the functional dependencies that can be inferred. This section investigates the inference rules that are used to discover all of the dependencies of a schema.

From your early training in arithmetic and mathematics you have encountered many examples of logical inference of logical expressions, which involves the application of inference rules. That is, from a set of true statements, we can infer other statements that are true. For example, if we know that Elizabeth is a sister of Mary and we know that Mary is a sister of Christina, then we can infer that Elizabeth is a sister of Christina. The transitive inference rule of logic supports that inference.

Let's begin with a formal statement of some inference rules, and proceed to see them in action. Six rules of inference for functional dependencies are typically used in schema development. Suppose that W, X, Y, and Z are sets of attributes and that XY is the union of X and Y.

Rule 1: Reflexivity, a set of attributes X determines a subset Y of itself:
   If $X \supseteq Y$, then $X \rightarrow Y$.

Rule 2: Augmentation, a set of attributes Z can be added to both sides of $X \rightarrow Y$:
   If $X \rightarrow Y$, then $XZ \rightarrow YZ$.

Rule 3: Transitivity, we can follow chains of dependencies from X to Y to Z:
   If $X \rightarrow Y$ and $Y \rightarrow Z$, then $X \rightarrow Z$.

Rule 4: Decomposition, we can remove a set of attributes Z from the right side of $X \rightarrow YZ$:
   If $X \rightarrow YZ$, then $X \rightarrow Y$.

Rule 5: Union, we can put two dependencies $X \rightarrow Y$ and $X \rightarrow Z$ together if they have the same left side Z:
   If $X \rightarrow Y$ and $X \rightarrow Z$ then $X \rightarrow YZ$

Rule 6: Pseudo-transitivity, a combination of augmentation by adding W to both sides of X → Y and transitivity in going from WX to WY to Z:

If X → Y and WY → Z, then WX → Z.

We already saw inference of a functional dependency in Figure 7.6 when we looked at these two rules:

```
FD6: accountId → {lastName, firstName, street, city, state,
zipcode}
FD7: {accountId, lastName} → (firstName, street, city,
state, zipcode}
```

FD6 is a functional dependency because the left side is a key. Section 7.3 included an informal argument that FD7 must also be a functional dependency. A formal argument would rely on two inference steps.

Inference 1: We use the augmentation rule (Rule 2) to add `lastName` to both sides of functional dependency FD6 and produce FD8. (Attribute `lastName` was already part of the right side.)

```
FD8: {accountId, lastName} → (firstName, street, city, state,
zipcode, lastName}
```

Inference 2: Then we use the decomposition rule (Rule 4) to remove `lastName` from the right side to infer FD7 and thus have finished the inference.

```
FD7: {accountId, lastName} → (firstName, street, city,
state, zipcode}
```

As another example of inference, suppose we have the following two declared functional dependencies for the `VideoMovie` schema (FD2 is repeated from earlier in the chapter).

```
FD9: videoId → (dateAcquired, movieId}
FD2: movieId → (title, genre, length, rating}
```

Applying decomposition (Rule 4) to remove `dateAcquired` from the right side of FD 9 yields FD10.

```
FD10: videoId → movieId
```

Applying transitivity (Rule 3) to FD10 and FD2 produces FD11:

```
FD11: videoId → (title, genre, length, rating}
```

VideoMovie:
(videoId, dateAcquired, movieId, title, genre, length, rating)

Finally, the union (Rule 5) of FD11 and FD9 produces FD12, a superkey rule.

```
FD12: videoId → (dateAcquired, movieId, title, genre,
length, rating}
```

VideoMovie:
(videoId, dateAcquired, movieId, title, genre, length, rating)

The closure of a set of functional dependencies is the largest set of dependencies that can be produced by repeated application of the inference rules to the original set. The closure of a set of dependencies describes every dependency that can be inferred from the dependencies that are declared as part of the schema. The closure is used to evaluate a schema for opportunities to improve its quality, especially with respect to redundancy and ease of maintenance.

7.5 DETERMINING KEYS FROM FUNCTIONAL DEPENDENCIES

The normal forms that are included here are all based on the keys of schemas. We know that keys are declared as part of the specification of a schema. In addition, we know that key constraints are functional dependencies. Hence, an alternative approach to determining keys is to specify all of the functional dependencies and then to use them to discover the keys.

If we know all of the functional dependencies of a schema, we also know the keys. First, list the superkeys by listing the left sides of the superkey dependencies. If a set of attributes is a superkey and no subset is also a superkey, then the set is a key. For `VideoMovie`, FD12 is a superkey rule and the determinant is a single attribute `videoId`. Thus, the specification of functional dependencies FD2 and FD9 for `VideoMovie` are sufficient to determine that `videoId` is a key.

The discovery of keys by analysis of functional dependencies supports the division of the attributes of the schema into two sets. An attribute that is part of any key of the schema is called a **key attribute**. An attribute that is not part of any key is called a **non-key attribute**.

7.6 NORMALIZATION

Normalization is the process of transforming some objects into a structural form that satisfies some collection of rules. In relation schemas, normalization is based on keys and functional dependencies. We analyze a schema to see if it conforms to the normal form and if not, modify the schema to make it conform.

Relation schema normal form rules are designed so that any schema that is in normal form is guaranteed to have certain quality characteristics. A tremendous amount of research and experimentation has been invested in defining normal form rules. This section covers rules that are concerned with turning functional dependencies into key dependencies. These rules provide the greatest benefits to fledgling database designers. As database schemas grow more complex, other rules become important. For details on the extensive literature on normal forms, please see the Further Reading section at the end of the chapter.

Two normal forms are covered in this chapter: third normal form (3NF) and Boyce-Codd normal form (BCNF). These are the two most important normal forms.

Each normal form has a rule that describes what kinds of functional dependencies the normal form allows. Normalization is the process of transforming schemas in order to remove violations of the normal form rules. It is applied independently to each relation schema in a database schema. Thus, a database schema is said to be *in normal form* if each of its relation schemas is in the normal form.

Not every functional dependency needs to be considered as a potential normal form violation. The general rule of thumb is to consider only those dependencies that have a minimal set of left-side attributes, a maximal set of right-side attributes, and no attributes that are part of both sides.

Concept

Schema Decomposition

Normal form violations can be removed from a schema by **decomposing** it into two schemas. Suppose the schema

R:(A, B, C, D, E, F) with key {A, B, C} has a functional dependency {A, B} →{E, F}.

The decomposition process removes the right-side attributes (E, F) of the dependency from the original schema to create a new base schema

S:(A, B, C, D).

All of the attributes of the dependency are combined to create a new related schema

T:(A, B, E, F).

The determinant of the dependency {A, B} forms the key of the new schema. Those attributes remain in the base schema (S) as a foreign key to the new schema (T).

S:(A, B, C, D, foreign key {A, B} references T).

Examples are given in the following sections.

7.7 THIRD NORMAL FORM (3NF)

Quite simply, a relation schema is in **third normal form (3NF)** if every functional dependency either has a superkey as determinant (left side) or the right side attributes are key attributes. Thus, in 3NF, non-key attributes are functionally determined only by keys or superkeys.

If we find that a schema is not in 3NF, we must decompose it into smaller relations.

Let's look at the `VideoMovie` schema of Figure 7.1. We know that `videoId` is the key of the schema. Further analysis would find that `videoId` is the only key and hence the only key attribute.

Earlier in the chapter, we found that `VideoMovie` has the following functional dependencies. Now we need to determine which ones are 3NF violations.

```
VideoMovie:(videoId, dateAcquired, movieId, title, genre,
length, rating)
FD1: movieId → title
FD2: movieId → {title, genre, length, rating}
FD9: videoId → (dateAcquired, movieId}
FD10: videoId → movieId
FD11: videoId → (title, genre, length, rating}
FD12: videoId → (dateAcquired, movieId, title, genre,
length, rating}
```

FD1 and FD2 have non-superkey determinants and the right-side attributes are non-key attributes. Hence, FD1 and FD2 are 3NF violations.

FD9, FD10, FD11, and FD12 all have `videoId`, the key, as determinant. None of these functional dependencies is a 3NF violation.

Because FD1 and FD2 are 3NF violations, schema `VideoMovie` is not a 3NF schema. We must decompose it using one of the violating functional dependencies in order to eliminate the violation.

We can choose either FD1 or FD2 for decomposition. However, normalization works best if we always decompose by the functional dependency with the fewest attributes in the determinant and the most attributes in the right side. In this case, FD2 is the better choice. The decomposition of `VideoMovie` by FD2 produces two schemas:

```
R1: (videoId, dateAcquired, movieId references R2)
R2: (movieId, title, genre, length, rating)
```

In this stage of the normalization the schemas have generic names `R1` and `R2`.

Notice that `R1` is created by removing the right-side attributes of FD2 from `VideoMovie` and making the determinant of FD2 a foreign key. `R2` is created from the attributes of FD2 with the determinant as key.

Both `R1` and `R2` are in 3NF because neither has a non-3NF dependency.

Can we pick better names for the schemas? `R2` has information that is strictly about movies and `R1` has information about videos. So we can rename them

```
Video: (videoId, dateAcquired, movieId references Movie)
Movie: (movieId, title, genre, length, rating)
```

Of course, these schemas are the ones that we defined in Chapter 5 when we transformed the E-R model into relational schemas. Look back at Figure 7.2 to make sure.

Let's continue with the example of the `Customer` schema with its functional dependencies.

```
Customer: (accountId, lastName, firstName, street, city,
state, zipcode)
FD3: zipcode → state
FD4: zipcode → {city, state}
FD5: {street, city, state} → zipcode
FD6: accountId → {lastName, firstName, street, city, state,
zipcode}
FD7: {accountId, lastName} → (firstName, street, city,
state, zipcode}
FD8: {accountId, lastName} → (firstName, street, city,
state, zipcode, lastName}
```

Dependencies FD6, FD7, and FD8 are not 3NF violations because they all have superkeys as determinants. Each left side includes the key attribute `accountId`.

Dependencies FD3, FD4, and FD5 are 3NF violations. To transform `Customer` into a 3NF schema, we must first choose one dependency to use in the first decomposition. We don't want to choose FD3 because it is extended by FD4. Both FD4 and FD5 can be used, so we'll try both, one at a time.

DAVID MCGOVERAN
Data Normalization

David McGoveran founded Alternative Technologies in 1976 and was among the first designers of commercial relational applications. Today, the company brings its relational database design experience to bear on commercial applications such as Wall Street online trading and portfolio management, digital telecommunications provisioning, and various B2B/e-commerce products.

FIRST DATABASE JOB It was data collection and analysis on portable kidney dialysis research for Dow Chemical.

CURRENT JOB *President, Alternative Technologies* Much of my work involves management and strategic technology consulting. I work extensively with business integration products, most of which have a DBMS at their core.

ON NORMALIZATION I've encountered a strong bias against, and lack of understanding of, normalization in the world of commercial applications development. The value of normalization has to be demonstrated, as do some of the fallacious benefits attributed to "denormalization." Most important is teaching that good design makes it easier to formulate meaningful queries and obtain the intended result.

> **"Teaching the benefits of separating logical and physical design, and the 'tricks of the trade' for achieving performance, rapid deployment, and flexibility is always rewarding."**

USING NORMALIZATION TECHNIQUES ON THE JOB—The Problem One project we consulted on involved printing masses of database-driven, custom reports for subscribers produced at the end of month. The processing window was insufficient to complete reports on time. Furthermore, volumes were expected to grow by several hundred percent over the next year.

On examining the database, I found that the "flat" tables contained many cases of multiple entities distinguished by a flag column, many nullable columns, repeating groups, and other problems. The DBMS almost always scanned the largest tables (it could not use indexes effectively) and the report application had to perform a great deal of conditional processing in order to accumulate related information. Designers had assumed that one large table was better than multiple small tables because it would "eliminate the need for joins."

The Solution Putting the tables in third normal form created a few extra tables, but simultaneously enabled each SQL retrieval to be precisely stated. In this way, table scans were all but eliminated and indexed access became very efficient. The combination of the newly required joins performed faster than the original table scans, and required no conditional processing of the result by the report application. The amount of I/O in the system dropped by well over 98%.

The Result After redesign, report generation was simplified, conditional processing—which was previously extensive—was all but eliminated, and performance ceased to be a problem (it was improved by orders of magnitude). The solution scaled (previously it did not), and to my knowledge, is still being used ten years later.

Teaching the benefits of separating logical and physical design, and the "tricks of the trade" for achieving performance, rapid deployment, and flexibility is always rewarding.

> **Concept**
>
> ### First and Second Normal Forms
>
> The development of normal forms for relation schemas began with three normal forms, first normal form (1NF), second normal form (2NF), and third normal form (3NF). The first two normal forms have ceased to be useful to schema developers and are of only historical interest.
>
> First normal form (1NF) simply says that each attribute of a schema must be atomic. You will recall from Chapter 5 that the definition of the relational model includes this requirement. Thus, all relation schemas are 1NF schemas. 1NF was defined early in the development of the relational model and was later incorporated into the standard model definition.
>
> Many presentations of normalization include a discussion of 2NF. However, including 2NF as part of normalization makes the entire process harder to understand. We can safely ignore 2NF because every 3NF schema is also 2NF and the goal of normalization is to produce 3NF schemas.

Decomposing `Customer` by FD4 produces two new schemas.

```
R3: (accountId, lastName, firstName, street, zipcode
references R4)
R4: (zipcode, city, state)
```

R3 is created by removing `city` and `state` from `Customer` and making `zipcode` a foreign key to R4. R4 has the attributes from FD4 with `zipcode` as the key.

Notice that decomposing `Customer` by FD4 changes the FD5 dependency. The determinate of FD5 is {`street, city, state`}. These attributes are no longer together in either R3 or R4. Hence, FD5 is not a functional dependency in either R3 or R4 and both schemas are in 3NF.

Decomposing `Customer` by FD5 produces two new schemas.

```
R5: (accountId, lastName, firstName, street, city, state,
foreign key {street, city, state} references R6)
R6: (street, city, state, zipcode, secondary key {street,
zipcode})
```

Schemas R5 and R6 were produced by decomposition in the usual way. The unusual thing is that because the determinant of FD5 has three attributes, so does the foreign key of R5 and the key of R6. The decomposition to R5 and R6 is inferior to the decomposition to R3 and R4 because multi-attribute keys and foreign keys are very difficult and expensive to work with.

We have to reconsider the keys of Schema R6. It is not too hard to see that we can infer from FD4 that {`street, zipcode`} is a key of R6.

We are not done with these schemas until we are sure that there are no 3NF violations. Notice that all of the attributes of FD4 are present in R6. However, the right-side attributes of FD4 are `city` and `state` and these attributes are key attributes in R6. Thus, R6 is in 3NF.

7.8 BOYCE-CODD NORMAL FORM (BCNF)

Another very important and useful normal form is called **Boyce-Codd Normal Form (BCNF)**. A schema is in BCNF if every functional dependency has a superkey as its determinant. To transform a schema into BCNF, we must remove all non-key dependencies even those with key attributes on the right side. Schema R6 of Section 7.7 is a 3NF schema that has a non-key dependency (FD4: zipcode → {city, state}) and therefore is not in BCNF.

Figure 7.7 shows the schema, functional dependency and decomposition of R6. The resulting schemas R7 and R8 are in BCNF. R7 was created by removing the right side attributes of FD4. However, because city and state were part of the key, zipcode was added to its key. Attribute street by itself is not an appropriate key because the many locations have the same street. Because zipcode determines city and state, zipcode provides an adequate substitute as a key attribute of R8.

Some experts prefer not to create BCNF schemas because of the way they split up keys. The BCNF problem with schema R6 was that it had two interdependent, multi-attribute keys. BCNF simply does not allow interdependent, multi-attribute keys.

7.9 CASE IN POINT: NORMALIZATION OF A CAR REGISTRATION

In this example, we will develop a relational schema without going through the data modeling described in Chapters 3 and 4. As has been emphasized, it is not good practice to skip data modeling. Nevertheless, this example clearly shows the power of functional dependency analysis and normalization.

Let's consider the record of automobile registrations that is maintained by a state's Department of Motor Vehicles. This agency issues car titles and keeps track of car ownership and license tags. Figure 7.8 shows a sample of the form that is issued by the State of Florida when a new owner first registers a car. It includes the fees paid to register the car and to transfer the title. The form also has information about the car, the title, the owners, the registration, and the license tag. Attributes for these entities are all mixed together on the form.

Our goal is to create a database schema in BCNF to store the information in the form. We do so by listing the attributes of a single relation containing this entity. Next, we determine an appropriate set of functional dependencies. We then go through the normalization process.

The first step in creating a schema is to list the attributes. From Figure 7.8, we find the following attributes:

```
decalNumber, year, sex, birthDate, expiresDate, tagIssued,
tagNumber, titleNumber, vehicleIdNumber, yearMake,
wtLength, class, make, type, color, ownerNameAddress,
ownerDL1, ownerDL2, pip, liability, creditAmt, refundAmt,
issuedDate, taxMonths, taxAmt, btMonths, btAmt,
tagSvcChargAmt, otherAmt, tagTotalAmt, titleFeeAmt,
titleLateFeeAmt, lienAmt, titleSvcChargeAmt, titleTotalAmt,
salesTaxAmt, grandTotalAmt
```

FIGURE 7.7

Non-BCNF Schema and Its Decomposition

R6: (<u>street</u>, <u>city</u>, <u>state</u>, zipcode, secondary key {street, zipcode})
FD4: zipcode → {city, state}

Decomposition of R6 by FD4 into R7 and R8:

R7: (<u>street</u>, <u>zipcode</u> references R8)
R8: (<u>zipcode</u>, city, state,)

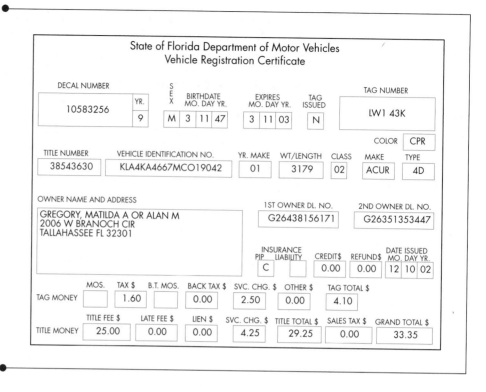

FIGURE 7.8

Sample Car Registration Form

The functional dependencies among these attributes come primarily from their organization into entities. From what we know of car registration, we expect to find that the entities represented by these attributes are the car, the title, the owners, and the registration. Functional dependencies should be defined that represent likely keys for these various entities. The car, owners, and title have obvious keys. The key for the registration is more difficult to analyze and requires some specific knowledge. In Florida, a new registration is issued for each car each year. A decal with the year is issued to the owner and must be attached to the license plate. The number on the decal is unique for the registration. Hence, we can use `decalNumber` as the key for the registration.

The following is a list of rules that includes each attribute. You will notice that some duplication of attributes occurs. This redundancy could have been avoided by more careful analysis, but is a typical situation and makes the normalization more interesting.

FD13: `VehicleIdNumber` → {`yearMake, wtLength, class, make, type, color`}

FD14: `TitleNumber` → {`yearMake, wtLength, titleFeeAmt, titleLateFeeAmt, lienAmt, titleSvcChargeAmt, titleTotalAmt, salesTaxAmt`}

FD15: {`ownerDL1, ownerDL2`} → {`sex, birthDate, ownerNameAddress`}

FD16: `decalNumber` → {`year, sex, birthMonth, birthDay, birthYear, expiresDate, tagIssued, tagNumber, pip, liability, creditAmt, refundAmt, issuedDate, taxMonths, taxAmt, btMonths, btAmt, tagSvcChargAmt, otherAmt, tagTotalAmt, grandTotalAmt`}

There are also dependencies between the entities. The registration has a single title, a single car, and one or two owners. The car has one or two owners. These rules can be represented by the following functional dependencies:

FD17: `decalNumber` → {`TitleNumber, VehicleIdNumber, ownerDL1, ownerDL2`}

FD18: `TitleNumber` → {`VehicleIdNumber, ownerDL1, ownerDL2`}

The normalization could be done informally or formally. As an illustration of the process, it's better to proceed formally. To do so, we begin with a simple renaming of the attributes, as described below.

So far, all of our examples of functional dependency and normalization have begun with an analysis of the meaning of relations and attributes. From these meanings, we infer functional dependencies, and normalization proceeds in the context of our understanding of those meanings.

Not surprisingly, the intuition of a designer may interfere with the normalization of schemas. For this reason, normalization is best seen as a formal process that applies specific syntactic rules to sets of attributes and functional dependencies. It is better that the attributes have names that are not meaningful, because attribute names may distract us from the process of normalization.

Figure 7.9 provides a renaming of the attributes and a restatement of the functional dependencies in terms of the new names. The relation that includes all of the attributes is called R.

FIGURE 7.9

Renaming of Registration Attributes and List of Functional Dependencies

Attributes of Relation R

New	Old	New	Old	New	Old
A	decalNumber	N	class	AA	btAmt
B	year	O	color	BB	tagSvcChargeAmt
C	sex	P	ownerNameAddr	CC	otherAmt
D	birthDate	Q	ownerDL1	DD	tagTotalAmt
E	expiresDate	R	ownerDL2	EE	titleFeeAmt
F	tagIssued	S	pip	FF	titleLateFeeAmt
G	tagNumber	T	liability	GG	lienAmt
H	titleNumber	U	creditAmt	HH	titleSvcChargeAmt
I	vehicleIdNumber	V	refundAmt	II	titleTotalAmt
J	yearMake	W	issuedDate	JJ	salesTaxAmt
K	wtLength	X	taxMonths	KK	grandTotalAmt
L	make	Y	taxAmt		
M	type	Z	btMonths		

FD13: I → {J, K, L, M, N, O}

FD14: H → {J, K, EE, FF, GG, HH, II, JJ}

FD15: {Q, R} → {C, D, P}

FD16: A → {B, C, D, E, F, G, S, T, U, V, W, X, Y, Z, AA, BB, CC, DD, KK}

FD17: A → {H, I, Q, R}

FD18: H → {I, Q, R}

Analysis for normalization begins with finding the closure of the set of functional dependencies. Some inferred dependencies follow:

FD19: A → {B, C, D, E, F, G, H, I, J, K, L, M, N, O, P, Q, R, S, T, U, V, W, X, Y, Z, AA, BB, CC, DD, EE, FF, GG, HH, II, JJ, KK}

FD20: H → {C, D, I, J, K, L, M, N, O, P, Q, R, EE, FF, GG, HH, II, JJ}

Dependency FD19 is a superkey dependency, as every attribute is included. Because the left side is a single attribute, it is a key. No rule includes A on the right side, so nothing determines A, and no other attributes are a key of the relation R.

The other functional dependencies (except FD16, a subset of FD19) represent 3NF violations. The first decomposition is made from dependency FD20, the largest violation. Decomposition using FD20 yields two relations:

R9: (<u>A</u>, B, E, F, G, H references R10, S, T, U, V, W, X, Y, Z, AA, BB, CC, DD, KK)

R10: (<u>H</u>, C, D, I, J, K, L, M, N, O, P, Q, R, EE, FF, GG, HH, II, JJ)

Dependencies FD13 and FD15 are 3NF violations in R10. Decomposing R10 according to dependency FD13 yields relations R3 and R4:

R11: (<u>H</u>, C, D, I references R12, P, Q, R, EE, FF, GG, HH, II, JJ}

R12: (<u>I</u>, J, K, L, M, N, O}

Dependency FD15 is now a violation in R11. Decomposition of R11 by dependency FD15 yields relations R13 and R14:

R13: (<u>H</u>, I references R12, Q, R, EE, FF, GG, HH, II, JJ, foreign key {Q, R} references R14)

R14: (<u>Q</u>, <u>R</u>, C, D, P)

The database schema {R9, R12, R14, R14} is in BCNF. Figure 7.10 shows the database schema with the original attribute names and reasonable schema names. You may notice that the duplication of non-key attributes has been eliminated and the attributes are in the correct relations.

FIGURE   7.10

BCNF Database Schema for Car Registration

Registration (R9): (<u>decalNumber</u>, year, expiresDate, tagIssued, tagNumber, titleNumber, pip, liability, creditAmt, refundAmt, issuedDate, taxMonths, taxAmt, btMonths, btAmt, tagSvcChargAmt, otherAmt, tagTotalAmt, grandTotalAmt, foreign key titleNumber references Title)

Vehicle (R12): (<u>vehicleIdNumber</u>, yearMake, wtLength, class, make, type, color)

Title (R13): (<u>titleNumber</u>, vehicleIdNumber, ownerDL1, ownerDL2, titleFeeAmt, titleLateFeeAmt, lienAmt, titleSvcChargeAmt, titleTotalAmt, salesTaxAmt, foreign key vehicleIdNumber references Vehicle, foreign key {ownerDL1, ownerDL2} references Owners)

Owners (R14): (<u>ownerDL1</u>, <u>ownerDL2</u>, sex, birthDate, ownerNameAddress)

> ### A Note about Having No Second Owner
>
> The key for the Owners relation in Figure 7.10 is the combination of the driver's license numbers of the two owners. In many cases, however, there will be no second owner. This situation causes a problem because database systems often require that key attributes must be non-null. Hence, for this schema, we must have a non-null value that means that there is no second owner.
>
> A solution to this problem is to designate a specific driver's license number, such as 11111111111, to stand for the null second owner. The database applications must recognize this designation and react appropriately.

CHAPTER SUMMARY

Once a relational model has been created, it must be subjected to analysis and modification to ensure that the final model is of an appropriate quality. The general criteria for quality are that each attribute and schema should have a simple meaning, redundant values in tables should be minimized, the presence of null values in tables should be minimized, and spurious or meaningless rows should be disallowed.

More formal measures of quality are based on functional dependencies and normal forms. Overall, the goal of normalization is to represent functional dependencies as key and foreign key dependencies, thereby reducing redundancy and making the functional dependency constraints easier to enforce.

A functional dependency is a constraint on a table that specifies that a certain set of attributes functionally determines another set. That is, any two rows that have the same values for their first set of attributes also have the same values for the second set of attributes. Inference rules can be used to find all of the dependencies that can be derived from a set of dependencies. The keys of a schema can be determined from the functional dependencies. A key declaration, in turn, defines a functional dependency.

Each normal form places a restriction on functional dependencies. If a relation schema contains a violation of the normal form, it must be decomposed into two schemas. The result of the decomposition is to transform a non-key dependency into a key dependency.

Database systems support the enforcement of some constraints, including primary and secondary key constraints and foreign key (referential integrity) constraints. Other constraints must be enforced by applications or other database programs.

KEY TERMS

Anomalous behavior. A situation in which an update to one value affects another value.

Boyce-Codd normal form (BCNF) schema. A schema in which every nontrivial functional dependency has a superkey on the left side.

Decomposition. The process of dividing a schema into two smaller schemas, often for the purpose of removing a normal form violation.

Deletion anomaly. A situation, usually caused by redundancy in the schema, in which the deletion of one row of a table results in the deletion of an unintended information.

Determinant. The attributes on the left side of a functional dependency that determine the attributes on the right side.

Functional dependency. The situation in which the values of one set of attributes determine the values of another set.

Insertion anomaly. A situation, usually caused by redundancy in the schema, in which the insertion of a row in a table creates an inconsistency with other rows.

Key. A superkey which is minimal in the sense that removing any attribute from it produces a set of attributes that is not a superkey.

Key attribute. An attribute in a relation schema that is part of some key of the schema.

Modification anomaly. A situation, usually caused by redundancy in the schema, in which the modification of a row of a table creates an inconsistency with another row.

Non-key attribute. An attribute in a relation schema that is not part of any key of the relation schema.

Normal form. A collection of rules that describes an acceptable form of a relation schema.

Normalization. A process of modifying a relation schema so that it conforms to certain rules called normal forms. Normalization is conducted by evaluating a relation schema to find violations of the particular rules, and then decomposing the schema into smaller, related schemas that do not violate the rules.

Redundancy. The duplication of information in multiple tables within a database.

Schema improvement. The modification of a schema to improve its design, especially so that each table will have a simple meaning, and so that the database will have less duplication of information and fewer null values.

Superkey. A set of attributes of a relation schema that together determine the rest of the attributes of the schema. Alternatively, the left side of a functional dependency that includes all of the attributes of a schema. Every key is also a superkey.

Superkey dependency. A functional dependency that includes every attribute of the schema.

Third normal form (3NF) schema. A schema in which every functional dependency has either a superkey as determinant or key attributes on its right side.

Update anomaly. A situation, usually caused by redundancy in the schema, in which an update to one value affects another value. An update anomaly may be a deletion anomaly, an insertion anomaly, or a modification anomaly.

QUESTIONS

1. Give three reasons why redundancy in schemas creates problems and provide an example of each reason.

2. Give an example (not from the book) of each type (deletion, insertion, modification) of anomaly for the `VideoMovie` schema and table shown in Figure 7.1.

3. Is it necessary to *declare* functional dependencies, or is it possible to infer them from sample tables? Which apparent functional dependencies can be inferred from the table of Figure 7.1 that are not functional dependencies?

4. What does it mean to violate a constraint on the contents of a database?

PROBLEMS

5. Suppose a student registration database has a table for student grades:

   `Grades: (studentId, lastName, firstName, courseId, courseTitle, sectionNumber, semester, numHours, meetingTime, meetingRoom, grade)`

   a. Give a sample table for the `Grades` schema that shows the redundancy inherent in the meaning of the information.

   b. Define appropriate functional dependencies for the `Grades` schema.

   c. Identify and remove any 3NF violations resulting from (b). Show the resulting schemas and tables.

   Suppose R: (A, B, C, D) is a relation. Answer problems 6–9 based on the functional dependencies given in each question.

6. With no functional dependencies defined, what is the key of R?

7. Suppose A is the key of R and B → {C, D}.

   a. Which dependencies represent 3NF violations?

   b. Eliminate the 3NF violations by decomposition.

8. Suppose A → {B, C} and B → {C, D}

   a. Which sets of attributes are the keys of R?

   b. Identify and eliminate any 3NF violations.

9. Suppose {A, B} → {C, D}, and C → B.

   a. Which sets of attributes are the keys of R?

   b. Identify and eliminate any 3NF violations.

   Suppose R: (A, B, C, D, E, F, G, H) is a relation. Answer problems 10–11 based on the functional dependencies given in each question.

10. Suppose {A, B} → {C, D, E, F, G, H}, and C → {A, B, E, F}.

    a. Which sets of attributes are the keys of R?

    b. Identify and eliminate any 3NF violations.

11. Suppose A → {B, C, D}, {A, E} → {G, H}, E → F, and F → E.

    a. Which sets of attributes are the keys of R?

    b. Identify and eliminate any 3NF violations.

FURTHER READING

Date's book [Date99], now in its seventh edition, contains a thorough treatment of how to create high-quality relational models and covers normalization in much more detail than provided in this chapter. Date includes comprehensive bibliographies of all major topics in rela-tional modeling. Silbershatz, Korth, and Sudarshan [SKS01] and Elmasri and Navathe [ElNa99] devote several chapters to discussions of normalization and schema improvement.

PART IV

Manipulating Relational Information

Now that you know how to specify and create databases, you are ready to learn how to create, access, and modify the content of those databases. Chapters 8 and 9 introduce three styles of manipulating relational information: a mathematical language called the relational algebra, the graphical style of Microsoft Access, and the SQL language.

In Chapter 8, we look into how to write extract information from relational tables. We start with the simplest manipulations of relational tables and gradually, step by step, progress to very complex manipulations. Each different operation, or *query*, is described in the simplest terms with a detailed example. Then the operation is described in a mathematical form that helps make the meaning very clear and precise. Finally, we consider how to express the query in the graphical user interfaces of Microsoft Access. By the end of the chapter, you will know how to express and understand even the most complex queries.

Chapter 9 brings us to the essence of manipulating relational databases, the SQL language. SQL is the language of choice for database professionals. Once you understand SQL, you will be able to create and manipulate any relational database. All of the queries of Chapter 8 are revisited, and the SQL versions are described in full detail. A few additional query types are introduced as well. Finally, you will learn how to modify the contents of tables using SQL and even how to create and modify the table definitions.

Once you've learned SQL, you'll be ready to move on to Part V and begin developing your own Web site applications.

CHAPTER 8

Manipulating Database Content with Relational Algebra and Microsoft Access

In this chapter, you will learn:

- How to access, use, and change information in a relational database

- What a relational database's main operations consist of

- How to create database queries in Microsoft Access

- How to create database user interfaces in Microsoft Access

Now that you understand how to design, specify, and construct relational databases, you're ready to learn how to *use* their information content. For example, once you've constructed a relational database, you'll probably want to search for specific information, combine information from various tables within the database, add new information to the database, and modify or delete existing information.

To access information in a database, you use what's called a **query**. In plain language, an example of a BigHit Video query might be, "How many customers have the zip code 32301?" You submit the query to the database software for processing, and in turn, the software finds the answer from the available tables in the database. In this example, the database would likely find the answer in the `Customer` table. The software reads the `Customer` table and counts how many rows in the table have the zip code you specified. Finally, it delivers the answer to you as a new table.

As with anything involving computers, you must specify your queries carefully to get useful answers from the software. To that end, programmers have developed a number of special languages for writing queries that both people and computers can understand.

Microsoft Access has a query wizard function that lets you submit queries relatively easily. However, good query writing follows a formal model based on the operations of **relational algebra**, a collection of mathematical operations that manipulate tables. In this chapter, you'll learn about the individual operations first and then discover how to use combinations of operations to create queries. To understand relational algebra expressions, you'll need to master some new notation. Why should you learn the notation if you don't need to use it in Access's query wizard? Familiarity with the notation will help you grasp the logic behind complex queries and clarify your own thinking as you begin creating queries.

This chapter focuses on using relational algebra and Microsoft Access to create and execute queries and display their results. In the next chapter, you'll learn about another language, SQL, or the Structured Query Language. Your knowledge of relational algebra will be particularly useful in learning SQL.

Your understanding of this chapter will be greatly enhanced by practicing with Access. Begin with the sample BigHit Video database. Whenever the book describes how to use Access, try it yourself. Follow each step of the explanation. With a little work, you should be able to reproduce all of the examples.

8.1 MANIPULATING INFORMATION IN RELATIONAL DATABASES

From the definition of the relational model that you saw in Chapter 5, you know that table in a relational database consists of a set of rows (also called **records**), and that each row in a table has the same number and types of attributes. When you send a query to the database, it finds the appropriate rows of information in the stored tables, performs the requested operations on the data, and presents the results in a new table. The database doesn't store the new table permanently in its files; rather, it delivers the **results table** to the user who submitted the query and destroys the table when the user no longer needs it.

As suggested above, users need to access and manipulate information in their relational databases in a number of ways. For example, a manager at BigHit Video might want to find relatively simple information, such as a list of all BigHit Video customers, the first and last name and address of a particular customer, or the number of hours a BigHit employee worked last week. The manager might also want to get more complex information, such as which videos a particular customer has rented and when those videos are due back at the store.

To retrieve simpler information, you would use one of three kinds of queries, all of which are based on relational algebra operations. The more complex information requires queries that *combine* several relational algebra operations. Below, we examine the three kinds of queries in more detail, and then explore how to combine them. For each example, we include the relevant tables from BigHit Video's database that the database software would access in order to address our queries.

Relational queries consist of combinations of operations. Each operation has one or two input tables. The operation reads the contents of its input tables and produces a new table. Relational operations can be classified into four types.

- A **projection** operation produces a new table that has only some of the columns of its input table.
- A **selection** operation produces a result table that has all of the columns, but only those rows of its input table that satisfy some criteria.
- A **join** or **product** operation produces a result table by combining the columns of two input tables.
- A **set** operation produces an output table whose rows come from one or the other of its input tables.

8.2 PROJECTION QUERIES

Suppose you worked as a manager at BigHit Video, and you wanted to get a list of the first and last names of all the company's customers. A projection operation could create such a list. A succinct way of writing this operation is *project* Customer *onto* (firstName, lastName).

The projection operation starts with the Customer table and creates a new table from the two requested columns. Table 8.1 shows a sample Customer table and Table 8.2 is the table that results from the projection.

The rows of the new relation are all of the firstName, lastName combinations that correspond to the values of those attributes from the Customer table. In the algebraic notation, we represent projection with the Greek letter pi (π) and write

$$\pi_{firstName, lastName}(\text{Customer})$$

This is our first example of a relational algebra expression. Relational algebra provides a concise and precise notation for describing queries. We'll see many more examples in the rest of the chapter. Learning this notation will give you confidence that you can understand any query language.

Notice that the sample Customer table has 8 rows, but the result of the projection has only 7. You may recall that a relational table is a set of rows and each row must be different from all others. Table 8.1 has two customers with the same first and last name. When we project the table onto these two attributes, any duplicate rows are

Table 8.1 Sample **Customer** Table

accountId	lastName	firstName	street	city	state	zipcode	balance
101	Block	Jane	345 Randolph Circle	Apopka	FL	30458-	$0.00
102	Hamilton	Cherry	3230 Dade St.	Dade City	FL	30555-	$3.00
103	Harrison	Katherine	103 Landis Hall	Bratt	FL	30457-	$31.00
104	Breaux	Carroll	76 Main St.	Apopka	FL	30458-	$35.00
106	Morehouse	Anita	9501 Lafayette St.	Houma	LA	44099-	$0.00
111	Doe	Jane	123 Main St.	Apopka	FL	30458-	$0.00
201	Greaves	Joseph	14325 N. Bankside St.	Godfrey	IL	43580-	$0.00
444	Doe	Jane	Cawthon Dorm, Room 642	Tallahassee	FL	32306-	$10.55

Table 8.2 Results of *project* **Customer** *onto* (*firstName*, *lastName*)

firstName	lastName
Anita	Morehouse
Jane	Block
Carroll	Breaux
Cherry	Hamilton
Catherine	Harrison
Jane	Doe
Joseph	Greaves

removed. Hence, because two customers are named "Jane Doe," the result table has a single row to represent both customers.

Thus, the relational operation *project Customer onto* `firstName, lastName` produces a table that does not have a row for each customer, but rather a row for each unique combination of `firstName, lastName`. A little later we'll see how to produce a projection operation that does not remove duplicates.

Projection operations are easy to create in Microsoft Access. Use the following steps, which are illustrated in Figure 8.1:

1. Click the `Query` tab at the left-hand side of the database window.
2. Double click on `Create query by using wizard`.
3. In the wizard dialog box (also shown in the figure), select `Customer` as the source table.
4. Move the `firstName` field into the `Selected Fields` area by clicking on `firstName` and then the select button (right arrow).
5. Move the `lastName` field into the `Selected Fields` area by clicking on `lastName` and then the select button.
6. Press `Finish` to save the query with the default name of `Customer Query`.

When you follow these steps in Access, you are asking the database software to go to the `Customer` table currently stored in the database and present the results of your query in the form of a new table listing all BigHit customers' first and last names, as shown in Figure 8.2. Thus, Access retrieves exactly the values shown in Table 8.1 into an internal table and displays them in the datasheet view of Figure 8.2. You will notice that Access has not eliminated the duplicates. You'll see below how to make this a proper projection query by eliminating duplicates.

Concept

Projection in Geometry

The relational operators are inspired by operations on multidimensional mathematical relations, but the meanings of the relational operators are much simpler. In mathematics, a relation is a table, just as it is in the relational model. Mathematical tables are used to store geometric images, among other things.

On a computer, a digital two-dimensional image is a set of pixels (dots of color), each represented by a triplet (x, y, c) where x and y are the horizontal and vertical coordinates and c is the color. Thus, an image can be stored in a table of three columns. A three-dimensional image would add a depth coordinate z and be a set of quadruples (x, y, z, c). An animation would add a time coordinate t and be a set of quadruples (x, y, c, t) in two dimensions and quintuples (x, y, z, c, t) in three dimensions.

Many of the projections that we use for geometrical images are complex numerical transformations, whereas relational projection simply removes columns from a table. No relational projection corresponds to a perspective drawing or a map of the globe. A relational projection that removes the z coordinate from a three-dimensional image produces a set of the (x, y, c) values. That is, the relational projection yields the set of all color values for each (x, y) coordinate. In contrast, a geometric projection from three to two dimensions is expected to produce a single color value for each (x, y) coordinate. Perspective projections, for instance, are created by complex mathematical formulas that give the illusion of three dimensions to a two-dimensional image.

We'll see more examples of relational operations and geometry later in the chapter.

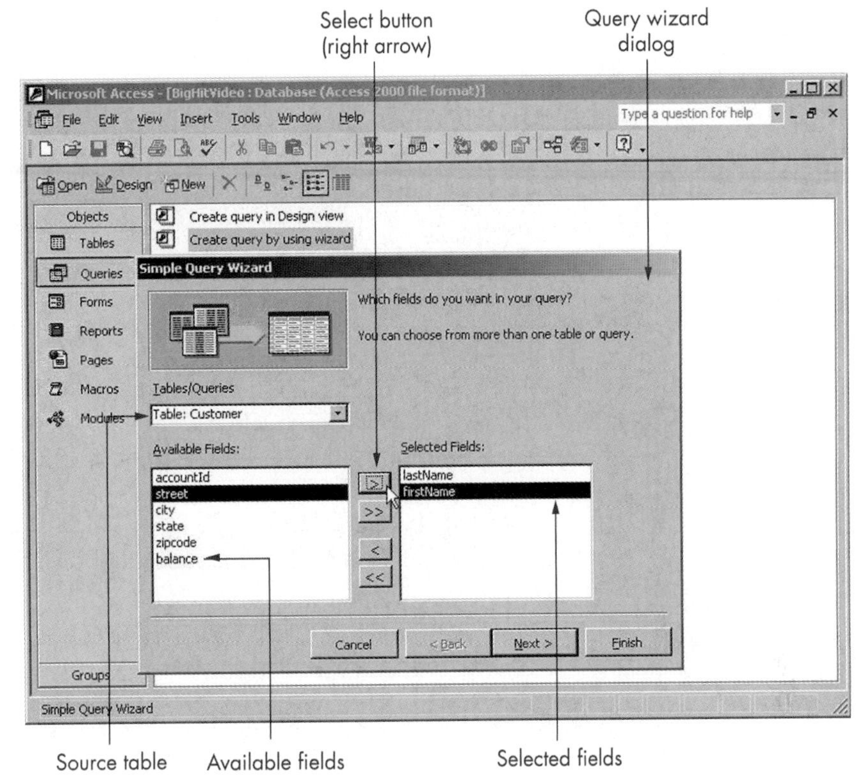

FIGURE 8.1

Using Access's Query Wizard to Create a Projection Query

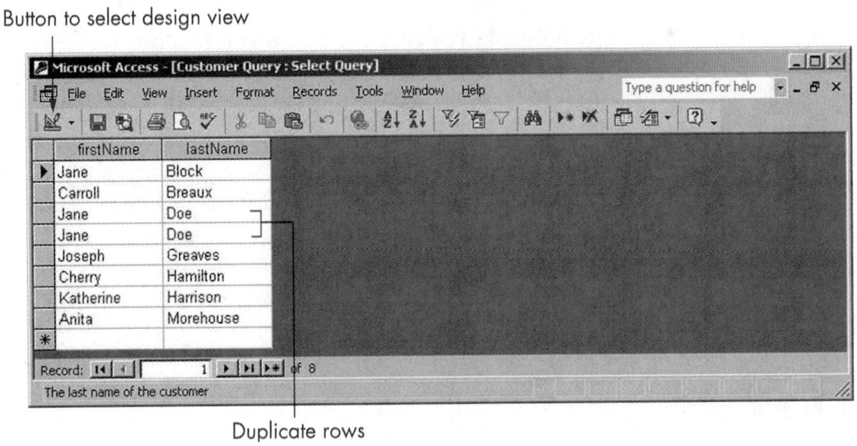

FIGURE 8.2

Access's Datasheet View of Results of a Projection Operation

Once you've created this projection query, you may want to modify it; for example, to eliminate duplicates or show the table in a certain order. To modify the query, use Access's query design view by clicking the design view icon, as shown by the comment box in Figure 8.3. You can also get to the design view from the `View` menu or by right clicking on the datasheet view. The design view of this query is shown in Figure 8.3.

Query design view is divided horizontally into two areas, as shown in Figure 8.3. In this example, the upper area lists all the attribute names from the `Customer` table,

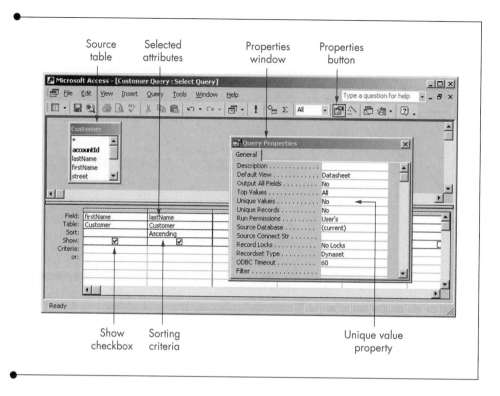

FIGURE 8.3

Design View of a Projection Operation

indicating that the results of the query are created from this table's rows. The lower area shows the two fields (`firstName` and `lastName`) from the source table that are used to create the results table. The `Show` checkboxes under both fields are selected, indicating that the query results include those fields.

You can also specify properties for your query by opening the query properties window. Either click the `Properties` button (as shown in the comment box of Figure 8.3) or select `Properties` from the `View` menu. The query properties window shown in Figure 8.3 depicts properties that may be of interest to you. For example, by selecting `No` in the `Unique Values` property field (the default), you would tell Access not to eliminate duplicates in the results table (thus, the name Jane Doe would appear twice in your results table, as in Figure 8.2). If you selected `Yes` in this field, Access would eliminate duplicates. Thus, Jane Doe's name would appear once in your results table, as shown in Table 8.2 and Figure 8.4.

FIGURE 8.4

Result of Projection without Duplicates, Ordered by `lastName`

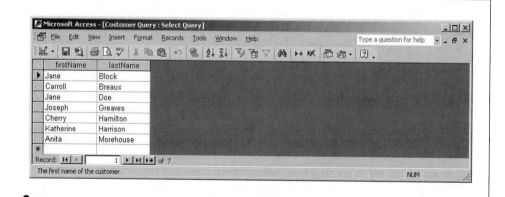

Figure 8.4 displays the result of the query sorted by `lastName` because the `Sort` field of the `lastName` attribute in Figure 8.3, as highlighted by the comment box, has value `Ascending`.

The presence or absence of duplicates in the projection queries illustrate the subtlety that is part of most queries. Table 8.2, with duplicates removed, lists all of the names of customers. No customer name is missing from this table. If you want to know if you have a customer with a particular name, you don't need duplicates. With duplicates, we might say the query produces "the first name and last name of *each* customer."

The table of Figure 8.2 shows the projection with duplicates. From this table, we know that we have two customers named Jane Doe, but we don't know anything else about these customers. The account ID, which uniquely identifies each customer, is missing because the projection removed it. We don't even know which row of the `Customer` table produced which Jane Doe row of the result.

As you'll see in the next sections, the query design view and the query properties window give you great flexibility in configuring queries.

8.3 SELECTION QUERIES

Now suppose you wanted to find all the information—such as account number, address, and balance owed to the store—relating to a particular BigHit customer. In this case, you would create what is called a **selection** query. BigHit Video's database would select all the rows from its `Customer` table that satisfy the criteria you specify in your query. For example, you could select all customers whose last name is "Doe." Table 8.3 shows the results of your query to *select from* `Customer` *where* `lastName` = *'Doe.'* The results table contains copies of the rows of `Customer` that have last name "Doe."

In relational algebraic notation, you would use the Greek letter sigma (σ) to represent the selection operator, and you would write this query as

$$\sigma_{lastName='Doe'}(\texttt{Customer})$$

To create this selection query in Access, use the following steps:

1. Click the `Query` tab of the database display.
2. In the `Design view` option, double click `Create query in Design view`. The system responds by opening the query design window and the table selection dialog, as shown in Figure 8.5.
3. Select the `Customer` table, then click Add and `Close`. The database responds with the window shown in Figure 8.6.
4. Now you need to tell the database that you want to see *all* information relating to customers with the last name "Doe." To do so, drag the asterisk shown in the `Customer` box in upper half of Figure 8.6 down to the `Field` entry of the first column in the lower half of the screen.

Table 8.3 Results Table for *select from* **Customer** *where* **lastName** = *'Doe'*

accountId	firstName	lastName	street	city	state	zipcode	balance
111	Jane	Doe	123 Main St.	Apopka	FL	34331	0.00
444	Jane	Doe	Cawthon Dorm, Room 642	Tallahassee	FL	32306	10.55

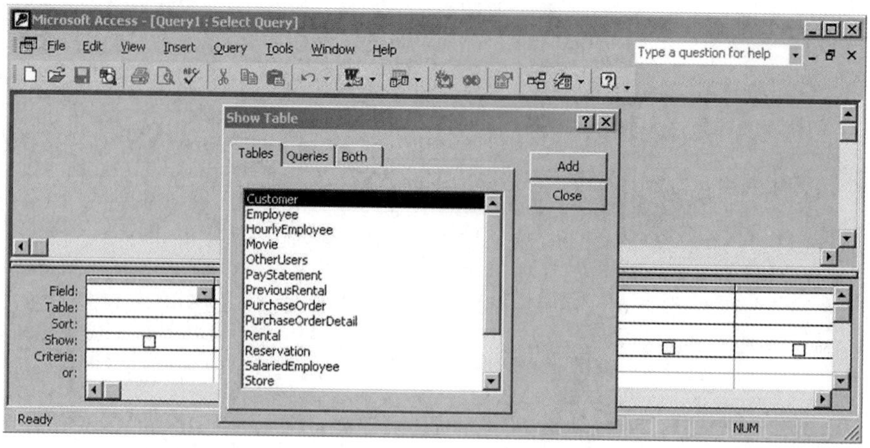

FIGURE 8.5

Query Design Window and Table Selection Dialog

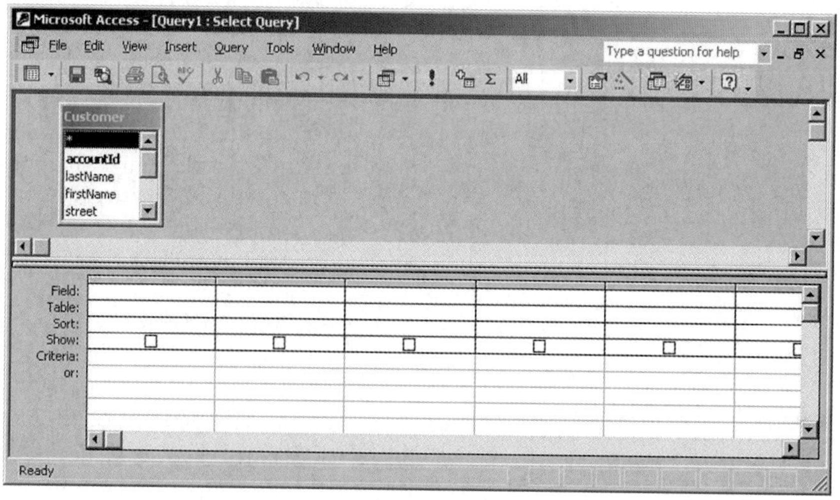

FIGURE 8.6

Query Design Window with **Customer** Table

Concept

Selection in Geometry

Relational selection can produce meaningful transformations of images. For instance, selecting all quadruples of a three-dimensional image with $z=5$ will produce the set of all quadruples $(x, y, 5, c)$, which is a two-dimensional slice of the original image at depth 5. We can take slices of images in any dimension. We can also find all places where the color is a particular value or range of values. This selection could be used to find hot or cold spots in an infrared picture, for instance.

Selection is particularly interesting in animations. Selecting all of the quadruples of a two-dimensional animation with $t=5$, for instance, will produce as set of $(x, y, c, 5)$ which is a single frame of the animation. Selecting for a range of t values will produce a sequence of frames—that is a clip of the animation. We can track the changes in color of a single pixel through time in an animation by selecting all pixels with a particular (x, y) to produce the set of (c, t) of a single spatial coordinate.

5. To specify the last name "Doe," drag `lastName` from the upper part of the screen down to the second column in the lower half. Click on the `Show` box to uncheck it, and type "`Doe`" in the `Criteria` entry. If you leave the `Show` box checked, the results would have an extra column containing a duplicate `lastName` field.

Figure 8.7 shows what you would see after performing these steps. Figure 8.8 shows the results table that Access would create after processing your query.

You could create a more complex selection query than the one shown in the above example. For instance, suppose you wanted a list of all the time cards submitted by a specific employee after a particular date. The employee's Social Security number is 376-77-0099, and you want to see all the time cards he has submitted since March 1,

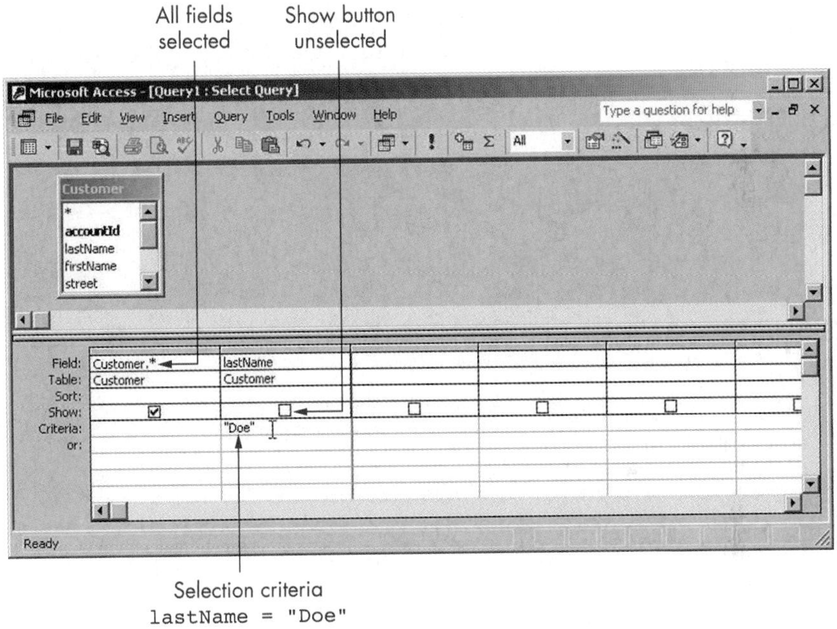

FIGURE 8.7

Selecting All Information for Customers with Last Name "Doe"

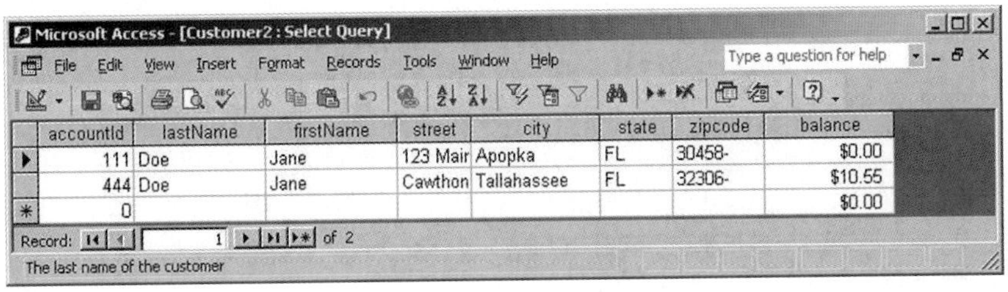

FIGURE 8.8

Access's Results Display for *select from* `Customer` *where* `lastName` = '*Doe*'

2002. You could express this query in English as *select from* `TimeCard` *where* `ssn` = *'376-77-0099' and* `date` *< '01-mar-2002'*. In relational algebraic notation, you would write this operation as

$$\sigma_{\text{ssn='376-77-0099' and date<'01-mar-2002'}}(\texttt{TimeCard})$$

Table 8.4 is a sample `TimeCard` table and Table 8.5 shows the results table for the operation *select from* `TimeCard` *where* `ssn` = *'376-77-0099' and* `date` *< '01-mar-2002'*.

Figure 8.9 shows you how to create this query in Access, again by using the query design view. After selecting the table `TimeCard` from the table selection dialog, as in Figure 8.5, you tell the database to add all of the `TimeCard` fields by dragging the asterisk from `TimeCard` down into the `Field` entry. You can drag `ssn` and drop it into the second column or use the drop-down menu attached to that field box to select the field, as shown in Figure 8.10. After selecting the field, uncheck the `Show` box, and type in the Social Security number of the employee in question.

In the third column, you select the `date` field. Once the field is selected, uncheck the `Show` box and type `<01-mar-2002` in the `Criteria` box. You can see how Access represents this date in the `Criteria` box of the third column. Access has replaced what you type by `<#3/1/2002#`. The date format has changed from day-month-year to month/day/year and Access has added pound signs (#) to delimit the date constant. The use of pound signs for date delimiters is just one of the strange features of Access. If you try to type single quote marks to delimit the date constant,

Table 8.4 Sample `TimeCard` Table

ssn	date	startTime	endTime	storeId	paid
145-09-0967	01/14/2002	8:15	12:00	3	yes
245-11-4554	01/14/2002	8:15	12:00	3	yes
376-77-0099	02/23/2002	14:00	22:00	5	yes
376-77-0099	03/21/2002	14:00	22:00	5	yes
145-09-0967	01/16/2002	8:15	12:00	3	yes
376-77-0099	01/03/2002	10:00	14:00	5	yes
376-77-0099	01/03/2002	15:00	19:00	5	yes

Table 8.5 Results Table for *select from* `TimeCard` *where* `ssn` = *'376-77-0099' and* `date` *< '01-mar-2002'*

ssn	date	startTime	endTime	storeId	paid
376-77-0099	02/23/2002	14:00	22:00	5	yes
376-77-0099	01/03/2002	10:00	14:00	5	yes
376-77-0099	01/03/2002	15:00	19:00	5	yes

Access will complain that the type of the value (a string type!) doesn't match the type of the attribute (date type). You would think that Access could figure out that a string can represent a date, but apparently it can't!

The datasheet view of this query, in Figure 8.10, shows the rows of Table 8.5.

8.4   PRODUCT QUERIES

Up to this point, the operators you've seen create a new table with the same number of attributes as the source table or fewer. Now we'll look at combining the attributes from two different tables to produce a new table with more attributes than either of the original ones. For instance, we may want to combine the `Employee` table, as shown in Table 8.6, and the `TimeCard` table to produce a new table that has all of the employee attributes *and* all of the time card attributes.

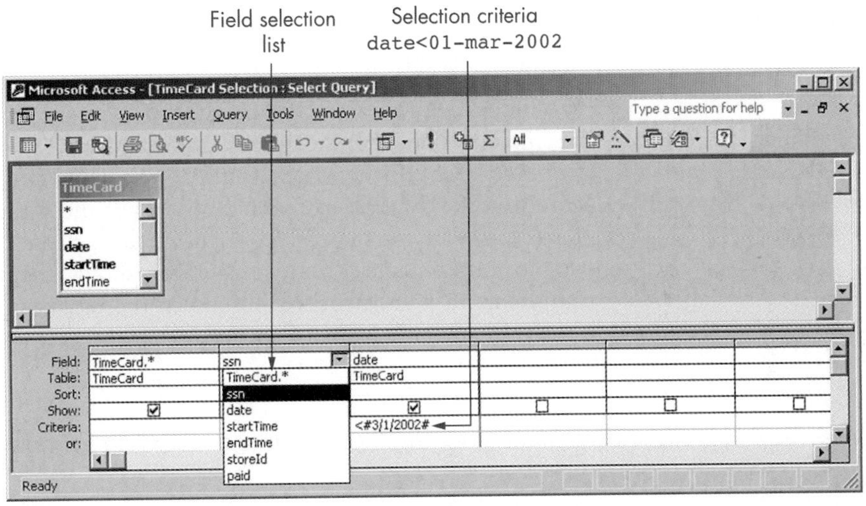

FIGURE 8.9

Design View of Employee Time Card Query

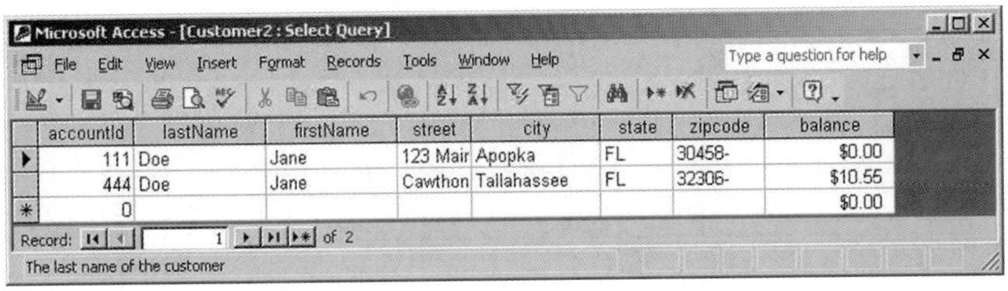

FIGURE 8.10

Access Datasheet View of *select from* `TimeCard` *where* `ssn` *= '376-77-0099' and* `date` *< '01-mar-2002'*

Table 8.6 Sample **Employee** Table

ssn	lastName	firstName
145-09-0967	Uno	Jane
245-11-4554	Toulouse	Jennifer
376-77-0099	Threat	Ayisha
479-98-0098	Fortune	Julian
588-99-0093	Fivozinsky	Bruce

To perform such an operation, you would use a **product** query. The simplest product operation would produce a new table that would contain a row for each combination of one row from one source table and one row from the other source table. Thus, in the employee and time card example, for each row in the original **Employee** table, the new table would contain as many rows as there are in the original **Time-Card** table. This results table would contain 30 rows, because the original **Employee** table has 5 rows and the **TimeCard** table has 6 rows.

In relational algebraic notation, you would write this operation using the **Cartesian product**: operator (×)

$$Employee \times TimeCard$$

A simple statement of the query is *product of Employee and TimeCard*.

Table 8.7 shows part of the results table you would get from this operation, using the employees of Table 8.6 and the time cards of Table 8.4. Note that each row has 9 attributes—3 from the original **Employee** table and 6 from the **TimeCard** table. Moreover, the database system had to change the names of the first and fourth attributes to produce the new table. Without these name changes, the table would show two attributes named **ssn**. This table shows the use of **qualified names**: Employee.ssn is the **ssn** attribute from the **Employee** table, and **TimeCard.ssn** is the **ssn** attribute from **TimeCard**.

Table 8.7 12 of the 35 Rows in the Result of *product of Employee and TimeCard*

Employee. ssn	last Name	first Name	TimeCard .ssn	date	startTime	endTime	storeId	paid	
145-09-0967	Uno	Jane	145-09-0967	1/14/2002	8:15:00 AM	12:00:00 PM	3	Yes	
245-11-4554	Toulouse	Jie	145-09-0967	1/14/2002	8:15:00 AM	12:00:00 PM	3	Yes	
376-77-0099	Threat	Ayisha	145-09-0967	1/14/2002	8:15:00 AM	12:00:00 PM	3	Yes	Rows from first time card
479-98-0098	Fortune	Julian	145-09-0967	1/14/2002	8:15:00 AM	12:00:00 PM	3	Yes	
579-98-8778	Fivozinsky	Bruce	145-09-0967	1/14/2002	8:15:00 AM	12:00:00 PM	3	Yes	
145-09-0967	Uno	Jane	145-09-0967	1/16/2002	8:15:00 AM	12:00:00 PM	3	Yes	
245-11-4554	Toulouse	Jie	145-09-0967	1/16/2002	8:15:00 AM	12:00:00 PM	3	Yes	
376-77-0099	Threat	Ayisha	145-09-0967	1/16/2002	8:15:00 AM	12:00:00 PM	3	Yes	Rows from second time card
479-98-0098	Fortune	Julian	145-09-0967	1/16/2002	8:15:00 AM	12:00:00 PM	3	Yes	
579-98-8778	Fivozinsky	Bruce	145-09-0967	1/16/2002	8:15:00 AM	12:00:00 PM	3	Yes	
145-09-0967	Uno	Jane	245-11-4554	1/14/2002	8:15:00 AM	12:00:00 PM	3	Yes	
245-11-4554	Toulouse	Jie	245-11-4554	1/14/2002	8:15:00 AM	12:00:00 PM	3	Yes	

INTERVIEW

JUDY BOWMAN
SQL As It Is Practiced

Judy Bowman is a best-selling author of various books on SQL. She has run her own consulting business since 1994, doing a mixture of training, writing, technical marketing, and project management.

CURRENT JOB Most of my jobs are connected to relational database management systems in one way or another. I've developed SQL and database administration/performance classes, written three books (two for Addison Wesley Longman, one for John Wiley and Sons), created documentation for applications, authored white papers, managed a corporate press, and created business plans for new products.

FIRST JOB I started out as a technical writer (the *first* technical writer) at Informix, after completing an MA in Oriental Languages, and I learned databases and SQL on the job. Not too hard for someone who'd been struggling with Japanese. After a year and a half with Informix, I moved to a local computer hardware company, and then to Sybase (another relational database management system company). There I went through a series of roles: tech writer, sales system administrator, project manager, product manager, engineering manager, internal training manager, and ended up directing joint development efforts with other companies.

MY INTEREST IS IN SQL AS IT IS PRACTICED rather than as a theoretical construct or a standards board product. [For this reason] I tend to run interesting problems on multiple systems. How does Oracle do this? Is SQL Server different? What about

IBM? I keep lots of books around, but mostly I learn by doing. That way, when I get a contract to document a database application or develop a custom class for a company, I can go in any direction—I'm not tied to a particular RDBMS vendor or version.

TURNING CLASS NOTES INTO BEST SELLING BOOKS I was doing a lot of teaching between 1996 and 1999, and got many requests for "advanced" SQL classes. I wasn't sure what that meant. Mostly, the level of database understanding I encountered at different corporate sites was either awful or pretty good. It seemed likely people wanted a way to make the transition from the first group to the second. I checked database newsgroups on the Web to see what kinds of questions were asked and began drafting exercises around them. After testing the materials in many classes and getting lots of feedback, I turned them into my third book, *Practical SQL: The Sequel*. The organizational structure was business problem solution, not feature, and I ran all the code on multiple systems. But . . . notes from the technical reviewers made it clear a book is different from a class. A class moves along in real time, and if a student gets lost, it's hard to get that person back on track. But a book sits still. Readers can go over sections more than once. I reorganized, cut, and added to the draft, and came out with a much better book. It was a lot of fun!

> **"I tend to run interesting problems on multiple systems. How does Oracle do this? Is SQL Server different? What about IBM? I keep lots of books around, but mostly I learn by doing."**

The data displayed in Table 8.7 show 12 of the combinations of employee and time card. Each row is the combination of information about an employee and information about a time card. You can see that the first five rows (highlighted in blue) show information about the five different employees but only a single time card. The next five rows (highlighted in red) are a different time card.

A more appropriate product would generate a row for each *combination of* Employee row and TimeCard row where the employee numbers in the two original rows are the same. That is, of all possible combinations of Employee and TimeCard, only those that have information about an employee and a time card for a particular employee are included in the results table. You can think of this product as a *selection* of those rows for which Employee.ssn equals TimeCard.ssn. If a particular employee worked a particular time period, we would get a row in the results table with all the information about that employee (Social Security number, last name, and first name) and all the information about the time card (Social Security number, date, start time, and end time).

In relational algebraic notation, you would express this product query as the selection of those rows in the product whose ssn fields match. Here's what the query would look like in this notation:

$$\sigma_{Employee.ssn=TimeCard.ssn}(Employee \times TimeCard)$$

This type of product is called a **join**. We express the join query in English as *join Employee and TimeCard where Employee.ssn = TimeCard.ssn*. The database combines from the two tables records that are connected by the relationships that the database designer defined in the database's original E-R model.

In this case, where the two tables are joined by attributes that have the same name, you would write the join expression in relational algebraic notation using the join operator ($\bowtie$) as

$$Employee \bowtie_{Employee.ssn=TimeCard.ssn} TimeCard$$

This type of join operation is called an **equi-join** (equality-join) because the join condition *Employee.ssn = TimeCard.ssn* specifies that the attribute values must be equal. Join operations can also be based on other comparisons: less than, greater than, etc.

Table 8.8 shows the result of this operation. The table has only 8 rows—one for each pair of matching rows of the two source tables.

Table 8.8 Results Table for *join Employee* and *TimeCard where Employee.ssn = TimeCard.ssn*

Employee. ssn	last Name	first Name	Timecard. ssn	date	start Time	store Id	paid	end Time
145-09-0967	Uno	Jane	145-09-0967	01/14/2002	8:15	3	no	12:00
145-09-0967	Uno	Jane	145-09-0967	01/16/2002	8:15	3	no	12:00
245-11-4554	Toulouse	Jie	245-11-4554	01/14/2002	8:15	3	no	12:00
376-77-0099	Threat	Ayisha	376-77-0099	02/23/2002	14:00	5	no	22:00
376-77-0099	Threat	Ayisha	376-77-0099	03/21/2002	14:00	5	no	22:00
376-77-0099	Threat	Ayisha	376-77-0099	02/23/2002	14:00	5	no	22:00
376-77-0099	Threat	Ayisha	376-77-0099	01/03/2002	10:00	5	no	14:00
376-77-0099	Threat	Ayisha	376-77-0099	01/03/2002	15:00	5	no	19:00

The information in Table 8.8 would be much more useful in creating paychecks than the information in Table 8.7. Each time card is associated with the correct employee and appears only once. This join operation combines entities that are associated by instances of the relationship type between entity classes `Employee` and `TimeCard`. The two source tables are joined on the key attribute of `Employee` and the foreign key attribute of `TimeCard`. The database designer specified this relationship type in the original data model so that the eventual user of the database could ask for precisely this join operation.

Note that the number of rows in the table shown in Table 8.8 is the same number as in the `TimeCard` table. This correspondence is no coincidence. The relationship type between `Employee` and `TimeCard` is one-to-many. Thus, there is exactly one employee for each time card, but there may be many time cards per employee. A join of a one-to-many relationship produces as many rows in the results table as there are rows in the source table that represents the "to-many" side of the relationship.

In this example, an employee would not appear in the join result unless at least one time card exists for that employee. For that reason, Julian Fortune, employee 479-98-0098, and Bruce Fivozinsky, employee 588-99-0093, are not represented in Table 8.8.

To program this join query in Access, begin with a new design window and select the tables `Employee` and `TimeCard`. Drag the asterisk from `Employee` to the `Field` entry of the first column and the asterisk from `TimeCard` to the `Field` entry of the second column. Figure 8.11 shows what you would see.

Notice that the two tables in the top half of Figure 8.11 are joined by a one-to-many (∞) relationship line. The line joins the `ssn` field of `Employee` and the `ssn` field of `TimeCard`. It tells Access to create the rows of the results table from a row of `Employee` and a row of `TimeCard` *only* if the values of the `ssn` fields in those two rows match. That is, the line specifies that the query is a join query.

There are two ways to create the join line.

1. If the two tables have been defined by the database designer as related, Access automatically creates the line between them. A database designer tells Access that two tables are related using the relationship window that was discussed in Section 6.5. In this case, the designer defined `Employee` and `TimeCard` as related in the original data model and therefore Access adds the join line as soon as you add the tables to the query.

2. As the query designer, you can create a join line by dragging an attribute from one table to an attribute of the other table. You can create a join between tables

FIGURE 8.11

Design View of a Join Query

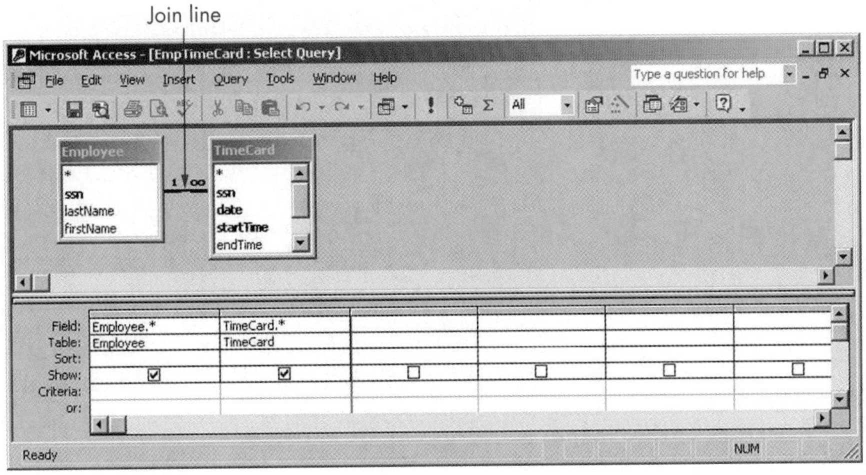

that have not been defined as related in the original data model, but that must be related for a query. For example, you might want to find combinations of BigHit stores and customers that have the same zip code, or locate all of the customers whose first and last names are the same as the first and last names of an employee. Figure 8.12 shows two query design windows, one for each of these ad hoc equi-joins.

You can create multiple join conditions on a single operation by adding more join lines, as shown in the lower query of Figure 8.12. In this case, the join lines connect `Customer.lastName` and `Employee.lastName`, and `Customer.firstName` and `Employee.firstName`, respectively. The results table will contain all pairs of customers whose names are the same. The result table will include an entry for each pair of customer and employee whose names are the same. Of course, we still don't know whether the customer and employee are the same person because a person's name is not unique.

An interesting case of equi-join is the **natural join**, which can be used when two tables have attributes with the same name. A natural join is an equi-join using equality on the common attributes as the join condition. In relational algebra, the natural join is written with the names of the shared attributes as the join condition as in these two expressions

$$\text{Employee} \bowtie_{ssn} \text{TimeCard}$$
$$\text{Customer} \bowtie_{lastName,\ firstName} \text{Employee}$$

In a natural join, the shared attributes appear only once in the results table. Table 8.9 shows the result of natural join of `Employee` and `TimeCard`. (Note that the

FIGURE 8.12

Two Ad Hoc Equi-join Queries

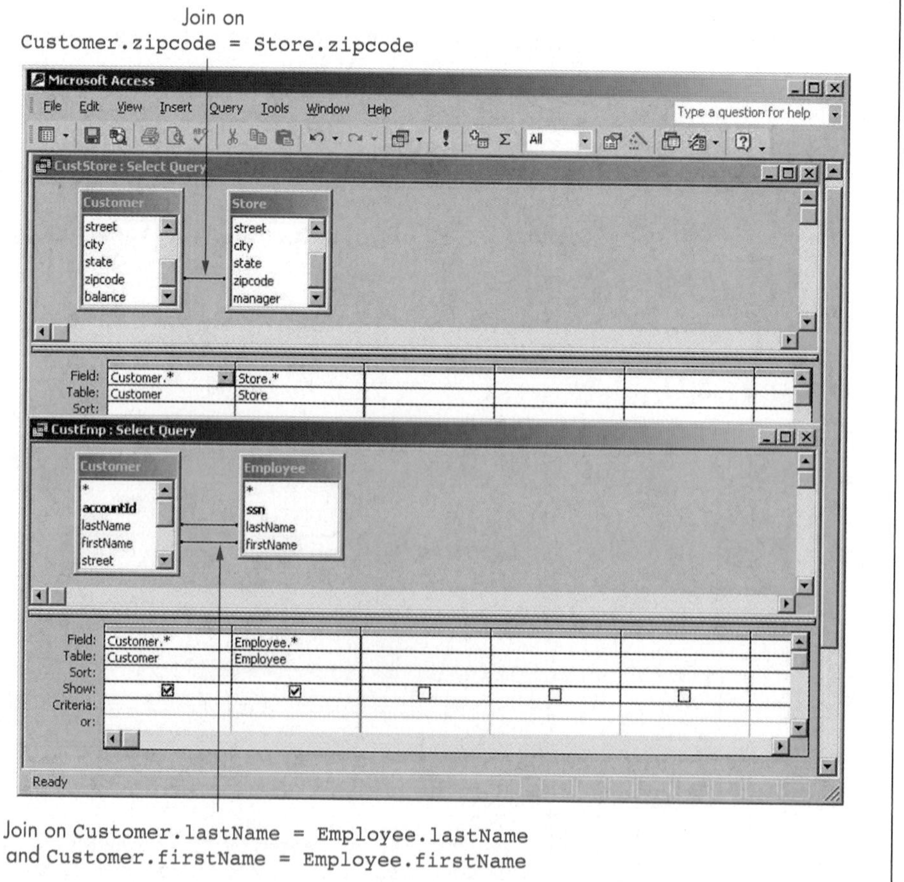

Join on
`Customer.zipcode = Store.zipcode`

Join on `Customer.lastName = Employee.lastName`
and `Customer.firstName = Employee.firstName`

ssn attribute appears only once.) Creating a natural join in Access is a little more difficult because you can't use the asterisk symbol for one of the source tables. Instead, you have to add each attribute individually. You'll learn more about this later in the chapter.

The join operation always compares the rows of one table with the rows of another. A join does not directly compare one row of a table with another row of the same table. But suppose you want to look at pairs of videos rented by a customer at the same time. To compare different rows from a single table, you use the same table twice in the relationship window of the design view. Figure 8.13 shows the design view of such a query with two copies of Rental in the upper part of the window. Notice that Access has renamed the second table to Rental_1 to distinguish it from the first table. The two copies of Rental are linked by two join conditions. Both accountId (same customer) and dateRented must agree for two rows to match. A

Table 8.9 Results Table for *Natural Join of* **Employee** *and* **TimeCard** *on* **ssn**

ssn	last Name	first Name	date	start Time	end Time	StoreId	paid
145-09-0967	Uno	Jane	01/14/2002	8:15	12:00	3	no
145-09-0967	Uno	Jane	01/16/2002	8:15	12:00	3	no
245-11-4554	Toulouse	Jie	01/14/2002	8:15	12:00	3	no
376-77-0099	Threat	Ayisha	02/23/2002	14:00	22:00	5	no
376-77-0099	Threat	Ayisha	03/21/2002	14:00	22:00	5	no
376-77-0099	Threat	Ayisha	01/03/2002	10:00	14:00	5	no
376-77-0099	Threat	Ayisha	01/03/2002	15:00	19:00	5	no

F I G U R E 8.13

Design View of a Join between Two Rows from One Table

Join on accountId and dateRented

Rental.videoId <>
Rental_1.videoID

further selection condition must be included: that the two related videos are different. Thus, the highlighted third column specifies that `Rental.videoId` is not equal to (<>) `Rental_1.videoId`.

The result of executing the query of Figure 8.13 is shown in Figure 8.14. You will notice that each pair of matching videos—113 and 114 match, and 90987 and 99987 match—are shown in two rows. The first row represents the rental of video 113 in `Rental` and video 114 in `Rental_1` and the second row is the reverse. You can eliminate this duplication by requiring that the lower numbered video be listed first. That is, change the condition on column 3 of Figure 8.14 to `Rental.videoId <` `Rental_1.videoId`. The result is the elimination of the first and third rows of Figure 8.15, leaving two rows, one for each matching pair of rentals.

You may not think these last few queries are very compelling examples. They don't seem very interesting and may not even make much sense. However, it is a feature of relational databases that just about any question you can think of can be expressed as a query, no matter how silly or meaningless it seems.

8.5 QUERIES WITH MULTIPLE JOINS

We can construct queries with joins between any number of tables. To see how this works, let's create a query to find out which videos are currently rented and when those videos are due. We need the `accountId`, `videoId`, `dateRented`, `dateDue`, and `cost` for each rental, plus the `title` of the video. To get the title, first join `Rental` and `Video` to get the `movieId`. Then join the result to `Movie` to get the title. Perform the following steps to create the query to fetch this information.

1. Join `Rental` and `Video` on `videoId`.
2. Join the result of Step 1 and `Movie` on `movieId`.
3. Project the `accountId`, `videoId`, `dateRented`, `dateDue`, `title`, and `cost` from the result of Step 2.

In relational algebraic notation, we would express these steps as follows:

$$\pi_{\texttt{accountId,videoId,dateRented,dataDue,title,cost}} \; (\qquad \text{Step 3}$$

$$(\texttt{Rental} \bowtie_{\texttt{videoId}} \texttt{Video} \qquad \text{Step 1}$$

$$\bowtie_{\texttt{movieId}} \texttt{Movie})) \qquad \text{Step 2}$$

The steps are out of order simply because of the way we write relational algebra expressions using parentheses. In relational algebraic notation, we would write the entire query as:

$$\pi_{\texttt{accountId, videoId, dateRented, dateDue, title, cost}}$$
$$((\texttt{Rental} \bowtie_{\texttt{videoId}} \texttt{Video}) \bowtie_{\texttt{movieId}} \texttt{Movie})$$

FIGURE 8.14
Result of Joining **`Rental`** with **`Rental`** in Figure 8.13

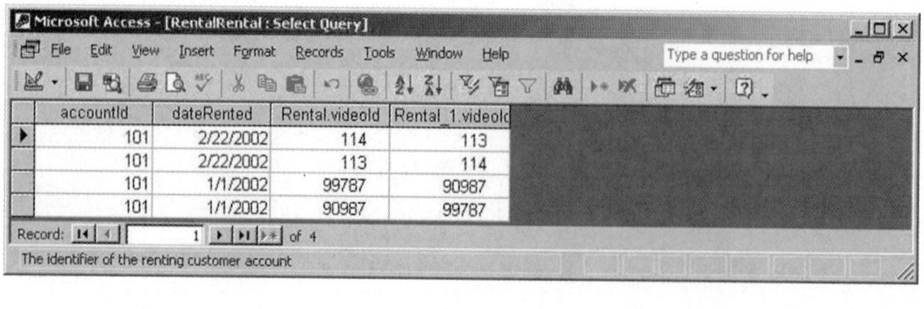

accountId	dateRented	Rental.videoId	Rental_1.videoId
101	2/22/2002	114	113
101	2/22/2002	113	114
101	1/1/2002	99787	90987
101	1/1/2002	90987	99787

Figure 8.15 shows the sample tables that form the input of the query. Figure 8.16 shows the Access query design view for this query. To construct this query, simply create a new query in design view, add all three tables to it, and select the appropriate fields.

FIGURE 8.15

BigHit Video's **Video**, **Movie**, and **Rental** Tables

Video

videoId	dateAcquired	movieId	storeId
101	1/25/98	101	3
111	2/5/97	123	3
112	12/31/95	123	5
113	4/5/98	123	5
114	4/5/98	189	5
123	3/25/86	123	3
145	5/12/95	145	5
77564	4/29/91	189	3
90987	3/25/2002	450	3
99787	10/10/97	987	5

Movie

movieId	title	genre	length	rating
101	The Thirty-Nine Steps	mystery	101	R
123	Annie Hall	romantic comedy	110	R
145	Lady and the Tramp	animated comedy	93	PG
189	Animal House	comedy	87	PG-13
450	Elizabeth	costume drama	123	PG-13
553	Stagecoach	western	130	R
987	Duck Soup	comedy	99	PG-13

Rental

accountId	videoId	dateRented	dateDue	cost
103	101	1/3/2002	1/4/2002	$1.59
101	113	2/22/2002	2/25/2002	$3.00
101	114	2/22/2002	2/25/2002	$3.00
103	123	12/1/2001	12/31/2001	$10.99
101	145	2/14/2002	2/16/2002	$1.99
101	90987	1/1/2002	1/8/2002	$2.99
101	99787	1/1/2002	1/4/2002	$3.49

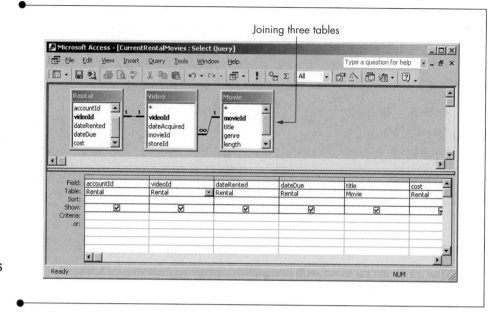

FIGURE 8.16

Query to Show Current Rentals by joining **Rental**, **Video**, and **Movie**

8.6   COMBINING RELATIONAL OPERATIONS

The relational operations you've learned about can be combined to produce much more complex queries. For example, combining selection and projection operations produces a restriction on both the number of rows and the number of columns of a results table.

To see how this works, let's create a query to find out which videos a particular customer has rented and when those videos are due. To do this, we must *select* the **Rental** rows for the customer in question and *project* the **videoId** and **dateDue** fields. We can express this query as *project* **videoId** *and* **dateDue** *from* **Rental** *where* **accountId=113**.

It would be helpful to also include the title of the video. Thus, we would need to add a join operation between **Rental** and **Video** and another between **Video** and **Movie**. In relational algebraic notation, we would write the entire query as:

$$\pi_{\text{videoId, title, dateDue}}((\sigma_{\text{accountId=113}}(\text{Rental}) \bowtie_{\text{videoId}} \text{Video}) \bowtie_{\text{movieId}} \text{Movie})$$

To make things even more complicated, suppose we want the BigHit database to give us a list of all comedy (**genre**) movies rented by customers since December 2001. We want the results table of this operation to show the customer names, movie titles, and dates the videos were rented. To produce this information, we must ask the database to perform join, selection, and projection operations on its **Customer**, **Video**, **Movie**, and **PreviousRental** tables, shown in Figure 8.17.

We want the database to perform the following steps:

1. Select the comedy movies.
2. Join the results of Step 1 and **Video** on **movieId**.
3. Select the previous rentals with a rental date that is after December 1, 2001.
4. Join the results of Steps 2 and 3 on **videoId**.
5. Join the results of Step 4 and **customer** on **accountId**.
6. Project the first name, last name, title, and date rented from Step 5.

PrevictousRental

accountId	videoId	dateRented	dateReturned	cost
101	101	12/9/2001	12/10/2001	$2.49
101	112	1/13/2002	1/4/2002	$1.99
101	113	1/15/2002	1/15/2002	$0.99
102	113	12/1/2001	12/3/2001	$2.49
111	101	12/4/2001	12/6/2001	$2.49
111	99787	1/1/2002	1/4/2002	$3.95
201	113	12/9/2001	12/14/2001	$3.99
201	77564	1/14/2002	1/24/2002	$3.35

FIGURE 8.17

Sample BigHit Video **PreviousRental** Table

In relational algebraic notation, we would express these steps as follows:

$$\pi_{\text{firstName, lastName, title, dateRented,}}(\qquad \text{Step 6}$$
$$((\sigma_{\text{genre='comedy'}}(\text{Movie}) \qquad \text{Step 1}$$
$$\bowtie_{\text{movieId}} \text{Video}) \qquad \text{Step 2}$$
$$\bowtie_{\text{videoId}} \qquad \text{Step 4}$$
$$\sigma_{\text{dateRented>'01-Dec-2001'}}(\text{PreviousRental})) \qquad \text{Step 3}$$
$$\bowtie_{\text{accountId}} \text{Customer}) \qquad \text{Step 5}$$

Thus, the entire expression would read:

$$\pi_{\text{firstName, lastName, title, dateRented}}(((\sigma_{\text{genre='comedy'}}(\text{Movie}) \bowtie_{\text{movieId}} \text{Video})$$
$$\bowtie_{\text{videoId}} \sigma_{\text{dateRented>'01-Dec-2001'}}(\text{PreviousRental})) \bowtie_{\text{accountId}} \text{Customer})$$

Table 8.10 shows the results table for this expression. Now let's examine how you would actually communicate this query to Access.

Table 8.10 Results Table for Comedy Movies Rented Since December 1, 2001

firstName	lastName	title	dateRented
Jane	Doe	Duck Soup	2001-12-04
Joseph	Greaves	Animal House	2002-01-14

DEFINING COMPLEX QUERIES
8.7 ## WITH MICROSOFT ACCESS

The query design window of Microsoft Access uses a variation on a technique called **Query by Example (QBE)**, which Moshe Zloof [Zlo77] developed as a way of defining queries graphically. As you've seen, Access's user interface lets you specify query source (input) tables, selection criteria, join criteria, and results-table attributes. A single query can represent a complex relational algebra expression.

Let's return to our `Employee—TimeCard` natural-join example (Table 8.9) to begin seeing how to create these queries in Access. Figure 8.18 shows how to create this query. Note that the results fields include all of the `Employee` and `TimeCard` fields except for `TimeCard.ssn`. (The fields of `TimeCard` are listed one by one across the Field column headings in the lower half of the figure.)

Figure 8.19 shows the more complex query that produces the table depicting comedy movies rented since December 1, 2001, as described in Section 8.7. Here, we have used four input tables. These tables are linked by lines and hence are joined in the query. The four fields specify the *projection* operation. Each field has the `Show` box checked. The `Criteria` field for `dateRented` shows that we are *selecting* only

FIGURE   8.18

A Natural Join Query in Access

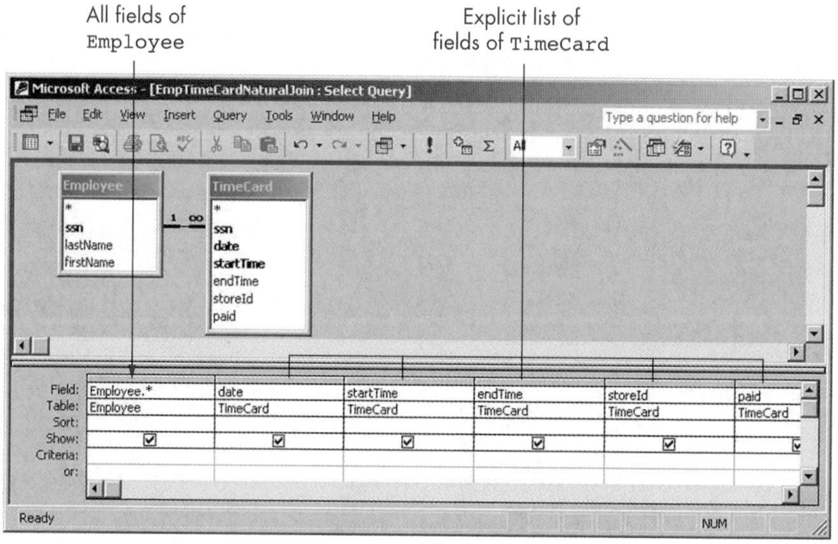

FIGURE   8.19

Access Query for Comedy
Movies Rented Since
December 1, 2001

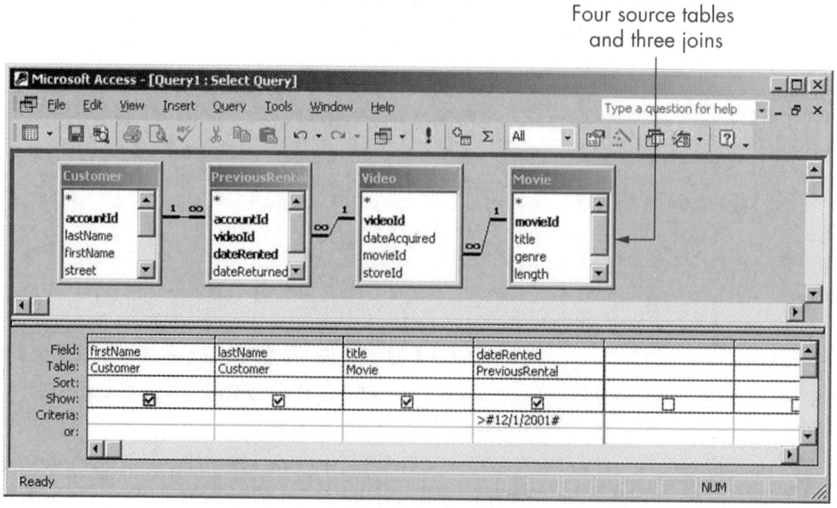

those rows for which date rented is after December 1, 2001. The `Show` box of `dateRented` is checked to indicate that `dateRented` is part of both the projected fields and the selection condition.

As you can see in the figures, Microsoft Access provides a flexible interface that experienced database programmers and inexperienced database users alike can easily learn.

8.8 APPLYING SET OPERATORS TO TABLES

The next set of operations we want to consider allows us to create tables that are composed of rows from more than one table. That is, we can create a new table with some rows from one input table and some rows from another input table. We might want to combine rows of the `Rental` table, which represent rentals of videos that have not yet been returned, with rows of the `PreviousRental` table, which represent videos that have been returned. By combining the rows of these two tables, we can analyze all of the rentals, both current and previous, together.

These operations are called **set operations** because they manipulate tables according to the mathematical set operations union, intersection, and difference. Before we look at the operations in detail, we must consider when the rows of two different tables are sufficiently alike that they can form the basis for a new table.

In the BigHit Video database, the tables `Rental` and `PreviousRental` have what's known as the same **shape**—that is, they have the same number and *types* of attributes. The schemas for these two tables are as follows:

```
Rental (accountId number, videoId number, dateRented date,
    dateDue date, cost currency)
PreviousRental (accountId number, videoId number,
    dateRented date, dateReturned date, cost currency)
```

The shape of each table is the list (`number, number, date, date, currency`). Each has five attributes, and the type of the first attributes matches, the type of the second attributes matches, etc. The fourth attribute has a different name in each table (`dateDue` and `dateReturned`, respectively), but that difference is irrelevant because the names of attributes are not part of the shape. Figure 8.20 shows the two tables.

When two tables have the same shape, we can apply *set operations* to them. Set operations are part of relational algebra and have their own notations. In the next sections, we consider the three kinds of set operations: *union*, *intersection*, and *difference*.

8.8.1 Union

The **union** of two tables is a new table that contains each row that is in at least one of the input tables. As with all relational operations, the output is a set with no duplicate rows, so some output rows may represent more than one input row. The union of `Rental` and `PreviousRental`, for instance, is the collection of all rows from `Rental` and all rows from `PreviousRental`, with duplicates, if any, eliminated. In the notation of relational algebra, we write this operation as

`Rental ∪ PreviousRental`

The result of the union is a table and thus must have a name for each of its attributes. When the names of the attributes of the two input tables are different, a query designer may have difficulty deciding what to call the attributes of the results table. Many database designers have adopted a simple convention that calls for the attribute names to be taken from the left-side table in the union expression. In this case, the attributes in the results table would have the same names as the attributes in the `Rental` table.

Rental

accountId	videoId	dateRented	dateDue	cost
103	101	1/3/2002	1/4/2002	$1.59
101	113	2/22/2002	2/25/2002	$3.00
101	114	2/22/2002	2/25/2002	$3.00
103	123	12/1/2001	12/31/2001	$10.99
101	145	2/14/2002	2/16/2002	$1.99
101	90987	1/1/2002	1/8/2002	$2.99
101	99787	1/1/2002	1/4/2002	$3.49

PreviousRental

accountId	videoId	dateRented	dateReturned	cost
101	101	12/9/2001	12/10/2001	$2.49
101	112	1/13/2002	1/4/2002	$1.99
101	113	1/15/2002	1/15/2002	$0.99
102	113	12/1/2001	12/3/2001	$2.49
111	101	12/4/2001	12/6/2001	$2.49
111	99787	1/1/2002	1/4/2002	$3.95
201	113	12/9/2001	12/14/2001	$3.99
201	77564	1/14/2002	1/24/2002	$3.35

Table 8.11 shows the rows in the results table of Rental ∪ PreviousRental. The table contains 15 rows—7 from Rental (highlighted in blue) and 8 from PreviousRental (highlighted in red). There were no duplicate rows in the input tables; therefore. the number of rows in the result is the sum of the numbers of rows in the input tables. Note that the attribute names come from Rental. This table represents the set of all rentals, current and previous, and would be useful to a manager who wanted to analyze all rental activity—even for videos that have not yet been returned. Using this table, the manager could figure out the number of rentals for each customer, or the number of rentals for each video.

This is the point in the section where you are expecting to learn how to create union queries in Access. Unfortunately, you can't define union and difference queries by using QBE in Access; rather, you must write these queries in SQL. Access's Query menu has an SQL Specific entry that lists Union as an option. If you select this menu item, Access presents a blank SQL entry screen. Thus, Access supports set operations, but you must write the proper SQL yourself. You'll learn more about writing set queries in SQL in Chapter 9.

8.8.2 Intersection

The **intersection** of two tables is the set of all rows that occur in both input tables. The intersection of Rental and PreviousRental is expressed in relational algebra as Rental ∩ PreviousRental.

Table 8.11 Results of `Rental` ∪ `PreviousRental`

accountId	videoId	dateRented	dateDue	cost
103	101	1/3/2002	1/4/2002	$1.59
101	113	2/22/2002	2/25/2002	$3.00
101	114	2/22/2002	2/25/2002	$3.00
103	123	12/1/2001	12/31/2001	$10.99
101	145	2/14/2002	2/16/2002	$1.99
101	90987	1/1/2002	1/8/2002	$2.99
101	99787	1/1/2002	1/4/2002	$3.49
101	101	12/9/2001	12/10/2001	$2.49
101	112	1/13/2002	1/4/2002	$1.99
101	113	1/15/2002	1/15/2002	$0.99
102	113	12/1/2001	12/3/2001	$2.49
111	101	12/4/2001	12/6/2001	$2.49
111	99787	1/1/2002	1/4/2002	$3.95
201	113	12/9/2001	12/14/2001	$3.99
201	77564	1/14/2002	1/24/2002	$3.35

Rows from Rental (first 7 rows); Rows from previousRental (remaining rows)

This operation would generate the set of all rentals that are both current and previous. We certainly would expect this set to be empty, because a particular video can't be both rented out and returned at the same time. A more interesting use of intersection would be to find the intersection between the `videoIds` of the two tables. This set would be the videos that are currently rented and have been rented before. Creating this relational algebra expression requires first *projecting* the `videoId` fields of the two tables and then taking the *intersection* of the results. The expression is written as:

$$\pi_{videoId}(\texttt{Rental}) \cap \pi_{videoId}(\texttt{PreviousRental})$$

The result of executing this query is shown in Table 8.12. The duplicates have been eliminated and what remains are the IDs of videos that are currently rented and that have been rented before.

Table 8.12 Result of $\pi_{videoId}(\texttt{Rental}) \cap \pi_{videoId}(\texttt{PreviousRental})$

videoId
101
113
99787

8.8.3 **Difference**

The **difference** between two tables is the set of all rows that appear in the first table, but not in the second. For example, the difference between the videos that are currently checked out and those that were previously checked out is exactly those videos that are currently checked out for the first time. The relational algebra expression would be written as follows:

$$\pi_{\texttt{videoId}}(\texttt{Rental}) - \pi_{\texttt{videoId}}(\texttt{PreviousRental})$$

The result of this expression is shown as Table 8.13.

Similarly, the set of all videos that have been rented previously, but are not currently rented is the reverse (or commutation) of the above expression:

$$\pi_{\texttt{videoId}}(\texttt{PreviousRental}) - \pi_{\texttt{videoId}}(\texttt{Rental})$$

Table 8.13 Result of $\pi_{\texttt{videoId}}(\texttt{Rental}) - \pi_{\texttt{videoId}}$ **(PreviousRental)**

videoId
114
123
145
90987

Concept

Set Operations in Geometry

Relational set operations are used extensively in image compression and animation. For example, suppose that we have a pair of two-dimensional images that are two adjacent frames of an animation. The difference between the images is the set of (x, y, c) where the color values have changed from one frame to the next. On the Internet, animations are typically transported from an animation server in a Web server to the animation display plug-in in the Web browser by sending only the changes in color values. Thus, the animation server performs set difference on each pair of frames in order to decide which pixels to send to the animation display. The animation display then uses set difference and set union to produce the next frame.

8.9   CREATING USER INTERFACES IN ACCESS

Access lets you specify how you want the database to display results tables. For example, Figure 8.21 shows one form you might create to make Access list all of the rentals for a particular customer. The top of the form displays information about the customer, Jane Block. The navigation buttons at the bottom let you see rentals and other information about other customers that appear before or after Jane Block in the `Customer` table. Thus, this form provides a tabular view of the `Customer` table.

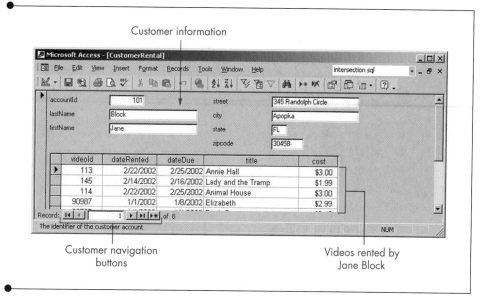

Customer navigation
buttons

Videos rented by
Jane Block

FIGURE 8.21

Form Showing Rentals for a
BigHit Customer

What makes this form interesting and useful is that it displays exactly those videos that are currently rented by the displayed user. That is, it shows those rows of the `Rental` table that are related to Jane Block. Figure 8.22 shows the same form, this time displaying customer Katherine Harrison, who has two videos checked out. Clicking the right navigation button moves the display from one record to the next.

The form shown in Figures 8.21 and 8.22 depicts related rows from two tables (`Customer` and `Rental`), but it displays these objects differently than a join query would. A join of `Customer` and `Rental` produces a table like that shown in Figure 8.23, which duplicates the customer information for each rental.

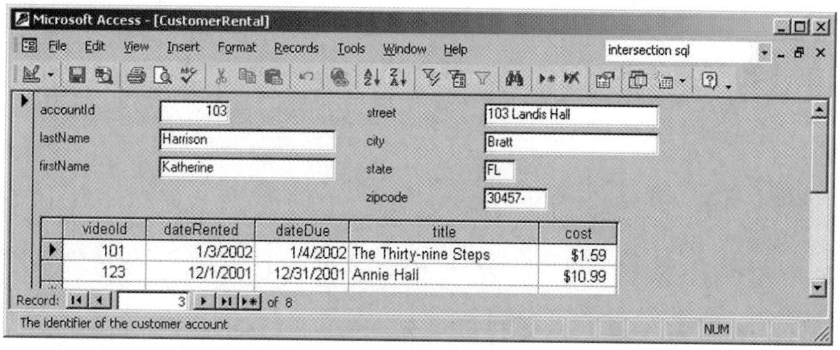

FIGURE 8.22

Form Showing Rentals for a
Different Customer

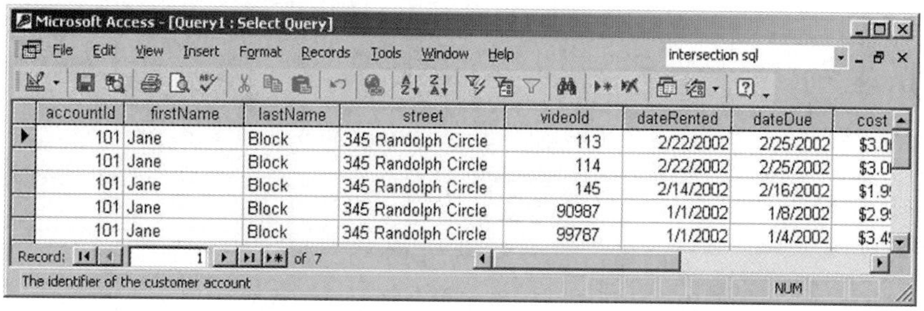

FIGURE 8.23

Results of *join Customer to
Rental on* `accountId`

You can create the customer part of the form of Figure 8.20 using `Create Form by Using Wizard`, as described in Section 6.3, to create a columnar view of the `Customer` table. The result is shown in Figure 8.24. Also in Figure 8.24 is the first step in creating the subform. First, open the toolbox by clicking on the toolbox icon in the query toolbar. Then, make sure the form wizard icon is selected and click the subform icon in the toolbox. Finally, position the cursor at the upper left of the area where you want to position the subform, drag to the lower right corner, and drop it. Once you release the cursor, the subform wizard will appear. In the first screen (not shown), choose the option to create a new subform, click `Next` and you'll see the second wizard screen, as shown in Figure 8.25.

The second subform wizard display asks you to choose a table or query as the source of the form and choose the fields to be added. In Figure 8.25, query `CurrentRentalMovies` has been selected and all of its fields have been added to the selected fields area. This query was created in Section 8.5 and displayed in Figure 8.16. When you click `Finish`, the subform wizard will create the subform and place it in the subform area of the main form.

With these operations, you've created two forms: one to display the customer information and one for the rental information. The design window of the resulting form is shown in Figure 8.26. The form created by the wizards will be little different from that shown in Figure 8.21.

A few minor adjustments will produce the final version. First, we need to get rid of the subform label. Simply select it and press `Delete`. Then change the size of the subform by dragging its resizing handle.

A final adjustment is to remove the `accountId` field from the subform display. You can see in Figure 8.21 that the `accountId` does not appear in the rental area of the form. After you delete the `accountId` field, the rental subform will not show

FIGURE 8.24

Creating a Subform with Drag and Drop

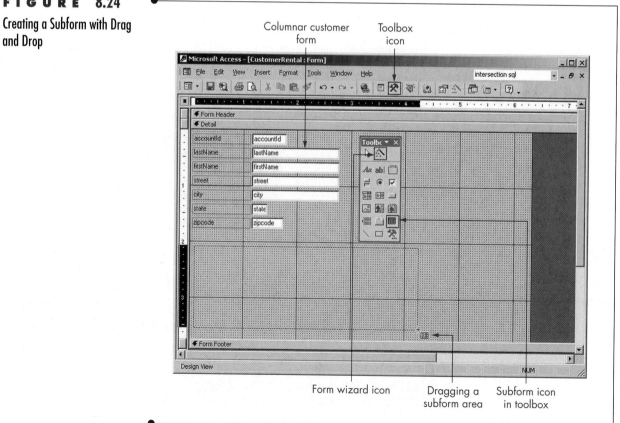

F I G U R E 8.25

Second Screen in the Subform Wizard: Table Selection

that field. We'll see in just a moment that the `accountId` is still part of the subform, but we don't want it to show.

Figure 8.27 shows the resulting design view of the form depicted in Figure 8.21. The form consists of a master form based on the `Customer` table. In Figure 8.27, the subform is shown in its design view inside the area reserved for it in the main form.

F I G U R E 8.26

Form Design Produced by Form and Subform Wizards with Needed Adjustments Marked by Comment Boxes

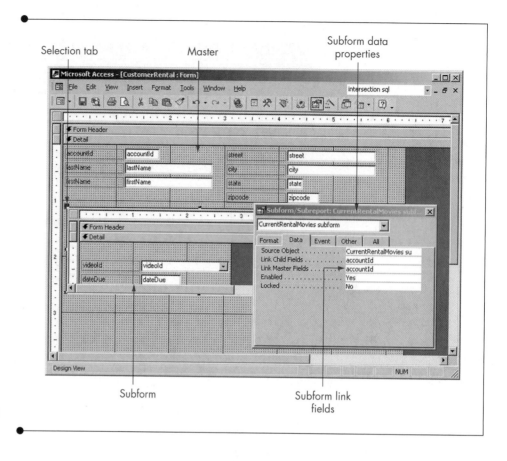

FIGURE 8.27

Design View of the Customer Rental Form Showing Subform Data Properties

You might wonder how the subform wizard arranges for the master form and the subform to be linked. Once the wizard is finished, the subform will display only those rental rows with the same `accountId` as the displayed customer. Changing which customer is displayed also changes which rentals are displayed. The wizard defines properties of the master form and subform that create this linkage.

The master form and the subform are linked together in Access so that the rows shown in the subform are only those that relate to the customer shown in the main form. Linking of master and subform is controlled by the `Link Child Fields` and `Link Master Fields` properties of the subform, as shown in Figure 8.27. In this form, these properties were set by the subform wizard so that each has the value `accountId`, which indicates that the value of the `accountId` field of the master form determines which subform rows Access will display. The user interface will display a row of the subform—that is, a rental—only if the `accountId` of the rental is the same as the `accountId` of the customer that is being displayed. You can see the link fields in the properties window only if the subform is selected. You will notice in Figure 8.25 that the selection tabs are surrounding the subform area as the properties are being displayed. You can also use the drop-down box at the top of the properties window to select the subform.

In addition to the linking, Access also needs to know the source of the information for the subform that is used to create the form shown in Figure 8.21. The fields displayed in Figure 8.21 are `videoId`, `title`, `dateRented`, `dateDue`, and `cost`. You might think that the `accountId` field would also show up in the subform, yet it doesn't. That's because the `videoId` comes from the `Video` table, the `title` comes from `Movie`, and the dates and `cost` come from `Rental`. Hence, the source table for the subform must be a *join* of the `Video`, `Movie`, and `Rental` tables.

The final details about how the subform works and where its information comes from in Access are shown in Figure 8.28, which shows the design view of the subform and its data properties. The value of the `Record Source` property of the form determines what table or query provides the information that gets displayed in the form. In the forms we've seen so far, the record source was a table. However, the record source can also be a query. That is, the information displayed in a form can be created by the database's execution of a query. The results table of the query is used as the source of information for the form.

As you can see in Figure 8.28, the value of `Record Source` is the name of the query `CurrentRentalMovies`. At the end of the query name are two icons: a down arrow and an ellipsis (…). The down arrow controls a drop-down box that lets you designate any of the tables or queries in the database as the source of information for the form. When clicked, the ellipsis opens the query design window so that you can create a new query to provide information for the form.

8.10 CASE IN POINT: A VIDEO RENTAL CHECKOUT FORM

The final example of this chapter shows you how to create a video rental checkout form for the BigHit Video rental system. In previous chapters, the closing example has come from the BigHit Online video purchase application. However, the video purchase example will be entirely online and thus all user interfaces will be developed as Web applications using HTML and Web browsers. We simply do not need Access forms for online applications. The BigHit Video rental system, however, will benefit from using Access to create user interfaces.

A rental checkout form should allow a clerk at the rental store to select a customer and display the customer information, to select videos for checkout, and calculate the cost of the rentals. The checkout form will be very much like the customer rental form of Section 8.9.

The customer rental form should be modified to show only the rentals from the current day and to add the total cost. Let's begin by making copies of the master and subforms for customer rental. Cutting and pasting forms in Access is simple enough.

FIGURE 8.28

Design View of Rental Subform with Properties

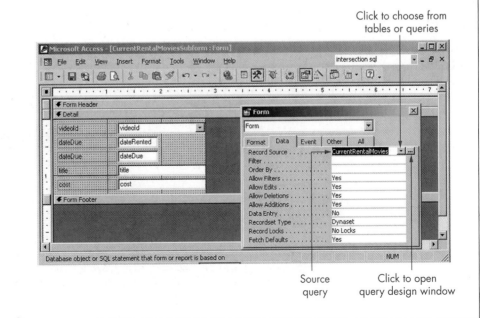

Click to choose from tables or queries

Source query

Click to open query design window

Select a form, choose `Copy` from the `Edit` menu and then choose `Paste`. Access responds with a dialog that requests a name for the new form. Name the forms `RentalCheckout` and `RentalCheckoutSubform`.

Begin by modifying the subform so that it will calculate the total cost of the rentals that it displays. Open the subform in design mode and open the toolbox. Select the text box icon and drag a new text box into the footer area of the form. The new text box has a default name and label, and the contents are shown as `unbound`. The text box is different from the others because they are all bound to fields of the record source of the form. Whenever the selected record changes, so do the values of the text boxes. An unbound text box has a value that is not directly linked to the record source. This new text box should always display the total cost, that is, the sum of the costs and not directly the value of any field.

Figure 8.29 shows the new box in the form after the name has been changed in the properties window. You can see in the figure that the `Control Source` property is set to `=Sum([cost])`. This expression represents the summation of all of the values of the cost field in the subform—exactly the value we need.

The new text box contains the total cost, but it will not be displayed in the form. We'll add a total cost box to the master form instead. Why? This is simply one of the tricks of the trade for Access programmers: Make the subform calculate the sum, but display the value directly on the master form.

Now that the subform calculates its own cost, we are ready to modify the master form. The form must include a field for today's date and a field to display the total cost. Finally, the linking between the master and the subform must be modified so that only today's rentals are displayed in the subform.

Figure 8.30 shows the new date rented and total cost text boxes. The value of `dateRented` is `=Date()`, a call on the Access function `Date` whose value is the current date. When the form is displayed, the function will be called by Access and the current date displayed in this field.

Most of Figure 8.30 is devoted to showing how to configure the `totalCost` text box. First, add a new text box to the form below the subform and change its name and label using the `Properties` window. Then, select the control source field and click the ellipsis to open the expression builder window, as shown in the middle of the figure. Select the highlighted row in each column, left to right, and click `Paste`. The correct expression will become the value of the `totalCost` text box. The expression

F I G U R E   8.29

Creation of Text Box to Contain Total Cost of Rentals

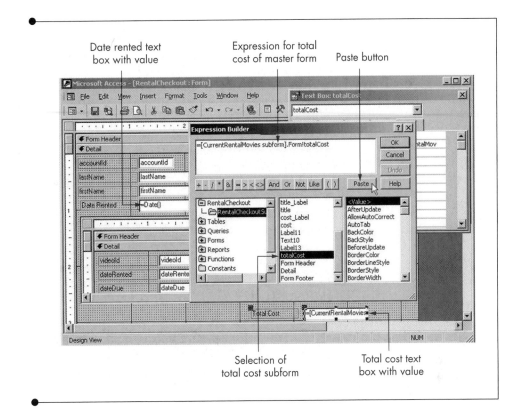

FIGURE 8.30

Modifications to Rental Checkout Master Form

value is =[RentalCheckoutSubform].Form![totalCost], which tells Access to look at the totalCost field of RentalCheckoutSubform for the master form total cost.

For the final major modification, you need to create the correct linkage between the master and child fields. Open the properties of the subform and click the Data tab. Figure 8.31 shows the properties of the subform after the linking fields have been modified. For both links, the value is accountId;dateRented, and thus, both the accountId and the dateRented fields are used to control the contents of the subform.

FIGURE 8.31

Subform Linking by accountId and dateRented

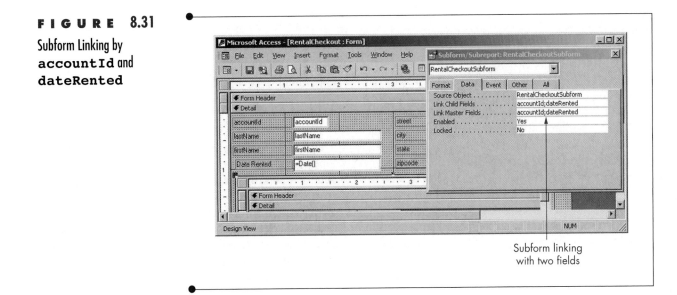

Figure 8.32 shows the resulting form with a couple of rentals selected. These rental rows are created by entering the `videoId`, the `dateDue`, and the `cost` fields. The `dateRented` and `title` will be filled in automatically by Access. For the last row, this information has not yet been entered.

Of course, this is a very primitive form: many enhancements would be appropriate in order to make a production-quality form. Access is a very powerful tool, and full use of its capabilities requires extensive knowledge of its companion programming language, Visual Basic. The Northwind sample database that is distributed with Access has many programming examples. You can learn many of Access's secrets by studying the Northwind sample database. Further study of Access can be enhanced by using one of the many excellent study guides. Some Access references are listed in the Further Reading section at the end of this chapter.

In this book, we are going to concentrate our programming activities on SQL programming and Web application development, which we'll begin in Chapters 9 and 10, respectively.

FIGURE 8.32

Rental Checkout Form

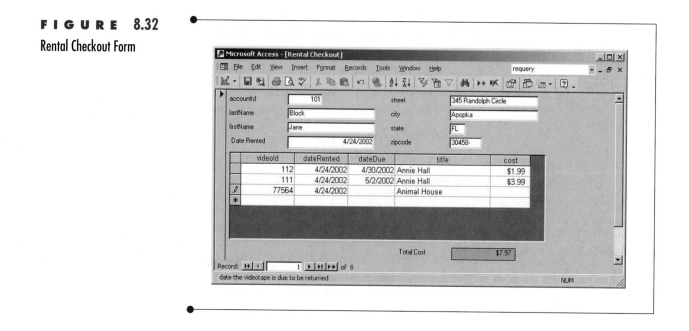

CHAPTER SUMMARY

This chapter presents two different methods of manipulating relational database tables. Relational algebra is a language for writing expressions that produce new tables from existing ones. Query by Example (QBE) is a graphical style of writing table manipulations that is used by Microsoft Access. In the next chapter, you will learn about SQL (Structured Query Language), a textual style of writing the same manipulations. All three of these styles are useful, each in its own way.

The fundamental benefit of the relational data model is that it lets users create new tables by writing and executing queries. Database designers do not have to describe all of the ways that data can be ex-

tracted from the database. Instead, they create tables and define the primary relationships among them. Users can then submit queries to the database that will construct new tables in a variety of ways.

Relational algebra is a collection of operations that transform input tables into results tables. The major operations are *selection*, *projection*, and *join*. The selection operator selects rows from a table according to a selection condition. The projection operator produces a new table with fewer columns than the original table. The join operator combines the attributes of one table with the attributes of another table to produce a new table that has more columns than its input tables. In a join, the database constructs the rows of the results table by combining a row of one table with a row of the other table. The join condition determines which combinations of input rows appear in the results table. A natural join is the join operator that combines tables having a common attribute.

Set operators support the combining of tables that are the same shape. These operations include union, intersection, and difference.

Relational algebra is most useful for understanding, specifying, and implementing complex queries. The algebraic characteristics of the operators include rules of equivalence; that is, rules that tell us when two relational algebra expressions produce the same results. Using these rules and expressions, database systems can transform relational expressions submitted by users into equivalent expressions that use different operations to achieve the same results. Query optimizers take advantage of these algebraic characteristics to determine how long it takes to execute queries.

QBE has been adapted for use in Microsoft Access and other graphical database tools to define queries. It lets users select input tables as well as specify projections and join and selection conditions. QBE is especially useful for displaying the structure of a query to make it easier for people to understand what it does.

Forms in Access can be used to create almost any presentation of database information. This chapter has given a brief overview of how you can develop forms that produce quite complex database applications.

KEY TERMS

Cartesian product. A relational product operation that produces a table that includes one row for each combination of a row from its left operand and a row from its right operand. The number of output table rows is the product of the number of rows in the left operand and the number of rows in the right operand.

Equi-join. A relational join operation whose join condition is an equality expression.

Join. The relational product operation that combines tables based on a join condition. The result table has a row for each pair of rows of the input tables for which the join condition is true.

Natural join. The relational join operation that combines two tables with a common attribute. The result of a natural join is a table with a row for each pair of rows in the input tables in which the common attribute has an equal value. The common attributes appear only once in the output table.

Product. The relational algebra operation that combines two tables to produce a new table whose attributes are the attributes of the input tables. Join and Cartesian product are both product operations.

Projection. The relational algebra operation that produces an output table consisting of selected columns from its input table. The number of rows in the results table may be less than the number of rows in the input table because of the removal of duplicate rows.

Qualified Name. The full name of an attribute that is the combination of the table name and the attribute name separated by a period.

Query By Example (QBE). A style of designing queries using a graphical user interface. QBE was developed at IBM and has been incorporated into a variety of database tools, including Microsoft Access.

Query optimization. A strategy for improving the execution performance of queries by exploiting the algebraic characteristics of relational operators.

Record. A row of a relational table.

Relational algebra. A collection of operations on relations including selection, projection, union, and join. The operations support a variety of equivalence rules for expressions. These rules, in turn, support the optimization of the algebraic expressions that represent database queries.

Relational algebra expression. An expression that consists of the application of relational operations to tables.

Results table. The temporary table that is created by a database server to hold the results of a query.

Selection. The relational algebra operation that selects all rows from a table that satisfy a selection condition.

Set operation. The relational algebra operations that combine tables of the same shape. The set operations include union, intersection, and difference.

Shape of a table. An ordered list of the types of the attributes of the table. Set operations can be performed on tables of the same shape.

QUESTIONS

1. Give an example, using a table in the chapter, of a projection operation that produces a table with fewer *rows* than its source table.

2. Explain why any projection operation that includes the key attributes of a table does not produce a table with fewer rows than its source table.

3. Which relational operators provide the following capabilities?

   a. Transform a relation into a new relation with fewer attributes.

   b. Transform a relation into a new relation with fewer rows and the same attributes.

   c. Combine two relations of the same shape into a new relation with the same attributes.

   d. Combine two relations into a new relation that has attributes from both input relations.

4. Show the relations that result from executing the following queries on the BigHit Video database of Tables 8.1, 8.4, and 8.6 and Figs. 8.15, 8.17, and 8.20.

   a. All customers who live in Louisiana.

   b. The names of employees who work at store number 3.

   c. The titles of all movies whose rating is "PG."

   d. The names of all customers who have rented a movie between February 1 and March 1, 2002.

   e. The employee name, date worked, and hours worked for each time card that has more than eight hours worked.

   f. All videos currently rented by customers who live in Florida.

   g. All customers whose last names are also the last name of an employee.

   h. All stores whose zip code is not the same as the zip code of any employee.

5. Write relational algebra expressions to represent the queries of problem 4.

6. Using the relations of the BigHit Video database of Tables 8.1, 8.4, and 8.6 and Figs. 8.15, 8.17, and 8.20, for each relational expression below, give an English description of the expression and the relations that result when it is executed.

   a. $\pi_{title,genre}(\sigma_{length > 110}(\texttt{Movie}))$

   b. $\pi_{firstName,lastName}(\sigma_{ssn='376-77-0099'}(\texttt{Employee}))$

   c. $\pi_{firstName,lastName,date}(\sigma_{ssn='376-77-0099'}$
     $(\texttt{Employee} \bowtie_{ssn\ TimeCard}))$

   d. $\pi_{id,price,quantity,movieId}(\sigma_{date>'01/01/99'}$
     $(\texttt{PurchaseOrder} \bowtie_{ssn}$
     $\texttt{PurchaseOrderDetail}))$

PROBLEMS

7. Use the BigHit Video sample database to implement the operations of Question 4.

8. Use the BigHit Video sample database to implement the operations of Question 6.

9. Modify the BigHit Video sample database query of Figure 8.9 so that it selects all of the time cards for all employees whose date is between Jan. 15, 2002 and Mar. 1, 2002.

PROJECTS

10. a. Improve the video rental form from the Case in Point section of this chapter. Make sure that you correctly detect and handle errors. Make the application more user friendly.

   b. Develop a video rental check-in form in Access using the sample database. Be sure to match each video check-in with a record in the `Rental` table and to delete the `Rental` entry and create a `PreviousRental` entry.

   c. Develop a video purchase application in Access using the sample database. The application should allow a clerk to create a new purchase order and select movies from a list to purchase. Use the order form of the Northwind sample database as a guide.

11. Develop a shipping application in Access to help a clerk with filling and shipping orders. The application should allow the clerk to choose an order and to mark the items that have been shipped. Be sure to allow for the partial shipment of an order. You should also create a bill to be submitted to the credit card company as soon as each item is shipped. This application requires both data modeling and application development.

12. Develop an Access application that allows a manager to edit customer information and to display all of the movies that have been seen by an individual member.

FURTHER READING

Relational algebra was introduced by Codd [Codd70] in his original presentation of the relational model. Extensive presentations of relational algebra, including proofs of its completeness, are presented in several database books, including [Date99, ElNa99, Ricc01, SKS01].

An alternative formal model of relational operations is relational calculus, which represents operations as declarative statements, rather than as the expressions of relational algebra. In 1971, Codd introduced the Alpha language [Codd71] for expressing a relational calculus. Ullman [Ull88] presents an extensive evaluation of relational calculus, including a sketch of a proof of its equivalence to relational algebra.

Books on Access abound. Some good ones are those by Irwin, et al [Irw02], Feddema [Fed02], and Litwin, et al [Lit02].

CHAPTER 9

Using SQL to Manipulate Database Content and Structure

In this chapter, you will learn:

- What SQL is
- How to represent relational algebra expressions with SQL statements
- How to use SQL statements to create projection, selection, and join queries
- How to write set operations in SQL
- How to use the SQL capabilities of Access

- How to combine rows and groups of rows with SQL
- How to modify a relational database's contents with SQL
- How to create and manipulate table definitions with SQL

Structured Query Language (SQL) is used by database programmers to define, query, and modify relational databases. In 1986, the American National Standards Institute (ANSI) and the International Standards Organization (ISO) standardized SQL; that is, they agreed on a definition for the language that would be the same all over the world [ANSI86]. The language includes statements that specify and modify *database schemas* (**data definition language (DDL)** statements) as well as statements that manipulate *database content* (**data manipulation language (DML)** statements). After researchers and developers extensively revised and expanded SQL, the language was standardized as SQL-2 (or SQL-92) in 1992 [ANSI92]. More recently, language designers have agreed on a new language, SQL:1999 [SQL1999], which extends and enhances the capabilities of the language. The term "SQL" is either pronounced "S-Q-L" or "sequel."[1]

The great advantages of SQL are:

1. Every relational database server understands SQL.
2. SQL statements can be executed without modification on database systems from many vendors.
3. All database operations can be carried out through a single language.
4. Many programming languages have been adapted to allow the creation and execution of SQL statements.
5. SQL makes database programming feasible.

---

[1]The Sequel language (Standard English Query Language) was a predecessor of SQL. It was developed as the query language of the System R project at IBM in the 1970s.

In this chapter, you'll learn how to write SQL query statements designed to extract information from a relational database as well as statements that modify database content and that define database tables. All the query examples you saw in Chapter 8 can be easily represented as SQL query statements and this chapter will show you how.

An SQL query always starts with the keyword `select` and resembles queries created through the Query By Example (QBE) user interface of Access. As with a QBE query, an SQL **select statement** specifies the results table that the database will return after executing the statement. It also specifies the results-table attributes, the source tables, and the conditions that determine which rows will be included in the results table.

The SQL language can be used with Microsoft Access, but more importantly, it can be used with all other relational database systems. It is truly the common language of all database developers. In this chapter, you will be exposed to many of the features of SQL. You can type SQL statements into Access for execution. As you'll see in Chapters 12–15, SQL is the only way to interact with databases for Web-site development applications.

Concept

Capitalization in SQL Statements

SQL is generally case insensitive. For example, it doesn't matter to SQL whether you write "SELECT" or "select" or call a table "Customer" or "customer." However, in naming tables and attributes, we'll continue to use the naming conventions of Java (see Chapter 2), which is a case-sensitive language. (As you've seen, table names start with a capital letter, and attribute names start with a lowercase letter.)

Throughout this book, keywords in SQL statements are shown in **boldface** and all lowercase letters.

9.1 CREATING QUERIES IN SQL

9.1.1 Simple Select Statements

SQL select statements let you extract information from a relational database. A single such statement can incorporate selection, projection, and join operations. As with all relational queries, the select query produces a table as its result. The basic select statement includes three clauses: a `select` clause, a `from` clause, and a `where` clause. Its syntax is

`select` `<attribute names>` **`from`** `<tables>` **`where`** `<condition>`

In the above format, the **select clause** specifies the attributes that go in the results table. The **from clause** specifies the source tables that the database will access in order to execute the query. The **where clause** specifies the selection conditions, including the join condition. By way of illustration, let's look at the SQL statements that would produce some of the results tables you saw in Chapter 8. Figure 9.1 shows several such statements and tables. Tables 9.1 and 9.2 repeat the sample `Customer` and `TimeCard` tables that are the inputs of the queries.

In Figure 9.1, statements (a) and (b) each represent a single projection operation. The `select` clause lists the names and sequence of the attributes that will appear in the results table. Note, however, that statement (b) uses the keyword `distinct`.

Table 9.1 Sample **Customer** Table

accountId	lastName	firstName	street	city	state	zipcode	balance
101	Block	Jane	345 Randolph Circle	Apopka	FL	30458-	$0.00
102	Hamilton	Cherry	3230 Dade St.	Dade City	FL	30555-	$3.00
103	Harrison	Katherine	103 Landis Hall	Bratt	FL	30457-	$31.00
104	Breaux	Carroll	76 Main St.	Apopka	FL	30458-	$35.00
106	Morehouse	Anita	9501Lafayette St.	Houma	LA	44099-	$0.00
111	Doe	Jane	123 Main St.	Apopka	FL	30458-	$0.00
201	Greaves	Joseph	14325 N. Bankside St.	Godfrey	IL	43580-	$0.00
444	Doe	Jane	Cawthon Dorm, room 142	Tallahassee	FL	32306-	$10.55

Table 9.2 Sample **TimeCard** Table

ssn	date	startTime	endTime	storeId	paid
145-09-0967	01/14/2002	8:15	12:00	3	yes
245-11-4554	01/14/2002	8:15	12:00	3	yes
376-77-0099	02/23/2002	14:00	22:00	5	yes
376-77-0099	02/23/2002	14:00	22:00	5	yes
376-77-0099	03/21/2002	14:00	22:00	5	yes
145-09-0967	01/16/2002	8:15	12:00	3	yes
376-77-0099	01/03/2002	10:00	14:00	5	yes
376-77-0099	01/03/2002	15:00	19:00	5	yes

The use of this term emphasizes one difference between relational algebra notation and SQL. The word `distinct` must be present for the database to produce the table of Figure 9.1(b), which has only one row to represent the two customers named Jane Doe. Without the keyword `distinct` (as in part (a)), the results table contains eight rows: one for each Jane Doe, and one for each of the other six customers.

In Figure 9.1, statements (c) and (d) each represent a single *selection* operation. The asterisk (`*`) in the `select` clause denotes that the results table will contain every attribute of the input table. In SQL, *string literals* (specific strings of letters or numbers) are enclosed in single quotation marks, as shown in statements (c) and (d). To indicate a single quotation mark inside a string literal, you type two consecutive single quotes (for example, `'Doe''s balance'`).

You may have noticed that relational algebra and SQL terminology are not consistent. For example, the *selection* operation is included in SQL's `where` clause, and the *projection* operation is specified by SQL's `select` clause.

(a) *Project* Customer *on* lastName, firstName with duplicates

select lastName, firstName **from** Customer

firstName	lastName
Anita	Morehouse
Jane	Block
Carroll	Breaux
Cherry	Hamilton
Catherine	Harrison
Jane	Doe
Joseph	Greaves
Jane	Doe

(b) *Project* Customer *on* lastName, firstName without duplicates

select distinct lastName, firstName **from** Customer

firstName	lastName
Anita	Morehouse
Jane	Block
Carroll	Breaux
Cherry	Hamilton
Catherine	Harrison
Jane	Doe
Joseph	Greaves

(c) *Select from* Customer *where* lastName *= 'Doe.'*

select * **from** Customer **where** lastName = 'Doe'

accountId	firstName	lastName	street	city	state	zipcode	balance
111	Jane	Doe	123 Main St.	Apopka	FL	34331	0.00
444	Jane	Doe	Cawthon Dorm, room 142	Tallahassee	FL	32306	10.55

(d) *Select from* TimeCard *where* ssn *= '376-77-0099' and* date *< '01-feb-2002'*

select * **from** TimeCard
  where ssn = '376-77-0099' **and** date < '01-feb-2002'

ssn	date	startTime	endTime	storeId	paid
376-77-0099	01/03/2002	10:00	14:00	5	yes
376-77-0099	01/03/2002	15:00	19:00	5	yes

The Results of `select` Statements

Unlike relational algebra statements, expressions, select statements in SQL do not automatically produce a set of values (that is, an unordered collection without duplicates). Rather, they produce an ordered list of values. In particular, there's no guarantee that an SQL results table won't contain repeated rows. If we know that a query will yield unique results, this SQL characteristic isn't a problem. However, if a user wants to ensure uniqueness, he or she must ask the database to produce distinct rows, as in the query of Figure 9.1(b). Producing distinct rows usually requires the database system to sort the input rows by some value and then compare them. Executing this operation can be quite costly for large tables. Thus, SQL leaves it to the developer to decide whether uniqueness is important. Adding the keyword `distinct` after `select` forces the SQL processor to produce a table with unique rows and to incur whatever costs are required to ensure uniqueness.

9.1.2 Simple Join Queries

Figure 9.2 shows two more select statements, each representing a single *join* operation for the query *join* `Employee` *and* `TimeCard` *where* `Employee.ssn = Time-Card.ssn`. The figure also shows the table that would result from these query statements using the employees of Table 9.3 and the time cards of Table 9.2. In statement (a), the join is specified in the `from` clause, which lists the two input tables (`Employee` and `TimeCard`), and the `where` clause, which lists the join condition (`Employee.ssn = TimeCard.ssn`). The phrase `select *` indicates that the results table will contain all the attributes of both input tables.

Table 9.3 Sample **Employee** Table

ssn	lastName	firstName
145-09-0967	Uno	Jane
245-11-4554	Toulouse	Jennifer
376-77-0099	Threat	Ayisha
479-98-0098	Fortune	Julian
588-99-0093	Fivozinsky	Bruce

Statement (b) demonstrates the same query, but uses an explicit join operator, which some versions of SQL (including that used in Microsoft Access) support. Note that statement (b) uses the `join` verb and that the join condition now appears after the `on` clause.

9.1.3 Outer Join Queries

Join queries can be divided into **inner joins**, where each output row represents a match between the two source tables, and **outer joins**, where rows that don't match are also included in the output. The previous section showed many examples of inner join queries. The word `inner` can be added to `join … on` queries, as in this example from Figure 9.2.

```
select * from Employee inner join TimeCard on Employee.ssn
= TimeCard.ssn
```

(a) **select * from** Employee, TimeCard
   where Employee.ssn = TimeCard.ssn

(b) **select * from** Employee **join** TimeCard
   on Employee.ssn = TimeCard.ssn

Employee. ssn	last Name	first Name	TimeCard. ssn	date	start Time	store Id	paid	end Time
145-09-0967	Uno	Jane	145-09-0967	01/14/2002	8:15	3	no	12:00
145-09-0967	Uno	Jane	145-09-0967	01/16/2002	8:15	3	no	12:00
245-11-4554	Toulouse	Jie	245-11-4554	01/14/2002	8:15	3	no	12:00
376-77-0099	Threat	Ayisha	376-77-0099	02/23/2002	14:00	5	no	22:00
376-77-0099	Threat	Ayisha	376-77-0099	03/21/2002	14:00	5	no	22:00
376-77-0099	Threat	Ayisha	376-77-0099	02/23/2002	14:00	5	no	22:00
376-77-0099	Threat	Ayisha	376-77-0099	01/03/2002	10:00	5	no	14:00
376-77-0099	Threat	Ayisha	376-77-0099	01/03/2002	15:00	5	no	19:00

F I G U R E   9.2

SQL Statements and Results Table for *join* `Employee` and `TimeCard` where `Employee.ssn = TimeCard.ssn`

We can express the outer joins most easily using the `join … on` SQL syntax, but we'll see later that this syntax is not required. There are three outer join operators: `left outer join`, `right outer join`, and `full outer join`. If the developer doesn't specify a modifier (`outer`, `left outer`, or `right outer`), the database automatically assumes an inner join, which produces an output row for each match between two input rows. This is the usual definition of join that we saw in the relational algebra of Chapter 8 and in the previous section.

Let's take a closer look at the three kinds of outer joins.

A **left outer join**, or just **left join**, produces all of the output of the inner join *plus* a row for each row of its left operand (the first source table listed in the query statement) that does not match any row of the right operand (the second source table listed). The output fields that are attributes of the right operand are given null values. For instance, the following select statement produces the table shown in Table 9.4:

select * from Employee **left outer join** TimeCard **on**
Employee.ssn = TimeCard.ssn

Actually, the word `outer` can be omitted. In this statement, `Employee` is the left operand, and `TimeCard` is the right operand. Note that Table 9.4 has two more rows in addition to those shown in the table of Figure 9.2. The two additional rows hold information about employees 479-98-0098 and 579-98-8778, who have no time cards. You can see that no values are listed for the `TimeCard` fields of these last two lines. The value of each of these attributes is the special null value.

A **right outer join**, or **right join**, is like a left join, except that it contains the inner join plus a row for each row of the *right* operand that does not match any row of the left operand. For instance, the right join of `TimeCard` and `Employee` (with the tables in the opposite order) produces Table 9.5. Notice that the attributes of `TimeCard` are now on the left and the attributes of `Employee` are on the right.

A **full outer join** is the *union* of the left and right joins. It has a row for each match, plus a row for each unmatched row of the left input table and one for each unmatched row of the right input table. For example, consider a join of `Customer` and `Store`

Table 9.4 Left Join of **Employee** and **TimeCard**

Employee. ssn	last Name	first Name	TimeCard. ssn	date	start Time	store Id	paid	end Time
145-09-0967	Uno	Jane	145-09-0967	01/14/2002	8:15	3	no	12:00
145-09-0967	Uno	Jane	145-09-0967	01/16/2002	8:15	3	no	12:00
245-11-4554	Toulouse	Jie	245-11-4554	01/14/2002	8:15	3	no	12:00
376-77-0099	Threat	Ayisha	376-77-0099	02/23/2002	14:00	5	no	22:00
376-77-0099	Threat	Ayisha	376-77-0099	03/21/2002	14:00	5	no	22:00
376-77-0099	Threat	Ayisha	376-77-0099	02/23/2002	14:00	5	no	22:00
376-77-0099	Threat	Ayisha	376-77-0099	01/03/2002	10:00	5	no	14:00
376-77-0099	Threat	Ayisha	376-77-0099	01/03/2002	15:00	5	no	19:00
479-98-0098	Fortune	Julian						
579-98-8778	Fivozinsky	Bruce						

Table 9.5 Right Join of **TimeCard** and **Employee**

TimeCard. ssn	date	start Time	store Id	paid	end Time	Employee. ssn	last Name	first Name
145-09-0967	01/14/2002	8:15	3	no	12:00	145-09-0967	Uno	Jane
145-09-0967	01/16/2002	8:15	3	no	12:00	145-09-0967	Uno	Jane
245-11-4554	01/14/2002	8:15	3	no	12:00	245-11-4554	Toulouse	Jie
376-77-0099	02/23/2002	14:00	5	no	22:00	376-77-0099	Threat	Ayisha
376-77-0099	03/21/2002	14:00	5	no	22:00	376-77-0099	Threat	Ayisha
376-77-0099	02/23/2002	14:00	5	no	22:00	376-77-0099	Threat	Ayisha
376-77-0099	01/03/2002	10:00	5	no	14:00	376-77-0099	Threat	Ayisha
376-77-0099	01/03/2002	15:00	5	no	19:00	376-77-0099	Threat	Ayisha
						479-98-0098	Fortune	Julian
						579-98-8778	Fivozinsky	Bruce

on zip code. An inner join would list all of the matching rows of `Customer` and `Store`—that is, each combination of a customer and a store that share a zip code. A full outer join would add a row for each customer that has no matching store (the left join) and a row for each store that has no matching customer (the right join).

The `join` verb is not required in the SQL-92 standard, and until very recently, the version of SQL in the Oracle database systems did not support the `join` verb. Oracle does have an extension that can be used to express left and right joins. You simply add (+) to one of the tables in the join. For example, in Oracle, we write the left join as

```
select * from Employee, TimeCard(+) on Employee.ssn
= TimeCard.ssn
```

Similarly, a (+) on the left table in a join signifies a right join. The popularity of the `join` verb has led Oracle to include it in the SQL for Oracle 9i.

In Access, you can express left, inner, and right joins through the query design window. To express a left join, click on the line connecting the two input tables, click the right mouse button, and click on `Join Properties`. The `Join Properties` dialog lets you choose an inner, left, or right join. Figure 9.3 shows the left join query of the table shown in Figure 9.2 and the `Join Properties` dialog with `left join` selected. Note that the option does not say "left join" but rather "Include ALL records from 'Employee' and only those records from TimeCard where the joined fields are equal." This is simply a long way of saying "left join." Access puts an arrowhead on the connecting left join line pointing to the `TimeCard` table.

To create an inner join through Access, choose option 1 in the `Join Properties` dialog (only the records where the joined fields match). This choice creates the default, an inner join. To create a right join, choose option 3 in the `Join Properties` dialog (all of `TimeCard` and only those of `Employee` that match).

Access has no simple way to express an outer join. It is possible to make Access produce an outer join, but not with the `Join Properties` window. The full outer join operator is not considered important enough to be worthy of special consideration. Most instances of outer joins are either left or right joins.

9.1.4 Queries with Multiple Relational Operators

As you saw in Chapter 8, some queries require multiple relational operators, such as the BigHit Video example in which a manager might want to produce a list of all comedy (`genre`) movies rented by customers since December 2001, with the results table including the customer names, movie titles, and dates the videos were rented. Figure 9.4 gives the select statement that produces this desired information. Figure 9.5 shows the input tables for `Video`, `Movie`, and `PreviousRental`. Table 9.6 shows the results table that this query would generate.

This statement contains three *join* operations, one *selection* operation, and one *projection* operation. It is difficult to see exactly where these operations are represented in the select statement, but the labels in Figure 9.4 help you identify them. As you may have noticed, the select statement describes the output table more clearly

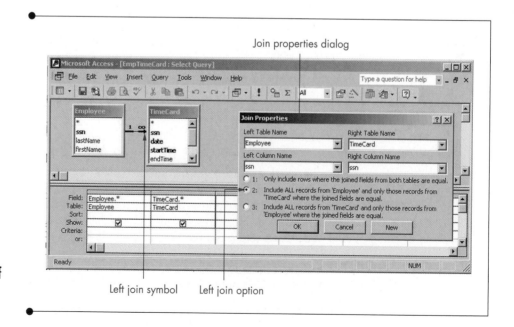

F I G U R E 9.3

Access Query for Left Join of **Employee** and **TimeCard**

```
1 select lastName, firstName, title, dateRented        Projection
2   from Movie, Video, PreviousRental, Customer          Source tables
3   where Movie.movieId = Video.movieId                  Join condition
4     and Customer.accountId = PreviousRental.accountId  Join condition
5     and Video.videoId = PreviousRental.videoId         Join condition
6     and dateRented > '2001-dec-1'                       Selection condition
```

F I G U R E 9.4

A Select Statement with Multiple
Relational Operators

Table 9.6 Results Table for Comedy Movies Rented Since
December 1, 2001

firstName	lastName	title	dateRented
Jane	Doe	Duck Soup	2001-12-04
Joseph	Greaves	Animal House	2002-01-14

than it describes the relational operations that produce the output. That is, an SQL statement describes *what* the user wants to do, not *how* the database should do it. We rely on the database server to process our queries. This **query processing** includes the translation of an SQL query into a relational algebra expression. The query processing also includes a query improvement step called **query optimization**, which finds an efficient strategy for executing the relational algebra expression.

To run the query shown in Figure 9.4 through Access, create a new query in design view and close the table selection dialog to produce a completely empty query. Then choose the SQL window option from the view menu. You will be presented with a window for typing SQL. Type the SQL statement of Figure 9.4 into the SQL window, as shown in Figure 9.6. The format of the data constant has been changed from the SQL standard '2001-dec-1' to #2001-dec-1# to conform to the way Access represents dates. No other change is required to make this an Access query.

Figure 9.7 shows how this SQL query looks in the Access query design window. You will notice that no lines connect the tables and the join conditions (`Movie.movieId=Video.movieId`, etc.) are explicitly listed in the field entries. Access does not seem to treat the SQL query of Figure 9.4 as a product query with selection operations. When this query appeared in Chapter 8, we produced the Access query design repeated here as Figure 9.8.

You can see the Access version of this query by changing from the design view of Figure 9.8 into the SQL view of the same query. The Access SQL query is shown in Figure 9.9. The primary difference between the SQL statements of Figures 9.4 and 9.9 is that the Access version uses `inner join ... on` to represent each join (highlighted in lines 3 and 4 of Figure 9.9). This join syntax makes the join operations more obvious and puts the selection condition in the `where` clause by itself. Note, too, that Access always includes the table name in the corresponding attribute name, even when the table name is not required, as for example in the highlighted section of line 9. The attribute names in Figure 9.4 are qualified with table names only when the names are required to resolve ambiguities. For instance, the name `accountId` in this query is ambiguous because it could be either `Customer.accountId` or `PreviousRental.accountId`, as we see in line 7 of Figure 9.9.

Video

videoId	dateAcquired	movieId	storeId
101	1/25/98	101	3
111	2/5/97	123	3
112	12/31/95	123	5
113	4/5/98	123	5
114	4/5/98	189	5
123	3/25/86	123	3
145	5/12/95	145	5
77564	4/29/91	189	3
90987	3/25/2002	450	3
99787	10/10/97	987	5

Movie

movieId	title	genre	length	rating
101	The Thirty-Nine Steps	mystery	101	R
123	Annie Hall	romantic comedy	110	R
145	Lady and the Tramp	animated comedy	93	PG
189	Animal House	comedy	87	PG-13
450	Elizabeth	costume drama	123	PG-13
553	Stagecoach	western	130	R
987	Duck Soup	comedy	99	PG-13

PreviousRental

accountId	videoId	dateRented	dateReturned	cost
101	101	12/9/98	12/10/98	$2.49
101	112	1/13/98	1/4/98	$1.99
101	113	1/15/2002	1/15/2002	$0.99
102	113	12/1/98	12/3/98	$2.49
111	101	12/4/98	12/6/98	$2.49
111	99787	1/1/2002	1/4/2002	$3.95
201	113	12/9/98	12/14/98	$3.99
201	77564	1/14/2002	1/24/2002	$3.35

F I G U R E   9.5

Sample Tables for `Video`,
`Movie`, and
`PreviousRental`

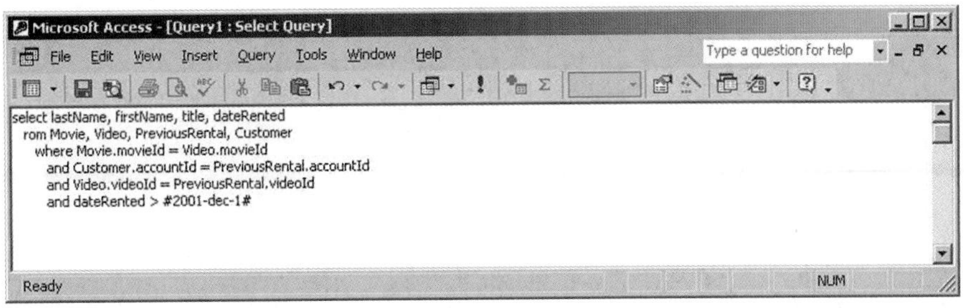

FIGURE 9.6

SQL Window in Access

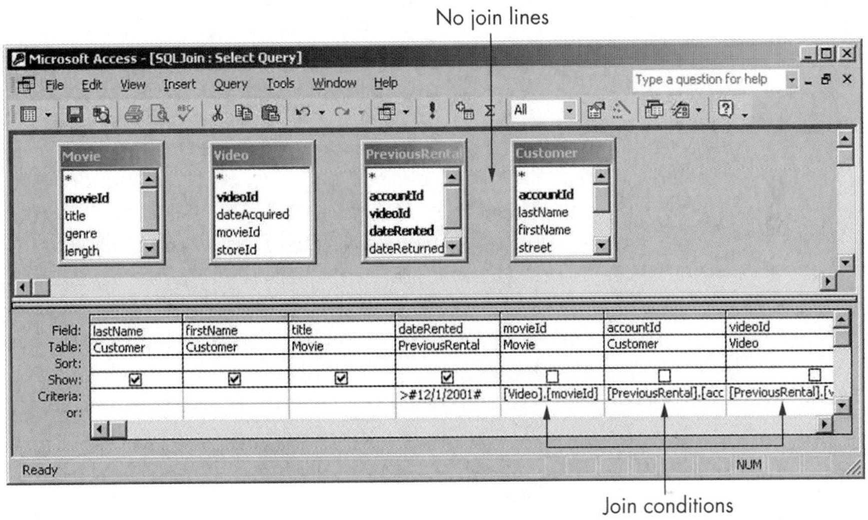

Microsoft Access - [Query1 : Select Query]

File   Edit   View   Insert   Query   Tools   Window   Help   Type a question for help

```
select lastName, firstName, title, dateRented
  rom Movie, Video, PreviousRental, Customer
    where Movie.movieId = Video.movieId
      and Customer.accountId = PreviousRental.accountId
      and Video.videoId = PreviousRental.videoId
      and dateRented > #2001-dec-1#
```

Ready   NUM

FIGURE 9.7

Query Design Window for
Query of Figure 9.4

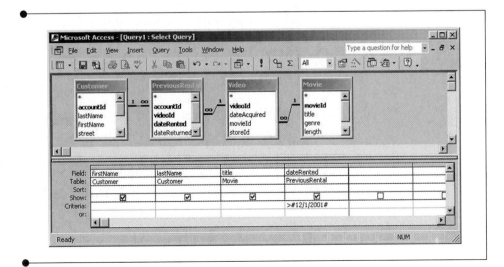

FIGURE 9.8

Query Design for Join Query

```
1  select Customer.firstName, Customer.lastName,
2     Movie.title, PreviousRental.dateRented
3  from (Movie inner join Video
4     on Movie.movieId = Video.movieId)
5     inner join (Customer
6        inner join PreviousRental
7           on Customer.accountId = PreviousRental.accountId)
8     on Video.videoId = PreviousRental.videoId
9  where (((PreviousRental.dateRented)>#12/1/2001#));
```

FIGURE 9.9

Microsoft Access Select Statement

9.1.5 String Pattern Matching and Ordering Results

If you were a clerk at BigHit Video, a customer might ask for a movie, but not know the exact title. The customer might say, "I know that 'alligator' is in the title." You would want to ask the database for any movie with "alligator" in the title. SQL supports **pattern matching** with the `like` operator and a simple alphabet using symbols such as % (the percent sign) and _ (the underscore sign). In a like expression, the percent symbol matches any arbitrary characters in an attribute value, and the underscore matches any single character in an attribute value.

For example, in Figure 9.10, statement (a) generates a list of all movies whose title attribute includes "alligator." Statement (b) generates a list of all movies whose title does *not* start with the word `The`. Pattern matching in SQL is case sensitive, so '`The %`' matches movie titles only if they begin with a capital T. Statement (c) generates a list of all employees whose Social Security numbers have "44" in the middle. It is difficult to read these underscore characters on the printed page, but the pattern in statement (c) has three underscores, a minus sign, the numerals 44, another minus sign, and four underscores. That's because each Social Security number consists of three digits, two digits, then four digits, separated by minus signs.

As noted in the Concept box in Section 9.1.1, each select statement returns a list of rows. If a select statement does not specify the desired order of the rows, the SQL processor may list the rows in any order. Often database users do care about the order of the rows in a results table. For example, we might want to generate a list of customer names that is ordered alphabetically by last name. To control the order of the rows, use SQL's `order by` clause, which directs the database to arrange the results-table rows in a specific order.

The first statement below produces a list of customers ordered alphabetically by last name and then by first name. The second statement adds the `desc` keyword to produce a list in descending order by account ID. The keyword `asc` lets you request a list in ascending order (the default). You can also mix these keywords within a single `order by` clause, as shown in the third statement below.

```
select * from Customer order by lastName, firstName
select * from Customer order by accountId desc
select * from Customer order by lastName desc, zipcode asc
```

FIGURE 9.10

Pattern Matching Examples

```
(a) select * from Movie where title like '%alligator%'
(b) select * from Movie where title not like 'The %'
(c) select * from Employee where ssn like '___-44-____'
```

9.1.6 **Expressions, Literals, and Aggregates**

The select statements we've seen so far all return values that occur as attribute values in the input tables. But we might also want to see entirely new values in a results table. For instance, we may wish to see the number of hours worked in employees' time-card reports. The BigHit Video database doesn't have any table containing this information, but we can use SQL to generate the data.

The number of hours worked is the difference between the ending time and starting time on a time card. In Microsoft Access, time calculations return numeric values represented as fractions of days. So, in an Access query, we have to ask the database to multiply the difference in ending and starting times by 24 to obtain the number of hours worked. We can include the expression `(endTime-startTime)*24` as a selected attribute, as in the following statement:

```
select lastName, firstName, Employee.ssn, date,
       (endTime-startTime)*24
  from Employee, TimeCard
where Employee.ssn = TimeCard.ssn
```

This statement produces a single row of output for each row in its input, which is the *join* of `Employee` and `TimeCard`. The database calculates the value of the expression for an output row from the values of the attributes `endTime` and `startTime` of the joined input row. Table 9.7 shows the results of executing this SQL statement.

In this table, the number of hours worked is listed under the attribute name `Expr1`. Result table attributes that are not simply an attribute of a source table are known as *expressions*. One difference between selecting an expression and selecting an attribute of a source table is that there is no obvious name for the selected results table attribute. After all, what would you call `(endTime-startTime)*24`? Every attribute of every table, including result tables, has a name, but SQL does not specify what the name should be for expressions. One SQL database system would call this attribute `column5`. Microsoft Access, which was used to generate the table in Table 9.7, calls the attribute `Expr1`. But we're not limited to these naming conventions. We can use SQL's **as** clause to name the resulting new attribute any way we like. For example, the following statement calls the calculated attribute `hoursWorked`.

```
select lastName, firstName, Employee.ssn, date,
       (endTime-startTime)*24 as hoursWorked
  from Employee, TimeCard
where Employee.ssn = TimeCard.ssn
```

Table 9.7 Results Table Showing Number of Hours Worked

lastName	firstName	ssn	date	Expr1
Uno	Jane	145-09-0967	1/14/2002	3.75
Uno	Jane	145-09-0967	1/16/2002	3.75
Toulouse	Jie	245-11-4554	1/14/2002	3.75
Threat	Ayisha	376-77-0099	2/23/2002	8
Threat	Ayisha	376-77-0099	1/3/2002	4
Threat	Ayisha	376-77-0099	2/23/2002	4

In a `select` clause, expressions can include string and numeric *literals* (for example, the number 100), values of attributes (for example, `lastName`), standard numeric operators (for example, /, *, +, and −), and function calls, which are small units of software that carry out specific operations.

SQL offers a wide variety of functions, including numeric functions, string manipulation functions, and date formatting functions. The usual syntax, rules of precedence, associativity, and numeric type conversion that you would find in mathematics also apply to SQL expressions. To see exactly which types, operators, and functions are available in your database system, it's best to consult an SQL reference manual. We'll see some examples of SQL functions when we develop our own SQL applications in Chapters 12–15.

In addition to expressions and literals, SQL also lets you ask for aggregates, collections of information extracted from more than one row of a source table. For instance, in Chapter 2 we defined a derived attribute, `numberRented` of `Customer`, that represented the number of videos currently rented by a particular customer. To create a value for this attribute in SQL, we must use an **aggregate operator**—one that puts together values from multiple rows of the `Rental` table. The following select statement returns the number of videos rented for the customer with account number 101:

```
select count(*) from Rental where accountId = 101
```

The `count` function returns the number of values of the attribute in the specified table. In this case, we use `count(*)` to ask the database to count the number of rows. To find the number of different last names of customers, we would write

```
select count(distinct lastName) from Customer
```

Each of the preceding queries returns a single row and a single column in its results table.

SQL includes aggregate functions to calculate the average, minimum, maximum, and sum of numeric attributes. For example, we can calculate the average number of hours worked on the time cards of employees as follows:

```
select avg((endTime-startTime)*24) as avgHoursWorked
   from TimeCard
```

Whenever an aggregate appears in a `select` clause, all other values in the `select` clause must either be aggregates or literals (numbers or strings). Other functions that can be used in an aggregating select statement include `min`, `max`, and `sum`. We'll see additional examples in the next section.

9.1.7 Group by and having Clauses

In many circumstances, we want an aggregating query to return more than one row—for instance, we want to select the average cost, the total cost, and the number of previous rentals for each video. In such cases, we would want to organize the source rows (previous rentals) into groups according to the value of the `videoId` attribute of each row, and see one aggregate for each group. SQL's **group by clause** lets us do that. The following query returns one row for each video ID. But each row contains the video ID, the average cost for that video, and the number of previous rentals for that video. Figure 9.8 shows the results of executing this query.

```
select videoId, avg(cost) as averageCost, sum(cost)
   as totalCost, count(*) as numRentals
from PreviousRental group by videoId
```

Table 9.8 Results of a **Group By** Query

videoId	averageCost	totalCost	numRentals
101	$2.49	$4.98	2
112	$1.99	$1.99	1
113	$2.49	$7.47	3
77564	$3.35	$3.35	1
99787	$3.95	$3.95	1

When we use group by, the database returns one row for each *group* of input rows. In the above query, the rows of the PreviousRental table are grouped by videoId. Within each group, all of the rows have the same value for videoId; in every other group, all the rows have a different value for videoId.

We can create the derived, or new, attribute numberRented of Customer for all customers by *joining* the Customer and Rental tables, *grouping by* accountId, and *counting* the number of rows. The following statement accomplishes this task:

```
select Customer.accountId, count(*) as numberRented
   from Customer, Rental
   where Customer.accountId = Rental.accountId
   group by Customer.accountId
```

The fields that we can select in a group by query are restricted to the attributes that appear in the group by clause, aggregate expressions, and literals. No attribute that does not appear in the group by clause can be listed in the select clause because those attributes are not guaranteed to have the same value for every row in a group. Consider Rental.videoId, for instance. Because we are grouping by accountId, all rows in a group have the same accountId, but each row has a different videoId. Hence, it is not possible for the database to uniquely determine a value of videoId that correctly represents all rows in the group, and so we cannot list videoId in the list of selected attributes.

If we want the query results to include the customer names, we must include lastName and firstName in both the select and group by clauses, as shown below:

```
select Customer.accountId, lastName, firstName,
      count(*) as numberRented
   from Customer, Rental
   where Customer.accountId = Rental.accountId
   group by Customer.accountId, lastName, firstName
```

Finally, we might want to restrict which groups produce output rows. For instance, we might not want to see information about customers with only one rental and return a row only for customers whose number of rentals is greater than 1.

SQL supports such queries through its **having clause**, which is a selection clause applied to groups. Any group that does not satisfy the having clause does not contribute a row to the results table. The values that can appear in the having clause are the same as those that can appear in the select clause. Consequently, we can restrict groups by size or other aggregate, or by the values of group by attributes. Figure 9.11 shows a query that selects the movie title and genre, the number of rentals, the average rental cost, and the total cost for all movies that have more than one rental.

```
1   select title, genre, count(*) as numRentals,
2       avg(cost) as average, sum(cost) as sum
3     from Movie, Video, PreviousRental
4     where Movie.movieId = Video.movieId
5       and Video.videoId = PreviousRental.videoId
6     group by Movie.movieId, title, genre
7     having count(*)>=1
```

title	genre	numRentals	average	sum
Annie Hall	comedy	4	$2.37	$9.46
The Thirty-Nine Steps	mystery	2	$2.49	$4.98

FIGURE 9.11

Using **Group By** and **Having** Clauses

The figure also shows the query's results table. As you can see in the table, only two movies satisfy this `having` clause.

To select the title and genre in this query, we have to include them in the `group by` clause. Yet their inclusion does not change the grouping, because `movieId` is a key attribute of `Movie`. That is, each movie has a single title and a single genre. These attributes appear to be superfluous in the `group by` clause, and perhaps they are. Nevertheless, SQL requires that we include them.

The `having` clause and the `where` clause both restrict the query. The `where` clause restricts the rows that become members of groups. Only rows that satisfy the `where` clause are used in forming the groups. Once the groups have been formed, the `having` clause determines which groups produce output rows. Only groups that satisfy the `having` clause produce output rows.

Figure 9.12 shows a Microsoft Access representation of the query depicted in Figure 9.11. Notice that the table contains a new row in the list of fields to hold a `Total`. We make this row appear by right-clicking on a field and clicking the Σ `Totals` button. This row has values `Group By`, `Sum`, `Avg`, and `Expression` for different fields. The list of `group by` fields (`title`, `genre`, and `Movie.movieId`) matches those given in Figure 9.11. The `having` clause is represented by the third field (`Expression`). The `Criteria` field of this column shows `>=2`; that is, at least two rentals for this movie. The last field indicates `group by movieId`.

9.1.8 Nested Select Statements

As you might have gathered by now, some SQL queries are so complex that they won't fit into the form of a single select statement. SQL allows a select statement to be used inside the `where` clause of another select statement. Such **nested select statements** can make complex queries easier to write *and* read. The following query demonstrates nested statements. This query selects all of the customers who rented a video in December 2001:

```
select * from Customer where accountId in
    (select accountId from PreviousRental
        where dateRented >='dec/1/2001' and
dateRented<'1/1/2002')))
```

Read from "the inside out," this query selects all previous rentals since December 2001, *then* selects all customers for those rentals. The query is the equivalent of a join of the two tables with a selection of rentals from December 2001. A good query op-

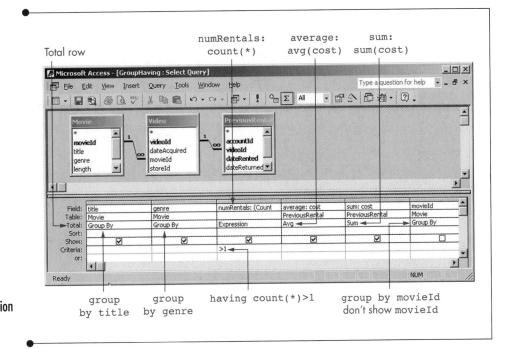

F I G U R E 9.12

Microsoft Access Representation
of a **group by** and
having Query

timizer recognizes the equivalence of the nested select query and the join query and
can produce the same execution strategy for both.

The nested select statement can also include references to fields of the containing
statement. For example, by using SQL's **not exists** operator, the following statement selects all customers who have not rented any video:

select * from Customer C **where not exists**
    (select * from PreviousRental P
        where C.accountId = P.accountId)

The operator **not exists** is true when its operand is an empty table (for example, when the customer has no previous rentals). The above statement also uses the
letters C and P as local names for tables, to simplify the query text. C stands for **Customer**, and P stands for **PreviousRental**.

As one acceptable execution of this select statement, the database query processor
could iterate through the rows of table C (that is, the **Customer** table). That is, for
each row in C, the query processor would execute the nested query with the account
number of the current row of C as the value for C.accountId. If the nested query
returns no rows, the database produces an output row for the main query. If the
nested query returns any rows, it does not produce an output row.

The operators and keywords that we can use in nested select statements include **in,
all, exists, unique, contains, union, not**, and **intersection**. The meaning of these terms is fairly obvious. A good SQL reference book will contain many examples of their use and we'll see more examples in later chapters.

Microsoft Access has no facility for building nested queries in QBE. Typing the
preceding query into an Access query window and switching to design view yields the
configuration shown in Figure 9.13. The nested select statement is shown in text
form in the second field. The **exists** operation of SQL has been turned into a function called **Exists**. The negation of the **exists** operation is represented by the
False in the second field in the **Criteria** row. So it's possible to write nested select statements in Access, but only by typing. The graphical query design window cannot be directly used for creating nested queries.

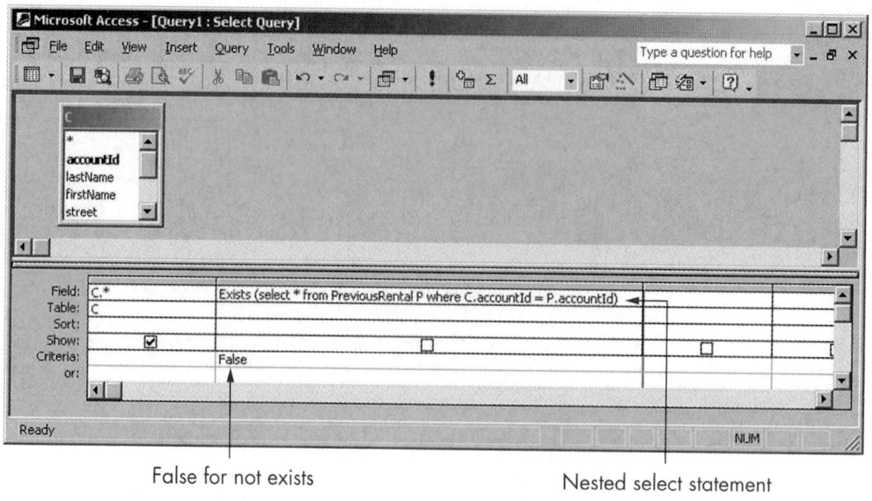

FIGURE 9.13

Microsoft Access Representation of a Nested Select Statement

9.1.9 **Set Operations**

In addition to all the preceding functions, SQL can perform union, intersection, and difference operations. For example, suppose we wanted a table containing all rentals, including both current and previous rentals. The following expression uses SQL's **union** operator to return the union of the source tables `Rental` and `Previous-Rental`:

```
(select * from Rental) union (select * from PreviousRental)
```

However, as we saw in Chapter 8, it is impossible for a user to determine the source of a row in the table produced by this union. If we don't care whether a video is currently rented or not, this query is the correct one. If, however, we need to be able to tell whether a row came from the `Rental` table or the `PreviousRental` table, the above query does not meet our needs. The following query adds a string value to each row to mark its source.

```
(select *, 'Rental' as sourceTable from Rental)
union
(select *, 'PreviousRental' as sourceTable from
    PreviousRental)
```

Table 9.9 shows the results table for this query. Note that the table has an extra column whose value is the name of the source table.

The intersection operation is called `intersect` in SQL, and the difference operator is called `except`. The following intersection query produces the list of the `videoId` values for the videos that are currently rented and have been rented before:

```
(select videoId from Rental)
intersect
(select videoId from PreviousRental)
```

The difference query below returns videos that are currently being rented for the first time:

```
(select videoId from Rental)
except
(select videoId from PreviousRental)
```

Table 9.9 Results of Union Query

accountId	videoId	dateRented	dateDue	cost	sourceTable	
103	101	1/3/02	1/4/02	$1.59	Rental	
101	113	2/22/02	2/25/02	$3.00	Rental	
101	114	2/22/02	2/25/02	$3.00	Rental	
103	123	12/1/01	12/31/01	$10.99	Rental	Rows from Rental
101	145	2/14/02	2/16/02	$1.99	Rental	
101	90987	1/1/02	1/8/02	$2.99	Rental	
101	99787	1/1/02	1/4/02	$3.49	Rental	
101	101	12/9/01	12/10/01	$2.49	PreviousRental	
101	112	1/13/01	1/4/01	$1.99	PreviousRental	
101	113	1/15/02	1/15/02	$0.99	PreviousRental	
102	113	12/1/01	12/3/01	$2.49	PreviousRental	
111	101	12/4/01	12/6/01	$2.49	PreviousRental	Rows from Previous Rental
111	99787	1/1/02	1/4/02	$3.95	PreviousRental	
201	113	12/9/01	12/14/01	$3.99	PreviousRental	
201	77564	1/14/02	1/24/02	$3.35	PreviousRental	

Finally, the difference query below produces a list of videos that have been rented before but are not currently rented:

```
(select videoId from PreviousRental)
except
(select videoId from Rental)
```

9.2 MODIFYING DATABASE CONTENT WITH SQL

All the queries we've seen so far have come in the form of select statements that let us retrieve and manipulate information from a database's tables. SQL also lets us modify the contents of a database's tables, through the use of statements other than select. Specifically, an insert statement adds new rows to a table. An update statement modifies one or more attributes of specified rows of a table. A delete statement deletes one or more rows from a table.

9.2.1 Insert Statements

Suppose BigHit Video gets a new customer and wants to add his or her name to the database's Customer table. To insert a row into a table, an SQL programmer needs to specify a value for each attribute of the table. The **insert statement** below gives a literal value for each attribute of one new row in BigHit Video's Customer table. The new customer, Jia Yu, has account number 555, street "540 Magnolia Hall," city "Tallahassee," state "FL," and zip code "32306." The values in the statement appear in the same order as the Customer table's attributes.

```
insert into Customer values (555, 'Yu', 'Jia','540 Magnolia
    Hall', 'Tallahassee', 'FL', '32306', 0.00)
```

We can specify the order and even the presence of the attributes by listing them, in parentheses, after the table name. One advantage is that this allows us to omit attributes whose values we don't know or would rather leave out. In the following statement, the order of attributes is different from the table definition, and no value is given for the address attributes:

```
insert into Customer (firstName, lastName, accountId)
    values ('Jia', 'Yu', 555)
```

Each of the missing attributes will take on its default value. If the database designer did not specify the default value during the table-definition process, the attribute takes the value `null`. If the `address` attribute was specified as non-null with no default value, this insert statement would fail and the database system would issue an error message.

An insert statement can contain a select statement to add multiple rows to a table—something we might want to do if we wished to create pay statements for BigHit's employees. To create such statements, we'd have to ask the database to collect all the time cards at the end of a pay period and calculate the number of hours each employee worked. Next, the database would have to multiply the hourly pay rate for each employee by the number of hours worked. Finally, it would create a new entity in the `PayStatement` table to record the amount to be paid.

The form of this kind of query is as follows:

```
insert into <table> <select statement>
```

To write the actual query, we would need to write a select statement that produces a table that has the same shape as the `PayStatement` table. The schema for `PayStatement` is as follows:

```
PayStatement (ssn, hourlyRate, numHours, amountPaid,
    datePaid)
```

The select statement must provide a value for every field, in the same order shown in the above table schema. We develop this select statement in a series of steps.

1. Write a select statement to select every pay statement that has not yet been paid (`paid = false`) and to perform the total hours worked calculation:

```
select TimeCard.ssn, sum((endTime-startTime)*24) as
    hoursWorked
from TimeCard where paid=false group by ssn
```

2. Add the pay calculation to the select statement. We'll need to use the `hourlyRate` field from the `HourlyEmployee` table in this part of the query. (Recall that some employees are paid by the hour. Thus, only those employees will be paid by time cards.) In this step, we must also include fields for the hourly rate and the pay date. We use the Access SQL constant `today` to represent the day that the statement is executed. This statement will create a table that has the same attribute types as `PayStatement` and hence can be used in the next step.

```
select TimeCard.ssn, hourlyRate,
    sum((endTime-startTime)*24) as hoursWorked,
    sum((endTime-startTime)*24*hourlyRate) as amountPaid,
    today
from TimeCard, HourlyEmployee
where TimeCard.ssn = HourlyEmployee.ssn and paid = false
group by TimeCard.ssn, hourlyRate
```

3. Write the insert statement. To write this part of the query, we add the insert information before the select portion of the query, as shown below:

```
insert into PayStatement(ssn, hourlyRate, numHours,
    amountPaid, datePaid)
select TimeCard.ssn, hourlyRate,
    sum((endTime-startTime)*24) as hoursWorked,
    sum((endTime-startTime)*24*hourlyRate) as amountPaid,
    today
from TimeCard, HourlyEmployee
where TimeCard.ssn=HourlyEmployee.ssn and paid = false
    group by TimeCard.ssn, hourlyRate
```

9.2.2 Update Statements

An **update statement** in SQL lets us change one or more rows of an existing table. An update statement has three clauses:

```
update <table> set <attribute>=<value> ...
    where <selection condition>
```

The update clause specifies which table to update. The set clause contains one or more assignments that specify which attributes to change and what their new values are. The where clause specifies which rows to change.

For instance, the following statement finishes the preceding pay statement example by marking all of the time cards as paid:

```
update TimeCard set paid = true
    where paid = false
```

An assignment can refer to attributes of the update table. For instance, if we wanted to give an hourly employee a 10% raise, we would write the following query:

```
update HourlyEmployee set hourlyRate = hourlyRate * 1.1
    where ssn = '145-09-0967'
```

In writing update statements, we need to make sure they affect the correct rows. For example, if we left out the where clause in the preceding statement, we'd give *every* employee a 10% raise!

The expression on the right side of an assignment (in this case '145-09-0967') can be very complex and may include nested select statements. Suppose, for instance, that we wanted to be generous with the BigHit Video employees and give each one a raise equal to 10% of the average hourly rate. We can calculate the average salary with a nested select statement and use it in the right side of the assignment:

```
update HourlyEmployee set hourlyRate =
    hourlyRate + 0.10 * (select avg(hourlyRate) from
        HourlyEmployee)
```

9.2.3 Delete Statements

To delete rows in a table, we must write a **delete statement** that specifies the table and a selection condition. Each row of the table that satisfies the condition is deleted when the statement executes. For instance, the following statement deletes every row of the `TimeCard` table where the employee is not an hourly employee:

```
delete from Timecard
    where not exists
        (select * from HourlyEmployee
            where TimeCard.ssn = HourlyEmployee.ssn)
```

INTERVIEW

PETER CHEN
The Importance of Theories That Solve Business Problems

CURRENT JOB I am M.J. Foster Distinguished Chair Professor of Computer Science at Louisiana State University in Baton Rouge. Whenever someone from the state sees my business card, they ask me about my relationship with Governor Foster. Interestingly enough, I did not know who Mr. Foster was until I met Mr. Murphy J. Foster, III (an attorney in Louisiana). His great grandfather was the governor of Louisiana from 1892 to 1900, and my position was set up in his honor. Furthermore, one of the previous governor's grandsons, another Murphy J. Foster, became the governor of Louisiana in 1996.

ON THEORIES THAT FIND THEIR WAY INTO EVERY-DAY BUSINESS **First**, if a model or technique does not solve a business problem, nobody will use it, not to mention spend time (and, possibly, money) to learn it. **Second**, if a model or technique is too complicated, the number of people who can master it is very small, and the model/technique does not have the critical mass to become popular. **Third**, natural concepts make the learning easier, the acceptance quicker, and the communication between different individuals more accurate. **Fourth**, no matter whether Confucius said it or not, it is an old saying that a picture is better than a thousand words. The E-R model solves a critical business problem. It is simple and to the point. The concepts of entity and relationships are very natural to human thinking and daily lives, and an E-R model can be expressed in an E-R diagram, a simple but yet powerful graphical representation of crucial semantic concepts.

ON GENERATING NEW IDEAS When I was a visiting professor of EECS at MIT from '86 to '87, I learned from Dr. Joel Moses there to think in inno-

> **"I see the E-R model becoming a core component of organizing data on the Web and for communicating the semantics of data through the Web. I see XML playing the role of a standard syntax for data transfer on the Web."**

vative ways, and that has been very helpful in my career. As a professor, I spend most of my time researching, teaching, and interacting with faculty members and students. I also participate in and organize professional conferences. I serve as editor of journals and referee for papers submitted to conferences and journals. In terms of research projects, I am working on: the relationship between the E-R model and XML, meta data modeling, information validity assessment techniques, and cyber security.

THE FUTURE OF THE E-R MODEL AND THE ADVENT OF XML XML is intended to be a major language for specifying data on the Web. It turns out that several main concepts of the XML family (such as XLink and RDF) are very similar to the main concepts of the E-R model. Currently, several research teams, including mine, are studying the relationships between the E-R model and the XML family and their Web applications. I see the E-R model becoming a core component of organizing data on the Web and for communicating the semantics of data through the Web. I see XML playing the role of a standard syntax for data transfer on the Web.

CREATING AND MANIPULATING 9.3 TABLE DEFINITIONS WITH SQL

In addition to letting you query and modify tables in an existing database, SQL also lets you create new tables and modify their characteristics. We can use `create table` statements to create new tables, `alter table` statements to modify attributes or constraints on tables, and `drop table` statements to delete tables.

9.3.1 Creating Tables and Defining Attributes

A **create table statement** specifies a table name and a list of attributes for a new table. The statement must specify a name and type for each attribute. Figure 9.14 shows an SQL statement that creates BigHit Video's `Customer` table. The attributes `lastName` and `firstName` are listed as variable-length text fields with a maximum of 32 characters in each one (for example, `varchar(32)`). We would expect the `street` field to be longer, so it has a maximum of 100 characters. The `accountId` field is an `int`, for integer. The `balance` field is `real`, for a number that may have a fractional part.

The SQL data types are extensive and somewhat interchangeable. For instance, a `varchar` type has a varying number of characters, up to some limit, and a `char` type has a specific fixed number of characters. That is, a `varchar(32)` attribute can have up to 32 characters, but will take up less space if the value is shorter. A `char(32)` will always occupy the same amount of space no matter how short or long its value is. When you expect that some values of a field are very long and some are very short, it's better to use `varchar`. If the values are short, it makes little difference.

SQL supports a specific collection of attribute types, listed in Table 9.10, and has several names for some types. Numeric attribute types include integers (such as `int`, `smallint`, and `long`), floating point types of various lengths (for example, `float` and `double`), and formatted numbers (such as `decimal`). A bit string is a list of binary (0, 1) values and is useful for storing a sequence of true/false values.

Date types include a date and a time (`datetime`), a date with no time (`date`), and a time with no date (`time`). In the BigHit Video database, we might use a `datetime` for the `dateDue` and `dateRented` of a rental, a `date` for the `date` of a time card, and a `time` for its `startTime` and `EndTime`.

F I G U R E   9.14

An SQL **Create Table** Statement

```
 1  create table Customer (
 2      accountId int,
 3      lastName varchar(32),
 4      firstName varchar(32),
 5      street varchar(100),
 6      city varchar(32),
 7      state char(2),
 8      zipcode varchar(9),
 9      balance real
10  )
```

Table 9.10 Some SQL Attribute Types

Numeric types	Integer	`integer, int, smallint, long`
	Floating point	`float, real, double precision`
	Formatted	`decimal(i,j), dec(i,j)`
Character-string types	Fixed length	`char(n), character(n)`
	Varying length	`varchar(n), char varying(n), character varying(n)`
Bit-string types	Fixed length	`bit(n)`
	Varying length	`bit varying(n)`
Date and time types		`date, time, datetime, timestamp, time with time zone, interval`
Large text types	Character	`long varchar(n), text, clob`
	Binary	`blob`

String attribute values that are longer than 256 characters are considered large text types. We define them as `longvarchar` or `text`, both of which can be unlimited in length. Many recent SQL versions also include `blob` (binary long object) and even `clob` (character long object) types. These types typically designate values that do not need to support searching; for example, a video clip (a `blob`) or a large document (a `clob`).

9.3.2 Key and Foreign Key Constraint Specifications

Attributes have characteristics other than simply a name and a type. For example, in Chapter 5, you saw that some attributes represent primary and secondary keys of tables. Other attributes represent foreign keys—relationships with other tables. These key characteristics of attributes determine which rows can be part of a relationship between two tables. Figure 9.15 shows three `create table` statements that declare key and foreign key constraints. (Note that the lines in this figure are numbered so that you can more easily find the various terms in the explanation of the figure.)

To declare a primary key (that is, a field that uniquely identifies a row), we use the `primary key` constraint, as in line 11. To declare a multiple-attribute primary key, we create a separate constraint clause using the same terminology, as in line 23. We can also use a separate constraint clause to declare a single attribute as a primary key, as in line 7.

We declare secondary keys, that is, additional sets of attributes that are unique within a table, by using the `unique` constraint for the attribute or set of attributes, as in lines 12 and 19.

For both primary and secondary keys, the relational database system will enforce the constraints and ensure that no violation occurs. Any attempt to insert or update a row that results in a constraint violation will result in an error.

To specify a foreign key (a representation of a relationship type as a reference to the key of another table), we create a **references clause**, as shown in line 8. In this line, the attribute `manager` of table `Store` is a foreign key whose value is the value of the primary key of a row of the `Employee` table. Lines 24 and 25 show the general form of a `references` clause. In these lines, the foreign key attributes are listed in the first pair of parentheses, and the primary key of the referenced table is listed in the second set of parentheses. This form allows the foreign key to consist of more than one attribute and to refer to attributes other than the primary key of the referenced table.

```
1  create table Store (
2      storeId int,
3      street varchar(100),
4      city varchar(32),
5      state char(2),
6      zipcode varchar(9),
7      primary key storeId,
8      manager int references Employee
9  )
10 create table Movie (
11     movieId varchar(10) primary key,
12     title varchar(100) unique,
13     genre varchar(32),
14     rating varchar(5),
15     accountId int,
16 )
17 create table Rental (
18     accountId int,
19     videoId varchar(10) unique,
20     dateRented datetime,
21     dateDue datetime,
22     cost real,
23     primary key (accountId, videoId),
24     foreign key (accountId) references Customer(accountId)
25     foreign key (videoId) references Video(videoId)
26 )
```

FIGURE 9.15

SQL **Create Table** Statements Declaring Key and Foreign Key Constraints

As with primary and secondary key constraints, the database system will enforce foreign key constraints by refusing to modify tables if the new values violate the constraints..

You may recall that `Rental` has a one-to-one relationship type with `Video` that is represented by the foreign key `videoId` of `Rental`. The `unique` constraint of line 19 requires the database system to ensure that no two rentals have the same `videoId`. Thus the combination of the `unique` constraint of line 19 and the `foreign key` constraint of line 25 enforces the one-to-one cardinality constraint.

9.3.4 Default Values, Nulls, and Constraints

Earlier in this chapter, you saw that it is often convenient to have default values for attributes. Specifying these values as part of the table definitions can often simplify the insert statements we use to add rows to tables.

It is not unusual to have attributes whose values must be supplied; in such cases, we give the `not null` characteristic to such attributes. For instance, a foreign key that represents a required relationship will be declared not null. The `movieId` attribute of `Video` is not null to enforce the participation constraint: That is, each video must be represented by a corresponding entity in the `Movie` table. This condition is specified in the following `create table` statement:

```
create table Video (
    videoId varchar(10) primary key,
    movieId varchar(10) not null references Movie,
    storeId int references Store
)
```

9.3.5 **Adding, Removing, and Modifying Attributes**

The **alter table** statement can also be used to add, modify, and remove attributes. For instance, we might want to add attribute `dateAcquired` to `Video`. This is the `alter table` statement:

alter table Video **add** (dateAcquired **date** = Today)

The table would be altered by adding a new column and setting all of the values of that column to today's date using the `Today` literal. If no default value is specified, all new attributes will have null values.

The `alter table` statement can also be used to drop attributes and to modify their characteristics. The following table makes some changes to `Video`, not all of them good.

```
alter table Video
    modify (storeId not null)
    drop constraint (primary key videoId)
    drop (movieId)
```

Line 2 requires that `storeId` be not null. If any row of the table has a null value, this change will not be allowed. Line 3 removes the primary key constraint. The table is left with no primary key, although the attribute `videoId` is not modified. Finally, line 4 removes the `movieId` attribute altogether.

These are very simple examples of `alter table` statements. You can see many more in SQL manuals. Look in the Further Reading section for some suggestions of where to find more information.

9.3.6 **Schemas and User IDs**

Tables and other definitions in a relational database are collected into schemas. The SQL use of schema is analogous to what we called a database schema in Chapter 5. A schema includes all of the definitions related to a particular user's database. Typically, each SQL connection to a database is made with a specific user ID and password. A schema is the set of definitions made by a single user. This user is referred to as the owner of the tables in the schema. When a user connects to the database, he can refer to an element of his schema as `schemaName.tableName` or simply as `tableName`.

Suppose our database has two user IDs: The owner of the BigHit Video database tables is called `bighit` and the owner of the BigHit Online tables is called `online`. When a user logs in as `bighit`, the rental table can be called `Rental` or `bighit.Rental`. When the `online` user logs in, the rental table must be called `bighit.Rental`. A database user can refer to tables in another schema, but only using the full name, including the name of the table owner. You'll see in Chapter 15 how database security is related to ownership of schemas.

Access databases do not have multiple users and hence also don't have multiple schemas.

9.3.7 **Drop Statements**

At times, we might want to remove (drop) a table from a database—for example, because it is no longer needed. Suppose the owner of BigHit Video decides to fire all of the employees and remove all information about them. He could use the **drop table** statement below to remove the `Employee` table.

drop table Employee

A serious problem occurs with the foreign key constraints of the `TimeCard` table when the Employee table is dropped. The value of the `ssn` attribute of each row of `TimeCard` must be the value of a row of `Employee` because `TimeCard.ssn` is a foreign key. Removing the `Employee` table will remove all of the rows of the table and thus the time cards will not refer to existing employees.

SQL offers two drop behavior options: `cascade` and `restrict`. The `cascade` option specifies that any foreign key constraint violations that are caused by dropping a particular table will cause the corresponding rows of the related table to also be deleted. The `restrict` option (the default) blocks the deletion of the table if any foreign key constraint violations would be created by the drop.

Suppose that we have rows in the `TimeCard` table and we execute the cascading drop statement:

drop table `Employee` **cascade**

All of the rows of the `TimeCard` table would be removed, and then the `Employee` table would be dropped. The `TimeCard` table would not be dropped, but it would be empty.

Suppose we execute the restricting drop statement:

drop table `Employee` **restrict**

This time, the presence of rows in the `TimeCard` table, each referring to an employee, will cause the database system to block the execution of the statement and issue an error message. The `Employee` and `TimeCard` tables would remain unchanged.

9.4 THE RULE OF 90/10

This chapter touches on just the basic operations and terminology of SQL. Chapters 12–15 describe additional aspects of SQL, including how to specify physical database properties. This chapter focuses on that part of SQL that is the most useful in producing Web databases and Web applications. This chapter also affirms the "rule of 90/10." In any computer science endeavor, there's a rule of thumb saying that 90% of a system's functionality is produced by 10% of the work of the developers. The other side of that coin is that the last 10% of the functionality requires 90% of the work. The "**rule of 90/10**" explains why many computer programmers optimistically expect to complete projects quickly!

The topics covered in this chapter represent the 10% of SQL that produces 90% of the utility of the language. You've learned most of what you'll need to implement database systems in SQL. However, the last 10% will be the most difficult part of your learning.

To truly master SQL, you need extensive additional study, lots of practice, and access to plenty of database books and SQL reference manuals. A sad fact of database systems is that, despite the standardization of SQL, every database system has its own version of SQL with its own differences from the standards. To create databases that suit your needs, you may well have to familiarize yourself with the nonstandard parts of the database. You've already learned some of the ways that Access SQL is non-standard.

9.5 CASE IN POINT: SQL STATEMENTS FOR BIGHIT ONLINE VIDEO SALES

Now we are ready to connect the BigHit Online relational model of Chapter 6 to the Web site of Chapter 2 by writing the SQL statements that will create the tables, add some rows to some tables, fetch data for use in Web pages, and update the database to reflect the user interactions.

Figure 9.16 repeats the Access database schema for BigHit Online and Figure 9.17 shows the `create table` statements for some of the tables. The rest are similar. We can execute these statements in an Oracle or SQL server database to create the tables for our system.

Before we can begin to sell videos, we need to add rows to the `Movie`, `DVD`, and `Video` tables. Figure 9.18 shows some sample insert statements. Lines 1–4 add four movies to the `Movie` table. Line 5 creates a `DVD` entry for each movie and specifies only the `movieId`, `cost`, and `quantity` (each has the same cost and the same quantity). The `videoFormat`, `languages`, and `captioning` attributes will be null. Lines 5 and 6 add `Videotape` entries for each movie. Since all of our videotapes are in the VHS format, the `format` attribute is given the string literal `'VHS'` as its value. You are invited to write your own SQL statements to create customers for the system.

FIGURE 9.16

Database Schema for Video Sales, Repeated from Figure 6.26

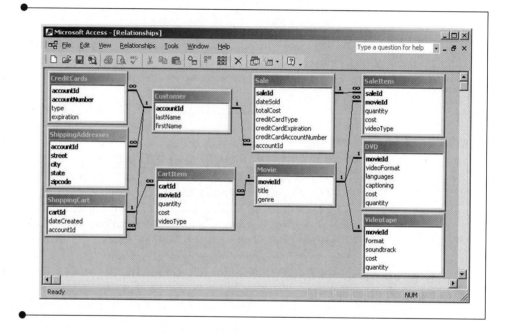

FIGURE 9.17

Create Table Statements for `Sale` and `SaleItem`

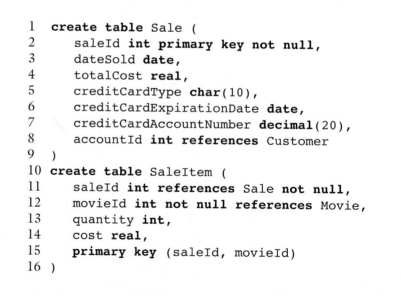

```
1   create table Sale (
2       saleId int primary key not null,
3       dateSold date,
4       totalCost real,
5       creditCardType char(10),
6       creditCardExpirationDate date,
7       creditCardAccountNumber decimal(20),
8       accountId int references Customer
9   )
10  create table SaleItem (
11      saleId int references Sale not null,
12      movieId int not null references Movie,
13      quantity int,
14      cost real,
15      primary key (saleId, movieId)
16  )
```

```
1   insert into Movie values (101,'The Thirty-Nine Steps','mystery')
2   insert into Movie values (123,'Annie Hall','romantic comedy')
3   insert into Movie values (145,'Lady and the Tramp','animated comedy')
4   insert into Movie values (189,'Animal House','comedy')
5   insert into DVD (movieId, cost, quantity)
6      select movieId, 15.99, 100 from Movie
7   insert into Videotape (movieId, format, cost, quantity)
8      select movieId, 'VHS', 15.99, 100 from Movie
```

FIGURE 9.18

Inserting Rows into **Movie**, **DVD**, and **Videotape**

Now that we have videos available for sale and customers to buy them, we want to be able to show a customer a list of what's available. For example, if the customer with `accountId` 101 asks to see comedy movies, he'll be presented with a Web page like the one in Figure 9.19. The SQL needed to find these movies is

```
select m.movieId, m.title, genre, rating, d.cost, v.cost
   from Movie m, DVD d, Videotape v,
   where m.movieId = d.movieId and m.movieId = v.videoId
   and genre like '%comedy%' order by title
```

We need the cost from both `DVD` and `Videotape`, so the query must join them both to `Movie`.

You'll notice that the customer has asked to purchase 3 copies of the DVD for movie 123 and 1 videotape of movie 987. To create a shopping cart and add these items to it requires the SQL statements of Figure 9.20. For this chapter, we'll omit the issues of how we create the IDs of the shopping cart and the sale, and concentrate on the rest of the information. We'll examine all of the details in Chapter 13. Lines 1 and 2 create the shopping cart and lines 3–6 add the items to it.

When our customer is ready to check out, we have to move the items from the shopping cart to the sale (with ID 234). Figure 9.21 shows the SQL statements

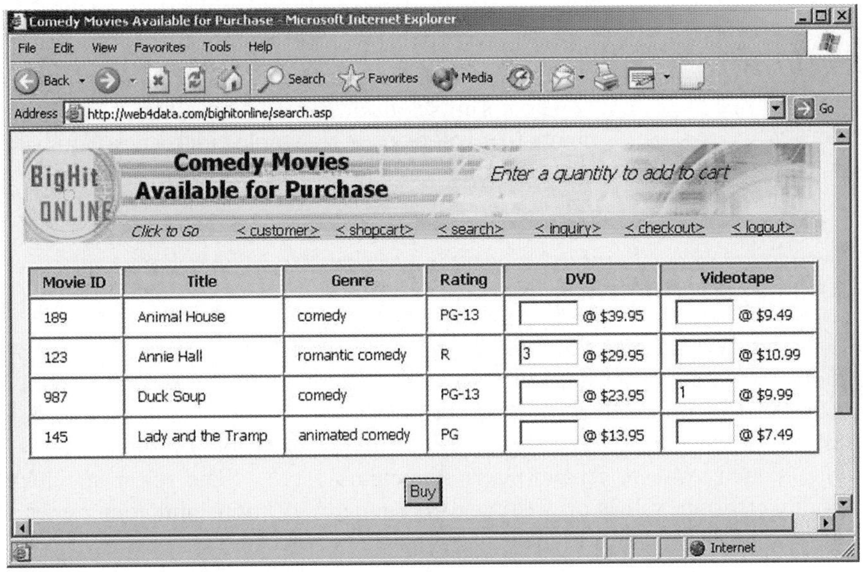

FIGURE 9.19

A Web Page Showing a Request to Add Comedy Movies to the Shopping Cart

```
1   insert into ShoppingCart (cartId, dateCreated, accountId)
2      values (13, now(), 101)
3   insert into CartItem (cartId, movieId, quantity, cost, videoType)
4      values (13, 123, 3, 29.95, 'dvd')
5   insert into CartItem (cartId, movieId, quantity, cost, videoType)
6      values (13, 987, 1, 9.99, 'videotape')
```

FIGURE 9.20

SQL Statements to Create
Shopping Cart and Cart Items

```
1   insert into Sale (saleId, dateSold, accountId)
2      values (234, now(), 101)
3   insert into SaleItem (saleId, movieId, quantity, cost, videoType)
4      select 234, movieId, quantity, cost, videoType
5         from CartItem where cartId = 13
6   update SaleItem
7      set totalCost = (select sum(cost) from SaleItem where saleId=234)
8      where saleId = 234
9   delete from CartItem where cartId = 13
10  delete from ShoppingCart where cartId = 13
```

FIGURE 9.21

SQL Statements to Create a Sale
from the Shopping Cart

needed to accomplish much of the sale. For the sake of brevity, the credit card and shipping information has been omitted.

Lines 1 and 2 of Figure 9.21 create a new sale for customer 101. You might notice that the `totalCost` field is not yet filled in. Lines 3–5 insert the sale items directly from the cart items. The only difference between a cart item and a sale item is its ID. So we put the sale ID (234) into the insert statement as a numeric literal and get the rest of the attributes from the cart item. Lines 6–8 update the `totalCost` field of the sale after the sale items have been recorded. Finally, the sale is properly recorded, so we can delete all the cart items and the shopping cart, in lines 9 and 10.

These samples from BigHit Online have demonstrated some of the SQL statements that will be used to handle video sales. You will be asked to fill in more details in the problems and projects that follow.

CHAPTER SUMMARY

SQL is a standard language for describing database definition, manipulation, and applications. The data manipulation language (DML) of SQL supports queries that extract data from databases (select statements), add new rows to tables (insert statements), and modify attribute values of existing rows (update statements). SQL is not an exact implementation of the relational algebra, as it does not guarantee the uniqueness of rows in a table, and it does impose an order on the rows.

The select statement combines selection, projection, and join operators into a single statement. A select clause contains the projection, the from clause lists the input tables, and the where clause contains the join conditions and the selection conditions. Additional clauses can be used to specify groupings of rows.

Update, insert, and delete statements describe modifications to a database table's content.

The data definition language (DDL) of SQL supports the definition of both the logical and physical structures of databases. The create table statement specifies a table schema; it describes the attributes, their types, default values, and constraints. It can also be used to define key and foreign key constraints. In addition, it supports the definition of physical characteristics of databases, as we'll see in Chapter 13.

KEY TERMS

Aggregate operator. A function that produces a single value from multiple rows of a table. SQL supports aggregate operators avg, count, max, min, and sum.

Alter table statement. An SQL statement that modifies the definition of a table by adding, modifying, or removing attributes or other characteristics.

Create table statement. An SQL statement that specifies the creation of a new table with specific attributes and constraints.

Data definition language (DDL). A language for specifying the structure of the components of a database system.

Data manipulation language (DML). A language for specifying operations that extract, insert, and update the contents of a database system.

Delete statement. An SQL statement that specifies the deletion of rows from a table.

Drop table statement. An SQL statement that removes a table from the database. Other drop statements remove indexes, users, and other objects.

From clause. A clause in an SQL select statement that specifies the source tables of the statement. Multiple source tables in a from clause represent product operations on those tables. Join conditions are specified in the where clause or in the on clause of a join verb.

Full outer join. A join operator that includes all the results of the left join and the right join.

Group by clause. A clause in an SQL select statement that specifies how select rows will be grouped. One output row is produced for each group of selected rows.

Having clause. A clause in an SQL select statement that specifies a selection condition on the groups. A having clause always appears in combination with a group by clause.

Inner join. The usual join of the relational algebra that returns only rows that match the join condition.

Insert statement. An SQL statement that specifies a set of rows to be added to a table.

Left outer join or left join. A join operator that includes the results of the inner join plus every row of the left input table that has no matching rows in the right input table.

Nested select statement. An SQL select statement that includes a subselect statement in the from or where clause.

Outer join. A join operator that includes all the results of the inner join plus some rows from right or left input tables that do not match. The three kinds of outer joins are full outer join, left join and right join.

Pattern matching. String operations that find substrings that match particular patterns. The SQL like operator performs pattern matching on string attributes.

Query optimization. The process of finding an efficient way to execute a query. Database servers use query optimization to improve execution performance.

Query processing. The execution of a query by a database server.

References clause. A clause in an SQL create table statement that declares a set of attributes to be a foreign key that reference a particular table.

Right outer join or right join. A join operator that includes the results of the inner join plus every row of the right input table that has no matching rows in the left input table.

Rule of 90/10. The rule of thumb for computing that says that 90% of the functionality of a system is produced by 10% of the work. Alternatively, understanding the last 10% of a system requires 90% of the effort.

Select statement. An SQL statement that fetches data from the database.

Select clause. A clause in an SQL select statement that specifies the projection operation of the statement. The select clause lists those attributes that are included in the result table.

SQL (Structured Query Language). The ANSI standard language for the definition and manipulation of relational databases. SQL includes both a data definition language and a data manipulation language.

Update statement. An SQL statement that specifies a modification of particular attributes in particular rows of a table.

Where clause. A clause in an SQL select statement that specifies a condition that determines whether particular rows will be included in the output table. The where clause includes the selection operation of the query and often includes the join condition.

QUESTIONS

1. What are the major differences between the relational data model and the SQL data model? Consider in particular the characteristics of attributes in the two models.

2. Which clause of the select statement is used to specify the following:
   a. Projection operation
   b. Selection operation
   c. Join operation

3. Write SQL statements to represent the queries of Problem 4 in Chapter 8.

4. Write SQL statements to represent the queries of Problem 6 in Chapter 8.

5. Write SQL queries to represent the following:
   a. Which customers have an "x" in their names?
   b. Which customers live in Florida (FL) or New Jersey (NJ)?
   c. Which customers currently have more than three videos rented?
   d. How many copies of *Elizabeth* have been ordered?
   e. How many previous rentals are there for customers whose first name is "Jane"?

6. Using the relations of the BigHit Video database, for each of the following SQL statements, give an English description of the statement and the relations that result when it is executed.

   a. ```
      select * from Customer where
      exists select accountId from
      Rental
      ```

   b. ```
      select title, genre from Movie,
      PreviousRental
      where Movie.movieId =
      PreviousRental.movieId
      and accountId = 101
      ```

   c. ```
      select movieId, title from Movie
      m, PurchaseOrderDetail p,
      PurchaseOrder d, Supplier s
      where m.movieId=d.movieId
      and d.id = p.id
      and p.supplierId = s.supplierId
      and s.state='LA'
      ```

7. Write relational expressions to represent the SQL statements in Problem 6.

8. Write an SQL statement to select all hourly employees who worked in (had a time card for) store number 3 during the week of Monday, February 22, 1999.

9. Write an SQL statement to select the title of every video that was previously rented by a customer whose last name is the same as the last name of an employee.

10. Write SQL statements for the following database update operations.
    a. Create a new hourly employee with your name. Be sure to give the employee all appropriate attribute values, and don't forget the row in `HourlyEmployee`.
    b. Record that this new employee works in store 3.
    c. Add a new store.
    d. Record a purchase order for five copies of *Elizabeth* and three copies of *Annie Hall* from Acme Video.
    e. Delete all previous rental records that are more than one year old.
    f. Delete all movies that have no rental copies.
    g. Delete all purchase order records that are more than one year old. Don't forget the purchase order detail records.

## PROBLEMS

11. Use the BigHit Video Access database to create and execute queries for the SQL statements of Question 3.

12. Use the BigHit Video Access database to create and execute queries for the SQL statements of Question 4.

13. Use the BigHit Video Access database to create and execute queries for the SQL statements of Question 5.

14. Use the BigHit Online Access database to create and execute SQL queries to
    a. Find the total value of all sales items.
    b. Find all sales items for the customer with `accountId 112`.

    c. Find the total and average value of all sales items for each customer.
    d. Record credit card information for a sale with ID 234.
    e. Record a shipping address for a sale with ID 234.

15. Use the BigHit Video Access database to create and execute SQL queries to represent the following:
    a. Which customers have an "x" in their names?
    b. Which customers live in Florida (FL) or New Jersey (NJ)?
    c. Which customers currently have more than three videos rented?
    d. How many copies of *Elizabeth* have been ordered?
    e. Which salaried employees work in store 5?
      ```

16. Using the BigHit Video Access database, create a query in the query design window for each of the following SQL statements. Turn in a printout of each.

   a. **select * from** Customer
      where exists select accountId
      from Rental

   b. **select** title, genre **from** Movie,
      PreviousRental **where** Movie.movieId
      = PreviousRental.movieId **and**
      accountId=101

   c. **select** movieId, title **from** Movie
      m, PurchaseOrderDetail p,
      PurchaseOrder d, Supplier s
      where m.movieId=d.movieId
      and d.id = p.id

      and p.supplierId = s.supplierId
      and s.state='LA'

17. Using the BigHit Video Access database, create a query in the query design window for each of the following update operations. Turn in a printout of each.

   a. Create a new hourly employee with your own name and other attributes.

   b. Record that you work in store 3.

   c. Add a new store.

   d. Delete all previous rental records that are more than one year old.

   e. Delete all movies that have no rental copies.

   f. Give a 10% raise to all salaried employees.

PROJECTS

18. Develop SQL statements for the rest of the operations needed for this application, including, but not limited to the following. Make up your own attributes, as appropriate.

   a. Creating a new customer.

   b. Modifying the attributes of a customer.

   c. Recording multiple shipping addresses for a customer.

   d. Creating a credit card for a customer.

   e. Defining all of the tables of the BigHit Online database.

20. Continue your extension to the book's BigHit Online project that you created for your project of Chapter 6. Develop SQL statements to create tables, add data to tables, and respond to user requests.

19. Continue your Movie Lovers project from Chapter 6 by developing the SQL statements that will be required to create the database tables, add data to the tables, and respond to user requests.

FURTHER READING

The standard for SQL-92 is published in [ANSI92]. Previous versions of SQL are Sequel 2, as described in Chamberlin et al [Cha76], and the standard SQL-89 [ANSI89]. The next version of the SQL standard, SQL:1999, has been accepted as an international standard. Information can be found at the ANSI and ISO Web sites. Texts on SQL include Cannan and Oten [CaOt93] and Date and Darwen [DaDa93]. SQL-1999 is discussed in Earp and Bagui [EaBa03], among many good books. Many Web sites have information about standard SQL and the various dialects from Vendors. The Microsoft developers site (http://msdn.microsoft.com) and the Oracle TechNet site (http://technet.oracle.com) have extensive online documentation. Each of these sites is free, but they require users to register. The O'Reilly site (www.ora.com) publishes considerable information online.

Creating Interactive Web Sites

Finally, we are ready to look at Web site development. We'll begin with an overview of HTML, progress to writing Web software that creates dynamic Web sites, and finally add database interaction to our Web sites.

In these chapters, you will be developing programming skills that enable you to create dynamic Web sites. Be careful with this material. Great care and attention to detail are required to be a successful programmer. The primary results of sloppy work in design and programming are many fruitless hours of wasted effort and even more hours spent in fixing mistakes.

Chapter 10 shows you how to create Web pages using the HTML language. You will focus on writing simple HTML documents and using Cascading Style Sheets (CSS) to control the format of pages. You will learn the principles of displaying information in Web pages, especially using HTML tables.

Chapter 11 adds action to Web servers by showing you a simple way of creating interaction between Web browsers and servers. Microsoft Active Server Pages (ASP) provide a simple environment for creating software applications that dynamically generate Web pages in response to user requests. You will learn to use the JavaScript programming language to build your ASP applications.

Chapter 12 is the final step in creating truly dynamic Web sites that interact with databases. You will learn how to connect your Web applications to database servers and how to make those applications query and update databases. The combination of JavaScript and SQL will provide you with all of the tools you need to make databases work for your Web sites. You also will learn additional programming skills and will emerge from Chapter 12 a competent Web site developer.

Presenting Information on the Web with HTML

- How to use basic HTML commands to create Web pages

- How to present information in HTML tables

- How to organize information on a Web page

- How to use tables and other formatting elements in designing Web pages

- How to design and use style sheets to control Web-page formatting

In this chapter, we take a break from database design and shift our focus to interactive Web sites—those increasingly essential (and proliferating) Internet-based pages that let visitors enter information, place orders, retrieve data, and so forth. As we saw in Chapters 1 and 2, interactive Web sites use databases extensively. For example, BigHit Video's Web site, which lets customers reserve movies and review their current rentals, retrieves and modifies information in BigHit's relational database.

To create such Web sites, designers use special software languages. Several languages exist, but in this chapter you'll begin learning about one called **HTML, the Hypertext Markup Language**.

This chapter introduces the basics of HTML. In subsequent chapters, you'll work with HTML-based programming tools that enable you to design Web sites that can interact with users and databases.

You may be wondering why you need to learn the details of HTML when so many good HTML editors, such as Microsoft FrontPage and Macromedia Dreamweaver, are available. These editors help you create and edit Web-site pages. However, the style of dynamic Web programming that you will learn beginning in Chapter 11 is based on direct manipulation of the HTML document. Your familiarity with HTML will be a great asset in creating Web sites. Nevertheless, HTML editors can simplify the programming of interactive Web sites, and most professional Web page developers make extensive use of them.

In a *dynamic* Web site, software programs generate new HTML pages on demand, that is, whenever users request them. For example, a customer of BigHit Video may request to see a page that lists all of her current rentals. As you start working your way through this and subsequent chapters in Part V, you'll gain exposure to advanced technologies that enable these pages to change in response to site visitors' requests and to the information in the databases with which the Web site is interacting.

In the next few chapters, you'll also develop programming skills that will let you create interactive Web sites. As you work through this material, keep this word of advice in mind: Successful programming hinges on great care and attention to detail. Sloppy work only wastes time. Pay close attention to the concept boxes and the examples in these chapters, and look for strategies that will help you minimize the amount of time you spend programming.

10.1   THE ARCHITECTURE OF WEB SITES

Figure 10.1 illustrates one way that Web browsers and Web servers interact. A user initiates the interaction by clicking on a link. In this case, the user has clicked on a reference to the document address `http://www.web4data.com/index.html`. The browser recognizes the click and sends a request for the page named `/index.html` to the server `www.web4data.com`. The server finds the file in its disk and sends it back to the browser. The browser is responsible for transforming the document into the formatted page that is shown to the user.

The request and response illustrated in Figure 10.1 use a Web page that has been created by some developer and stored in the server's file system. Such a page is called a *static page* to reinforce the contrast between a page that is stored in a file system, and one that must created by the Web server in response to the query. A page that is generated by the server is called a *dynamic page*, and a Web site with dynamic pages is called a *dynamic Web site*. In Chapters 11 and 12, we'll be increasing the complexity of this picture by adding the capability for dynamic pages.

FIGURE 10.1

Requesting and Displaying a
Page in a File

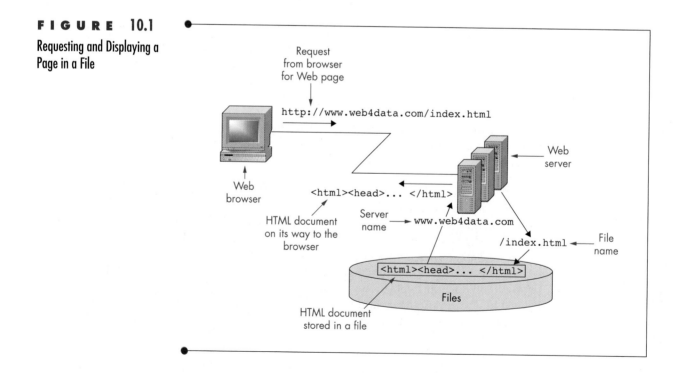

10.2 INTRODUCTION TO HTML

The World Wide Web was originally proposed by Tim Berners-Lee in 1989 at CERN, the European Laboratory for Particle Physics. Berners-Lee believed that the Web could serve as a much-needed resource for people all over the world who wanted to create multimedia, integrated electronic documents and share them over the Internet. HTML was first described by Berners-Lee in a 1992 document that sought to provide a standard way for people to create documents for the Web. Since that time, the Web development community has standardized and modified the language extensively. In 1999, the Internet Engineering Task Force standardized HTML 2.0. The current version of the language—called HTML 4.0—proposed by the World Wide Web Consortium (W3C), forms the basis for the examples in this book.

How does HTML work, in basic terms? An **HTML document** consists of lines of text with embedded *markup tags* that specify Web-page formatting and links to other pages. The vast collection of HTML documents distributed over many sites on the Internet became known as the World Wide Web. Most HTML documents are created by designers using special editing tools and are stored in files on Web servers.

In 1993, students, faculty, and staff of the National Center for Supercomputing Applications (NCSA) at the University of Illinois recognized HTML's potential to create a worldwide community of people exchanging information over the Internet. HTML was in wide use by that time, but the utility of the Web was restricted by the lack of graphical Web browsers and the limited capabilities of Web server software. The Web browsers were simple text displays without the integrated formatting and color that makes Web pages so appealing now.

The group began developing what became known as the Mosaic Web browser and Web server. These systems revolutionized the Web. The Mosaic browser gave users a very appealing and natural interface and point-and-click interaction. The Web server made it easy for individuals with a computer connected to the Internet to install their own Web servers to publish their own Web sites. The ready availability and high quality of the Web browsers and servers made it possible for the Web to expand far beyond anyone's expectations. The Web experienced vast increases in the number of users, the amount of information, and the variety of types of information. The Web expanded beyond the scientific community and into a broad range of organizations and industries. With more advanced browsers, servers, and search engines, thousands of companies, large and small, could now serve their customers more speedily and inexpensively than ever—with spectacular financial returns.

10.3 A CLOSER LOOK AT HTML DOCUMENTS

An HTML document specifies text, formatting instructions, links to other Web pages, instructions for retrieving and displaying graphics on Web pages, and other information. A Web *browser* formats a page according to the instructions in the HTML document and displays the page on a Web site. In addition, the browser supports interaction between HTML documents and a variety of information servers. When site visitors click on a document reference, or link, the browser issues a request to the appropriate server and then displays the Web page the server returns.

The HTML document has formatting instructions, but does not directly specify how the page will be displayed. The browser, under the user's control, selects font sizes, colors, and other style elements and produces the format of the HTML document that is shown to the user. When you use your browser to look at the HTML documents on this book's Web site, they will probably not match the screen shots in the book. Differences in font sizes, whether links are underlined, and even browser window size affect the exact presentation of each page. You will definitely see differences between the different browsers. The pictures in the book come from Microsoft Internet Explorer 5.5, but they can be viewed equally well with Netscape Navigator 6 and Internet Explorer 6.

In HTML, a markup tag, or simply **tag**, is a string of characters that begins with < and ends with >. The text between these symbols consists of a tag name and a series of attributes and their values. HTML is called a markup language because the tags place markers within a document. HTML tag names are case insensitive, but the preferred style is to use lowercase tag names.

The simplest tags are formatting marks such as the paragraph tag `<p>` and the break tag `<br>`. Each occurrence of `<p>` in a document marks the beginning of a paragraph. The browser will break a paragraph at this point and add a little extra space before the following text. A break tag is similar, except that no extra space is added.

Tags often come in pairs. An **end tag** is a tag that starts with `</` and whose tag name matches an earlier tag. A begin tag and an end tag delimit a section of the document. A paragraph end tag is `</p>` and a break end tag is `</br>`. When tags come in pairs, they mark a section of the document—the text between the two tags.

HTML has several heading tags. The largest heading tag is `<h1>`. The following shows how `<h1>` is used.

```
<h1> BigHit Video </h1>
```

This line shows two tags (`<h1>` and `</h1>`) that surround the text `BigHit Video`. The two tags form a pair with `<h1>` as the begin tag and `</h1>` as the end tag. The meaning of this line is that the text "BigHit Video" is to be formatted as a heading with a large font size.

Although HTML standards suggest that each tag be paired with an end tag, most Web browsers allow some end tags to be omitted. A tag can be its own end tag if it ends with `/>`. You'll see an example in line 23 of Figure 10.3, below.

To see examples of Web-page sections, consider Figure 10.2. The figure shows the welcome page that BigHit Video's customers would see if they used Internet Explorer to visit the company's Web site. The dotted lines in the figure are not part of the Web page, but are there to show how the page can be divided into three sections.

FIGURE 10.2

BigHit Video Welcome Page

```
1   <html>
2     <head>
3       <title>BigHit Video Online Reservation System</title>
4     </head>
5     <body bgcolor="white">
6       <table border="0">
7         <tr>
8           <td><img src="bighit.jpg" alt="BigHit Video logo"/></td>
9           <td valign="middle">
10            <font face="Arial" size="24pt">BigHit Video, Inc.</font>
11            <br><h1><em>Online Reservation System</em></h1>
12          </td>
13        </tr>
14      </table>
15      <!-- body of page -->
16      <center>
17        <a href="reservation.html"><h2>
18          Enter Video Reservation System
19        </h2></a>
20      </center>
21      <!-- footer of page -->
22      <center>
23        <img src="hbar.gif"/>
24        <p><font face="Arial" size=+0><b>
25          <a href="http://localhost/bighit/index.html">
26            BigHit Video home page
27          </a>
28        </b></font></p>
29          <p><font face="Arial">
30            Developed and maintained by
31            <a href="mailto:riccardi@cs.fsu.edu">
32              riccardi@cs.fsu.edu
33            </a>
34          </font></p>
35      </center>
36    </body>
37  </html>
```

F I G U R E 10.3

HTML Source Code for the
BigHit Video Welcome Page

The upper part of the page contains what's known as a header. It consists of the BigHit's logo (a picture) and company name (text), and the page title, "Online Reservation System." The center of the page contains the working portion, or body, of the page—in this case, a single (underlined) link to BigHit's video reservation system. The bottom of the page contains a footer, which consists of a horizontal line, a link to BigHit's home page, and a link to the e-mail address of the person who maintains the Web site.

This page also serves as the style standard for all the pages that make up this Web site. That is, to maintain a consistent "look and feel" throughout the site, the site designer has made sure that every page on the site contains BigHit's logo at the upper left, a title next to the logo, and a footer. Consistent styling has many benefits. Once a user has seen one of the pages, others will be familiar. If we're careful with our design, we'll put standard links and images in consistent places so that a user who learns how to use one page will be able to quickly use any other. In the case of BigHit Video, for instance, the footer always has links to both the main page of the site and the site developer.

Figure 10.3 shows the HTML document used to create BigHit's welcome page. Lines 1–14 created the page's header. Lines 15–20 created the body. Lines 21–37 created the footer. Lines 15 and 21 are comment tags. Any tag beginning with `<!--` and ending with `-->` is a comment tag and is ignored by the browser when it formats the document for display.

Note that this source code begins with an HTML start tag `<html>` and ends with an HTML end tag `</html>`. Every HTML document should have these tags, although many browsers do not require them. The beginning and ending **head** tags (lines 2 and 4) bracket the page section specifying the text "BigHit Video Online Reservation System," which is defined by begin and end **title tags** and is displayed in the browser's title bar, which is the area at the top of the window above the browser menus and buttons.

The BigHit Video logo and the page title are contained in an HTML table, a structure that guides document formatting and is defined by a variety of **table tags**. This table, created by lines 6–14 in Figure 10.3, begins with a `table` tag. The `table` tag contains an *attribute* `border` with value 0. Attributes serve to add information to tags. The value of the `border` attribute specifies the width of the border around the table. In this case, the border has width zero and thus is invisible. The header is organized into a table in order to control the format. Tables are made up of rows, marked with the table row tag `<tr>` and table elements, marked with table header `<th>` and table data `<td>` tags.

The information to be displayed in this borderless table row begins with a table row tag in line 7. The first table-data element (line 8) begins with a table data tag `<td>` and consists of an **image tag** `<img>`. The image tag refers to the BigHit Video logo that's contained in a file called `bighit.jpg`. (You'll learn more about image tags in the next section in this chapter.) The second element in the table row (lines 9–12) specifies the page title, which includes BigHit's company name and the words "Online Reservation System." This element contains a break tag `<br>` (line 11), which forces a line break after the words "BigHit Video, Inc."

Concept

Unknown Tags and Poorly Formed Documents in HTML Browsers

When a browser is formatting an HTML document for display, it may encounter tags that are unknown to it, that is, tags whose names are not recognized as HTML tag names. It may also encounter improper HTML, such as a `td` tag that is not in a table row, text within a table that is not contained in a `td` or `th` tag, or an end tag that has no matching begin tag.

Most browsers are very forgiving about accepting poorly formed documents. In most cases, missing end tags and tags that are out of place are ignored and the browser simply formats the document as well as it can. In the case of text within a table that is not in a table element, the text is usually placed before the table. Other elements that simply cannot be understood are ignored by browsers.

Non-HTML tags are perfectly legal in HTML. The HTML standard defines many tag names, but does not exclude additional tag names. Browsers typically ignore all tags that are not recognized.

URLS, ANCHOR TAGS, AND
10.4 DOCUMENT REFERENCES

HTML lets you include references to *objects* (other pages on a site, external Web sites, or images) and Web services (such as e-mail) on any page. These references make HTML a powerful tool indeed. For example, they enable site designers to retrieve and display pictures and other elements to create attractive and useful Web sites. And they let visitors jump to other Web sites of interest and send e-mail messages, among other things.

The HTML source code shown in Figure 10.3 includes such references. Specifically, line 8 contains a reference to BigHit's logo, line 17 contains a reference to a reservation page, and line 23 refers to an image that is the multicolored line that separates the body from the footer. Line 25 refers to the homepage of the site, and line 31 to the e-mail address of the person who maintains the site.

A reference in one HTML-generated page to another object or Web service is represented by a **URL (Uniform Resource Locator)**, something you learned about in Chapter 2. Each URL tells the browser how to access the referenced object or service.

For example, the image (`img`) tag in line 8 of Figure 10.3 caused the browser to add BigHit Video's logo in the upper left corner of its welcome page. This tag directs the browser to fetch and display the referenced image. Line 8 contains the `src` attribute, which tells the browser where to get the image. In this case, the value of `src` is `bighit.jpg`. Whenever the browser displays the welcome page for a site visitor, it must get a copy of the logo to include in the displayed page.

A URL describes how and where to get any object (whether it's another document, an image, or another Web page). Consider the URL shown in Figure 10.4. This URL refers to a document describing HTML 4.0. If you wanted to know more about the latest version of HTML, you could type this URL into your Web browser and check out the document.

A URL has three components:

- A **protocol**, a mechanism used to fetch the desired object. For most information searches conducted by Web servers, the protocol is **http** (which stands for **Hypertext Transfer Protocol**). The protocol might also be `https`, which is a more secure version of HTTP.

- The **host machine**, the computer that contains the requested object. In this case, the host computer is `www.w3.org`.

- The **object name**, in this case, `/TR/REC-html40/`.

If you typed this URL into your Web browser, the browser would contact the computer `www.w3.org`, fetch the named document, and send it back to your computer. A URL with protocol, host machine, and object name is called an **absolute URL**.

The URL on line 8 in Figure 10.3 is `bighit.jpg`. This is a **relative URL**, meaning that the protocol and the host computer have been omitted. A relative URL is a reference to a document that is on the Web server that delivered the page that contains the URL.

FIGURE 10.4

URL Referencing an HTML Document

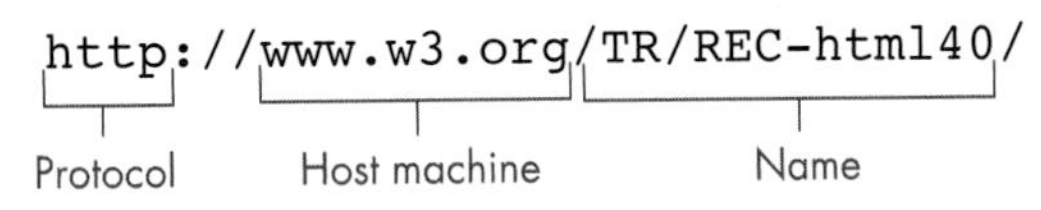

```
http://www.w3.org/TR/REC-html40/
```
Protocol   Host machine   Name

To turn a relative URL into an absolute URL, first determine the URL of the document that contains the relative URL. From the location field of the Internet Explorer page shown in Figure 10.2, we know that the URL of the containing page is

In this URL, the protocol is `http`, the host computer is **localhost** (the name that many computers use as a reference to themselves) and the object name is `/bighit/index.html`. Here, the name `localhost` refers to a Web server that's running on the same computer as the Web browser.

Once you determine the URL that contains the reference, you append the relative URL to the *base URL* of the page. In BigHit's welcome page, the base URL is

`http://localhost/bighit/`

Therefore, the absolute URLs that correspond to the relative URLs in lines 8, 17, and 23, respectively, of Figure 10.3 are

`http://localhost/bighit/bighit.jpg`
`http://localhost/bighit/reservation.html`
`http://localhost/bighit/hbar.gif`

A major advantage of relative URLs is that a collection of Web objects can be moved from one server to another without changing the relative URLs that link them. The absolute URL of a document changes if the document is moved to another server or to another location on the same server. If a document contains absolute URLs as references, the document must be modified whenever a linked document is moved. Relative URLs help to make the contents of documents less sensitive to their locations.

The `alt` attribute of the image tag in line 8 defines the text that the browser displays while the image is loading. With extremely large images, there may be a considerable delay before the image appears. During this delay, the browser represents the image by an area of the correct size, and displays the `alt` text in that area.

Clickable Web-page links, such as "Enter Video Reservation System" in Figure 10.2, let visitors jump to other Web pages. These links are underlined (if the user chooses), and are created by **anchor tags**. See lines 17–19, 25–27, and 31–33 in Figure 10.3 for examples of these tags. All anchor tags use tag name `a`. Also, the text between an anchor tag and its end tag is called a **hyperlink**. The use of the term "hyper" predates HTML and was used in the Apple Macintosh Hypertext system, among others. The term *hyperlink* refers to users' ability to jump from one page to another.

Lines 17–19 in Figure 10.3 contain a phrase bracketed by beginning and ending anchor tags (`<a>` and `</a>`). The `href` attribute of an anchor is a reference to another document, or another place within the same document. The value of `href` is a relative URL, like the image source URL in of Figure 10.3.

The footer of BigHit's welcome page was created by an image tag that produced the separating horizontal line (line 23 in Figure 10.3), a hyperlink to BigHit Video's Web-site home page (lines 25–27), and a `mailto` hyperlink (lines 31–33) by which site visitors can send e-mail messages to the site developer. The `href` of the anchor tag in line 31 uses the `mailto` rather than the `http` protocol. When site visitors click this link, the browser creates an e-mail form that lets the visitor send mail to the specified address. The e-mail form will be created in whatever mail software this browser is linked to. This may be Microsoft Outlook or some other e-mail package.

10.5 PRESENTING INFORMATION IN HTML TABLES

The HTML table gives Web sites a convenient way to show users and visitors the contents of a database table or the result of a database query. For example, a visitor to BigHit Video's Web site might want to check the due dates on the videos she is currently renting. Figure 10.5 depicts the current video rentals for a particular BigHit customer.

The table in Figure 10.5 uses a format consistent with the relational data model. A name for the table appears at the top, and the first row contains the names, or column headings, of the displayed fields. The remaining rows contain data values. Each row contains attribute values of a single object, in this case, a video rental.

The first row is formatted with a beige background and midnightblue boldfaced font. These visual clues indicate that the values displayed in the first row are not data values, but rather column headers. These headers are attribute names.

Each data row consists of information about a single rental. The video ID field has a beige background to indicate that this is the row's key, or identifier. The other values of the data rows are displayed against a lightcyan background with a normal (not boldfaced) font.

The HTML source for the table, as shown in Figure 10.6, begins by defining the table title (line 3). Lines 6–32 define the table. Line 6 specifies that the table will have a border that is 2 pixels wide and that each cell will have a default background color (attribute `bgcolor`) of `lightcyan`. This background color is used for the two data rows.

Lines 7–11 create the table's title (called a *caption* in HTML) and define all of its type specifications (font, use of color, and type size). For example, line 8 specifies that the caption is to be two sizes larger than the table text's default font and that the text color is `midnightblue`. The bold tag (<b>) specifies that the caption type is to be set in boldface.

Lines 12–17 create the first row of the table (a header, not a data row). The table row (<tr>) tag in line 12 begins the row. With the `bgcolor` attribute, this tag specifies a `beige` background color for the row. Table header tags (<th>) imply a bold font for the header text. Because the site designer set the background color for the whole row with the `bgcolor` attribute of the `tr` tag, each field within that row has a `beige` background. Each entry has its own `font` tag to specify its text as `midnightblue`.

Lines 18–24 and 25–31 specify the two data rows in the table. The first field in each of these rows contains a table header (in this case, a video ID number). The remaining three fields contain table data. The table's overall style calls for `beige` background for header elements and `lightcyan` for data elements. This style is created by the various tags' `bgcolor` attributes.

FIGURE 10.5
A Simple HTML Table

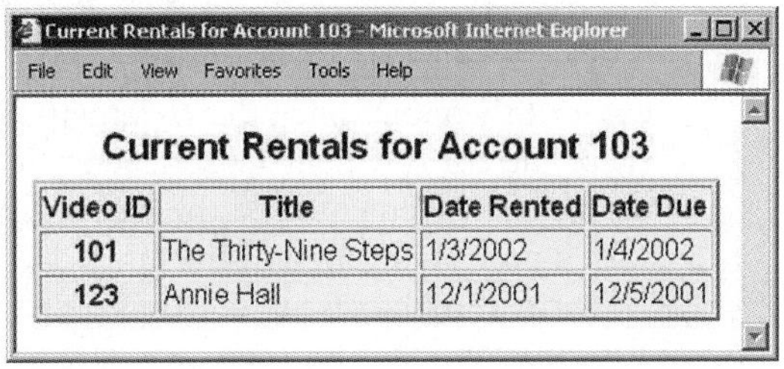

Video ID	Title	Date Rented	Date Due
101	The Thirty-Nine Steps	1/3/2002	1/4/2002
123	Annie Hall	12/1/2001	12/5/2001

```
1   <html>
2      <head>
3         <title>Current Rentals for Account 103</title>
4      </head>
5      <body>
6         <table border="2px" bgcolor="lightcyan">
7            <caption>
8               <font size="+2" color="midnightblue"><b>
9                  Current Rentals for Account 103
10              </b></font>
11           </caption>
12           <tr bgcolor="beige">
13              <th><font color="midnightblue">Video ID</font></th>
14              <th><font color="midnightblue">Title</font></th>
15              <th><font color="midnightblue">Date Rented</font></th>
16              <th><font color="midnightblue">Date Due</font></th>
17           </tr>
18           <tr>
19              <th bgcolor="beige">
20                 <font color="midnightblue">101</font></th>
21              <td>The Thirty-Nine Steps</td>
22              <td>1/3/2002</td>
23              <td>1/4/2002</td>
24           </tr>
25           <tr>
26              <th bgcolor="beige">
27                 <font color="midnightblue">123</font></th>
28              <td>Annie Hall</td>
29              <td>12/1/2001</td>
30              <td>12/5/2001</td>
31           </tr>
32        </table>
33     </body>
34  </html>
```

F I G U R E   10.6

HTML Source for a Table

You can see that lines 19 and 26 define the first element of each data row as a table header (note the th tag). Hence, each of these elements will have a bold font. The background color of these header elements is given in the th tag that defines each element. Because HTML does not support setting background colors of columns, the site designer must repeat formatting attributes (in this case, bgcolor) and font tags for each element.

The default background color of the data elements in each row is the background color of the table, since these elements' tr tags do not define bgcolor. That is, because the last three entries for each row (lines 21–23 and 28–30) are table data (note the td tags) elements and the bgcolor attribute is not defined, the elements appear with a non-bold font and the table-default lightcyan background color.

Formatting tables in HTML is quite complex, and site designers must specify many attributes and tags for each table element. Fortunately, enhancements to HTML have created a far superior way to define formatting styles. As you'll see below, you can use an HTML feature called **style sheets** to enforce consistent table styles. When you use style sheets, you can write far simpler HTML code to define table formatting. For ex-

Concept

XML, the Extensible Markup Language

XML is a variation of HTML and uses tags to mark up documents. XML is emerging as the best method for representing information that moves around the Internet. An XML document uses tags just like HTML, but whereas HTML tags are intended to describe the formatting of a document, XML tags are intended to describe the organization and meaning of a document. We can expect that XML will replace HTML in many Web sites in the near future.

The designer of an XML document is free to use any tag names that are appropriate for the document. XML has no predefined tag names. The following is an XML document that contains the same information as the first line of rental of Figure 10.5:

```
<?xml version="1.0" encoding="ISO-8859-1"?>
<rentals>
    <account> 103 </account>
    <rental>
        <videoId> 101 </videoId>
        <title>The Thirty-Nine Steps</title>
        <dateRented>1/3/2002</dateRented>
        <dateDue> 1/4/2002</dateDue>
    </rental>
</rentals>
```

You can see that the tag names `rentals`, `account`, `rental`, `videoId`, `dateRented`, and `dateDue` express the meaning of the data items. It is much easier to figure out what this document means than to figure out what the HTML document of Figure 10.6 means.

The XML version of HTML is called **XHTML**. The major differences between HTML and XHTML are that in XHTML, all HTML tag and attribute names must be lowercase, attribute values must be delimited by double quotes, and every tag must have a matching end tag. All HTML documents that satisfy these three conditions are XHTML documents. Most of the documents in this book satisfy the XHTML requirements.

Several software tools are available to help you check your HTML documents to see if they are in proper XHTML form. The XML Tidy tool that was developed by Dave Raggett is available on the Web. See the Further Reading section for a reference.

ample, you can define the background color and text color attributes for the various table elements in the style sheet and then omit them from the lines of code.

10.6 CONTROLLING HTML TABLE FORMAT WITH STYLE SHEETS

One standard method of using style sheets is through an HTML 4.0 software feature known as **Cascading Style Sheets (CSS)**. All Web browsers support CSS, although the evolution of browsers and CSS make certain versions of CSS incompatible with some browsers. The CSS examples presented in this section have been displayed with Microsoft Internet Explorer 5.5.

With CSS, you can define a default presentation style for each element of a table. Each instance of a particular element will take on the attributes of that element's defined style. The incorporation of style definitions significantly simplifies HTML documents. For example, consider the HTML code shown in Figure 10.7, which produces the page shown in Figure 10.8. Lines 3–10 contain style definitions for the table, the table caption, the table headers, and table data. Note that the remaining lines of code in Figure 10.7 have no formatting tags or attributes. Instead, the style definitions at the beginning of the document completely define the presentation of the table.

The style definitions in lines 3–10 of Figure 10.7 define default styles for the `table`, `caption`, `th`, and `tr` tags. Each occurrence of one of these tags in the actual table will be presented according to the corresponding defined style. Of course, the site designer could modify any of these styles by adding formatting tags or attributes to individual HTML elements.

FIGURE 10.7

Simplified HTML Source
Using CSS

```
1   <html>
2     <head>
3       <style type="text/css">
4         table{border-collapse:collapse}
5         caption{color:midnightblue; background-color:beige;
6             font-weight:bold; font-size:24px}
7         th{color:midnightblue;border:ridge;background-color:beige}
8         td{color:midnightblue;border:ridge;
9             background-color:lightcyan}
10      </style>
11      <title>Current Rentals for Account 103</title>
12    </head>
13    <body>
14      <table>
15        <caption>Current Rentals for Account 103</caption>
16        <tr>
17          <th>Video ID</th>
18          <th>Title</th>
19          <th>Date Rented</th>
20          <th>Date Due</th>
21        </tr>
22        <tr>
23          <th>101</th>
24          <td>The Thirty-Nine Steps</td>
25          <td>1/3/2002</td>
26          <td>1/4/2002</td>
27        </tr>
28        <tr>
29          <th>123</th>
30          <td>Annie Hall</td>
31          <td>12/1/2001</td>
32          <td>12/5/2001</td>
33        </tr>
34      </table>
35    </body>
36  </html>
```

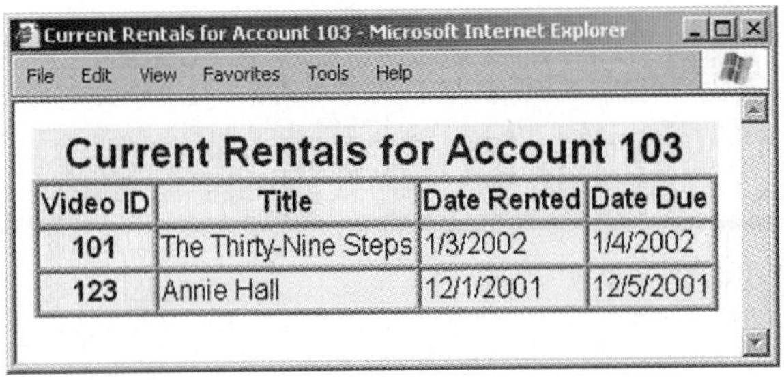

FIGURE 10.8

Results of HTML Code in Figure 10.7 Displayed in Internet Explorer

Note the `style` begin and end tags in lines 3 and 10 of Figure 10.7. Also note that each `style` tag must include the `type` attribute so that the browser knows how to interpret the style definitions.

Each style definition (lines 4–9) consists of a tag name and a set of attributes contained in set braces ({ and }). Each attribute name is followed by a semicolon and a value. Finally, each attribute is separated from the next by a semicolon.

Line 4 in Figure 10.7 defines the default style for all tables in the HTML document. This line does not include a background color, because the designer has defined the color of each table element in subsequent lines. In line 4, the attribute `border-collapse` indicates that the borders around adjacent table elements will be fused together. Without the value `collapse`, each table element would have its own border, and the borders will be separated by white space.

Clearly, the HTML code shown in Figure 10.7 is much simpler than that depicted in Figure 10.6. The designer didn't need to specify individual parts of the table or include font tags in the table elements. However, this code produces a table (see Figure 10.8) that differs in a few respects from the table in Figure 10.5. For example, the table caption in Figure 10.8 has a beige background, and the font for the table data elements is midnightblue instead of black. The designer accomplished these changes easily by using styles.

To see an example of the differences between browsers, look at Figure 10.9, which shows the Netscape 6.2 display of the HTML document of Figure 10.7. The most obvious difference between Figures 10.8 and 10.9 are the table borders. Netscape 6 does not recognize the `border-collapse` attribute of line 4 of Figure 10.7 and puts space between the cell borders. Internet Explorer would add the space between the table cells if `separate` was the value for `border-collapse`.

FIGURE 10.9

Results of HTML Code in Figure 10.7 Displayed in Netscape Navigator 6

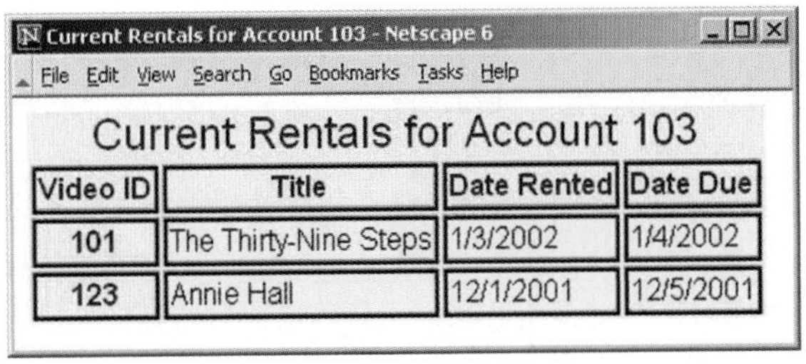

CSS2 Style Attributes

The names and meanings of style attributes in CSS2 are quite different from the names of tag attributes in HTML 4.0. For instance, the font family is specified in the HTML `font` tag with the `face` attribute, but in CSS it is done with the `font-family` attribute. Similarly, background color is `bgcolor` in HTML, but `background-color` in CSS.

The following table shows just a few of the attributes that can be specified with CSS styles. It is not surprising that books have been written about CSS. The CSS of this chapter is enough to control our pages, but full appreciation will require lots more study.

CSS2 Attribute	Meaning and Effect	Examples
Font Properties		
`font-family`	Allow the browser to choose the first font in the list that it supports	`font-family: Arial, Helvetica, sans-serif`

`font-size`	Determine the font size	`font-size: 14pt`
		`font-size: +2`
		`font-size: medium`

`font-style`	Specify the slant	`font-style: normal` `font-style: italic`
`font-weight`	Specify bold or normal	`font-weight: bold`
`font`	Specify all font attributes at once	`font: bold 12pt Arial, Helvetica`
Color and Background Properties		

`background-color`	Specify color behind the text	`background-color: blue`
		`background-color: transparent`
		`background-color: #FF0000`

`background-image`	Put an image in the background	`background-image: url(images/bighit.jpg)`

`color`	Specify foreground font color	`color: black`
		`color: rgb(255, 0,0)`
		`color: rgb(100%, 0, 0)`

Table Properties		
`caption-side`	Positions the caption at top, bottom, or either side	`caption-side: top` `caption-side left`
`border-collapse`	Specifies whether the table cell borders are combined	`border-collapse: collapse` `border-collapse: separate`

`border-style`	Specifies the style of cell borders	`border-style: ridge`
		`border-style: groove`
		`border-style: none`

`border-width`	Specifies width of cell borders	`border-width: 3px`

10.7 USING EXTERNAL STYLE SHEETS AND STYLE CLASSES

In addition to using styles to control tables, you would also want to create and be able to modify a style for all pages and all HTML elements in an entire Web site. To do that, you would have to be able to store the style description separately from the Web pages and create different presentations for different kinds of information.

External style sheets let you do all of this. As the first step in creating an external style sheet, write the style elements into a separate CSS file. Figure 10.10 shows the file `bighit.css`, which contains the four style settings created in the HTML code shown in Figure 10.7. This `bighit.css` file contains any settings that we might want to apply to all pages in BigHit Video's Web site. To define these style settings for the page shown in Figure 10.8, you would simply replace lines 3–10 of Figure 10.7 with the single `link` tag shown below:

```
<link rel="stylesheet" type="text/css" href="bighit.css">
```

This `link` tag specifies that the file `bighit.css` contains style elements for the page shown in Figure 10.8. The Web page will look the same regardless of whether we use the `link` tag or the embedded style elements shown in Figure 10.7.

Figures 10.5 and 10.8 show a customer's current rentals in a table all by itself. But most companies would want every page in their Web site to have a consistent design and to contain the company's name and logo, as shown in Figure 10.11. But in adding this customer rental page to the Web site's standard page, we would create a conflict in the formatting of the two tables. If you recall, the header of BigHit's stan-

FIGURE 10.10

The External Style Sheet
bighit.css

```
1    table {border-collapse:collapse}
2    caption {color:midnightblue; background-color:beige;
3        font-weight:bold; font-size: 24px}
4    th {color:midnightblue; border:ridge; background-color:beige}
5    td {color:midnightblue; border:ridge;
6        background-color:lightcyan}
```

FIGURE 10.11

A Borderless and Bordered
Table on One Web Page

dard page is formatted as a borderless table, and it doesn't share the specified background color, font size, and other attributes of the customer rental table. (See lines 6–14 of Figure 10.3 for the code that creates the BigHit Video header.)

If we did nothing about this conflict, we would see a page like that shown in Figure 10.12. In this figure, the lightcyan background and border styles of the `td` tag have been applied to the borderless header table—something we don't want. To keep the background of the header table white, we must tell the browser to use a different style for the header table. CSS supports the creation of style classes to make this possible.

A *style class* in CSS lets us define different presentation styles for two kinds of tables. For example, to create the page shown in Figure 10.11, we need to specify that the table entries (`td` elements) in the standard BigHit page heading have a different background and border from those of the table entries in regular information tables. Figure 10.13 shows how to define several style classes. For instance, line 2 in the figure causes any element that is defined as class `header` to have a white background and no border.

To define an element as class `header`, we simply add the `class` attribute, as in lines 7, 8, 9, and 12 in Figure 10.13. The HTML code that generates the heading shown in Figure 10.11 is in lines 1–6 of Figure 10.13. Note: These lines would normally be included in the `bighit.css` file, but they're shown here to make it easier for you to see the whole example.

INTERVIEW

JAKOB NIELSEN
Better Design for a New Medium

DESIGNING FOR A NEW MEDIUM The most universal mistakes on Web sites are:

1. Wrong balance in designing "look-and-feel," resulting in something that looks great but feels sluggish and unwelcoming.

2. Wrong information architecture that reflects the company's structure rather than the way users think about things.

3. Not giving sufficient priority to the users' top three tasks (often because the site doesn't even know the top reasons people visit the site—without knowing, you can't prioritize these top goals).

4. Being vague about what the site is about or what the company does. For example, having a tagline that could have been equally good for millions of other companies.

5. Bad search engine.

THINKING FOR A NEW MEDIUM Web design is completely different from traditional graphic design for print publications because the Web is interactive. Thus, Web design is interaction design first and foremost. In 1994 and 1995, it was misery every time we got a new graphic designer on a Web project, because we *knew* that he or she would spend the first several months creating designs that could not be used. It takes some time to retrain a designer to understand the characteristics for a new medium.

Luckily, there are now many graphic designers who have extensive experience with Web design and who can create designs that emphasize interaction and speed of download and are still aesthetically pleasing. It is a myth that usability requires sites to look bad. Usability simply requires designers to think about two problems: both how the site looks *and* how it will be used and to balance these two considerations. Creativity has nothing to do with excessive technology: Some of the best sites use the

FIGURE 10.12

Unwanted Application of Styles to the Header Table

The table tags in lines 7, 8, 9, and 12 of Figure 10.13 all have the attribute `class` with the value `header`. This specifies that all of these tags are in the class `header` and therefore should have a white background and no border.

simplest technologies on the actual pages, even though they often have very fancy stuff in the back room where users don't see it. Consider, for example, the feature on Amazon.com that says "people who bought this book also bought these four books." This feature looks like a simple bullet list of text-only hypertext links and yet it is one of the most creative designs in the history of the Internet, both in terms of user appeal and in terms of increased sales for the Web site.

A LIST OF THE TWENTI-ETH CENTURY'S BIGGEST THINKERS INCLUDES VANNEVAR BUSH AND BUGS BUNNY: Vannevar Bush invented the Web. At least, he has more claim to it than Al Gore :-) Seriously, Vannevar Bush wrote an important article in 1945, where he proposed a system for interlinking information so that professionals would have all the information they need at their fingertips. Two main differences between the system described by Bush and the Web: The Memex (as Bush called his "memory extender") was a very personalized sys-

> **"Bugs Bunny was a pioneer in being better than reality and showing what can be done when physics is no longer a constraint. . . .I view him as the patron saint of the Internet. To do really well on the Web requires us to stop thinking in terms of old media."**

tem that was focused on information that was relevant to you and your colleagues. Also, it was supposed to be implemented with microfilm, which was the best storage medium Bush could envision in 1945. Even though the system would be completely impractical to build with the *technology* that was known to Bush in 1945, the *ideas* were revolutionary and we are still quite far from having anything as useful or powerful as the Memex.

Bugs Bunny was a pioneer in being better than reality and showing what can be done when physics is no longer a constraint. Thus, I view him as the patron saint of the Internet. To do really well on the Web requires us to stop thinking in terms of old media. Don't make the Web like television. Don't blindly automate the way things were done in the physical world when you live in a virtual world. Just like Bugs Bunny was neither Humphrey Bogart nor the Barber of Seville, even when starring in a cartoon spoofing the opera. (For the rest of Nielsen's list visit: www.useit.com)

```
1   <style type="text/css">
2     .header {background-color: white; border:none}
3     td.header {text-align:left; vertical-align:center; font-size:28px}
4     .bighit {font-family: Arial; font-weight:bold}
5     .subtitle {font-style:italic; font-size: 24px}
6   </style>
7   <table class="header" summary="BigHit header">
8     <tr class="header">
9       <td class="header">
10        <br><IMG SRC="images/Bighit.jpg" alt="BigHit Video logo">
11      </td>
12      <td class="header" valign="middle">
13        <span class="bighit">BigHit Video, Inc.</span><br>
14        Outstanding Rentals<br>
15        <span class=subtitle>for customer Jane Block</span></td>
16    </tr>
17  </table>
```

F I G U R E 10.13

HTML Code Showing Class
Selectors

The style elements in lines 2–5 of Figure 10.13 further simplify the HTML code
that defines the header table. The `td.header` style element (line 3) creates the 28-
pixel font (`font-size: 28px`) and the vertical and horizontal alignment of the text
in the header.

Note the new tag, `span`, in lines 13 and 15. These tags specify different font styles
for the first and third lines in the header. A `span` tag and its end tag surround text
that would not otherwise be delimited by begin and end tags. The `span` tags divide
the HTML code for the header text into three sections that correspond to the three
lines of text we want to see on the displayed page. In this case, we can specify that the
header text "BigHit Video, Inc." is to be set in the Arial font family and bold font
weight by setting its `class` attribute to `bighit`. The `class` attribute in line 15 in
Figure 10.13 puts the header's subtitle ("for customer Katherine Harrison") in the
`subtitle` style class. According to the definition of `.subtitle` in line 5, the subtitle will appear in italic style and a smaller (24 pixel) font.

Learning to use CSS styles takes some practice. Once you've familiarized yourself a
bit more with styles, you can begin designing your own Web sites. By faithfully using
styles, you can create sites whose pages have a consistent look and feel—something
that your site visitors will greatly appreciate. You can also easily change the site's overall look by modifying external style sheets.

CASE IN POINT: DEFINING
10.8 **A STYLE FOR BIGHIT ONLINE**

In this chapter, we'll look at the basic design of the BigHit Online Web site by looking at a sample Web page. You'll be asked to produce your own Web site design as
your project for this chapter. Figure 10.14 is a customer information page for BigHit
Online. Some of the stylistic elements are highlighted by comment boxes. All of the
major components of the Web site are shown in this page. All of the pages will follow
this same basic look.

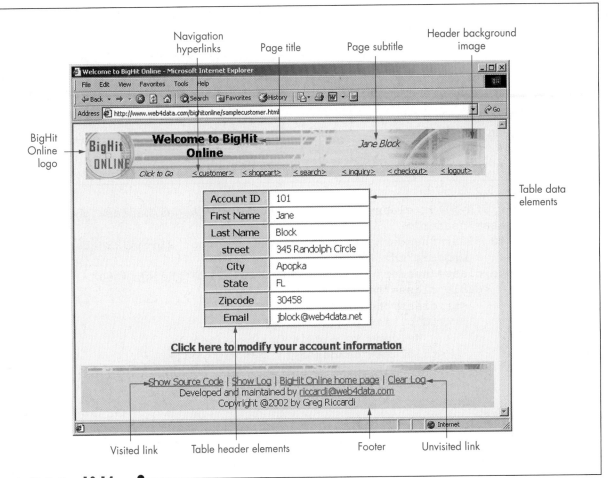

Navigation hyperlinks

Page title

Page subtitle

Header background image

BigHit Online logo

Table data elements

Visited link

Table header elements

Footer

Unvisited link

FIGURE 10.14

Sample Web Page for BigHit Online

The header of the customer information page contains a background image, as shown in Figure 10.15. This image was created from images that appear on the book's cover, with text added in the image of a DVD at the left. Adobe Photoshop was used to create the image.

The header text elements, including title, subtitle, and navigation buttons, are formatted inside a table with no borders. Figure 10.16 shows what the header looks like with visible borders. The logo is in a table element that is all of the rows of the first column. The rest of the first row of the table contains two elements, the title and the subtitle. The second row has 7 elements: a label "Click to Go" and 6 hyperlinks to other pages of the Web site. Part of the HTML code that produces the header is shown in Figure 10.17.

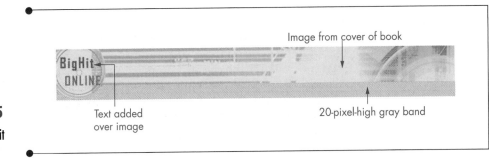

Image from cover of book

Text added over image

20-pixel-high gray band

FIGURE 10.15

Background Image for BigHit Online Header

F I G U R E 10.16

Header of BigHit Online Page
with Visible Table Borders

```
1    <table width="715" class="header" background="images/banner.jpg">
2     <tr class="header">
3         <td class="header" rowspan="2" valign="top" width="88" height="80">
4              </td>
5         <td class="header" valign="top" width="627" height="60">
6             <table class="header">
7                 <tr class="header">
8                     <td class="bighit" width="40%">
9                         Welcome to BigHit Online </td>
10                    <td class="header">
11                        <span class="subtitle">Jane Block</span></td>
12                </tr>
13            </table>
14        </td>
15     </tr>
16     <tr class="button"><td class="button">
17        <table class=header colspan=2 width="610">
18            <tr><td class="click" width="14%">Click to Go</td>
19                <td align="center" class="button" width="14%">
20                    <a href="customer.asp">&lt;customer&gt;</a>
21                </td>
22                <td align="center" class="button" width="14%">
23                    <a href="shopcart.asp">&lt;shopcart&gt;</a>
24                </td>
```

F I G U R E 10.17

Partial HTML Code for Header

It requires very precise formatting to control the location of the text on the images. The various table tags are given width and height attributes with exact numbers of pixels. Line 1 specifies the width of the table as 715 pixels and the background as the image of Figure 10.15. An image width of 715 pixels is very good because on the printed page it is 6.5 inches, which fits nicely on 8.5 by 11 paper. This image also fits inside the typical minimum-sized 800 by 600 pixel computer screen that people use.

The area of the table over the logo is described in lines 3 and 4. Attribute `rowspan="2"` specifies that this table element occupies 2 rows of the table. The `height` and `width` specify how much space to leave, and the ` ` on line 4 is a *non-breaking space*. The importance of a non-breaking space is that it occupies a little space, so that the table entry is not empty, but can't be seen.

The rest of the first row, given in lines 5–15 is a table element (`td`) that contains a table. This nested table effectively controls the spacing of the area that contains the title and subtitle. The title is 40% of the width of the nested table (line 8) and the subtitle (lines 10 and 11) is the rest of the width. The height of this row is 60 pixels, leaving 20 pixels for the gray area that contains the navigation links. The gray area at the bottom of the background image is exactly 20 pixels high.

The second row of the table begins to the right of the logo and is 20 pixels high. It also contains a nested table; each element occupies 14% of the whole width. The < and > that surround the hyperlinks (line 20) are created using < and > which are the HTML names of these symbols. We cannot simply write <customer> in line 20 because that would be the definition of a tag with name customer and would be ignored by the browser because it is not a recognized HTML tag name.

The style document for the sample page is shown in Figure 10.18. The first four lines define the font as 14 pt Tahoma and the background color as #f5f7c8, which is the light yellow. The color is expressed as three pairs of hexadecimal values, for the red, green and blue intensities. The value was determined by sampling the background picture for a good color and then using color selection software to lighten it until it was unobtrusive, but still colorful.

The default table style is defined in lines 6–12. The background color of the table headers (line 9) is the light gray of the bottom band on the header. The table data elements have a white background (line 11). This gray and white call attention to the tables with a clean crisp look.

FIGURE 10.18

CSS Style Document for
BigHit Online

```
1   /*style for whole document
2       body {font-family:tahoma; background-color:#f5f7c8; font-size:14pt}
3       .footer {background-color:#d8d8d8; border:none;}
4       h2 {font-size:18pt}
5   /* default styles for table elements */
6       table {background-color:black; border-collapse:collapse;}
7       caption {color:black; background-color:#d8d8d8;
8           font-weight:bold; font-size: 18px}
9       th {color:black; border:ridge; background-color:#d8d8d8;
10      padding: 3px 12px 3px 12px}
11      td {color:black; border:ridge; background-color: white;
12          padding: 3px 12px 3px 12px}
13  /* styles for other tables classes */
14      .header {border: none; color:black; padding: 0px 0px 0px 0px;
15          background-color:transparent}
16      td.header {text-align: center; vertical-align: center;
17          font-size: 20px; background-color:transparent}
18      .bighit {border:none; text-align: center; vertical-align: center;
19          font-size: 20px; font-weight:bold; background-color:transparent;
20          padding: 0px 0px 0px 0px}
21      .subtitle {border:none; font-style:italic; font-size: 16px;
22              background-color:transparent; padding: 0px 0px 0px 0px}
23      td.click {border:none; font-size: 10pt; color:black;
24          background-color:#d8d8d8; text-align:left; font-style:italic;
25          padding: 0px 0px 0px 0px}
26      td.button {border:none; font-size: 10pt; color:black;
27          background-color:#d8d8d8; text-align:center;
28          padding: 0px 0px 0px 0px}
29      td.button a:link {color:black}
30      td.button a:visited {color:black}
```

As we saw previously in the chapter, the `header` style class (lines 14–17) has no border. The padding, defined on line 14, specifies no extra space around table elements. This is necessary to make the precise sizes of the header elements work just right. The `bighit` style class (line 18–20) is used for the title area and the `subtitle` class (lines 21–22) for the subtitle area.

Finally, the `click` class (lines 23–25) is for the `Click to Go` label and the `button` class (lines 26–30) is used for the navigation links. These have no borders, no padding, and a 10 pt font.

Lines 29 and 30 show how to define the colors of hyperlinks using a compound style. The notation `td.button a:link` refers to the characteristics of an anchor (`a`) tag within an element with a `button` style. Style elements `link` and `visited` and `active` are used to specify the colors of the different kinds of links. An active link is one that is currently being clicked.

Lines 29 and 30 force the colors of the hyperlinks in the header to remain black even when they are visited. The hyperlinks in the footer of Figure 10.14 are either blue or purple. The blue ones have not been visited recently, and the purple link has been visited. These are the default colors for link states.

CHAPTER SUMMARY

This chapter explains how to present information in Web pages by using basic HTML conventions. The simple guidelines you learned here will help you understand how to create dynamically generated pages in the next few chapters.

An HTML document contains simple text and tags that organize the presentation of information for display by a Web browser. A tag consists of a less-than symbol (`<`), a tag name, a list of attributes and their values, and a greater-than symbol (`>`). A tag and its end tag (the matching tag that has the same tag name and starts with `</`) delimit a section of a Web page.

The chapter presents a variety of useful tags, including `table`, `tr`, `td`, `th`, `img`, `a`, `br`, `p`, `center`, `font`, `title`, `html`, `body`, and `caption`. These tags enable site designers to specify the format of various Web-page elements, including tables and their headings and data, as well as page headers.

An anchor tag (tag name `a`) creates a link to another page within a particular Web site or to an outside Web site, object, or Web service. The `href` attribute gives a location for another site, object, or service as a URL (Uniform Resource Locator). The HTML code lines delimited by the anchor tag and its end tag create a clickable link to the other site, object, or service. When visitors click on the link, the browser issues a request to access the site.

A URL consists of a protocol (usually `http`), a host machine, and a resource name. In many cases, the resource name is the name of a file that is stored on the host machine. Web browsers and servers use the `http` protocol to retrieve and display documents requested by site designers and visitors.

HTML's table tags enable designers to organize information in a tabular style. Most designers use table header (`th`) tags to identify the column or row headers and table data tags (`td`) to identify the table's data elements.

Cascading style sheets (CSS) let designers define the style characteristics of tables and other page elements with simpler code than through HTML. CSS also produces a more consistent style when all pages within a Web site use the same CSS documents.

CSS lets designers define style classes, which allow Web-page elements to appear in different formats for different situations. For example, the `header` style in the BigHit style sheet provides an alternative style for tables that are part of a document header.

KEY TERMS

Absolute URL. A URL that contains a protocol, host machine, and object name.

Anchor tag. An HTML tag that references another document; also called a *hyperlink*.

Cascading style sheet (CSS). A collection of style descriptions that specify the format of tagged information in an HTML document. CSS is a language for describing formatting. A style sheet may be included in an HTML document or stored as a separate document and referenced from HTML documents.

End tag. A tag that begins with `</`. A tag may be its own end tag if the tag ends with `/>`.

External style sheet. A cascading style sheet that is stored in a file and referenced from HTML documents with a `link` tag. An external style sheet is typically shared by many HTML documents.

Host machine. A computer that has a Web server. Also the portion of a URL that gives the name of the computer that hosts the resource.

HTML (Hypertext Markup Language). A standard language for representing text, formatting specifications, and hyperlinks.

HTML document. A text document that contains HTML source code.

HTTP (Hypertext Transfer Protocol). The standard for requesting and transmitting information between a browser and a Web server.

Hyperlink. A reference in an HTML document to another document or other object, possibly on another server.

Image tag. A tag that specifies a link to an image document that is to be displayed as part of the Web page.

Localhost. The name in a URL for the host machine that is running the browser.

Object name. The last part of a URL that designates a specific resource.

Protocol. A strategy for communicating between computers.

Relative URL. A URL that does not contain a protocol or a host machine, but only the name of a document. It is converted to a URL by appending the protocol and host machine of the page that contains the URL. The full URL also includes the directory path of the containing document, if the relative URL does not start with slash (/).

Style class. A collection of style elements in a CSS style sheet that is applied to tags through the use of `class` attributes.

Style sheet. *See Cascading Style Sheet.*

Table tags. A collection of several tags in HTML that specify the organization and format of tabular information. Tag names include `table`, `caption`, `tr`, `td`, and `th`.

Tag. A markup notation within an HTML document. Each tag begins with a less than symbol (<), has a name and a sequence of attributes, and ends with a greater than symbol (>). Each tag should have a matching end tag.

Title tag. The HTML tag that defines the title of the document that is shown in the header bar of the browser window.

URL (Uniform Reference Locator). A text string that is used as a reference to a Web resource. A URL consists of a protocol, a host name, and a document name.

XHTML. A version of HTML that conforms to the requirements of XML. Every begin tag must be matched by an end tag, every attribute value must be delimited by quote marks, and all HTML tag names must be lowercase.

XML. (Extensible Markup Language). An extension of HTML that is being extensively used for transmitting information on the Internet.

QUESTIONS

1. What URL is displayed in the address area of Figure 10.2? What URL is associated with the hyperlink in the body?

2. State which HTML tag accomplishes each of the following. Give an example of each.
   a. Specify the text to be included in the title bar of the browser window.
   b. Specify that text is to be displayed in bold face.
   c. Specify that text is to be displayed in italics.
   d. Specify that a picture is to be included in a document.
   e. Define a clickable reference to another document.
   f. Define a table header element.

3. What is a URL? Give an example. Then identify the protocol and the name of the Web server in your example.

4. What is the difference between a static Web page and a dynamically generated Web page? Give two reasons why a Web-site designer would create static pages. Give two reasons why a designer would create dynamic pages.

5. Consult an HTML reference. For each type of tag below, list each attribute that can be included and give its purpose.
   a. Anchor tag
   b. Base tag
   c. Title tag
   d. Paragraph tag
   e. Meta tag
   f. Table tag
   g. Table row tag
   h. Table header tag

6. Suppose that the following anchor tags are part of a page that has URL http://www.cs.fsu.edu/database/. Give the full URL for each anchor tag.
   a. `<a href="index.html">`
   b. `<a href="/bighit/login.html">`
   c. `<a href="http://www.awl.com">`
   d. `<a href="homeworks/hw1.html">`
   e. `<a href="mailto:riccardi@cs.fsu.edu">`

7. Consult a CSS2 reference. For each type of attribute below, list four attributes (not described in this chapter) that can be included and give their purposes.
   a. Font attributes
   b. Border attributes
   c. Table attributes
   d. Color attributes

8. What is the purpose of style classes in CSS? Give an example of the use of a style class.

PROBLEMS

9. Look at the source code for a major Internet retailer. Find the image tags that appear in the page. Create a simple HTML document that displays those images with image tags. Save the document in a file called exercise109.html on your Web site. Submit the source code and the URL of the document.

10. Modify the HTML document of Figure 10.2 so that your name and e-mail address is included as the title and subset and appears in the footer. Save the revised document in a file called exercise1010.html on your Web site. Turn in the source code and the URL of your new document.

11. Modify the style of the document of Figure 10.6 so that the background and foreground colors are different and so that all table header (th) elements are presented in bold and italic. Save the document in a file called exercise1011.html on your Web site. Turn in the source code for the document and its URL.

12. Create a simple HTML document that uses a table to display your name and address. Save the document in a file called exercise1012.html on your Web site. Submit the source code and the URL of the document.

13. Write an HTML document that uses a table to create a header with an image on the left and a page title on the right. Make sure that the page title appears both within the page and in the header of the browser window. Save the document in a file called exercise1013.html on your Web site. Submit the source code and the URL of the document.

PROJECTS

14. Design a new style for your own BigHit Video Web site.
    a. Select a color palette, font, background image, and a logo.
    b. Create a style sheet and save it in a file called mybighit.css
    c. Revise the document of Figure 10.11 to use the new style.
    d. Save the document in a file called mybighitsample.html. Turn in the source of the style sheet and the HTML document along with the URLs of the two documents.

15. Design a new style, a welcome page, and a style for your own BigHit Online Web site.
    a. Select a color palette, a background image, and a logo. Design a header and footer for the site.
    b. Create a style sheet and save it in a file called mybighitonline.css.
    c. Create a welcome page as an HTML document. Include a header and footer in the style defined in part (a) and a sample table showing the names and dates of some new movie releases (you can make up the content). Also include a link to the page created for part (d).
    d. Create a sample page showing information about a purchase by a particular customer based on your Movie Lovers database. Save the page as samplepurchase.html.
    e. Save the document in a file called mywelcome. html.
    f. Turn in the source of the style sheet and the HTML document along with the URLs of the two documents.

16. Design a new style, a welcome page, and a style for your own Movie Lovers Web site.
    a. Select a color palette, a background image, and a logo. Design a header and footer for the site.
    b. Create a style sheet and save it in a file called mymovielovers.css.
    c. Create a welcome page as an HTML document. Include a header and footer in the style defined in part (a) and a sample table showing the names and dates of some new movie releases (you can make up the content). Also include a link to the page created for part (d).
    d. Create a sample page showing member information for a customer based on your Movie Lovers database. Save the page as samplemember.html.
    e. Save the document in a file called mywelcome. html.
    f. Turn in the source of the style sheet and the HTML document along with the URLs of the two documents.

FURTHER READING

A wealth of information about HTML and CSS is available on the W3C (World Wide Web Consortium) Web site at http://www.w3.org. The definition of HTML 4.0 and of CSS 2 are included, along with many commentaries and references. The books by O'Reilly and Associates are uniformly helpful. Of particular interest are the HTML guide [MuKe00] and the CSS guide [Meyer00]. The Addison-Wesley Web Wizard series (http://www.aw.com/info/webwizard/) includes an excellent introduction [Leh02]. Many other excellent HTML books are available at every bookstore.

XML information can be found at the W3C site (http://www.w3.org). The Microsoft XML site (http://www.microsoft.com/xml) is truly worthwhile. Microsoft is making significant contributions to XML development. The HTML Tidy program for checking HTML documents for conformance to XHTML standards is available from http://tidy.sourceforge.net.

Creating Interaction between Users and Servers with ASP and JavaScript

- How dynamic Web sites are organized
- How HTML allows user input with forms
- How user input is sent from browser to server

- How Web servers produce dynamic Web pages
- How to write programs that accept user input and produce Web pages in response

We are ready to add dynamically generated Web pages and user interaction to our Web sites. In this chapter, you will learn to create Web pages that allow users to enter data. You will also learn to create Web applications that respond to each user request by generating an HTML document.

The HTML documents of the previous chapter were all written by a developer and stored in files. A particular collection of pages was available, and users were able to choose among them. After studying that chapter, you have learned the skills necessary to write HTML documents for use as static Web pages.

Of course, many Web sites are not static. Truly interactive Web sites allow users to enter information that is collected by the browser and sent to the Web server. The Web server then determines which application should respond and sends the user's information to that application.

In this chapter, you will learn how to create interaction between users and Web servers. You will see many examples, and design and develop your own. By the end of the chapter, you will have learned how to write simple programs. You will understand how to decide what a program should do and how to write it so that it works.

You will be able to fully appreciate the material in this chapter only if your reading is accompanied by practice. You will see practical examples of programming discussed in detail. However, without trying for yourself, you will not be able to master the material, or even to learn enough to understand the subsequent chapters. You will encounter the basics of Web applications programming through a series of examples. Each example program introduces new programming techniques at the same time that it shows how to solve specific problems in Web-site development.

If you have no previous experience with computer programming, this may be the hardest chapter in the book for you to master. You certainly will have to pay very close attention to detail and you will have to practice writing programs. The chapter includes several concept boxes that explain some of the basic principles of programming. Don't skip those concepts.

The programming examples in the chapter are fragments of larger programs. The full text for all of the examples can be found on this book's Web site at http://www.web4data.com/bighit. You should install these applications on your own Web site and experiment with them. The Web site includes detailed installation instructions and all of the software you need to make your own Web sites.

This chapter begins by describing the basic strategies that browsers and Web servers use to communicate. Extensive examples demonstrate the capabilities of Web servers and show the details of how we can develop Web applications. In the next chapter, we'll look at how these services can be integrated with databases.

11.1   THE ARCHITECTURE OF DYNAMIC WEB SITES

When a user clicks a button on a Web page, the browser begins an interaction with a Web server that results in a new page appearing on the user's screen. Figure 11.1 illustrates the steps in that interaction. The outer boxes represent the two computers involved and the inner boxes represent the execution of software programs that interact to process the user's request.

When the user enters data into fields of a Web page and clicks on a button (Step 1), the browser collects that data from the Web page and sends it to the Web server (Step

FIGURE 11.1

Architecture for Dynamic Web Site Request

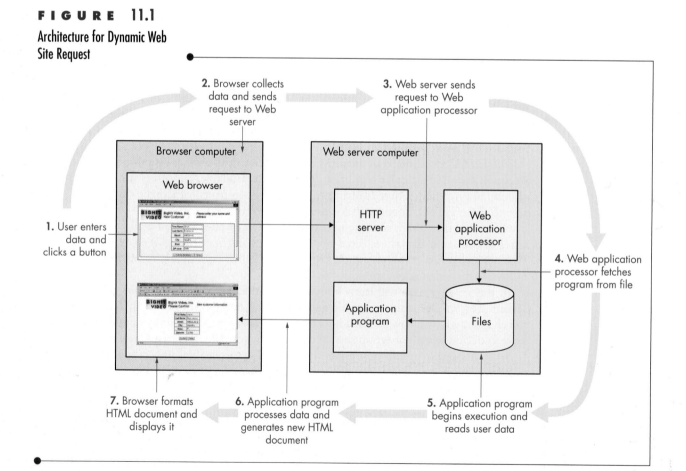

2). The browser and server send information back and forth using a protocol called HTTP. The HTTP protocol specifies a dialog between the browser and server. In essence, the browser says "hello" and the server says "what do you want" and so on. Of course, this dialog is carried out not in English, but in some esoteric computer-speak. You do not need to know the details of this dialog. You do need to understand what happens as a result.

The browser gives the Web server all of the information collected from the Web page. The Web server does not process the information, but must hand it off to some Web application processor (Step 3). The **Web application processor** is a program that knows how to execute certain kinds of requests. Later, you will be learning about the Microsoft ASP (Active Server Pages) processor.

The application processor then analyzes the request and decides which application program, called a **Web application**, it must execute to service this request. The person responsible for the Web page must have provided the Web server with a program to handle this request. In Step 4, the application processor fetches the application program from where it is stored in a file and initiates its execution (Step 5).

The application program reads the user's data and generates an HTML document as its response (Step 6). The document is sent back to the browser, which formats the document and displays it for the user (Step 7).

In this architecture, a Web site is a collection of Web pages and many of the pages are created dynamically by Web applications. Thus, the Web site is essentially a collection of static HTML documents and Web applications.

As you study this chapter, you will learn how to

- Create Web pages that allow users to enter data and click buttons
- Create requests for the execution of specific programs
- Develop your own programs to service user requests
- Generate HTML documents as responses to user requests
- Create a Web site by defining a collection of Web applications

Once you've learned these fundamental skills, you will be ready to add databases to your Web sites.

11.2 DESIGNING HTML FORMS FOR USER INPUT

Forms in HTML, like the Microsoft Access forms discussed in Chapters 6 and 8, are graphical interfaces that allow users to enter data. The forms we developed in Access contain a variety of input elements, including text boxes, check boxes, drop-down lists, and buttons. The same variety of input elements is available in HTML. Your challenge in this section is to learn the capabilities of HTML forms and to understand how to design HTML forms that are intuitively easy for users.

Our first example of an HTML form is a Web page that collects personal information from a new customer of BigHit Video. We'll look at a sample form and analyze the HTML that defines it. Then we'll investigate how to write an application program that reads the customer information and shows it back to the user in a new page.

11.2.1 Creating a Customer Information Form in HTML

An **HTML form** collects data from users for transmission to a Web server. Consider the simple form shown in Figure 11.2. A new customer has entered her name and address. The page has a new header style from the page shown in Figure 10.2. The layout of the header has been reduced in height to make the pages more compact. The title and subtitle are now laid out horizontally instead of vertically. The footer of the page is below the edge of the browser and is not shown.

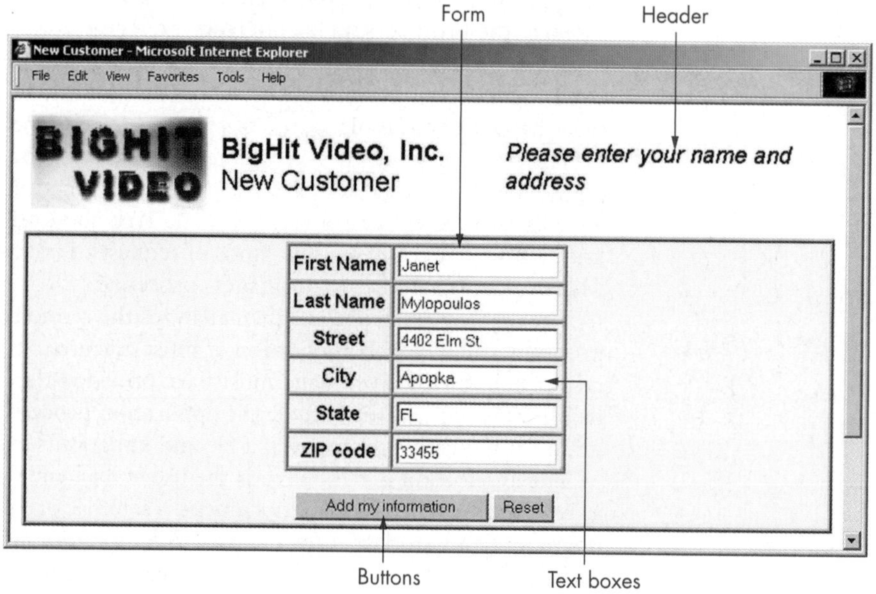

FIGURE 11.2

BigHit Video Page with
Customer Information Form

The form on this page consists of the table in the center of the page and the two buttons. A border and background color surrounding the form were added to the page for emphasis. The form has 6 text boxes, one for each field in the name and address, and 2 buttons.

The HTML source for the body of the form is shown in Figure 11.3. Line 1 begins the form with a `form` tag. The `action` attribute specifies the URL of the program that processes the information collected by the form. The URL is a relative

FIGURE 11.3

HTML Source for the Form of
the Page of Figure 11.2

```
1   <form method="GET" action="newcustomer.asp">
2      <table>
3         <tr><th>First Name</th>
4            <td><input type="text" size="20" name="firstName"></td></tr>
5         <tr><th>Last Name</th>
6            <td><input type="text" size="20" name="lastName"></td></tr>
7         <tr><th>Street</th>
8            <td><input type="text" size="20" name="street"></td></tr>
9         <tr><th>City</th>
10           <td><input type="text" size="20" name="city"></td></tr>
11        <tr><th>State</th>
12           <td><input type="text" size="20" name="state"></td></tr>
13        <tr><th>ZIP code</th>
14           <td><input type="text" size="20" name="zipcode"></td></tr>
15     </table><br>
16     <input type="submit" value="Add my information">
17     <input type="reset">
18  </form>
```

reference to a program called `newcustomer.asp` in directory `bighit`. Because the relative URL begins with `/`, it is relative to the root directory of the Web server and not to the directory that contains the HTML source document of the page.

The form contains a table, several text input fields, and two buttons. As described in Chapter 10, the table format is specified by an external style sheet. Each row consists of a table header element (`th` tag) with a text label and a table data element (`td` tag) with a text input box.

The text input box in the first row is defined by line 4 of Figure 11.3. The **input tag** specifies that a form element should be placed in the table. Its `type` attribute, with value `text`, designates this as a one-line text field. The `size` attribute, with value `20`, tells the browser to allocate enough space to display 20 characters. The `size` attribute does not put a limit on the number of characters that can be entered, only on the number displayed.

The `name` attribute, with value `firstName`, gives a name to the value entered in the text field. This name and the value are transmitted by the browser to the server as part of the HTTP protocol.

When a user clicks the **submit button** (line 16) on the form, the browser collects all of the information in the input fields, encodes and formats it in a specific style, and transmits it to the Web server as an **HTTP request**. The `action` attribute of the `form` tag in line 1 defines the URL of the Web application that will receive this request. The Web server, in turn, initiates the execution of the specified application and makes the input information available to that program.

The information made available to the application program includes much more than just the inputs. The HTTP request has quite a few attributes, including the browser type, URL of the request, the name of the Web server, and the request action, as represented by the `action` attribute of the `form` tag. The book's Web site contains a Web application (`showrequest.asp`) that displays many of the attributes of an HTTP request. (Try it!)

The `method` attribute of the form tag in line 1 of Figure 11.3 has value `GET`. In the HTTP specification, a **GET method** is translated into a URL that includes the input information from the form. A GET method transmits the program name and the information in a single step. The alternative is a **POST method**, in which the program name is part of the URL and the input information is transmitted separately. In most cases it doesn't matter whether a form uses `GET` or `POST` for interaction. You'll see some of the differences in these two methods in the next section.

Eight form elements are listed in the body of this form—each has `input` as its tag name. The first, on line 4, is named `firstName` and is a single-line text box with room to display 20 characters. The `input` tag of line 4 of Figure 11.3 produces the text box in Figure 11.2 that contains the value "Janet." The value is not part of the page specification, but has been typed into the text box by the user.

The form elements on lines 16 and 17 represent the two buttons on the form. The `submit` input type is the special input that when clicked causes the form information to be submitted to the Web server. The `reset` input type, when clicked, clears the values in the form fields. The `value` attribute of the `submit` input on line 16 is the text that appears as the label of the button.

11.2.2 Understanding Browser-Server Interaction with HTTP

HTTP describes two methods of transmitting information from a browser to a server. The `GET` method appends the form contents to the URL given in the `action` attribute and sends the result to the server. The `POST` method sends the information in two steps. First, the browser contacts the server specified in the action attribute. Once contact is made, it sends the form contents.

The form contents are formatted as a sequence of name–value pairs, with each pair separated from the next by an ampersand (&). We call this sequence a **query string**.

The format of the query string is called the *Internet Media Type* `application/x-www-form-urlencoded`. For the form of Figure 11.2, the contents are represented as follows:

```
firstName=Janet&lastName=Mylopoulos&street=4402+Elm+St.
    &city=Apopka&state=FL&zipcode=33455
```

The query string contains a sequence of names and values. The names come from the `name` attributes of the input elements. The values come from the input fields on the form. One effect of the encoding can be seen in the pair with value `street`:

```
street=4402+Elm+St.
```

In the value portion of this pair, each space that was typed into the form has been replaced by a plus sign (+). This part of the encoding is necessary because blanks are not allowed in query strings. Details about query string encoding are included in the next section.

When Janet Mylopoulos clicks the `submit` button on this form, the actual URL is put together as the base URL, the relative URL from the `action` attribute, a question mark (?) that separates the program locator from the data, and the form contents, encoded as above. The result is the following URL:

```
http://localhost/bighit/newcustomer.asp?firstName=Janet
    &lastName=Mylopoulos&street=4402+Elm+St.&city=Apopka
    &state=FL&zipcode=33455
```

We call a URL that represents a GET request an **active URL**.

An active URL can be used directly as a hyperlink by making it the value of the `href` attribute of an anchor tag. It can also be typed directly into the location field of a browser. Pasting the preceding active URL into the location text area of a browser will have the same effect as clicking the `submit` button on this form. We'll see later in the chapter how active URLs can be used in hyperlinks.

When you click the `submit` button on a form, a new Web page is displayed in the browser. The address field of the browser will show the URL of the HTTP request. With a GET request, the address field of the browser will include the full query string. This can be very convenient to users. For instance, if you modify the URL in the ad-

---

Concept

HTTP POST Method

With a POST method, the URL does not include the question mark and query string. The HTTP interaction for POST starts with the browser sending the application name to the server. After the server responds, the browser sends the query string. Thus, the POST method separates the name of the application program from the query string.

The POST method has major advantages for developers. Because the URL does not include the query string, neither does the address field of the browser. Thus, the user does not get to see the details of the request. By removing the query string from the URL, the POST method also bypasses restrictions that servers or browsers place on the length of a URL.

One disadvantage of the POST method is that it requires browsers to clear the form elements when the page is reloaded. You may have had the experience of making mistakes filling in a complicated form. If you press `submit` and the resulting page is not what you wanted, you'd like to use the browser's Back button to return to the form. With a POST method, however, you'll find all of the fields of the form returned to their default values.

dress field and press the `Enter` key, the new URL will be interpreted as a `GET` request by the Web server.

As we will see later, it is possible in an HTML form to have multiple values for the same variable. The query string represents this situation by having the same variable represented in multiple name–value pairs, one for each value of the variable. We'll see examples later.

Concept

Encoding HTML Form Data

The data that are transmitted from the browser to the server are encoded in a simple style—one that relies on a collection of delimiters, including `?`, `=`, and `&`. **URL encoding** also requires that all information be represented as printable characters that can be part of a URL. These two constraints demand that HTTP information be encoded. An encoding strategy must be used to represent delimiter characters used as data and nonprintable characters. This encoding is included in the Internet Media Type `application/x-www-form-urlencoded`. Spaces are replaced by plus signs (+). Each delimiter or nonalphanumeric character is replaced by the three-character sequence `%XX`, where `XX` is the hexadecimal representation of the ASCII code for the character.

The following table shows a text string and its encoding. The digits, letters, and period (.) are not modified. The spaces are encoded by pluses (+) and the symbols +, &, <, and / are encoded as the hexadecimal values `%2B`, `%26`, `%3C`, and `%2F`, respectively.

The Encoding of a Text String as a URL

		Character-by-Character Encoding									
String	`104 x+& </.`	1	0	4		x	+	&		<	/	.
Encoding	`104+x%2B%26+%3C%2F.`	1	0	4	+	x	&2B	&26	+	&3c	&2F	.

Fortunately, we don't have to worry about explicitly encoding or decoding HTTP strings. The browser extracts the information and encodes and formats it. All of the standard Web application programming languages, including ASP, have modules that perform encoding and decoding.

WRITING WEB APPLICATIONS IN ASP AND JAVASCRIPT

We are ready to write the Web application to accept the customer information from the new customer form and process it. From Figure 11.1, you can see that the Web server sends the HTTP request from the form to an application processor that initiates the execution of the Web application. Before we can proceed further, we need to choose a specific application processor from the many that are available.

The early developers of Web technology defined the **Common Gateway Interface (CGI)** protocol to describe how Web servers and Web applications can interact. CGI is designed primarily for Web servers that run with the Unix operating system and does not work very well with the Microsoft Windows operating system. The development of CGI moved the Web from static to dynamic Web sites. CGI is a very useful tool and is the foundation of many dynamic Web sites.

The Microsoft **Internet Information Server (IIS)** is a Web server for Windows that includes an alternative to CGI. IIS is distributed as part of the Windows NT, Windows 2000, and Windows XP operating systems. The Internet Server Application Programming Interface (ISAPI) makes it easier for Windows application developers to create Web applications. Software developers use ISAPI to build the application processors that provide the interface between the Web server and the Web applications that handle dynamic requests.

Early in the development of IIS, Microsoft designers introduced the **Active Server Pages (ASP)** Web development technology. ASP is both an application processor that knows how to run Web applications and a language for writing Web applications. We are primarily concerned with the ASP language, and you will write many Web applications using ASP. Figure 11.4 shows how dynamic pages are processed using IIS and ASP.

ASP programs are written in a **scripting language** that mixes program code and HTML. An ASP program, also called an **ASP script**, is an HTML document that has programming language statements interspersed within the HTML statements. The HTML statements create the basic structure of the page and the programming language statements fill in the details. Figure 11.5 shows a sample ASP script. We'll begin by looking at the structure of ASP scripts and then look at what they mean.

An ASP document is divided into simple HTML code (black text) and ASP programming code (highlighted text). In Figure 11.5, the symbols <% and %> delimit ASP programming code. Everything not surrounded by these symbols is simple HTML. In Figure 11.5, lines 1 and 4–6 are ASP code and lines 7, 9, and 12 contain pieces of ASP code. All the rest is regular HTML. ASP code in figures in this book is always shown using blue type.

The ASP script begins in line 1 with a special ASP tag that specifies which programming language is used in the program. The programming code in an ASP script can be written in any of several programming languages. Many ASP scripts use VBScript, which is an adaptation of the Microsoft Visual Basic programming language. In this book, we will use JavaScript, a language that was originally developed by Netscape and has subsequently become an international standard language.

FIGURE 11.4

Dynamic Web Site Architecture with IIS and ASP

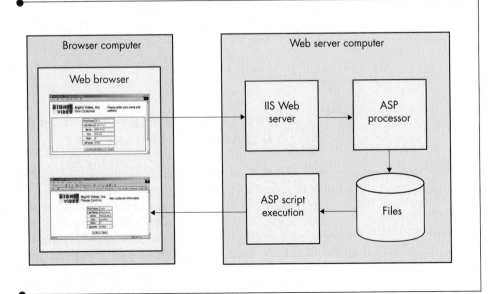

```
1   <%@LANGUAGE="JavaScript"%>
2   <html>
3       <link rel="stylesheet" type="text/css" href="bighit.css">
4       <% // begin javascript code
5           var id;
6           id = 459;
7       %>
8       <title>Account ID: <%= id %> </title>
9       <center><table>
10          <caption>Account ID: <%= id %> </caption>
11          <tr>
12              <th>Account ID</th>
13              <td> <%= id %> </td>
14          </tr>
15      </table></center>
16  </html>
```

FIGURE 11.5

ASP Document
simple.asp That
Prints an Account ID

Line 4 starts with `<%` to mark the beginning of a code segment. The rest of the line is a JavaScript comment. The two slashes (`//`) mean that the rest of the line is ignored by the ASP processor.

JavaScript, like any programming language, has the ability to create and manipulate **variables** which are named locations that store values. Line 5 is a **variable declaration**, which serves to declare that a variable named `id` will be used in the program.

Concept

The JavaScript Programming Language

JavaScript was originally designed for use within Web browsers to add dynamic behavior to Web pages. JavaScript is loosely based on the Java programming language and shares many of Java's programming styles. With JavaScript, Web page developers can create animations and other special behaviors. JavaScript programs that run in Web browsers are called **client-side programs** because the Web browser is the client in the client-server Web environment. We'll see examples of client-side JavaScript programs in Chapter 15.

Our major concern is with writing JavaScript programs that execute within the Web-server environment. These programs are called **server-side programs**. If you are looking for a reference book on JavaScript to help you study Web application development, be sure to look carefully at the table of contents to see how much of the book is devoted to server-side programming. Most JavaScript books are completely client-side and thus won't be very useful for us on the server side.

JavaScript has been standardized under the name **ECMAscript** by the ECMA, an industry association dedicated to the standardization of information and communication systems. ECMAscript includes both client-side and server-side programming tools. Server-side JavaScript is supported in the Netscape Web server and in IIS. Don't be confused by references that talk about JScript, which is simply Microsoft's name for JavaScript.

Line 6 assigns the value `459` to that variable using an **assignment statement**. An assignment statement consists of a variable name (in this case `id`), an equal sign, and a value (in this case `459`). The value of the variable `id` can be used in any subsequent JavaScript code within the document and appears in lines 8, 10, and 13. The statements in lines 5 and 6 end with semicolons to satisfy syntactic rules of JavaScript. As a general rule of thumb, each JavaScript statement should be terminated by a semicolon.

You'll have to be careful when typing JavaScript because it is a case-sensitive language. In JavaScript `id` is not the same as `ID`. It is possible, but not good practice, to create two different variables, one called `id` and one called `ID`.

The purpose of this little ASP script is to produce the page shown in Figure 11.6. The number `459` appears in three places in the page. It appears in the title bar of the browser, in the caption of the table, and in the right-hand table element. You will also notice that the URL of the page is a reference to the script `simple.asp`.

Figure 11.7 illustrates the behavior of the ASP application processor, which is a program that runs inside the Web server. The ASP application processor reads the ASP document and executes the ASP code segments (shown in blue), in their order from top to bottom and left to right. Then it removes the ASP code and replaces it by any results of that execution. Lines 1 and 4–7 simply disappear, since they have no results. They have an effect on later execution, but do not directly produce output.

The code segments in lines 8, 10, and 13, however, do have results. Each of these code segments is the same.

```
<%= id %>
```

The contents of the code segments (`= id`) seem to be saying that the value of the variable `id` should be assigned, or copied, somewhere. It looks like an assignment statement with no left-hand side. It actually means that the value of `id` is to be copied into the surrounding HTML code. The arrows in Figure 11.7 show that replacement of ASP code by values.

Figure 11.8 shows the HTML source for the page of Figure 11.6. Most of the HTML is the same as Figure 11.5 with the ASP code removed. The line numbers have changed because of the removal of original lines 4–7. The real difference can be seen in the new lines 3, 5, and 8, where ASP code has been replaced by the (highlighted) value `459`. That is, it has been replaced by the value of the variable `id`.

Now you know a major characteristic of ASP scripts. Values that are created and stored in variables can be used later in the program. In the case of the script of Figure 11.5, the value `459` is stored in the variable `id` and used three times to produce content in the HTML output.

F I G U R E 11.6

Browser View of the Result of Executing the Script of Figure 11.5

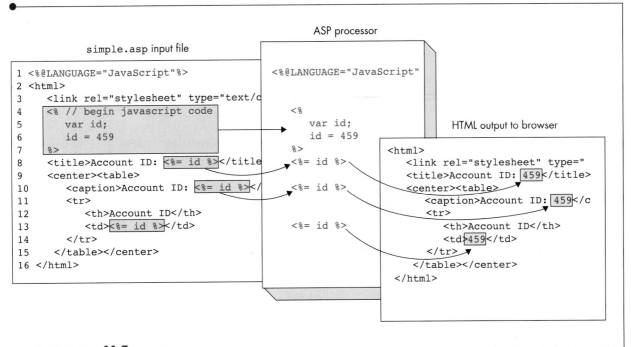

FIGURE 11.7

Transformation of ASP Script
into HTML

```
1   <html>
2     <link rel="stylesheet" type="text/css" href="bighit.css">
3     <title>Account ID: 459</title>
4     <center><table>
5       <caption>Account ID: 459</caption>
6       <tr>
7         <th>Account ID</th>
8         <td>459</t>
9       </tr>
10    </table></center>
11  </html>
```

FIGURE 11.8

HTML Code That Produces the
Display of Figure 11.6

11.4 PROCESSING FORMS WITH ASP AND JAVASCRIPT

Let's continue the example of the previous section by allowing the value of the variable **id** to be specified by a request variable, as would happen if the value had been entered in an HTML form in a browser. We want to make the ASP script fetch the value of the request variable and put that value into the HTML output.

Editing ASP Scripts

ASP scripts are simple text files that can be created and edited with any text editor. Microsoft WordPad could be used, for instance. The Microsoft Script Debugger is a very helpful tool that allows the editing of ASP scripts and also provides help in finding and fixing errors. The picture below shows the ASP script of Figure 11.5 as it is displayed by the script debugger. You can see that the ASP code is highlighted in yellow and the HTML parts are displayed in various colors. We'll see more of the script debugger later. The script debugger can be downloaded from the Microsoft Web site.

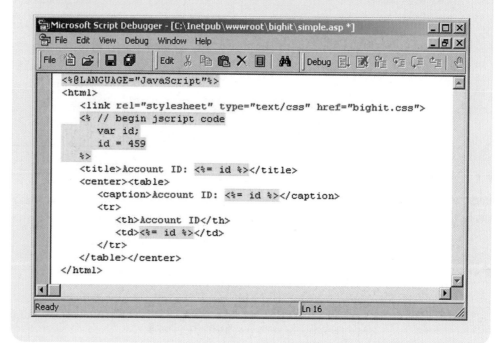

Let's suppose that we have a form with a text input field with name `accountId` and the value `459` has been entered into the text field. Pressing the `submit` button will result in a request like this:

```
http://localhost/bighit/simpleaccount.asp?accountId=459
```

This request is for an ASP script called `simpleaccount.asp` using a variable called `accountId` with a value `459`. The query string is `accountId=459`.

ASP stores the query string and other information in an object called `Request`. (You'll read about objects in Section 11.5.) We can get the value of the variable `accountId` from the `Request` object with the following statement:

```
id = Request("accountId");
```

In this JavaScript statement, the `Request` object is asked to produce the value of the `accountId` request variable.

We need only modify the script of Figure 11.5 by replacing line 6 with the above line to produce the script `simpleaccount.asp`. You can look at `simpleaccount.asp` on this book's Web site.

We are now ready to look at an ASP script that processes the information of the new customer information form of Figure 11.2. A person who wants to become a customer will fill out the form of this figure. The Web server will respond by displaying

Concept

Hidden Input Elements in HTML Forms

Hidden input elements are used by Web designers in HTML documents to store information that will not be shown to users. Some information is hidden so that it cannot be modified and some is hidden so that users will be unaware of it.

Hidden elements are used in Figure 11.9 because the information is being sent from one Web application to the next. The new customer information that was entered in the form (Figure 11.2) is displayed in Figure 11.9 as simple HTML text (lines 22–26 of Figure 11.10). The user cannot change this information since it is not displayed as form elements. Without the hidden input elements, the customer information would not be included in the query string that is sent with the request created by clicking the submit button. Thus, the customer information is repeated in the hidden elements and included in the next request.

In other Web pages, hidden fields are included so users will be unaware of it. A Web site may track information about users and store it in hidden fields. As a sophisticated Web user, however, you can look at the page source and see any hidden values.

the information that has been entered. Once the user confirms that the information is correct, an application will add the new customer to the database. The response to the form of Figure 11.2 should look like Figure 11.9. We will defer issues of how to put this new customer into the database until Chapter 12.

Figure 11.10 has a portion of the ASP script that produces the page of Figure 11.9. The first thing to notice about this code is that again it is a combination of HTML and ASP. Lines 1–8 are ASP code, delimited by <% and %>, and lines 10–26 are HTML, with some <%= blocks included.

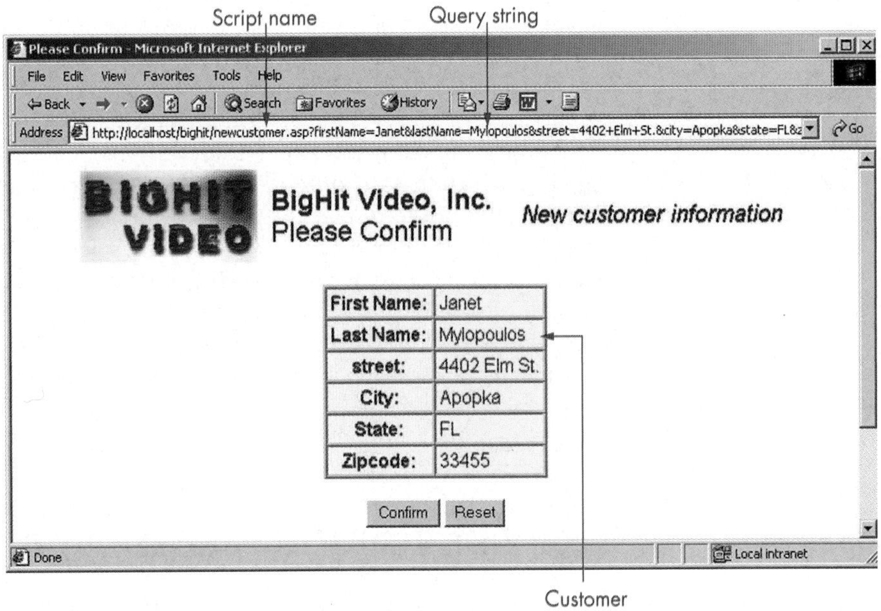

FIGURE 11.9

Confirmation Form for a New Customer

```
1  <% var firstName, lastName, street, city, state, zipcode;
2     firstName = Request("firstName");
3     lastName = Request("lastName");
4     street = Request("street");
5     city = Request("city");
6     state = Request("state");
7     zipcode = Request("zipcode");
8  %>
9  <form method="GET" action="addcustomer.asp"><center>
10    <table>
11       <tr><th>First Name: </th><td> <%=firstName%> </td></tr>
12       <tr><th>Last Name: </th><td> <%=lastName%> </td></tr>
13       <tr><th>street: </th><td> <%=street%> </td></tr>
14       <tr><th>City: </th><td> <%=city%> </td></tr>
15       <tr><th>State: </th><td> <%=state%> </td></tr>
16       <tr><th>Zipcode: </th><td> <%=zipcode%> </td></tr>
17    </table><br>
18    <input type="submit" value="Confirm"> <input type="reset">
19    <!-- hidden fields to hold customer info-->
20    <input type="hidden" name="firstName" value="<%=firstName%>">
21    <input type="hidden" name="lastName" value="<%=lastName%>">
22    <input type="hidden" name="street" value="<%=street%>">
23    <input type="hidden" name="city" value="<%=city%>">
24    <input type="hidden" name="state" value="<%=state%>">
25    <input type="hidden" name="zipcode" value="<%=zipcode%>">
26 </center></form>
```

FIGURE 11.10

Partial ASP Script That Produces
Figure 11.9

The block of code in lines 2–7 fetch the values of the request variables and store them in JavaScript variables of the same name. The output table is produced by lines 10–17. No muss, no fuss. However, the rest of the script (lines 19–25) may be unfamiliar.

Line 9 shows the beginning of an HTML form, line 18 defines submit and reset buttons, and lines 20–25 contain input elements. Although the buttons appear on the form of Figure 11.9, no input elements are obvious. The reason is *hidden* in the types of the input elements of lines 20–25. The type of these input elements is hidden, which tells the browser to keep track of the request variables for these input elements, but not to display them. The values of hidden input fields are stored in the browser and submitted to the Web server with any other request variables.

In this form, the new customer information is displayed as simple text values in the table, and hidden in input fields for use by the ASP script that processes the form. From line 9, we know that a script called addcustomer.asp will process the new customer confirmation. That script appears as Figure 12.14 and is explained in Chapter 12.

11.5 USING OBJECTS IN ASP AND JAVASCRIPT

An **object** in a programming language is very much like an entity in a database. An object is a collection of attributes and their values. Just like an entity is a member of an entity class, an object is a member of an **object class**. Each object in the class has the same collection of attributes, which we'll call **fields**, but the attributes values are different from one object to another.

An object-oriented programming environment adds functionality to object classes by allowing developers to create units of code, called *functions* or *methods*, that are part of the object class. A programming language such as JavaScript provides a way of creating objects and a way of initiating the execution of methods.

In this section, you will learn about how to use objects in your programming. We're not going to see the full capabilities of object classes, but just enough to get started. Additional object classes and capabilities will be introduced as they are used in the programming examples of this and subsequent chapters.

The examples in this section are based on some of the predefined object classes that are available to ASP and JavaScript programmers. We'll start with objects that store text values and move on to the objects that allow programmers to interact with the Web server.

11.5.1 Strings in JavaScript

A `String` object in JavaScript has a value that is simple text. The values of the request variables are text, for instance. You will recall that we encountered strings in SQL when we used string literals in Chapter 9. Both SQL and JavaScript provide extensive mechanisms to create and manipulate text information. Table 11.1 shows some JavaScript examples of string literals, assignment statements, and string-valued expressions. We will see many more as we explore JavaScript.

The first 2 rows of Table 11.1 are simple assignment statements that assign a string literal to a variable. The literal is enclosed in double quote marks (row 1) or single quote marks (row 2). In contrast, SQL requires single quotes and does not allow double quotes to enclose a string literal. Row 3 of the figure shows the use of the plus sign (+) to concatenate strings. Here we concatenate the first and last name with a space in between.

Rows 4 and 5 of the table demonstrate how we can embed quote marks within a string literal. Row 4 uses a single quote to delimit the string literal. The double quotes inside the literal are treated just like any other character. In row 5, the backslash (\) before a double quote means that the quote mark is to be included in the string. Without the backslash, the quote mark would denote the end of the string. As we saw in Chapter 9, quote marks in SQL literals are created by replacing each embedded (single) quote mark by two quote marks.

Other special symbols are also created by preceding a character with a backslash. The end-of-line character is \n, as in row 6, the tab character is \t, etc.

Table 11.1 String Expressions in JavaScript

	String expression	Result
1	firstName = "Janet";	variable `firstName` has value `Janet` (double quotes)
2	lastName = 'Mylopoulos';	variable `lastName` has value `Mylopoulos` (single quotes)
3	firstName + " " + lastName;	the string `Janet Mylopoulos`
4	'name="lastName"'	the string `name="lastName"` including quote marks
5	"name=\"lastName\""	the string `name="lastName"` including quote marks
6	"</td>\n"	the string `<td>` followed by an end-of-line character

JavaScript supports an extensive collection of methods for manipulating strings. So far, you've seen string literals, string concatenation, and string assignment. Later on, you'll learn how to determine the length of a string and how to look inside strings to find and extract text that matches a variety of patterns.

11.5.2 **The `Request` and `Response` Objects in ASP**

The ASP environment includes several predefined objects. The most important of these to us are the `Request` and `Response` objects. The **Request object** has attributes and methods that represent the HTTP request that initiated the execution of the script. The **Response object** has attributes and methods that allow the script to create the response that will be returned to the browser.

We have already seen a simple example of the `Request` object when we extracted request variables. `Request` has several fields, including `QueryString`, `Form`, and `ServerVariables`. The `QueryString` field contains the variables from a GET request and the `Form` contains the variables from a POST. Figure 11.11 shows part of an ASP script that displays a table of information from the `Request` object and Figure 11.12 shows the resulting Web page. You can see this code in action at this book's Web site using the script `customerrequest.asp`.

Lines 1–6 display information from the `QueryString` field of `Request`. You create a JavaScript reference to a field of an object by giving the name of the object, then a period, then the name of the field. In line 2, the reference is `Request.QueryString`. In line 4, `Request.QueryString.Count` is a reference to a field of a field of `Request`. In essence, `Request.QueryString` is an object with its own field named `Count`.

Line 6 shows a call on a method of `Request` that gets the value of the `street` request variable. You create a method call by giving the name of the object, then a period, then the name of the method then a list of values in parentheses. In line 6, the

FIGURE 11.11

Part of an ASP Script to Display Information from the **Request** Object

```
1   <tr><th>QueryString</th>
2      <td> <%=Request.QueryString%> </td></tr>
3   <tr><th>QueryString.Count</th>
4      <td> <%=Request.QueryString.Count%> </td></tr>
5   <tr><th>QueryString("street")</th>
6      <td> <%=Request.QueryString("street")%> </td></tr>
7   <tr><th colspan="2">Server Variables </th>
8   <tr><th>HTTP_ACCEPT_LANGUAGE </th>
9      <td> <%=Request.ServerVariables("HTTP_ACCEPT_LANGUAGE")%> </td></tr>
10  <tr><th>HTTP_REFERER </th>
11     <td> <%=Request.ServerVariables("HTTP_REFERER")%> </td></tr>
12  <tr><th>HTTP_USER_AGENT</th>
13     <td> <%=Request.ServerVariables("HTTP_USER_AGENT")%> </td></tr>
14  <tr><th>REQUEST_METHOD </th>
15     <td> <%=Request.ServerVariables("REQUEST_METHOD")%> </td></tr>
16  <tr><th>REMOTE_HOST </th>
17     <td> <%=Request.ServerVariables("REQUEST_METHOD")%> </td></tr>
```

11.6 USING OBJECTS AND METHODS TO IMPROVE CODE

As programmers, we can create our own objects and our own functions. In the presentation of JavaScript programming in this and the next chapters, you will discover many benefits of organizing programs into objects and functions. In this section, we look at scripts that produce the header and footer for our pages and ones that help in processing customer information.

The BigHit Video Web site that is emerging from this chapter is created by a collection of ASP scripts. Each ASP script defines a Web application that services specific requests and produces a particular type of page. We've seen an example in the script `newcustomer.asp` that services the request to accept new customer information and produces the new customer confirmation page. Each additional type of page—rental check out, rental check in, employee time card, purchase order, etc.—will have its own ASP script.

Now you are ready to learn how you can share JavaScript code between these scripts.

11.6.1 Defining Functions That Produce the Page Header and Footer

We want to make sure that every page in the BigHit Video Web site has the same style of header—the same layout, font, and image. Only the title and subtitle are different from one page header to another. We certainly do not want to write JavaScript code to generate the header and add that code to every Web page. Fortunately, JavaScript provides the function definition and function call mechanisms to allow this code to be written once and used in many places.

A **function** in JavaScript is a group of statements that perform a designated task. Lines 1–25 of Figure 11.13 show the complete definition of function `printHeader`, whose task is to print the HTML code needed for the header area of a page, and a portion of `printFooter`, whose task is to print the footer of BigHit Video pages.

Each function definition begins with its header, consisting of the keyword `function`, the name of the function (`printHeader`), a list of variable names enclosed by parentheses, and an opening set brace (`{`). A function definition ends with the matching closing set brace (`}`). Set braces are used in many places in JavaScript to enclose sections of code.

As you can see in function `printHeader`, JavaScript functions can have HTML sections embedded within the function. Line 3 ends the JavaScript section with `%>` and starts an HTML section, which continues until line 20. Notice that the closing set brace for `printHeader` (line 22) is part of the ASP code, not the HTML.

Functions can have **parameters**, which are variables used to pass values into functions. The parameters are listed between parentheses in the header of the function. Function `printHeader` has two parameters named `title` and `subtitle`. Function `printFooter` (line 23) has no parameters. Its parentheses enclose no parameter names.

The parameters are variables of the function and can be used just like any other variables. For instance, in line 6, the `title` parameter is inserted into the output using a JavaScript section to produce the title of the Web page.

A function is used in a script by the execution of a **function call**, which is an expression that consists of the name of the function and a list of values for its parameters, separated by commas. These values are called the **arguments of the function call**. Lines 27–29 contain sample calls on functions `printHeader` and `printFooter`. The call on `printHeader` in line 27 has string literals as the values for both `title` and `subtitle`. The call in line 28 has a string concatenation expression for the value of `subtitle`. The subtitle of the page is to be the word `Welcome`, a space, the first name of the customer, another space, and the last name of the customer.

```
1   <%
2   function printHeader(title, subtitle) {
3   %>
4       <head>
5           <link rel="stylesheet" type="text/css" href="bighit.css">
6           <title> <%=title%> </title>
7       </head>
8   <body bgcolor="white">
9   <!Header block>
10      <center><table class="header" summary="BigHit header">
11          <tr class="header">
12              <td class="header">
13                  <IMG SRC="images/Bighit.jpg" alt="BigHit Video logo"></td>
14              <td class="header" valign="middle">
15                  <span class="bighit">BigHit Video, Inc.</span><br>
16                  <%=title%> <br>
17              <td class="header" valign="middle">
18                  <span class=subtitle> <%=subtitle%> </span></td>
19          </tr>
20      </table></center>
21      <%
22  }
23  function printFooter () {
24      // printFooter has no parameters, its body goes here
25  }
26  // sample calls on functions printHeader and printFooter
27  printHeader("New Customer","Please enter customer information");
28  printHeader("New Customer Receipt","Welcome "+firstName+" "+lastName);
29  printFooter();
```

FIGURE 11.13

Definition of Function
printHeader, Part of
printFooter, and
Two Function Calls

In the BigHit Video Web site directory, the definitions of `printHeader` and `printFooter` are in a file called `bighittools.js`. This file is used by all of the ASP scripts. Each script has an `include` statement that tells the ASP processor to include the function definitions of file `bighittools.js`:

```
<!-- #include file="bighittools.js" -->
```

One more important characteristic of functions is that they can return values to the caller. We'll see an example in the next section.

11.6.2 Creating and Manipulating Objects

JavaScript is a rich language with many features. You will need considerable study and practice to become expert in its use. This chapter tries to present a few of the most useful features so that we can use JavaScript for our BigHit Video Web site. The use of functions, as in the previous section, can greatly simplify our code and reduce programming effort. We are able to create groups of statements, name each group as a function, and easily use the functions in multiple contexts.

This section presents the next logical step, which is to create a group of variables as a single object. An **object** in JavaScript is a collection of variables and functions (also called **methods**).

We have already made extensive use of the `Request` and `Response` objects of ASP. We've fetched request variables from `Request` and used the `write` method of `Response` to generate HTML. It's time to create our own objects.

In the ASP scripts of this chapter, we use the fields of the customer as a group of values. It would simplify and organize our programs if we had a customer object that contains a variable for each of the customer's data fields. Figure 11.14 contains function `makeCustomer` that creates such an object from the request variables of the `Request` object.

The first step in creating and populating the customer object is to create a general purpose object using the `new` operator (line 2). JavaScript defines class `Object` for this purpose. `Object` is a class whose objects can have any fields that they are assigned. The `new` operator asks JavaScript to create a new object. Lines 3–8 assign values to fields of the object, and at the same time create those fields. You may have noticed that line 2 is a single statement that combines the declaration of variable (`var`) `customer` and an assignment of a value to the variable. This is allowed in JavaScript and is considered good practice.

Function `makeCustomer` creates an object, populates its fields, and then returns it to the caller in line 9. A call to `makeCustomer` might be contained in an assignment statement:

```
cust = makeCustomer();
```

When this statement is executed, a new object would be created and its value stored in the variable `cust`.

Figure 11.15 illustrates an object as it would be created by a call to `makeCustomer` for the customer Janet Mylopoulos shown in Figures 11.2 and 11.9. The whole object is shown as a table with a rounded border. At the top we have the name of the variable that contains the object. The left column contains the names of the fields and the right column the values of the fields.

An illustration of the use of customer objects is given in Figure 11.16. Here we have a function called `writeCustomer` that extracts the values from the fields of a customer object and writes those values as 3 lines of HTML. A pair of function calls are included in lines 8 and 9. The call on line 8 creates a new customer object and stores it in variable `cust`. In line 9, that customer object is passed to function `writeCustomer`, where it becomes the value of parameter `c`.

FIGURE 11.14

Function **makeCustomer** That Creates a Customer Object from Request Variables

```
1   function makeCustomer() {
2       var customer = new Object();
3       customer.firstName = Request("firstName");
4       customer.lastName = Request("lastName");
5       customer.street = Request("street");
6       customer.city = Request("city");
7       customer.state = Request("state");
8       customer.zipcode = Request("zipcode");
9       return customer;
10  }
```

customer	
firstName	"Janet"
lastName	"Mylopolous"
street	"4402 Elm St."
city	"Apopka"
state	"FL"
zipcode	"33455"

FIGURE 11.15

An Object Created by
makeCustomer

```
1  // definition of function
2  function writeCustomer(c) {
3      Response.write(c.firstName+" "+c.lastName+"<br>\n");
4      Response.write(c.street+"<br>\n");
5      Response.write(c.city+", "+c.state+" "+c.zipcode+"<br>\n");
6  }
7  // call on functions
8  var cust = makeCustomer();
9  writeCustomer(cust);
```

FIGURE 11.16

Using Customer Objects
and Function
writeCustomer

Within the function `writeCustomer`, the value of parameter `c` is used as a customer object. In line 3, for instance, the expression `c.firstName` is used to extract the value of the `firstName` field of the object. You can see this code in action in the ASP script `simplecustomer.asp`.

11.6.3 Using `with` Statements to Simplify Code

You can reduce the use of object names in your programs by using the `with` statement in JavaScript. You may have noticed that we often use the same object over and over again within a section of code. In lines 3–8 of Figure 11.14, for instance, each line begins with `customer`. Lines 3–5 of Figure 11.16 feature repetitions of the objects `Response` and `c`. We can introduce a `with` statement to eliminate this repetition.

Figure 11.17 is a revision of function `writeCustomer` that takes advantage of the capability of `with` statements. Lines 2–6 show the general form of the `with` statement. It begins with the keyword `with` and an object enclosed in parentheses. The body of the statement (lines 3–5) is enclosed in set braces. The meaning of the `with` statement is that any variable in the body may be associated with the object named in the statement. In this case, all of the variables in the arguments of the calls to `Response.write` are considered fields of the object `c`. Line 3, for instance, uses the shorthand `firstName` to refer to `c.firstName`. and `lastName` to refer to `c.lastName`.

We can also put more than one `with` statement together. Figure 11.18 shows the revision of function `writeCustomer` to shorten references to `Response.write` in addition to the previous use of `with (customer)`.

After studying this chapter and practicing JavaScript programming with the examples and exercises, you will be ready to add database interactions to your dynamic Web sites.

11.7 CASE IN POINT: WRITING JAVASCRIPT CODE FOR BIGHIT ONLINE

In this case study, we'll look at a new customer form for BigHit Online and some of the HTML and programming issues that must be addressed to create the Web applications.

The new customer form is shown in Figure 11.19. The only new HTML in it is the password input elements. The HTML for these is

```
< input type="password" size=20 name="password">
< input type="password" size=20 name="repeatpwd">
```

FIGURE 11.17

Revised Function
writeCustomer
Simplified by a **with**
Statement

```
1   function writeCustomer(customer) {
2      with (customer) {
3         Response.write(firstName+" "+lastName+"<br>\n");
4         Response.write(street+"<br>\n");
5         Response.write(city+", "+state+" "+zipcode+"<br>\n");
6      }
7   }
```

FIGURE 11.18

Writing a Customer Using Two
with Statements

```
1   function writeCustomer(customer) {
2      with (Response) {
3         with (customer) {
4            write(firstName+" "+lastName+"<br>\n");
5            write(street+"<br>\n");
6            write(city+", "+state+" "+zipcode+"<br>\n");
7         }
8      }
9   }
```

The HTML form input type `password` creates a text input field whose value is not shown. We can see how many characters have been typed, but not the values. Be careful, though, because the value is obscured but not secure. With simple HTML forms like these, the values of password fields are transmitted in plain text between browser and server. To get a secure password facility we must use the secure HTTP (HTTPS) protocol or some other security tool. The Further Reading section includes references to Web site security information.

You've already seen the page style of Figure 11.19 in Chapter 10 (Figure 10.14) so we don't need to discuss all of the details of creating the `printHeader` function. For the most part, we simply plug the HTML of the header into the `printHeader` method of Figure 11.13 and then substitute `<%=title%>` wherever the title appears in the HTML code, etc. However, we'll take a little extra care with the navigation hyperlinks that appear in the gray bar at the bottom of the header.

Software developers all know that any program that has users will have to be changed, and probably changed often. People who use software are always demanding changes and we want to identify places where changes are likely. Good software developers try to anticipate changes and write programs that are easy to change. These navigation hyperlinks are a prime candidate for modification, so let's build a function to generate them that will be easy to change. The HTML code for the first two navigation links of Figure 11.19 is shown in Figure 11.20. The other four links are the same.

What is likely to change? The names of the links might change, the targets might change, and the number of links might change. The JavaScript code to generate this HTML must be flexible so that if the number of links changes, the code reacts automatically. You can see in line 2 of Figure 11.20 that the width of each link is

FIGURE **11.19**

New Customer Form for
BigHit Online

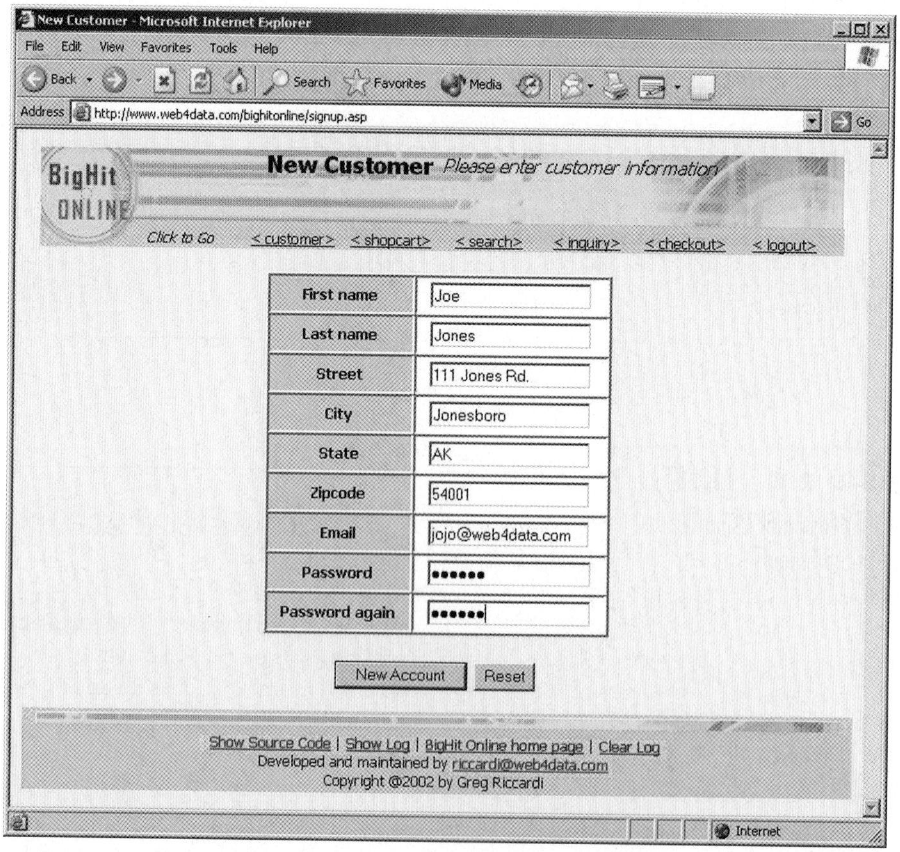

14.2857142857143% of the width of the entire table. This value, with all of its decimal digits, is the JavaScript result of dividing 100 by 7, the number of elements in the table.

So let's begin by looking at the JavaScript code in Figure 11.21 that defines the items that are likely to change. Each of the two variables holds a list of values in a type of object called an **array**. Variable `links` is a list of the targets of the hyperlinks and the variable `labels` is a list of the text that should appear on the page.

The list of fields in an array object are referenced by their position in the list. That is, the reference is by the number of the element. Each array also has a field called `length` whose value is the number of elements in the list.

The code to print the navigation links is shown in Figure 11.22. It has several new JavaScript features, including numerical calculations and looping—that is, executing a block of code several times. Lines 2 and 3 create variables to hold the number of links and the width of each link as a percentage. The expression `links.length` is the number of elements in array links. In this case, `numLinks` is 6. The number of elements in the navigation table is 7 because the table includes the links plus the label `Click to Go`. Thus, the variable `widthLink` is set to 100/7.

Now that we know how many links we have and how wide each should be, we need to generate the hyperlnks by going through the array one element at a time. Looping through the elements of an array is accomplished using the `for` statement of JavaScript, as shown in lines 7–12. The general form of a `for` statement is

```
for (initialization ; condition ; increment) {
    body of loop
} // end of loop
```

The italics marks those parts of the `for` statement that vary from one to the other. The `for` statement in line 7 has `i=0` for the *initialization*, `i<numLinks` as the *condition*, and `i++` as the *increment*. The body of the loop is in lines 8–11.

The execution of a `for` statement begins by executing the initialization. This sets the value of the variable `i` to 0. Next, the condition is executed. In this case, we are

FIGURE 11.20

HTML Code for the First Two Navigation Hyperlinks for BigHit Online Header

```
1   <table class="header" colspan=2 width="610">
2      <tr><td class="click" width="14.2857142857143%">Click to Go</td>
3      <td align="center" class="link" width="14.2857142857143%">
4         <a href="customer.asp">&lt;
5            customer&gt;</a>
6      </td>
7      <td align="center" class="link" width="14.2857142857143%">
8         <a href="shopcart.asp">&lt;
9            shopcart&gt;</a>
10     </td>
```

FIGURE 11.21

Declaration of Variables to Hold Hyperlink Information

```
1   var links = ["customer.asp","shopcart.asp","search.asp",
2      "inquiryform.asp","checkout.asp","logout.asp"];
3   var labels = ["customer","shopcart","search","inquiry",
4      "checkout","logout"];
```

```
1   function printButtonBar() {
2       var numLinks = links.length;
3       var widthLink = 100/(numLinks+1);
4   %> <table class=header colspan=2 width="610">
5       <tr><td class="click" width="<%=widthLink%>%">
6           Click to Go</td>
7       <% for (i=0; i<numLinks; i++) { %>
8           <td align="center" class="link" width="<%=widthLink%>%">
9               <a href="<%=links[i]%>">&lt;
10                  <%=labels[i]%> &gt;</a>
11          </td
12          <%}// end of for loop %>
13      </tr></table>
14  <%}
```

FIGURE 11.22

Function **printButtonBar** That Prints the Navigation Hyperlinks

testing to see if the value of i is less than 6 (the value of numLinks). Since i has value 0 from the initialization, the condition is true.

After the condition evaluates to true, the body of the loop (lines 8–11) is executed and then the increment is executed. After the first execution of the body of the loop, the increment statement i++ adds one to the variable i, resulting in a new value of 1. Then the condition is evaluated again, and again it is true (1<6). The execution continues with the body, then the increment, and again the condition.

The loop continues execution until the condition is false. In this loop, the condition is false when i has the value 6. The body is executed 6 times.

Each execution of the body generates one table data element. The first execution generates lines 3–6 of Figure 11.20 and the second execution generates lines 7–10. Each time through, the value links[i] is used for the target of the link and labels[i] is used for the label of the link. The square brackets are used to identify an element of an array.

We can now change the navigation links in the header by simply changing the declaration of variables links and labels.

We'll see more about arrays and for statements in the next chapter when we use them for iterating through the columns and rows of database tables.

The full details of generating the BigHit Online header and footer can be found in the bighitonline directory of this book's Web site.

CHAPTER SUMMARY

HTTP (Hypertext Transfer Protocol) supports interactions between browsers and Web servers. The browser can collect user input, encode it according to the URL encoding standard, and create requests for the Web server. The application program can accept a request, process it, and write a new HTML document. The Web server sends the output HTML document back to the browser.

HTML forms provide a means for browser users to enter information that can be transmitted to a Web server as part of a request. A form is defined by form

begin and end tags. The action attribute of the form tag defines the URL of the application program that will process the form. The value of the method attribute specifies which of the two request methods (GET or POST) is used by the form.

A GET request is processed by a URL that consists of the action parameter followed by a question mark (?), followed by the request variables, suitably encoded. A POST request is implemented by a two-stage process: The URL is sent to the Web server and then the encoded request variables are sent.

A variety of form input elements are placed within the form. The `input` tag has several types, including `text` for a single line text field, `submit` for a button that submits the form, and `reset` for a button that returns the form to its default values. Each form element has a `name` attribute that defines a request variable. It is possible for many form elements to share a single name.

The request variables are sent to the Web application program as a sequence of name–value pairs separated by ampersands (`&`). The variable names and values are encoded using URL encoding in which a blank is replaced by + and special characters such as =, &, and + are replaced by hexadecimal codes. The forms processor in the browser encodes the values automatically. Modules within the ASP execution environment decode the values for the application program.

A GET request can be used directly as a hyperlink by creating a string consisting of the URL of the application program, followed by ?, followed by the encoded request variables.

Microsoft Active Server Pages (ASP) is a Web programming tool that embeds programming code in HTML documents. The code is placed between symbols `<%` and `%>` to separate it from the HTML portion of the program. An ASP document can contain any number of code segments.

The Microsoft IIS Web server contains a module that processes ASP scripts. The ASP processor reads the ASP file, extracts and executes the code segments, and puts the HTML segments together with the HTML produced by the code segments. The resulting HTML document is delivered to the browser as the response to its request.

JavaScript is an international standard programming language that can be used within ASP to create Web applications. This use of JavaScript is called server-side programming. JavaScript is better known as a client-side programming language in which JavaScript code is added to an HTML document to create Web pages with special behaviors.

Forms processing in JavaScript is enabled by the use of the `Request` and `Response` objects. The `Request` object contains the request variables and their values. The `Response` object has a `write` method that is used to write HTML output.

Functions in JavaScript collect a group of statements into a single unit that is executed by a function call. Functions may have both parameters and local variables. Function definitions are often collected in files and included in ASP scripts.

Objects in JavaScript are created by the `new` operator and can have their own fields and values. `String` objects are of particular importance for storing and manipulating text. Objects support a particular type of function, called a method. Methods of `String` objects include concatenation, pattern matching, and equality.

KEY TERMS

Active URL. A URL that specifies a GET request. An active URL typically has a question mark followed by the request variables and values, suitably encoded. An active URL with no request variables does not have to include a question mark.

Argument of a function call. An expression that is included in a function call and specifies a value for a parameter of the function.

Array. A list of values that are referenced by their position.

ASP [Microsoft] (Active Server Pages). A Web programming style that adds code segments to HTML documents. The code segments are executed in the Web server in response to requests.

ASP script. An HTML file that contains a mixture of HTML and code segments in accordance with the ASP style. An ASP script defines a Web application.

Assignment statement. A JavaScript statement that changes the value of a variable.

Client-side programming. The use of programming language code within HTML documents in which the code is executed by the browser as part of the user interaction.

Common Gateway Interface Specification (CGI). A standard interface for supporting interaction between Web servers and Web applications.

ECMAscript. The international standard for the JavaScript language.

Field. An attribute of an object.

for statement. A JavaScript statement used for repeated execution of a block of statements that includes the incrementing of an index variable. The statement is repeated and the variable incremented until the variable satisfies some condition.

Function. A collection of JavaScript statements that perform a designated task and are executed as a unit through a function call. A function can include parameters that receive initial values as part of the function call.

Function call. A JavaScript code segment that initiates the execution of the statements of a function. Values can be included for the function parameters.

GET method. An HTTP request that uses the URL to transmit the CGI query string.

Hidden form element. An HTML input form element that contains a name and value, but is not displayed by the browser.

HTTP Request. A request initiated by a browser for service by a Web server application.

HTML form. A part of an HTML document that contains input areas. Clicking on a `submit` input button on a form initiates a request.

Input tag. A form tag that defines a user input element.

Internet Information Server (IIS). The Microsoft Web server for Windows operating systems that supports dynamic Web content using ASP.

JavaScript language. A programming language that is used for both server-side and client-side scripting. JavaScript is the basis for the server-side scripting throughout this book.

Method. A function that is part of an object class.

Object. A collection of fields and methods in a JavaScript program.

Object class. The specification of the fields and methods of a set of objects of the same type.

Parameter. A variable that is used to pass a value into a function.

POST method. An HTTP request that uses a two-step process to transmit the query string and other information.

Query string. The URL-encoded string that contains the arguments and values of an HTTP request.

Request variable. A named value that is transmitted to the Web application as part of the HTTP request.

Request object. An ASP/JavaScript object that contains information about the request, including the names and values of the request variables.

Response object. An ASP/JavaScript object that contains information about the response, including a `write` method that is used to create HTML output.

Scripting language. A programming language that embeds code statements in HTML documents. The code is executed within the Web server in order to service a request.

Server-side programming. The use of programming language code within ASP documents in which the code is executed by the Web server.

Submit button. An input form element which, when clicked, causes the browser to collect the information from the form and send it to a Web server as a request.

URL encoding. The translation of query strings to replace characters with special meaning by their hexadecimal codes.

Variable. A named location in a JavaScript program that is capable of storing a value. A variable can contain a simple value such as a number or an object like a `String`.

Variable declaration. A JavaScript statement that declares the name of a variable.

Web application. A program that is executed by a Web application processor in response to a request.

Web application processor. A program that interacts with a Web server to execute applications in response to requests.

QUESTIONS

1. Consult an HTML reference. For each type of tag below, list each attribute that can be included and give its purpose.
   a. Form tag
   b. Input tag with `type = text`
   c. Input tag with `type = select`
   d. Option tag
   e. Submit tag
   f. Input tag with `type = radio`
   g. Input tag with `type = checkbox`

2. What is a hidden input in an HTML form? Why might a designer designate an input as hidden? Give an example of an appropriate use of a hidden input in an HTML document.

3. What is the difference between a `GET` method and a `POST` method in an HTML form? Give two advantages of each method.

4. Search the Web for an HTML page that utilizes forms. Determine the `method` and `action`. List all variables appearing on the form and the values that are produced by clicking the `submit` button.

5. What is Internet Media Type `application/x-www-form-urlencoded`? How does it encode text strings? What special characters must be encoded in this type?

6. Create a simple text entry form using the `GET` method whose action is the ASP script `request.asp` of Figure 11.11. Use this form to translate the following strings to Internet Media Type `application/x-www-form-urlencoded`:
   a. `I've fallen! and "I can't get ^^"`
   b. `103 S. Main St.`
   c. `You & Bobbie need $2.00.`

7. Consult a reference on ASP programming.
   a. List a property of the `Server` object and give examples of its use.
   b. List two methods of the `Server` object and give examples of their use.
   c. List two properties of the `Application` object and give examples of their use.
   d. List two methods of the `Application` object and give examples of their use.
   e. List two properties or collections of the `Request` object not included in Figure 11.12 and give examples of their use.
   f. List two methods of the `Request` object or its collections and give examples of their use.
   g. List two properties of the `Response` object and give examples of their use.
   h. List two methods of the `Response` object (not `write`) and give examples of their use.

PROBLEMS

8. Create an HTML document that uses each tag of problem 11.1 to accept user input. Store the HTML document in file `problem1108.html` in your Web site. Turn in the file and the URL.

9. Write an ASP script that produces an HTML document that shows the values of the variables used in the document that you created for problem 8. Store the script in file `problem1109.asp` in your Web site. Turn in the files and the URL.

10. Write an ASP script that echoes the query string so that it is displayed in the browser. Create an active URL in a Web page that references your ASP script. Store the script in file `problem1111.asp` and the HTML document in `problem1110.html` in your Web site. Turn in the files and the URLs.

11. Modify the ASP script of Figure 11.5 so that is creates variables `firstName` and `lastName`, initializes them to your own names, and displays the values of these variables in a table. Save the script in your Web site as `problem1111.asp`. Turn in your ASP source code and the URL of the script.

PROJECTS

BIG HIT VIDEO

12. a. Implement the site design for your BigHit Video Web site that you created in your project of Chapter 10. Write JavaScript functions `printHeader`, `printFooter`, and other methods to enforce your style. Test these functions by writing ASP scripts to generate the sample pages you created for Chapter 10 in the style of the BigHit Video pages of the book's Web site. Store the ASP test scripts in directory `bighit` in your Web site.

   b. Write an ASP script to generate a new member form for your BigHit Video site. Write another ASP script that responds to the submission of the new member form and creates an HTML page that shows the information entered in the form. Use the style of function `makeCustomer` (Figure 11.11) and script `customer.asp` (see BigHit Video Web site) to create and use objects in your scripts.

BigHit ONLINE

13. a. Implement the site design for your BigHit Online Web site that you created in your project of Chapter 10. Write JavaScript functions `printHeader`, `printFooter`, and other methods to enforce your style. Test these functions by writing ASP scripts to generate the sample pages you created for Chapter 10 in the style of the BigHit Video pages of the book's Web site. Store the ASP test scripts in directory `bighitonline` in your Web site.

   b. Write an ASP script to generate a new member form for your BigHit Online Web site. Write another ASP script that responds to the submission of the new member form and creates an HTML page that shows the information entered in the form. Use the style of function `makeCustomer` (Figure 11.11) and script `customer.asp` (see BigHit Video Web site) to create and use objects in your scripts.

Movie Lovers

14. a. Implement the site design for your Movie Lovers Web site that you created in your project of Chapter 10. Write JavaScript functions `printHeader`, `printFooter`, and other methods to enforce your style. Test these functions by writing ASP scripts to generate the sample pages you created for Chapter 10 in the style of the BigHit Video pages of the book's Web site. Store the ASP test scripts in directory `movielovers` in your Web site.

   b. Wite an ASP script to generate a new member form for your Movie Lovers Web site. Write another ASP script that responds to the submission of the new member form and creates an HTML page that shows the information entered in the form. Use the style of function `makeCustomer` (Figure 11.11) and script `customer.asp` (see BigHit Video Web site) to create and use objects in your scripts.

FURTHER READING

The World Wide Web Consortium Web site (http://www.w3.org) has all of the history of who did what and when for creating dynamic Web sites and also extensive information on Internet security. The O'Reilly ASP books [Wei00, Mit00, LiHu02] are excellent resources and provide extensive information about ASP objects and ASP processing. Additional ASP books abound; see especially [HoSu02, Lov00]. When selecting a book, be careful to get one with extensive coverage of JavaScript; many cover only VBScript.

The use of forms in HTML is covered in all of the HTML references of Chapter 10 and many others.

The trouble with JavaScript books is that almost all of them concentrate on client-side programming. The basics of JavaScript—syntax, use of functions and objects, basic data types and statements—are found in all JavaScript books. Excellent examples are the Addison-Wesley Web Wizard series book [Estr01] and books by Flanagan [Fla01] and Goodman and Eich [GoEi01]. Wyke et al [Wyke02] is a thorough reference to the ins and outs of server-side JavaScript.

Developing Database Applications for the Web

In this chapter, you will learn:

- How to query and modify databases using ASP and JavaScript
- How to create dynamic Web pages through database programming

- How to create complex JavaScript programs
- How to create complex HTML forms

In Chapter 11, you learned how to use ASP and JavaScript to interact with Web servers and HTML forms. In this chapter, you'll discover how to do basic database programming—that is, how to use SQL to query and modify databases—through ASP and JavaScript. You'll take a closer look at the use of JavaScript as a programming language and learn more about the advantages of object-oriented programming.

This chapter walks you through the execution of database queries using three BigHit Video examples: getting current rental information for a BigHit customer, executing an SQL select statement that was typed into an HTML form by users, and inserting a new row in the database's `Customer` table. The examples increase in complexity. However, along the way, you'll learn several new aspects of JavaScript, including if-then-else statements, looping statements, and error handling.

As you work your way through this chapter, it's vital that you use the example Web sites provided with this book or by your instructor, or a Web server on your own computer. As in previous chapters, the examples in the book have been simplified to demonstrate the concepts more clearly. The book's Web site (http://www.web4data.com) shows the full implementation of all of the examples you'll encounter in this chapter and will help you begin developing ASP scripts of your own.

12.1   CONNECTING TO DATABASES WITH ASP

ASP includes the Microsoft **ActiveX Data Object (ADO)** library, which supports database interaction in ASP with a variety of programming tools. The ADO library contains a variety of object classes that can be used by programmers. ADO is particularly well adapted to the ASP environment and JavaScript programming. Our Web applications will use JavaScript code with ADO objects to interact with databases.

The ADO library is a part of the Microsoft Windows operating system, and is not available to programmers who develop code for other operating systems. If you were programming for a Web server that runs on a Unix operating system, you would have to use different data access object classes. However, most database interaction tools support the same basic operations, and the programming style that you will learn in this chapter is easily adapted to other programming environments.

Figure 12.1 illustrates how an application program can communicate with a database server. The outer boxes represent computers, the inner boxes represent programs, and the ovals represent objects. Your applications will interact with a database through a special **connection object** that has the ability to connect to a database on a database server computer. The application program can create an SQL query and hand it off to the connection, which sends it to the database for processing. The results of the query, which are typically a set of table rows, are sent back from the database through the connection object and are made available to the application for processing.

In ASP, the connection object comes from a class called ADODB. **Connection**, which is one of the classes in the ADO library. The name of the class implies that `Connection` is one of several classes in the `ADODB` portion of the ADO library. The `ADODB` library also includes classes to manipulate query results.

The first step in connecting an ASP application to a database is to make sure that the database is available. This chapter will use a strategy called **ODBC (Open Database Connectivity)** to connect to databases. ODBC is a Microsoft standard for database interaction that is part of the Windows operating system. Users can register data sources with ODBC so that applications can easily access them. We are most interested in data

FIGURE 12.1

Interaction Between an
Application and a Database

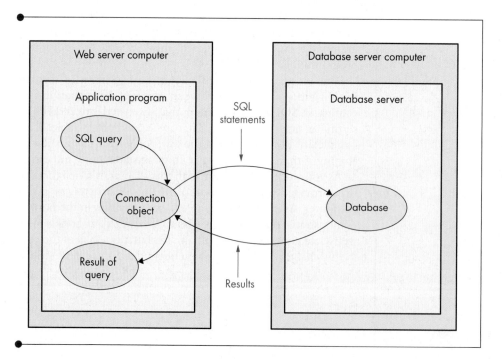

sources that are relational databases, but ODBC also allows data sources to be spreadsheets or text files.

For a Web application to use an **ODBC data source**, the source must be registered on the Web server computer. So far in this book, we've been assuming that the Web server is on the same computer as the Web browser. We've used `localhost` for the computer name in all of our URLs so far. If you are using a Web server on the same computer as your browser, you will need to register your database on that computer. Once the database is registered, the Web applications on the computer will have access to the database.

In this chapter, we'll create Web applications that use an Access database that is stored in a file on the Web server computer. In the next chapter, we'll discuss how to create Web applications that use databases on separate computers.

Data sources are registered by using the ODBC data-source administrator. Under Windows, you'll find the ODBC administration tool in the Control Panel, or possibly in the Administrative Tools directory of the Control Panel, depending on which Windows operating system is running on your computer. Figure 12.2 shows the ODBC administration tool. After opening the tool, click on the `System DSN` tab; then click `Add`. In the resulting menu, enter a name for the data source. (In this case, the data source's name is `bighitmdb`.) Then click the `Select` button and select the file that contains the Access database that you want to register. In this case, the database is `BigHitVideo.mdb`. Then click the `OK` buttons in each window. Now you can interact with the database through ASP scripts.

In order for a JavaScript program to interact with a database, it must create an ADO `Connection` object and connect to the database. The following two lines of JavaScript code can be added to an ASP script to create a `Connection` object, store the object in a variable named `conn`, and open a connection to the database named `bighitmdb`.

```
conn = Server.CreateObject("ADODB.Connection");
conn.Open("bighitmdb");
```

F I G U R E   12.2

Using the ODBC Administration Tool to Register a Data Source

The first line calls the `CreateObject` method of the `Server` object. The `Server` object in ASP provides a way of creating ADO objects. The parameter to the method call is the name of the class. The value returned by the method call is an object of that class. After the execution of the first line, the variable `conn` contains the `Connection` object. The second line calls the `open` method of the `Connection` object and passes the name of a database as its argument. Once the connection is open, the program can ask the `Connection` object to execute SQL statements.

12.2 EXECUTING SQL SELECT QUERIES WITH ASP

Remember the rental information page you saw in Chapter 10? That page is shown here as Figure 12.3. It looks different than it did in Chapter 10 because we've changed the page style. Although Chapter 10 focused on HTML, the rental information page was actually created by an ASP script. In the `Address` area of the Internet Explorer image in Figure 12.3, you can see the URL of the `GET` request. In the URL, the name of the script appears as `rentals.asp`. The script has a single parameter—`accountId`—which in this case has been defined as 103.

To generate this page, the Web application would need to create and execute two SQL select queries: One fetches the first and last name of the customer from BigHit's `Customer` table. The other fetches the list of all that customer's rentals from the `Rental`, `Video`, and `Movie` tables.

The code for `rentals.asp` contains two database interaction sections, one for each query. Let's take a closer look at these sections below.

12.2.1 Fetching and Displaying the Customer's Name

Figure 12.4 shows the code that is contained in `rentals.asp` and used to fetch the name of the customer and to create the page header that includes the customer's name. The code begins in line 1 by declaring two variables and then in line 2 fetches the value of the `accountId` request variable and stores it in the `accountId` JavaScript variable.

In Figure 12.4, lines 4 and 5 create the SQL select query. The program constructs the query by concatenating the string literals highlighted in lines 4 and 5 and the

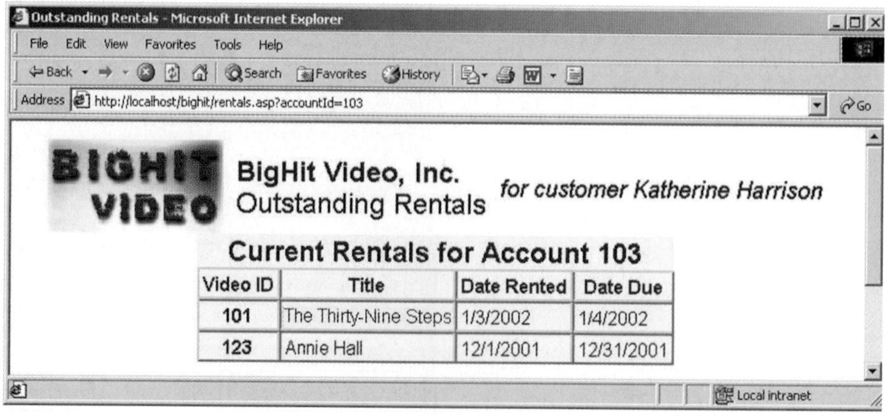

FIGURE 12.3

Rental Information for Account 103, Generated by `rentals.asp`

```
1   var accountId, customer;
2   accountId = Request.QueryString("accountID");
3   // construct SQL query to fetch customer name
4   customerQuery = "select lastName, firstName from Customer"
5       + " where accountId = " + accountId;
6   // execute the query
7   customer = conn.Execute(customerQuery);
8   // get the first and last names from the query result
9   var firstName = customer("firstName");
10  var lastName = customer("lastName");
11  customer.close();
12  printHeader("Outstanding Rentals",
13      "for customer "+firstName+" "+lastName);
```

FIGURE 12.4

Getting a Customer's Name
from a Database

value of the `accountId` variable. The resulting SQL statement, as stored in variable `customerQuery`, reads as follows:

```
select lastName, firstName from Customer where
    accountId = 103
```

Line 7 executes the query by calling a method of the `Connection` object. The **Execute method** of the `Connection` object sends the SQL query statement to the database server and receives the results of the query. The results are stored in the variable `customer` (defined in line 1).

We expect the results to be a single row with two fields: `lastName` and `firstName`. Why does the query return only one row? The query is a selection of all rows of the `Customer` table that have a particular account ID. Because `accountId` is the key of the `Customer` table, no more than one row can match a particular account ID.

The value of variable `customer` is an object of yet another ADO type: `Recordset`. A **Recordset** object represents a database table. In this case, the `Recordset` is a table of two columns and one row. Class `Recordset` includes a variety of methods to allow applications to access the contents of a table that is produced by the execution of an SQL query. We'll begin our look at `Recordset` objects with a brief introduction and study it in much more detail in Section 12.4.

Lines 9 and 10 fetch the values of the two fields of the first row from the `Recordset`. The method called `customer("firstName")` fetches the string value of the `Recordset` attribute named `firstName` of the current row (the first row).

Line 11 calls the `close` method of the `Recordset` object to tell the database connection that the object is no longer needed. Closing the `Recordset` object prepares the `Connection` to process the next query.

Lines 12 and 13 concatenate the customer's first and last name with a space between, and print the header with the customer's name included in the subtitle.

12.2.2 Gathering Rental Information from Three Database Tables

The JavaScript code that fetches the rental information has the same basic form as that for fetching the customer name. First construct a string object whose value is the SQL query, then execute the query, and then process the results. Both the SQL query and the results processing are considerably more complicated this time, however.

The code to fetch and process the rental information is shown in Figure 12.5. The select statement (created in lines 2–5) must join the `Rental`, `Video`, and `Movie` tables to get all of the required fields. Line 6 causes the database server to execute the statement and store the resulting `Recordset` object in variable `rentals`.

We expect to see several rows in the resulting `Recordset` because this customer may currently be renting many videos. In fact, we know from the Web page shown in Figure 12.3 that there are two rows. That is, customer 103 has two videos rented.

The processing of the query results will begin by extracting the values of the `videoId`, `title`, `dateRented`, and `dateDue` attributes of the first row of the results. After printing those rows in the appropriate form, the program will move on to the next row of the result table. After the values are extracted and printed, the program goes to the next row. This continues until no more rows are left to process.

Thus, we need to write some kind of repeating structure in the program so that the program will repeat the processing, one row at a time, and stop only when no more rows are left. Although the example of the Web page of Figure 12.3 has 2 rows, other customers will have different numbers of rows. That is, some customers will have no rentals and some will have many. The program should use information in the query results to decide when to stop.

Look at lines 14–22 in Figure 12.5. These lines form a repeating structure, a **while** loop, which causes the program to iterate through the rows of the result table until none are left. A `while` loop executes some statements repeatedly until a termination condition is met. As we've seen in Chapter 11, a **condition** is a JavaScript ex-

F I G U R E 12.5

Fetching and Printing Rental
Information for a Customer

```
1   <%// get rentals for account and print as table
2   rentalQuery = "select v.videoId, title, dateRented, dateDue"
3       + " from Rental r, Video v, Movie m "
4       + " where v.videoId = r.videoId and v.movieId = m.movieId"
5       + " and r.accountId = "+ accountId;
6   rentals = conn.Execute(rentalQuery);
7   %>
8   <center><table border=2>
9       <caption>Current Rentals for Account <%=accountId%> </caption>
10      <tr>
11          <th>Video ID</th><th>Title</th>
12          <th>Date Rented</th><th>Date Due</th>
13      </tr>
14      <% while(!rentals.eof){ %>
15          <tr>
16              <th> <%=rentals("videoId")%> </th>
17              <td> <%=rentals("title")%> </td>
18              <td> <%=rentals("dateRented")%> </td>
19              <td> <%=rentals("dateDue")%> </td>
20          </tr>
21          <% rentals.movenext();
22      }
23  rentals.close();
24  conn.close();
25  %>
```

pression that evaluates to true or false. In this case, we want to repeatedly process a row of the table and advance to the next row. We want to stop only when all rows have been processed. Thus, the termination condition would be "no rows remain."

In JavaScript, the general form of a `while` loop is

```
while (condition) {
    body of loop
} // end of loop
```

To write a `while` loop, replace the phrases in italics by the appropriate JavaScript code. In Figure 12.5, the *condition* is `!rentals.eof` in line 14, and the **body of the loop** is the code between the opening set brace in line 14 and the closing set brace in line 22.

The condition in line 14 checks to see if more rows remain to be processed by checking the `eof` field of the `rentals Resultset`. The name **eof** is an abbreviation for *end-of-file* and comes from a programming term used in reading files. It has been accepted among programmers to mean the end of data and so is used here.

The value of **eof** is false if rows remain to be processed and true if not. The exclamation point (`!`) in line 14 means "not" in JavaScript. Thus, the expression `!rentals.eof` is true if no more rows remain and false if more rows are available. When this expression is false, the execution of lines 14–22 ends and the execution picks up in line 23.

The program begins executing the `while` loop by evaluating the condition. If the condition is true, the body of the loop executes once. Then it checks again whether the condition is still true. If it is, the program executes the body of the loop once more. This continues until the condition is false.

The body of the `while` loop (lines 15–21) contains HTML text with embedded references (in lines 16–19) to the fields of the current row of rentals. These lines produce a single row in the table.

The last line of the body (line 21) calls the **movenext** method of `results` in order to move the `Recordset` to the next row of the table. After the first execution of `movenext`, the values of the fields of the `Recordset` will come from its second row. To produce the Web page shown in Figure 12.3, the program will execute the body of the `while` loop twice, once for each of the two rentals. After the second call on `movenext`, the `Recordset` will have no more rows and its `eof` property will be true.

The script in Figure 12.5 ends by closing the results of the second query (line 23) and closing the connection to the database (line 24). Now the ASP script can terminate properly and send the requested page back to the browser.

12.3 CREATING OBJECTS FROM QUERIES

We can organize the processing of query results by writing functions to process queries that will occur in many Web applications. You will recall from Chapter 11 that a function is a block of code that can be used many times without writing it more than once. You learned how to store function definitions in a JavaScript code file (we called ours `bighittools.js`) so that many ASP scripts can use them.

In Chapter 11, you saw some of the benefits of creating objects to contain customer information. In general, objects hold the fields of complex data. Figure 11.14 showed you how to use a JavaScript function to create a customer object from a GET request. In this section, we add a function that lets you create a customer object from information stored in BigHit Video's database. This book's Web site contains a Web application that uses this function to generate a Web page that displays customer information. The script `custlookupform.asp` displays a customer lookup form. You can enter a customer account ID, click the `submit` button, and the script `get-customer.asp` will return a Web page that shows information about that customer.

Figure 12.6 shows the JavaScript code for the function `lookupCustomer`. The function has two parameters: It expects the caller to provide it with (1) an open connection to BigHit's database and (2) the account ID of a customer. The function begins executing the function at line 2, which creates a new object to hold the requested information about the customer. This part of the function follows the example of function `makeCustomer` from Chapter 11 (Figure 11.14) that creates a customer object from an HTTP request.

Line 3 contains the simple SQL select statement. The program executes the statement and stores it in the variable `custSet`, defined in line 4. Since the account ID is the key attribute of the `Customer` table, we can expect this query to return one row if the specified customer exists, or no rows if that customer does not exist.

Lines 6–8 form an **if statement** that causes the program to test whether there is a row and, if not, to return the empty customer object with no fields.

In JavaScript, the `if` statement has two forms—`if-then` and `if-then-else`:

```
if (condition) { // if-then statement
    statements to be executed if condition is true
} //end of if-then statement
if (condition) { // if-then-else statement
    statements to be executed if condition is true
} else {
    statements to be executed if condition is false
} // end of if-then-else statement
```

The `if-then` statement of lines 6–8 has `custSet.eof` as its *condition* and line 7 as the statement that is executed if the condition is true.

The program begins executing an `if` statement by evaluating the condition. If the condition is true, the program executes the first block of statements. If the condition is false, it executes the second block of statements. In Figure 12.6, lines 6–8 form an `if-then` statement. If the condition `customer.eof` is false, the `program` skips executing the rest of the statement.

F I G U R E   12.6

Function **lookupCustomer** That Fetches Customer Information from a Database

```
1   function lookupCustomer(conn, id) {
2       customer = new Object();
3       customerSQL = "select * from Customer where accountId="+id;
4       custSet = conn.Execute(customerSQL);
5       // check to see if
6       if (custSet.eof) { // no customer with this accountId
7           return customer; // return empty object
8       }
9       customer.accountId = custSet("accountId");
10      customer.firstName = custSet("firstName");
11      customer.lastName = custSet("lastName");
12      customer.street = custSet("street");
13      customer.city = custSet("city");
14      customer.state = custSet("state");
15      customer.zipcode = custSet("zipcode");
16      return customer;
17  }
```

The condition of the `if` statement in line 6 is `custSet.eof`. The `eof` property of any query result is true if there are no rows left in the result. In this case, if the `eof` property is true, the query execution returned no rows. That is, there is no customer with the account ID that was supplied as the value for parameter `id`.

Line 7 introduces a new use for JavaScript's `return` statement. The execution of a `return` statement ends the execution of the `lookupCustomer` function. The program sends the empty object created in line 2 back to the caller of the function. The program does not execute the rest of the body of the function, lines 9–16.

If the execution reaches line 9, then the program extracts the row of the query result, one field at a time. In lines 9–15, the program extracts the fields of the customer from the query result and adds them to the new object. You'll learn more about this method later in the chapter.

12.4 A GENERAL PURPOSE QUERY EXECUTION SCRIPT

Now that you know how to create, execute, and process the results of simple SQL statements, you are ready to consider a more general problem. Suppose that we create an HTML form that allows users to type an SQL select statement and submit a request for it to be executed, as shown in Figure 12.7. When the user clicks the `submit` button, he will expect the result to be a Web page that displays the results of executing the select statement as an HTML table.

By the time you have finished studying this section, you will know everything required to process any SQL select statement in your JavaScript code. From now on, any time you need to extract information from a database, you'll be able to use the techniques of this section and the two before it to write your own JavaScript solution.

The Web page of Figure 12.7 has a text area for entering SQL. The multi-line text input field is constructed using the HTML **textarea** tag:

```
<textarea cols="40" rows="6" name="sqlQuery"></textarea>
```

This tag describes a text area that is 40 characters wide and 6 lines long. The initial value for the field is any text that appears between the **textarea** begin and end tags.

FIGURE 12.7

Web Page with HTML Form to Enter SQL Select Statement

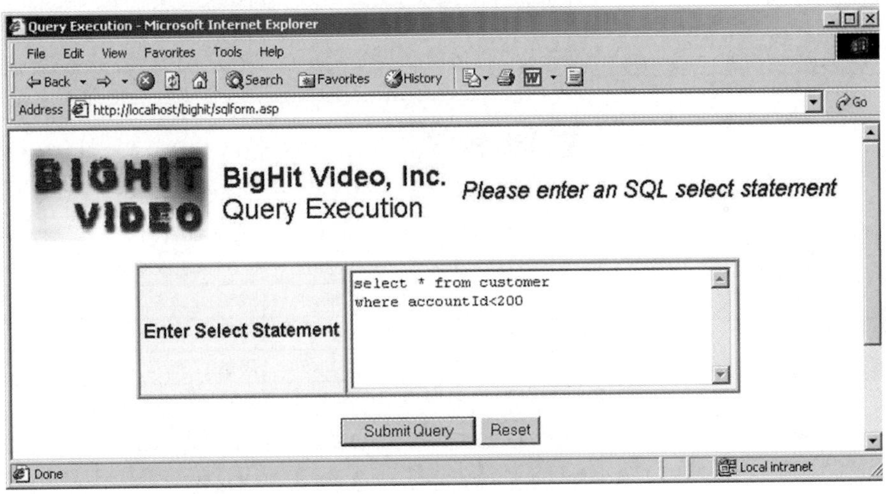

In this case, the initial value is empty. The query `select * from customer where accountId<200` has been typed in by the user.

When the user clicks the `submit` button, the Web application should return an HTML document that displays the results of executing the query, as shown in Figure 12.8. The text of the query is displayed in the subtitle of the header.

The body of the Web page is a table containing the query results. The column headings are the names of the attributes. Each row of the result table is shown as a row of the HTML table.

You have already encountered most of the JavaScript code required to produce this table. You have learned how to extract the request variables and how to execute SQL statements. In `rentals.asp` of Figure 12.5, a `while` loop was used to iterate through the rows of the `Recordset` object that is the result of an SQL execution. What you haven't seen yet is how to determine how many columns are in a `Recordset` and what their names are.

The code to produce the rentals information (Figure 12.5) expected the SQL result to have exactly 4 fields named `videoId`, `title`, `dateRented`, and `dateDue`. The columns were named accordingly (lines 11 and 12 of Figure 12.5) using string literals, and the values were fetched by name (lines 16–19).

We must develop a script for producing Figure 12.8 that discovers the attribute names using properties and methods of the `Recordset` object that is the result of executing the query.

Figure 12.9 shows the first part of the ASP script that executes the query and displays the results. The script starts with an HTML comment tag (line 1) that identifies the script by name. It is followed by the opening `html` tag and an `include` command for the `bighittools.js` file that contains many helpful functions including `printHeader` and `printFooter`.

Processing the HTTP request begins, as usual, with fetching the value of the request variables, in this case `sqlQuery`, as shown in line 7, and generating the header. Line 8 calls `printHeader` to produce the header of the HTML document.

The script continues by creating and opening a database connection (lines 10–11). The query execution in line 13 stores the resulting table in the `results` variable. Line 14 passes the query result to a function called `printTable` that has the responsibility for printing the results.

F I G U R E 12.8

Results of Executing the Query of Figure 12.7

```
1   <!-- sqlexec.asp -->
2   <html>
3      <!-- #include file="bighittools.js" -->
4      <%
5      // get parameter values
6      var conn, sqlQuery, results;
7      sqlQuery = Request("sqlQuery");
8      printHeader("Execution of Query",sqlQuery);
9      // connect to database
10     conn = Server.CreateObject("ADODB.Connection");
11     conn.Open("bighitmdb");
12     // execute query
13     results = conn.Execute(sqlQuery);
14     printTable(results,Response);
15     printFooter(); %>
16  </html>
```

FIGURE 12.9

JavaScript Code That Processes a Query Submitted by Figure 12.6

Before looking at the code for `printTable`, you need to understand some more of the characteristics of query results. You first encountered the `Recordset` objects that are returned as query results in Section 12.2. These objects have a variety of properties and methods that make it easy to get the information needed to create the Web page of Figure 12.8. Figure 12.10 illustrates the structure of a `Recordset` object. The objects are shown as rectangles, methods as rounded rectangles, and properties and variables as ovals.

The figure represents the state of the program just after the execution of the query. The `Recordset` contains the first row of the query result. The oval in the upper left represents the variable `results` whose value is the `Recordset` object. The `Recordset` object has a collection called `fields` that contains one `field` for each column. Each **field object** contains the name, type, and value of a single attribute. You've already seen and used method `movenext` and property `eof` of the `Recordset`. Object `fields` has a property called `count` with value 8—the number of fields in the row. Each `field` has two properties, a `name` and a `value`.

Of course, the ADO objects are much more complex than illustrated in Figure 12.10. Each object has many more fields, as well as many objects. For more details, see the references listed in the Further Reading section at the end of the chapter.

The information needed to generate the Web page is shown in Figure 12.10. The number of columns in the result is the value of `fields.count`. The name of the first column is `fields(0).name`, and the value of the first column is `fields(0).value`. All of the fields and methods of `Recordset` that are needed are included in Figure 12.11.

Function `printTable` is shown in Figure 12.11. On the Web site, this function is part of the `bighittools.js` file. This function can process any select statement, so we can expect it to be quite useful in many Web applications.

The code that processes the query result in `printTable` is very different from that of our previous scripts, primarily because `printTable` doesn't know how many fields are in the result and doesn't even know the names of the fields. Hence, `printTable` must determine the number of fields and find their names.

The code of Figure 12.11 accesses information in these objects. Line 3 uses the expression `results.fields.count` to fetch the number of fields in the query result

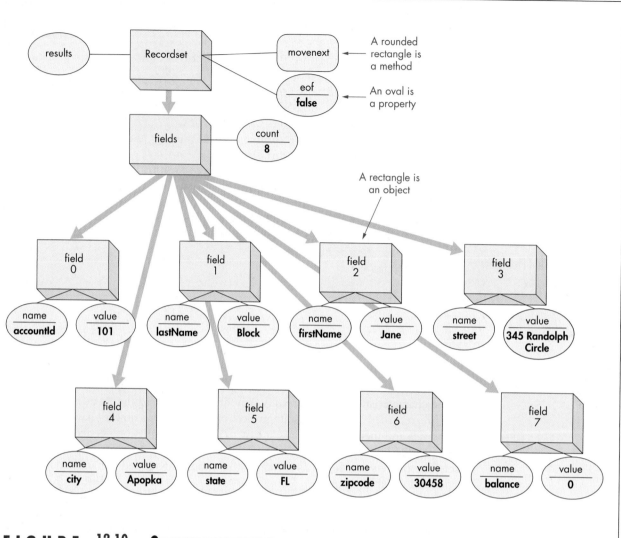

FIGURE 12.10

A **Recordset** Object for Figure 12.7 Positioned on the First Row

and store it in variable `numCols`. Line 7 uses the expression `results.fields(col).name` to fetch the name of a `field`. Line 14 uses `results.fields(col)` to fetch the value of a field. These expressions could also be written using the shorthand expressions `results(col).name` and `results (col).value`.

Iteration through the fields of a row is accomplished using JavaScript `for` statements in lines 6–8 and lines 13–15. We originally encountered `for` statements in the Case in Point section at the end of Chapter 11.

The `for` statement in lines 6–8 has `col=0` for the initialization, `col<numCols` as the condition, and `col++` as the increment. The body of the loop is in line 7.

The execution of the `for` statement of lines 6–8 begins by executing the initialization. This sets the value of the variable `col` to 0. Next the condition is executed. In this case, we are testing to see if the value of `col` is less than 8, the value of `numCols` as assigned in line 3. Since `col` has value 0, the condition is true.

After the condition evaluates to true, the body of the loop is executed and then the increment is executed. After the first execution of the loop of lines 6–8, the increment statement `col++` adds one to the variable `col`, resulting in a new value of 1. Then

```
1  function printTable(results) {
2      // print the rows of the query result as an HTML table
3      numCols = results.fields.count;
4      Response.write("<center><tr>\n");
5      // write names of columns
6      for (col=0; col<numCols; col++) {
7          Response.write("<th>"+results.fields(col).name+"</td>\n");
8      }
9      Response.write("</tr>\n");
10     // write rows of data
11     while (!results.eof) {
12         Response.write("<tr>");
13         for (col=0; col<numCols; col++) {
14             Response.write("<td>"+results.fields(col)+"</td>\n");
15         }
16         results.movenext();
17         Response.write("</tr>");
18     }
19     Response.write("</table></center><br>\n");
20 }
```

FIGURE 12.11

JavaScript Function to Print a
Query Result as a Table

the condition is evaluated again, and again it is true (1<8). The execution continues with the body, then the increment, and again the condition.

The loop continues its execution until the condition is false. In this loop, the condition is false when col gets the value 8. The body is executed 8 times.

Each time the body executes, col has a different value. First 0, then 1, 2, ... 7. Thus, the first time through the loop, the expression results.fields(col).name refers to results.fields(0).name, that is, the string "accountId". The second time through the loop col is 1 and the expression refers to results.fields(1).name, which is the string "lastName", etc.

The execution of the for loop of lines 6–8 produces the header row of the HTML table of Figure 12.8. Each execution of the for loop of lines 13–15 produces one data row of the table.

The while loop of lines 11–18 iterates through the rows of the table. Each iteration of the while loop includes an iteration through the fields of one row in lines 13–15. At the end of the body of the while loop, method movenext is called to advance the Recordset to the next row.

By the end of the execution of printTable, all of the rows have been processed and the HTML table has been generated.

You now have all of the tools necessary to execute and process any select statement for any database. It doesn't matter whether the database server is Access or if it is one of the more powerful servers such as Oracle 9i, IBM DB2, or Microsoft SQL Server. No change in this code is required to make it work for any database. For evidence, you can investigate the BigHit Online Web site, which is powered by a SQL Server database. It includes ASP scripts sqlform.asp and sqlexec.asp. Those scripts and function printTable are identical to the scripts that we've just studied.

The rest of the chapter is devoted to processing other SQL statements, especially insert, update, and delete statements.

INTERVIEW

VICTOR VIANU
Database Ideas for Tomorrow

Currently Professor in the Computer Science and Engineering department at U.C. San Diego. "I am still on my first job!"

RESEARCHING NEW IDEAS My main current research interests are in static analysis of XML queries, processing streaming data, and e-services.

PROGRAMMING THE OLD WAY As a high school student in Romania, I followed a special pilot program in mathematics and computer science. We learned programming in Fortran, logic, and discrete mathematics. It was not very high-tech: Our programs were punched on cards and carried in a large suitcase to a nearby computer center. But I enjoyed it a lot. And thinking back to then, it is thrilling how things have changed!

DATABASES AND THEIR ROLE ON THE WEB The Web represents an opportunity of an entirely different scale, and databases have a crucial role to play. You can view the Web as one big database. After all, the Web is a global source of information

> **"...classical databases are well-polished artifacts. The Web is closer to a natural ecosystem. So the Web scenario requires reinventing many aspects of the database paradigm."**

that begs to be queried! In the past 20 years, the database area has generated a highly successful, multi-billion dollar industry.

THE WEB AND ITS INFLUENCE ON FUTURE DATABASE RESEARCH Viewing the Web as a database raises tremendous challenges. Data is no longer neatly formatted and centralized. It is instead heterogeneous, semi-structured, and globally distributed. Access to the database is no longer controlled by transactions, but instead by a very flexible protocol. And the Web is highly dynamic and impossible to capture completely as a consistent snapshot. At the bottom of it, classical databases are well-polished artifacts. The Web is closer to a natural ecosystem. So the Web scenario requires reinventing many aspects of the database paradigm. It also requires increased interaction with adjacent areas, such as information retrieval.

12.5 INSERTING NEW CUSTOMER INFORMATION

In this section you will learn how to create and execute insert and update statements in JavaScript. We continue to use the `Connection` object and its `Execute` method for processing queries. Most of the complications of this section are related to the difficulty of generating SQL to modify the database, rather than the intricacies of JavaScript or the ADO library.

Chapter 11 included a presentation of the first step in processing the new customer information form in Section 11.4. ASP script `newcustomer.asp` processed the request to add the customer information. The result page of that request showed the information to the user and asked him to confirm that it was correct. Figure 12.12 shows the confirmation page.

The HTML code that produces the table, form, and button of Figure 12.12 is shown in Figure 12.13. The crucial code is in lines 12–17. As explained in Section 11.4, the hidden input entries serve to transmit the customer information fields from the script (`newcustomer.asp`) that generated the confirmation to the `addcustomer.asp` script that creates the new database entry for the customer.

F I G U R E **12.12**

Customer Confirmation Page,
Repeated from Figure 11.9

F I G U R E **12.13**

Partial HTML Document for the
Customer Confirmation Page

```
1   <form method="GET" action="addcustomer.asp"><center>
2     <table>
3        <tr><th>First Name: </th><td>Janet </td></tr>
4        <tr><th>Last Name: </th><td>Mylopolous</td></tr>
5        <tr><th>street: </th><td>4402 Elm St.</td></tr>
6        <tr><th>City: </th><td>Apopka</td></tr>
7        <tr><th>State: </th><td>FL</td></tr>
8        <tr><th>Zipcode: </th><td>34455</td></tr>
9     </table><br>
10    <input type="submit" value="Confirm"> <input type="reset">
11    <!-- hidden fields to hold customer info-->
12    <input type="hidden" name="firstName" value="Janet">
13    <input type="hidden" name="lastName" value="Mylopolous">
14    <input type="hidden" name="street" value="4402 Elm St.">
15    <input type="hidden" name="city" value="Apopka">
16    <input type="hidden" name="state" value="FL">
17    <input type="hidden" name="zipcode" value="34455">
18  </center></form>
```

Concept

Autonumber Fields in Databases

The creation of an account ID for the new customer is complicated and could be simplified by allowing the database server to choose the account ID. All database systems allow the primary key of a table to be created by the server as part of the insert operation. In Access, you can set the type of a field to `autonumber`. In SQL Server, the `identity` property of a table controls the autonumbering.

If you set the type of the primary key to autonumber, the insert statement will not need to specify a value for the primary key. The database server will create it automatically. Autonumbering has some advantages to database programmers, but also some disadvantages. Section 15.3 investigates some of these issues.

The ASP script `addcustomer.asp` that creates the new customer is shown in Figure 12.14. When the customer clicks on the `Confirm` button of the page of Figure 12.12, the hidden variables are collected and passed to `addcustomer.asp` for processing. Line 2 uses the `makeCustomer` method from the tools collection (discussed in Section 11.6.2) to create an object containing all of the fields of the customer.

So far, this customer has no account ID, and one must be created. A simple way to create a new account ID is to determine the largest account ID that is currently used and let the new ID be one larger. Lines 9 and 10 accomplish this task. Line 9 executes

FIGURE 12.14

Script
addcustomer.asp
That Adds a New Customer to the Database

```
1  var customer, newId;
2  customer = makeCustomer(Request);
3  with (customer) {
4      printHeader("New Customer Receipt","Welcome "+firstName+" "+lastName);
5      // connect to database
6      conn = Server.CreateObject("ADODB.Connection");
7      conn.Open("bighit");
8      // get new account ID as maximum current account ID plus 1
9      maxId = conn.Execute("select max(accountId)from Customer");
10     newId = maxId(0) + 1;
11     // insert customer
12     newCustSQL = "insert into Customer "
13         +"(accountId, firstName, lastName, street, city, state, zipcode)"
14         +" values ("+newId+", '"+firstName+"', '"+lastName+"', '"
15         +street+"', '"+city+"', '"+state+"', '"zipcode+"')";
16     conn.Execute(newCustSQL);
17  } // end with customer
18  // fetch customer information from the database
19  customer = lookupCustomer(conn,newId);
20  customer = makeCustomer(Request);
21  printCustomerTable(customer);
```

a query that fetches `max(accountId)`, the maximum account ID in the `Customer` table, and stores the result table in variable `maxId`. Line 10 extracts the value of the first field (number 0) from the first row of the result table, adds 1 to it, and stores the new ID number in `newId`.

Now we have the account ID for our new customer and can create the SQL insert statement. Lines 12–15 construct the insert statement using the values of the customer object created in line 2, that is, the values that came from the hidden fields of the confirmation page. The attribute names for the insert statement are listed in the large string literal in line 13. The values for those attributes are extracted from the customer object and added to the SQL statement in lines 14 and 15. The resulting insert statement for the request of Figure 12.12 is:

```
insert into Customer (accountId, firstName, lastName,
    street, city, state, zipcode) values (447, 'Janet',
    'Mylopolous', '4402 Elm St.', 'Apopka', 'FL', '33455')
```

We have to be careful with our SQL statements to make sure that they conform to SQL conventions. In particular, we must be careful that all string literals are enclosed in single quotes. Lines 14 and 15 include single quotes that delimit the attribute values. Between each pair of values in lines 14 and 15 is a single quote, a comma, and another single quote. The quote marks end up delimiting the string literals in the above insert statement.

The account ID does not have to be quoted because its value is an integer and not a string. In the next section we'll address the problem of what happens when a string literal contains a single quote.

Figure 12.14 shows the receipt page that is generated by lines 19–21 of `addcustomer.asp`. Notice that the script fetches the customer information from the database (line 19) using the `lookupCustomer` function of Section 12.3. This simply ensures that the results as reported reflect exactly what ended up in the database. It's an important principle that after a database update, the result of the update should be reported by querying the database. Otherwise, we are reporting on what should have been done, rather than what was done.

FIGURE 12.15

Result of Adding a New
Customer to the Database

12.6 HANDLING QUOTE MARKS IN SQL STATEMENTS

The script of Figure 12.13 will produce an error if any field contains a single quote mark. Suppose, for instance, that our new customer's name is "Janet O'Connell." The script will produce the following SQL insert statement:

```
insert into Customer (accountId, firstName, lastName,
    street, city, state, zipcode) values(485, 'Janet',
    'O'Connell', '4402 Elm St.', 'Apopka', 'FL', '33455')
```

The quote marks in the last name field are no longer balanced. The execution of this request results in the page shown in Figure 12.16. The error message is rather cryptic and says that there is a "Syntax error (missing operator)." Of course the real cause of the error is the extra quote mark, but we cannot expect very good error analysis from the SQL processor. We need to clean up the value of the last name before creating the insert statement.

Function `sqlString` of Figure 12.17 uses JavaScript pattern matching to double the single quote marks. This function is included in the `bighittools.js` file. The crucial step is in line 5. String objects have a method `replace` that finds and replaces substrings that match a particular pattern. Pattern matching in JavaScript is based on the Perl programming language and provides a very powerful mechanism for string manipulation. In this example, we simply replace every occurrence of a single quote by a double quote.

Line 4 of Figure 12.17 makes a new `String` object from the parameter `str`. This line of code guards against a possible JavaScript error. Method `replace` must be ap-

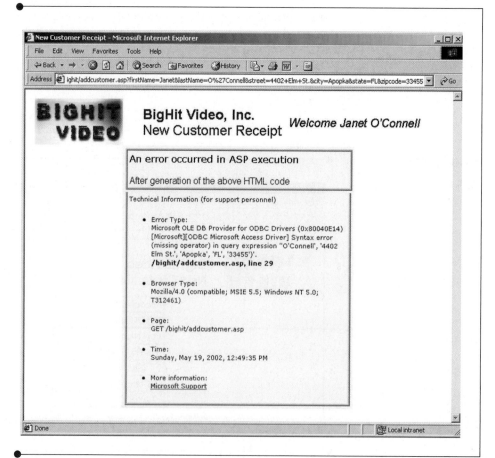

F I G U R E 12.16

Error Page Produced by Insert Statement with Unbalanced Quote Marks

```
1   function sqlString(str) {
2       // convert str into an SQL string literal
3       //  by doubling any embedded single quotes
4       tmp = new String(str);
5       newStr = tmp.replace(/'/, "''");
6       return newStr;
7   }
```

F I G U R E 12.17

Function to Double the Quote Marks in SQL String Literals

plied to a **String** object and cannot be applied to a string literal. If the value of **tmp** is a string literal and not a **String** object, the call to **tmp.replace** in line 5 will result in an error. Making a new **String** object in line 4 simply ensures that the value of **tmp** is a **String** object and thus eliminates this possible JavaScript error.

The first argument to the call of method **replace** in line 5 of Figure 12.17 is the pattern **/'/**. A pattern in JavaScript matches whatever is delimited by the slashes. In this case, the single quote is the only character between the slashes, so the pattern matches each single quote in the parameter.

The second argument to the call in line 5 is the string that is to replace the matched strings. This replacement string consists of two single quotes.

The string that is returned in line 6 is the original string parameter modified so that every single quote has been doubled. In the case of the string value **O'Connell**, the new string in variable **newStr** is **O''Connell**.

To use **sqlString** in creating the insert statement for **addcustomer.asp**, we simply add calls to **sqlString** in the creation of the insert statement. We can replace lines 14 and 15 of Figure 12.14 with these:

```
+" values ("+newId+", '" +sqlString(firstName)+"','"
   +sqlString(lastName)+"', '"+sqlString(street)+"', '"
   +sqlString(city)+"', '"+sqlString(state)+"', '"
   +sqlString(zipcode)+"')";
```

The insert statement that results from this change is:

```
insert into Customer (accountId, firstName, lastName,
   street, city, state, zipcode) values (485,'Janet',
   'O''Connell', '4402 Elm St.', 'Apopka', 'FL', '33455')
```

This doubling of quote marks to eliminate errors is just one example of the pains we must take in programming. We'll see many more examples in the more complex Web sites developed in Chapters 13 and 14.

12.7 DEBUGGING ASP AND JAVASCRIPT

When errors occur in your ASP and JavaScript code during development, you will be pleased to know a few tips to help you find them. Two techniques are most helpful: printing debug messages and using debugging software. In Chapter 14 you will learn about how to catch and handle errors within ASP scripts. This section discusses how to report errors to a developer so that he can find and fix the errors.

All of the Web page examples in the last three chapters have used a Web server on the same computer as the browser—all of the URLs are to computer `localhost`. When the Web server is on your computer, you will find that editing your code and especially debugging it is simpler. Once the Web applications are working properly, they can be moved to a production Web server.

The book's Web site has detailed instructions for configuring your local Web server to make debugging feasible. The two most important configuration changes are to enable custom error message and to enable debugging.

Every IIS server has an ASP script called `500-100.asp` that is executed whenever an ASP script commits a serious error. You should modify your server configuration by replacing the standard error script with one that produces better error messages. The book's Web server has a custom `500-100.asp` script that produced the error page of Figure 12.16. You can use this script for your error processing. It makes sure that all output that was produced by the Web application appears in the output page and then adds the ASP error messages.

With this custom error script installed, anything your Web application outputs before it commits its error will appear in the Web browser in the result page. When your application has a problem that results in an error page, you can modify the program so that it prints extra information to help you find the source of the problem. That extra information will be displayed in the Web browser along with the ASP error message.

The ASP error message in Figure 12.16 includes the file name and line number of the ASP file where the error was found. By adding calls to `Response.write` just before the error, you can make the program tell you the values of its variables just before it quits. For example, if you have an SQL error like the one in Figure 12.16, print the text of the SQL statement that is being executed. Then you can see what's wrong with it, or even cut and paste it into an Access SQL query window for execution. Once you see what's wrong with the SQL statement, you can change the code that creates the statement.

The Microsoft Script Debugger that you saw in Section 11.3 is a debugging tool for ASP scripts. You can download a copy from the Microsoft Web site and install it on your computer. To take full advantage of the script debugger, you need to configure IIS to enable server-side script debugging. Once this is done, any error in a `localhost` ASP script will start the debugger and show exactly where the program stopped. The debugger allows you to look at the values of all variables, and even to modify the code.

You can also use the debugger to execute your code one line at a time. When you are having a problem with some part of a Web application, add `debugger` as a line of code to the script. When the script's execution reaches that line, the script debugger will pop up with execution paused at that point. You can then execute a single line of code, look at variables, modify the program, or resume execution.

Script debugging can be very helpful, but it can also be a terrible waste of time. The best debugging strategies start with analyzing the code and the error messages to pinpoint the source of the problem. Printing is most helpful and direct. If printing doesn't help, or you cannot tell what might have happened, the debugger will be your best hope.

12.8 CASE IN POINT: ADDING AND UPDATING CUSTOMERS IN BIGHIT ONLINE

In this chapter's Case in Point, we'll look at creative ways to share code among Web applications. Software developers must find methods to increase the effectiveness of their programming efforts. A great way to do this is to define functions that can be used in several different places.

Let's look at the two customer information forms of Figure 12.18 and try to find a single function that can generate both Web pages. The page on the left accepts information about a new customer and the page on the right allows an existing customer to modify her customer information. These two pages are almost identical.

The only visual differences between the pages are the header, the contents of the input elements, and the labels on the `submit` buttons. With this much similarity, we ought to be able to find a way to have the two Web applications that generate these pages use a single page-generation function.

Before we try to share the code, let's make sure we know what it should do. The program `customereditform.asp` that generates the customer update form starts with the account ID, extracts the current customer information from the database and then generates the HTML form that displays the information. Figure 12.19 shows part of the HTML code that defines the form.

The initial value of each input element of the form carries the customer information as its value `attribute`. You can see the examples in lines 4 and 7. Pushing the `reset` button on this form will restore the input elements to those initial values.

The JavaScript code that generates the HTML form of Figure 12.19 is quite simple. If we have already established a database connection in variable `conn` and variable `accountId` has the account ID 101, the following code generates lines 3–8.

```
1   <%var cust = lookup(conn,accountId)%>
2   <tr><th>First name: </th>
3     <td><input type="text" size="20" name="firstName"
4     value="<%=cust.firstName%>"></td></tr>
5   <tr><th>Last name: </th>
6     <td><input type="text" size="20" name="lastName"
7       value="<%=cust.lastName%>"></td></tr>
```

FIGURE 12.18

Forms to Create and to Update
Customer Information

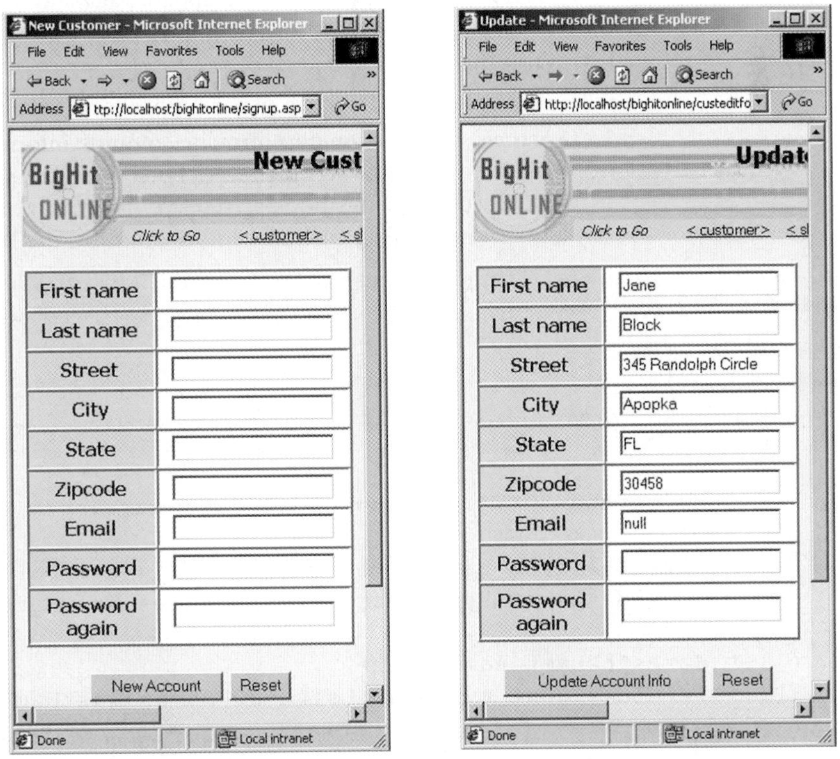

```
1    <form method="GET" action="updatecustomer.asp">
2    <table>
3        <tr><th>First name </th>
4            <td><input type="text" size="20" name="firstName" value="Jane"></td>
5        </tr>
6        <tr><th>Last name </th>
7            <td><input type="text" size="20" name="lastName" value="Block"></td>
8        </tr>
```

FIGURE 12.19

Part of the HTML Code for the
Customer Update Form of
Figure 12.18

This code simply extracts a customer object (variable `cust`) from the database using function `lookup` and generates the HTML code with `value` attributes initialized from the customer fields.

What would happen if the fields of the `cust` object were all blank? If `cust.firstName` and `cust.lastName` were blank, the HTML of Figure 12.20 would be generated. The differences between Figures 12.19 and 12.20 are highlighted. The values of the input elements of Figure 12.20 are blank, just like the initial values of the fields of the new customer form. The code of Figure 12.20 is the HTML source of the new customer page. We ought to be able to generate both of these forms with a single function.

The function that generates both pages must have arguments that tell it how to make the differences in the form. Figure 12.21 shows much of function `printCustomerEditPage`. The three parameters of the function are:

- `update`, which is true for the update page and false for the new customer,
- `cust`, which contains the customer object with the initial values (blank for new customer)
- `scriptname`, the name of the script that is used for the action of the form

Together, these parameters provide enough information to generate the correct pages. You will find the function defined in file `customer.js` in the `bighitonline` directory of this book's Web site. File `customer.js` is a collection of functions that manipulate customer information for the BigHit Online Web site.

FIGURE 12.20

Part of the HTML Code for the
Customer Update Form of
Figure 12.18

```
1    <form method="GET" action="updatecustomer.asp">
2    <table>
3        <tr><th>First name </th>
4            <td><input type=text size=20 name="firstName" value=""></td>
5        </tr>
6        <tr><th>Last name </th>
7            <td><input type=text size=20 name="lastName" value=""></td>
8        </tr>
```

The first parameter, `update`, is used in the `if-then-else` statement of lines 3–7 to initialize the title and subtitle that are used in the header.

The second argument to the function is the customer object that is used to initialize the input elements. A blank object creates an empty form and an object from the database creates an update form.

The final argument, `scriptname`, is simply the name of the script that will service the requests from the generated page.

The final piece of this Case in Point is the scripts `signup.asp` and `custeditform.asp` that use the function to generate the pages of Figure 12.18. The scripts are shown in Figure 12.22. The actual JavaScript code takes only two lines for `signup.asp` and four lines for `custeditform.asp`.

Script `signup.asp` creates an empty customer by calling function `makeEmptyCustomer` (located in file `customer.js`) and passes the customer to `printCustomerEditPage` with `false` as the value for parameter `update`.

Script `custeditform.asp` begins by making a database connection (line 5). The function `makeConnection` is included in `bighittools.js` to create a database connection. The script then gets the account ID from the request variable (line 5), extracts the customer information from the database (line 7) and calls `printCustomerEditPage` with `true` as the value for `update`.

The process of generating the new customer form and the process of generating the customer edit form are so similar that combining them has cut the amount of code nearly in half. Without function `printCustomerEditPage`, the code to generate the pages would have been duplicated in the two ASP scripts.

You have seen a clear example of the advantage of thinking creatively about programs and organizing our code. The next two chapters will put together all of the parts of the BigHit Online Web site. We'll start from scratch, develop the data models, the database, and finally the Web applications. Your understanding and appreciation of JavaScript will increase as we see more features and more complicated code.

FIGURE 12.21

Function **printCustomer EditPage** That Prints Pages to Add or Update Customer

```
1  function printCustomerEditPage(update,cust,scriptname) {
2     var title, subtitle
3     if (update) { // update if true, new customer if false
4         title="Update Customer"; subtitle="Please update your information";
5     } else {
6         title="New Customer"; subtitle="Please enter your information";
7     }
8     printHeader(title, subtitle);%>
9     <form method="GET" action="<%=scriptname%>">
10    <table>
11       <tr><th>First name: </th>
12          <td><input type=text size=20 name="firstName"
13             value="<%=cust.firstName%>"></td></tr>
14       <tr><th>Last name: </th>
15          <td><input type=text size=20 name="lastName"
16             value="<%=cust.lastName%>"></td>
17       </tr>//rest of function omitted
18 <%} // rest of function omitted
```

```
1   <%@LANGUAGE="JScript"%>
2   <!-- signup.asp -->
3   <!-- #include file="bighittools.js" -->
4   <html> <%
5       var customer = makeEmptyCustomer();
6       printCustomerEditPage(false, customer, "signup.asp");
7   %>
```

```
1   <%@LANGUAGE="JScript"%>
2   <!-- custeditform.asp -->
3   <!-- #include file="bighittools.js" -->
4   <html> <%
5       var accountId = Request("accountId");
6       var conn = makeConnection();
7       var customer = lookupCustomer(conn,accountId);
8       printCustomerEditPage(true, customer, "custeditform.asp");
9   %>
```

FIGURE 12.22

ASP Scripts That Generate the
Customer Pages

CHAPTER SUMMARY

ASP and JavaScript support database interaction through the Microsoft ActiveX Data Objects (ADO) library. The `Connection` class supports connecting to databases and executing SQL statements. The Microsoft ODBC package allows data sources to be easily created on Windows systems and used by `Connection` objects.

This chapter explains the BigHit Video Web site that supports the execution of arbitrary SQL queries and the display of customer rental information. All of the components of this Web site are explained, including all of the ASP scripts and JavaScript programming.

The `Execute` method of the `Connection` object is used to execute SQL queries and retrieve the results. The result of executing an SQL select statement is an ADO `Recordset` object that contains the names of all the columns of the table produced by the statement. The values in a single row of the table are available. Method `movenext` moves the result to the next row of the result table. The `Execute` method

will also execute SQL statements that modify database content.

Functions and objects are extremely useful in simplifying database interaction programs. This chapter includes functions that create customer objects from both request variables and SQL queries. It also includes the example of using a single function to generate both new customer entry forms and customer update forms. A primary goal of using functions is to simplify programs by minimizing code duplication.

The JavaScript language includes `if` statements that support conditional execution of statements and `while` and `for` statements that support repeated execution of statements. A `while` statement executes its body repeatedly until some condition is true. A `for` statement executes its body a specific number of times that is determined by the increment and test operations of the indexing variable.

The ASP script `sqlexec.asp` is a complete script to execute arbitrary SQL queries. It accepts an SQL query that has been entered in an HTML form, executes the query, and outputs the result table as an HTML table. The SQL form uses an HTML `textarea` input, which is a multi-line form element for entering text.

The BigHit Video ASP scripts use a strategy of dynamically generating SQL statements for execution.

Each SQL statement is created using values that are passed into or generated by the script.

The chapter includes the details of how to generate and execute SQL statements that create new customer objects in the BigHit database that query the database for the information needed to generate the BigHit Video Web site.

KEY TERMS

ActiveX Data Object (ADO). The Microsoft data access library that is used in ASP programming.

Body of a loop. The block of statements within a `for` or `while` statement that is executed repeatedly.

Condition. A JavaScript expression that evaluates to true or false. Conditions are used to determine the execution patterns of `if`, `for`, and `while` statements.

Connection. The ADO class that is used to establish connections between ASP scripts and database servers.

Connection object. An object that is used by a program to interact with a database server.

eof property. A property of a `Recordset` object that is true if all of the rows have been processed and false otherwise.

Execute method. A method of the `Connection` class that is used to execute SQL statements.

Field object. An ADO object that holds a field of a `Recordset` object.

If statement. A JavaScript statement that has a condition and one or two blocks of statements. If the condition evaluates to true, the first block is executed and

the second block is skipped. If the condition is false, the first block is skipped and the second block is executed.

movenext. The method of `Recordset` that advances it to the next row.

ODBC (Open Database Connectivity). The Microsoft standard for communicating between applications and data sources in the Microsoft Windows environment.

ODBC data source. A source of data, which may be a SQL database server, that has been registered on a computer and can be used by applications on that computer.

Recordset. The ADO class that is used to access data that has been created by the execution of an SQL select statement.

Textarea tag. A multi-line HTML form element used for entering text.

While loop. A JavaScript statement used for repeated execution of a block of statements. The block of statements, or body, of the `while` loop is executed repeatedly until the condition of the loop is false.

QUESTIONS

1. Briefly describe how a Web application can access a database in ASP. What are the steps in connecting to a database? What method is used to execute queries? What type of object is returned by the execution of a select statement?

2. What does the + operator of JavaScript do with its string arguments?

3. What method of `Recordset` is used to fetch the value of a field in a row of a table? Give an example of fetching the value of a field by name. Give an example of fetching a value by it position in the list of fields.

4. What method of `Recordset` is used to change the row?

5. Describe the JavaScript `while` statement. What controls how many times it iterates?

6. Compare the different ways that quote marks can be embedded in string literals in SQL and JavaScript. Give an example of an SQL string literal that contains a single quote. Give an example of a JavaScript string literal that contains an embedded double quote.

7. Consult a Microsoft ActiveX Data Object (ADO) reference, such as the ADO Web site (http://www.microsoft.com/data/ado/). List the following

   a. Three properties of the `Connection` class.

   b. Three methods of the `Connection` class.

   c. Three properties of the `Recordset` class.

   d. Three methods of the `Recordset` class.

PROBLEMS

8. Add your own copy of the BigHit Video Access database to your computer and register it as an ODBC data source. Modify scripts `sqlform.asp` and `sqlexec.asp` to use your own page style and your database. Test your new scripts by executing SQL select statements. Turn in printouts of sample Web pages.

9. Modify the `rentals.asp` script so that it lists all of the videos for a particular movie. The new script (to be named `problem1209.asp`) should accept a CGI variable `movieId` that specifies the movie.

10. Write ASP and JavaScript code for the following.

   a. A script that creates an HTML page containing a table with a single column and 10 rows. The values 1 through 10 are to appear, one in each row. Use a `for` loop that iterates from 1 to 10 and prints each value of the variable as a separate row of the table. Store the script in file `problem1210a.asp` and turn in the source code and the URL.

   b. A script that creates an HTML page containing a table with two columns. The script should accept a single request parameter called `max`. The values 1 through `2*max` are to appear, two in each row. Use a `for` loop that iterates from 1 to the value

of the parameter and prints the correct two values in a row of the table. Store the script in file `problem1210b.asp` and turn in the source code and the URL.

   c. A script that creates an HTML page containing a table. The script should accept two request parameters called `cols` and `rows`. The values 1 through `rows*cols` are to appear. The table should have as many columns as the value of `cols`. Use two nested `for` loops to produce the values. The outer loop (variable `rownum`) should iterate through the rows and the inner loop (variable `colnum`) through the columns. The value printed by the inner loop should be `rownum*cols+colnum`. Store the script in file `problem1210c.asp` and turn in the source code and the URL.

11. Modify the ASP scripts `sqlform.asp` (producer of Figure 12.7) and `sqlexec.asp` of Figures 12.9 and 12.11 so that they use your own header and footer methods and connect to your own database. Store the scripts in files `problem1211form.asp` and `problem1211exec.asp` in your course Web site. Turn in the source code and the URLs.

PROJECTS

12. Modify the BigHit Video Web site by constructing scripts that allow clerks to check out and check in videos. For checkout, your site should present a page that allows the clerk to select the customer and several videos. The response to this page should be to create entries in the `Rental` table and to generate a receipt page that displays the details of the rental. The check-in page should allow the clerk to select a customer and display that customer's current rentals. The clerk should be able to check in the videos that have been returned. The result page should display a receipt that identifies any overdue videos.

13. a. Expand the add and update customer ASP scripts of this chapter to allow the user to provide multiple shipping addresses and multiple credit cards. You must also create ASP scripts that display this information.

   b. Expand your BigHit Online Web site to allow customers to register their movie preferences. They might like movies that have certain actors or directors, certain genres, or certain ratings. Decide exactly what preferences you will support, and develop a conceptual model and database tables for these preferences. Finally, develop the ASP scripts that create these capabilities for customers.

14. a. Write an ASP script in the style of `rentals.asp` that displays the list of movies seen by a member of your Movie Lovers Web site.

   b. Develop scripts to allow users of your Movie Lovers Web site to record which movies they have seen and to view the lists. Store the scripts in your Web site and turn in the URL of the main page of the site.

   c. Develop scripts to allow users to create information about new movies that are not in the database. Also allow the users to view and manipulate information about actors in the movies.

FURTHER READING

The Microsoft ASP Web site (http://www.microsoft.com/data/ado) is filled with documentation, tips, and examples. The ADO Programmer's Guide and Programmer's Reference are particularly helpful. Look for the "ADO Section of the MDAC SDK" in the documentation page of the ADO site.

The ASP books listed in the Chapter 11 Further Reading section all have documentation on the ADO library. Most do not have extensive coverage of using JavaScript, but they still provide information that you can use. *ASP in a Nutshell* [Wei00] is a particularly good source of information on database interaction.

The Web provides a wealth of information from other programmers about how to use ASP with JavaScript. The Google search engine (http://www.google.com) will provide many references to help answer your questions.

JavaScript books for server-side database programming with ASP were not too helpful at the time of publication of this book. You can find references to database access in JavaScript using the Netscape Web server. Unfortunately, the Netscape data access objects are very different from the ADO objects. The principles are the same, but the details are confusingly different. We can expect ASP/JavaScript books to appear soon, and you should use the Web to check on their progress.

At the time of publication of this book, Microsoft was distributing its ADO.Net systems. The changes for our programming style are not significant, but you should check the Microsoft Web site for differences between ADO version 2.7, which is featured in this book, and more recent versions.

Developing and Managing Web-Database Interaction

The last part of the book will help you to review the content of the first five parts, to apply the techniques you have learned to develop a whole system, and to master some additional techniques and concepts. The Case in Point sections of previous chapters covered issues and solutions for BigHit Online. Now we'll see how they all fit together.

Chapter 13 takes you through the creation of an information system for BigHit Online from its initial conception to the design of the Web site. We will review the Case in Point material from previous chapters and look for opportunities for improvement. At each step in information system design and implementation, we must review the previous steps to identify problems and make potential improvements. This chapter provides an opportunity to do just that. This review will enable us to make sure that we've designed an information system that accomplishes its goals.

Chapter 14 offers you a much more detailed understanding of how you can produce interactive Web applications in JavaScript. It shows you step by step how to develop interactive Web applications, while increasing your knowledge of programming techniques. You will learn how to organize your applications programs to make programming easier and more productive. This chapter will also help you to learn many new capabilities of the JavaScript language that are crucial for Web applications developers.

Chapter 15 completes the book by looking at important concepts and techniques for making high-quality, useful information systems. You'll learn several new techniques for making your databases and Web applications less sensitive to both user error and a variety of system failures. You'll find out the best way to allow many users to access the Web site at the same time and how to protect it from breaches in security.

These three chapters open the door to further study. This book sets the stage for you to develop excellent information systems. Your commitment to study beyond the scope of this book will make it happen.

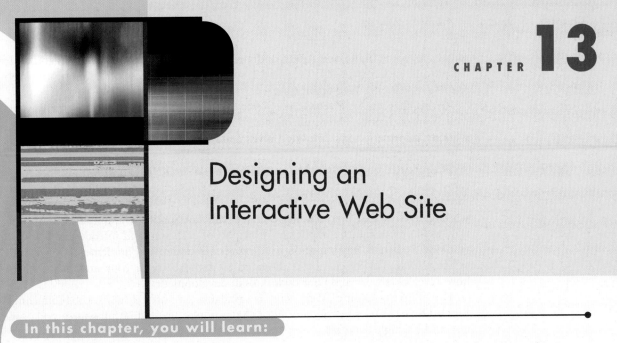

Designing an Interactive Web Site

In this chapter, you will learn:

- How to design and develop a complex information system
- Additional strategies to assist in conceptual modeling

- How to use SQL Server with Web applications
- How to design and evaluate SQL statements for a complex information system

By now, you have all of the skills you need to construct a video purchase Web site for BigHit Online. In the Case in Point sections of each chapter, you have already seen large pieces of this Web site. The purpose of this chapter is to work our way through the development of a complete information system, from the idea of the system and what it should be through to the Web applications that provide user interfaces.

The major topics of the book have been explained using the BigHit Video, Inc. information system as the primary example. You have learned how an information system can keep track of the business activities of a retail company. The information system database and user interfaces are tailored to the activities of the employees of the company. The employees register new customers, check videos in and out, purchase videos, and make sure the staff gets paid.

The BigHit Online information system is primarily intended for use by customers of the company. Customers access the information system directly. They remember their own account IDs, choose movies, and arrange to pay for them. BigHit Online still needs employees who will purchase the movies from their suppliers and who will ship movies to clients and respond to customer inquiries.

In the Case in Point sections of previous chapters, we considered some of the issues in the development of the BigHit Online information system. In Chapter 3 we listed entity classes, attributes, and relationship types. In Chapter 4, we drew an E-R diagram. In Chapter 5, we developed a relational model, and in Chapter 6 we created a Microsoft Access database. In Chapter 8, we wrote Access and relational algebra

325

queries for some of the operations, and in Chapter 9, we wrote SQL queries and table definitions. In Chapters 10, 11, and 12, we began the process of designing the Web site and developing Web applications.

In this chapter, we'll review the work of previous chapters and look for ways to make improvements. The result of all of this effort will be the design for a complete, working information system. We'll investigate the development of the Web applications in Chapter 14.

This chapter begins with data modeling and Web site organization and proceeds through the creation of the relational schema, the database, and finishes with the Web site design and SQL programming. Chapter 14 will show you how to produce the working Web site by investigating the ASP and JavaScript programming. Along the way, we'll emphasize the important principles of each step and introduce a few new wrinkles. Be sure to pay attention to the *process* of design and implementation as well as the results. This discussion is intended to reinforce both your understanding of how developers work and your own skills in development.

The BigHit Online Web site is available at http://www.web4data.com/BigHitOnline. This site contains all of the examples, including full source code listings and a sample database.

13.1 COMPONENTS OF THE BIGHIT ONLINE WEB SITE

The statement from Chapter 4 of the purpose of the information system is

> *BigHit Video Inc. wants to create an information system for online sales of both DVD and videotape format. People will be allowed to register as customers of the online site and to update their stored information. Information must be maintained about customers' shipping addresses, e-mail addresses and credit cards. In a single sale, customers will be allowed to purchase any quantity of videos. The items in a single sale will be shipped to a single address and will have a single credit card charge.*
>
> *A customer will be provided with a virtual shopping cart to store items to be purchased. As each item is selected, it is added to the shopping cart. When the customer finishes shopping, he will be directed to a checkout area where he can purchase all of the items in the shopping cart. At this time, payment and shipping information is entered. Once the sale is complete, the shopping cart will be deleted and the customer will be sent a receipt by e-mail.*

We want customers to use the BigHit Online Web site to order movies online; employees will use it to interact with customers, process orders, and maintain information about the business. The basic organization of the site follows that of most Internet retailers.

The customer side of the Web site must provide these major capabilities:

- *Customer information*: allow customers to create and edit their own profiles, and to login and logout
- *Shopping*: allow customers to search for movies to buy, select movies and place them in a shopping cart, and view and modify the contents of the shopping cart
- *Checkout*: allow customers to purchase items in the shopping cart, specify shipping and method of payment, and receive both an online and an e-mail receipt
- *Inquiry*: allow customers to inquire about the status of orders, see records of their past purchases, and comment on services

The business side of the Web site provides employees with the information services they need:

- *Orders*: allow employees to evaluate orders and record their status as it changes
- *Inventory*: allow employees to evaluate the inventory on hand, add new movies, update movie prices, and update the quantities as new movies arrive
- *Business activity*: allow employees to analyze the purchasing behavior of customer and evaluate the popularity of movies

In this chapter, we will evaluate at the information requirements of the BigHit Online information system, create a database to record this information, and develop the necessary Web applications. We will consider the buying activity of customers and leave the renting, and possibly downloading, of movies as exercises.

13.2 DATA MODELING FOR BIGHIT ONLINE

The analysis of the information requirements for BigHit Online from Chapters 3 and 4 led to the conceptual model represented by the E-R diagram of Figure 13.1. This diagram represents the entity classes and their attributes and relationships, and shows us what information can be represented by our system. An entity, often a row of a database table, always belongs to one of the entity classes and has values for all of the attributes of the class. An entity of one class may be related to an entity of another class by one of the relationship types that joins the two classes.

As you recall, rectangles (e.g., `Customer`) represent entity classes, ovals (`accountId`) represent attributes, and the diamonds and connecting lines (`Purchases`) represent relationship types. The underlined attributes of an entity class (`accountId`) form the key of the class. A double oval (`creditCards`) is a multi-valued attribute, and an attribute with its own attributes (again `creditCards`) is a composite attribute.

A double line between a relationship type and an entity class (between `Purchases` and `Sale`) means that an entity in the class must participate in this relationship. That is, a `Sale` entity (a sale) cannot exist without being related to a `Customer` entity (a customer). A single line means that an entity doesn't have to participate. A customer does not have to have any sales.

The `1` and `M` cardinality marks tell us how many entities may be related to one entity. The `1` on the line between `Purchases` and `Customer` means that a sale is purchased by one customer. The `M` on the line between `Purchases` and `Sale` means that customer may purchase many sales.

13.2.1 Evaluating the E-R Diagram

Can you find anything missing? It appears that all of the requirements on the customer list have been met. If you review the Case in Point sections of Chapters 3 and 4, you'll find that analysis paid careful attention to customer requirements.

Some issues in evaluating the capability of a conceptual model are quite subtle. For instance, we want customers to come to the Web site and login. How will the customer identify himself? Compare the online customer with the BigHit Video store customer. What happens when you want to rent a video at your local store? You take your movie to the counter and the clerk requests to see your membership card, or asks, "Do you know your account number?" The typical customer has lost the card and never knew the number, but has a driver's license or other picture ID. The clerk uses the computer system to look up the account by name or driver's license number and looks at the picture on the ID to verify the customer's identity. Will this strategy work for Web access? There's no clerk and no picture ID.

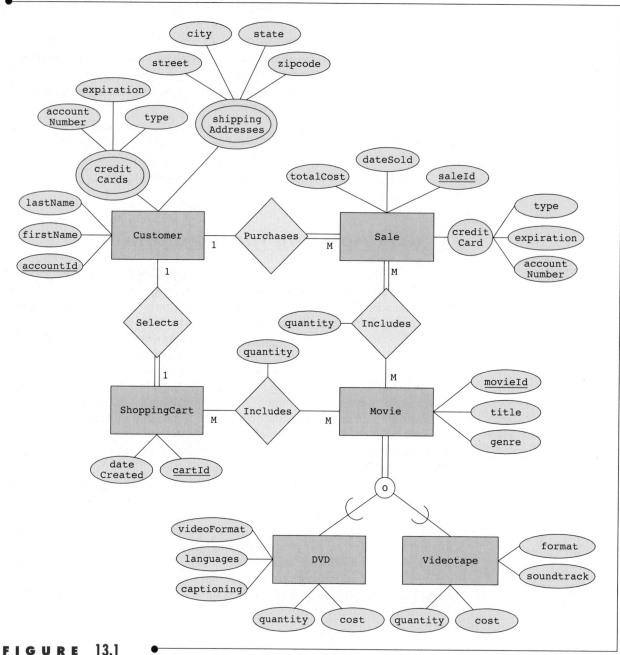

FIGURE 13.1

E-R Diagram for BigHit Online
from Figure 4.25

On the Web, we must expect the customer to remember his account ID. Most Web sites choose one of two strategies: Use the customer's e-mail address or let the customer choose his own account ID. Both require non-numeric identifiers. In Figure 13.1, the key of the `Customer` class is the integer `accountId` attribute. We must either change the type of the ID or add secondary keys to uniquely identify customers. If the e-mail address is used to identify the customer, it must be unique.

Let's change `accountId` to a text field and allow the customer to choose its value. The customer registration Web application will have to verify that no one else is using the ID before adding the customer. We'll make the account ID case insensitive by storing it as a lowercase string. It won't matter whether the customer types the account ID with uppercase or lowercase letters. The applications will turn it into lowercase.

The customer requirements are satisfied, but what about the employee requirements? We can turn some of the requirements of Section 13.1 into questions.

1. Can an employee evaluate a sale to determine how many items it includes and how much it costs?
2. Can a shipping clerk tell where to ship the items of a sale?
3. Is there any way for an employee to record information about packaging and shipping?
4. Can an employee determine inventory information such as quantity on hand of particular items?
5. Can a manager extract information about purchasing behavior of customers?
6. Can a manager determine the rate of sales of movies?

These are just a few of the questions we must ask to determine whether the design meets the system needs.

The answers to these questions allow us to conclude that the E-R diagram meets some, but not all of the system requirements. The answers are:

1. **Yes and no.** The `Sale` table is related to `Movie` and thus records the quantity of each movie that is purchased. However, we cannot tell whether a particular sale item is a DVD or videotape. Each sale is related to a movie, but a movie, with overlapping inheritance, can be both DVD and videotape.
2. **No.** The customer has several shipping addresses, but a sale has no record of which address to use.
3. **No.** The `Sale` table has no information about the status of the order. We know that the presence of a `Sale` entity means that something has been sold. It has a customer and quantities of movies, but no attributes or relationships to represent shipment. There is no way to tell whether an item has been shipped.
4. **Yes.** Each of the classes DVD and Videotape has a quantity attribute that records the quantity in inventory.
5. **Yes.** As long as all sales entities are kept and never deleted, we can analyze sales.
6. **Yes.** The rate of sales can be determined by correlating the dates of sales and the quantities of movies sold. The `Sale` class has a `dateSold` attribute and its relationship to `Movie` has a `quantity`.

You should write your own questions based on the requirements of Section 13.1. Can you find other issues that must be addressed?

13.2.2 Improving the E-R Diagram

Figure 13.2 shows the E-R diagram that has been modified to meet the missing requirements identified above. Table 13.1 shows the modified list of constraints. New attributes represent crucial information about status, shipping, and the type of each sale-movie combination and each shopping cart-movie combination. A `name` attribute was added to the shipping address so that an order may be shipped to someone other than the purchaser.

New `videoType` attributes on the two `Includes` relationship types add crucial information to the relationships. Now the clerk will be able to tell which type of video to ship for each sale. A customer will be allowed to order both a DVD and a videotape for a single movie.

Two new attributes represent information about the status of sales: the status attribute of a sale and the `qtyShipped` attribute of the `Includes` relationship type. The status of a sale is either `pending`, `complete`, or `partial`. The `qtyShipped` of a sale-movie relationship records the number of items that have been shipped. A realistic view of mail-order sales is that customers are allowed to buy items that are not in stock. The company will immediately ship items that are in stock and ship others as they become available. A pending sale is one that has been recorded, but no items

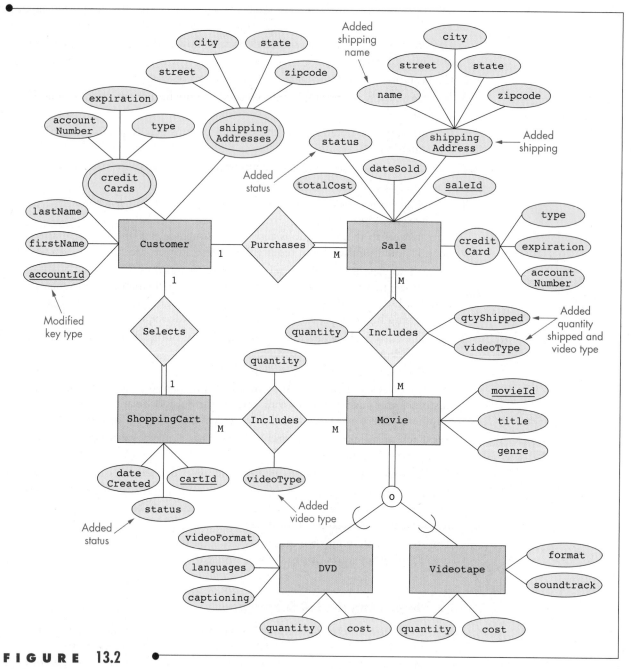

have been shipped. A partial sale is one that has some items shipped, but not all. Only if all items have been shipped is the sale considered complete. Thus, the combination of `status` and `qtyShipped` record sufficient information for a full determination of the status of a sale.

13.2.3 Using Weak Entity Classes for Many-To-Many Relationship Types

Many information system developers don't like many-to-many relationship types, and they especially don't like many-to-many relationship types with attributes because re-

Table 13.1 Modified Attributes and Constraints for BigHit Online Conceptual Model

Entity Class	Attribute	Constraints or Further Description
Customer	accountId	Key of type text, all lowercase letters and digits
Sale	shippingAddress	Composite attribute includes name
	status	Value from {pending, partial, complete}
ShoppingCart	status	Value from {new, newitems, updated}
ShoppingCart IncludesMovie	videoType	Value from {dvd, videotape}
SaleIncludesMovie	qtyShipped	Must be ≤ quantity
	videoType	Value from {dvd, videotape}

Concept

Choosing Key Attributes

The choice of keys for tables can have significant impact on the performance of databases. Single attribute numeric keys have the best performance because a numeric value can be stored in a single word (4 bytes) of memory and the value of two numbers can be compared with a single operation. Thus numeric keys are both compact and fast. Text keys require significantly more space and take longer to compare. A string of 10 characters takes at least 10 bytes to store and several operations to compare with another string. Comparison operations are particularly important for join queries. Reducing the size of a key can be crucial when many foreign keys reference it.

Professional designers often choose to create artificial keys for tables that would naturally have text keys. The additional trouble of maintaining the artificial keys is insignificant compared to the reduced cost of query execution when tables are very large.

---

lational database schemas do not directly support many-to-many relationship types. You know from Chapter 5 that each many-to-many relationship type in a conceptual model must be translated into a table in a relational database. Hence, many developers prefer to make the transformation in the conceptual model (E-R diagram).

Figure 13.3 shows the Includes relationship type between Sale and Movie represented as a weak entity class SaleItem. A similar diagram should be drawn for the ShoppingCart-Includes-Movie relationship type. Most attributes have been removed from the diagram. The SaleItem weak entity class is identified by its Has relationship types to both Sale and Movie. The identifying relationship types are both one-to-many, and each sale item must be related to one sale and one movie. We can express these relationship types as

- A sale item must have exactly one sale.
- A sale item must have exactly one movie.
- A movie may have many sale items.
- A sale may have many sale items.

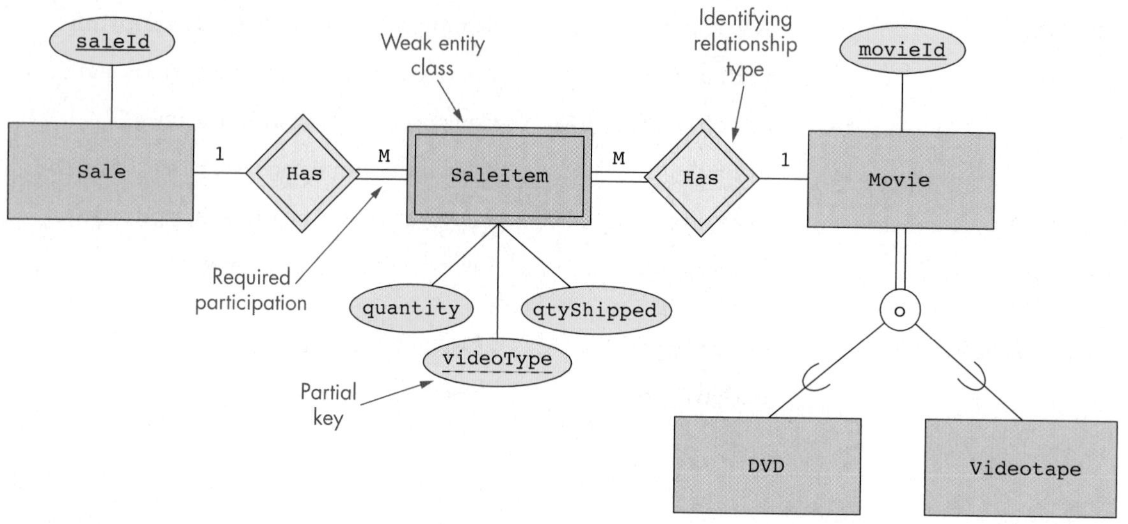

FIGURE 13.3
E-R Diagram with Weak Entity Class **`SaleItem`**

The entity classes with double borders (`SaleItem`) are weak entity classes. The relationship types with double borders (`Has`) are the identifying relationship types of the weak entity class. Entities of a weak class have no keys of their own and cannot exist unless they are related to at least one other entity. An attribute with a dashed underline (`videoType`) is a discriminator, or partial key, of its weak entity class. In this case, an entity of class `SaleItem` must be related to a sale and a movie. The key of the sale item will be the combination of the keys of its related sale and movie, plus the value of attribute `videoType`.

The `videoType` attribute of `SaleItem` is shown as a partial key (or discriminator) of the entity class. Thus, each sale item is identified by its relationship to a sale and a movie and its video type. Two sale items cannot have the same sale, movie, and video type. Thus, customer Jane Block may buy 2 DVDs and 1 videotape of *Annie Hall* in a single sale, but cannot have two sale items in a single sale for DVDs of *Annie Hall.*

The diagram of Figure 13.3 is more explicit about sale items than the original many-to-many relationship type of Figure 13.1. We have added a constraint to eliminate multiple items for a single type of video. This change improves the conceptual model.

A problem with the diagram of Figure 13.3 is that the key of the `SaleItem` table in the relational model will have three attributes. A simpler key would be better. Figure 13.4 shows how the diagram changes when we add an artificial partial key line to `SaleItem`. Now the sale item is identified by both its sale and its line number. The meaning of the diagram has changed, since the combination of sale, movie, and `videoType` is no longer guaranteed to be unique. Fortunately, it will be simple for us to enforce this restriction. We'll use the conceptual model of Figure 13.4 for the final E-R diagram.

13.2.4 **Modeling Shopping Carts and Wish Lists**

If you have used online retail sites, you are probably familiar with shopping carts. Do Web sites keep shopping carts intact between customer sessions? Some do and some don't. Some retail sites keep shopping carts for days or weeks and some delete them

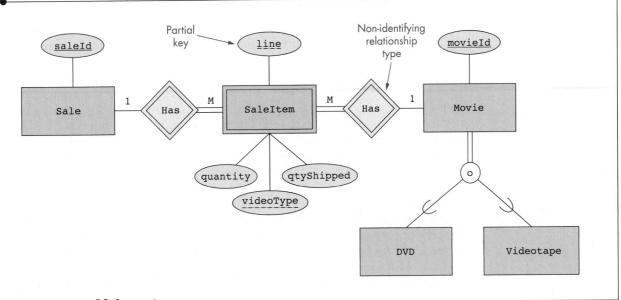

F I G U R E   13.4

Alternative with an Artificial
Partial Key

as soon as the customer leaves the site. If you go to the site one day and select items but don't buy them, you may find those items still selected when you return.

Keeping shopping carts is easy for the retailer, but may be burdensome for the customers. If you truly do not want items that you selected at a previous session, you must delete them before you can buy what you want.

The managers of the business will certainly want to be able to adjust the length of time to keep shopping carts. As designers, we must ensure that the managers' policy about retention of shopping carts can be modified without changing the E-R diagram. This is a place in the design where we recognize that a feature of the system (keeping shopping carts) is a policy and is subject to change. We need to evaluate the design to see if it restricts our ability to change this policy.

We are safe here. Nothing in the conceptual model specifies how long to keep the shopping cart. The `dateCreated` attribute of `ShoppingCart` allows the system to keep track of the age of a cart. We could add `dateModified` and `dateAccessed` fields to give additional flexibility. For instance, we could enforce a policy of deleting shopping carts after three days of inactivity.

We can also improve the customer's experience at the site by providing a way for customers to express interest in an item without committing to buy it. Many online retailers provide customers with a mechanism for keeping track of items that they hope to buy. Auction sites, for example, provide a way for customers to track the activity on specific items. We could add a wish list feature to allow customers to choose items that they are interested in purchasing in the future. We could track the price or availability of items and use e-mail to send notices to customers. Another advantage of wish lists is that they might be shown to another customer who is looking to buy a gift for the person who created the wish list.

Much of the utility of shopping carts and wish lists is related not to the data model but to the applications that use it. Shopping carts might be deleted, for instance, by a program that runs every night at midnight and looks at all the shopping carts in the system. Similarly, wish lists would be supported by offline applications that users would never see.

One of the problems at the end of the chapter asks you to add wish lists to the conceptual model.

13.2.5 **Modeling to Support Searching for Movies**

Each person who rents or buys movies has his or her own preferences. A movie Web site should maintain information about the people who acted in or created each movie. We also might want to have more information about plots and genres so that we can search for keywords. A customer might want to find movies that have certain historical characters, that take place at a certain time in history, or that feature certain kinds of actions.

Much of the consideration of searching is left as exercises and projects, but we can build a data model that relates people to movies, as in Figure 13.5. People are now included in our database and can have a variety of positions in their relationships with movies. A person could act in, direct, or write a movie. Woody Allen has all of these relationships with *Annie Hall*, for instance. The approach of Figure 13.5 allows us to identify individuals who play more than one role in creating movies.

The attributes of `Person` are few, and certainly incomplete. The key of `Person` is an artificial `personId`. We cannot expect that peoples' names are unique, even in the movie business where names are carefully protected. Other attributes could be added to aid in searching.

The diagram does not allow different positions to have different attributes. Can we record the name of Woody Allen's character in *Annie Hall*? Can we find all the movies in which Harrison Ford played a character named Indiana Jones? A more helpful diagram would add character names for actors. Of course, other positions do not have character names.

If we modify the diagram of Figure 13.5 so that `IsPartOf` is a weak entity class, we could use inheritance to model the variations in roles. Figure 13.6 shows some details of this approach. The positions are divided into cast and crew. Inheritance is required and disjoint so that a position must be either cast or crew and cannot be both. The `Position` class has a defining attribute `type` that specifies which subclass a particular position belongs to. Attribute `type` is the discriminator of the weak entity class. Each position is identified by the combination of its person, movie, and type. In the subclasses, cast members have roles, that is, character names, and crew members have titles: Key Grip, Best Boy, etc.

13.2.6 **Final Evaluation of the Conceptual Model**

Figure 13.7 shows the full E-R diagram for BigHit Online. Is there anything in the list of activities of Section 13.1 that requires additional information? Let's go through them one by one.

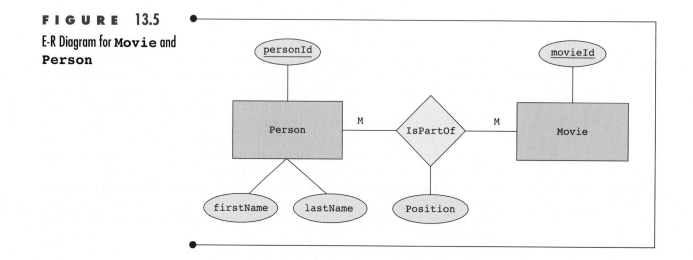

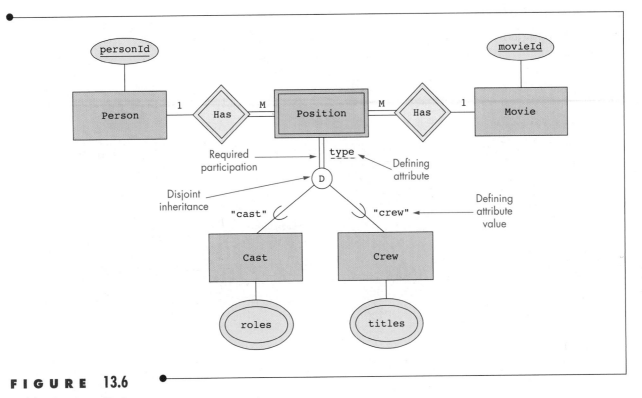

F I G U R E   13.6

Modeling Positions in Movies with Inheritance

The customer information management activities will create and modify `Customer` entities, but will have no direct impact on other classes. The login activity could be seen as modifying the customer and thus would require an attribute to store the login state for the customer. However, we will treat the login as a characteristic of the application and hence will not maintain information in the database about the login status of customers.

Shopping will involve searching for movies and placing items into the shopping cart. We have provided attributes of `Movie` that support searching and attributes of class `ShoppingCart` that store the shopping cart information.

Checkout will fetch `ShoppingCart` and `CartItem` entities and create `Sale` and `SaleItem` entities. Once the `Sale` and `SaleItem` entities have been created, the corresponding `ShoppingCart` and `CartItem` entities will be deleted. Hence, the relationship between `ShoppingCart` and `Sale` is not a persistent one. A brief relationship is created by the checkout application, but by the end of the checkout activity, no relationship endures.

Inquiry activities involve queries of information stored in classes that are included in Figure 13.7. No further information is required unless we want to record information about the inquiry activities themselves. A customer will not be able to ask, "What was the last sale I asked about?"

The models of this chapter certainly simplify the information requirements for online retail sales. A thorough investigation of the Amazon site, for instance, would yield many opportunities for increasing the utility and user-friendliness of the site.

On the business side of the information system, we will be able to evaluate sales and modify their status. We can determine the e-mail address of customers to enable sending notices of various kinds. Because we save the sales entities, even after they have been shipped and paid for, we have many opportunities to evaluate buying and selling patterns.

FIGURE 13.7

Improved E-R diagram for
BigHit Online

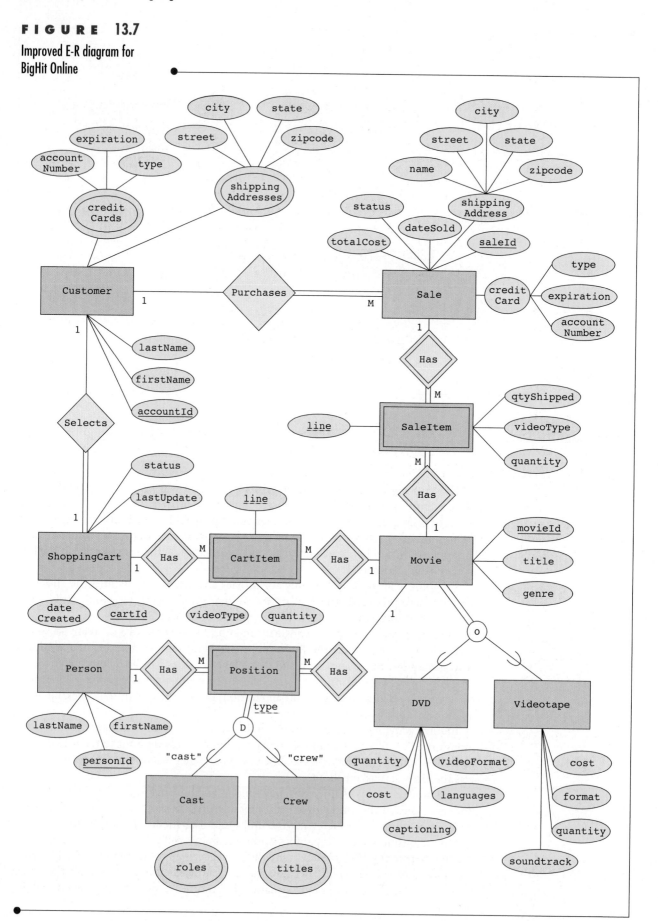

We have not, however, included any employee information in the data model, nor have we made arrangements for recording the results of analysis. A full information system would need enhanced capabilities on the business side.

13.3 RELATIONAL MODEL FOR BIGHIT ONLINE

We create the relational model for BigHit Online by a direct application of the E-R diagram transformation rules of Chapter 5, with a little additional analysis and simplification. Figure 13.8 is a snapshot of the relational model showing the tables, attributes, and relationships as displayed in the Microsoft SQL Server Enterprise Manager. An **enterprise manager** is a graphical user interface provided as part of a database system that allows users to create, modify, and view database objects.

This diagram shows the relationship types as lines with either a yellow circle or a double white circle on each end. The yellow circle denotes a to-one relationship role and the double circle a to-many role. So the relationship type between `Customer` and `ShoppingCart` is one-to-one and the relationship type between `Customer` and `Sale` is one-to-many. The diagram does not identify which attributes are related

FIGURE 13.8

Database Schema for
BigHit Online

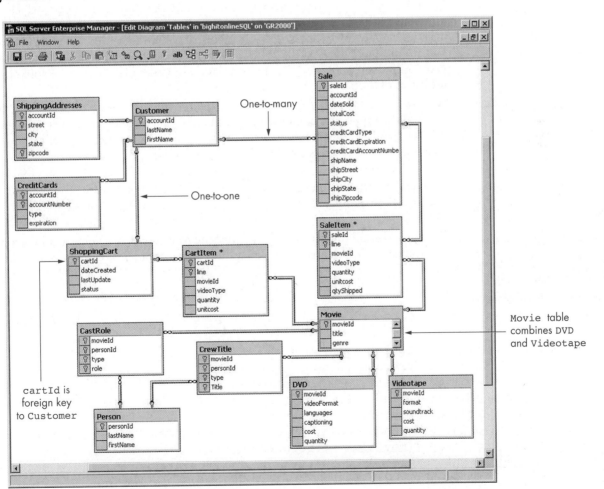

to which others. In Access, the relationship lines connected attributes of tables, but in the Enterprise Manager, the lines connect tables.

The schema for `ShoppingCart` uses the `cartId` as key and as foreign key to `Customer`. That is, the ID of a shopping cart takes its value from the account ID of the related customer. A shopping cart has to be related to a customer and the cart ID is intended to be an artificial key. So if we use the account ID of the customer as the key of the shopping cart, we have one fewer attribute in `ShoppingCart` and thus one fewer value to manipulate.

The `Movie`, `DVD`, and `Videotape` entity classes were transformed into a single `Movie` table by combining the attributes of the three classes. The `quantity` and `salePrice` attributes of the `DVD` entity class became the `dvdQty` and `dvd-SalePrice` attributes of the `Movie` table. This strategy for representing superclass and subclasses as a single table is embodied by Rule 8b of Section 5.9.

Rule 8b: For each superclass C, create a new relation schema using the appropriate rules. For each specialization of C that has a defining attribute, add that attribute to the schema for C. For each subclass S of C, add the simple and composite attributes of S to the schema for C.

This representation is particularly appropriate because not only can each movie be both DVD and videotape, but in most cases, movies are available in both formats. Hence, for most movies none of the attributes will be null.

The representation of the `Position` entity class and its subclasses is hardly recognizable in Figure 13.8. The final table definitions come from transformation and analysis of the entity classes.

The first step in the transformation is to select which of the transformation rules should be applied. The only attribute in the `Position` class is the `type`, which determines the subclass. Because `Position` has so few attributes and each position must be a member of a subclass, we can represent the classes with a table for each subclass and no table for `Position`, as in Figure 13.9, which also includes tables for their multivalued attributes. The representation of `Cast` and `Crew` is an application of Rule 8c of Section 5.9.

Rule 8c: For each subclass S, create a new relation schema. For each superclass C of S, add the simple and composite attributes of C and S to the new schema, as in Rules 2 and 4. Declare the key of the schema to be the combination of the key attributes from the superclasses. For each superclass C that has a partial specialization, create a new relation schema and add all of the attributes of C.

Tables `CastRole` and `CrewTitle` of Figure 13.9 represent the multivalued attributes `roles` and `titles`, respectively, as required by Rule 7 of Section 5.8.

Rule 7: For each multivalued attribute M of an entity class C, define a new relation schema M. Add the components of attribute M to the new schema. Add the key attributes of the schema that contains the other attributes of C to M as a foreign

FIGURE 13.9

Initial Table Definitions for Cast and Crew and Their Multivalued Attributes

```
1  Schema: Cast (movieId int references Movie,
2     personId int references Person, type text)
3  Schema: Crew (movieId int references Movie,
4     personId int references Person, type text)
5  Schema: CastRole ((movieId int references Cast,
6     personId int references Cast, type text references Cast, role text)
7  Schema: CrewTitle ((movieId int references Crew,
8     personId int references Crew, type text references Crew, title text)
```

key. Define the key of the new schema to be the combination of all of its attributes.

Look closely at the differences between `Cast` and `CastRole` and between `Crew` and `CrewTitle`. Each `CastRole` has all of the attributes of `Cast` and each `CrewTitle` has all of the attributes of `Crew`. Suppose that each cast member has at least one role and each crew member has at least one title. Then no entity in `Cast` can exist without at least one entity in `CastRole` that duplicates all of its attributes. Does each cast member have to have a role name? The answer is yes, even if the role name is "Extra." The same analysis can be applied to `Crew` and `CrewTitle`.

Thus, we can completely eliminate `Cast` and `Crew` without losing any information. As a result, the database schema of Figure 13.8 has no tables for entity classes `Position`, `Cast`, or `Crew`.

More details are available from the SQL statements that create these tables. Figure 13.10 shows the `create table` statement for `ShoppingCart` and `CartItem`. The `cartId` (line 2) of the shopping cart is a foreign key reference to the account ID of the customer. The type of this field is `varchar(16)`. This allows our customer to select an ID of up to 16 characters. The information system will reject the key if it is the same as another customer's.

We must also anticipate the various searches and provide indexes to make queries run faster. SQL databases always provide indexes on primary keys. We will add indexes to all foreign keys and also to the fields of `Movie` that we expect to use in searching. Of course, we will be searching by movie title and the names of people and customers. Figure 13.11 shows some of the `create index` statements.

FIGURE 13.10

SQL **create table** Statements for BigHit Online Tables

```
1   create table ShoppingCart (
2       cartId varchar(16) not null primary key,
3       startDate datetime not null,
4       status varchar(16) not null,
5       lastUpdate datetime not null,
6       foreign key cartId to Customer(accountId)
7   )
8   create table CartItem (
9       cartId varchar(16) not null,
10      line int not null,
11      movieId int not null references Movie(movieId),
12      quantity int not null,
13      videoType char(4) not null,
14      unitcost money not null,
15      foreign key cartId references ShoppingCart(cartId),
16      primary key (cartId, line)
17  )
```

FIGURE 13.11

SQL Statements to Create Indexes

```
1   create index MovieTitle on Movie (title)
2   create index PeopleLastName on People (lastName)
3   create index SaleAccount on Sale (accountId)
```

13.4 CREATING A SQL SERVER DATABASE

We want our BigHit Online database to be robust and efficient. If we anticipate very much customer activity, a Microsoft Access database will not meet our requirements. We need to create a database on a more powerful database system, but still be able to write applications in ASP and JavaScript. Fortunately, every database system can be accessed from the ASP programming environment. We can choose IBM DB2, Oracle 9i, or Microsoft SQL Server (pronounced "sequel server") to name but a few.

The BigHit Online Web site that is described in this chapter uses the version of SQL Server that is distributed with Microsoft Office Professional. Microsoft refers to this version as the Microsoft Data Engine (MSDE). You can install it on your system from the MSDE directory of the Office Professional CD.

In the Case in Point section in Chapter 6, we created an Access database for BigHit Online. It needs to be updated to be consistent with the relational schema of Figure 13.8. Once we've made the necessary changes, we can use a tool called the **upsizing wizard** that is part of Access to create a SQL server database directly from the Access database.

Once you've opened your Access database, you should select the `Tools` menu, then `Database Utilities` and `Upsizing Wizard`, as shown in Figure 13.12. The wizard will take you through a series of steps in which you select a server, a database name, and the tables you want to transfer. When you answer all of the questions, the wizard will transfer your database to SQL Server. The results will include a new Access file `bighitonline.adp` (an Access project file) and a SQL Server database.

The Access project file is connected to the SQL Server database to allow you to use Access as your user interface. You can modify tables, add and remove data, and create Access forms and Queries.

However, the database can also be accessed using other programming tools. If you register the SQL Server database as an ODBC data source, as described in Section 12.1, you will be able to use this database from your Web applications.

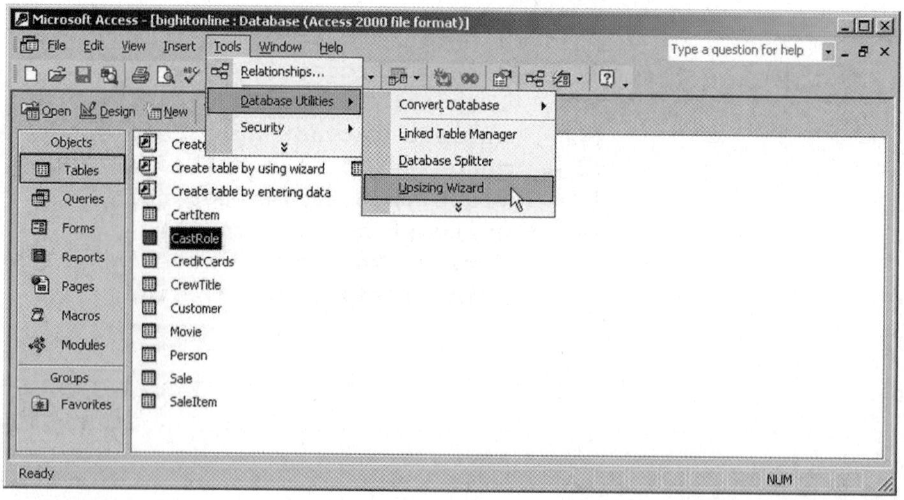

FIGURE 13.12

Selecting Upsizing Wizard from the Tools Menu

INTERVIEW

MARY RICCARDI

Merging the Needs of the Client with the Ability of the Technology

Mary Riccardi became interested in Web development at Florida State University (FSU), where she did work as a Web master for various FSU associations. She graduated with a minor in Computer Science in the Spring of 2001, and worked as a Web developer at a local Tallahassee company. In Fall 2002, Mary entered the Masters in Internet Technology program at University of Georgia.

FIRST EXPERIENCE WITH WEB WORK I think the only way you can learn is to try to do it yourself. One of the best things I did was to get involved with school organizations and do Web work for them, which gave me first-hand experience on what it was like to build a Web page to meet people's needs.

FIRST JOB/CURRENT JOB "This is my first real job. My days consist of designing and programming Web sites. I spend a great deal of time maintaining these and making sure the clients' Web sites most efficiently meet their needs. This includes making sure that they can access data in the most efficient way possible and making the collecting of data conducive to their individual needs.

> ❝I think the only way you can learn is to try to do it yourself. One of the best things I did was to get involved with school organizations and do Web work for them, which gave me first-hand experience on what it was like to build a Web page to meet people's needs.❞

FROM COLLEGE TO THE REAL WORLD—ON CURRENT JOB TRENDS From what I am seeing at my job, almost every aspect of data is moving from shared computers to online access of data. Here is an example: Today most employees access company data by connecting to the server through a LAN connection. Companies are now moving toward accessing that same data via the Internet or intranet. In years to come, Web developers, like myself, will be working to improve access and security of online data and working with various different types of handheld computers (phones, handhelds, etc.) to access this data.

ON CURRENT JOB CHALLENGES I think one of the hardest obstacles is working with the client to come to a compromise between what is efficient and technically correct and how the client thinks things should be done. In other words, finding ways to achieve what the client wants while still maintaining proper Internet protocol. This involves explaining to the client, in non-technical terms, a lot of technical "can'ts" or security "shouldn'ts" and it involves them explaining to me a lot more of why they need certain functionality. There is a trend to make certain parts of Web sites that can be updated and maintained by people who have limited technical knowledge. For example, in our office the human resources assistant updates that contact page on our Web site through an online administrator login which allows her to change/add employees' contact information. Whatever the project is, in the end, we need to find a way that both our wants are met.

ON CONTINUING EDUCATION Always look at a lot of Web sites. If you go to a site and you think it is a really good page that is either a good design, cool programming, or has a great navigation system, then bookmark it or print it out. Also, if you think something is really cool about a Web site, check out the source code and see how the page was created. One of the best ways to learn is to learn through example.

13.5 WEB SITE DESIGN, PAGES, AND FLOW

Now that you've created your database, you are ready to begin designing and implementing Web applications. As much as we'd like to, it will be impossible in this book to cover all of the details of building a commercial Web site. We'll make some simplifications and refer you to the Web site for many of the details.

Several simplifications will make the site implementation straightforward and easier to understand. Chapter 14 discusses many of the simplifications and addresses additional issues in security and other important concepts.

The first simplification we'll make is to require that every customer begins interacting by logging in or enrolling. Commercial retail sites allow unknown people to browse through the site and even choose items for their shopping carts, but only registered customers can buy. We'll simply avoid the additional complications of non-customer interaction. Every Web application will expect to know who the customer is.

We'll be following a user, Joe Jones, beginning with his login and continuing through selection and purchase of videos. After logging in, Joe will see his customer information. He will access the page that shows his shopping cart, which is empty. Next, he will search for comedy movies, view a list of them, and select some to put in his shopping cart. He will go to the checkout area, view a list of the items to be purchased, and confirm his purchase. Finally he will log out.

We'll go through this sequence of actions from three perspectives. Joe Jones sees the interaction as a sequence of Web pages. The database server sees the interaction as a sequence of SQL statements. Finally, the Web applications developer sees this interaction as a sequence of requests for the execution of ASP scripts.

The first trip through Joe Jones's video purchase will look at the Web pages and SQL statements. You will see exactly which SQL statements are executed by the Web applications in order to create the pages and update the database. Chapter 14 will address the issues of how the ASP/JavaScript programs are organized and show some of the programming strategies and difficulties that are encountered.

13.5.1 Login and Customer Information

Joe Jones begins at the home page of the Web site—the login page that is shown in Figure 13.13. It features a button bar that allows the customer to go to the customer information page, the shopping cart, the search page, the inquiry page, the checkout page, or the logout page. This button bar has been incorporated into the `print-Header` function and so will appear on every page in the site. The site supports freedom of movement rather than a predetermined access sequence.

The customer entered the account ID `JoJo` and a six-letter password. The HTML input tag with type `password` does not show the text typed by the user. When Joe clicks the `submit` button the on the form, the account ID and the password will be passed to the Web application through HTTP request variables. Checking the account ID and password can be done after the execution of

```
select * from Customer where accountId=lower('JoJo')
```

The function `lower` is used to force a string to lowercase. Here, we have a string `JoJo` that has been entered by the user. Since we are using case-insensitive account IDs, we allow the user to use uppercase or lowercase, but look up the account ID in the database using its lowercase equivalent.

After logging in, Joe Jones is shown the customer information summary page as shown in Figure 13.14. Of course, the password is not shown. The previous select statement provides the information for the summary page. Joe is now logged in and can move through the site by clicking the navigation links in the header.

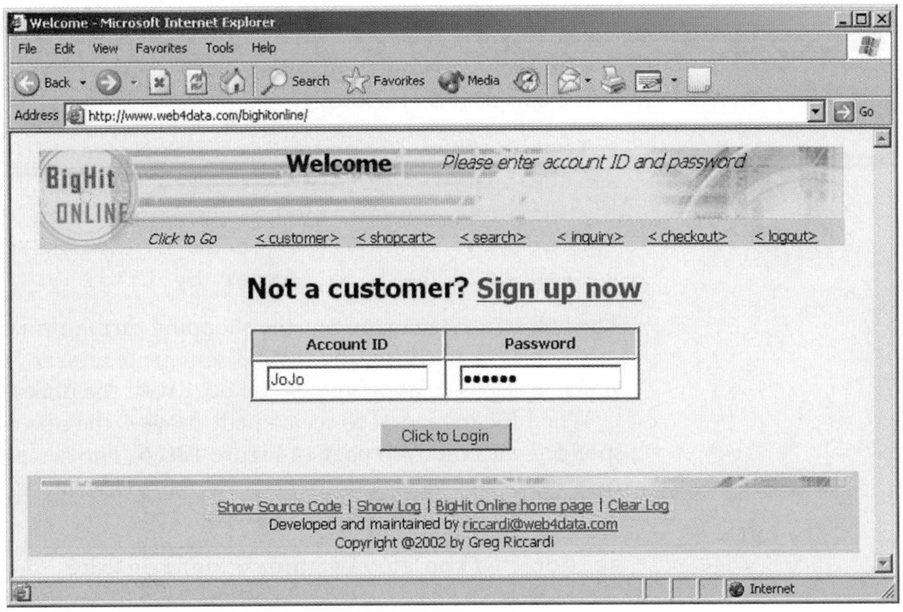

FIGURE 13.13
Login Page for BigHit Online

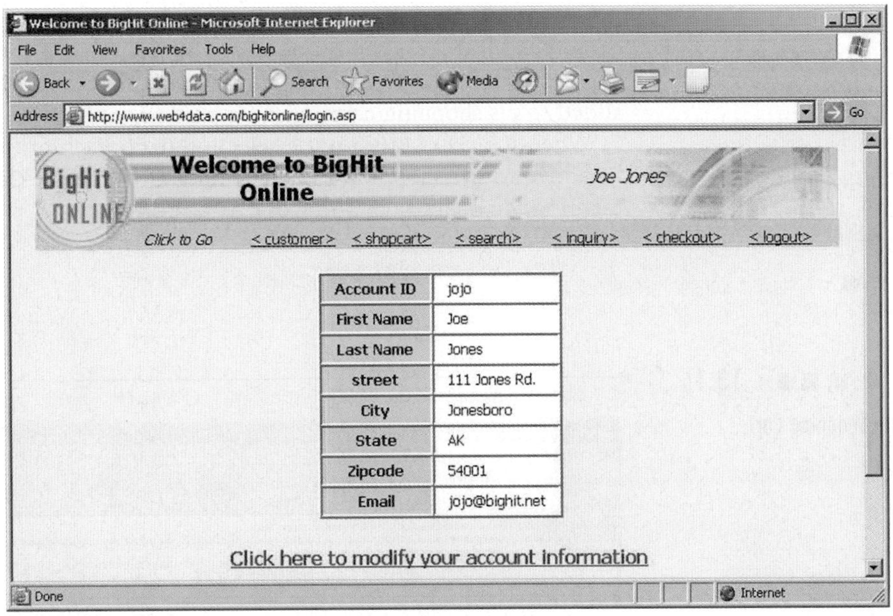

FIGURE 13.14
The Customer Information Page

13.5.2 **Shopping Carts, Searching, and Selecting Items**

When Joe clicks the `shopcart` link in the button bar, the Web application responds by displaying the shopping cart status page, as in Figure 13.15. The shopping cart is empty, since no items have been added. The new shopping cart was created by the execution of

```
insert into ShoppingCart (cartId, startDate, status,
    lastUpdate) values ('jojo', getdate(),'new', getdate())
```

The SQL Server function `getdate` produces the system date on the server. The same value is used for the start date (second value in the list) and the date of the last update (fourth value in the list).

The Web application that produced Figure 13.15 executed the following SQL statements to fetch the displayed information.

```
select * from ShoppingCart where cartId = 'jojo'
select line, c.movieId, title, quantity, videoType,
    unitCost, quantity*unitCost as totalCost from
    cartItem c, Movie m where c.movieId=m.movieId
    and cartId='jojo' order by title
```

The first select statement gets the shopping cart information, and the second gets the cart items. In this case, the second statement returns an empty table with no rows, which is displayed accurately in the page with the phrase "No items in your cart."

When Joe requested to see comedy movies, the `search.asp` Web application responded with the Web page of Figure 13.16. The details of searching are left as exercises. The Web application executed the following SQL statement to extract the information on this page.

```
select * from Movie where genre like '%comedy%' order by
    title
```

The details of how this information is printed on the page are deferred to Section 13.6. We can see that the page shows information about the movie in the first four columns followed by a column with DVD information and a column with videotape information.

Joe can use the input elements on this page to select items to add to his shopping cart. When Joe clicks the `Buy` button, he will request that the Web application add 2 copies of the DVD of *Animal House* and 3 copies of the videotape of *Duck Soup* be added to his shopping cart.

When Joe clicks `Buy` on the selection page, each of the two requested items must be added to the shopping cart by adding a row to the `CartItem` table, or by incrementing the quantity in a row of `CartItem`.

FIGURE 13.15

Empty Shopping Cart

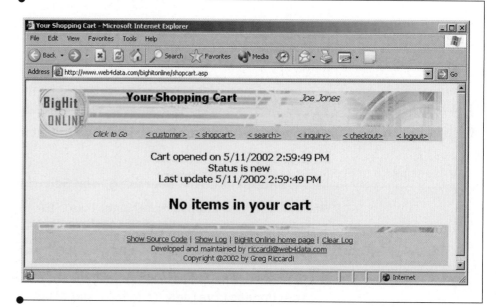

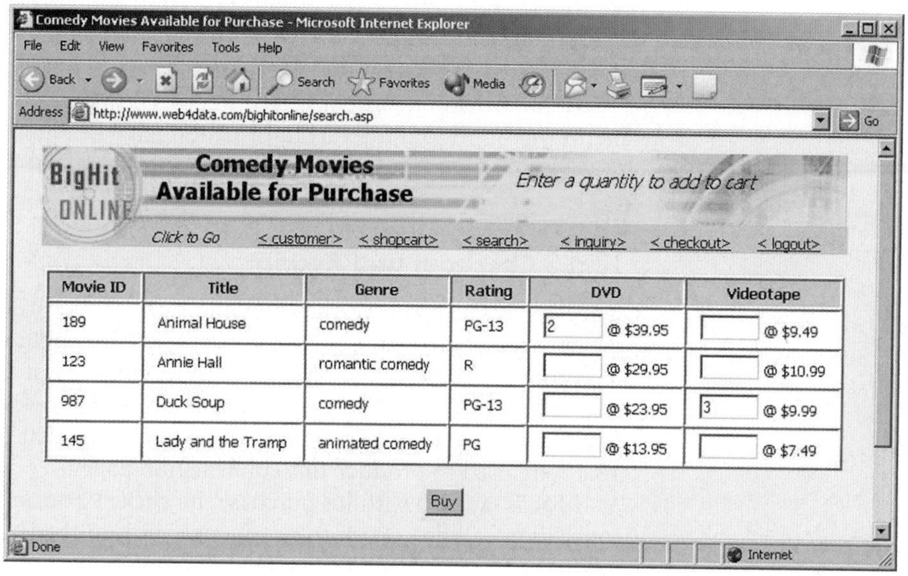

Selecting Movies to Put in the Shopping Cart

Before adding a new row to `CartItem`, the Web application must check to see if the item is already in the cart. If it is, the application should increment the quantity of the proper row of the `CartItem` table. If the customer does not already have this item in the cart, a new entry is required.

For the first item, which is a DVD with `movieId` 189, the Web application executes this query, which will return a row if the selected item is already in the cart.

```
select line from CartItem where cartId='jojo' and
    movieId=189 and videoType='dvd'
```

Suppose the query reports that line 1 of the cart holds a copy of the DVD with `movieId` 189. The following update statement adds 2 copies of the movie to the cart.

```
update CartItem set quantity=quantity+2
    where line=1 and cartId='jojo'
```

If the selected items are not already in the cart, they must be added with SQL insert statements. The key of each entry must be the combination of the cart ID (the customer's account ID) and a line number. Execution of this SQL statement will determine the maximum line number currently in use.

```
select max(line) from CartItem where cartId='jojo'
```

Because Joe's cart is empty, the Web application will execute these two insert statements to add the items selected in Figure 13.16 to the empty cart.

```
insert into CartItem (cartId, line, movieId, videoType,
    quantity,unitcost)
    values ('jojo','1','189','dvd',2,39.95)
insert into CartItem (cartId, line, movieId, videoType,
    quantity,unitcost)
    values ('jojo','2','987','vhs',3,9.99)
```

After updating the database, the Web application generates the shopping cart information and update page of Figure 13.17. Joe can either modify the quantities of items in the cart and click `Modify Shopping Cart` or use the button bar to return to shopping or go to checkout.

The information content of Figure 13.17 was produced by the same SQL statements that produced the cart information page of Figure 13.15. This time, however, two items are in the cart and are displayed in the table.

13.5.3 **Checkout and Receipt**

Once Joe is satisfied with the shopping cart, he can proceed to checkout by clicking the checkout button in the button bar. The Web application responds with the page of Figure 13.18, which shows the current contents of the shopping cart, much like that of Figure 13.17. This is a confirmation page, however, and will not support any modification of items. The same select statements that produced Figures 13.15 and 13.17 are used to produce this confirmation page.

If Joe is satisfied with his purchase, he clicks `Proceed to Checkout`. The Web application will first check to see if anything is in the shopping cart by executing the following.

```
select count(*) from CartItem c where cartId='jojo'
  and quantity>0
```

The query reports on how many rows of Joe's shopping cart have non-zero quantities. If this query returns zero, there is nothing to be purchased. In the present case the query returns 2 because two rows have non-zero quantities.

The `checkout.asp` Web application must create new entries in the `Sale` and `SaleItem` tables and produce a receipt page for the customer. The `Sale` and `SaleItem` entries are very similar to the `ShoppingCart` and `CartItem` entries.

F I G U R E 13.17

Shopping Cart Status and
Update Page

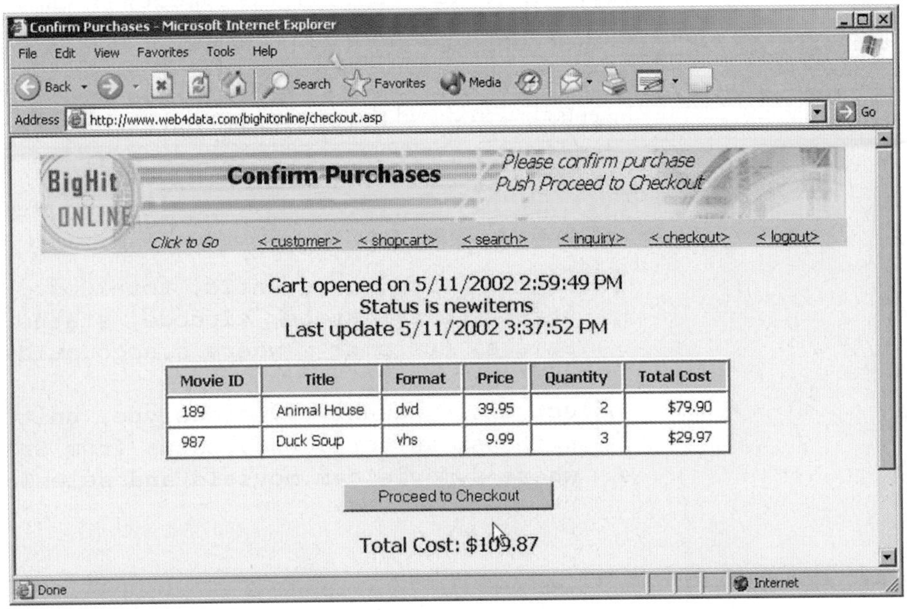

FIGURE 13.18

Checkout Confirmation Page

Before adding information to the tables, the Web application must find a sales ID for the new `Sale` entry that will be added. The execution of this `select` statement will find the largest current sales ID.

select max(salesId) **from** Sale

Suppose that the max(`salesId`) is 65. The Web application can add the new row to the `Sale` table with

insert into Sale (salesId,accountId,saleDate,status,total
    Cost) **values** (66,'jojo',getdate(),'sold',0)

The sales ID is 66 (the next one after 65), and the `totalCost` is set to 0. The application will update `totalCost` after creating the sales items.

The `SaleItem` entries are created directly from `CartItem` entries with

insert into SaleItem **select** 66, line, movieId, quantity,
    videoType, unitCost, 'pending' **from** CartItem
    where cartId='jojo' and quantity<>0

Each new value for `SaleItem` is created from the line number, movie ID, quantity and video type of the corresponding `CartItem`, plus the sales ID (`66`) and the status (`'pending'`).

Now that the sales items have been created, the Web application can calculate the total cost and update the row of the `Sale` table.

select sum(quantity*unitCost) **from** SaleItem
    where salesId=61
update Sale **set** totalCost=112.87 **where** salesId=66

Next, the Web application removes the items from the available inventory by updating the `Movie` table.

```
update Movie set dvdQty=dvdQty-2 where movieId=189
update Movie set tapeQty=tapeQty-3 where movieId=987
```

The last update step is for the Web application to delete the shopping cart and its items.

```
delete from CartItem where cartId='jojo'
delete from ShoppingCart where cartId='jojo'
```

Finally, the Web application generates the receipt page, shown in Figure 13.19. The information on this page is produced with

```
select salesId, s.accountId, totalCost, firstName, lastName,
    street, city, state, zipcode, status, saleDate from
    Sale s, Customer c where s.accountId=c.accountId
    and salesId=66
select title, quantity, videoType, unitCost, quantity*
    unitCost as totalCost,status from SaleItem s, Movie m
    where s.movieId=m.movieId and salesId=66 order by title
```

FIGURE 13.19

Receipt for Purchase

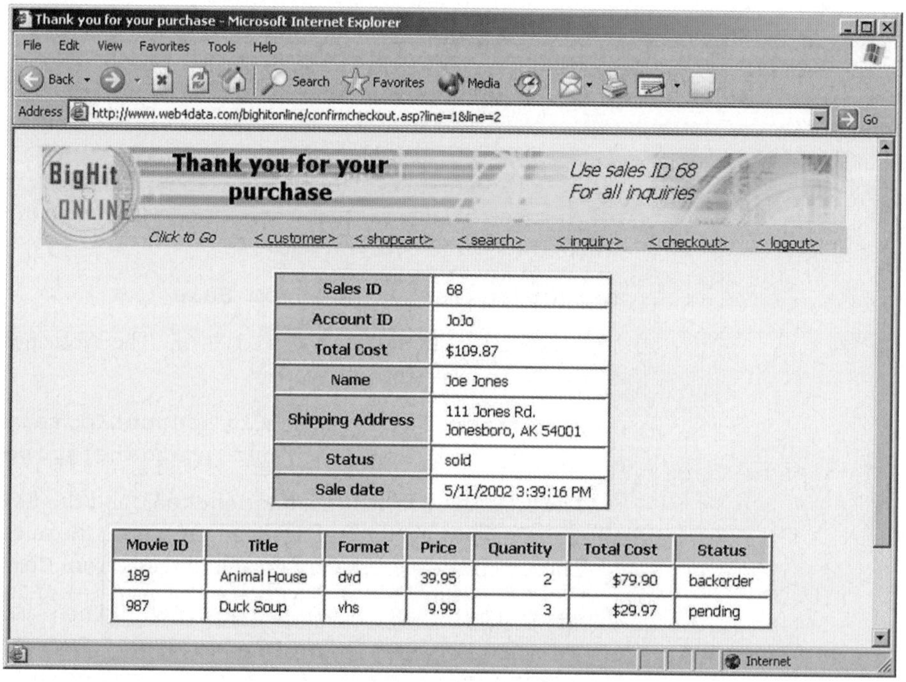

CHAPTER SUMMARY

This chapter presents much of the design and implementation process for information systems as it applies to creating an online video purchase Web site. It demonstrates E-R modeling, translation to relational schema, Web-site design, and application development.

The components of the information system are associated with customer processing, searching for movies and selecting items for purchase, purchasing and paying for items, and inquiries into the status of orders and shopping carts.

The E-R modeling included the creation of entity classes to represent sales and shopping carts and to add information to the basic movie attributes in order to record information about the people who participate in the production of the movies.

The E-R modeling also included a review of the information requirements to ensure that everything that was needed was included. This review identified several areas where extensions are appropriate.

The production of the relational schema for BigHit Online is mostly very straightforward. Keys were created for weak entities, and foreign keys were added to represent relationships. The inheritance relationships between `Movie` and its subclasses `DVD` and `Videotape` were represented by a single `Movie` table with all of the attributes of entity classes `Movie`, `DVD`, and `Videotape`.

The first step in creating the application is to decide on the types of pages that will be included and the flow between pages that will be supported. The basic navigation strategy is to use a button bar that supports arbitrary movement between the major sections. Other pages such as the order confirmation page can only be reached from some specific page.

The next step in the design and implementation is to determine exactly what information is required for each page and design the SQL statements that will fetch that information. A parallel activity is the determination of what database updates are required for processing each form and the design of the SQL statements that create those updates.

Section 13.5 shows all of the SQL and all of the pages that are involved in the purchase of several videos by a customer.

KEY TERMS

Enterprise manager. A graphical user interface for interacting with database servers. An enterprise manager can be used to create and modify database objects.

Upsizing wizard. The Microsoft Access process that creates a SQL Server database from an Access database.

QUESTIONS

1. What is the difference between a strong entity class and a weak entity class?
2. What is the difference between a relationship type and a relationship?
3. Write SQL statements to use the BigHit Online database of Figure 13.8 for the following customer activities.
   a. Register yourself as a BigHit Online customer. That is, add a row to the `Customer` table.
   b. Modify your profile by changing your zip code.
   c. Add a credit card to your customer profile.
   d. Add a shipping address to your customer profile.
   e. Find all of the movies with "black" in the title.
   f. List the items in your shopping cart.
   g. Update the status of your shopping cart to "newitems."
   h. Remove the rows from your shopping cart.
   i. Create a sale from your shopping cart items.
   j. Calculate the total cost of the sale items
4. Write SQL statements to use the BigHit Online database for the following business activities.
   a. Calculate the total value of all shopping carts.
   b. Calculate the total value of all sales with status "pending."
   c. Make a list of all items for pending sales
   d. Make all changes necessary to ship 2 DVDs for line 3 of the sale with `saleId` 2144.
   e. Add one of your favorite recent movies to the `Movie` table.
   f. Add 10 DVDs and 5 videotapes to the quantities of the movie you added in part e.
   g. Find the movie IDs and titles of all movies with fewer than 10 DVDs in inventory.

h. Find the movie IDs and titles of all movies with fewer that 10 total tapes plus DVDs.

i. Calculate the total value of all sales in the past month.

j. List the customer name, account ID, and total sales for each customer, ordered by maximum total sales.

5. Write SQL statements to search the movie and person information of Figure 13.8.

a. List each movie that has Cameron Crowe as director.

b. Which movies had a character named Buzz Lightyear?

c. Which movies had Helen Hunt in the cast?

d. Which movies had Jodie Foster in the crew?

e. Which movies were more than 150 minutes long and had Kevin Costner in the crew?

f. Which movies had some person in both cast and crew?

6. Write SQL table definitions for these tables of Figure 13.8.

a. `Customer`

b. `CreditCards`

c. `ShippingAddresses`

d. `SaleItem`

e. `Movie`

f. `CrewTitle`

PROBLEMS

7. Draw an E-R diagram for a wish list as an addendum to Figure 13.7. Base your response on the description of wish lists in Section 13.2.4.

8. Create table definitions in SQL for the wish list you created in problem 7.

PROJECTS

9. a. Extend the Web site design of this chapter to include customer information update pages. Be sure to include credit card and shipping addresses. Give sample SQL statements to extract and modify database information as required by your new pages.

b. Extend the Web site design of this chapter to include wish list processing according to the design of problem 7. Give sample SQL statements to extract and modify database information as required by your new pages.

c. Extend the Web site design by adding payment and shipping information to the checkout interaction. Give sample SQL statements to extract and modify database information as required by your new pages.

d. Extend the Web site design by creating an interface for a shipping clerk. The shipping clerk needs to be able to find all items in pending or partial sales that have items in inventory. Give sample SQL statements to record when items are shipped and to check for sales that have status pending or partial, but all items have been shipped.

10. a. Extend your Movie Lovers Web design to include pages that allow members to find which movies other customers have watched and what they prefer. Give sample SQL statements to extract and modify database information as required by your new pages. Update your E-R model and your database to include whatever changes are required to support this activity.

b. Extend your Movie Lovers Web design to allow members to rate movies and to write reviews. Add ratings to the movie display pages. Add a section to your home page that shows the top ten highest rated movies and the top ten most watched. Update your E-R model and your database. Give sample SQL statements to extract and modify database information as required by your new pages.

FURTHER READING

The Access upsizing wizard is described in detail in the Microsoft Web site at http://www.microsoft.com/office/access. Information about the SQL Server Enterprise Manager can be found at http://msdn.microsoft.com. The Oracle Enterprise Manager is described in Oracle database administrator guides, such as the excellent ones by Loney and Theriault [LoTh99, LoTh01] and at the Oracle Technet Web site at http://technet.oracle.com.

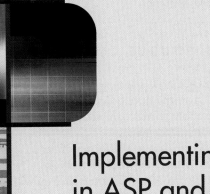

Implementing BigHit Online in ASP and JavaScript

- How to design and develop complex Web applications
- How to organize your programs into modules
- How to make your applications simpler by using objects and arrays

- How to generate and process complex HTML forms
- How to display HTML source code in Web pages

This chapter will show you how to produce the working Web site by investigating the ASP and JavaScript programming that defines the Web applications. Along the way, we'll emphasize the important principles of each step and introduce a few new wrinkles. Be sure to pay attention to the *process* of design and implementation as well as the results. The discussion is intended to reinforce both your understanding of how application developers work and your skills in JavaScript programming.

In essence, this chapter is a series of programming examples, each one with a theme. Each programming example also contributes to the BigHit Online Web site. The programming examples emphasize: the need to organize programs into small modules that can be used by many applications; the use of arrays and objects to organize and simplify applications; the processing of complex HTTP requests; and the use of SQL in applications.

As with previous chapters, the full details are off-line. You will not fully appreciate the subtlety of the JavaScript application components unless you study the complete implementation that is available in the Web site and carry out your own information system development.

The BigHit Online Web site is available at http://www.web4data.com/ BigHitOnline. This site contains all of the examples, including full source code listings and a sample database.

You will find many new programming techniques and language characteristics in the following sections. It may be tedious to study code, but it will help if you follow along with the Web site as you read.

14.1 VIEWING SOURCE CODE AND SQL STATEMENTS

In this section, you will see how a simple idea and a small amount of programming can have a major impact on the development environment for a Web site. Along the way, you'll learn a little about string manipulation in JavaScript and about ways to display HTML source code in Web pages.

The simple idea is to add links to the footer of each page that will allow the developer and anyone else to easily see how the site works. The original intention of these links was to help the author produce Chapter 13. You will recall that Chapter 13 presents the flow of information in the Web site as a sequence of SQL statements. The basic idea was to make the Web applications show their own SQL, which could then be cut from the Web site and pasted into the manuscript. The result of adding the links is a terrific enhancement in the Web site.

The footer of each page in the Web site contains links to allow users to see the source code of the page and to view a record (a log) of executions of the Web applications that includes all of their SQL statements. A **log** is a list of activities in the order in which they took place. Figure 14.1 shows a typical Web page with its footer. This particular page shows the source code for one of the Web applications.

14.1.1 Displaying ASP Source Code in a Web Page

If you click on the Show Source Code link in a page, you'll see a page like Figure 14.1. This Web page displays the full source code for the Web application called showlog.asp. (You'll hear about showlog.asp in a moment.) The name of the

FIGURE 14.1

Web Page with Web Application
Source Code

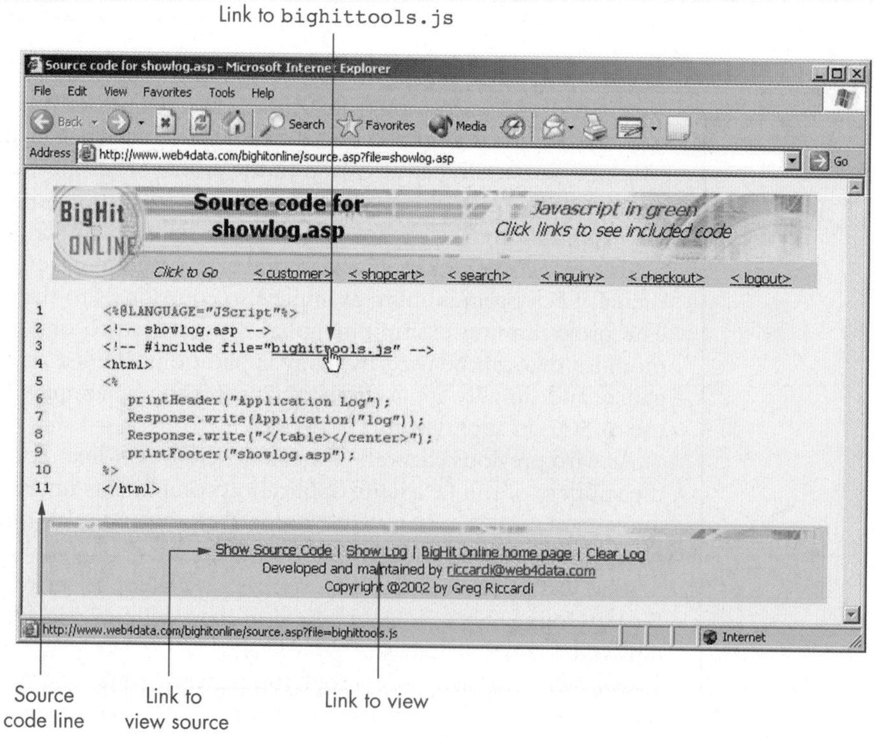

code file appears in the header. The ASP and JavaScript code is shown in green and the HTML in black.

If you want to see the source code of the application that produced the page of Figure 14.1, you can click the `Show Source Code` link in the source code page. You'll be shown the source for a script called `source.asp`—the Web application that formats code files as Web pages. (Try it!) You can also click on the link to `bighit-tools.js` (like the pointing hand in Figure 14.1) in the third source code line to see code in that file.

The source has to be displayed carefully. The < and > symbols in the text must be modified so that the browser will not interpret them as tag delimiters and so that the ASP processor will not treat `<%` and `%>` as delimiters of ASP code. If these symbols are not modified, the browser and the ASP processor will interfere with the display.

Figure 14.2 shows part of the HTML code of the page of Figure 14.1. The numbers are confusing. The figure follows the example of all code listings in the book by having line numbers. The HTML also has line numbers, as you can see from Figure 14.1. So the first column of numbers is line numbers of the listing and the second column is part of the HTML.

These 10 lines display source code lines 3-10 of Figure 14.2. Line 1 is a `pre` tag and is matched with its end tag in line 10. `Pre` is the HTML tag that tells the browser that the text is preformatted. Browsers use a fixed-width font for `pre` and include all of the spaces and line breaks. The first three source code lines are omitted. They include some additional complexity that you can see if you look at the Web site.

Line 2 of Figure 14.2 shows how the HTML code tells the browser to display `<html>`. The special HTML code `&lt;` is for < and `&gt;` is for >. These symbols tell the browser to display less than and greater than symbols and not to treat them as tag delimiters of an `html` tag. Line 3 shows the beginning of a block of ASP code. The code is surrounded by the `span` tag in line 3 and its end tag in line 8. Also on line 3 is `&lt;%` the transformed `<%` that starts the ASP code. Thus, the HTML of lines 5–8 will display preformatted text formatted according to the rules of the CSS `code` class. The CSS definition of this class is `span.code{color: green}`. That is, make the text green.

The Web application `source.asp` that produces the source code listing is surprisingly simple. Figure 14.3 shows the code that produces the lines of Figure 14.2. The majority of the transformation is performed in line 3 by the call to `Server.HTMLEncode`, which changes < to `&lt;`, & to `&amp;`, " to `&quot;` and whatever else is required to make the browser ignore the HTML tags.

Line 4 of Figure 14.3 uses the `String` method `replace` to mark the beginning of a code block by replacing `<%` by `<span class=code><%`. Method `replace`

F I G U R E   14.2

Partial HTML Code for
Figure 14.1

```
 1  <pre>
 2   4  &lt;html&gt;
 3   5  <span class=code> &lt;%
 4   6      printHeader(&quot;Application Log&quot;);
 5   7      Response.write(Application(&quot;log&quot;));
 6   8      Response.write(&quot;&lt;/table&gt;&lt;/center&gt;&quot;);
 7   9      printFooter(&quot;showlog.asp&quot;);
 8  10  %&gt; </span>
 9  11  &lt;/html&gt;
10  </pre>
```

```
1   <pre>
2   <% while (!file.AtEndOfStream) {
3       strIn = Server.HTMLEncode(file.ReadLine());
4       strTemp = strIn.replace(/&lt;%/, "<span class=code>&lt;%");
5       strTemp = strTemp.replace(/%&gt;/,"%&gt;</span>");
6     }
7     Response.write(line+"\t"+strTemp+"\n"); line++;
8   }%> </pre> <%printFooter("source.asp"); %>
9   </html>
```

F I G U R E 14.3

JavaScript Code to Print
Application Source Code

changes a string by replacing anything that matches the pattern of its first argument by the string of its second. Because the < has been replaced by < in line 3, the actual pattern for the replace method is /<%/.

The only part of source.asp that has been omitted from this example is the code that handles references to other scripts, such as the reference to bighittools.js in line 3 of Figure 14.1. The code is not too complicated, but it is a bit tedious. You can see it in the Web site.

14.1.2 Recording and Displaying the Application Log

When you click Show Log in the footer of a page, you will see a page that displays a log of the Web applications. Figure 14.4 shows the log after customer jojo has logged into the site. In this page, you see a record of the start of Web application default.asp, the script that produces the welcome page that we saw as Figure 13.13. The next log entry shows the end of default.asp; the third row of the table shows Web application login.asp starting; and the fourth row shows that it executed a single SQL statement:

```
select * from Customer where accountId=lower('jojo')
```

F I G U R E 14.4

Web Page with Application Log,
Including SQL Statements

Special Symbols in HTML

You can add special symbols to your HTML code with the HTML character-entity sequence &name; where name is one of the predefined HTML character names. You can add any symbol, even if it has no HTML name, by using its three-digit character number. A numeric character description is shown as &#nnn;. The character number comes from the International Standards Organization (ISO) character coding.

This table shows some of the HTML symbols.

Symbol	HTML name	Description
"	&quot;	quotation mark
£	&pound;	British Pound
&	&amp;	ampersand
¥	&yen;	Japanese Yen
<	&lt;	less than
©	&copy;	copyright
>	&gt;	greater than
€	&euro;	Euro
		non-breaking space
Ä	&Auml;	German A umlaut
¢	&cent;	cent sign
‡	&#135;	double dagger
®	&reg;	registered trademark
…	&#133;	ellipsis

The source code for the Web application that produces the log page was shown in the source code page of Figure 14.1. This very simple application prints a header for the page (line 6), then uses `Response.write` to print the value of `Application("log")` (line 7), and finishes by printing some HTML code (line 8) and a footer (line 9). The value of `Application("log")` is a string that contains the HTML code of the log table of Figure 14.4.

The entries in the log are kept in a `String` variable called `Application("log")` that is shared by all of the applications of the Web site. All of the other variables we've seen have been part of a single application. ASP includes an object called **Application** that is shared by all Web applications. When a Web application adds a field to `Application`, the field can be used in all Web applications in the site. The expression `Application("log")` refers to the `log` field of the `Application` object. This field contains all of the log entries, formatted as an HTML table.

Web applications record entries in the log at the beginning and ending of their executions and when they execute SQL statements. File `bighittools.js` includes several functions that help applications record log entries. Two of the functions are shown in Figure 14.5. Function `appendLog` in lines 1–4 adds an entry to the log.

Line 2 includes the operator += that adds its right argument to the value of its left. Lines 2 and 3 are equivalent to the following:

```
Application("log") = Application("log") +
    "<tr><th>"+title+":</th><td>"+str+"</td></tr>\n";
```

Function executeSQL of lines 5–8 of Figure 14.5 adds its SQL statement to the log (line 6) and then executes the SQL statement using the Execute method of a Connection object (line 7).

Each BigHit Online Web application executes SQL statements with a statement such as

```
result=executeSQL("select * from Customer where
    accountId=lower('jojo')")
```

With these very simple methods, all SQL statements executed by Web applications are added to the log for viewing by users. Each time you display a new Web page, you can click Show Log in the footer and see which SQL statements have been executed to produce the page.

In your own applications, you can use method appendLog to record additional information. Simply add calls to appendLog anywhere in an application. Whenever the call is executed, another row will be added to the log.

14.2 LOGIN AND CUSTOMER INFORMATION

In this section, you'll see examples of how the BigHit Online Web site includes functions that are used by many Web applications. You'll also learn more about how to manipulate string values in JavaScript.

You will recall that Chapter 13 followed the Web interaction of user Joe Jones as he logged in and purchased videos. He enters the BigHit Online Web site through the login page that you saw as Figure 13.13 and types in his account ID and password.

When Joe clicks the submit button on the login page, Web application login.asp produces the customer information page of Figure 14.6. It simply compares the account ID and password with the contents of the customer table, as in Figure 14.7. As in previous code listings, the particularly interesting parts of the scripts are highlighted. Of course, many details must be added to make this work properly. Additional functions have been added to our tools scripts (bighittools.js) to make the code more modular. These functions are part of the support code for BitHit Online Web applications and are available for your use.

FIGURE 14.5

Log Functions from **bighittools.js**

```
1  function appendLog(title, str) {
2      Application("log") +=
3          "<tr><th>"+title+":</th><td>"+str+"</td></tr>\n";
4  }
5  function executeSQL(sqlStr) {
6      appendLog("Execution of SQL", sqlStr);
7      return conn.Execute(sqlStr);
8  }
```

FIGURE 14.6

The Customer Information Page

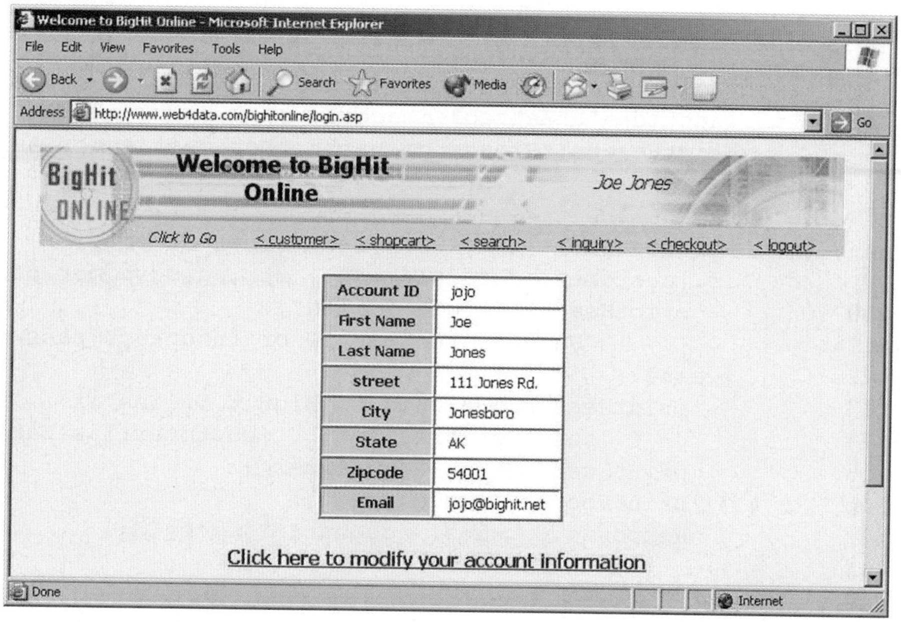

The first new function, in line 2, is `makeConnection`. This very simple function, shown in lines 21–25 of Figure 14.7 encapsulates the creation of the database connection so that every ASP script can easily connect to the same database. Most of the ASP scripts in the Web site begin by connecting to the database with `makeConnection`.

Function `trim` (defined in `bighittools.js`) in line 3 removes any leading and trailing spaces from the account ID. It's a simple step that makes it easier to login. We will not allow any spaces in account IDs.

In line 4, the script tests to make sure the user typed in an account ID. The first test is for the special value `"undefined"` that is the value used by JavaScript whenever a value is unknown or a variable undefined. As long as this HTTP request came from the welcome page, a request variable `accountId` will be included and this condition will be false. The vertical bar in line 4 is the JavaScript symbol for the **or** operator. The `if` statement of line 4 is true if either condition is satisfied. If the HTTP request did not include a valid account ID, the script prints an error message (line 5).

If a value of `accountId` is given, the script gets the `password` request variable (line 7) and calls `lookupCustomer` to create a customer object from the database. We saw `lookupCustomer` for BigHit Video in Section 12.3. The details are found in the JavaScript file `customer.js`, which contains several functions that help Web applications manipulate customer information.

The highlighted condition in line 9 tests to see if the password from the database (`customer.password`) is different from the password entered in the login form (`passwd`). The condition includes a call on a function `String`. The purpose of calling `String` is explained in the accompanying Concept box.

Once the login application has determined that the account ID and password match, the application generates the customer information page. The application calls function `printCustomerTable` (line 15) to produce the table of customer information at the bottom of Figure 14.8. This function is also included in `customer.js`.

```
1   // code from login.asp
2      conn = makeConnection();
3      acctId = trim(Request("accountId"));
4      if (acctId=="undefined" | acctId=="") {
5         printHeader("Please go back","You must enter an accountId");
6      } else {
7         var passwd = Request("password");
8         var customer = lookupCustomer(conn,acctId);
9         if (customer.accountId=="" | String(customer.password)!=passwd) {
10           printHeader("Login failed",
11                 "Unknown account ID or incorrect password");
12        } else {
13           printHeader("Welcome to BigHit Online",
14                 customer.firstName+" "+customer.lastName);
15           printCustomerTable(customer);
16           printFooter ("login.asp");
17           Response.Cookies("accountId")=acctId;
18        }
19     }
20  // code from bighittools.js
21  function makeConnection () {
22     conn = Server.CreateObject("ADODB.Connection");
23     conn.Open("DSN=bighitonline");
24     return conn;
25  }
```

FIGURE 14.7

Part of the ASP Script
`login.asp` and Function
`makeConnection` of
File `bighittools.js`

The Web is designed so that the user enters his account ID once and then is logged in for the rest of his interaction. The Web applications must be able to keep track of the account ID. The design of the Web applications must include some mechanism for remembering which user is logged in from a particular browser. We are expecting to have several users interacting with the site at the same time, so the applications must keep track of several users at once.

Fortunately, the HTTP protocol allows Web servers to store information in Web browsers for later access. A piece of information stored this way in a browser is called **cookie**. The login application can store the account ID in a cookie in the browser. When another request comes from that browser, the application that responds to the request can fetch the account ID from the cookie.

Cookies in JavaScript are manipulated through the `Request` and `Response` objects. A Web application can create or modify a cookie, as shown in line 17 of Figure 14.7, and repeated in the first line below. The second line retrieves a cookie value from the browser.

```
Response.Cookies("accountId")=acctId; // save a cookie
acctId = Request.Cookies("accountId"); // get a cookie
```

The name of the cookie is accountId and the value saved is the value of variable `acctId`.

Concept

Comparing Strings in JavaScript

`String` is a standard JavaScript function that converts a value into a `String` object. String values and `String` objects are somewhat different. In particular, the equality (and inequality) operators of `String` objects compare strings letter by letter. In other cases in JavaScript, comparisons are done on the basis of memory addresses. Figure 14.8 illustrates the difference between character and address comparisons.

The diagram in Figure 14.8 shows four variables on the left and two objects on the right. The objects have the same string value, but are stored in different locations. Variables `var1` and `var2` both contain a reference to a string object as their values. Variables `var3` and `var4`, on the other hand, contain simple string values. As with `var1` and `var2`, the address of these values is different.

The table on the right of Figure 14.8 lists four expressions that compare string variables that feature two different definitions of what makes values equal. Either the addresses of the two values are the same or the values themselves are the same. In the first and second lines, the *values* of the variables are tested for equality and since both have value "Jane", the tests are true. The third test is the unusual one. Since neither value is a `String` object, JavaScript tests for equality of the *locations* of the values. Since the two variables `var3` and `var4` are in different locations, the test returns `false`. The last comparison forces JavaScript to convert one of the values (`var3`) into a `String` object, and thus allows JavaScript to use the equality by value test, which results in `true`.

As long as we make sure that one value in a comparison is a `String` object, we can be sure that we'll get equality of value and not address.

FIGURE 14.8

String Values and Equality Tests

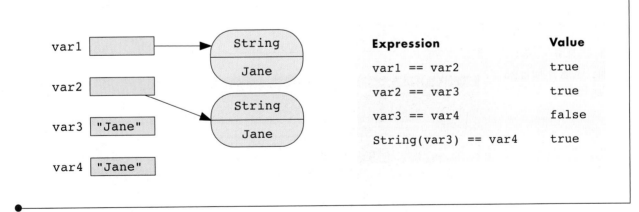

14.3 SEARCHING AND ADDING ITEMS TO A SHOPPING CART

Understanding the shopping cart Web applications will help you to increase your skills in writing applications that generate and process HTML forms. You will also learn more about how to create and manipulate arrays and objects in JavaScript. Your ability to put data into complex objects and arrays will allow you to greatly simplify your programs. As Web applications become more and more complicated, your skill at organizing the variables and objects will make your programs better and your programming efforts will be more effective.

When user Joe Jones requested to see comedy movies, the movie search Web application responded with the Web page of Figure 14.9. The details of searching are left as exercises. The page includes an HTML form presented as a table. In the Web page, Joe has requested the purchase of 2 copies of the DVD of *Animal House* and 3 copies of the videotape of *Duck Soup*.

The first two rows of the table in Figure 14.9 are produced by the browser display of the HTML code of Figure 14.10. Each row has several form input elements. You will notice that both rows of the table define input elements with similar names. For example, you see hidden inputs named `movieId0` in line 2 and `movieId1` in line 10, and text inputs named `dvd0` in line 4 and `dvd1` in line 12. The request variables in each row include the row number.

This form uses a familiar strategy for representing information. In line 2, for instance, the movie ID is stored in hidden variable `movieId0` for use by the Web application and placed in a table data element (`td`) for the user to see.

Function `printMoviesForm` produces movie selection tables like the one of Figure 14.10. Part of the code is shown in Figure 14.11. The full code is part of the JavaScript utility file `shopcart.js` in the Web site. Lines 2 and 3 show the definition of this simple search query. The condition `genre like '%comedy%'` was used to produce this page.

Each data row of the form table is printed by lines 8–23. Lines 9 and 10 add the movie ID as a hidden value and a table data element. Lines 15–18 put in the DVD input area. The input named `dvd<%=row%>` is the space for entering the quantity of DVDs for this movie. The actual name of the input element, as you saw in lines 4 and 11 of Figure 4.10, is also `dvd` concatenated with the row number. The price is displayed preceded by @ $ and is included as a hidden input. The tape quantity and price are included in the same style.

F I G U R E   14.9

Selecting Movies to Put in the Shopping Cart

```
1   <tr> <!-- row 0 -->
2       <input type="hidden" name="movieId0" value="189"><td>189</td>
3       <td>Animal House</td><td>comedy</td><td>PG-13</td>
4       <td><input type="text" name="dvd0" size="5"> @ $39.95
5           <input type="hidden" name="dvdPrice0" value="39.95"></td>
6       <td><input type="text" name="tape0" size="5"> @ $9.49
7           <input type="hidden" name="tapePrice0" value="9.49"></td>
8   </tr>
9   <tr> <!-- row 1 -->
10      <input type="hidden" name="movieId1" value="123"><td>123</td>
11      <td>Annie Hall</td><td>romantic comedy</td><td>R</td>
12      <td><input type="text" name="dvd1" size="5"> @ $29.95
13          <input type="hidden" name="dvdPrice1" value="29.95"></td>
14      <td><input type="text" name="tape1" size="5"> @ $10.99
15          <input type="hidden" name="tapePrice1" value="10.99"></td>
16  </tr>
```

FIGURE 14.10

HTML Code for Item Selection
Table of Figure 14.10

```
1   function printMoviesForm(conn, condition)
2       var movieSQL="select * from Movie where "+condition+"
3           order by title";
4       var movies = conn.Execute(movieSQL);
5       // table header here
6       var row = 0;
7       while(!movies.eof) { %>
8           <tr><!-- row <%=row%> -->
9               <input type="hidden" name="movieId<%=row%>"
10                  value="<%=movies("movieId")%>">
11              <td> <%=movies("movieId")%> </td>
12              <td> <%=movies("title")%> </td>
13              <td> <%=movies("genre")%> </td>
14              <td> <%=movies("rating")%> </td>
15              <td><input type="text" name="dvd<%=row%>" size="5">
16                  @ $<%=movies("dvdSalePrice")%>
17                  <input type="hidden" name="dvdPrice<%=row%>"
18                      value="<%=movies("dvdSalePrice")%>"></td>
19              <td><input type="text" name="tape<%=row%>" size="5">
20                  @ $<%=movies("tapeSalePrice")%>
21                  <input type="hidden" name="tapePrice<%=row%>"
22                      value="<%=movies("tapeSalePrice")%>"></td>
23          </tr>
24          <%movies.movenext(); row++;
25      }%>
26      <input type="hidden" name="numMovies" value="<%=row%>">
27      // rest of function
```

FIGURE 14.11

Selected Code from the
Production of the Search Form

When the `Buy` button is pushed, the resulting query string is

```
movieId0=189&dvd0=2&dvdPrice0=39.95&tape0=&tapePrice0=9.49&
    movieId1=123&dvd1=&dvdPrice1=29.95&tape1=&tapePrice1=
    10.99&movieId2=987&dvd2=&dvdPrice2=23.95&tape2=
    3&tapePrice2=9.99&movieId3=145&dvd3=&dvdPrice3=13.95
    &tape3=&tapePrice3=7.49
```

That is, the request includes four sets of variables. Some values are empty, as in the value of `tape0`.

The script that responds to the request (`additem.asp`) must make sense of these complex request variables. We can think of the variables as a collection of four objects, each with fields `movieId`, `dvd`, `dvdPrice`, `tape`, and `tapePrice`. We need to organize the data within the script as a collection of objects. We also must allow the number of objects in the collection to vary according to the number of rows in the form.

Figure 14.12 shows a collection of objects that represent the information in the request variables. Each rounded box in the figure represents an object. The name at the top is the name of the JavaScript type of the object. Three types are shown `Array`, `Object`, and `String`. The names of the fields of each object are in boxes below the type name. An **Array** object is a standard JavaScript object that has integer field names. The pointers in the figure are used to show that a field of an object points to another object.

The basic organization of the information in Figure 14.12 is as a collection (array) that points to four objects, each with information about a movie. Each movie object has five fields, with appropriate names. Each field has a `String` value. This figure shows exactly the information in the request variables that has been reorganized to make it easy for the application to use.

The code to produce the objects of Figure 14.12 is a function `getMovies` in file `shopcart.js`, as shown in Figure 14.13. The function begins its execution in line 3 by creating an `Array` object and storing it in variable `movies`. Next, it gets the number of movies from request variable `numMovies` in line 4. The function needs to be able to use the value of `numMovies` as an integer to control a `for` loop, but the values of all request variables are text. The JavaScript function `parseInt` in line 4 creates an integer value from a string.

The `for` loop of lines 5-12 iterates through the rows of the form. The body of the loop begins in line 6 by creating a new `Object` to hold the movie information. In its four executions, it will create four objects, as was shown in Figure 14.12. Lines 7–11 add the fields and their values. In the first iteration, line 7 gets the value of request variable `movieId0` and stores it in `movies[0].movieId`. At the end of the loop, all of the objects of Figure 14.12 have been created and linked together.

Now that we know how to organize the request information, we are ready to look at the Web application `additem.asp` (Figure 14.14), which processes the information and adds items to Joe's shopping cart. Line 1 calls function `getMovies` from Figure 14.13 to fill the structure of Figure 14.12. The `for` loop of lines 3–16 uses the number of elements in the array (`movies.length`) as the number of iterations.

The body of the loop includes a `with` statement in line 4 that simplifies the code. For instance, the reference to the `movies[i].dvd` in line 5 is written simply as `dvd` because the JavaScript system adds `movies[i]`.

The body of the loop (lines 4–15) begins by checking to see if the customer has requested to buy any DVDs from this row of the table. In particular, the question is whether the value of field `dvd`, which is the quantity of DVDs requested by the customer, is a non-zero number. Two operations are required to make this test. First, the script converts the text of `dvd` to a number in line 5 and stores the number in variable `qty`. Next, in line 6, the script tests to see if the conversion succeeded. The function `isNaN` accomplishes this test. The name of the function comes from the computer term **NaN** (pronounced "nan"), which stands for "Not a Number." If the value of

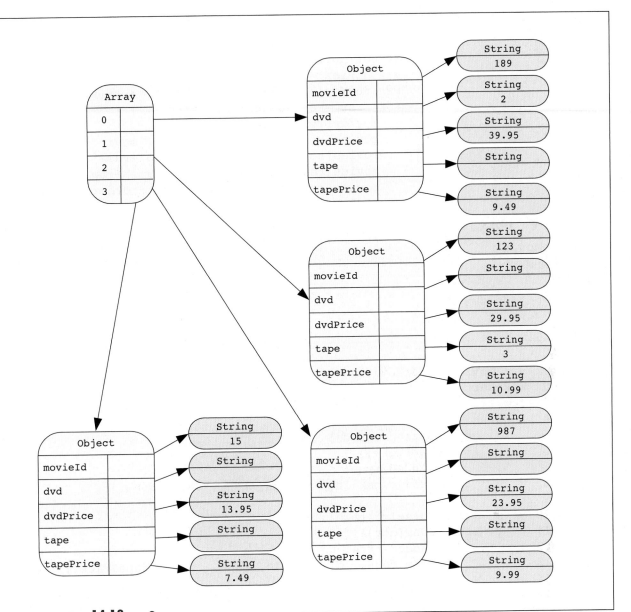

FIGURE 14.12

Illustration of Objects in JavaScript

`qty` is a number, the script calls function `addItem` to add the item to the shopping cart.

The body of the loop continues in lines 10–14 with the processing of the videotape request.

Function `addItem` (called in lines 8 and 13) does the work, using an SQL insert statement. A typical statement is

```
insert into CartItem (cartId, line, movieId, videoType,
        quantity, unitcost)
    values ('jojo',1,189,'dvd',2,39.95)
```

The code of `addItem` has two ways to make its update. If the item is already in the customer's shopping cart, `addItem` increments the quantity. If not, `addItem` simply determines the next unused line number for the shopping cart for this customer

```
1  function getMovies() {
2     // get movie quantity info from Request
3     var movies = new Array();
4     var numMovies = parseInt(Request("numMovies"));
5     for (row = 0; row<numMovies; row++) {
6        movies[row] = new Object();
7        movies[row].movieId = Request("movieId"+row);
8        movies[row].dvd = Request("dvd"+row);
9        movies[row].tape = Request("tape"+row);
10       movies[row].dvdPrice = Request("dvdPrice"+row);
11       movies[row].tapePrice = Request("tapePrice"+row);
12    }
13    return movies;
14 }
```

FIGURE 14.13

Function **getMovies** That Creates the Objects of Figure 14.12

```
1  var movies = getMovies();
2  makeCart(conn,id);
3  for (i = 0; i<movies.length; i++) {
4     with (movies[i]) {
5        qty = parseInt(dvd);
6        if (!isNaN(qty)) {
7           itemAdded=true;
8           addItem(conn, id, movieId, dvd, "dvd", dvdPrice);
9        }
10       qty = parseInt(tape);
11       if (!isNaN(qty)) {
12          itemAdded=true;
13          addItem(conn, id, movieId, tape, "vhs", tapePrice);
14       }
15    }
16 }
17 printCart(conn,id, true,"cartupdate.asp","Modify Shopping Cart");
```

FIGURE 14.14

Part of the Code to Add Items to the Shopping Cart

and adds the next line. The full code is included in `shopcart.js`, the shopping cart tools file.

Web application `addItem.asp` finishes its execution (line 17) by calling `print-Cart` to print the new shopping cart as shown in Figure 14.15. This page shows the shopping cart as a form that allows the customer to modify his choices. You can see function `printCart` in file `shopcart.js`.

The final shopping cart application is `cartupdate.asp`, which responds when the customer clicks `Modify Cart Contents` on the page of Figure 14.15. This application simply updates the shopping cart entries with the new quantities entered by the customer. If the customer enters 0 for a quantity, the application will delete the line from the cart.

INTERVIEW

DAVID MCGOVERAN
Transaction Processing and Performance

DATABASES WITH SLOW TRANSACTION PROCESSING In the early days of databases (the 1960s) database work was very physical and design was really file design. I worked extensively with databases throughout the 1970s. Recognizing their deficiencies from experience, I followed relational database literature and commercial developments, becoming one of the first designers of commercial relational applications. Today, evaluating technology products for vendors and consumers alike often involves reviewing database designs or the ability to support an application with today's DBMS technologies. Designers of Web-based products often have little formal database design training and do not differentiate between logical and physical design. It is not uncommon during either a design audit or performance tuning to find examples of poor logical design.

One past project involved financial transaction processing for a large international bank. Among the problems: an account number appeared only in the transaction history table along with a foreign key to the account owner. This meant that an account could not exist unless transactions were posted against it and that long transaction histories could not be completely archived for active accounts. Various "works-around" had been used, all of which complicated maintenance and the understandability of the database. Tasks like obtaining the total number of accounts or altering characteristics of the account were expensive, often interfering with or even preventing other transaction processing.

USING BASIC DATABASE CONCEPTS TO ACHIEVE BETTER PERFORMANCE Normalization is primarily a semantic, rather than a structural, process and is intended to clarify meaning that would otherwise be obscured from the DBMS and therefore from users. A common logical design

> **"After redesign, transaction processing performance improved by a factor of ten..."**

problem is failing to have a primary key which fully determines non-key column values. Another common problem that is easily remedied is the use of intelligent or compound keys in a single column.

In the case above, although the database schema was ostensibly in second normal form, it was not in third normal form. Putting the tables in third normal form created an accounts table that existed independently of the transactions table. This permitted aged transactions to be archived periodically in a straightforward manner and had the side effect of eliminating redundant account data and an integrity hole. After redesign, transaction processing performance improved by a factor of ten, several errors (due to the integrity hole) were found and fixed, and both new account processing and account totals were no longer in conflict with transaction processing. The in-house design team is now charged with following the principles of documented normalized logical design, optimized physical design, and data independence.

14.4 CHECKOUT PROCESSING

This section refocuses our attention on using SQL to make complex queries and updates and also shows how to use other HTML input elements. When our customer Joe clicks the checkout link in the header, he will see the checkout confirmation

FIGURE 14.15
Shopping Cart Status and Update Page

page of Figure 14.16. If he decides that he wants the items shown, he'll click on `Proceed to Checkout` to finalize the purchase. The Web application that receives his request will have to create a new row in the `Sale` table, transfer the items in his shopping cart to this new sale, and create a receipt for Joe.

FIGURE 14.16
Checkout Confirmation Page

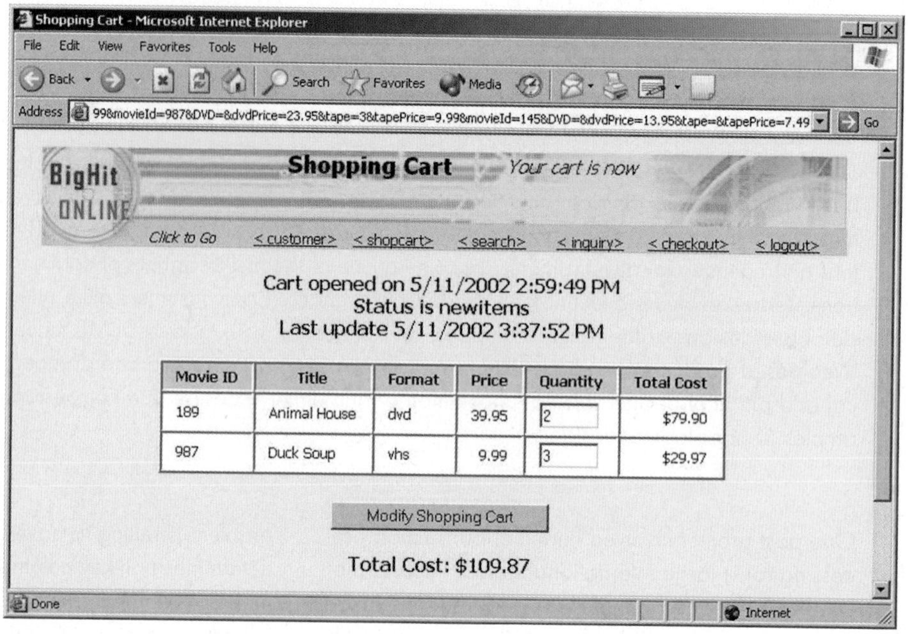

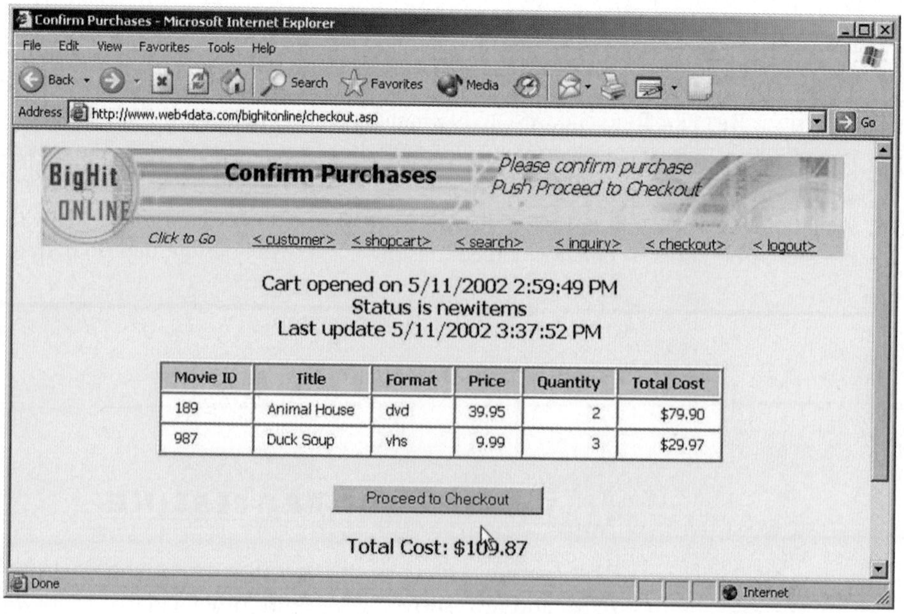

The checkout confirmation page is a display of the contents of the shopping cart. You can see that no modifications are allowed once Joe has started to check out. Of course, Joe can abandon the checkout process at this point. As long as he doesn't click `Proceed to Checkout` (the `submit` button of the form), he will not commit to buying the objects.

When Joe clicks the `submit` button of the page of Figure 14.16, he should be shown a page to allow him to specify his method of payment and shipping address. These steps are not part of the book's Web site, but have been left for you as projects. Instead, when Joe clicks the `submit` button, the purchase will be finalized.

The checkout processing script `confirmcheckout.asp` is the longest script in the Web site. We've already seen in Section 13.5.3 that the script must execute many SQL statements to perform all of its database updates. Once the updates are completed, the application produces the customer receipt page of Figure 14.17.

The major difference between the purchase confirmation form and the receipt form is that the receipt form displays information from the `Sale` and `SaleItem` tables after the sale is completed. The purchase confirmation form shows the information from the `ShoppingCart` and `CartItem` tables before the sale.

The Web application `confirmcheckout.asp` that responds to Joe's request to complete the purchase is long, but not complicated. Once you know exactly which SQL statements must be written and executed, writing the script is simple. Section 13.5.3 shows the SQL statements that were executed in response to Joe's request.

Once a customer has made a purchase, he can inquire about its status by clicking the inquiry link in a page header. The status of Joe Jones's order is shown in Figure 14.18. The page shows an open drop-down box that is being used to select sale number 66, the sale that was described in this chapter. The drop-down box is called a *selection* box in HTML and is an example of the use of `select` and `option` tags. Figure 14.19 shows the HTML code that describes the first two entries and the last entry in the selection box.

FIGURE 14.17

Receipt for Purchase

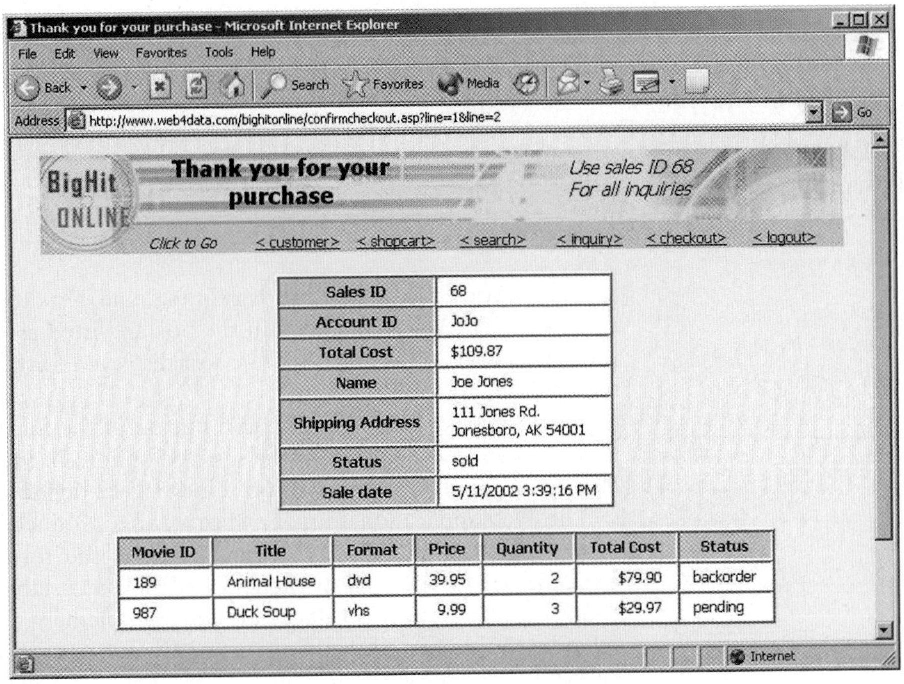

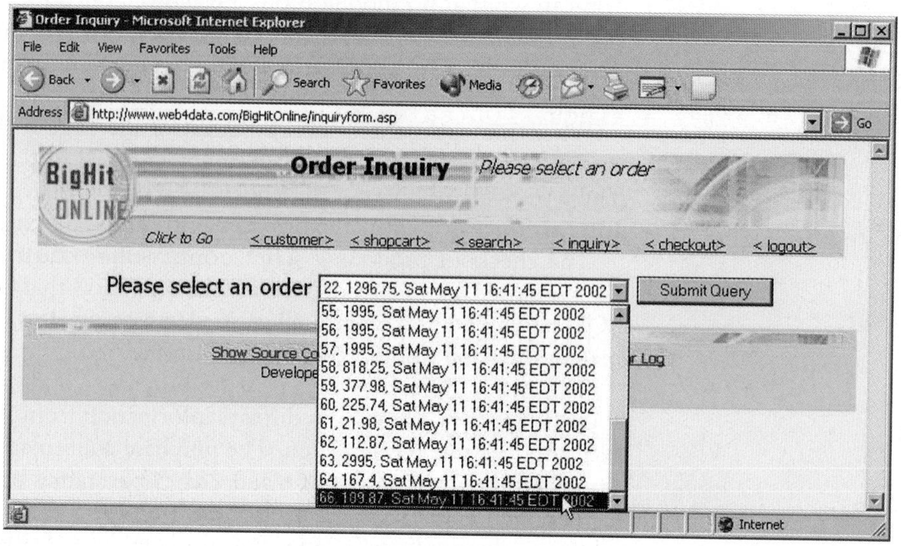

FIGURE 14.18

Inquiring about a Sale with a Selection Box

```
1   Please select an order
2   <select name="salesId">
3      <option value="22">
4         22, 1296.75, Sat May 11 16:41:45 EDT 2002
5      </option>
6      <option value="23">
7         23, null, Sat May 11 16:41:45 EDT 2002
8      </option>
9      <!-- rest of options follow -->
10     <option value="66">
11        66, 109.87, Sat May 11 16:41:45 EDT 2002
12     </option>
13  </select>
```

FIGURE 14.19

HTML Code to Produce a Selection Box

The select tag and its end tag (lines 2 and 13) define the input element named salesId. The values included in the box are listed as option tags. Line 3 defines the first option, with value 22. The text displayed for the option is the text between the option tag and its end tag.

When the user clicks the submit button of the form, the value of the input element salesId is the value of the selected option. In Figure 14.18, the user is selecting the option that begins with 66. Lines 10–12 define this option with value 66.

The Web application inquiryform.asp produced the page of Figure 14.18. Figure 14.20 shows the code that produces the form. The application uses the accountId to select all of the rows of the Sale table (lines 1–4). Then, in lines 8–14, the application produces an option element for each row by making the value be the salesId of the row (line 9) and the text of the option (lines 10–11) be the concatenation of the sales ID, the total cost, and the date of the sale. The processing of the sale inquiry produces a page that looks just like the sales receipt of Figure 14.17.

```
1    <% var salesSQL =
2        "select salesId, saleDate, totalCost from Sale where accountId='"
3           +id+"'";
4    var sales = executeSQL(salesSQL); %>
5    <center><form method="GET" action="inquiry.asp">
6        Please select an order
7        <select name="salesId">
8        <% while (!sales.eof) { %>
9           <option value="<%=sales("salesId")%>">
10              <%=sales("salesId")+", "+sales("totalCost")+", "
11                  +sales("saleDate")%>
12          </option>
13          <% sales.movenext();
14      } %>
15      </select>
```

FIGURE 14.20

JavaScript Code to Produce
Selection Box

CHAPTER SUMMARY

This chapter examines the design and implementation process for Web applications for an online video purchase Web site. It reinforces the principles of good design and programming that you studied in Chapters 10–12. It also presents several new features of JavaScript.

The BigHit Online Web site includes Web applications that display the source code of every application and display the list of all SQL statements executed by the applications. The presentation of source code relies on method `Server.HTMLEncode`, which changes < to <, & to &, " to " and whatever else is required to make the browser ignore the HTML tags. New pattern matching operations are introduced in the presentation of this material.

The division of applications into reusable modules is one characteristic of good application design. The BigHit Online JavaScript tools files `bighit-tools.js`, `customer.js`, `movie.js`, and `shop-cart.js` contain many functions that facilitate application development. A prominent example is function `makeConnection`, which is used by every Web application in the Web site to connect to the database. By creating this function, we've made it easy for an application to connect to the database and easy for us to change which database is used by the applications. Any change in this function will affect every Web application that uses it.

The application that responds to requests to add items to a shopping cart takes good advantage of the organization of data into complex objects. The list of movies that is created by the HTTP request is very complicated, and the application organizes this list into an array of objects. Because of the organization, the processing of the request for information is quite simple.

Checkout processing in BigHit Online is an example of the power of SQL. The checkout application must make a series of complicated database updates. However, the application is not complicated. It simply creates and executes each SQL statement in the proper order. The difficult part of creating the checkout application was determining which SQL statements to execute. Once that was done, the programming was not hard.

You now know how to design databases and Web applications to create high-quality dynamic Web sites. The next chapter will show you how to improve the ability of your Web applications to respond to errors, both from users and from outside sources. It will also emphasize the need for security in our systems and show you how to take advantage of the security capabilities of database servers and Web servers.

KEY TERMS

Application. An ASP object that is shared by all applications within a Web site.

Array. A JavaScript object whose fields are selected by numeric indexes instead of field names.

Cookie. A piece of information that a Web server places in a Web browser so that it can fetch it later. The HTTP protocol includes a strategy that allows Web servers to store and retrieve cookies.

Log. A list of activities in the order they took place. An SQL log is a list of the SQL statements executed by an application.

NaN (Not a Number). A special value that is produced by an attempt to convert from string to a number when the string does not correctly represent a number. NaN is also produced when a number is divided by 0.

QUESTIONS

1. Consult a JavaScript reference and describe the parameters and functionality of the following methods.
   a. `String.replace`
   b. `String.match`
   c. `String.split`
   d. `parseInt`
   e. `parseFloat`

2. What is the HTML representation of the value: "£5 & 67¢?

3. What is a cookie? Consult a reference to determine how to show the cookies that are stored on your browser. Look at the cookies in your browser.
   a. List the browser name and its version number.
   b. How does your browser store cookies?
   c. How many cookies (approximately) are stored in your browser?

4. What methods in ASP and JavaScript allow a program to store and retrieve cookies?

5. Consult a JavaScript reference.
   a. What are the properties of an `Array` object?
   b. What method allows two arrays to be concatenated?
   c. What method allows a new element to be added to the beginning of an array?
   d. What method allows an element to be deleted from the end of an array?

6. Draw a picture, like that of Figure 14.12, of the object created by the following JavaScript code.

```
var arr = new Array();
arr[0] = new Object();
arr[0].num = 1;
arr[0].str = "abc";
arr[1] = new Object();
arr[1].fld1 = "eieio";
arr[1].fld2 = "hello";
arr[0].fld3 = 25;
```

7. Write an SQL statement to delete all rows of the `CartItem` table in which the quantity is 0.

8. Consult an HTML reference. Describe each of the following input elements and give an example of its use
   a. `<input type="radio">`
   b. `<input type="image">`
   c. `<button>`
   d. `<input type="checkbox">`
   e. `<input type="button">`
   f. `<select>`
   g. `<option>`

PROBLEMS

9. Design a Web page to allow a customer to search for movies in the BigHit Online Web site. Begin by making a list of all of the search criteria you want to include. Make a sample HTML document and put it in your Web site as `searching.html`.

10. Design a Web page to allow a customer to specify the method of payment and shipping address for a sale. Make a sample HTML document and put it in your Web site as `payment.html`.

11. Design a Web page to allow a customer to send a message to BigHit Online. Include input elements for a name and address, an account ID, an e-mail address, a sales ID, and a comment.

PROJECTS

12. a. Implement Web applications to support the movie search Web page that you designed for problem 9. Create all of the functions required to support searching and put them in file `search.js` in your Web site.

b. Implement Web applications to support the credit card and shipping information Web page that you designed for problem 10. The Web applications should make all required database updates.

c. Implement Web applications to support the messaging Web page that you designed for problem 11. Design relation schemas to store the messages and the responses of the BigHit employees. Create the tables in your database.

d. Extend the `confirmcheckout.asp` application described in Section 14.4 to send e-mail to a customer when the sale is confirmed. Consult an ASP reference to determine how to send mail with ASP and JavaScript.

13. a. Use the design and development principles of this chapter and the BigHit Online tool files to create your own utility functions for your Movie Lovers Web site. Create a tools file for each major component of your site, as was done here for customers, shopping carts, and movies.

b. Continue the development of your Movie Lovers site by adding an e-mail capability. Allow a member of the site to send e-mail to another member through an HTML form.

FURTHER READING

Information about ASP and JavaScript is found in the references cited in previous chapters. The Microsoft .Net software makes very little change in the behavior of the Web applications described in this book. However, the .Net Web site, which can be found from http://msdn.microsoft.com, is full of information about its latest capabilities. You will find information about e-mail capabilities at that site.

CHAPTER **15**

Advanced Issues in Web Site Design and Implementation

In this chapter, you will learn:

- How to increase the reliability of your information systems
- How to check for user errors in the browser
- How to handle errors in JavaScript applications
- How to control the interactions of multiple users

- How database systems can recover from a variety of failures
- How to create secure databases and database applications

This concluding chapter addresses several issues that are crucial to the successful design and implementation of information systems. The primary theme is error checking, error recovery, and error prevention through the use of database and programming technologies. The primary goal is for you to learn how to improve the reliability and security of your information systems.

Users make mistakes. Computers crash. Programmers write faulty code. One of our jobs as Web site developers is to anticipate errors of various kinds. We must design applications that help users correct their mistakes, but still protect the computer system from malicious tampering. For example, if a user is trying to login but enters an incorrect account ID or password, the login application should respond with a gentle message and another login screen. If a user attempts to login every 10 seconds for several minutes, it is likely an attempt by some computer program to break into the system. A secure Web application would respond by refusing to process further login attempts.

The topics begin with how to write JavaScript code that checks for errors and inconsistencies in what users type into browser forms. The chapter ends with how to move application code into database servers to increase security and reliability. In between, you will learn the general strategy for error handling in JavaScript, the ways that database servers prevent users from interfering with each other, how database servers can recover from failures of many kinds, and. the ways that database servers keep users from inappropriately accessing or modifying database content.

375

FORMS CHECKING WITH
15.1 CLIENT-SIDE JAVASCRIPT

Suppose a user begins registering as a new customer at the BigHit Online Web site, fills out part of the customer information form, and clicks the `submit` button. The browser collects the (incomplete) form contents and sends it to the Web server as an HTTP request. The Web application `addcustomer.asp` receives the HTTP request, but does not have enough information to add the new customer. The Web application can only reply by returning a new page to the user's browser with an error message. This style of error checking complicates Web applications and frustrates users.

The alternative to this scenario is **data validation**, in which the browser checks the form before it becomes an HTTP request. Any error in the contents of the form would be reported to the user without disturbing the page displayed in the browser.

You can add data validation to your Web pages by adding JavaScript code to HTML documents. That is, you can write client-side JavaScript applications that are part of the HTML documents sent to the browser. With client-side forms checking, each time the user clicks the `submit` button, the browser checks the form for completeness and reports errors to the user.

15.1.1 Validating Form Data

When a user completes a customer information form properly, as shown in Figure 15.1, all of the fields have values, the account ID is at least 6 characters in length, the e-mail has the proper format, and the two password fields match. The best time to check all of these details is before the form is submitted.

FIGURE 15.1

The BigHit Online Customer Information Form

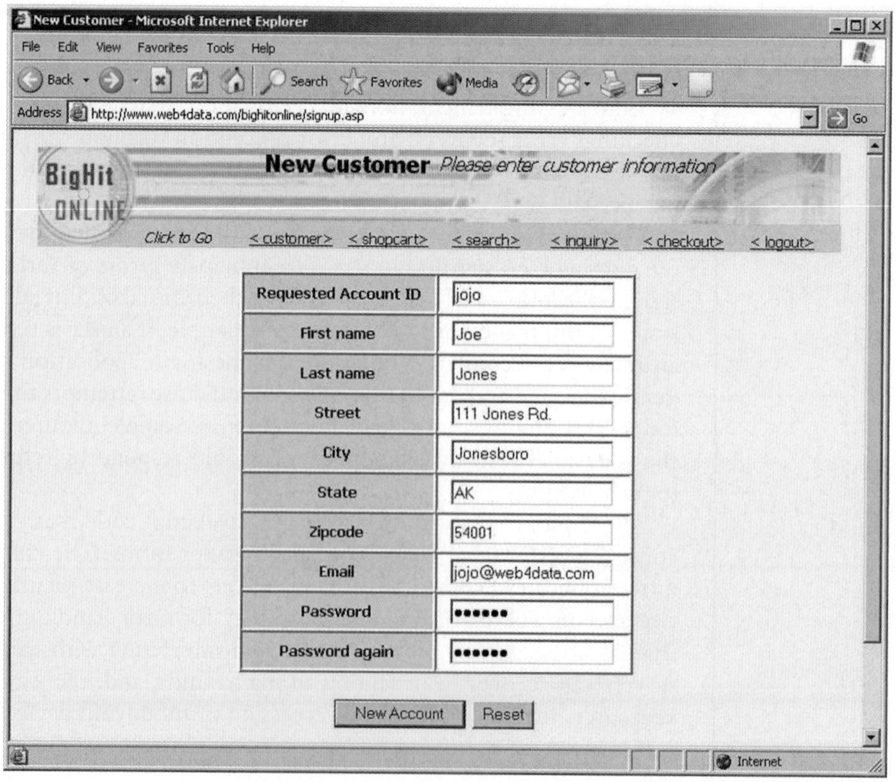

The form of Figure 15.2 has no fields filled in. Clearly, this is an incomplete form. The first problem is that the account ID is empty. The figure shows a warning instructing the user that the account ID field must be between 6 and 16 characters long. The warning, called an **alert** in JavaScript, is easily generated by client-side programming.

Figure 15.3 illustrates the way that a Web browser uses client-side JavaScript. The browser contains a software package that executes the JavaScript code–identified in the figure as the JavaScript processor. When the browser receives an HTML document that contains JavaScript, the JavaScript portions are stored and the HTML portions are formatted and displayed. When the user clicks the submit button, the browser sends the JavaScript code to the JavaScript processor, which executes the appropriate code. In the case of Figure 15.2, the code tells the browser to display an alert window. When the user clicks OK to close the alert, the browser closes the window and allows the user to resume interacting with the page.

Client-side JavaScript applications are written in the same language as server-side JavaScript applications. Many of the classes you've become familiar with are available on both server and client sides. Classes `Array`, `Object`, and `String` are part of the core language and are available to all JavaScript programs. All of the basic language features of variables, functions, assignments, method calls, loops, and `if` statements are part of the core language.

The main differences between server and client sides are in the classes and predefined objects that are available. The server side includes objects `Server`, `Request`, `Response`, `Application`, and `Session`. None of these objects are available to server-side applications. Database connections are also server side.

On the client side, JavaScript applications have objects `document`, `window`, and `cookies`, among others. Client-side applications can use their objects to manipulate

FIGURE 15.2

New Customer Form with Alert

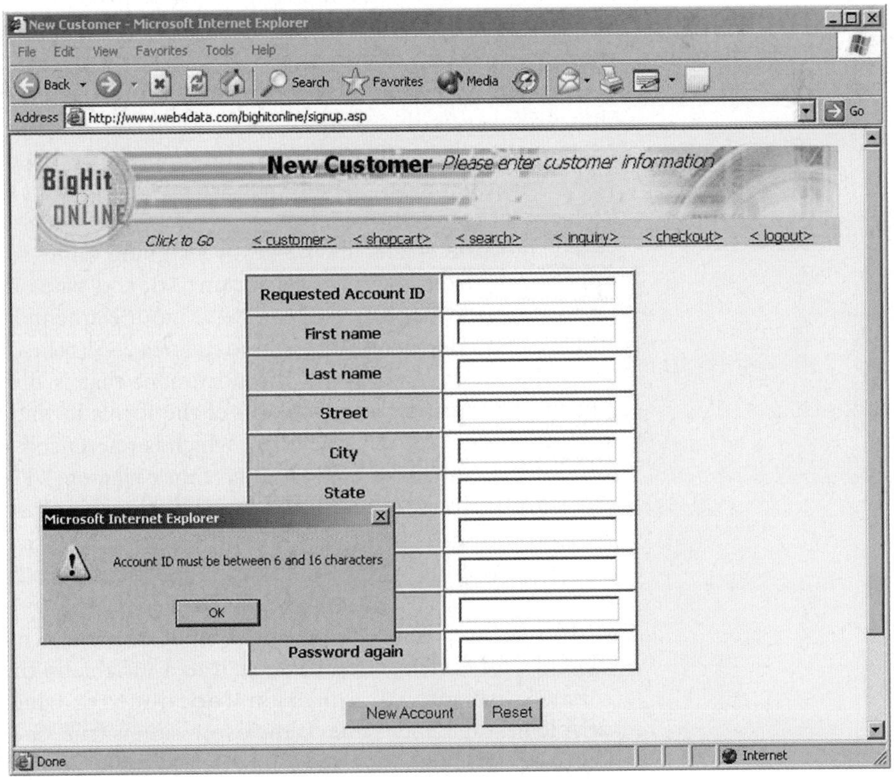

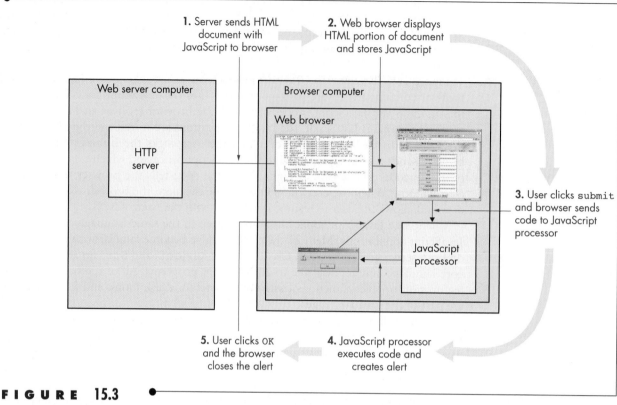

1. Server sends HTML document with JavaScript to browser

2. Web browser displays HTML portion of document and stores JavaScript

3. User clicks submit and browser sends code to JavaScript processor

4. JavaScript processor executes code and creates alert

5. User clicks OK and the browser closes the alert

F I G U R E **15.3**

Execution of a Client-Side JavaScript Application

the displayed document. They can modify the contents of form input elements; create windows and alerts; and change what happens when users click buttons and links. A forms validation application will need to read the values that users type and react to them.

You have to write JavaScript functions to carry out forms validation. Figure 15.4 shows a function that you can use to validate the customer information form. We'll begin our study of client-side programming with this function that can perform the necessary form validation, and then see how we can get the function to be called when the user clicks the submit button.

The function begins (lines 2–5) by assigning values to four variables. The values assigned come from the form's accountId, and email text input elements, and the password and repeatpwd password input elements.

The object document that is used in lines 2–5 is the client-side object that contains all of the information about the document that is displayed in the browser. Array document.forms has a list of all of the forms in the document. The customer information page has only one form, which is referenced as document.forms[0]. A form object contains a field for each input element. The names of the fields are the names of the input elements. Thus, document.forms[0].accountId is the input field with name accountId in the first form of the document.

The accountId field of the form object has type Text. The password field of the form has type Password. Each of these types has a value method that can be used to get and set the value of the input element. Thus, each of lines 2–5 gets the value of a form element and assigns it to a variable in the function.

Line 6 includes the expression !accountId, which is true if the accountId variable has an empty value. If the expression is true, as it is in the empty customer information form of Figure 15.2, line 7 creates the alert popup. This same test could be applied to all of the other fields of the form in order to ensure that all fields are not empty.

```
1  function validateCustomer() {
2     var accountId = document.forms[0].accountId.value;
3     var email     = document.forms[0].email.value;
4     var password  = document.forms[0].password.value;
5     var repeatpwd = document.forms[0].repeatpwd.value;
6     if(!accountId) {
7        alert("Account ID must be between 6 and 16 characters");
8        document. forms[0].accountId.focus();
9        return false;
10    }
11    if(accountId.length<6) {
12       alert("Account ID must be between 6 and 16 characters");
13       document. forms[0].accountId.focus();
14       return false;
15    }
16    if(!email.match(/.+@.+/)) {
17       alert("Email address must be user@host");
18       document. forms[0].email.focus();
19       return false;
20    }
21    if(!password) | !(password == repeatpwd)) {
22       alert("Passwords must be non-empty and match");
23       document. forms[0].password.value="";
24       document. forms[0].repeatpwd.value="";
25       document. forms[0].password.focus();
26       return false;
27    }
28    return true;
29 }
```

F I G U R E 15.4

A Portion of the Client-Side
Function
validateCustomer

Line 8 changes the focus of the browser window to the `accountId` input element. That is, it puts the cursor of the browser window in the `accountId` text input element. Line 8 sets the focus by calling the `focus` method of the `Text` object that represents the `accountId` input field. The purpose of setting the focus is to draw the user's attention to that field and make it easy for him to modify the value.

If the test in line 6 is true, line 9 ends the execution of the function and returns value `false` to the caller. When the function is called by the browser, the `false` value will tell the browser to abort the submission of the form. The customer information form will remain in the browser and the user will have the opportunity to correct the error. We will discuss this in more depth later in the chapter.

The test in line 11 (`accountId.length<6`) is true if the number of characters entered by the user is less than 6. Every `String` object in JavaScript has a `length` property that is the number of characters in the string.

In line 16, we test the format of the value entered in the `email` field with the expression `!email.match(/.+@.+/)`. The `match` method matches a pattern against a string. The pattern in line 16 is

`/.+@.+/`

The period (`.`) matches any character and the plus (`+`) matches one or more instances of the previous symbol. That is, `.+` matches one or more characters. The at sign (`@`) matches itself. The last `.+` matches at least one character. Thus, the pattern matches one or more characters followed by an at sign, followed by one or more characters. This is a very simple view of valid email addresses.

Method `match` returns the string that is matched by the pattern. If no string matches, `match` returns `false` and the condition of line 16 is true. An alert will be posted and the form submission cancelled.

Finally, line 21 tests to make sure that the `password` field is not empty and the two passwords match.

If none of the conditions in lines 6, 11, 16, or 21 is satisfied, no alert will be posted. The function executes all the way to line 28 and returns `true` to signal that the browser should continue with the form submission.

The pattern matching operations and methods of JavaScript can also be used to perform numeric validation. The following pattern matches strings that are completely composed of numeric digits

```
/^[0-9]+$/
```

The caret (`^`) matches the beginning of the string and the dollar sign (`$`) matches the end of the string. In between, `[0-9]` matches a single digit and the plus sign (`+`) matches one or more of the previous match. Hence, all of the characters in the string must be digits, and there must be at least one of them.

15.1.2 Calling the Validation Function During Form Submission

If we want form validation in the browser, we must ensure that `validateCus-tomer` is called whenever the user clicks the `submit` button. We make the browser perform the validation by adding the **onsubmit attribute** to the `form` tag.

```
<form method="POST" action="newcustomer.asp" onsubmit=
    "validateCustomer()">
```

With this attribute, the browser will call `validateCustomer` before it starts the HTTP request. If the function returns `true`, the HTTP submission continues. If the function returns `false`, the HTTP request is not made and the browser remains unchanged.

One problem with client-side JavaScript that executes in the browser is the difficulty of keeping errors out of the scripts. If function `validateCustomer` has any problems such as syntax errors or references to nonexistent methods, it is the same as if it returned `true`. A function with errors has no effect on the submission of the script.

Fortunately, browsers provide error logs or debugging tools for client-side JavaScript code. The Netscape 6 browser, for instance, has a JavaScript console that shows all of the JavaScript error messages and warnings. To see the JavaScript console, choose `Tools` on the `Tasks` menu, and select `JavaScript Console`. Netscape also has a JavaScript debugging tool that may help in finding errors in client-side JavaScript.

Internet Explorer uses the Microsoft Script Debugger to help users with JavaScript errors. You must download and install the script debugger to enable debugging. When Internet Explorer finds an error in a JavaScript function, it alerts the user with a message window that asks "Do you wish to debug?" along with an error message. If you click "Yes," the script debugger will open and display the source code. You can also open the debugger from the Internet Explorer `Tools` menu.

15.1.3 Installing Form Validation in ASP Scripts

The final step in using client-side JavaScript in the customer information page is to modify the Web application that generates the page. The tricky part is to include the client-side JavaScript code in the ASP script, but to tell the ASP processor to send the client-side code to the browser as part of the HTML document. We have to make sure that the server-side code is executed by the ASP processor and the client-side code is not.

An important difference between server-side and client-side programming is in the way JavaScript code is embedded in HTML documents. On the server side, we embed our JavaScript code in ASP scripts. The special tags `<%` and `%>` delimit JavaScript code in ASP scripts.

On the client side, `script` begin and end tags delimit JavaScript code. A `script` tag marks the beginning of a code segment and also identifies the script type and language: Figure 15.5 shows part of the file `client.js` that is included in the HTML document that produces the customer information Web page.

When an ASP document is processed by the ASP processor, the JavaScript code between `<%` and `%>` is executed, but the JavaScript between begin and end `script` tags is not. The ASP processor recognizes that script tags delimit client-side code and transmits the `script` tag and its contents to the browser.

The BigHit Online Web site includes the JavaScript file `client.js` that contains the code for function `validateCustomer`. To use the JavaScript function, the ASP code simply adds an `include` directive for `client.js` and sets the `onsubmit` attribute of the form tag.

We can embed server-side code in `script` begin and end tags by using attribute `runat="server"` in the `script` tag. This attribute tells the ASP processor to execute the code between the tags. You must be careful, however, because the ASP processor will move all code in `script` tags to the end of the ASP script. Function definitions may be included in `script` tags, but other JavaScript code must be delimited by `<%` and `%>`.

15.2 ERROR HANDLING IN SERVER-SIDE JAVASCRIPT

Among the many sources of errors we can expect in our ASP JavaScript applications are errors caused by the execution of improperly formed SQL statements. We can reduce SQL errors by client-side data validation as described in the previous section. Data validation will reduce SQL errors by making sure that values entered by users are reasonable, for example checking to see that numeric values are numeric, that all values are present, and so on. However, there are still situations in which errors will occur.

The easiest place to see the need for error processing is in the SQL query execution form that was discussed in Chapter 12. This form, shown here as Figure 15.6, allows a user to type any string and have it submitted to the database server for execution as an SQL statement. Because the Web site has no control over what the user enters, we must expect that SQL execution errors will occur.

FIGURE 15.5

Part of File `client.js` Showing Script Tags

```
1  <!-- client.js -->
2  <script type="text/javascript" language="javascript" >
3  function validateCustomer() {
4      var accountId = document.customer.accountId.value;
5      // rest of function follows
6      return true;
7  }
8  </script>
```

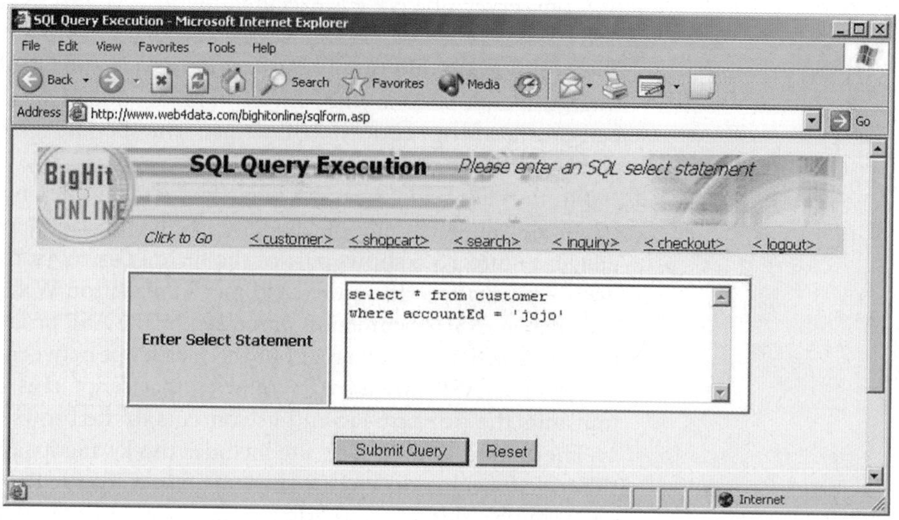

You might want to use this form to test your own SQL statements. You can type an SQL statement into the form and submit it for execution. If the statement you type is not correct, you'd like the response page to show you the error.

The SQL statement shown in the text input area of Figure 15.6 is not correct for the database. The name of the account ID field is misspelled. The attribute of the table is `accountId`, but the user has mistyped the `I` as an `E`. There is no field in the table named `accountEd`. The query execution engine will detect the error in this SQL statement.

The script `sqlexec.asp` that processes the form submission should recognize when an error has occurred and create a response page that reports an error message to the user. Figure 15.7 shows the page produced by `sqlexec.asp`, after it has been modified to handle errors properly.

The error message shown in Figure 15.7 is very specific. SQL Server, the database server for this Web application, reported that the name `accountEd` is not the name of a column of the source table of the query. The rest of the message might be meaningful to the developer of the site, but is not much use to the person who wrote the query.

FIGURE 15.7

Error Page in Response to the
Query of Figure 15.6

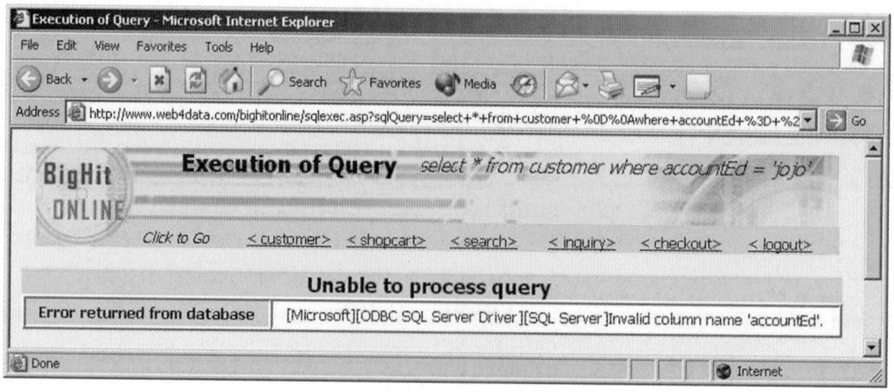

In order for you to understand error handling in JavaScript, or in any other programming language, you must know some terminology. In JavaScript we call an error an **exception** and deal with error through **exception handling**. An exception is an object that is created by a part of the program that detects some exceptional condition.

In this case, the part of the JavaScript system that interacts directly with the database receives a message that an error has occurred in SQL execution. The JavaScript system code creates an exception object that contains the error message from the SQL server, along with additional information about what the JavaScript program was doing when the error occurred.

Once an exception has been created, it is *thrown* into the system, the normal execution of the program is interrupted, and the exception handling part of JavaScript takes over. JavaScript searches for a block of code that can deal with, or *handle*, the exception. Once it finds such a block of code, called an **exception handler**, it resumes execution in the handler.

An exception handler is created using a JavaScript statement called a **try-catch statement**. The general form of the **try-catch** statement is

```
try {
    // begin by executing these statements (try block)
} catch (exception) {
    // if exception occurs execute these statements
    //(catch block)
} finally //optional
    // always execute these statements (finally block)
}
```

The execution of the **try-catch** statement begins by executing the statements of the **try** block. If no exception is thrown during their execution, the exception handler is skipped and the **finally** block is executed.

If an exception is created and thrown during the execution of the statements of the **try** block, execution of that block of code terminates and execution resumes in the statement of the exception handler. Once it completes, the **finally** block is executed. The **finally** block is optional and should only be included when necessary.

The statements of the **finally** block are executed regardless of whether an exception happens during the execution of the **try** block. An exception that happens during the execution of the **catch** block is not handled by this **try-catch** statement, but rather causes termination of the whole statement. The **finally** block is still executed.

Consider the script **sqlexec.asp** shown in Figure 15.8. Line 2 gets the SQL statement from the request variable and stores it in variable **sqlQuery**. Then it opens a connection to the database in line 5.

Lines 7–16 are the **try-catch** statement. Lines 8–9 are the **try** block and lines 11–15 are the **catch** block. The **finally** block was not needed here and so has been omitted from this statement.

In our example, the execution of the SQL statement in line 8 results in a thrown exception. The execution of the **try** block is terminated. No assignment occurs to variable results in line 8 and the call to **printTable** in line 9 is not executed.

Because the exception happened in a **try** block, execution resumes at line 11, the first line of the exception handler. The **catch** block statements create the HTML table of Figure 15.7 to show the error message to the user. The error message is written by line 14, which prints the **description** property of the **exception** object.

Once the exception handler is finished, the next line, line 17, is executed to print the page footer and the script finishes normally. After a handler is found for an exception, the exception is removed from the system and normal execution resumes.

A function may have multiple **try-catch** statements, either nested or in sequence. If an exception is raised but not handled during the execution of a function, the function execution is terminated and the exception thrown back to the calling

```
 1  var conn, sqlQuery, results;
 2  sqlQuery = Request("sqlQuery");
 3  printHeader("Execution of Query",sqlQuery);
 4  // connect to database
 5  conn = makeConnection();
 6  // execute query
 7  try {// we may get an error in executing the query
 8     results = conn.Execute(sqlQuery);
 9     printTable(results,Response);
10  } catch (exception) {
11     Response.write("<table><center>\n");
12     Response.write("<caption>Unable to process query</caption>\n");
13     Response.write("<tr><th>Error returned from database</th><td>");
14     Response.write(exception.description+"<br>\n");
15     Response.write("</tr></table></center>\n");
16  }
17  printFooter();
```

FIGURE 15.8

Part of the ASP Script
sqlexec.asp That
Handles Error in SQL Execution

code. The search for an exception handler continues at the point of call. If the calling code has an exception handler, it is invoked. Otherwise the search for an exception handler continues.

Whenever an exception occurs and no handler can be found, the script execution terminates with an error condition. The ASP processor recognizes this situation and invokes its own error handler. The exception description will be printed to the HTML output page by the ASP processor, just as was shown in Figure 12.16.

15.3   TRANSACTIONS AND TRANSACTION MANAGEMENT

Whenever a database is accessed by multiple users or applications at the same time, those users can interfere with each other. We call these multiple accesses **concurrent** because their actions happen within a single time period. One user accesses the database, and then the second user, then the first user again, and so on.

We can see an example of concurrent interference in a video store. Suppose that two customers in a store are trying to rent the same two movies, and only one copy of each is available. One customer looks at the shelves of movies and sees that both are available and then reaches for one movie. Concurrently, the other customer looks at the shelves and then reaches for the other movie. Now each customer has one movie but not the other.

At the beginning to the selection process, both customers evaluated what was available and decided what they wanted. Either customer could have been satisfied. However, because of the ordering of the actions of the customers, neither customer was satisfied. Both were stuck holding one movie and not the other.

What happens next? Both customers put their movies back and then reach for the other? Both customers refuse to release a movie? Because customers are people and people are reasonable, either one will give the other the movie, or they will modify their rental decisions.

Computer applications that interact with databases concurrently have similar problems. The actions of one application will interfere with the actions of another. The solutions to problems like these involve cooperation between applications and support from the database server.

15.3.1 Example of Concurrent User Interference in BigHit Online

Several situations in the BigHit Online information system of Chapter 13 could result in errors when more than one application is interacting with the database. In particular, errors may occur in these situations when more than one application is updating the database.

Consider the creation of a new sale entity for customer `jojo`, as was described in Section 13.5.2. The following two SQL statements must be executed to create the sale. The first determines an appropriate sales ID and the second creates the `Sale` entity.

```
select max(salesId) from Sale
insert into Sale (salesId,accountId,saleDate,status,total-
Cost) values (66,'jojo',getdate(),'sold',0)
```

If the first statement returns the value 65 as the maximum current sales ID, the second statement will use 66 as the sales ID of the new row of the `Sale` table.

Suppose we have another customer, with account ID `hannah`, attempting to purchase items at the same time. The application will execute statements like those above for both transactions. One possible sequence of actions is shown in Table 15.1. Because of the order of their actions, both customers find the same value as the maximum sales ID (65) and hence try to use the same sales ID (66) for the new row of the `Sale` table. Whichever customer inserts the new entity first (in this case `hannah`) succeeds and the other customer (`jojo`) fails.

We can prevent this problem, but we need a few new ideas first.

15.3.2 Database Transactions

Database experts developed the notion of a **transaction**, or *atomic transaction*, as a logical unit of database activity that consists of a single user or application executing several SQL statements. The term *atomic* is used in the same way as it was for physicists when they described the atom: a unit that cannot be broken into smaller pieces. The atomic nature of transactions is most important when a transaction includes several update, delete, or insert statements. If an error occurs in any statement of the transaction, none of the database modifications will take place. A transaction either executes completely or it does not change the database.

A transaction is also a declarative unit. That is, an application designer declares a collection of SQL statements to be a transaction. The application will execute these

Table 15.1 Two Customers Buying at the Same Time

Customer	Action	Result
jojo	**select** max(salesId) **from** Sale	Value 65 returned
hannah	**select** max(salesId) **from** Sale	Value 65 returned
hannah	**insert into** Sale **values** (66, 'hannah', ...	New Sale entity created
jojo	**insert into** Sale **values** (66, 'jojo', ...	Insert fails because of duplicate key

---

Concept

Autonumber Keys and Interference between Users

We could eliminate some problems with assigning sales IDs to concurrent requests by making the `salesId` field an autonumber key, as described in Section 12.5. An autonumber key is one whose value is assigned by the database as part of the insert operation. With autonumbering, the two sales could be created by insert statements:

```
insert into Sale (accountId, saleDate, status, shipDate,
    totalCost, shippingAddress) values ('hannah', ...)
insert into Sale (accountId, saleDate, status, shipDate,
    totalCost, shippingAddress) values ('jojo', ...)
```

These statements eliminate the problem with assigning the same sales ID. But, how do we know which sales ID goes with which customer? The sales processing application needs to determine the sales ID in order to create the `SaleItem` entries. The obvious way to find out the sales ID is to ask the database for the highest numbered entry with a select statement.

```
select max(salesId) from Sale
```

Suppose the order of execution of the statements is: insert sale for Hannah; insert sale for Jojo; request sales ID for Hannah; request sales ID for Jojo. Both customers will think they have the same sales ID.

So, although autonumbering removes some of the problems associated with concurrent sales processing, it does not remove them all. Transactions, as described in this section, must be used to eliminate interference.

---

statements as a unit. If any problem is encountered in completing the entire collection, all of the modifications created by the statements will be cancelled and the previous state of the database restored.

Database servers include software to manage the transaction behavior of their client applications. This software is called a **transaction manager**. Whenever a client submits an SQL statement to the server for execution, the transaction manager will check to make sure that the rules of transaction processing are followed.

Each access to databases and especially each modification to a database is executed as part of a transaction. This situation has remained hidden in our applications so far. All of our database updates have been executed one statement at a time. That is, each SQL statement has been a transaction by itself.

The default transaction behavior of an SQL server is to execute each SQL statement as a single transaction. Thus whenever an SQL statement is presented for execution, the transaction manager creates a new transaction. Once the execution of the statement is complete, the server terminates the transaction. This mode of execution is called **autocommit** mode.

The more general strategy for SQL statement execution, **explicit commit mode**, is for an application to connect to a database server and request that a new transaction be created, or *opened*. The application can then execute any number of queries and updates within the open transaction.

The application can then choose to **commit** the transaction, making all of the updates permanent, or **rollback** the transaction, canceling all of the updates and returning the database to its previous state. There is no middle ground. Either all of the updates are applied to the database, or the state of the database is not affected by the transaction at all. Once the transaction is closed as a result of a commit or rollback operation, the application must open a new transaction to continue its database access.

One of the most important responsibilities of the transaction manager is to reduce or eliminate interference between concurrent transactions. For example, if one transaction reads a row of a database table, other transactions will be allowed to read the row, but no other transaction will be allowed to modify it until the first transaction is closed.

Concurrency control is the process of managing the interactions of concurrent transactions. The transaction manager is responsible for implementing concurrency control in a way that optimizes the sometimes conflicting requirements of isolating transactions from each other, and allowing as many transactions as possible to execute concurrently. The transaction manager must keep track of all of the objects read and written by the concurrent transactions so that it can find and block actions issued by one transaction that will interfere with some other transaction. You can find many references to concurrency control and transaction managers in the Further Reading section of this chapter.

15.3.3 **Using Transactions in BigHit Online**

Concurrent database interaction can be very complicated. In the example of this section, we combine sales and payment to show what can happen and how transactions can help. Later on we'll see a specific example of programming with transactions.

Sales and payments in BigHit Online provide a good opportunity for using transactions. A complicated relationship exists between creating a sale and the corresponding sale items, and processing a payment for those items. In particular, we can't bill someone for items that are not available for sale, but we also cannot sell items to someone who cannot pay.

Suppose we have only 3 copies of the DVD for the movie *Elizabeth* and we have 2 customers, Joe and Jane, who each want to purchase 2 copies and pay by credit card. We cannot deliver all of the items to both customers. However, we could sell 2 copies to Joe and 1 copy to Jane. We can bill both customers for the appropriate amount and tell Jane that we'll bill and send her second copy when it is available.

The sale to Joe has two parts: update the database to show that Joe has bought the DVDs (create `Sale` and `SaleItem` objects) and bill Joe's credit card account for the items. We can do these actions in either order.

Table 15.2 shows three different ways in which we can try to sell these items to Joe alone (scenario 1) and to both Joe and Jane.

The first scenario shows the importance of allowing a transaction to be cancelled in a single operation. Action 1a determines that the 2 copies for Joe are available. Item 1b updates the database to record our intention to sell these items to Joe. Unfortunately, in item 1d, Joe's request for credit is rejected and the previous state of the database must be restored. The `Sale` and `SaleItem` objects must be removed from the database and the DVD quantity of the movie restored to 3.

If the actions are executed as within a single transaction, the application can invoke the abort (rollback) operation and the database will be restored. If the updates have been executed as separate transactions, we must create new SQL `delete` statements that put the database back. It is clearly easier on the application if the actions are executed as a single transaction.

In scenario 2, we see the effects of the interaction of two concurrent updates. The first three steps (2a, 2b, 2c) are identical to those of scenario 1. Action 2d, however, introduces the second customer. While waiting on the approval of credit for Joe, the processing of Jane's purchase begins. In step 2d we find that only 1 DVD is available for sale to Jane, since the others are held for Joe. We process Jane's purchase and deliver 1 DVD to her. When Joe's credit is again rejected (action 2i) we have to return the 2 DVDs that were held for Joe. We have missed the opportunity to sell one copy to Jane.

Table 15.2 Three Scenarios for Selling DVDs to Joe and Jane Including Problems with Transaction Management

	Person	Action	Result
Scenario 1, Joe tries to buy but payment rejected			
1a	Joe	Check for availability of 2 DVDs	Yes, 2 copies are available
1b	Joe	Update database	`Sale` and `SaleItem` objects created Quantity of DVDs reduced from 3 to 1
1c	Joe	Request approval for Joe's credit card	Waiting for approval
1d	Joe	Receive denial of credit	Must put back database so that `Sale` and `SaleItem` objects are removed and quantity is restored to 3
Scenario 2, Joe and Jane try to buy with reserving copies, Joe's payment rejected			
2a	Joe	Check for availability of 2 DVDs	Yes, 2 copies are available
2b	Joe	Update database	`Sale` and `SaleItem` objects created quantity of DVDs reduced from 3 to 1
2c	Joe	Request approval for Joe's credit card for 2 DVDs	Waiting for approval
2d	Jane	Check for availability of 2 DVDs	No, only 1 copy is available
2e	Jane	Update database	`Sale` and `SaleItem` objects created Quantity of DVDs reduced from 1 to 0 2nd DVD put on backorder
2f	Jane	Request approval for Jane's credit card for 1 DVD	Waiting for approval
2g	Jane	Receive approval of credit	Record payment
2h	Jane	Deliver 1 DVD	Sale missed because Jane's order could not be filled
2i	Joe	Receive denial of credit	Must put back database so that `Sale` and `SaleItem` objects are removed and quantity restored to 1
Scenario 3, Joe and Jane try to buy without reserving copies			
3a	Joe	Check for availability of 2 DVDs	Yes, 2 copies are available
3b	Joe	Request approval for Joe's credit card	Waiting for approval
3c	Jane	Check for availability of 2 DVDs	Yes, 2 copies are available
3d	Jane	Request approval for Jane's credit card	Waiting for approval
3e	Joe	Receive approval of credit	Record payment
3f	Joe	Update database	`Sale` and `SaleItem` objects created Quantity of DVDs reduced from 3 to 1
3g	Jane	Receive approval of credit	Record payment
3h	Jane	Update database	`Sale` and `SaleItem` objects created Quantity of DVDs reduced from 1 to −1 Update fails because quantity <0 Final result, no items sold

The two transactions have interfered with each other. If the actions for Jane had not overlapped the actions of Joe, we would have been able to sell 2 DVDs to Jane.

In scenario 3, the actions of updating the database and processing the payment are reversed. Now we check (actions 3a and 3c) for the availability of the DVDs. Because we do not reserve DVDs for Joe, we find that both can have 2 DVDs. Of course, this is not correct.

When action 3e finds that Joe's credit is accepted, we can sell 2 items to Joe, record the payment, and update the database. Unfortunately, when Jane's payment is also approved in action 3g, only 1 DVD remains and we cannot sell 2 items.

Action 3h, the attempt to sell 2 DVDs, fails and Jane's payment, which has already been collected, must be refunded to Jane's credit card.

Notice that scenario 3 would have worked if Joe's credit had been rejected, just as scenario 2 would have been proper if Joe's credit had been accepted. Neither of these scenarios is inherently bad. The problem is that the actions on behalf of the two customers interfere with each other.

15.3.4 General Theory of Database Transactions

Database theory and practice have identified four crucial properties of transactions: the **ACID** (atomicity, consistency, isolation, and durability) properties.

- **Atomicity**: All of the updates of a transaction are successful, or no update takes place.
- **Consistency**: Each transaction should leave the database in a consistent state. Properties such as referential integrity (foreign key consistency) must be preserved.
- **Isolation**: Each transaction, when executed concurrently with other transactions, should have the same effect as if it had been executed by itself.
- **Durability**: Once a transaction has completed successfully, its changes to the database should be permanent. Even serious failures should not affect the permanence of a transaction.

Each database server has a transaction manager that helps create **ACID transactions**—that is, create transactions that satisfy the ACID properties. The transaction manager keeps track of all of the active transactions in the system as well as which database objects have been read or written by which transactions.

The examples of Section 15.3.3 illustrated some of advantages of ACID properties.

Scenario 1, if executed with all actions as a single transaction, takes advantage of the atomic property by cancelling all of the updates in one simple request to the transaction manager to rollback.

Scenarios 2 and 3 featured transactions that were interdependent, and thus violated the isolation property. A transaction manager would not allow the actions to proceed in the order listed. In scenario 2, for example, once Joe has begun to update the database, all requests by Jane to access the database would be refused, or blocked, by the transaction manager until Joe's transaction was completed.

15.3.5 Transaction Management in ASP with SQL Server

The ActiveX Data Object library that is used in JavaScript with ASP scripts supports transactions through the `BeginTrans`, `CommitTrans`, and `RollbackTrans` methods of the `Connection` object.

Unless a `BeginTrans` method has been called, the ASP database connection executes SQL statements in autocommit mode. Each call to `Connection.Execute` is treated as a new transaction.

When an application executes `BeginTrans`, a new transaction is opened in explicit-commit mode. The transaction remains open until the application executes `CommitTrans` or `RollbackTrans`, or closes the database connection.

Figure 15.9 shows the code for creating `Sale` and `SaleItem` objects in script `confirmcheckout.asp` as a single transaction. The code incorporates a `try-catch` statement to test for any error in SQL.

The block of code begins with a call to `BeginTrans` to open a transaction. The `try` block of lines 2–18 surrounds the execution of the select and insert statements in lines 8, 11, and 17. If all of these statements execute successfully, the transaction is committed by the call to `CommitTrans` in line 18. If there is any problem in executing the SQL statements, an exception is thrown and the `catch` block of line 20 is executed. The call to `RollbackTrans` in line 20 cancels all of the effects of the update statements, no matter what happened, and restores the database just as it was before the execution began.

15.3.6 Analyzing Interference with Concurrent Updates

In Section 15.3.1, we looked at how two users trying to create sales concurrently could cause one of the applications to fail. In essence, each user finds the next sales ID and both users try to create a sale with the same sale ID. The SQL code of lines 4-10 solves this problem.

Lines 4–8 create a new sale item with this SQL.

```
insert into Sale (salesId, accountId, saleDate, status,
    totalCost) select max(salesId)+1, 'jojo', getdate(),
    'pending', 0 from Sale
```

The select statement nested inside the insert statement creates a table with a single row. The value for `salesId` in the new row is one more than the maximum value for `salesId` that is in the table before the insert. Thus, the application inserts a new row

F I G U R E 15.9

Create `Sale` and
`SaleItem` Objects in a
Transaction

```
1   conn.BeginTrans();
2   try {
3       // create Sale object
4       var insertSales =
5           "insert into Sale(salesId,accountId,saleDate,status,totalCost)"
6           +" select max(salesId)+1,'"+accountId+"',getdate(),'pending',0"
7           +" from Sale";
8       conn.Execute(insertSales);
9       // get new salesId
10      var maxSQL = "select max(salesId) from Sale";
11      var maxSQLResult = conn.Execute(maxSQL);
12      var newSalesId = parseInt(maxSQLResult(0));
13      // add sale items from cart items
14      var makeItems = "insert into SaleItem select "+newSalesId+", line,"
15          +" movieId, quantity,format,unitCost,'pending'"
16          +" from CartItem where cartId='"+id+"' and quantity<>0";
17      conn.Execute(makeItems);
18      conn.CommitTrans();
19  } catch (exception) {
20      conn.RollbackTrans();
21  }
```

into `Sale` with the appropriate sales ID. Then, in lines 10–12, the application extracts `max(salesId)`, which is the sales ID of the new row, and stores it in variable `newSalesId`. The insert of items into `SaleItem` (lines 14–17) uses this new sales ID.

You might wonder what happens with this new SQL code when two customers try to add a sale concurrently. Both customers record their sales with the application code shown in Figure 15.9. Table 15.3 shows a possible sequence of actions by the two customers.

The customer (jojo) who arrives first at line 8 adds a new row to the `Sale` table. The other customer (hannah) will try to execute line 8, but will be blocked by the transaction manager. That is, the transaction manager will refuse to allow another row to be added to `Sale` until the first transaction finishes. Thus, jojo will be allowed to fetch the `salesId` of the new row and insert the rows into `SaleItem` table without interference.

As soon as jojo's transaction is complete, hannah will be unblocked. The transaction manager will allow hannah to add a new row to `Sale` and finish her transaction.

This works so well that you should wonder why we didn't use the SQL of Figure 15.9 in the code without transactions of Section 15.3.1? A possible sequence of actions is shown in Table 15.4.

Table 15.3 Two Customers Buying at the Same Time with the SQL Statements of Figure 15.9

Customer	Action	Result
jojo	`insert into Sale(...)` `select max(salesId)+1, 'jojo', ...`	New `Sale` entity created with ID 66
hannah	`insert into Sale(...)` `select max(salesId)+1, 'hannah', ...`	Action blocked by transaction manager
jojo	`select max(salesId) from Sale`	Value 66 returned
hannah	`insert into Sale (...)` `select max(salesId)+1, 'hannah', ...`	Action allowed: New `Sale` entity created with ID 67
hannah	`select max(salesId) from Sale`	Value 67 returned

Table 15.4 Two Customers Buying at the Same Time with the SQL Statements of Figure 15.9

Customer	Action	Result
jojo	`insert into Sale(...)` `select max(salesId)+1, 'jojo', ...`	New `Sale` entity created with ID 66
hannah	`insert into Sale(...)` `select max(salesId)+1, 'hannah', ...`	New `Sale` entity created with ID 67
hannah	`select max(salesId) from Sale`	Value 67 returned
jojo	`select max(salesId) from Sale`	Value 67 returned

The execution starts in the same order as Table 15.3. First `jojo` inserts a row into `Sale` with sale ID 66. Then, `hannah` tries to insert a row. This time, however, no transaction manager blocks `hannah`'s attempt. Hence, `hannah` will be allowed to insert a row with sales ID 67. In the third step, `hannah` finds the proper sales ID (67).

In step 4, `jojo` asks for his sales ID and is given 67—the wrong number. When `jojo` continues and adds the content of his shopping cart to sale 67, the items will go into `hannah`'s sale.

Both customers think they have the same `salesId`. The error caused by interference is worse in this case than in the previous one. In Section 15.3.1, one of the customers was unable to create a sale. The error was detected by the database server and reported to the application. The application is free to try again to create a sale.

With the code of Fig. 15.9 and no transactions, both customers appear to have recorded their sales correctly, but the update is done incorrectly. The applications will be unaware of the mistake because no SQL error was committed.

Transaction management was created to address the types of problems we've seen in this section. Of course, mastery of transaction management will require a considerably more detailed study of the subject.

15.4 BACKUP AND RECOVERY FROM FAILURES

Possibly the most important aspect of commercial DBMSs is their support for recovering from failures. Here, we must consider the broadest interpretation of failure. Imagine that you are responsible for a database that is running on a computer system located in the basement of a building near the Mississippi River. The river rises, a levee breaks, your basement is flooded, and your computer system is destroyed! What happens to the database? This failure is catastrophic. Most failures are less severe, but they still can have a significant effect on the consistency and availability of databases.

Database systems and applications must be designed for recovery after failures. Unfortunately, we cannot design systems so that failures will never occur. Instead, designers must anticipate the potential failures and create plans for reacting when these failures occur.

The goal of a **recovery** plan is to restore the database to a state that is known to be correct and then put it back in service as quickly as possible. Recovery plans must include what people should do to keep their business operations functioning while the database is unavailable. If the system is unavailable for an extended period, there must be a plan for updating the database to incorporate the activities that took place during its absence.

Many potential sources of database failures exist. Examples include:

1. *The database server computer crashes.* In this case, the database server will become unavailable for some time. The information content may be corrupted because of information that is stored in memory and has not been transferred to the more permanent disk storage.

2. *The database server program crashes.* This failure should never happen. An important characteristic of a commercial database server is that it never fails catastrophically without some external cause. The effect is the same as that in failure 1.

3. *A database client computer crashes.* The state of the client application will be lost and any open transactions will stop.

4. *A client program crashes.* This failure is just like failure 3, except that the computer executing the client program continues running and may be able to inform the database server that the client crashed.

5. *The network connection between client and server fails.* This failure is similar to failure 3 in that the client computer is unavailable and its transactions are stopped. The major difference is that the client may reappear at any time.

6. *A transaction executes a rollback operation.* The transaction has voluntarily canceled itself and its updates must be removed from the database.

7. *A transaction executes an illegal operation.* The transaction manager detects that a transaction has violated some protocol. The server must be able to abort the transaction and recover through a rollback.

8. *One or more transactions introduce errors into the database.* This situation occurs when an application program runs incorrectly and updates the database in ways that introduce nonfactual or inconsistent information to the database. The integrity of the database has been compromised.

9. *Data on a disk drive is corrupted.* A hardware error causes some of the database information to become unavailable.

The primary tool for supporting recovery is keeping multiple copies of information. A database transaction manager, for example, might keep the old values of objects modified by open transactions. Then, when a transaction fails and must be rolled back, it can simply copy the old values back into the database. This strategy uses redundancy to accomplish recovery from transaction failures.

Another redundancy strategy is creating and maintaining backup copies of the database and putting those copies at a remote site. With proper off-site backups, even catastrophic losses of computer systems don't have to cause the loss of data.

Let's begin with catastrophic failures. In this case, something happens and the database becomes completely unavailable for some period of time. The first response must be to continue business functions in an offline or manual mode. A retail store, for instance, typically has cash registers that function as database clients. Each sale is recorded in the database as it is made. If the database is unavailable, the cash register must save the sale records. This goal can be accomplished by the paper record that is created by the cash register or by the local storage of the cash register.

When the database becomes available again, the cash registers must be brought back online as database clients, and the sales that were recorded during offline operations must be recorded in the database. This operation can be done immediately when the database comes up, or it may be deferred until later. If the sales were recorded on paper, there must be a capability to enter those sales at a later time.

The examples of retail sales and backups to mitigate physical problems show us that the physical and manual activities of recovery must be carefully planned in advance. No amount of computerized redundancy will be able to compensate for not having plans for physical failures.

15.4.1 Backups and Checkpoints

A **backup** is a copy of the contents of a database at a specific time. It contains sufficient information to allow the restoration of the database. A database that has been restored from a backup has the same contents that it had at the time the backup was created. Of course, all updates that occurred after the creation of the backup are not part of the contents of the restored backup. As mentioned earlier, it is crucial to store backups in a different location than the system itself. It is not unusual for a company with more than one office to have each location keep the backups for another location. With this practice, a catastrophe in any one site will not cause the loss of information.

A **checkpoint** is an operation that forces the database on the disk to be in a state that is consistent with all of the committed transactions. It includes flushing the contents of disk caches so that the disk is up to date. Checkpoints are needed because database systems try to keep files in memory and only update the disk when necessary. The contents of a file on the disk may be inconsistent because changes made to the in-memory copy of the file are not automatically applied to the disk copy.

If the DBMS crashes and the disk is not corrupted, the database on disk will contain all of the changes that were committed before the checkpoint. It is not guaranteed that changes committed after the checkpoint will be on the disk.

When a DBMS fails, recovery can take advantage of backups and checkpoints. If the disk is not corrupted, the database server can be restarted in the state it was in at the last checkpoint. If the disk was corrupted, the state can be restored to the last available backup.

Our goal, however, should be to recover to the state when the system crashed, or at least so that all updates performed by committed transactions are included. If the system crashes when transactions have been committed since the last checkpoint, we cannot be sure that all of the committed updates are in effect.

Recall that the durability property of a transaction states that once a transaction has been committed, its effects are permanent. If a database becomes corrupted and is restored from backup, the transactions that ran after the backup are not included. Thus, these transactions are not durable. Durability cannot be achieved without a mechanism that goes beyond backups and checkpoints.

15.4.2 Transaction Logs

In order to create systems that can recover from failures with no loss of information, database servers must maintain careful records of every update. The records are kept in log files. As mentioned before, a log is a record of actions in the order they happened.

Each DBMS maintains several log files that record significant activity within the server. A **transaction log** is a file that records the actions of all transactions as they occur. An entry in a transaction log consists of the following items:

- The unique transaction ID that is automatically assigned to a transaction when it starts execution
- The name of the action performed
- The object that is referenced by the action, if any
- The value of the object before the action
- The value of the object after the action

Transaction logs play a crucial role in achieving durability. For example, recovery systems use these logs to recreate the state of the database after failures.

A transaction cannot finish its commit operation until the transaction log has been permanently recorded. Thus, the minimal condition for permanence is that the entries in the log have been force-written to the disk drive. To increase reliability, the transaction log should be copied to multiple disks. The ultimate reliability can be achieved only when a copy of the transaction log is force-written to a remote location, usually through a network connection.

With proper use of backups, checkpoints, and logs, database systems can recover from most failures.

15.5 SECURITY IN INFORMATION SYSTEMS

Security in information systems is designed to place controls on what information users can see and what they can modify. For instance, in the BigHit Online Web site, we might want to enforce these rules:

1. Each user must be registered as a customer.
2. A customer is allowed to fetch information about his purchases.
3. A customer is allowed to modify the database through the Web applications.
4. A customer is not allowed to fetch information about other customers.
5. A customer is not allowed to modify the database except through the Web applications.
6. A customer is not allowed to see information about inventory or employees.

The first rule simply establishes that users must be known to the system and that unknown users are not allowed any access to it.

The other rules about customers describe things that users are allowed to do (rules 2 and 3) and things that users are not allowed to do (rules 4–6). You can probably think of lots of other rules for customers. A security model for BigHit Online would also have rules about what different employees can do.

We might say that an information system is secure if no unauthorized users can gain access and authorized users can access information that they are supposed to and cannot access information they are not supposed to.

A Web site is secure if the site can control user logins, can ensure that all access to the database systems is through the Web applications of the site, and that the Web applications cannot be modified by users. Much of the security of Web sites lies in the security of the Web server. Web server security is beyond the scope of the book. As Web developers, we can take advantage of the great progress that is taking place in Web security. It is not unreasonable to expect that some form of universal user authentication will become available for Web servers in the future.

This section is primarily about how database servers can be made secure, but it also applies to making our Web sites secure. The Web applications of our Web site are users of the database and must be given access to the database. The list of restrictions and access rights for customers could just as well be a list for the Web applications. For example, no customer Web application is allowed to access information about inventory or employees.

15.5.1 Security in Database Management Systems

We are interested in the role of DBMSs in creating reliable and secure systems. The previous sections on data validation, error handling, transaction processing, and recovery addressed reliability in servers. We have seen how minimizing the probability of failure and maximizing the probability of full recovery when failure does occur helps produce reliable systems.

Controls on access to information by users and applications help increase the reliability of the content of databases. That is, reliability is increased by reducing the likelihood that data has been modified improperly.

Information stored in databases has enormous value, and that value is derived from the accuracy of the information and its availability. The more valuable the database becomes, the more vulnerable it is to misuse and corruption, however. The information content of a database must therefore be protected from being altered or stolen.

Database security begins with physical security for the computer systems that host the DBMS. No DBMS is safe from intrusion, corruption, or destruction by people who have physical access to the computers. After physical security has been established, database administrators must protect the data from both unauthorized users and unauthorized access by authorized users. No DBMS can be used for valuable databases unless it has support for three types of security:

- Account security for the validation of users
- Access security for protection of database objects
- Operating system security for database and file protections

The goals of database security are to protect the integrity of the database and to prevent unauthorized use of the information. The system configuration must ensure that only authorized users and programs can access the data and the operations of the database. Fortunately, the SQL standard includes strong support for security and all commercial DBMSs include security controls.

15.5.2 User Authorization for Database Servers

A commercial DBMS stores user identifiers and passwords in system tables in the database. SQL has commands to create, alter, and drop users. Each connection by a user or client program must be authenticated as a valid database user.

Figure 15.10 gives a variety of SQL statements that manipulate users. These statements are used by most commercial DBMSs, including Oracle. Lines 1 and 2 use the `create user` statement to add `Dick` and `Jane` to the list of database users. The `identified by` clauses define their initial passwords. Line 3 shows how the `alter user` statement can give user `Jane` an unlimited quota on the segment; that is, no limit on the size of Jane's tables. The `drop user` statement of line 4 removes `Jane` from the database.

Using line 5 of Figure 15.10, a database administrator can lock an account so that the user cannot login. In line 6, the password of user `Dick` is changed. After the execution of line 7, his password has expired and he will be prompted for a new password at his next login.

A profile is a list of limitations that can be shared by many users. Line 8 shows the creation of a profile with a limit of 10 minutes on any database connection. In line 9, a new user is created using this profile to limit his connection time. The `OPS$` in front of the `hannibal` account name identifies it as an operating system account. This operating system user will be allowed to connect to the database without the use of a password; instead, we rely on the operating system to authenticate the user. Operating system users can also be identified by database passwords. The statement on line 10 allows any other operating system user to connect as `hannibal` by entering the password `use-this-password`.

Unfortunately, Microsoft SQL Server does not support the SQL statements of Figure 15.10. Creating users in SQL Server is most easily done with the enterprise manager. The SQL Server version of SQL has command `sp_addlogin` that creates a database login account and `sp_adduser` that allows a login account to be a user of a database.

15.5.3 Protection of Database Objects

Now that you know how to create users, you will want to specify what they can do with the database. You need know both how to grant them access to database resources and how to deny them access.

FIGURE 15.10

Sample SQL Statements That Manipulate User Accounts

```
1   create user Jane identified by crockette;
2   create user Dick identified by go-man-go;
3   alter user Jane quota unlimited on USERS;
4   drop user Jane;
5   alter user Dick account lock;
6   alter user Dick identified by stop-please;
7   alter user Dick password expire;
8   create profile LimitedUser limit CONNECT_TIME 10;
9   create user OPS$hannibal profile LimitedUser;
10  alter user OPS$hannibal identified by use-this-password;
```

SQL databases define a collection of **privileges** that may be granted to users, including those to read, update, append, create, and drop access to databases, schemas, tables, and views. The `grant` and `revoke` statements are used to allow and disallow privileges, respectively. Access privileges restrict (and allow) access by specific users to specific operations on specific objects. By default, full access to objects is granted to the creating user and no access to other users.

If you login to the database and create tables, you will have full privileges to access them. No one else will be granted any access. If you want another user to have privileges to access your tables, you have to explicitly grant them those privileges. You can specify the privileges of other users in great detail using SQL statements. SQL Server supports all of the standard SQL statements described below.

Figure 15.11 shows some SQL statements that affect database privileges. The privilege to insert new rows in the `Customer` table is given to user `Jane` by the statement of line 1. After the execution of line 2, every database user (`public`) will be allowed to perform select statements on the `Customer` table. Line 3 grants all privileges on the `Employee` table to `Jane`, but line 4 denies her the privilege to delete rows. The `on` clause can refer to a variety of system resources, including databases, schemas, tables, views, and columns. Line 5 allows `Jane` to update specific columns of `Customer`, but not the other columns.

The assigning of privileges to users may quickly become very time-consuming for database administrators. Lines 6 and 7 of Figure 15.11 show how the role capability can be used to describe a collection of privileges that may be granted to many users. Line 6 creates the role and line 7 gives all clerks access to the `Sale` and `SaleItem` tables. In line 8, a specific user is allowed to be a clerk. When `Dick` is acting as a clerk, he has all the privileges of the `Clerk` role and can manipulate the `Sale` and `SaleItem` tables. The database administrator can assign a collection of privileges to users according to their roles. Each user can be a member of many roles.

It is also appropriate to allow a role to be a member of another role. Line 9 of Figure 15.11 creates a floor manager role with a password. A user who is granted the `FloorManager` role must give a password to assume that role. In line 10, the floor manager is given all of the privileges of the `Clerk` role.

Privileges in SQL Server are stored in system tables and are most easily viewed and modified with the enterprise manager. Figure 15.12 shows the properties for the `Movie` table of the BigHit Online database. User `Dick` has been granted the privilege to insert rows but not to select, update, or delete them. User `Jane` has been granted the privilege to select and insert rows, but not to update or delete them. User `public` has the right to select rows. This view does not show the privileges of the owner of the table, who has full rights.

FIGURE 15.11

Examples of `Grant` Statements

```
1  grant insert on Customer to Jane;
2  grant select on Customer to public;
3  grant all on Employee to Jane;
4  revoke delete on Employee from Jane;
5  grant update on Customer(street, city, state, zip) to Jane;
6  create role Clerk not identified;
7  grant all on Sale, SaleItem to Clerk;
8  grant role Clerk to Dick;
9  create role FloorManager identified by ImInCharge;
10 grant role Clerk to FloorManager;
```

F I G U R E 15.12

Setting and Displaying
Privileges with Enterprise
Manager

15.6 STORED PROCEDURES AND FUNCTIONS

Database developers often find themselves writing a particular sequence of SQL statements that will be used in many different applications. In application development, you encapsulate sequences like that into a function, as you've seen many times in the previous chapters. Database developers have the option of defining a function out of these SQL statements and storing that function in the database server.

Commercial databases allow developers to add functionality to database servers by defining and storing complex operations. Each **stored procedure** or function has a name that can be used in SQL statements. For example, a derived attribute can be added to a table by defining a function that calculates and returns the attribute value. In this way, several complex database manipulations can be encapsulated into a single procedure. The syntax of stored procedures and functions varies from one database system to the next. The examples in this section use the style and syntax of SQL Server.

For example, the derived attribute `numberRented` of entity class `Customer` of the BigHit Video system is the number of videotapes currently rented by the customer. It can be represented in SQL by the stored procedure definition shown in Figure 15.13. The value of the derived attribute can be extracted in a select statement such as the following:

```
select *, numberRented(accountId) from Customer;
```

Stored procedures and functions can be used to increase system reliability by moving an operation out of the client application and into the database server. This approach improves reliability by placing the operation inside the database, where any changes are tracked and controlled by database security.

```
1   create function numberRented (@accId int)
2       return int
3   as select count(*) from Rental
4       where Customer.accountId = @accId;
```

As an example, consider the processing required to check in a videotape. A `Rental` record must be deleted and a `PreviousRental` record must be inserted. These two operations can be encapsulated into a stored procedure, as shown in Figure 15.14.

Concept

Inserting Sale Entries with a Function

We have seen in Section 15.3.1 that problems arise when multiple users are trying to purchase items concurrently. The discussion in Section 15.3.1 illustrates the difficulty of assigning a sales ID to a new sale. Figure 15.9 shows how to use the transaction model to solve this problem. An even better approach is to use a database function to create the new `Sale` entry.

```
1   create function newSale (@accountId varchar) returns int
2       as begin
3           declare @newId int;
4           set @newId = (select max(salesId)+1 from Sale);
5           insert into Sale (salesId, accountId)
6               values (@newId, @accountId);
7           return @newId;
8       end newSale;
```

The sales processing application can call this function to create a new `Sale` entry. The function returns the sales ID of the new row. Once the application has received the new sales ID, it can proceed to update the rest of the sale information and add the sale items.

The function will always execute as a transaction and therefore will not create problems with duplicate sales IDs.

```
1   create procedure checkIn (@vidId int, @cost double)
2       as begin
3           insert into PreviousRental
4               select accountId, @vidId, dateRented, now(), @cost
5                   from Rental where videoId = @vidId;
6           delete from Rental where videoId = @vidId;
7       end checkIn;
```

INTERVIEW

VICTOR VIANU
Database Research and the Web

A DAY IN THE LIFE OF A PROFESSOR The "average" day is split between teaching, research, departmental meetings and administration, and outside professional duties such as refereeing and journal editorial work—all of it punctuated by an occasional espresso. My main current research interests are in static analysis of XML queries, processing streaming data, and e-services.

THE LINKS BETWEEN DATABASE RESEARCH AND THE WEB The database theory community has played a major role in establishing the foundations for many developments related to the Web. The work on the semi-structured data model and query languages did the groundwork for the emergence of XML as a standard for data exchange on the Web. Then, database theoreticians developed much of the formal foundations for XML. This includes a wide range of aspects, from static analysis techniques for XML queries, typechecking, XML constraints, and query language expressiveness, all the way to storage and indexing techniques.

This has had a practical impact, but they also generated some very elegant theory. One of my favorites is a surprising and elegant connection between XML and the classical theory of tree automata. There were many other important contributions on data integration, handling inconsistent and incomplete information, and algorithms used in search engine technology.

There is every reason to believe that database theory will continue to be an important contributor to formal foundations for the Web. After all, database theory has developed a considerable body of knowledge on data models, query languages, and data management in general. These will remain central issues in the larger context of the Web. We can also expect increased interaction with other areas such as information retrieval, data mining, and cryptography.

> **"Database theory has developed a considerable body of knowledge on data models, query languages, and data management in general. These will remain central issues in the larger context of the Web."**

SQL allows stored procedures and functions to have their own privileges, thereby ensuring that access to objects can be granted for specific operations. For example, it is appropriate to allow a store clerk to perform the check-in operation, but not to delete records from `Rental` or add records to `PreviousRental`. The following grant statements allow the database to enforce this security plan:

```
grant execute on checkIn to clerk;
revoke delete on Rental to clerk;
revoke insert on PreviousRental to clerk;
```

Even though the clerk role has no privilege to modify the tables, the clerk's privilege to execute the procedure allows the procedure to make those modifications.

CHAPTER SUMMARY

This chapter presented a variety of new techniques for improving the quality of information systems and Web sites. Topics included client-side programming in JavaScript, data validation in HTML forms, error handling in JavaScript, transaction management techniques, and security in database servers.

JavaScript is easy to use for validating form data. A validation `function` is invoked just before the HTML form is submitted as an HTTP request. The validation function should check for the consistency and format of request variables and return `false` if any problem exists. When the validation function returns `false`, the browser does not submit an HTTP request. The pattern matching operations of the JavaScript `String` class are particularly useful for validating form data.

A validation function can be installed in an HTML page by placing the function between `script` begin and end tags and defining a function call as the value of the `onsubmit` attribute of the form tag.

Error handling in JavaScript is based on `try-catch` statements and the throwing of exception objects. The `try-catch` statement is composed of a `try` block of statements and a `catch` block of statements and a `finally` block of statements. If an exception occurs during the execution of the `try` block, its execution is terminated and the `catch block` is executed. If no exception occurs during the execution of a `try` block the `catch` block is skipped. An exception that is thrown outside of a `try` block is thrown into the calling function, and if it is not handled, results in the termination of the program. Exception handling is particularly useful in catching errors caused by the execution of SQL statements.

A transaction is a logical unit of database activity that must be completed as a whole or not at all. A transaction begins with an open operation and remains open until it executes a commit or rollback (abort) operation. If a transaction executes a rollback, all the database updates that were part of the transaction are cancelled and the state of the database is restored as though the transaction never occurred.

Database servers include modules called transaction managers that ensure that transactions execute independently of each other so that the changes made by one transaction cannot be seen by another transaction until it commits.

The BigHit Online information system of Chapters 13 and 14 has several blocks of SQL statements that should be executed as single transactions. This chapter discussed the creation of sales and sale items, and the processing of payments. Executing these operations as transactions ensures that mistakes caused by interference between transactions cannot occur.

The ACID properties of proper transaction processing are atomicity, consistency, isolation, and durability. Transactions that do not satisfy these properties lead to errors in both applications and database content.

The ADO Connection class supports `Begin-Trans`, `CommitTrans`, and `RollbackTrans` methods to control transaction processing.

Database servers support backup and recovery tools that enhance security by assuring that information that is added to a database is never lost. Full database security requires, in addition, both physical security of the computer systems and networks, and careful analysis of possible failures.

User security in database servers supports the creation of user identities and the granting and denying of privileges to access database objects. Stored programs can be created and privileges can be assigned to them.

KEY TERMS

ACID transaction. A transaction that is atomic, consistent, isolated, and durable.

Alert. A message box that a browser displays to alert the user to some problem or to convey information in a demanding way.

Atomicity. The property that the updates of a transaction are either all successful or have no effect at all.

Autocommit mode. A mode of processing SQL statements in which each statement is a transaction that is committed when the statement processing finishes.

Backup. A copy of the state of a database at a specific time. Also, the process of creating such a copy.

Checkpoint. A partial backup that can be used to recover the state of the database from a full backup.

Commit operation. The operation that brings a transaction to a successful close and makes its updates permanent.

Concurrency. A situation in which multiple independent processes are executing on one or more processors.

Concurrency control. The process of managing multiple interacting programs so that errors are minimized or reduced.

Consistency. The property that if a database is in a consistent state before the execution of a transaction, it is in a consistent state afterwards.

Data validation. The process of the checking the data entered on a form before the values are submitted for processing.

Durability. The property that once a transaction is committed, all of its updates are permanent.

Exception. A JavaScript object that represents the detection of an error or exceptional condition.

Exception handler. A block of code in a JavaScript program that is executed in response to an exception.

Exception handling. The error handling mechanism used by JavaScript and other programming languages to handle unexpected or unusual errors.

Explicit commit mode. A mode of processing SQL statements in which a sequence of statements is executed as a transaction.

Isolation. The property that one transaction is not affected by database updates made by any other active transaction.

OnSubmit attribute. An attribute of a form tag that specifies a function to call to perform data validation.

Privilege. A right granted to a user to manipulate specific database objects.

Recovery. The process of bringing a damaged database back to a former, consistent state.

Rollback operation. A database operation that restores a database to a previous state. A transaction can be rolled back to remove its updates. A database may be rolled back to a state that existed previously.

Stored procedure. A complex operation that is written in a database programming language and stored in a database and can be invoked from SQL. Stored procedures can have their own privileges.

Transaction log. A file that contains a record of each transaction action. Each entry in the log identifies the transaction, the action, the object referenced by the action, and the values of the object before and after the action.

Transaction manager. The software within a database server that monitors the behavior of transactions and decides whether each action can be executed. The transaction manager is charged with enforcing restrictions on the way transactions interact.

try-catch statement. A JavaScript statement that incorporates exception handling.

QUESTIONS

1. Pick one of the Web forms from the BigHit Online Web site (not the customer information form) and describe validation rules that should be enforced.

2. Consult a client-side JavaScript reference. Describe the methods and properties of these objects
   a. `document`
   b. `document.forms`
   c. `document.images`
   d. `document.links`

3. Consult a HTML 4.0 reference. List the attributes besides `onsubmit` that can be added to HTML forms and that link the forms with JavaScript code. Give a brief description of when each attribute becomes active.

4. Write JavaScript patterns that match the following
   a. A string consisting of letters and digits.
   b. An e-mail address: the only symbols allowed are letters, digits, period (`.`) and hyphen (`-`). An e-mail address must have one @ that is not the first character and have at least one period in the characters that follow the @ and no two periods together.
   c. A zip code is five digits, optionally followed by a hyphen and four more digits.
   d. A state is two capital letters.

5. Define and give a brief justification for each of the ACID characteristics of transactions.

6. What is a transaction manager? Describe two major responsibilities of a transaction manager.

7. How does an ASP/JavaScript application open a new transaction? How does an ASP/JavaScript application commit a transaction?

8. How do the backup and recovery capabilities of a DBMS contribute to the atomicity of a transaction? To its durability?

9. Give four examples of failures in DBMSs. For each one, describe how recovery from this failure may be accomplished.

10. What is the difference between a backup and a checkpoint? Give a scenario in which both backups and checkpoints are required for recovery from a failure.

11. Write SQL statements to perform the following security actions:
    a. Create a new user named "Janet" with an initial password of "hi-ho".
    b. Give Janet an unlimited quota.
    c. Give Janet permission to perform all actions on the `ShoppingCart` table.
    d. Revoke Janet's permission to insert objects into the `CartItem` table.
    e. Allow Janet to use the Clerk role.

12. Answer the following questions about access to a database after the execution of these SQL statements:

```
grant all on Customer to Clerk;
revoke delete on Movie from Eric;
grant update on Customer(street,
    city, state, zip) to Dieter;
create role Buyer not identified;
grant all on Sale, SaleItem, Movie
    to Buyer;
grant role Buyer to Dieter, Eric;
```

a. Can the user Eric insert a row into the `Movie` table?

b. Can the table `CartItem` be updated by the user Eric?

c. Can the user Dieter assume the role of Buyer?

d. Can Eric assume the role of Buyer?

13. What are the default permissions on a table for the owner of the table? For a user who is not the owner?

PROBLEMS

14. Write a JavaScript function to perform the validation described in your answer to question 1. Add the function to the `client.js` file and modify the HTML document so that it invokes your function when the user clicks the `submit` button.

15. Write a JavaScript function `validateSelection` that will validate the movie selection form of Figure 14.9. Install the function in application `additem.asp`.

16. Using the syntax of Figures 15.13 and 15.14, define a stored function or procedure that:

a. Produces the number of items in sales to a specific customer.

b. Produces the total cost of all items in shopping carts.

c. Creates a new row in the `Sale` table

d. Adds an item to a shopping cart.

PROJECTS

17. a. Write client-side JavaScript functions for the forms of the Web site. Install the functions in the appropriate ASP scripts so that all forms are checked before submission.

b. Evaluate the error-handling capabilities of the Web applications. Modify the applications so that all errors are processed correctly.

18. a. Design and implement a security model for the BigHit Online SQL server database. Identify each role that users can take on. Give a description of both the role and the privileges the role will have. Be sure to include a read-only role for those Web applications that do not modify the database. Add the roles to the database and write SQL statements to create the privileges. Execute those statements.

b. Modify the Web applications so that each one logs in as the appropriate user. If a Web application is not supposed to modify the database, then it should connect as the read-only user.

19. Design an error-handling model for your Movie Lovers Web site. Identify each form that should have client-side error checking. Implement the form validation functions and install them in the Web applications. Evaluate your Web applications for potential SQL errors and use `try-catch` statements to detect and recover from any errors.

FURTHER READING

Client-side JavaScript is the topic of many excellent books. It is used extensively in Web sites and has had much attention from publishers. Excellent examples are the Addison-Wesley Web Wizard series book [Est01] and books by Flanagan [Fla01] and Goodman and Eich [GoEi01]. Wyke et al. [Wyke02] is a thorough reference to understanding the ins and outs of server-side JavaScript. These books include extensive discussions of error handling of all kinds.

The database topics of this chapter are covered in much more depth in more advanced database textbooks, including Riccardi [Ric01], Elmasri and Navathe [ElNa99] and Date [Date99].

Much of the earliest work on transactions, backup and recovery, and security was conducted as part of the IBM System R database development. Recovery mechanisms in the System R database are addressed in detail in Gray et al [GMB81]. Security in System R is described in Griffiths and Wade [GrWa76]. General tutorials can be found in Denning and Denning [DeDe79] and in Denning's book [Den83].

Strategies and mechanisms for database administrators working with Oracle databases are presented in [Lon98, Lon01] and for SQL Server in Woody [Woo01] and Garbus [Gar01].

References

BOOKS, JOURNALS, DOCUMENTS

[ANSI89] "The Database Language SQL with Integrity Enhancement," *ANSI X3,135–1989*, American National Standards Institute, New York, 1989. Also available as ISO/IEC Document 9075:1989.

[ANSI92] "The Database Language SQL," *ANSI X3,135–1992*, American National Standards Institute, New York, 1992. Also available as ISO/IEC Document 9075:1992.

[Ber1999] Berners-Lee, Tim, *Weaving the Web*, New York, Harper Collins, 1999.

[CaOt93] Cannan, S., and G. Otten, *SQL—The Standard Handbook*, Maidenhead, UK: McGraw-Hill International, 1993.

[Cha76] Chamberlin, D. D., M. M. Astrahan, K. P. Eswaran, P. P. Griffiths, R. A. Lorie, J. W. Mehl, P. Reisner, and B. W. Wade, "Sequel-2: A Unified Approach to Data Definitions, Manipulation, and Control," *IBM Journal of Research and Development*, 20:6, November 1976, pp. 560–575.

[Chen76] Chen, P. P., "The Entity—Relationship Model: Toward a Unified View of Data," *ACM Transactions on Database Systems*, 1:1, January 1976, pp. 9–36.

[Codd70] Codd, E. F., "A Relational Model of Data for Large Shared Data Banks," *Communications of the ACM* 13:6, June 1990, pp. 377–387. Republished in Milestones of Research—Selected Papers 1958–1982, CACM 25th Anniversary Issue, 26:1, January 1983.

[Codd71] Codd, E. F., "A Data Base Sublanguage Founded on the Relational Calculus," *Proceedings of the ACM SIGFIDET Workshop on Data Description*, Access and Control, November 1971, pp. 1–17.

[Codd82] Codd, E. F., "The 1981 ACM Turing Award Lecture: Relational Database, a Practical Foundation for Productivity," *Communications of the ACM*, 25:2, February 1982, pp. 109–117.

[Codd90] Codd, E. F., *The Relational Model for Database Management Version 2*, Boston, MA: Addison-Wesley, 1990.

[Date99] Date, C. J., *An Introduction to Database Systems*, 7th ed., Boston, MA: Addison-Wesley, 1999.

[DaDa93] Date, C. J., and G. Darwen, *A Guide to the SQL Standard*, 3rd ed., Boston, MA: Addison-Wesley, 1993.

[Den83] Denning, D. E., *Cryptography and Data Security*, Boston, MA: Addison-Wesley, 1983.

[DeDe79] Denning, D. E., and P. J. Denning, "Data Security," *ACM Computing Surveys*, 11:3, September 1979, pp. 227–250.

[ElNa99] Elmasri, R., and S. B. Navathe, *Fundamentals of Database Systems*, 3rd ed., Boston, MA: Addison-Wesley, 1999.

[Est01] Estrella, Steven G., *Web Wizard's Guide to JavaScript*, Boston, MA: Addison-Wesley, November 2001.

[Fed02] Feddema, Helen, *Microsoft Access Version 2002 Inside Out*, Redmond, WA, Microsoft Press, 2002.

[Fla01] Flanagan, David, *JavaScript: The Definitive Guide*, Sebastopol, CA: O'Reilly & Associates, 2001.

[Fri01] Friedrichsen, Lisa, *New Perspectives on Data-Driven Web Sites with Microsoft Access 2000: Tools for E-Commerce*, Cambridge, MA: Course Technology, 2001.

[Gar01] Garbus, Jeffrey R., Alvin T. Chang, and Penny Garbus *Learn SQL Server 2000 Administration*, Plano, TX, Wordware Publishing, 2001.

[GoEi01] Goodman, Danny and Brendan Eich, *JavaScript Bible*, 4th Ed., New York: J. Wiley, 2001.

[GMB81] Gray, J. N., P. R. McJones, and M. Blasgen, "The Recovery Manager of the System R Database Manager," *ACM Computing Surveys*, 13:2, June 1981, pp. 232–242.

[GrWa76] Griffiths, P. P., and B. W. Wade, "An Authorization Mechanism for a Relational Data Base System," *ACM Transactions on Database Systems*, 1:3, September 1976, pp. 242–255.

[Gup2001] Gupta, Uma G., *Information Systems: Success in the 21st Century*, 2nd ed., Englewood Cliffs, NJ: Prentice-Hall, 2001.

[Hal99] Halpin, Terry, *Information Modeling and Relational Databases: From Conceptual Analysis to Logical Design*, San Mateo, CA: Morgan Kaufmann Publishers, 1999.

[Her97] Herbst, H., *Business Rule-Oriented Conceptual Modeling*, Berlin, Germany: Springer Verlag, 1997.

[HoSu02] Homer, Alex, and Dave Sussman, *Professional ASP.NET 1.0*, San Mateo, CA: Morgan Kaufmann Publishers, 2002.

[Hob01] Hoberman, Steve, *Data Modeler's Workbench: Tools and Techniques for Analysis and Design*, New York: J. Wiley, 2001.

[Irw02] Irwin, Michael R., Cary N. Prague, and Jennifer Reardon, *Access Microsoft Access 2002 Bible Gold Edition*, New York: J. Wiley, 2001.

[JeVa1999] Jessup, Leonard M., and Joseph S. Valasich *Information Systems Foundations*, Englewood Cliffs, NJ: Prentice-Hall, 1999.

[Leh02] Lehnert, Wendy G., *Web Wizard's Guide to HTML*, Boston, MA: Addison-Wesley, 2002.

[LiHu02] Liberty, Jesse, and Dan Hurwitz, *Programming ASP.NET*, Sebastopol, CA: O'Reilly & Associates, 2002.

[Lit02] Litwin, Paul, Ken Getz, and Mike Gunderloy, *Access 2002 Developer's Handbook*, Alameda, CA: Sybex, Inc., 2002.

[Lov00] Lovejoy, Elijah, *Essential Asp for Web Professionals*, Englewood Cliffs, NJ: Prentice-Hall, 2000.

[LoTh99] Loney, K and Marlene Theriault, *Oracle8 DBA Handbook*, Berkeley, CA: Osborne/McGraw-Hill, 1999.

[LoTh01] Loney, Kevin, and Marlene Theriault, *Oracle9i DBA Handbook*, Berkeley, CA: Osborne/McGraw-Hill, 2001.

[Mel96] Melton, J. (ed.), "An SQL-3 Snapshot," *Proceedings of the International Conference on Data Engineering*, November 1996, pp. 666–672.

[Meyer00] Meyer, Eric A., *Cascading Style Sheets: The Definitive Guide*, Sebastopol, CA: O'Reilly & Associates, 2001.

[Mit00] Mitchell, Scott, *Designing Active Server Pages*, Sebastopol, CA: O'Reilly & Associates, 2000.

[MuKe00] Musciano, C., and B. Kennedy, *HTML & XHTML: The Definitive Guide*, 4th ed., Sebastopol, CA: O'Reilly & Associates, 2000.

[Mul01] Muller, Robert J., *Database Design for Smarties: Using UML for Data Modeling*, San Mateo, CA: Morgan Kaufmann Publishers, 2001.

[ReMo02] Reynolds, Janice, and Roya Mofazali, *The Complete E-Commerce Book:Design, Build & Maintain a Successful Web-based Business*, Gilroy, CA: CMP Books.

[Ricc01] Riccardi, Greg, *Principles of Database Systems with Internet and Java Applications*, Boston, MA: Addison-Wesley, 2001.

[Sel01] Silverston, Len, *The Data Model Resource Book: A Library of Universal Data Models for All Enterprises*, Revised Edition, Volume 1, New York: J. Wiley, 2001.

[SKS01] Silberschatz, A., H. F. Korth, and S. Sudarshan, *Database System Concepts*, 4th ed., New York, NY: McGraw-Hill, 2001.

[St2001] Stair, Ralph M., and George Walter Reynolds, *Principles of Information Systems*, 5th ed., Cambridge, MA: Course Technology, 2001.

[Teo94] Teorey, T. J., *Database Modeling and Design: The Fundamental Principles*, San Francisco, CA: Morgan Kaufmann, 1994.

[Wei99] Weissinger, A. K., *ASP in a Nutshell*, Sebastopol, CA: O'Reilly & Associates, 1999.

[Woo01] Woody, Buck, *Essential SQL Server 2000: An Administration Handbook*, Boston, MA: Addison Wesley, 2001.

[Wyke02] Wyke, R. Allen, Jason D. Gilliam, Charlton Ting, and Sean Michaels, *Pure JavaScript*, Indianapolis, IN: Sams Publishing, 2001.

WEB SITES

Addison-Wesley Web Wizard Series: http://www.aw.com/info/webwizard

Google search engine: http://www.google.com

Gregory Gromov's *History of Internet and WWW: The Roads and Crossroads of Internet History*: http://www.netvalley.com/intval1.html

HTML Tidy software to test for XHTML conformance: http://tidy.sourceforge.net

Internet economy: http://www.internetindicators.com

Internet history: http://www.w3history.org

Internet news: news.com.com

Microsoft Access: http://www.microsoft.com/office/access

Microsoft ADO: http://www.microsoft.com/data/ado

Microsoft Developer Network: http://msdn.microsoft.com

Microsoft SQL Server: http://www.microsoft.com/sql

Microsoft XML: http://www.microsoft.com/xml

Oracle TechNet: http://technet.oracle.com

O'Reilly Internet resources: http://www.ora.com

Powersoft PowerBuilder: http://www.powersoft.com

Web cookie information: http://www.cookiecentral.com

World Wide Web Consortium: http://www.w3c.org

World Wide Web Consortium XML : http://www.w3.org/xml

Index

A

Absolute URL 245–246, 260
Access database system,
  Microsoft 7
  Creating tables 123–128
  Date literals 214
  Defining queries 168–171, 185–186
  Design view 138, 169–170, 172–175,
    179–182
  Join properties 210
  Join queries 210, 213
  SQL 211–214
  Subforms 194
  Time calculations 215
ACID transaction properties 389, 401
ActiveX Data Object library. *See* ADO
Active Server Pages. *See* ASP
Active URL 291
Administrator, database 10, 15
ADO (ActiveX Data Object Library) 296, 319
ADO object classes
  `Connection` 319, 389
  `Field` 305–307, 319
  `Recordset` 299–300, 304–307, 319
Aggregate operators 216–219, 233
Algebra, relational. *See* relational algebra
Alert 401
Alter table statement 233
Amazon.com 5, 19
American National Standards Institute (ANSI)
Anchor tag 24, 32, 260
Anomalies in database schemas 144–145, 161
Anomalous behavior 161
Apache Web server 20
Application, Web 292
Application developer 10, 15
Application processor, Web 292
Argument of a function call 283, 291
ARPANET 4
Array 291. *See also* JavaScript
ASP (Active Server Pages) 267, 272–275. *See*
    also JavaScript
  Editing scripts 276
  Execution errors 312–313
  Files. *See* Web application files
  Processor 274–275
  Tags 272
ASP script 291
Assignment statement 274–275, 291
Atomic attribute domains 115
Atomicity transaction property 385, 389, 401

Attribute 26–27, 40–47, 54–55, 57, 63–64,
    225–226
  Atomic 93, 115
  Compared with relationships 49
  Component 111–112
  Composite 43, 57, 93, 96–97, 111–112
  Constraints 63
  Defining 82–83, 334
  Derived 63, 99
  Foreign key 100–103, 115, 226–227
  HTML 32
  Key 43–45, 94, 110, 125, 152, 161
  Multivalued 43, 54, 58, 63, 93, 97–99, 107,
    114
  Non-key 152, 161
  Relationship types 100–103
  Single-valued 42, 58, 63, 93, 96
  Value 40, 42, 57
Augmentation of functional dependencies
    150–151
Autocommit 386, 389, 401
Autonumber keys 310, 386

B

Bachman, C. 13
Backup and recovery 392–394, 401
Back-end database 131–134, 138
Bagui, S. 235
Berners-Lee, Tim 4, 17, 241
Bit 8, 15
Body of a loop 290, 307, 319
Bowman, J. 177
Boyce-Codd normal form (BCNF) 156–157,
    161
Bridge table 115
Browser. *See* Web browser
Byte 8, 15

C

Cannan, S. 235
Car registration example 157–161
Cardinality 49
Constraints 49–50, 52–53, 57, 64–65, 68, 70
  Over specifying 70
  Ratio 49–51, 57
  Symbols 65, 327
Cartesian product operator 199
Caruso, M. 56
Cascade
  Delete 137–138
  Update 137–138, 140

Cascading style sheet (CSS) 248–260
  Attributes 252
  External 253–254
  Classes 254–256, 261
CERN, the European Center for Particle Physics 4, 241
CGI (Common Gateway Interface) 271–272, 291
Chamberlin, D. D. 235
Charron, S. 113, 127
Checkpoint 393–394, 401
Chen, P. P. 13, 81, 87, 224
Client-server system 8–9, 15
Client-side programming 291, 376–382
Closure of functional dependencies 152
CODASYL 13
Codd, E. F. 13, 118, 201
Columnar form 138
Commit transaction 386, 401
Common Gateway Interface Specification. *See* CGI
Communication protocol 25. *See also* HTTP
Composite attribute 43, 57
Conceptual
  Data model 38, 57, 327. *See also* Entity-
    Relationship model
  Schema 38, 57
Concurrency 384–385, 387, 390–392, 401, 402
Condition 319
Conference on Data Systems Languages (CODASYL) 13
Connection to a database 319, 389
`Connection` object 319, 389
Consistency property of a transaction 402
Constraint 12, 41, 57, 94, 115, 329–331
  Cardinality 49–50, 57, 64–65, 68, 70
  Domain 42
  Foreign key 100–104, 115, 135, 226–227
  Key 45, 57, 149–150, 226–227, 327
  Participation 50, 58, 64–65, 327
  Referential integrity 115
Controls in Access 138
Convention, naming 41
Cookie 360, 372, 377
Count function in SQL 216–217
Create table statement in SQL 9, 233
Currency data type 46
Customer requirements for BigHit Online 326–327

D

DARPA, Defense Advanced Research Projects Agency 4
Darwin, G. 235
Data 8, 15
  Analysis of 7
  Dictionary 63, 86

Validation 376–381
Data definition language (DDL) 8, 233
Data manipulation language (DML) 8, 233
Data model 8, 15, 38–39, 48
  Conceptual 38, 57
  Entity relationship 13, 61, 86, 91
  Goals 68
  Logical 38–39, 58
  Object-oriented 78–83, 86
  Physical 38, 58
  Relational 91, 115
Data types. *See* JavaScript data types
Data validation 376–382, 402
Database 6, 15, 52
  Administrator 10, 15
  Back-end 138
  Connections in ASP 319, 389
  Creating in Access 122–124, 138
  Designer 10, 15
  Engine 8
  Failure sources 392–393
  History 13
  Importance to economy 6–7
  Languages 8
  Physical 8
  Privileges 397, 402
  Queries. *See* Queries
  Relational 8
  Representing information in 8–9
  Schema 8, 11–12, 16, 115
  Server 20, 32, 395
  Splitter 131–134, 138
  State 11–12
  Structure. *See* Schema, Database Schema
  Transactions 385
Database management system (DBMS) 6, 15
  History 13
  Security 395–396, 398–400
  User authorization 396–398
Datasheet view in Access 126–127, 138
Date as attribute domain 94, 211
Date, C. J. 13, 87, 118, 162, 235, 403
DB2 database system 15
Debugging 313–314, 380
Decomposition 161
  Functional dependencies 150–151
Defining attribute 82–83, 334
Degree of a relationship type 52–53
Deletion anomaly 145, 161
Denning, D. 403
Denning, P. 403
Dependency. *See* Functional dependency
Design view in Access 138, 169–170, 172–175, 179–182
Derived attribute 63, 99
Determinant 146, 161

Difference operation 190
Discriminator 72, 78, 86, 106–107, 332
Discovering requirements 39–40, 49, 54
Disjoint inheritance 82
Domain of data values 57
Drop table statement 233
Drop-down box in HTML 369–371
Duplication of values 98, 168
Durability of a transaction 389, 394, 402
Dynamic Web page 26, 32, 239–240

E

Earp, R. 235
eBay.com 3–4, 19
ECMAscript 273, 291. *See also* JavaScript
eof property 300–303, 319
Eich B. 293, 403
Electronic commerce 10
Eliminating duplicates in queries 168
Elmasri, R. 59, 87, 162, 403
Employee requirements of BigHit Online
    328–329
Encoding 270–271, 292
End user 9, 15
Enterprise manager 121, 349, 337, 351, 396–398
Entity (instance) 40–43, 57
Entity class 40–47, 54–55, 57, 63
    Instance 63. *See also* Entity
    Owner 69
    Representing as relation 95–96
    Strong. *See* Entity class
    Weak 67–69, 72, 75–78, 86, 98–99, 104–107,
        330–332, 334
Entity-Relationship diagram 62–65, 86, 327–337
Entity-Relationship (ER) model 13, 61, 86, 91
    Translation to relational model 94–95
Equi-join operator 178, 199
E-R. *See* Entity Relationship
Ethernet 4
European Center for Particle Physics (CERN) 4
Exception 383–384, 402
    Handler 383–384, 402
Execute method 299–300, 302, 305, 308, 310,
    319
Explicit commit mode of a transaction 386, 402
External
    Schema 38–39, 57
    Style sheet 261

F

Feddema, H. 201
Field 279, 291, 319. *See also* Attribute
Files, storing information in 123
First normal form (1NF) 156
Flanagan, D. 293, 403
Font conventions in book 41

for statement 289, 291, 306–307
Foreign key attribute 100–104, 115, 135,
    226–227
    Enforcing constraints 227
    Names 102
Forms in HTML 267–269, 292
    Processing with ASP 275–278
Forms in Access 128–132, 138
Friedrichsen, L. 33
from clause 204–205, 233
Front-end database in Access 131–134
Full outer join 233
Function 279, 283–284, 291
Function call 291
Functional dependencies 146–148, 158, 161
    Inference 150–152
    Keys 150, 152
    Maintaining 148
    Non-key 153–156, 162
    Superkey 162

G

Garbus, J. 403
Generalization. *See also* Specialization
Geometry and relational operations 168, 172, 190
Get method 269–271, 282, 291
Goodman, D. 293, 403
Google Web search engine 25
Gray, J. N. 403
Greenspun, P. 14, 281
Griffiths, P. 403
Gromov, G. 17
Group by clause 216–219, 222–223, 233

H

Halpin, T. 59
Having clause 216–219, 233
Herbst, H. 87
Hidden form element in HTML 291
History of database systems 13
Hoberman, S. 59
Host computer 21, 245–246, 261
Href attribute of hyperlink tag 24
HTML (Hypertext Markup Language) 20–24, 32,
    239, 241, 261
    Document 241, 261. *See also* Web page
    Document references 245–246
    Extending with new tags 244
    Forms 267–269, 292
    Non-breaking space 258
    Poorly formed documents 244
    Special symbols 357
    Tables 247–252, 258
    Unknown tag names 244
    Validating form data 376–382, 402
HTML forms 292

HTML tag attributes 23, 32
  `action` 267
  `background` 258
  `bgcolor` 23
  `border` 244
  `color` (font color) 248
  `class` 256
  `href` 24
  `onsubmit` 380–381, 402
HTML tags 22–24, 32, 261
  Anchor <a> 24, 26, 32, 245–246, 260, 270
  `body` 23
  Break
 242, 244
  `caption` 247–248
  Comment <!-- --> 243
  End 22–23, 32, 242, 260
  `font` 248
  `form` 267–269, 292
  Heading 242
  `hidden` input type 277–278, 291
  `html` 242
  Image <img> 244, 261
  `input` 269, 292
  `link` 253
  `option` (drop-down elements) 369–371
  Paragraph <p> 242
  `password` input type 287–288, 342–343
  `select` (drop-down box) 369–371
  `script` 381
  `span` 256, 355
  `style` 251
  `submit` input type 269, 292, 303–304
  Start tag 244
  Table data <td> 247
  Table header <th> 247
  Table row <tr> 247
  Table tags 261
  `textarea` 303, 319
  `title` 23, 32, 244, 248, 261
  Unknown tags 244
HTTP (Hyptertext Transfer Protocol) 21–22,
    25–26, 32, 245–246, 261
  Encoding data 270–271, 292
  Get method 269–271, 282, 291
  Post method 269–271, 292
  Protocols 245–246, 261
  Query string 269–270, 276, 280–282, 292, 299
  Request 24–26, 292
  Request variable 275–277, 292, 364
Hyperlink 26, 242, 261. *See also* Anchor tag

I

IBM 13, 15
Identifying relationship type 67–69, 86
IDS. *See* Integrated Data Store.

IIS (Internet Information Server) 272, 292
`if` statement 302–303, 316, 319
Image tag 261
IMS. *See* Information Management System
Indexes 339
Inference rules for functional dependencies
    150–152
Information 8, 15
  Organization of 40–43
  Representing in databases 38
  Storing in tables 43
  Server 20, 25, 32
  System 4–6, 15
Information Management System (IMS) 13
Information system 4–6, 15
Inheritance 80–83, 107–110, 334, 338–339
  Disjoint 82
  Overlapping 82
  Relationship type 86
Inner join 207, 210, 211, 233
`input` tag 269, 292
Insert statement 30, 221–223, 230–232, 233,
    308–311, 345, 347, 386
Insertion anomaly 145, 161
Instance 11–12, 15, 26
Integrated Data Store (IDS) 12
Internal schema 39
International Standard Book Number (ISBN) 44
Internet 3–5, 15
Internet Explorer 10, 19, 20, 32, 242
Internet Information Server. *See* IIS
Internet Server Application Programming Inter-
    face (ISAPI) 272. *See also* ADO, ASP
Intersection operation 188–189
Is-a relationship 80. *See also* Inheritance
Isolation property of a transaction 389, 402
Irwin, M. R. 141, 201

J

JavaScript 272–274, 292. *See also* ASP
  Alert 377
  Arguments 283, 291
  Assignment statement 274–275, 291
  Backslash character 279
  Body of a loop 290, 307, 319
  `catch` block 383–384
  Comparing strings 361
  Condition 300–301, 319
  Debugging 313–314, 380
  Exception handling 383–384
  Files. *See* Web application files
  `finally` block 383
  `for` statement 289–291, 306–307
  Functions 283–284, 291
  `if` statement 302–303, 316, 319

Literals 279
new operator 285
Objects 278–282, 284–286, 301–303
Parameters 283
Pattern matching 379–380
Quote marks 279
return statement 302–303
Server-side 273, 377
Strings 279–280, 361
Transactions. *See also* ADO transactions
try block 383–384
try-catch statement 383–384, 402
Variable 273–275, 292
Variable declaration 292
while loop 300–301
with statement 286–287
JavaScript API classes and objects
Application 357–358, 372, 377
Array 292, 364, 372, 377
Connection 319, 389
cookies 377
document 377–379
Field 305–307, 319
Form 280
Object 285, 292, 365, 377
QueryString 280–282, 299
Recordset 299–300, 304–307, 319
Request 276–277, 280–282, 292, 299, 360, 377
Response 280–282, 287, 292, 314, 360, 377
Server 298–299, 377
ServerVariables 280
String 279–280, 361, 365, 377, 379
Text 378–379
window 377
JavaScript fields, functions and methods
addItem 365
appendlog 358
BeginTrans 389–390
CommitTrans 389–390
Cookies 360
CreateObject 298–299, 360
eof 300–303, 319
execute 299–300, 302, 305, 38, 310, 319, 358
executeSQL 358
getMovies 366
HTMLEncode 355–356
lookup 315
lookupCustomer 302–303, 359
makeCustomer 285, 287, 310
makeConnection 307, 359
match 379–380
movenext 300–301, 319
printButtonBar 289–290
printCart 366

printCustomerEditPage 316
printCustomerTable 359
printFooter 283–284
printHeader 283–284, 288–289
printMoviesForm 362–363
printTable 304–307
RollbackTrans 389–390
sqlString 312–313
trim 359
validateCustomer 379–381
write 282, 287, 314, 357
writecustomer 285–286
Jessup, L., 17
Jet database engine. *See* Access
Join operators 166, 178–184, 199, 207–211, 213,
    Equi-join 178, 199
    Inner join 207, 210, 211, 233
    Left join 208–210, 233
    Natural join 180–181, 199
    Outer join 208–210, 233
    Right join 208–209, 233
JScript. *See* JavaScript
Junction table 115

K
Kennedy, B. 33
Key 26–27, 43–45, 57, 67, 69, 94, 113, 161, 328,
    338–339
    Attribute 43–45, 94, 110, 125, 152, 161
    Choosing 331
    Combination 45
    Constraint 45, 57, 149–150, 226–227
    Declaration 45, 125
    Defined by functional dependency 150, 152
    Foreign 100–104, 115, 135, 227
    Multiattribute 126, 226
    Partial 72, 78, 86, 106–107, 332
    Primary 45, 58
    Secondary 45
    SQL
Korth, H. K. 162

L
L. L. Bean Company 6–7
Lehnert, W. 33
Left join 208–210, 233
Link. *See* Hyperlink
Linked tables in Access 138
Literal 215, 279
Litwin, W. 201
Localhost 246, 261, 276
Log 354, 372, 394, 402
Logical
    Data model 38–39, 58
    Schema 38–39, 58
Loney, K. 351

M

Mailto protocol 246
Mandatory participation constraint 50, 58, 65
Many-to-many cardinality ratio 50–52, 57, 103–104, 330–332
Many-to-one cardinality ratio. *See* One-to-many cardinality ratio
Market-basket analysis 7
Markup tag. *See* HTML tag
Master form in Access 194
McGoveran, D. 155, 367
Metadata 115
Method 279, 292
Microsoft
   Access. *see* Access
   Active Server Pages (ASP). *See* ASP
   Internet Explorer. *See* Internet Explorer
   Internet Information Server 272, 292
   JScript. *See* JavaScript
   Script Debugger 314
   SQL Server database system. *See* SQL Server
   VBScript. *See* VBScript
Model. *See* Data model
Modification anomaly 145, 161
Mofazali, R. 87
Mosaic Web browser 4, 241
movenext function 300–301, 319
Muller, R. 59
Multivalued attribute 43, 54, 58
Musciano, C. 33

N

NaN (Not a Number) 364–365, 372
National Center for Supercomputing Applications (NCSA) 4, 241
Natural join operator 180–181, 199
Navagation buttons 126, 191
Navathe, S. B. 59, 87, 162, 403
Netscape Navigator Web browser 4, 19, 20, 32, 242, 380
New York Times Company 10, 19, 24–25
Nielsen, J. 30, 254–255
Nonbreaking space in HTML ( ) 258
Non-key attribute 161
Normal form 145, 153, 161
  Boyce-Codd (BCNF) 156–157, 161
  First (1NF) 156
  Second (2NF) 156
  Third (3NF) 153–156, 162
Normalization 145, 152–153, 161
  Car registration example 157–161
Null value 46–47, 58, 109, 227

O

Object class in JavaScript 292
Object in JavaScript 285, 292, 365, 377
Object name in a URL 245–246, 261
Object-oriented
  Data model 78–83, 86
  Inheritance 80–83, 107–110, 334, 338–339
  Representing entity classes 107–110
ODBC (Other Database Connectivity) 134, 296–298, 319
  Data source 297, 319, 340
One-to-one cardinality ratio 50–51, 57, 67, 74, 100–101, 104, 137, 179
One-to-many cardinality ratio 49–50, 56–57, 74, 101–103, 112, 227
onsubmit attribute 380–381, 402
Optional participation constraint 50, 58, 65
Oracle database system 7, 15
Other Database Connectivity. *See* ODBC
Oten, G. 235
Outer join 208–210, 233
Overlapping inheritance 82–83
Owner entity class 69

P

Packages. *See* Java packages
Parameter 292
Partial key 72, 78, 86, 106–107, 332
Participation constraint 50, 58, 64–65, 327
Pattern matching 215, 233, 362, 379, 380
People in database systems 9–10
Physical
  Data model 38, 58
  Schema 38, 58
Post method 269–270, 292
Primary key. *See* Key
Privacy issues 75
Privilege in a database 397–402
Processes in data modeling 56
Product operations 166, 175–182, 199
Projection operations 166–171, 186, 199, 205–206
  In geometry 168
Property. *See* attribute
Protocol in a URL 245–246, 261
  Mailto 246
Pseudo-transitivity of functional dependencies 151

Q

QBE. *See* Query by example
Qualified name 199
Query 9, 12–13, 15, 27, 165. *See also* Relational algebra, Relational calculus, SQL
  Defining with Access 168–171, 185–186
  Optimization 199, 211, 233
  Processing 211, 233, 299–301
Query by example 185
Query design view in Access 169–170, 179–182

Query string, HTTP 269–270, 276, 280–282, 292, 299

R
Record 166, 199
`Record Source` property in Access 195
`Recordset` in ADO 319. *See also* ADO objects
Recovery 392–393, 402
Redundancy in database systems 393
Redundancy in relation schemas 144–145, 162
References clause 226–227, 233
Referential integrity 115
Reflexivity in functional dependencies 150–152
Relation 91, 115, 187, 199
Relation schema 92–96 115
  Constraints 94
  Redundancy 144–145, 162
Relational algebra 165–166, 199
  Expressions 184–185, 199
  Join operations 166, 178–184, 199, 207–211, 213
  Product operations 166, 175–182, 199
  Projection operations 166–171, 186, 199, 205–206
  Representing expressions with Access 168–171, 185–186
  Selection operation 166, 171–175, 178, 186, 199, 205
  Set operations 166, 187–190, 199
Relational database management system (RDBMS) 8, 16
Relational model 91, 115
Relationship (instance) 12, 48–53, 58
  Instance 48
  Sentences 48–49, 54, 65, 67, 70
  Three-way 52–53
Relationship Type 48–53, 55–56, 58, 64, 135–138
  Compared with attribute 49
  Constraints 49–50, 57, 64–65
  Higher degree 51-53
  Identifying 68, 86, 104–106, 331–332
  Inheritance 80–83, 86
  Is-a 80
  Many-to-many 50–52, 57, 103–104, 330–332
  One-to-many 50–51, 57, 67, 74, 100–101, 104, 137, 179
  One-to-one 49–50, 56–57, 74, 101–103, 112, 227
  Representing as attributes 100–103
  Roles 69–71, 74–75
  Specifying in Access 135–138
Relative URL 245–246, 261, 267–269
Rents relationship type 48–49
Request, HTTP 24–26, 292
Request object in JavaScript 292

Request variable 292
Response object in JavaScript 292
Results table 166, 199
Reynolds, G. 17
Reynolds, J. 87
Riccardi, G. 59, 87, 403
Riccardi, M. 341
Right join 233
Role in a relationship 48–50, 59, 69–71, 74–75
Rollback operation 386, 402
Row of a table. *See also* Entity
Rule of 90/10 229, 233

S
Sabre airline reservation system 13
`Sale` table 26–27, 30–31
Schema 8, 11–12, 16, 58
  Conceptual 38, 57. *See also* E-R model
  Database 8, 11–12, 16, 115
  External 38–39, 57
  Improvement 162
  Internal 39
  Logical 38–39, 58
  Physical 38, 58
  Quality measures 143
  Relation 92–96, 115
  Table 8
Script debugger 314
Scripting language 272, 292
Second normal form (2NF) 156
Security 394–398
`select` clause 204–205, 215–216, 233
Select statement 30–31, 204–205, 233, 303–304
  Executing in JavaScript 299–300, 302, 305, 308, 310, 319, 358
  Processing the results in JavaScript 207
Selection operations 166, 171–175, 178, 186, 199, 205
Server-side programs 273, 377
Servers
  Database 20, 32, 395
  Information 20, 24–26, 32
  Web 20, 24, 32, 240, 266–267, 276–277
Set operations 166, 187–190, 199, 220–221
Shape of relations 187, 199
Shopping cart 83, 85, 332–333, 335
`Show` box in Access 173
Silberschatz, A. 162
Silverston, L. 59
Single-valued attribute 42, 58, 63, 93, 96
Specifying application requirements 326–329
SQL, or SQL- 13, 16, 27, 166, 224, 233
  Access 211–214
  Aggregates 216–219, 233
  Alter table statement 228, 233

as clause 215
Attributes 225–226
Capitalization in 204
count function 216, 217
Create index statement 339
Create table statement 9, 225, 230, 233
Create user statement 396
Delete statement 223, 348
distinct operator 204–207
DML statements 225–229
Drop statement 228–229, 233, 396
Errors 381–382
except operator 220–221
Executing with JavaScript. *See also* ADO
Expressions 215–216
Foreign key constraints 226–227
from clause 204–205, 233
getdate function 344
Grant statement 397
group by clause 216–219, 222–223, 233
having clause 216–219, 233
Insert statement 30, 221–223, 230–232, 233,
    308–311, 345, 347, 386
intersect operator 220
join operator 207–209
Key constraints 226–227
like operator 214, 362
Literals 215
Nested select statements 218–219, 233
order by clause 214, 231
Pattern matching 214–215, 233, 362
primary key clause 226–227
Quote marks 312–313
references clause 226–227, 233
Results of select statements 207
Revoke statement 396
Roles 397, 400
select clause 204–205, 215–216, 233
Select statement 30–31, 204–205, 233,
    303–304
Set operations 220–221
Standards 13
Stored procedure 398–399, 402
union operator 220–221
unique constraint 227
Update statement 223, 232, 233, 345, 347–348
Users 228
where clause 204–205, 218, 233
SQL Server database system 337, 340, 382,
    396–398
Social Security number 44–45
Splitter, database 138
Stair, R. 17
Stored procedure in SQL 398–399, 402
Style class 254, 261
Style sheet. *See* Cascading Style Sheet

Structured query language. *See* SQL
Subclass and superclass 107–110, 338
Subform in Access 192–198
submit input type in HTML 269, 292, 303–304
Sudarshan, S. 162
Superkey 149–150, 160, 162
System R group at IBM 13

T

Table 91. *See also* Relation
    Linked in Access 138
    Results 199
Tags in HTML. *See* HTML tags
Teory, T. J. 87
Theriault, M. 351
Third normal form (3NF) 153–156, 162
Toolbox in Access 138, 192
Transaction 384–392
    ACID properties 389, 401
    Atomicity 385, 389, 401
    Autocommit mode 386, 389, 401
    Commit 386, 401
    Consistency 389, 402
    Durability 389, 394, 402
    Explicit commit mode 386, 402
    Interference 384–387, 389–392
    Isolation 389, 402
    Logs 394, 402
    Manager 386, 402
    Management 389–390
    Processing 367
    Rollback 386, 402
    Scenarios 387–388, 391–392
Transitivity of functional dependencies 150–152

U

Ullmann, J. 201
Unbound text box in Access 196
Unique identifier. *See* Key
Union of functional dependencies 150, 152
Union operation 187–189, 220–221
Universal Product Code (UPC) 44
Universal resource locator. *See* URL
Update anomaly 144–145, 162
Update statement 223, 232, 233, 345, 347–348
Upsizing wizard 340, 349
URL 21–22, 24, 32, 245, 261, 267–269
    Absolute 245–246, 260
    Active 291
    Encoding 270–271, 292
    Protocol 261
    Relative 245–246, 261, 267–269
User authorization 396–398
User interfaces 128–132, 138
    Access 190–95
Users of database systems 9–10, 70–71, 396

V

Valasich, J. 17
Variable declaration in JavaScript 292
VBScript 272
Vianu, V. 308, 400
View. *See* external schema
Video rental form 195–198

W

Wal-Mart Company 6–7
Wade, B. 403
Weak entity class 67–69, 72, 75–78, 86, 98–99, 104–107, 330–332, 334
Web (World-Wide Web) 3–4, 16
  Application 26, 29–30, 32, 267, 272, 292, 296–298, 342, 362, 395
  Application developer 10, 16
  Application processor 274–275, 292
  Architecture 240–241, 266–267
  Browser 4, 10, 19–20, 22, 24, 32, 241
  Consortium (W3C) 22, 33
  Dynamic page 26, 32
  Pages 19–23, 32
  Server 20, 24–26, 32, 240, 266–267, 276–277
  Site 10, 342
  Site designer 10, 16
  Static page 240
Web application files
  `500-100.asp` 314
  `addcustomer.asp` 277–278, 310–311, 376
  `additem.asp` 364, 366
  `bighit.css` 253
  `bighittools.js` 284, 304, 307, 355–360
  `cartupdate.asp` 366
  `checkout.asp` 346
  `confirmcheckout.asp` 369, 390

  `custeditform.asp` 317
  `custlookupform.asp` 301–302
  `customer.js` 316, 359
  `customerrequest.asp` 280–282
  `default.asp` 356
  `inquiryform.asp` 370
  `login.asp` 356, 360
  `newcustomer.asp` 277–278, 283, 308–310
  `rentals.asp` 298–299, 304
  `search.asp` 344
  `shopcart.js` 362, 366
  `showlog.asp` 354
  `signup.asp` 315–316
  `simple.asp` 272–274
  `simpleaccount.asp` 276–277
  `simplecustomer.asp` 286
  `sqlexec.asp` 307, 382–384
  `sqlform.asp` 307
  `source.asp` 355–356
  `updatecustomer.asp` 316
`where` clause 233
`while` loop 319
Wide area network (WAN) 4
Wizard in Access 122, 128–132, 138, 192, 349
Woody, B. 403
World-Wide Web. *See* Web
Wyke, R. 293, 403

X

XHTML, the Extensible Hypertext Markup Language 249, 261
XML, the Extensible Markup Language 249, 261

Z

Zloof, M. M. 185

V

Valasich, J. 17
Variable declaration in JavaScript 292
VBScript 272
Vianu, V. 308, 400
View. *See* external schema
Video rental form 195–198

W

Wal-Mart Company 6–7
Wade, B. 403
Weak entity class 67–69, 72, 75–78, 86, 98–99,
    104–107, 330–332, 334
Web (World-Wide Web) 3–4, 16
    Application 26, 29–30, 32, 267, 272, 292,
        296–298, 342, 362, 395
    Application developer 10, 16
    Application processor 274–275, 292
    Architecture 240–241, 266–267
    Browser 4, 10, 19–20, 22, 24, 32, 241
    Consortium (W3C) 22, 33
    Dynamic page 26, 32
    Pages 19–23, 32
    Server 20, 24–26, 32, 240, 266–267, 276–277
    Site 10, 342
    Site designer 10, 16
    Static page 240
Web application files
    500-100.asp 314
    addcustomer.asp 277–278, 310–311, 376
    additem.asp 364, 366
    bighit.css 253
    bighittools.js 284, 304, 307, 355–360
    cartupdate.asp 366
    checkout.asp 346
    confirmcheckout.asp 369, 390

custeditform.asp 317
custlookupform.asp 301–302
customer.js 316, 359
customerrequest.asp 280–282
default.asp 356
inquiryform.asp 370
login.asp 356, 360
newcustomer.asp 277–278, 283, 308–310
rentals.asp 298–299, 304
search.asp 344
shopcart.js 362, 366
showlog.asp 354
signup.asp 315–316
simple.asp 272–274
simpleaccount.asp 276–277
simplecustomer.asp 286
sqlexec.asp 307, 382–384
sqlform.asp 307
source.asp 355–356
updatecustomer.asp 316
where clause 233
while loop 319
Wide area network (WAN) 4
Wizard in Access 122, 128–132, 138, 192, 349
Woody, B. 403
World-Wide Web. *See* Web
Wyke, R. 293, 403

X

XHTML, the Extensible Hypertext Markup Language 249, 261
XML, the Extensible Markup Language 249, 261

Z

Zloof, M. M. 185